Oracle Press™

Oracle Power Objects Handbook

Bruce Kolste
and
David Petersen

Osborne **McGraw-Hill**

Berkeley New York St. Louis San Francisco
Auckland Bogotá Hamburg London Madrid
Mexico City Milan Montreal New Delhi Panama City
Paris São Paulo Singapore Sydney Tokyo Toronto

Osborne **McGraw-Hill**
2600 Tenth Street
Berkeley, California 94710
U.S.A.

For information on translations or book distributors outside the U.S.A., or to arrange bulk purchase discounts for sales promotions, premiums, or fundraisers, please contact Osborne **McGraw-Hill** at the above address.

Oracle Power Objects Handbook

234567890 DOC 998765

ISBN 0-07-882089-8

Publisher
Lawrence Levitsky

Acquisitions Editor
Scott Rogers

Project Editor
Janet Walden

Proofreader
India Echo

Computer Designer
Lance Ravella

Illustrator
Marla Shelasky

Series Design
Jani Beckwith

Quality Control Specialist
Joe Scuderi

Cover Design
Ted Mader Associates

About the Authors...

Bruce Kolste is a writer and editor for Larson-Davis Laboratories. He is responsible for their marketing database operations and works as a database consultant.

David Petersen is a programmer and an Oracle database administrator for Larson-Davis Laboratories. In addition, he maintains customer Oracle databases and coauthors user manuals.

Contents at a Glance

Contents

Acknowledgments

We would like to thank Oracle Corporation for providing us with the opportunity to write this book, and especially thank Matthew Bennett at Oracle for his technical reviews. Thanks also to Ron Lashaw for his technical support on the inner workings of Oracle Power Objects, and John Stroud who helped us get information for the Macintosh version of the program.

We also want to thank those at Osborne/McGraw-Hill who have made this book possible—Jeff Pepper and Ann Wilson for their editorial reviews of the first chapters, Brad Shimmin and Scott Spanbauer for their developmental reviews, and Scott Rogers and Daniela Dell'Orco for editing and technical reviews. Thanks also to Kathryn Hashimoto, India Echo, and Janet Walden for their copyediting, proofreading, and review of the final chapters.

And, we would like to thank our wives and children for their patience while we worked late evenings and weekends on the book. Bruce wants to thank his wife, Sabra, for all of her encouragement and help in editing chapters, and for her ideas on how to present complicated concepts in an understandable manner. He's grateful to his children, Kristian, Tyler, Kolbein, Nils, Erik, and Kasja, for their encouragement on the book and for their constant questioning of "Are you done yet, Dad?". David wants to thank his wife, Pat, for her patience and encouragement, and especially for making his lunches while he worked. He wants to thank his children, Wade, Troy, Ryan, Melinda, and Brandon, for their interest in how the book was coming along and for their ideas on how to spend any royalties.

Introduction

Welcome to Oracle Power Objects and the *Oracle Power Objects Handbook*! Oracle Power Objects is one of those rare programs that is easy to use and includes an easy-to-use programming language (Oracle Basic) for customizing your database. Oracle Power Objects is the first low-cost database application development program, which runs on both the Microsoft Windows and Apple Macintsoh operating systems, to provide users the ease of drag-and-drop methods for creating stand-alone databases and applications for individual or corporate databases. Oracle Power Objects also reduces development time with its object-oriented design and libraries of reusable objects (classes and bitmaps).

About this Book

This book is designed to provide a one-volume solution to creating database applications with Oracle Power Objects. We have attempted to cover all of the features of Oracle Power Objects and to provide you with tips, helpful hints for some applications that are difficult to create in the program (such as cross-tab reports), and a complete reference to Oracle Power Objects properties and methods with real-life examples that you can use in your applications. The book shows screenshots from both the Windows and Macintosh versions of Oracle Power Objects, and is based on a prerelease version of the product.

How this Book Is Organized

The *Oracle Power Objects Handbook* is intended for individuals new to database application development and for experienced designers trying to quickly master Oracle Power Objects. If you are an experienced database designer, you may choose to skip Chapters 1 and 2. These chapters are an introduction to Oracle Power Objects, with an emphasis on object-oriented design and database design. Chapters 3 through 6 introduce using Oracle Power Objects' interface, Chapters 7 through 9 delve deeper into the heart of Oracle Power Objects, explaining how to use Oracle Basic and offering detailed explanations and examples of modifying and setting properties and methods. Chapter 10 explains using SQL (structured query language) with Oracle Power Objects and Chapter 11 covers advanced Oracle Power Objects topics.

The following is a brief outline of the chapters in this book.

Chapter 1 provides a description of object-oriented design, and explains how Oracle Power Objects incorporates object-oriented design in contrast to other similar products, such as Microsoft Access, Microsoft Visual Basic, and PowerBuilder.

Chapter 2 covers the fundamentals of relational databases and proper database design methods. Topics include basic definitions, proper preparation for designing the database, and interface design.

Chapter 3 defines Oracle Power Objects concepts and provides a quick overview of Oracle Power Objects' menus, windows, and toolbars.

Chapter 4 describes starting Oracle Power Objects, connecting to a local or remote database, and creating database sessions, tables, indexes, views (to relate tables), synonyms, and sequences.

Chapter 5 explains creating forms with Oracle Power Objects' Designer, linking tables to forms, using controls (such as text fields, check boxes, push buttons, etc.), setting properties of controls, running completed forms, and querying the database from a running form. Properties are introduced here, but a more complete explanation of using the power of properties is covered in Chapter 8.

Chapter 6 discusses adding subforms, repeater displays, and classes to forms, and explains how to create and print reports.

Chapter 7 provides an introduction to Oracle Basic (with examples of using Oracle Basic in Oracle Power Objects), and shows how to debug an application.

Chapter 8 provides a detailed overview of object properties. Object properties control the look and feel of objects.

Chapter 9 provides a detailed overview of object methods. Object methods incorporate Oracle Basic subroutines and functions.

Chapter 10 explains use of embedded SQL in Oracle Power Objects.

Chapter 11 covers and advanced reporting techniques such as cross-tab reports and Avery label reports; using OLE, dynamic link libraries, and OCX controls (in Windows); and customizing run-time menus and status bars.

Appendix A illustrates how to set up the client-server relationship between Oracle Power Objects and Oracle7 Server using TCP/IP and SQL*Net.

Appendix B is a complete Oracle Basic reference.

Appendix C provides a list of Oracle reserved words.

Typographical Conventions Used in this Book

This book uses the following special formatting conventions:

- Boldface type specifies user input.
- Keys on the keyboard, such as ENTER, SHIFT, and TAB, are in small caps.
- Simultaneous keypress combinations are indicated by hyphens (ALT-C).

Using Oracle Power Objects

Historically, sophisticated database applications have been difficult to develop and maintain. With the advent of form and report generators, and database graphical user interfaces (GUIs), some of the difficulty is eased. It still takes, however, considerable knowledge and training to design and maintain databases. PC-based databases have been easier to develop because of easily used GUIs, but only for relatively simple and small databases. They cannot handle the large corporate databases that reside on workstations and mainframe servers.

Oracle Power Objects is a database application development environment that provides the tools to rapidly create and maintain sophisticated Windows and Macintosh database applications for databases of any size. Oracle Power Objects also helps those who need a good, easy to create and maintain Windows or

Macintosh relational database, by using its own internal database (called Blaze); in this way, Oracle Power Objects provides a database application development environment that can change as the needs of the company change. Oracle Power Objects' Blaze database can grow from a local database to one on a database server. Then, if the need arises, the Blaze database data can be moved to an Oracle 7 or SQL (which stands for "structured query language" and is pronounced like "sequel") Server database (such as Microsoft's SQL server or Sybase System 10 that is accessed through the DBLIB Library) without any loss in application development.

Oracle has developed Oracle Power Objects to fill several strategic areas of its product line. Oracle Power Objects adds an entry-level relational database, a graphical object-oriented application development environment, and a cross-platform application development system. This chapter will introduce you to the following topics: rapid application development tools, object-oriented programming (OOP), Oracle Power Objects as an object-oriented development system, comparing Oracle Power Objects to other rapid application development tools (like Visual Basic and PowerBuilder), and an overview of Oracle Power Objects' database connectivity. Terms used throughout this book to describe Oracle Power Objects and its various capabilities will be described in this chapter, to help you as you move on to the more detailed chapters in the rest of the book.

Oracle Power Objects Features

Following is a summary of the Oracle Power Objects features that will be described in more detail in this chapter.

- **Object-oriented design** The Oracle Power Objects application development environment creates reusable objects. These objects include all of the characteristics that define a development environment as being object-oriented: encapsulation, inheritance, and polymorphism. These concepts will be explained later in the chapter in the section "Object-Oriented Programming." The concept of object orientation is central to understanding and using Oracle Power Objects.
- **Graphical design tools** The user interface to a database is created using Oracle Power Objects' drawing tools. These tools let you quickly create forms and reports by dragging and dropping objects (like database fields, buttons, or bitmaps) onto forms.
- **OLE 2** Using Microsoft's OLE (object linking and embedding) technology, you can link and embed objects from other applications, like Microsoft Word or Excel, on Oracle Power Objects forms.

- **Local relational database engine (Blaze)** Oracle Power Objects includes its own relational database. The Blaze database can be used for either prototyping databases or for creating databases that don't need all of the features of larger, more expensive server-based databases.
- **Support for remote relational databases** Oracle Power Objects provides tools for easily connecting to and manipulating data stored in most of the major databases. Databases supported by Oracle Power Objects include Oracle7 Server and SQL Server (DBLIB).
- **Programming language** Oracle Power Objects includes Oracle Basic, a full-fledged programming language. Similar to Microsoft's Visual Basic, it allows you to control the actions of your application.
- **Cross-platform application design** You can create database applications on either the Microsoft Windows or Macintosh platforms and you can recompile the application for the other platform. Employees can then use their computer platform of choice for accessing data.

Because of its graphical nature and ease of use, Oracle Power Objects enables nonprogrammers to rapidly develop powerful applications without having to understand the complexities of normal programming languages like C/C++, Pascal, and other procedural computer languages. Oracle Power Objects provides the tools for visual application design, object-oriented programming (OOP), and the use of compilers to create stand-alone applications. These tools include prebuilt controls and objects to paint the user interface. The Oracle Power Objects developer doesn't have to write code for drawing windows or lines, placing items on windows, creating menus, etc. These are all taken care of by Oracle Power Objects.

Rapid Application Development

Oracle Power Objects is the most recent and powerful of what are known in the programming world as *rapid application development* programs. HyperCard, the first rapid application development program, provided an environment where nonprogrammers could quickly create windows, place objects, and attach small pieces of hypertalk code to the windows and objects. Objects like buttons, for example, could be copied, pasted, and reused in other HyperCard stacks with little or no changes. Developers quickly added XCMDs (external commands) to HyperCard to extend its functionality. With these tools, many nonprogrammers started developing their own personal applications (called *stacks*) to meet specific needs, and many programmers used HyperCard to prototype an application to see how it would look and act. HyperCard stacks, however, have their limitations, as they cannot be compiled into stand-alone applications and, because they are not compiled, are extremely slow.

Microsoft Visual Basic was the first widely used object-oriented rapid application development tool for Windows. Visual Basic, like HyperCard, is a system for rapidly developing applications. Visual Basic allows you to create a window with the click of a button. Also, objects such as buttons and database entry fields can then be placed on the window, and code added to each object. Visual Basic added a richer variety of controls (prebuilt objects such as data entry fields, buttons, and combo boxes that are placed onto forms) and added a powerful compiled Basic language that could be used to control the applications. Third-party developers have added many Windows function extensions to Visual Basic through the use of DLLs (dynamic link libraries) and custom controls with Visual Basic extensions (.VBXs), which Visual Basic developers can purchase.

More recently, many expensive rapid application development programs have been specifically designed to create graphical user interfaces to supported databases. Programs such as PowerBuilder Enterprise 4.0 and SQLWindows Corporate Edition 5.0 are among the best of this new breed. Most of these programs are object-oriented in nature and provide tools for graphically developing application user interfaces. They also contain a database for prototyping database applications. Thus, a developer can create a database application and database on his or her development computer and not have to be physically attached to and using a company's database. These programs usually contain a fourth-generation language (4GL) that is easier to learn and use than traditional computer languages like C/C++ and Pascal, which are third-generation languages (3GL).

Where Oracle Power Objects Fits In

Oracle Power Objects is an extremely easy-to-use program, similar to Visual Basic and Access in its use of prebuilt controls to graphically create database applications. However, it extends the use of object-oriented programming techniques far beyond that of Visual Basic and Access, by letting you create objects (called *classes*) that can be reused on many forms. Oracle Power Objects also provides all of the tools for the creation of database front ends (like PowerBuilder Enterprise and SQLWindows) or for the creation of its own internal (Blaze) databases. Oracle Power Objects includes Oracle Basic, a fourth-generation language that is very similar to Visual Basic, and a powerful subset of Oracle7's SQL to query either its own Blaze database or other supported databases.

Oracle Power Objects is a program designed to shorten the development time of your application, especially *client/server database* systems (the database and its data are stored on a company server computer, which can be accessed by employees, or clients, on personal computers).

With Oracle Power Objects' features, developers can quickly create database applications with the Blaze database. Oracle Power Objects let you create tables, views, indexes, sequences, sessions, forms, classes, libraries, and reports as objects by clicking on toolbar icons or by selecting menu items. Controls, such as check boxes, radio buttons, text, and text fields, are placed onto forms simply by selecting the appropriate control tool from a palette of objects.

Oracle Power Objects uses drag-and-drop techniques to simplify and shorten the creation of database applications. You can place objects by clicking and dragging them between windows. For example, table fields can be placed on a form by clicking on a field or fields in a table window and dragging onto the form that will contain that database field. Oracle Power Objects places both the field and its name on the form and automatically links the form to the appropriate table.

Because of the way you can visually create your applications, you and your clients can review the progress of the project through the entire development cycle. For example, you can drag the fields from a table onto a form, add a scroll bar to scroll through the table's records, and press the Run button to have a working application for inputting data into a form. Forms and reports can be run at any time from within Oracle Power Objects, allowing continuous input from your clients. Of course, once your boss or your clients see how easily changes can be made, you may find yourself with endless requests to "tweak" the database application.

Object-Oriented Programming (OOP)

Object-oriented programming is currently the fashionable term used for various programming languages and programming tools. Object-oriented programming can reduce application development time because it allows you to create reusable objects (classes) that are easily maintained. If you have never developed an application before, don't worry—novice programmers often have an easier time learning object-oriented programming techniques than experienced programmers, because object-oriented programming is so different from traditional programming. Programmers using traditional languages like C or Pascal have to worry about the development of their programs from beginning to end. With an object-oriented approach, you create smaller pieces of code that can be reused throughout the program and treated as objects.

In addition to *reusability*, object-oriented also means that an object's properties can be *inherited* from another base object, and that different attributes can be added or removed to create a new object based on the original. This inheritance feature is the foundation of object-oriented programs.

Oracle Power Objects is a truly object-oriented application development tool. Most, if not all, of the rapid application development programs today claim to be object-oriented, but not all of them meet the criteria of true object-oriented programs. Even high-end application development programs like PowerBuilder and SQLWindows, which have many object-oriented characteristics, are not completely object-oriented in their application design. Because object-oriented programming is central to Oracle Power Objects, it is important to understand just what defines a program as object-oriented. Object-oriented programming involves applying the three main concepts of encapsulation, inheritance, and polymorphism. We begin our discussion of these three concepts by first defining objects, properties, and methods.

Objects

An object is an entity that has a clearly defined set of public (or external) behaviors and a private (or hidden) internal state (data and function). The external behavior of an object includes how messages sent to an object (e.g., clicking on a close button) result in an anticipated behavior (closing the open form). Another external behavior of a button is how it looks. The Close button has a rounded rectangle shape, a gray background, and text on the button (Close) that describes its use. However, the means by which the Close button performs its specific task—closing the form—is private or inaccessible to the end user.

The external behaviors of an object are called its *properties*. For example, properties can control the background color, size, record source (database table), and name of a form. *Methods* are what control the action performed by an object in response to events like a single or double mouse click. Each of these properties and methods can be manipulated by a property sheet associated with the object or by Oracle Basic. All rapid application development programs are at least object-oriented in that they treat windows, buttons, fields, etc., as objects that contain properties and that can be referenced by methods (3GL or 4GL code used to define or control the behavior of the object).

To reduce the amount of actual programming you have to perform, Oracle Power Objects sets default methods and properties for all its objects. For example, when you can drag and drop a field from a table onto a form, the record source property is set to the appropriate table.

Properties

Properties control the external behavior of objects in Oracle Power Objects (such as forms, classes, fields, etc.). They include physical attributes and control properties. *Physical properties* include items such as the color of the form or the horizontal and vertical position of a button on a form. *Control properties* control how objects behave. They include properties such as if a field is visible, if a button is enabled or disabled, and the record source (the name of the table from which data is retrieved and displayed) for a form or subform. Each property contains a value within Oracle Power Objects (though the value may be NULL) which you can change with a property sheet or with an Oracle Basic script.

A simple example of a physical property is the HasBorder property, which can be turned on or off depending on if you want the form or subform you are defining to have a border drawn around it. Another simple example is whether the HasScrollBar property of a field is set to True or False. If it is set to True, the field will have a scroll bar. Properties are listed on the property sheet. Whenever an object (such as an application or form) is opened, its property sheet (see Figure 1-1) is automatically displayed next to the object . Each object in Oracle Power Objects

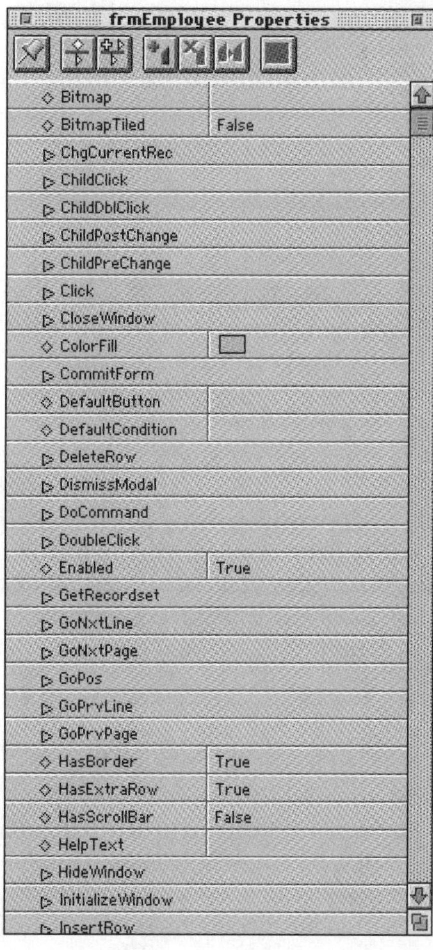

FIGURE 1-1. *Property sheet for a form, showing some of the form's properties and methods*

has its own unique set of properties and it has a property sheet associated with it. You can edit any of the properties in the property sheet. Some simple objects may have just a few properties, while other objects, such as forms, have many properties and methods.

Some of the properties, such as name, are common to all objects. Other properties are unique for that type of object. For example, session objects contain specific properties such as DesignRunConnect for connecting to databases. Properties are described in detail in Chapter 8.

Methods

Methods determine how an object will respond to an event or call to the object. For example, all forms have a method called OpenWindow. There is a predefined action for this method that causes a window containing the form to open. However, you can override the existing method, using Oracle Basic, to perform some other action. If you wish, you can use the default action as well as your newly defined action by including the following line in the method you write with Oracle Basic:

```
inherited.method_name
```

There are many methods defined in Oracle Power Objects, and each is described in detail in Chapter 9. Different methods are attached to the various objects defined within Oracle Power Objects. Some objects in Oracle Power Objects have no methods associated with them. Methods enable the application designer to customize the actions that are performed in the various forms and reports created.

Oracle Power Objects has a rich set of predefined programs and utilities incorporated in the methods for creating many different applications. However, no single program can anticipate, let alone incorporate, all the features that you may need. Therefore, Oracle Power Objects lets you create your own methods to add desired features, through procedures and functions written in Oracle Basic. Defining new methods is described in Chapter 9.

Encapsulation

Encapsulation is the ability to encapsulate or attach properties and methods in self-contained objects. For example, when you define a button, all the properties of the button (font characteristics, fill color, fill pattern, button name, etc.) and the methods attached (what happens when the button is pushed or the mouse cursor passes over it) are contained or attached to the button. If the button is reused (for example, copied and pasted into a different application or form), the copied button retains the attached or encapsulated properties and methods. Therefore, future developers using the button only need to understand how to use the object and are insulated from how you, the designer, defined and coded the object.

Inheritance

Every time a class is placed on a form or a report, it is an *instance* of the class. Each separate instance has the same properties and methods of the master class. This is called *inheritance.* For example, you could create a class that contains your company's name, address, phone number, and logo, which you could then drag and drop on all of your reports or forms (thus creating a new instance of the class). These instances, and all of the objects they contain (the name, address, phone number, and logo), inherit *all* of the characteristics of the master class. Therefore, your company's information will appear exactly the same on every form and will save you valuable time from having to create the same company header over and over. Also, any changes that need to be made to the company information (such as changing the address or adding a fax number) are only made once to the master class—these corrections are then inherited by all the instances on the various forms. Inheritance is covered in more detail in Chapter 6.

Polymorphism

Polymorphism is the ability to create a *subclass* that inherits only *some* of the attributes from the master class. To continue the company information class example from the previous section, you create a subclass by highlighting the original class and then selecting Create Subclass from the Edit menu. You can then redefine any of the attributes of that subclass—you might decide to change the color of the company information text from blue to red to make a subclass which you would place on a form that displays all delinquent payments. Also, some of your subclasses may require more functionality than is contained in the master class. For example, you may need a subclass that includes not only the company information, but also objects to display the customer's phone and fax numbers. This subclass inherits all attributes of the master company information class, plus it includes the ability to display customer information.

Oracle Power Objects and Object-Oriented Programming

As we mentioned earlier, Oracle Power Objects offers the same type of object-oriented programming power made popular by Microsoft Visual Basic. You can develop database applications by creating and manipulating objects with

Oracle Power Objects and Oracle Basic. In Oracle Power Objects, everything is an object. Databases, database sessions, applications, tables, forms, classes, reports, form controls (such as combo boxes, text fields, etc.) are all objects. The properties and methods of each of these objects can be accessed and manipulated by Oracle Basic.

Objects in Oracle Power Objects

When you start Oracle Power Objects, a Main window appears, like the one shown in the following illustration, that displays the database session, application, and library objects.

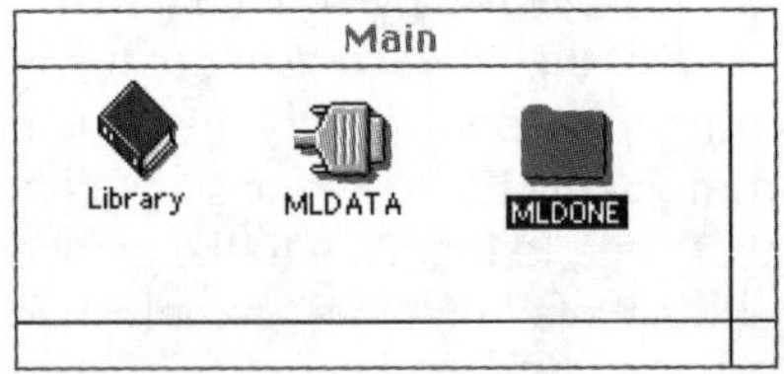

Every database session, application, and library is an Oracle Power Objects object, and each of these objects is stored as a separate file in the operating system. These main objects consist of other objects that comprise your database application. Following is a breakdown of the major objects of Oracle Power Objects.

Database Session Object A database session object controls the communication between your application and the database. When a database session is connected, its window displays all of the database's objects (tables, views, sequences, and indexes), like the ones shown here:

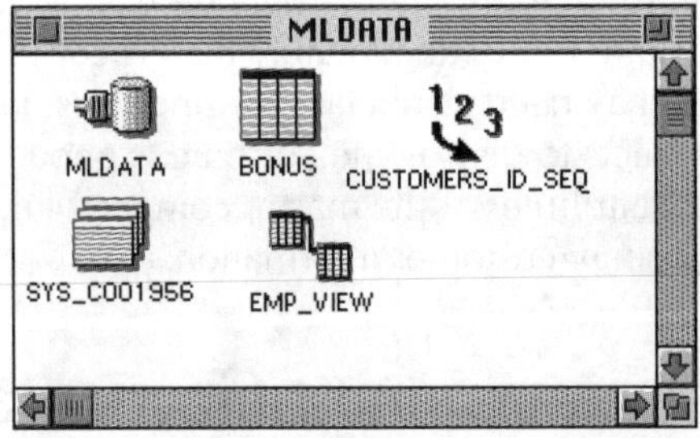

Application Object An application object is the user interface to the database, and it contains classes, forms, reports, OLE objects, and bitmap objects, like the ones shown in the following illustration. (Each of these objects can contain other objects like buttons, fields, and combo list boxes.)

Library Object The library object contains the same types of objects as an application. However, library objects, like the ones shown here, can be accessed by multiple applications.

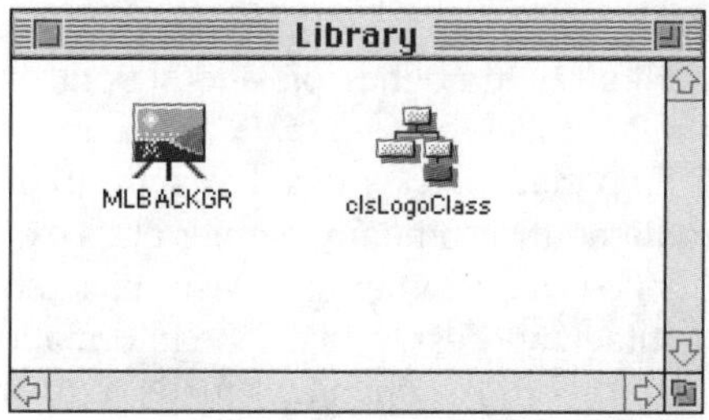

You create a library object to contain the classes and bitmaps for distribution or sharing. You can drag classes, bitmaps, and other objects from the library and drop them onto forms in different applications. Oracle Power Objects stores an internal name and path for each object, so applications using that object will not lose track of the library object even if you later change its name. Therefore, library objects can be created and used by developers on either Windows or Macintosh platforms and by individuals on networks who have different path directories to the library. The construction and use of libraries is covered in Chapter 6.

Inheritance and Classes

When you create a new form or button, you are creating what is called an *instance* of an Oracle Power Objects object. As we mentioned earlier, inheritance is the ability of an instance of an object to inherit the properties and methods of its object class. Whenever you create a database session, the database session inherits a set of default properties and methods associated with controlling the interaction between applications and database objects. By using the property sheet associated with an object and Oracle Basic, you can override the default properties, user-defined Oracle Power Objects properties, and methods. This ability to override properties and methods is an example of polymorphism.

With Oracle Power Objects, you can create the user-defined objects called classes. As we described earlier, a class consists of the methods (specifications of the internal actions, e.g., what happens when a mouse is clicked on an object) and the properties (external behaviors, e.g., the color of an object) of a set of objects. Oracle Power Objects' classes are bindable containers for placing static objects and controls (static text, fields, buttons, repeater displays, etc.). A *bindable container* is any object that can be tied to a record source (table) by its record source property. Once you define a class, you can add instances of it to multiple forms throughout an application (and with the library object, to multiple applications). All instances of the classes inherit the methods and properties of the master class.

While all of this sounds very complicated, it is really quite simple in practice. To summarize, classes are objects that you can reuse on any form or report in your application. When a class is placed on a form or a report, it is called an *instance* of the class. Instances inherit all of the behaviors and actions of the master class. A class can consist of a single object (button) that can be used on any form, or a set of objects (buttons, fields, etc.) that can be placed as a group on a form or report.

We've already introduced the company banner class example. Another example of a practical class is a customer class. This class could display the customer's company, contact, address, and phone information, to be placed onto an order form and invoice report. If a change is made to the manner in which the customer information is displayed or the information to be displayed for a customer, it only needs to be changed once to update all instances of the customer class.

To go a step further, you might create a control button class that performs some generic functions and consists of unique properties such as color and size. You can then use the control button as a master class to create subclasses called exit button, cancel button, and OK button, which all perform the operations defined in the base control button as well as additional operations relevant to the specific button. Classes are discussed in detail in Chapter 6.

It is the use of true classes with inheritance that sets Oracle Power Objects apart from most other rapid application development programs. Most database front-end programs like Visual Basic, Access, and PowerBuilder don't provide true classes and the ability to have subclasses that inherit the properties and methods from a master class.

OLE Support

Oracle Power Objects supports Microsoft's OLE, an object-oriented approach to using the same object across applications. OLE lets you embed an object from one application into another application. When you double-click on an embedded OLE object, the original application is launched and its menus and tool palettes appear for editing the object right in the object in which it is embedded. Any changes made to an embedded object automatically updates the original object (only if it is linked, not embedded).

For example, you could place an Excel chart OLE object on an Oracle Power Objects form. Any changes made to the original spreadsheet will automatically update the chart object. Oracle Basic can then be used to control how OLE objects will react to double-clicking and how they will react at both design time and run time.

Oracle Power Objects Database Connectivity

One advantage Oracle Power Objects has over other database application development tools is its ability to create user interfaces for local or remote databases that run on both Windows and Macintosh platforms.

Oracle Power Objects and Remote Database Servers

Servers for remote databases, like Oracle7 Server, can reside on a remote server machine (such as a UNIX-based machine or a Novell PC network server) or on the host's own computer if you are using a product like Personal Oracle7. Therefore, developers of database applications can create remote databases on UNIX, Windows, or Macintosh platforms, and users will be able to access the database using an Oracle Power Objects application on either a Macintosh or Windows computer.

Oracle Power Objects database applications automatically manage remote server database activities and support all of the features and capabilities of Oracle7 servers. Oracle Power Objects, however, doesn't provide tools for creating and administrating server databases. But, once an Oracle7 database has been created, you can add and make changes to tables, views, indexes, and sequences.

Oracle Power Objects applications automatically handle activities such as locking database records. Locking records ensures that the first person to select a record is the only one who can modify the record. This ability to control remote databases elevates Oracle Power Objects and high-end programs like PowerBuilder and SQLWindows over programs like Visual Basic, which require extensive programming to ensure data integrity.

Oracle Power Objects and ODBC Databases

Oracle Power Objects connects to most of the major external databases that support Microsoft's ODBC (open database connectivity) database standard. If your company has already developed a company database in a PC-based program like Paradox, dBASE, or Microsoft Access, you can use Oracle Power Objects to develop a database application for both Windows and Macintosh platforms that can access those databases. Not only does Oracle Power Objects offer you multiplatform access to company PC databases, but it provides tools for more easily developing powerful database applications than most DOS- and Windows-based databases.

Oracle Power Objects' Internal Database—Blaze

Oracle Power Objects creates an efficient and compact internal relational database, called a Blaze database. Blaze databases contain most of the features of larger server databases like Oracle7, and they consist of tables, views, indexes, sequences, and synonyms. While having many of the capabilities of larger databases, Blaze databases require significantly fewer system resources, so they will effectively run on either Macintosh or Windows machines. Data stored in a Blaze database is accessed through a subset of the Oracle7 SQL.

The Blaze database is intended for personal and small-company needs and works effectively for the following uses:

- **Prototyping** Because the Blaze database is a subset of Oracle7, it makes a great prototyping tool for any SQL database and especially for companies using Oracle7. You can develop and test your database and database application with the Oracle Power Objects database engine on your development system, without having to interface with a network SQL server database.
- **Small applications** Blaze provides all of the features necessary to create databases smaller than 4GB (gigabytes), which have a relatively small number of concurrent users. Databases over 4GB or databases that will be accessed by a large number of concurrent users need the extra database horsepower of databases like Oracle7.
- **Local lookup tables** Applications that call for the use of tables and views that change infrequently, such as your company's vendors, employees, etc., are perfect for Blaze. Applications like these will actually run faster using Blaze than using a server database.

- **Offline client access** You can develop Oracle Power Objects applications that download data from a large database and place them in a Blaze database. You can then analyze the data or make any data modifications and upload the data to the original database.

Blaze databases unfortunately provide no method to manage memory structures or processes. The Blaze database file contains all of the information, such as record locking, needed by Oracle Power Objects to control the database. The Blaze database engine also handles all necessary in-memory operations like interpreting and responding to SQL statements.

Blaze Database Specifications

Blaze has the following database specifications:

- A maximum file size (counting both the application and the database) of 4GB
- A maximum table size of 4GB
- A maximum long column size of 4GB (smaller column sizes are more efficient)
- A maximum short column size of 32K
- A maximum total size of all short columns of 1MB
- A maximum of 8,192 columns per row
- A 512-byte database sector size
- A four-sector (2K) database block size
- A maximum of 250 simultaneous *read-write* sessions (database sessions to which you can both view data and modify data)
- A maximum of 100 concurrent *read-only* sessions (database sessions to which you can view data but cannot modify data)
- A maximum of 350 total concurrent read-write and read-only sessions
- Unlimited sessions to read-only databases
- A maximum of ten concurrent *object locks* (the ability to lock a record in a table so only one individual can make changes to the record) per read-only session
- Text fields of 2,000 characters

Oracle Basic Language

As with other rapid application development programs, Oracle Power Objects uses a programming language to control the actions of the applications it creates. PowerBuilder uses PowerScript, a Basic-like programming language. Other rapid application development programs like SQLWindows allow the developer to compile the application into C code. Oracle Power Objects uses Oracle Basic, a programming language very similar to Visual Basic. Oracle Basic should be extremely easy for Visual Basic programmers to learn.

The ability to visually create forms and controls on the forms makes the creation of applications extremely easy. In most programming environments, it is the creation of the user interface to an application that takes the most time to develop. It actually takes longer to make the menus, windows, and to follow the user's mouse and keyboard actions than it does to create the functions to be performed by the application. With Oracle Power Objects, the interface to your applications is easy to create in the Form Designer window (see Figure 1-2).

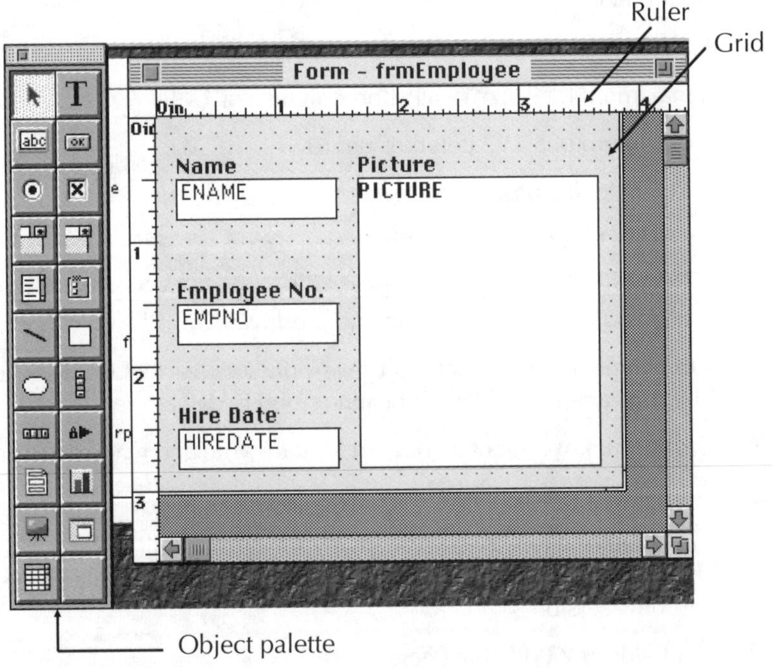

FIGURE 1-2. *The Form Designer window and Object palette*

Objects created in Oracle Power Objects automatically recognize events like mouse clicks, but how the objects react to those events depends upon the Oracle Basic code you attach to the object. Note that every object has predefined methods that handle these events, but you can modify the action of the object by writing Oracle Basic code.

The following are two examples of how a window is created, automatically opened at the application's startup, and designed to watch for movements of the mouse. The first example shows an abbreviated version of a C program in Windows, and the second example shows the Oracle Basic code that could be placed in any method to open a window. Let's start with the C program:

```
/* This opens a blank window with a small event handler */
#include <windows.h>
#include <stdlib.h>
#include <string.h>

long FAR PASCAL _export WndProc( HWND hWnd, UINT iMessage,
                                 WPARAM wParam, LPARAM lParam );

int PASCAL WinMain (Handle hInstance, HANDLE hPrevInstance,
                    LPSTR lpszCmdLine, int nCmdShow)
{
    static char szClassName[14];
    HWND     hWnd;
    MSG      msg;
    WNDCLASS wndclass;
    if (!hPrevInstance)
       {
        wndclass.style          = CS_HREDRAW | CS_VREDRAW;
        wndclass.lpfnWndProc    = ::WndProc;
        wndclass.cbClsExtra     = 0;
        wndclass.cbWndExtra     = 0;
        wndclass.hInstance      = Main::hInstance;
        wndclass.hIcon          = LoadIcon (NULL, IDI_APPLICATION);
        wndclass.hCursor        = LoadCursor( NULL, IDC_ARROW );
        wndclass.hbrBackground = (HBRUSH)GetStockObject( WHITE_BRUSH );
        wndclass.lpszMenuName   = NULL;
        wndclass.lpszClassName = szClassName;
        if ( ! RegisterClass( &wndclass ) )
            exit( FALSE );
        }
     hWnd = CreateWindow( szClassName,
            szClassName,
```

```
            WS_OVERLAPPEDWINDOW,
            CW_USEDEFAULT,
            0,
            CW_USEDEFAULT,
            0,
            NULL,
            NULL,
            Main::hInstance,
            (LPSTR) this );
    if ( ! hWnd )
            exit( FALSE );

    ShowWindow( hWnd, nCmdShow );
    UpdateWindow( hWnd );
    while( GetMessage( &msg, NULL, 0, 0 ) )
      {
       TranslateMessage( &msg );
       DispatchMessage( &msg );
       }
    return msg.wParam;
};
/* If this were a complete program you would need many more case statements
   to process the many Windows events. */
long FAR PASCAL WndProc( UINT iMessage, WPARAM wParam, LPARAM lParam )
{
     switch (iMessage)
     {
          case WM_CREATE:
        break;
          case WM_PAINT:
             Paint(); //This function needs to be predefined for this to work.
             break;
         case WM_DESTROY:
             PostQuitMessage( 0 );
             break;
         default:
             return DefWindowProc( hWnd, iMessage, wParam, lParam );
     }
     return 0;
}
```

As you can see, even in its abbreviated form, the C program in Windows required a good deal of coding. In contrast, the following Oracle Basic example opens a window named SalesReps when the application loads. This piece of Oracle Basic code is placed on the application's property sheet (in a method named OnLoad) for the selected application.

```
SalesReps.OpenWindow()
```

The true power of Oracle Basic lies in its ability to control all of the physical attributes of objects (properties) and actions to be taken when messages are received by an object in an application (methods) with a relatively small amount of coding. The functions to handle the mouse events are prebuilt. Additional actions are easily added by using the properties and methods of the object.

Oracle Basic Debugger

Oracle Power Objects has a full-featured debugging system to help find errors in your applications and a compiler that will compile either stand-alone applications or applications that will work with the run-time version of Oracle Power Objects. In Oracle Power Objects, if an error occurs when you are running an application or form in the Design mode, the debugger opens the object in which the error occurred and its accompanying property sheet, and selects the line of code that contains the error. With the Oracle Power Objects Debugger window, shown in Figure 1-3, you can set breakpoints (to stop the flow of the program) and step through a script. The debugger window lets you list all the objects used by the application being run in Design mode. Selecting an object from the object list displays its associated properties and methods. Selecting an object's method displays its associated method code. A watch window is used to view the values of variables, properties, and the result of expressions.

System Requirements for Windows and Macintosh Developers

Oracle Power Objects combines the programming power of Visual Basic with the relational database capabilities of many PC and Macintosh computer systems. Therefore, it is recommended that your development computer system meet the *recommended* and not the minimum system requirements. You need a fast processor for fast development, sufficient hard disk space for both Oracle Power Objects and for the desired database. Also, a high-resolution monitor is helpful

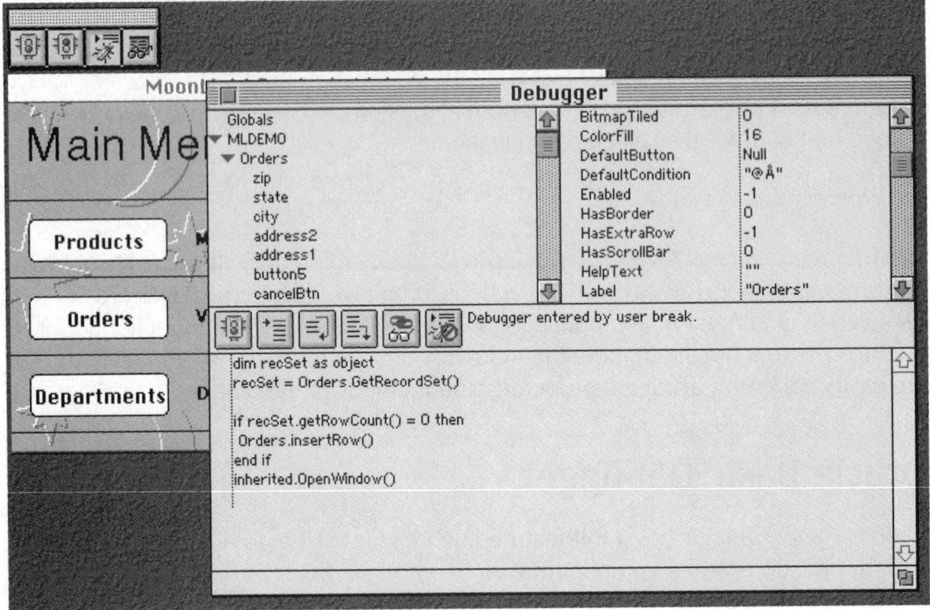

FIGURE 1-3. *The Debugger window displaying the Oracle Basic code added to the OpenWindow method*

when trying to view the form and report design windows and their accompanying property sheet.

PC Configuration

The following are the minimum and recommended system configurations for the Windows version of Oracle Power Objects.

- An 80386 running in Enhanced Mode Windows 3.1; 80486 or higher IBM-compatible PC is recommended
- 4MB of RAM; 8MB are recommended for development (especially with SQL*Net drivers) and 16MB are required if you will be using OLE 2.0 or running Oracle7
- 13MB of available hard disk space; 8MB if you don't install the sample applications
- An EGA display; VGA or higher is recommended

- MS-DOS version 3.1 or later
- Microsoft Windows version 3.1 or later
- A Microsoft-compatible mouse
- SQL*Net to connect to a remote Oracle7 server (optional)

Macintosh Configuration

The following are the minimum and recommended system configurations for the Macintosh version of Oracle Power Objects.

- A 68030- or 68040-based Macintosh; PowerMac-based PowerBooks or desktop models are recommended (for development purposes, you should avoid a small-screen Macintosh)
- 4MB of RAM; 8MB to 16MB are recommended if you will be using OLE 2.0
- 15 MB of available hard disk space; 10 MB if you don't install the sample applications
- System 7.0 or later
- MacTCP and SQL*Net to connect to a remote Oracle7 server (optional); MacTCP comes standard now with System 7.5

How Does Oracle Power Objects Measure Up?

Oracle Power Objects is clearly on the leading edge of the object-oriented development environment with its use of encapsulation, inheritance, and polymorphism. Programs such as Access and Visual Basic don't take advantage of inheritance and polymorphism, so each form and report has to be recreated from scratch; if you go back and make a change that impacts each form or report, you have to manually make that change. Most rapid application development programs like SQLWindows allow inheritance, encapsulation, and polymorphism, but they only provide single inheritance.

Oracle Power Objects is equipped with powerful tools for connecting to remote and local databases. Oracle Power Objects applications can have multiple sessions running at the same time; they provide the ease of clicking and dragging tables, indexes, views, etc. between the open databases; and they control database functions such as record locking. Oracle Power Objects has built-in reporting and graphing capabilities that include detail and group-by reports. Reports can contain first-page headers and footers besides the normal headers and footers. In comparison, Visual Basic requires extensive coding to manage connections to databases and database management and requires add-on packages for reporting and graphing data. These add-on packages often have their own distinctive properties for their custom controls, creating a hodgepodge user interface. Also, the add-on packages of Visual Basic may come with their own interesting set of quirks and bugs.

Oracle Power Objects' programming language, Oracle Basic, is similar to Microsoft's Visual Basic language and PowerBuilder's PowerScript. It is easy to learn and requires little coding to accomplish most programming tasks, and it lets you call DLLs and external Oracle Basic extensions. While not as fast as the C code that can be created with SQLWindows, Oracle Basic can be compiled to create reasonably fast stand-alone applications. Oracle Power Objects is one of the few programs to provide cross-platform development tools.

Oracle Power Objects does have a few deficiencies, as can be expected with any new product. For example, it doesn't have the project management tools of higher-end programs like PowerBuilder and SQLWindows, or the breadth of nice wizards of Access. However, any Visual Basic or PC database developer should take a hard look at Oracle Power Objects and its extensive set of tools for application development. Also, anyone looking to develop for both the Macintosh and Windows platforms or anyone using Oracle7 as the database server should look first to Oracle Power Objects.

Understanding Database Management

Because Oracle Power Objects creates front ends to relational databases, this chapter is designed to help you learn the fundamentals of good relational database design and to emphasize the need for careful planning. Proper database planning and design will save you time, energy, hours of frustration, and money. When planning your database, two factors are vital in preparation. First, analyze your present and future database needs; second, decide what database will meet those demands. For example, you may only need a stand-alone (as opposed to a client/server) database right now, but you must consider whether the database can handle increased amounts of data and whether multiple users will access the database in the future. Consider the following scenario:

> A startup company that sells and installs whirlpools wants to keep track of their orders and invoices on the computer. They hire an individual to create the database in a simple, inexpensive "works" program like Microsoft Works. After a few months of tremendous growth, the owners of the company find that the program is unable to meet their increasing demands. Besides keeping track of orders and invoices, they now need to track inventory and scheduling.
>
> Their database has become a nightmare to run. The program is slow and is designed for a single user (i.e., only one user can enter and look at data at a time), and it can't keep track of all the information needed. They have to purchase a new database program, create a new database from scratch, and transfer all of the back information into the database. This time, the whirlpool company selects a much better database, which meets their immediate needs more efficiently.
>
> But the owners, who have minimal computer experience, haven't consulted with anyone with database experience before purchasing a flat-file database. Though the new database is light years better than the first program, it isn't really designed to meet all of the needs of their company. Even more time and energy is wasted because of a lack of planning for their real long-term database needs.

Unfortunately, this is how too many databases are designed and created. The original database is built to meet a simple, immediate need and then increasing functionality is added a little at a time in an ad hoc manner. The resulting database is poorly designed and may never fully meet the future needs of the individual or company using it.

Proper database design begins with accurate planning of your personal or company needs, along with an understanding of *how* to design your database to meet those needs. In this chapter, you will be introduced to the purpose of a database, differences between relational and flat-file databases, a definition of relational databases, components of a relational database, rules for relational database design, and the preliminary steps to follow to design a database.

Purpose of a Database and the User Interface

A database is used to store small to very large amounts of information about a particular subject or group of subjects. For a database to be of use, the data needs to be easy to enter. Also, the creation of forms and reports must be uncomplicated, so that information can be retrieved and presented in a readable manner. Whether your needs involve a list of customers, a printout of the inventory on hand, research notes for a book or professional paper, or a customer order form, each case requires special planning to store, retrieve, and present the information. A good way to think of a database is as a file cabinet that holds data for a particular company, household, or other entity.

A relational database management system (RDBMS) like Oracle7 is a system that stores and retrieves data. One of the strengths of Oracle Power Objects is its ability to easily create complex forms and reports that act as "windows" to the data. These windows can be used to view information in Oracle Power Objects' Blaze database, a local database on your own computer, or a remote database (a database residing on a company server).

This flexibility of Oracle Power Objects to view and manipulate data stored in different locations is one of its strongest features. For example, you can easily store customer information, order information, and line items for an order in different locations (tables) of the company database. Then you can create forms, reports, or tabular views that integrate all of this data together. You can create an order entry form to display long lists of items in scrolling windows instead of viewing all items at once. And you can create a report to print the order as a regular order form.

The formats that Oracle Power Objects can create are of an infinite variety, including data lists, order forms for salespeople to fill out as they take orders from customers, and various types of reports. Oracle Power Objects knows where to find the information requested and how to present the data in the correct form for whomever needs it.

Flat-File vs Relational Databases

There are two main types of databases: flat-file and relational. As we compare flat-file and relational databases, the advantages of relational database design will become evident.

A *flat-file database* consists of only one file or table, with each entry containing all the required data defined within it. This is similar to a file cabinet in which there is only one folder—the folder has many pages in it, each page containing all the information for that specific entry. This makes it easy for the user to know where to find requested entries and all the data associated with them. The user copies only the desired parts of the entry to create the type of report needed at the moment.

Because all of the data is in one location, flat-file databases are extremely easy to put together and they can be very fast, if small, uncomplicated data sets are involved. However, if the data set is large and complicated, you face a potential redundancy of data and difficulty in maintaining the database. Consider the example of a flat-file database in which every order record includes the name, address, and phone number of a customer. You can see how this database can become overrun with duplicate data, which increases the size of the file (database) needed to store the information. If managed poorly, the database could contain many fields with duplicate data in each entry. Also, maintenance problems occur if customers change their addresses: the operator needs to go through the entire database, find every record for that customer, and update the address.

In addition, creating and analyzing reports on certain aspects of data in a flat-file database can be difficult. For example, line items in an order form are stored in many separate fields in the database. It is therefore extremely difficult to create a report based on the total sales of different products for the quarter, because they aren't in one location (field).

A *relational database,* on the other hand, is like a file cabinet with several folders, each containing only one type of data, for example, a folder for customer names and addresses, a folder for methods of payment, etc. In addition, some folders contain entries with information on how to retrieve associated data from other folders. This additional information is the *relational* part of the database. Because of this association of data between folders, relational databases avoid the typical problems encountered when using flat-file databases.

For example, in the order folder, each order entry has information pointing to a particular customer entry in the customer folder. Now, if the customer moves, the operator has to change the customer's address in the customer folder just once. File space is saved and redundancy of data is minimized, because the information pointing to the customer entry takes up much less space than spelling out the entire customer name and address for each order. In addition, reports that analyze the total sales of any or all items listed in the order are easy to construct because you only need to create a query on one field in a table. (There will be more on fields and tables in the next section.)

The cost of making the relational database more compact and easier to maintain is a slight increase in retrieval time over the flat-file databases. The relational database must find the order entry, retrieve the location of the customer entry from the field pointing to the customer entry, and then retrieve the customer entry from that location. This action is performed very quickly in electronic databases, however, and the advantages of having the associated data far outweigh the slightly longer retrieval time. A more detailed definition of a relational database and its components follows.

How Relational Databases Work

Once again, consider a relational database as a file cabinet with drawers that contain folders. The folders contain information that describes only one subject, and they also contain information pointing to related data in other folders.

A file cabinet not only contains your files, it also provides labels on the drawers and on the files to make locating information as easy as possible. In relational database terminology, your company's file cabinet would be called a database. A manager requesting an employee to retrieve an invoice from the file cabinet would be called an application. When you develop an application, you are developing the interface to the information in the database (an application written to create a user interface to a company's SQL server database is called the *SQL front end*). Your application is usually compiled into a stand-alone program that provides all of the methods necessary to query the data in your electronic file cabinet, enter information with customized entry forms, analyze information, and provide the desired reports.

In database terms, the collective files in your file cabinet containing related information form a *database*. A company database could include information about its employees, customers, vendors, orders, company products, and product pricing. Or, as another example, a library database could include information about the library cardholders, authors, publishers, titles of books, journals, magazines, and so on.

The individual files in a file cabinet correspond to *tables* in a computer database. A table contains information about one subject. For example, a company database might contain a table with information about each of its customers. In a relational database, you create separate tables for different types of information or data, such as customer information, vendor information, company products, and inventory on hand.

Each piece of information in a table is called a *field,* or *column*. For example, a customer table could contain fields for company name, contact, company street address, city, state, ZIP code, phone number, and so on.

A table also contains *records*. In the example above, each customer in the company database has an associated record. All records contain the same set of fields, but each record contains different information. In the customer table, the information for each customer appears as a separate record.

Tables also contain key fields. A *key* field contains information that establishes relationships in the database and how the records are sorted. A key field that uniquely identifies each record in a table, such as a customer id number, an order number, or a part number, is called the *primary* key for the table. Sometimes a combination of fields that make that record unique can be used as a key for the table. A field containing a primary key from another table is called a *foreign* key.

By using these key fields, data in different tables are related. For example, a record in an order table contains the primary key "orderid" to uniquely identify the order. A foreign key called "custid" references the customer information located in the customer table. The following illustration shows how the customer number in a record in the order table relates to, or identifies, the customer who made the order.

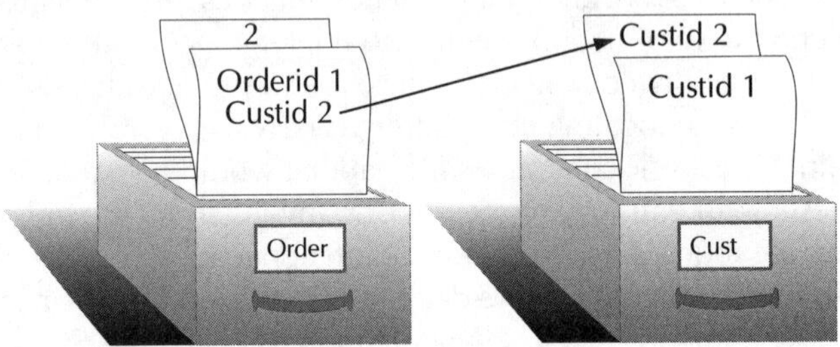

The components of a relational database are discussed in more detail in the following section.

Components of a Relational Database

Each database is comprised of the following components, which are either data or the constructs to manage the data.

Fields (Columns)

As mentioned before, data is contained in information blocks called fields, or columns. Each separate piece of data is declared to contain a specific type of data (called a *datatype*). There are many different types of data, but only four are of general use. These four types of data are presented in Table 2-1. Datatypes are important because they are used (in part) to protect the integrity of the data.

Various constraints may be placed on a field so that data integrity can be preserved. Some of these constraints are listed in Table 2-2.

Assigning these constraints and field sizes is part of designing the database and must be done with forethought. For example, let's say a column assigned to hold city names in an address table is defined as a string field containing ten characters; when Oregon City is entered, the database reports an error and disallows the entry.

Datatype	Description
String	Character data, such as names, addresses, comments
Integer	Whole numbers, such as 1, -5, 234
Float	Decimal numbers, such as 1.5, -2.68, 0.03
Date	Calendar dates, such as 10-21-47, Nov. 7, 1994

TABLE 2-2. *The Four Most Commonly Used Datatypes*

Tables

A table contains a group of fields of related pieces of information that define a single category, much like a spreadsheet. A table stores data in the fields (columns). Each set of fields that define one entry in a table is a record (row). In Figure 2-1, a library database uses a book table with fields for book title, publication date, number of pages, and a foreign key pointing to a record in the author table. The data for a single book makes up one record in the book table.

Other examples of tables include the following:

- Vendor information, such as phone numbers and addresses
- A list of your company's inventory
- Company products with a description of the products and their pricing
- Customer orders
- Book authors
- Serial numbers of items in your home

Type Of Constraint	Description
Size	The data must be of a specific size. For example, a string may be defined to contain no more than 30 characters, or a number field may contain only eight digits.
Not Null	The field cannot be empty.
Unique	The data in this field must be unique within the table. This is one way to specify a key field (i.e., two records won't have the same identifying data).

TABLE 2-1. *Constraints on Fields and the Data Entered into Them*

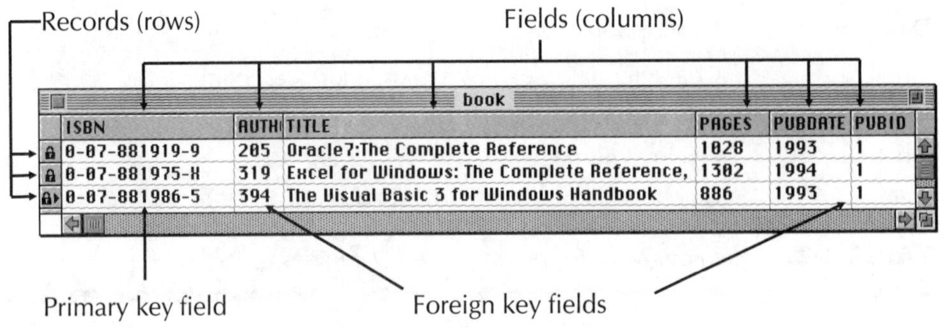

FIGURE 2-1. *A sample table with fields and records*

Internal Database Tables

Fields, keys, tables, and database constructs (discussed in the next section) combine to define a database. In addition to the tables that you define, some databases create tables that keep track of what is being done with the data. One example is a table of statistics covering the amount of storage available. In another example, a table keeps track of all editing done to a database during a user's session; if the user decides that a mistake was made, then the database can undo, or *roll back*, the latest changes to the database and restore the database to its original state. Using this type of table, however, can take up considerable space so you should save, or *commit*, the work as often as possible to conserve space in the database. When the work is committed, the database can no longer roll back what was done.

Once you decide how to organize your database tables, you need to create *database constructs.* With database constructs, you can optimize the database for quick access, create relationships between the tables, and specify who can access different types of data.

Database Constructs

There are many database constructs that help to define and efficiently manage your database. Indexes help locate data quickly; keys help tie data together; and authorizations restrict the editing of data to authorized users. A discussion of these three constructs follows.

Indexes

Indexes provide quick access to data in large tables; without indexes, data retrieval can take a very long time. For example, a query on a table with nearly two million records can take hours if the table has no indexes. However, with an appropriately designed index based on the key fields and the most used fields, the query time can be reduced to only a few minutes. Indexes are discussed further in Chapter 4.

Keys

Key fields enable the quick retrieval of information for a specific record in a table, and enable the database engine to combine information stored in separate tables. A key must be unique. As we discussed earlier in "How Relational Databases Work," a primary key is a single unique field (or a group of nonunique fields forming a unique combination) that uniquely defines a record in a table. The primary key can simply be an ID number, such as an employee ID number, an ISBN book number, or a part number. When you create a primary key field or declare a field to be unique, Oracle Power Objects prevents you from accidentally duplicating information in that field.

Key fields are used to relate tables together. For example, you can relate the customer table to the order table by placing a field in the order table that corresponds to the primary key field (e.g., "customerid") in the customer table.

Authorizations

A database can be designed to limit access by using *authorizations*. For example, all employees can access the inventory table, but only the personnel department can access the salary table in a corporate database. This is accomplished by assigning database user names, which may be associated with an individual, a department, or just a general class of users, and an associated password for each user name. When tables are subsequently created, one of the defined users is designated the *owner* of the table, which means only that person can view the data it contains, unless that person grants view, select, or other privileges to other users. See your database manuals for information on setting authorizations in your particular database.

Relational Database Rules

There are certain rules you should follow when creating and relating tables in a relational database. These rules govern how to relate data and prevent redundancy of data in the database. The first set of rules ensures that the database *is* a relational database (relational rules); the second set of rules simplifies the database and reduces the redundancy of data (normalizing rules).

Relational Rules

There are three major rules for relational databases that, when applied to tables in a relational database, distinguish them as relational.

Relational Rule #1 Each table contains only one record type (category of information). In other words, a table cannot contain information about a car in one record and an address in another record.

Relational Rule #2 Every record in the table has the same number of fields. No table can contain a variable number of fields or a set of repeating fields. Oracle Power Objects enforces this rule.

Relational Rule #3 Each table has a unique identifier (primary key). These fields are used to link related data from different tables. When you create an Oracle Power Objects table, you must identify one or more fields as a primary or unique field. You can set key fields to automatically enter sequential numbers or you can manually enter unique data into the field.

Normalizing Rules

Normalizing rules help reduce redundancy of data, make future changes to the table structure easier, and minimize the impact of these changes on the user's interface to the database. In general, these rules are easy to understand and are based on common sense. The first part of designing a database is to find out just what is needed, how items are related, and what constraints exist on the data. One example of a constraint dictated by the data is the use of several methods of payment (cash, check, credit card). The constraint is that the customer can only use one of these methods per order. In this case, you should create a separate table for the methods of payment.

Once you have collected the data and you know the constraints that need to be set on it, you create the necessary tables and link them with key fields. The constraints on the data are used to guide you as you build the tables. The general objective is to decrease redundancy of data and prevent loss of unrelated data if a value is deleted. After creating the necessary tables, you should be able to combine the data into the original set of fields.

We have compressed the five normal forms into two simple rules that will help you with your design of tables:

Normalizing Rule #1 Whenever data has a one-to-many relationship, you should create multiple tables.

For example, in an orders table, a field for the method of payment may consist of three different methods (cash, check, credit card). This is a *one-to-many relationship,* so the types of payment could be entered in a separate table called Paymethod (see Figure 2-2) rather than in the orders table. Notice that the primary key indicator is selected and the Not Null attribute is checked for the primary key field PayMethid. This forces the user to enter a unique number as the primary key to each record in the table. It cannot be left blank if data is entered in the Method field, which contains the types of payment. By selecting the primary key indicator, the user tells Oracle Power Objects that the PayMethid is the primary key field for the Paymethod table. The orders table then has a foreign key field containing an ID that corresponds to an entry in the Paymethod table.

Normalizing Rule #2 Each row (record) in the table must contain a primary key field (or a group of fields that acts as a primary key because it uniquely identifies the record). Each row must also contain associated fields that are mutually independent and describe an attribute of the entity that the table describes.

For example, a table of hot tubs consists of one field called Tub# and four fields describing its name, color, water capacity, and cost. Each field is independent of the other, and all describe one item, a hot tub. However, if the cost of a tub depends on the quantity purchased or on a wholesale versus retail purchase, then the tub cost must be placed in another table, because the cost is dependent on what is entered in another field.

These rules are guidelines only. It is not always advisable to place some fields into separate tables even though they may be multivalued or mutually dependent. For example, it is generally not necessary to break down a set of fields describing an address into separate address and ZIP code tables. This is because only one ZIP code is assigned to an address, and ZIP codes rarely change. It does not make sense to enter a ZIP code ID to reference a ZIP code table. This is called a *many-to-one relationship,* which means that many addresses may point to one ZIP code, but each address has only one ZIP code.

In addition to one-to-many and many-to-one, relationships can be classified as one-to-one and many-to-many. A one-to-one relationship is the matching of husbands and wives (at least in our society), so that each husband has one unique

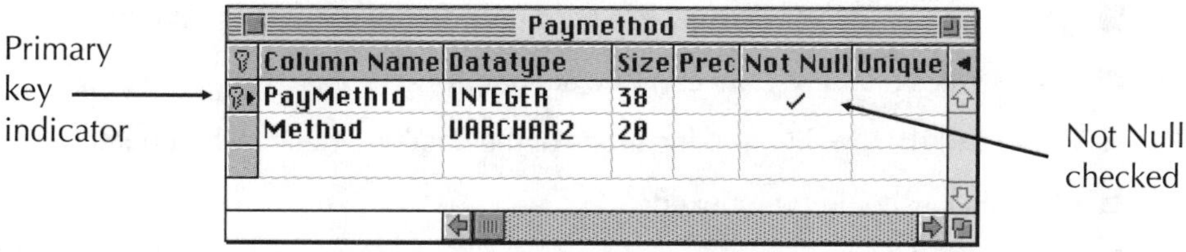

Paymethod

Column Name	Datatype	Size	Prec	Not Null	Unique
PayMethId	INTEGER	38		✓	
Method	VARCHAR2	20			

Primary key indicator

Not Null checked

FIGURE 2-2. *The primary key and null field indicators in the Paymethod table*

wife and each wife has one unique husband. Several makes of cars matched to a set of colors is a many-to-many relationship: each make of car can be in several colors and each color can be used by several different makes of cars. A many-to-one (children to parent) relationship can be just the reverse of the one-to-many (parent to children) relationship, such as an order number and all of the items for that order. It is up to you as the database designer to decide when it is appropriate to create a new table for a field or set of fields, based on data, relational, and normalizing constraints.

Planning and Designing Your Database

The first step of designing a database is to define the set of data that is needed to prepare reports, keep track of inventory, set up orders, etc. This set of data can best be obtained through a thorough investigation of what the individuals using the database really need. Problems will be encountered if you design a database based upon an interview with just one individual. Therefore, when deciding what information must be stored, interview the office managers who will be writing the reports and analyzing the business. Talk to the sales personnel who need to locate products, enter quotes, or track information about their clients. Ask the people in the order entry department how they presently enter the information into the database and what they like and don't like about their present system. All of these individuals have different needs that must be addressed to make the database effective for them to use.

Your interviews with different office personnel should include the following questions:

- What information does each employee need to store?
- How are these various pieces of information related?
- If information exists now, what form is it in?
- What kind of forms are presently being used and what changes are needed to make them more effective?
- What type of reports do they use right now and might want in the future?
- What types of analyses need to be accomplished?
- How will data in different locations of the database need to be updated?
- What data should be indexed?
- What type of computers and operating systems do they intend to use?
- What is their wish list for the perfect database system?

Once you have interviewed the personnel and studied their present forms and reports, create sketches or mock-ups (Figure 2-3) of the new forms and reports for review. From these forms, you can list the fields that will be needed for the form and make preliminary groupings of data into similar units. These groupings can then be stored in logically ordered files in the database, just as you would file similar items of information in the same folder in a file cabinet.

Once you obtain the information on what data is required, you must decide how to access that data with Oracle Power Objects. Because this list of information to store or retrieve can be quite long, you need to decide the best way to organize this information to effectively fulfill your database needs. If the data is currently stored in file cabinets, you will need to organize the database and create data entry windows to import all of the information from the file cabinet. If the data is currently stored in a corporate database such as Oracle7, you can use Oracle Power Objects to create a front end to that database with the necessary data entry, query, and report windows.

Creating a Database: An Example

Following is a real-world example of how the relational database rules and design concepts discussed above can be applied to create a simple order-entry system. Let's return to the small whirlpool tub manufacturing company we introduced at

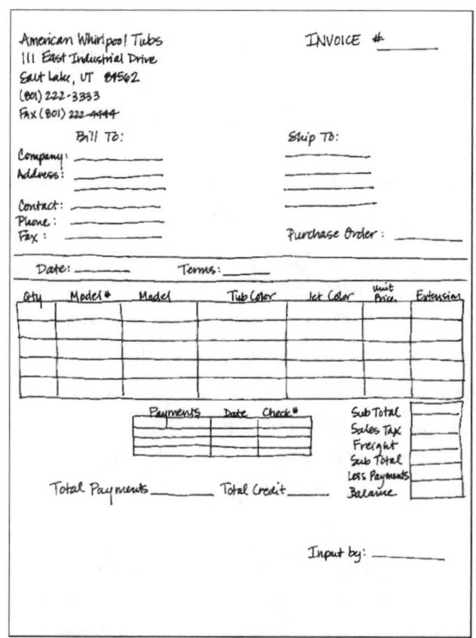

American Whirlpool Tubs
111 East Industrial Drive
Salt Lake, UT 84562
(801) 222-3333
FAX (801) 222-4444

INVOICE #

Bill To:
Company:
Address:
Contact:
Phone:
Fax:

Ship To:

Purchase Order:

Date: Terms:

Qty	Model #	Model	Tub Color	Jet Color	Unit Price	Extension

Payments	Date	Check #

Sub Total
Sales Tax
Freight
Sub Total
Less Payments
Balance

Total Payments Total Credit

Input by:

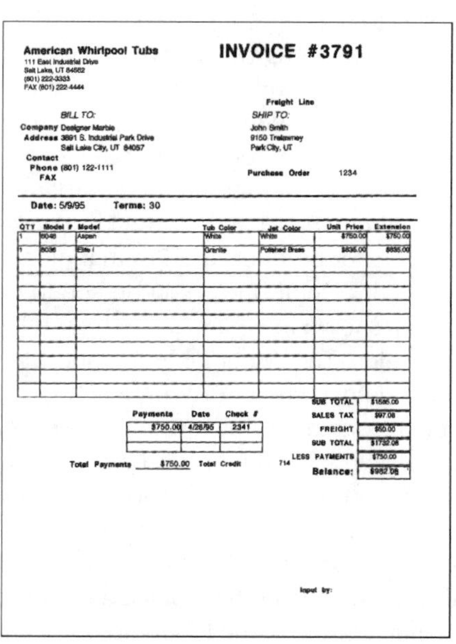

American Whirlpool Tubs
111 East Industrial Drive
Salt Lake, UT 84562
(801) 222-3333
FAX (801) 222-4444

INVOICE #3791

BILL TO:
Company Designer Marble
Address 3891 S. Industrial Park Drive
Salt Lake City, UT 84057
Contact
Phone (801) 122-1111
FAX

Freight Line
SHIP TO:
John Smith
9150 Trelawney
Park City, UT

Purchase Order 1234

Date: 5/9/95 Terms: 30

QTY	Model #	Model	Tub Color	Jet Color	Unit Price	Extension
1	8048	Aspen	White	White	$750.00	$750.00
1	8036	Elite I	Granite	Polished Brass	$836.00	$836.00

Payments	Date	Check #
$750.00	4/28/95	2341

Total Payments $750.00 Total Credit 714

SUB TOTAL	$1586.00
SALES TAX	$97.08
FREIGHT	$50.00
SUB TOTAL	$1732.08
LESS PAYMENTS	$750.00
Balance:	$982.08

Input by:

FIGURE 2-3. *A preliminary sketch of an invoice and its mock-up*

the beginning of this chapter. This example shows how using Oracle Power Objects can help fulfill the long-term needs of the company.

Let's say you have been hired to redo the company's database The first thing you need to do is visit with the various employees who work for the tub company. Discuss with all those involved their perceptions of what the database will do for them and the types of information they need to be able to enter and retrieve. Next, ask to see the computerized forms and paper forms they are using right now for entering orders, work-in-progress, invoices, employee records, product catalogs, etc. Now, armed with a basic knowledge of all the information they want to enter and how they want to view and retrieve that information, you can begin to analyze the tables that will be needed, what information to track in each table, and how to relate the tables.

Because the company uses a flat-file database, it currently has separate databases to track customers, products, orders, and vendors. One of the constraints placed on the present database (because it is a flat-file database) is that no more than twelve tubs can be entered in an order. The manager wants to track the work-in-progress of each line item on the order form. So 12 different work-in-progress forms have been created, one for each of the twelve tub detail lines on the order form. Each work-in-progress form has 28 different fields that uniquely identify the tub on the order form for an order of 12 tubs. Therefore, even though the information to be tracked is identical for each tub and the forms look identical, each form has to be created separately and must have 28 totally different fields (see Figure 2-4).

Using your Oracle Power Objects database, you can replace these 13 forms (the order form and 12 detail forms) with two forms (an order form and a detail form), and you will spend a fraction of the time designing the forms. There is no limit on the number of tubs that can be placed on an order. You can also offer to provide other services to the company that were impossible to implement with the present database, such as tracking product inventory levels and tracking multiple vendors for products used to manufacture tubs.

After careful study, you decide to design the relational database with eight tables, shown in Figure 2-5, which relate to each other using primary and foreign key fields. The Order table includes items that directly describe an order, such as order date, company, invoice number, and promised date. The Order table also contains fields to link it to the Custs table, Employee table (for the salesperson who makes the sale and for those who work on each tub), the Payment table (for a record of payments), and the TubDetail table (for information about each tub on an order).

A major constraint is requested by the plant manager: on the tub order-entry database, you can only place a quantity of one tub for each detail line. Because the manufacturing of the tub includes so many variables, it is undesirable to order more than one tub for each detail line. These variables include tub color, jet color,

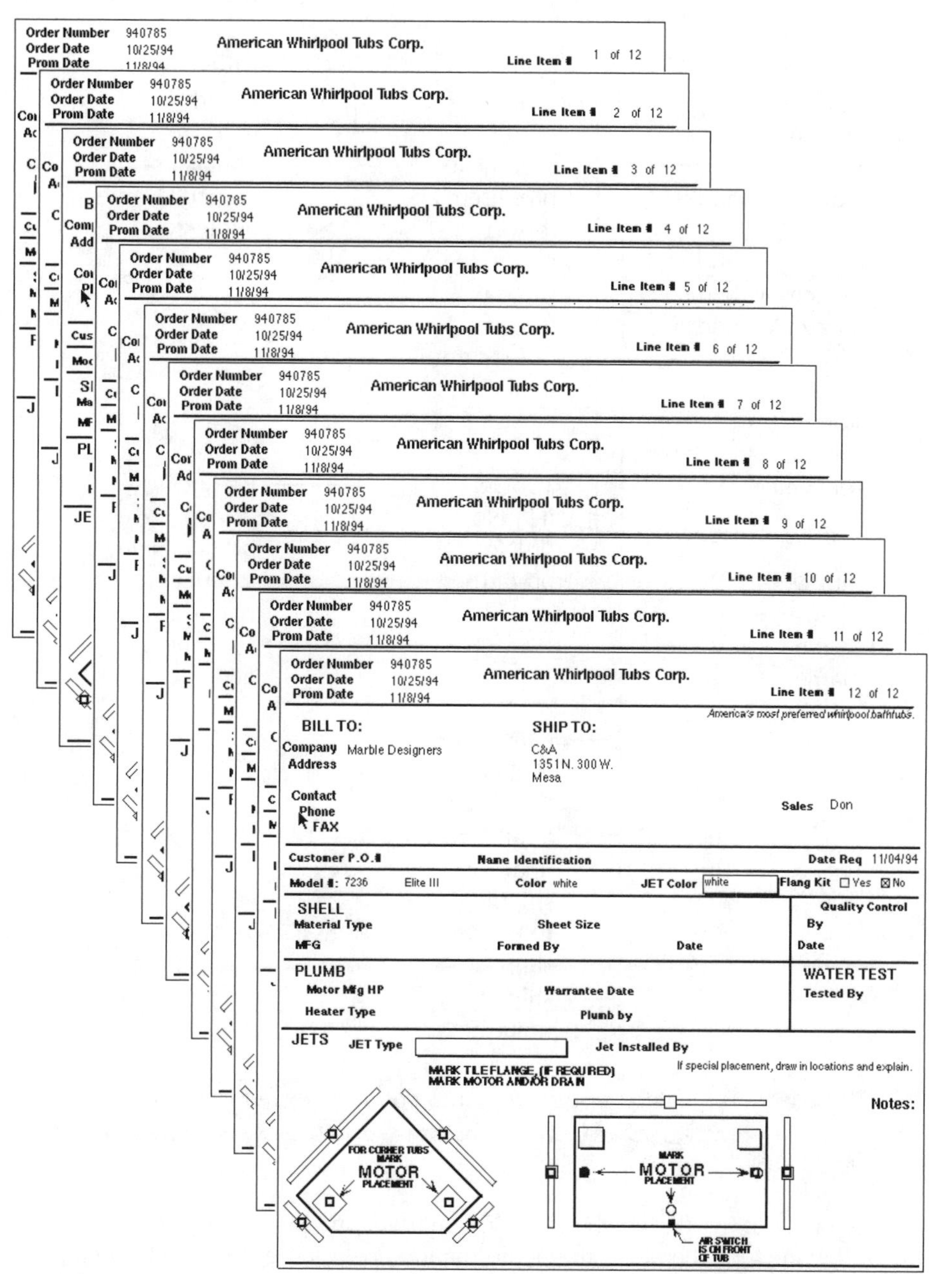

Order Number 940785
Order Date 10/25/94
Prom Date 11/8/94

American Whirlpool Tubs Corp.

Line Item # 12 of 12

America's most preferred whirlpool bathtubs.

BILL TO:
Company Marble Designers
Address
Contact
Phone
FAX

SHIP TO:
C&A
1351 N. 300 W.
Mesa

Sales Don

Customer P.O.# | Name Identification | Date Req 11/04/94

Model #: 7236 Elite III | Color white | JET Color white | Flang Kit ☐ Yes ☒ No

SHELL
Material Type | Sheet Size
MFG | Formed By | Date

Quality Control
By
Date

PLUMB
Motor Mfg HP | Warrantee Date
Heater Type | Plumb by

WATER TEST
Tested By

JETS JET Type | Jet Installed By

MARK TILE FLANGE, (IF REQUIRED)
MARK MOTOR AND/OR DRAIN

If special placement, draw in locations and explain.

Notes:

FIGURE 2-4. *Multiple work-in-progress forms created in a flat-file database*

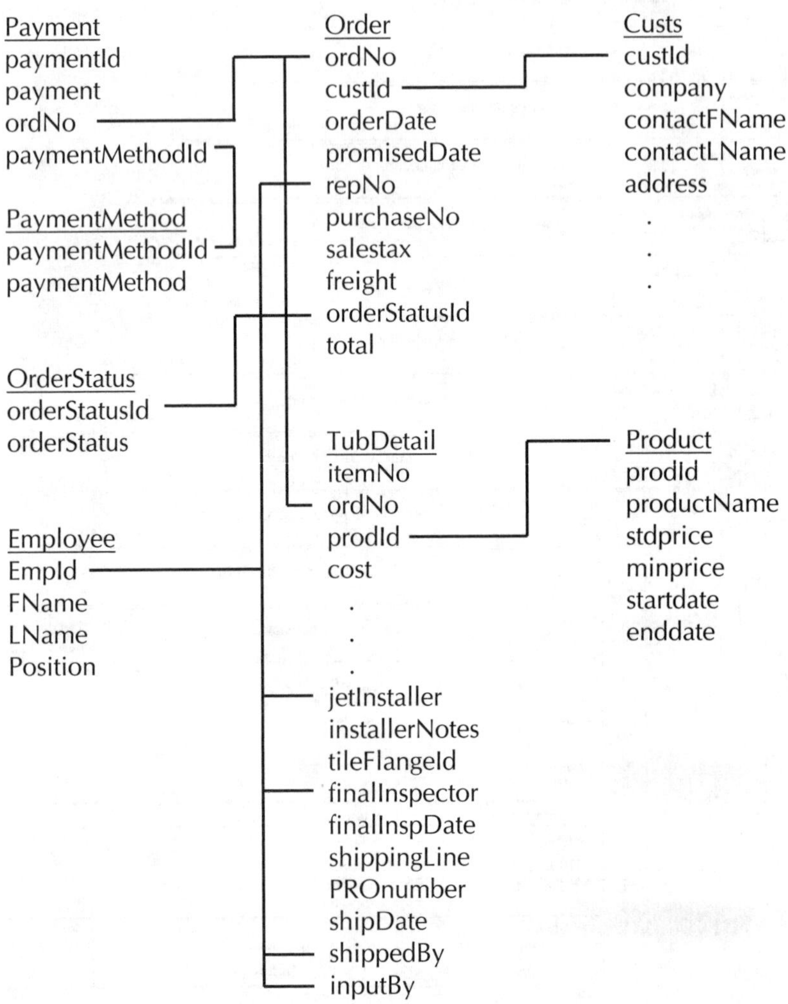

FIGURE 2-5. *Tub database structure (lines connect key fields in each table)*

number of jets to install, which motor will be used, and the employees who worked on the tub. Therefore, more information needs to be stored in the detail line area than in most order-entry systems, and the system needs to be able to handle numerous line items. Each tub is entered on its own detail line on the order form. Each detail line on the order form is tied to the tub detail item by the primary key, ItemNo. A separate pop-up form is used to enter detail information for each tub, and a separate manufacturing form is used to enter the work-in-progress detail for each tub.

The order-entry personnel ask that the forms for entering orders be reduced in size for ease of entry. Because all detail lines in the flat-file database had to be shown in their entirety (you couldn't scroll through separate fields in a single record), order entry staff had to scroll to enter data in different sections of the order form. With Oracle Power Objects, you can easily create a repeater display (covered in Chapter 6) that lists all of the tubs in a scrolling window.

This is a simplified example, but it illustrates the basic features of designing a relational database. Designing tables, fields, forms, users, authorizations, indexes, and more will be discussed in more detail as the various features of Oracle Power Objects are covered.

CHAPTER 3

Oracle Power Objects Overview

This chapter provides an overview to the Oracle Power Objects user interface, illustrating the rich functionality of its menus, toolbars, and windows. Regardless of the type of application being developed with Oracle Power Objects, the menus, toolbars, and other controls are the same and each will be described in this chapter. Oracle Power Objects runs on both the Windows and Macintosh operating systems and soon on the OS/2 operating system. We will assume that you are acquainted with the operating system in which you are working. Differences in operating systems are noted wherever there are significant variances in the interface or operation of Oracle Power Objects.

Oracle Power Objects Main Screen

When Oracle Power Objects is first started, it displays the Main application window, title bar, status bar, menu bar, and toolbar. In Windows, these are displayed in the Desktop Manager window, which is shown in Figure 3-1. On the Macintosh, these are displayed on the main screen as shown in Figure 3-2.

The Main application window can contain icons representing applications, sessions, and libraries. The title bar, at the top of the Desktop Manager window in Windows, helps identify that you are in Oracle Power Objects when switching between programs. There is no title bar in the Macintosh version of Oracle Power Objects. With the Macintosh, the active program's icon is displayed in the upper-right corner of the screen. The status bar (or status line) shows a brief help message when you pass the cursor over various parts of the Desktop Manager, and it also shows the status of operations in progress. On Windows it shows the status of the NUM LOCK, CAPS LOCK, and SCROLL LOCK keys.

Oracle Power Objects' menu bars and toolbars are context-sensitive, which means they change depending on whether you are working with sessions of the database, developing an application, or running an application. Menus provide

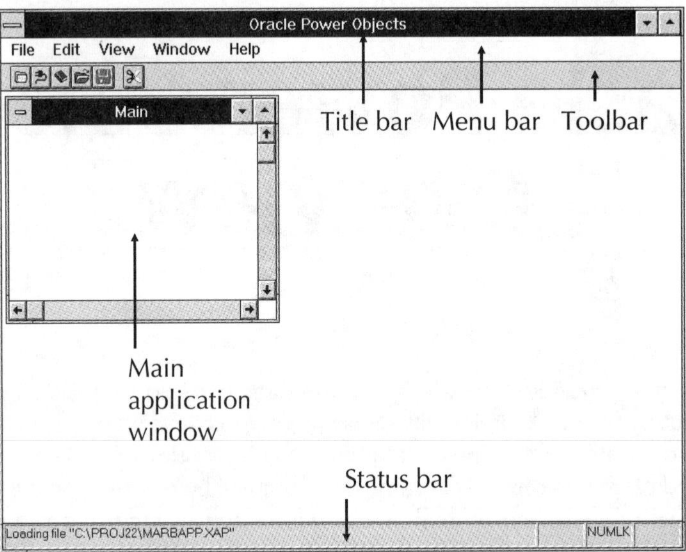

FIGURE 3-1. *Oracle Power Objects' main screen, as displayed in Windows*

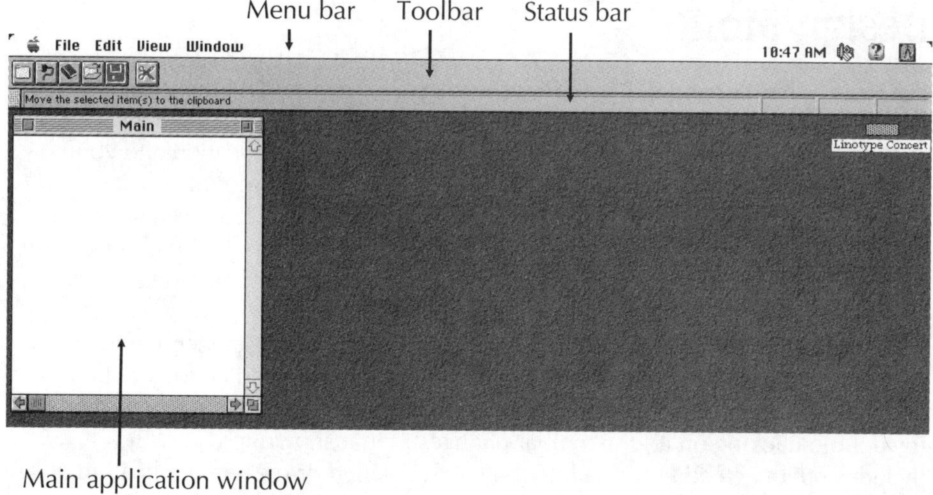

FIGURE 3-2. *Oracle Power Objects' main screen, as displayed on the Macintosh*

an easy way to access all of the features of the Oracle Power Objects database development program without having to memorize keystrokes or commands. You can click on the pull-down menus to browse the menu items. The menus are covered in detail under each of the following modes discussed in this chapter:

- Design mode
- Form, Class, and Report Designer modes
- Run-time mode
- Print Preview mode
- User Properties Edit mode (Prop Edit mode)

Toolbars display a set of buttons, which changes as the mode of operation changes. Many buttons on the toolbar correspond to a menu item in one of the pull-down menus. You can invoke an action by selecting a menu item or by pressing a toolbar button. As each menu item is discussed in the following sections, its corresponding toolbar button will be displayed next to it. Note that not all menu items have a toolbar button associated with them, and not all toolbar buttons have corresponding menu items. These "orphan" toolbar buttons will also be described in the following sections.

Design Mode

Figures 3-1 and 3-2 show Oracle Power Objects in the Main window, the state in which Oracle Power Objects comes up when first started. Select the New Application menu item or toolbar button to create a new application and go into Design mode. If you have previously defined an application, double-click on its icon to open it and go into Design mode. In this mode you create, read in, or open the highest level objects in Oracle Power Objects— application, library, and session objects. These objects are each stand-alone objects in which other lower level objects are added.

All of the menus that are available in Design mode are discussed in the following sections. When creating (by clicking on the appropriate toolbar button or selecting the appropriate menu item) or opening an existing application or library (by double-clicking on it), the toolbar changes to that shown in Figure 3-3. It includes buttons to add objects into the newly opened or created application or library. When creating a new session by clicking on the New Session button or selecting New Session from the File menu, the toolbar changes to that shown in the section "Database Editing" later in the chapter. (Creating sessions and applications is discussed in detail in Chapters 4 and 5. Creating and working with libraries is covered in Chapter 6.)

Each of the menus and toolbar buttons used in Design mode is discussed below.

File Menu

When developing applications, the File menu lists the actions that can be performed with existing or new files such as creating, saving, or printing applications, sessions, and libraries used by Oracle Power Objects. It is also used to import or export Windows BMP files or to exit Oracle Power Objects. The following briefly describes each of the items on the File menu and shows the toolbar button (where applicable) related to that specific menu item.

File
- New Application... Ctrl+N
- New Session...
- New Library...
- New Form
- New Report
- New Class
- New Blaze DB...
- Open... Ctrl+O
- Close Ctrl+W
- Save Ctrl+S
- Save As...
- Print... Ctrl+P
- Print Setup...
- Print Preview
- Read from File...
- Write to File...
- Import BMP...
- Export BMP...
- Exit Ctrl+Q

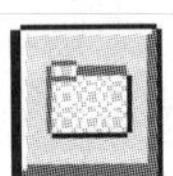

New Application This menu item displays a dialog box used to create and name a new Oracle Power Objects application in the Main window. It is within the application that you create your project's classes, forms, and reports. After naming the new application and pressing the OK button in the New Application dialog box, an empty window for a new application is opened and a new application icon labeled with its name is added to the

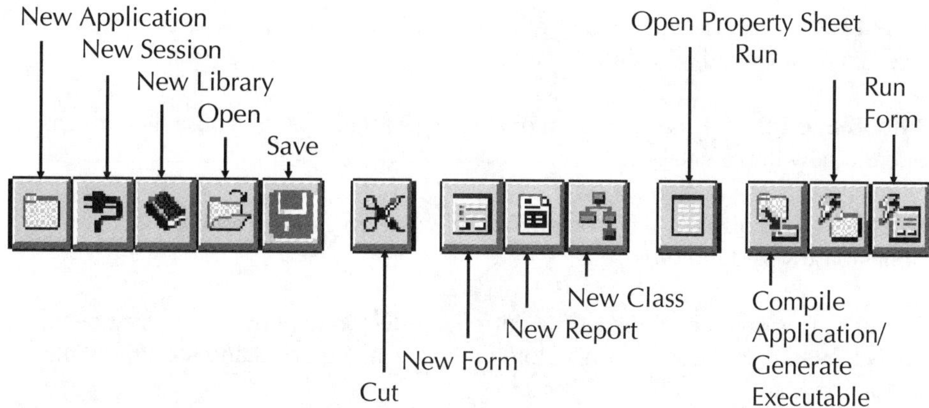

FIGURE 3-3. *Design mode toolbar*

Main application window. See Chapters 5 and 6 for more information on creating applications.

New Session A session is used to connect Oracle Power Objects to a selected database, whether a stand-alone database, a local database, or a remote database. Selecting this button first displays a dialog box, or "wizard," where you select the database to which you want to connect, as well as a text field in which to enter the connect string. After selecting the OK button, Oracle Power Objects displays another dialog box for creating and naming a new Oracle Power Objects database session, using the connect string that was entered in the previous dialog box. A window for a new session is opened and a session icon with its given name is added to the Main application window. See Chapter 4 for more information on creating and using sessions.

New Library New Library displays a dialog box used to create and name a new Oracle Power Objects library for storing objects that can be reused by different applications. After naming the new library and pressing the OK button in the New Library dialog box, an empty window for a new library is opened and a new library icon labeled with its name is added to the Main application window. See Chapter 6 for more information on using libraries.

New Form This button creates a blank form and places it in the currently selected and opened application window.

New Report This button creates a blank report and places it in the currently selected and opened application window.

New Class This button creates a blank class and places it in the currently selected and opened application window.

New Blaze DB This menu item opens the Create Blaze database file, which opens a new Blaze database.

Open Open displays a dialog box for selecting an existing application, library, or database session to open.

Close This menu item closes the currently selected window in Oracle Power Objects, which is shown by the colored title bar in Windows and the striped title bar on the Mac.

Save This item is used to save the changes made in the currently opened object, whether an application, form, class, etc. The first time a new object is saved, a Save As dialog box appears so you can name the object.

Save As You use this to save the currently opened application, library, or session to a differently named application.

Print Selecting this item sends the opened form, class, or report to the printer. This menu item is grayed out until a form, class, or report is opened.

Print Setup This item displays a dialog box in which you select parameters used to print the form, such as landscape or portrait mode, percent of enlargement or reduction, size of paper, etc. This menu item is grayed out until a form, class, or report is opened.

Print Preview Print Preview displays the selected form in a preview window just as it will look when printed to paper. Selecting this menu item causes Oracle Power Objects to go into Print Preview mode (see the "Print Preview Mode" section later in this chapter), with its own menus and toolbar. This menu item is grayed out until a form, class, or report is opened.

Read from File This powerful feature of Oracle Power Objects is used to read in a file containing an entire application or just a form, class, or report written out by Oracle Power Objects, perhaps from a remote site. Thus, a particularly useful form or class can be developed at one site and used at another site simply by reading in the file containing the form or class.

Write to File This menu item is used to write the selected form, class, report, or entire application to the named binary file. Oracle Power Objects can then read in the file to reuse the saved object and insert it into the currently opened application or in the case of an application, into the Main window.

Import BMP This item is used to import a Windows BMP bitmap file into an application. The bitmap can then be dragged and dropped into a form to be the backdrop for the form or other objects.

Export BMP This item exports a Windows BMP bitmap file used in an application to a named file.

Exit Selecting this menu item quits the Oracle Power Objects program. Oracle Power Objects will prompt you if there are any unsaved changes and ask if you want to save the changes before exiting.

Edit Menu

Edit
Can't Undo
Can't Redo
Cut
Copy
Paste
Paste Special...
Insert Object...
Select All
Create Subclass

The Edit menu contains items that are used to edit the contents of the various windows and to create subclasses. You can cut, copy, and paste items from one application to another, select all objects in a window, and undo or redo actions from this window.

Undo Selecting this item undoes the last changes made to the currently active window, which may be a form, class, report, or application. This item changes to Can't Undo when there are no changes.

Redo This item cancels the Undo you just did. Use it when you get carried away undoing changes and you go too far. This item changes to Can't Redo when no changes have been undone.

Cut Selecting this item cuts the currently selected object from the application and places it on the Clipboard. This works as a delete for the top-level objects, applications, forms, classes, and libraries. You can tell when Cut will act as a delete because the Copy menu item is grayed out. You cannot use the Cut button to remove selected text from a text entry window, it applies only to objects. To delete text, highlight it and press the DELETE key or press CTRL-X (COMMAND-X on the Mac). To copy text, highlight it and press CTRL-C (COMMAND-C on the Mac). To paste copied text into a text entry window, press CTRL-V (COMMAND-V on the Mac).

Copy This item copies the currently selected object from the application window and places it on the Clipboard. The menu item is grayed out unless the selected object is a low-level object or there is no selected object.

Paste Selecting this item pastes the most recent object placed on the Clipboard into the currently active application window. The menu item is grayed out unless the selected object can accept an object from the Clipboard.

Paste Special At times you may have created a picture or some other object using OLE-compliant programs that you can also use in Oracle Power Objects. You can copy the object onto the Windows or Mac Clipboard and then use this menu item to paste the copied OLE object from Windows or Mac Clipboard into the currently opened form.

Insert Object Selecting this item causes Oracle Power Objects to display the Insert Object dialog box. You then select the appropriate OLE application to create an object to insert into the currently opened form or application.

Select All Use this item to select each item in the currently active window. The next action you take will apply to each of the items. For instance, after performing Select All, if you select the Cut menu item, every object in the application window is deleted from the application.

Create Subclass Click on this menu item to create a class using the selected existing class as the master class (base). A *class* is a reusable object that can be dropped into other forms. For more information, see the section "Object-Oriented Programming (OOP)" in Chapter 1 and "Classes" in Chapter 6.

View Menu

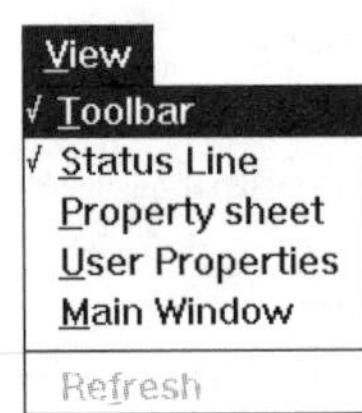

The View menu is used to display or hide the toolbar and/or status bar, select which windows to move to the front, and display the user-defined property sheet.

Toolbar The toolbar menu item toggles the Oracle Power Objects toolbar on and off. Turn it off to increase the window space in which to work.

Status Line This item toggles the Oracle Power Objects status bar on and off. The status bar informs you of the progress of loading files and offers brief help messages. Turn it off when you need more window space in which to work.

Open Property Sheet This button opens the property sheet associated with the currently selected object for editing or review. This is discussed in detail in Chapters 8 and 9.

User Properties This item is used to display the user-defined properties list so you can edit or create a property or method to be used in various objects (see the end of Chapters 7 and 8).

Main Window This menu item displays the Main application window, which shows icons of your applications. This menu item is necessary to redisplay the Main window after you close it to unclutter the screen while working on other applications.

Refresh This menu item requeries the database for new tables, views, etc., to add an opened session window. The new objects may have been added through a SQL program such as sqldba after the session window was opened.

Run Menu

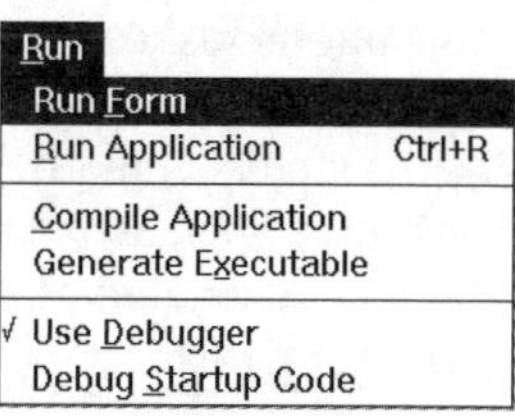

The Run menu is displayed on the menu bar in Design and Form Designer modes. It is used to run the application in test mode, to run the currently active form, compile the application, and to set up debugger options.

Run Form Selecting this menu item or pressing the associated toolbar button compiles and runs just the opened and selected form or report object in the currently opened application. This menu item and associated button is grayed out in this mode and is active only in the Form Designer mode.

Run Application Selecting this menu item or pressing the associated toolbar button compiles and runs the currently selected and opened application in Oracle Power Objects. It is used to periodically run the full application to test it as more functionality is added to the application.

Compile Application Use this menu item to compile an application to be run using Oracle Power Objects' run-time program. If this menu item is selected while in Form Designer mode, the application to which the opened form belongs will be compiled. In Windows, the compiled application will have a .POA suffix. This menu item and the Generate Executable menu item are combined in the one Compile Application button on the toolbar. When the button is pressed a second window is displayed. You then select whether to compile the application or generate an executable.

Generate Executable Use this menu item to generate a standalone executable program from the currently opened and selected application. This can generate a fairly large file. If this menu item is selected while in Form Designer mode, the application to which the opened form belongs will be compiled. In Windows, the compiled application will have a ".EXE" suffix. This menu item and the Compile Application menu item are combined in the one Compile Application button on the toolbar. When the button is pressed a second window is displayed. You then select whether to compile the application or generate an executable.

Use Debugger This menu item is selected by default (indicated by the check mark). This enables the Debugger palette to be displayed when the application or form is run. If you do not want the Debugger palette to be present, click on the menu item to turn the option off. When not checked, Oracle Power Objects returns directly to the designer windows and generally highlights the statement that caused the error upon encountering run-time errors. (This does not always work.)

Debug Startup Code There may be times that your newly developed application crashes on startup and gives you no chance to start the debugger. Selecting this menu item will invoke the debugger at the very first line of Oracle Basic code executed by Oracle Power Objects when the application is started. This gives you a chance to debug code entered in the OpenWindow or OnLoad methods which are executed as the program starts up and before a window and the Debugger palette are displayed.

Window Menu

Window
New Window
Cascade
Tile
Arrange Icons
√ 1 Main

You use the Window menu to create new windows and to arrange the placement of application windows on the Desktop Manager window (Windows) or the Main screen (Macintosh). The Window menu also contains a list of the application windows as they are created or opened. They can then be activated by selecting them from this menu. Initially, only the Main application window is listed in this menu, unless it was closed when exiting Oracle Power Objects. If the Main application window is not listed in the Window menu, select Main Window from the View menu to redisplay it. The order of the following menu items varies slightly between the Windows and Macintosh platforms. The Window menu is the same in all modes and is described in this section only.

New Window By selecting New Window, a window with the currently selected application is displayed. If a window is already open, it opens a second window with the selected application.

Cascade When several editor windows are open in Oracle Power Objects, this menu item can be used to place them in order, on top of each other, each slightly offset lower and to the left.

Tile When several editor windows are open in Oracle Power Objects, this menu item can be used to place each window in its own space in the Desktop Manager window in Windows or the Main screen on the Macintosh. Oracle Power Objects will change the size of the windows so that all will fit.

Arrange Icons If several windows are minimized, selecting this menu item arranges the icons at the bottom of the Desktop Manager window in Windows. This menu item is in the Windows version only.

[Open Windows] The names of currently opened application windows are numbered and displayed below a solid line in the menu. Selecting the window name activates that window and brings it to the top of the stack if more than one window is opened.

Help Menu

Help
Contents
Using Help
About Oracle Power Objects...

The Help menu is only on the Windows version of Oracle Power Objects. (Help is invoked on the Macintosh by selecting Help from the "apple" menu.) In the Windows version, select the Help menu to display Oracle Power Objects' online help, instructions on using Help, and the usual Windows dialog box that describes Oracle Power Objects. The online help uses Microsoft's Help engine and includes instructions on how to use Oracle Power Objects, a general reference to Oracle Power Objects, and a technical reference to methods, properties, the Oracle Basic language, and the SQL language.

Contents Displays the table of contents of the online help for Oracle Power Objects.

Using Help Gives instructions on how to use the online help feature, which is based on Microsoft Windows Help engine.

About Oracle Power Objects Displays the copyright notice and other information about Oracle Power Objects.

Database Editing

Generally, but not always, an application is associated with an underlying existing database. There are times when you will need to edit existing tables or add new tables, views, synonyms, sequences, and indexes to the database. This is done through a session (created by selecting the New Session menu item or pressing the New Session toolbar button). A *session* is an object in Oracle Power Objects that stores the information (such as the server and database to which you are connecting and the connection string) to establish a connection to a database. When you open or create a new session, the menu bar is nearly the same as in Design mode though many of the pull-down menu items will be grayed out. The File menu and the toolbar do change. When you open a table or view, or open a table to browse or edit a table's data, the toolbar again changes appropriately. The toolbar buttons and menu items displayed when editing a database are described below. See Chapter 4 for more information on creating tables, views, etc.

Opening a Session

When the session is opened, all of the defined tables, views, synonyms, indexes, and sequences currently defined in the database will be shown as icons in the session window. The toolbar associated with an open session is shown in Figure 3-4. Most of the buttons on the toolbar correspond to the items on the File menu—only the new menu items are described here.

The first six buttons on the toolbar are the same as those described earlier for the Design mode toolbar. The next five buttons, used for creating new tables, views, synonyms, sequences, and indexes, are described below. The last button on the toolbar, Open Property Sheet, opens the property sheet for the session. It is described in the "Form, Class, and Report Designer Modes" section of this chapter. The File menu changes to include menu items to create new database objects as described below.

New Table This menu item or button creates a table. New Table opens a blank table entry screen in which you define the fields, datatypes, etc. for a new table in the database to which the session is connected. The table name is given in the Name property in the property sheet. Upon saving, the table will be added to the attached database.

New View You create a new view in the attached database by selecting this menu item or button. A view is created by selecting a combination of fields from one or more tables and placing them into an object that can be used as a new table by Oracle Power Objects.

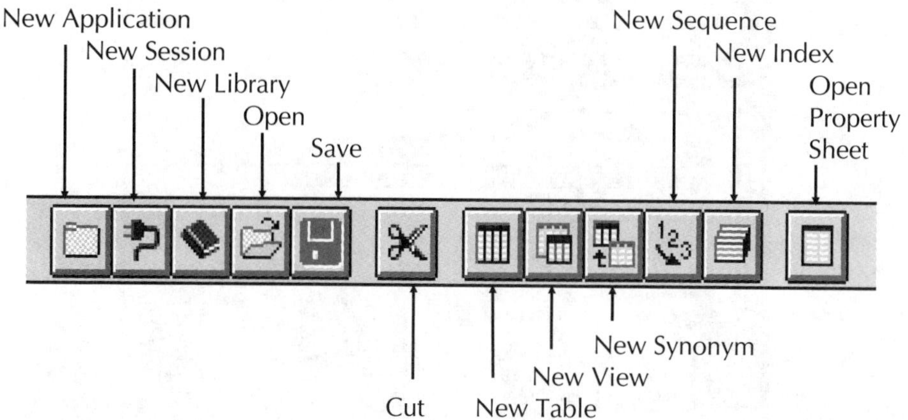

FIGURE 3-4. *Database Session toolbar*

New Synonym This menu item or toolbar button allows you to create a new synonym for an existing object in the attached database. The synonym name can then be used instead of the object's actual name in all transactions with the database.

New Sequence This menu item or button is used to create a sequence object in the attached database. A sequence generates unique integers to create unique values in the primary key field in a table.

New Index When a table contains many entries (in a large database, tables can contain millions of entries), it is necessary to create an index on that table, as described in Chapters 2 and 4. This menu item or button is used to create an index on the given table using the given fields as the keys.

Opening or Creating a Table

Figure 3-5 shows the windows in Oracle Power Objects (in Windows) that are opened when a table is to be edited. The toolbar associated with editing the table is shown in Figure 3-6. All of these icons have been described before, except the Cut, Copy, and Paste actions now apply to fields (columns) in a database. Thus, you can copy and then paste a common type of field several times and then just change its name, to avoid having to repeatedly enter all the information for each field. The Run Table button, which looks just like the Run Form button, is used to start Oracle Power Objects' Table Editor/Browser.

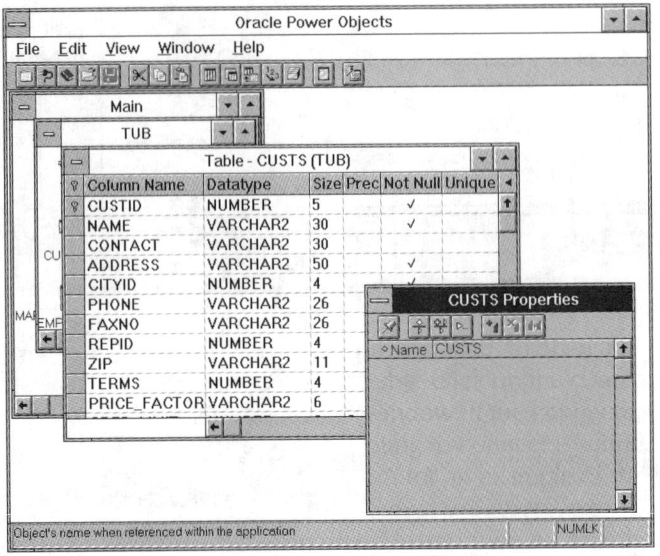

FIGURE 3-5. *Table opened for editing*

Editing Data in a Table

Database
- **Insert Row**
- **Delete Row**
- Query App
- **Commit Work**
- **Rollback Work**

After pressing the Run Table button, the currently selected table's data will be displayed for viewing or editing in the Table Editor window. The toolbar changes to that shown in Figure 3-7. A database menu is added to the menu bar with menu items corresponding to the buttons on the toolbar. This toolbar is similar to the toolbar described later in the chapter in "Database Menu" (within the "Run-time Mode" section). Use these icons to insert or delete rows of data from the

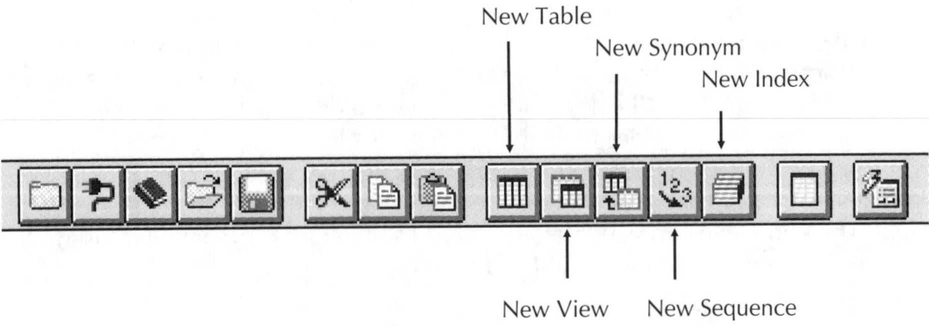

FIGURE 3-6. *Edit Table toolbar*

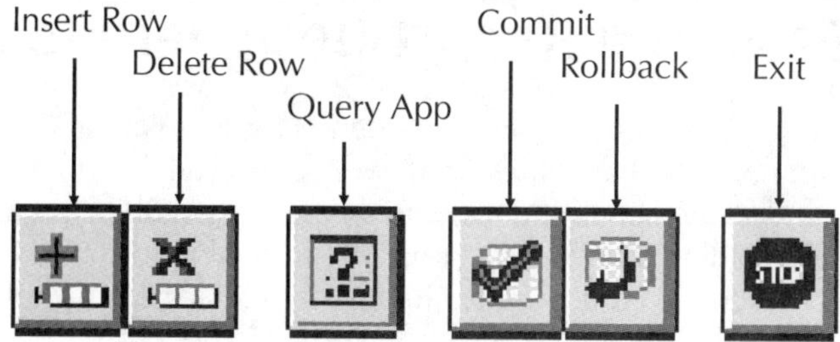

FIGURE 3-7. *Edit Table Data toolbar*

opened table, remove or make permanent the changes made, query the database for more information, and close the Table Editor window.

Insert Row This button or menu item is used to insert a row into the database above the currently selected row. This is used only if the order of the data in the table is important. Generally, you add new rows to the table by entering the data in the blank row at the end of the list of data.

Delete Row Use this button or menu item to delete the currently highlighted row. Oracle Power Objects will query if you really want to delete the row.

Query App There are times that you may have a Table Browser window open while running a separate application that may change the contents of the table from which the Table Browser displays data. Press this button or menu item to update the display in the Table Browser by requerying the database.

Commit As explained in Chapter 2, some databases keep track of changes made to the database but don't actually make the change until told to do so. This button or menu item, Commit, causes the data to be stored.

Rollback This menu item or button allows you to cancel all changes made to the database that have not been committed.

Exit Closes the Table Editor window. It corresponds to the Close item in the File menu.

Form, Class, and Report Designer Modes

When a form, class, or report is created or opened for editing, the Oracle Power Objects menu bar and toolbar change from what was available in Design mode. The File, Edit, and View menus change, and a new menu, Object, is added. Each menu is described in the following sections. The Run, Window, and Help menus are the same as described earlier in the chapter. An expanded view of the Form Designer mode toolbar is shown in Figure 3-8. The Compile Application, Run, and Run Form button functions were described under "Run Menu" in the "Design Mode" section earlier in the chapter.

File Menu

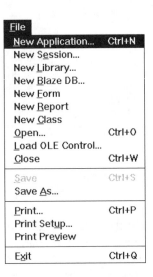

File
New Application... Ctrl+N
New Session...
New Library...
New Blaze DB...
New Form
New Report
New Class
Open... Ctrl+O
Load OLE Control...
Close Ctrl+W
Save Ctrl+S
Save As...
Print... Ctrl+P
Print Setup...
Print Preview
Exit Ctrl+Q

There are relatively few changes in the File menu in this mode than from what was available for Design. The menu items to read in or write out files are deleted, and the print features are activated, so you can print your working forms. (Now that the print features are activated, there are two buttons at the end of the toolbar that correspond to the Print and Print Preview menu items.) The Load OLE Control item is added and is described below. All the other items for this menu are the same as those described in the "File Menu" section earlier in the chapter under the Design mode.

Load OLE Control This item loads an OCX control into the Object tool palette, which allows you to place the OLE control object into active forms just as you place embedded forms, repeater displays, etc., into the active form. OCX controls are usually created with Microsoft's Visual Basic or its OCS CDK programs. OCX controls are described in more detail in Chapter 11. The Object tool palette is briefly described below and in more detail in Chapters 5 and 6.

Print This item compiles and runs the currently selected form and then prints the form. If it is a report, it will be printed as expected, i.e. several items per page. If it is a form, a page for each record in the recordset for the form will be printed. For example, if you have a form in which you enter a customer's name, tub selection, method of payment, etc., the printout will consist of a page with a "picture" of the form as it looks on the screen for each customer in the database. This is useful for invoices.

Print Preview This item displays the selected form in a preview window just as it will look when printed to paper.

Edit Menu

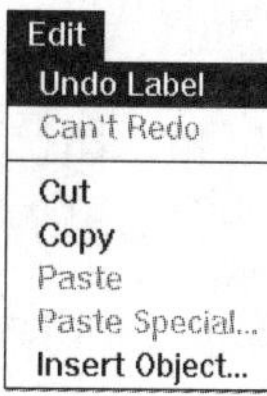

The Edit menu simply drops two menu items, Select All and Create Subclass. The rest of the menu stays the same and is described earlier in the "Edit Menu" section under the Design mode. However, there are now toolbar buttons that correspond to the Copy and Paste menuitems.

Copy This menu item copies the currently selected object to the Clipboard.

Paste This item pastes a copy of the last item placed on the Clipboard to the currently opened form, class, or report.

Object Menu

When in Form Designer mode, the Object menu (shown on the following page) is added to the menu bar. It is used to position or align the currently selected object(s) in the form, place the selected object(s) on top or behind other objects, edit the object's properties, or open a superclass (see Chapter 6). All of the menu items related to alignment require that more than one object be selected. This is done by

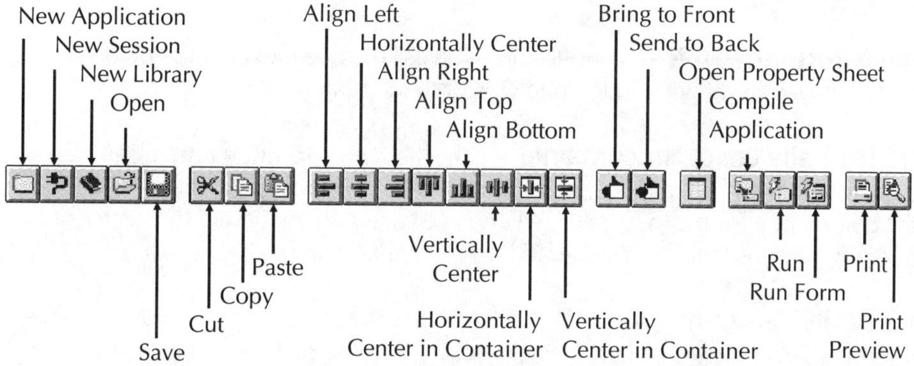

FIGURE 3-8. *Form Designer mode toolbar*

pressing the left mouse button outside the objects and then dragging the displayed box outline across all objects to be included in the alignment. Alternatively, you can click on one object and then click on the other required objects while holding down the SHIFT key (SHIFT-click).

Object
Align Left
Horizontally Center
Align Right
Align Top
Vertically Center
Align Bottom
Horizontally Center in Container
Vertically Center in Container
Further front
Bring to front
Further back
Send to back
View in own window
Open Superclass

Align Left Clicking this menu item causes all selected objects in a form to align themselves according to their left edge. All the objects are aligned with the left edge of the object furthest to the left on the form.

Horizontally Center Clicking this menu item causes all selected objects in a form to align themselves according to their horizontal centers. In other words, Oracle Power Objects places objects in rows with the objects' centers aligned. Oracle Power Objects calculates the average of the center point of all the nonaligned selected objects and uses that point to align the horizontal centers of the selected objects.

Align Right This item works the same as Align Left, except the objects' right edges are aligned to the one furthest to the right.

Align Top This item acts the same as Align Left, except the objects' top edges are aligned to the one closest to the top of the form.

Vertically Center This item is the same as Horizontally Center, except the vertical center of each object is used for alignment. This is used to align the centers of objects in columns.

Align Bottom This item works the same as Align Left, except the objects' bottom edges are aligned to the one closest to the bottom of the form.

Horizontally Center in Container This item centers one or more selected objects with the horizontal center of the form. For example, a single exit button at the bottom of a form can be selected and automatically moved to the center of the form, by selecting the exit button and then this menu item.

Vertically Center in Container This item is the same as Horizontally Center in Container, except Oracle Power Objects moves the selected objects to the vertical middle of the form.

Further Front This menu item moves the selected object one level closer to the top of the form. Picture a desk with four file folders stacked on top of each other. If the bottom folder is selected, Further Front exchanges the bottom and next to bottom folder. If the selected object is on top of the other objects, this menu item is grayed out.

Bring to Front Bring to Front moves the selected object to the top of all the objects in the form. For example, the folder on the bottom of the stack is moved to the top of the stack.

Further Back This item is similar to Further Front, except it moves the selected object one level towards the bottom. If the selected object is on the bottom, this menu item is grayed out.

Send to Back Send to Back is similar to Bring to Front, except it places the selected object on the bottom.

View in Own Window This menu item opens an edit window for the selected object. The selected object must be a class, embedded form, or other object that has its own edit window. For example, if you have a class with an exit button that you have placed in a form, then you can select the exit button in the form being edited and then select this menu item to display the exit button in its own form editor. Any changes made to the class here will not be inherited by other forms containing the class.

Open Superclass The Open Superclass item opens the master class (not the *instance* of the class in the current selected object) in an edit window. It is very similar to View in Own Window, except you edit the master class itself, which affects all applications that use the class being edited.

View Menu

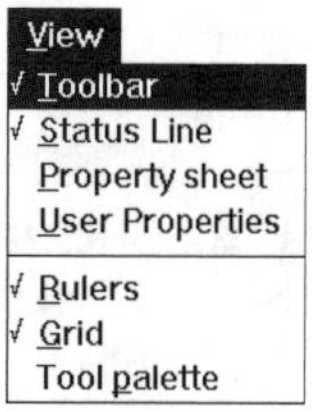

The View menu in Form Designer mode retains the same first four items (Toolbar, Status Line, Property Sheet, and User Properties) described earlier in the "View Menu" section under the Design mode. It also adds the ability to show or hide rulers, a grid, and the appropriate tool palette.

Rulers Selecting Rulers toggles on and off the display of the rulers along the top and left side of the form, which show the actual dimension of the form being edited.

Grid This item toggles on and off the display of the points defining the grid on a form. It does not turn off the grid snap. The grid is used to orient objects placed in the form. If you move an object, it will automatically align its top and left side with the grid when you release the mouse button. You can override the snap-to-grid action by pressing the CTRL button while dragging the selected item to the desired location on the form. There is no option to turn off the grid snap.

Tool Palette The Tool Palette item toggles on or off the display of the Object tool palette used to add controls to a form. The icons in the palette are described below, and a detailed description of each tool or painter in the Object tool palette is presented in Chapter 5.

The Object Palette

In Form Designer mode, Oracle Power Objects displays a palette to add controls to the object opened for editing. The Object palette is shown in Figure 3-9. A brief description of the tools follows. A complete description of this Object palette is in Chapter 5.

You use the Object palette whenever you are in the Form, Class, and Report Designer modes. This floating palette provides an easy method for adding controls to the selected Oracle Power Objects object. These controls include the ability to add static text, text fields, graphic objects, repeater display, and subforms to the current form being edited. These tools are described in detail in Chapters 5 and 6.

Pointer Arrow This tool simply changes the cursor to the arrow pointer which is used to select, move, or resize objects in Oracle Power Objects. Use this button to change the cursor back to the pointer if you inadvertantly select the wrong control.

Static Text This tool places static text for labels, instructions, etc., onto forms, classes, or reports, which cannot be changed at run time.

Text Fields Text fields can be added onto a form, report, or class, in which the end user can input data. The end user can also view data retrieved from the database or calculated by other methods.

Push Button This tool adds a push button onto a form, report, or class. A push button is clicked to accomplish some user-defined action, such as exiting the application.

Radio Button Radio buttons (option buttons generally in a group) can be added onto a form, report, or class. You use radio buttons to limit the user to select

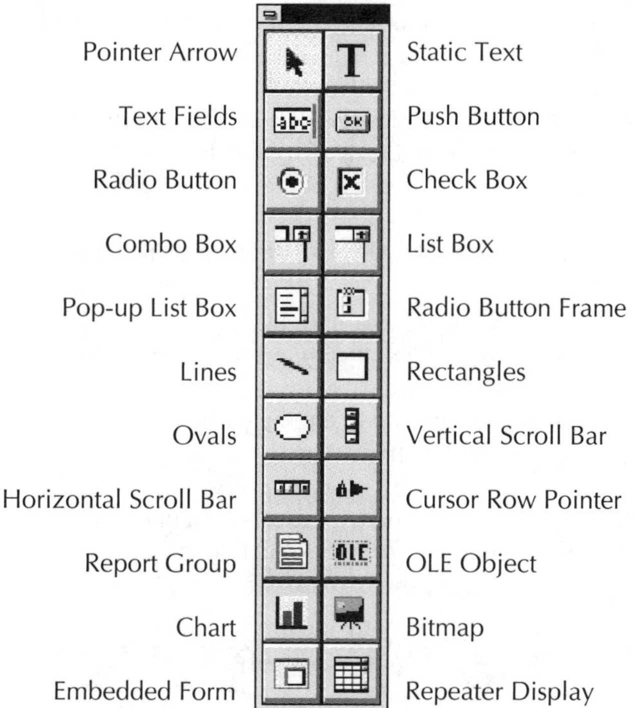

FIGURE 3-9. *Object palette*

only one item from the group. When a radio button option is selected, any previously selected options are deselected. For example, radio buttons might be used to specify what color of tub a customer is ordering.

Check Box This tool provides a check box that toggles on or off. You can use check boxes instead of radio buttons to provide multiple selection of related options. For example, multiple options for a tub could be selected at one time.

Combo Box This tool adds a combo box, which combines a text box (the end user can enter a value) with a pull-down list of values or options (the end user can select a value). One example is a list of cities from which to choose when filling in an address. A new city can be added, if necessary.

List Box This tool adds a nonresizable (in Run-time mode) list box of choices to the open object. The list box is always open and may have scroll bars to enable the end user to view all values in the list.

Pop-up List Box The Pop-up List Box tool adds an object similar to the combo box from which to select a value, except it does not contain an editable text box.

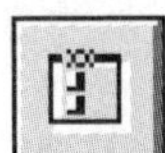

Radio Button Frame This tool adds a bindable control to the selected form, class, or report in which radio buttons are grouped together. Selecting a radio button from the group deselects all other buttons in the frame.

Lines This tool adds a straight line to the open form. You can modify the length and position of the line.

Rectangles This tool adds a resizable rectangle to the open object.

Ovals The Oval tool adds an oval to the open object. You adjust the size and shape to what is required for the application.

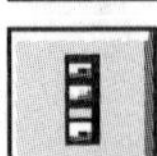

Vertical Scroll Bar This tool adds a vertical scroll bar to the open object. You then attach it to a repeater or form to scroll through data, or you use it to generate values.

Horizontal Scroll Bar This tool adds a horizontal scroll bar to the open object.

Cursor Row Pointer The Cursor Row Pointer tool adds little arrows to the edge of a row in a detail view, to show the status of the row: whether it is active (black), the current row but not active (gray), or neither (white). A "lock" displayed in the pointer control indicates the value in the row has been changed.

Report Group This tool adds a group header and footer to a report form. This is used to group similar items together in the report.

OLE Object This powerful feature of Oracle Power Objects allows you to add an OLE object to the currently open form. How to use this function is described in Chapter 11.

Chart You add a chart using one table column as the x axis and one or more table columns as the y axis by selecting this icon.

Bitmap This is an alternative method of adding a bitmap to a form. The first method is to import a bitmap file into an application and then drag it onto the form. Use this control to add a bitmap stored in the database (as a long raw) directly to a form. (Also called a Picture object.)

Embedded Form The Embedded Form tool adds a subform to an open object. The subform can any objects that a main form can contain.

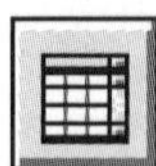

Repeater Display This tool adds a repeater display to the form. A repeater display consists of a primary container in which various objects are placed, secondary panels to show the number of records to be displayed at a time, and an optional vertical scroll bar. A different record of the data retrieved by the objects in the primary container is displayed in the selected number of repeater panels. This can be used to show a list of all items being purchased on an order form, for example.

Run-time Mode

The menu bar and toolbar displayed when Oracle Power Objects is in Run-time mode is shown in Figure 3-10. The main use of the menus is to work with information in the database.

The File and Edit menus are the same as in Form Dsigner mode, except most of the File menu is grayed out and all of the Edit menu is grayed out. The Window and Help menus are the same as those for the other modes. The new menu, Database, is discussed below.

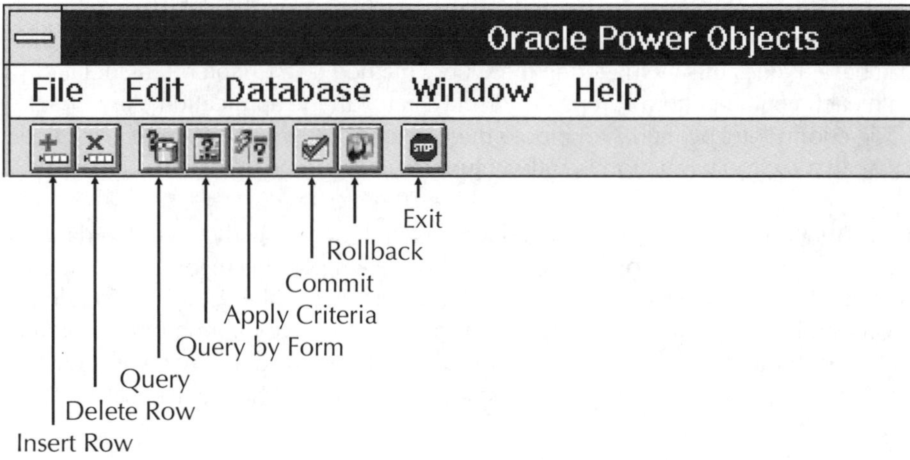

FIGURE 3-10. *Run-time mode menu bar and toolbar*

Database Menu

This menu, shown here, contains items that add or delete data from the database, update the forms being displayed, and save or undo any changes made to the data in the database.

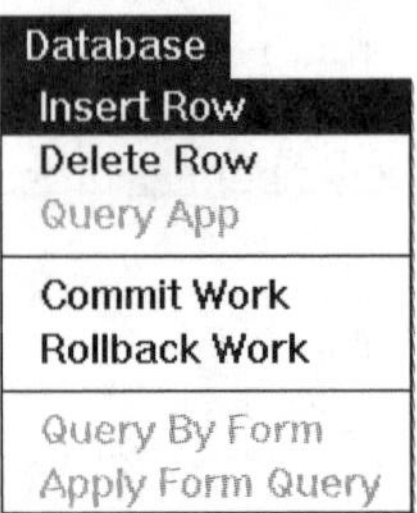

Insert Row This item inserts a new row or record into the table. This item is grayed out until a row is selected in the form displaying data from the database in a repeater object. (See Chapter 6 for descriptions of this object). When you select a row and select this menu item, a row is inserted into the database above the selected row.

Delete Row This item deletes the selected row or record from the database.

Query App Query App forces Oracle Power Objects to update the data in the currently running form. It is used if the data has changed in the database while the form is running. This item simply has the form reload the necessary data from the database. It does this by triggering the Query method (see Chapter 9) associated with each container (forms, repeater displays, etc.) in the application. Any Oracle Basic code added by the developer to the container's Query methods is executed. (Note that the toolbar button is called Query.)

Commit Work After you have added, deleted, or changed data in the database using the running form, you save the work by clicking on this menu item or toolbar button. This item is grayed out until you make changes to the database. Oracle Power Objects will prompt you to commit your work (save information) if you try to close a form in which you have added data but not saved it. Once you save the data, this menu item will once again be grayed out. (Note that the toolbar button is called Commit.)

Rollback Work This is the undo feature for the database. As long as you have not committed the work, you may select this item to restore the database to its original configuration. If the work was previously committed, or no changes have been made to the database, this item is grayed out. (Note that the toolbar button is called Rollback.)

Query by Form Oracle Power Objects displays a query window for the currently opened form. You can then enter criteria, specified constraints, filters, etc., that Oracle Power Objects uses to find the rows containing data that fits the criteria.

Apply Form Query After filling in the desired criteria in the Query window, selecting this button or menu item applies it to the active form to display the retrieved data that fits the criteria. (Note that the toolbar button is called Apply Criteria.)

Debugger Palette

When you go into Run-time mode (which includes running only a form), a small debug palette is displayed. This palette is shown in Figure 3-11 with each button labeled. You use the icons in the palette to open the debug windows to debug an application. See Chapter 7 for a full description of using Oracle Power Objects' Debugger. A brief description of each button on the palette is given below.

Resume After you have reached a breakpoint in running your application and have examined the method code under question, you press this button to resume the execution of the application.

Stop If you have reached a point in debugging the application where you need to revise the method code, press this button to abort the application and return to Form Designer mode.

Start Debugger Press this button to open the Debugger Main window.

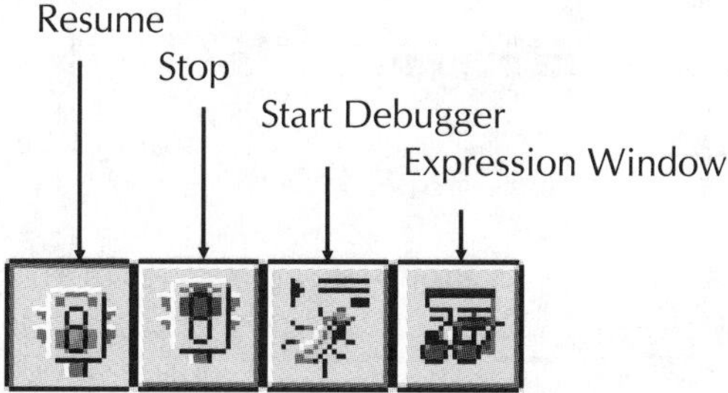

FIGURE 3-11. *The Debugger palette, used to help debug your applications*

Expression Window Press this button to open both the Debugger Main window and the Expression window.

After pressing the Start Debugger button, the Main debugger window is displayed. It includes a toolbar with buttons to navigate through the application. The Main debugger window (with the Debugger toolbar) and the Expression window is shown in Figure 3-12. An expanded labeled view of the debug toolbar is shown in Figure 3-13. A brief description of each toolbar button is given below.

Resume This button is the same as the Resume button on the Debugger palette. It tells Oracle Power Objects to resume execution of the application.

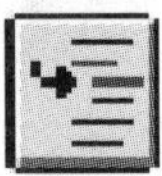

Step Into After you have reached a break point in the Oracle Basic code in a method of your application, press this button to execute one line of method code at a time.

Step Over As you execute one line of Oracle Basic code at a time in a method, there may be some lines of code that trigger other methods in the application. Press this button to execute the line of code but stay in the current method rather than stepping into the called method.

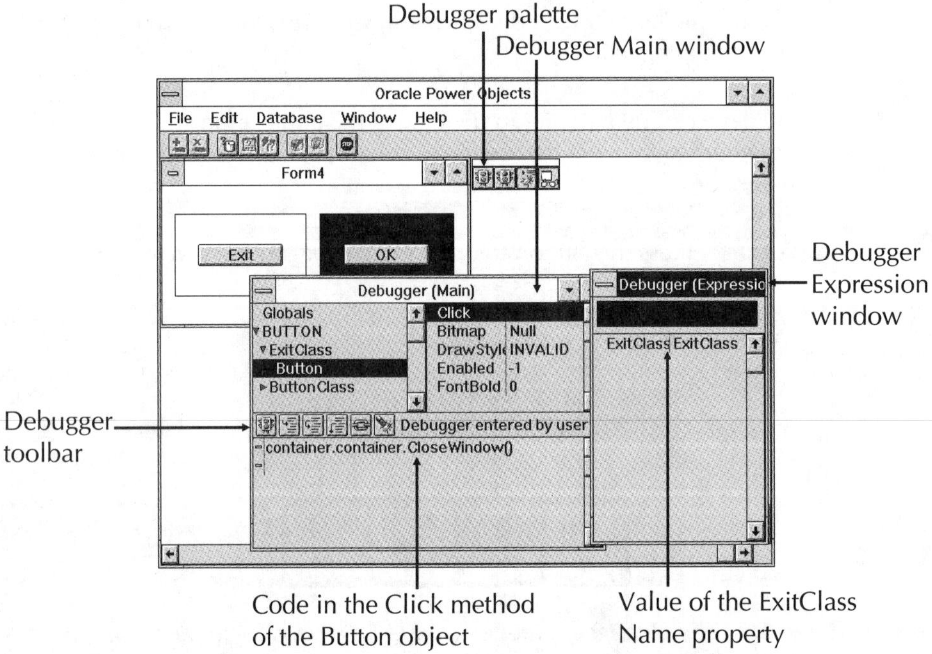

FIGURE 3-12. *The Debugger Main window and the Expression window*

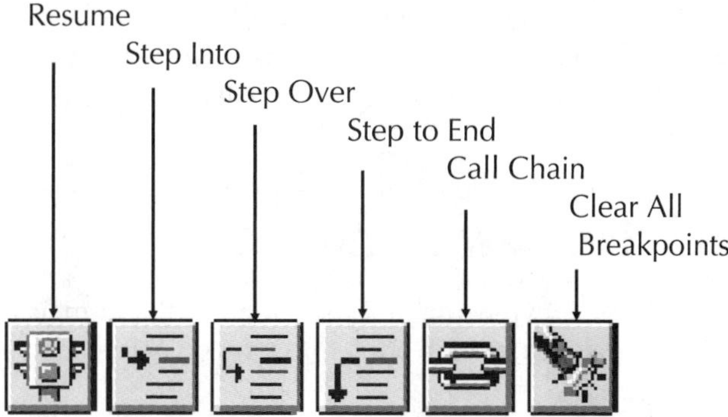

FIGURE 3-13. *The Debugger toolbar*

Step to End Press this button to execute all the remaining code in the current method and stop at the end of the method.

Call Chain Within an application, one method can call another method, and that method can call even a different method, etc. Press this button to display the hierarchy of called methods and then select which method you would like to examine more closely.

Clear All Breakpoints As explained in Chapter 5, you can set breakpoints in the Oracle Basic code in the methods. This means that when the Oracle Power Objects reaches this point while executing the application, it will stop and open the Main debugger window. Press this button to clear all breakpoints that have been set so the execution of the code can continue uninterrupted.

Print Preview Mode

Print Preview mode is activated when the Print Preview menu item is selected from the File menu or the Print Preview button is selected on the Form Designer toolbar. It is used to view the currently selected form as it will appear when being run. If the form includes objects that retrieve data from a database, you must have the database running (if the database is not Blaze). Oracle Power Objects runs the form and retrieves the data. The data is inserted into the fields and Oracle Power Objects presents a view of the running application. Figure 3-14 shows the menu bar and toolbar for the Print Preview mode.

The File, Edit, Window, and Help menus are the same as those in Design mode, though several menu items in Print Preview mode are grayed out. In Print Preview mode, a Preview menu is added. The items on the Preview menu are discussed below.

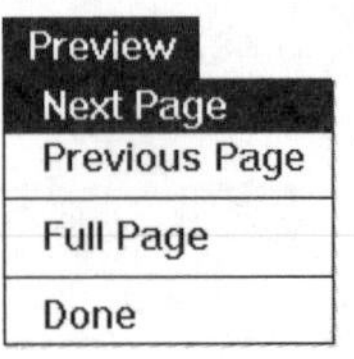

Preview Menu

The Preview menu is used to view the form as it will look if the report or form is printed to paper. Each menu item is discussed below.

Next Page Because Print Preview is actually running the form, application, etc., selecting this item fills the form with the next full set of data from the database. It is grayed out if there is no more data to review. If the form or report does not include *bound controls* (objects with values retrieved from a database), it will have only a single page.

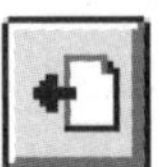

Previous Page Select this item to go back one full screen of data from the database. This item is grayed out if the record set is at the beginning of the data.

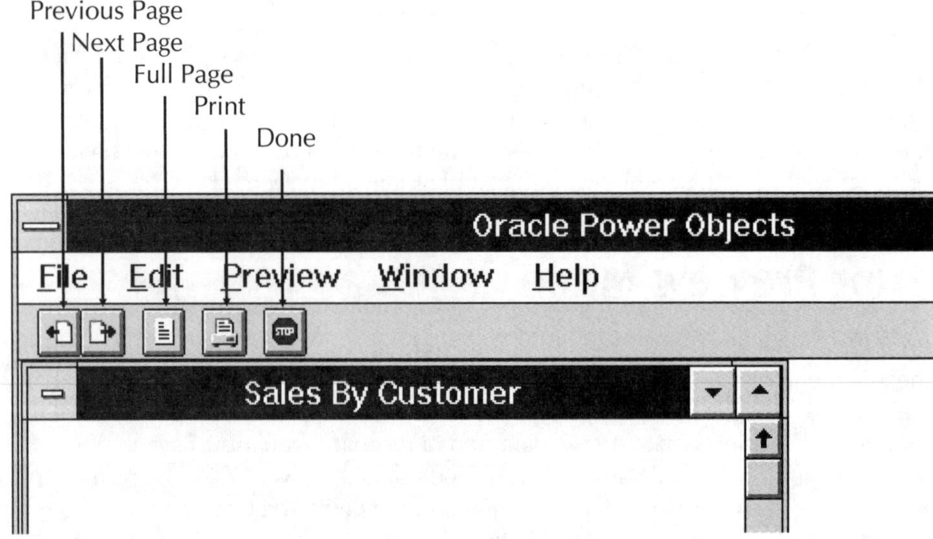

FIGURE 3-14. *Print Preview mode menu bar and toolbar*

Full Page This item displays the report or form on a screen scaled to represent an 8½-by-11-inch sheet of paper.

Done Select this item to exit Print Preview mode.

Property Sheet and Property Sheet Toolbar

The previous sections have described the menus and toolbars for Oracle Power Objects in its different modes of operation. One constant in all but the Run-time mode is the display of the property sheet that is associated with the currently highlighted object.

Each object in Oracle Power Objects has a property sheet with a toolbar at the top of it, as shown in Figure 3-15. Every time you open an application, form, library, class, etc., the object's property sheet is displayed. The property sheet changes to show the methods and properties associated with each selected object, but its overall appearance and toolbar are the same. The following section describes the Property sheet and its associated toolbar. (Property sheets are covered in more detail in Chapters 7 and 8.)

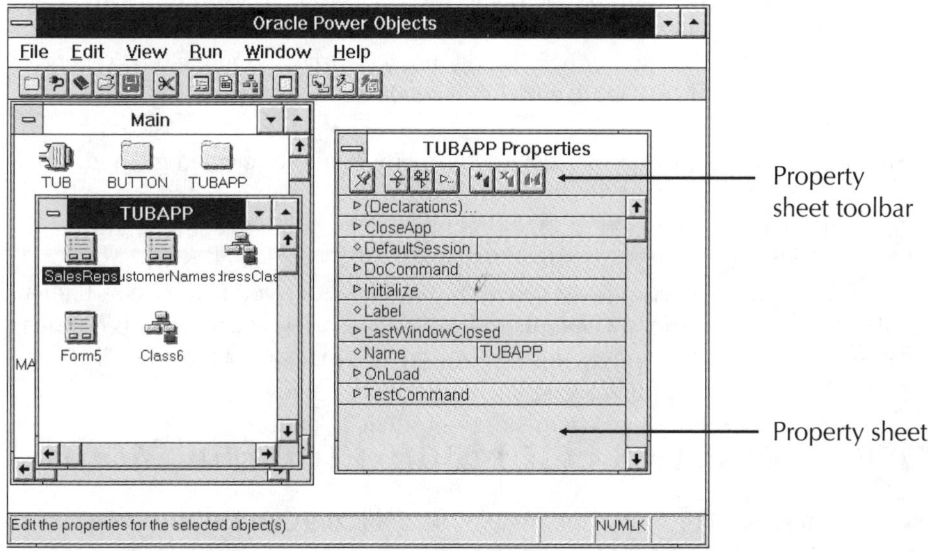

FIGURE 3-15. *An open application, TUBAPP, with its associated property sheet*

The following property sheet toolbar buttons allow you to keep the focus of the property on a selected object, change the order of the properties and methods, hide or show user-defined properties, add or delete a user-defined property, and create a separate window in which you can edit the selected method.

Push Pin Generally, when you select different objects, the property sheet changes to show the properties of the selected object. By selecting this button, the property sheet for the currently selected object remains displayed even when other objects are selected.

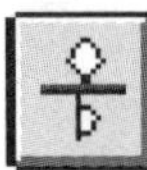

Property Order Property Order toggles the order of how the properties and methods are listed in the property sheet. Default lists the properties and methods in alphabetical order. Pressing the button rearranges the list to first list the properties in alphabetical order and then list the methods in alphabetical order.

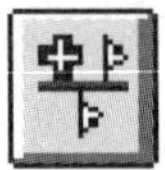

Custom/System Property This button displays or hides user-created properties in the property list. Default is to show all properties.

Hide Unusual Methods Pressing this button will hide all the currently active object's methods, except those in which you have added Oracle Basic code.

Add User Property This button opens the User Properties window, which allows you to create your own property to be associated with object instances in Oracle Power Objects. User Properties Edit mode is discussed in the next section and the description of creating user-defined properties is in Chapters 7 and 8.

Remove This removes a user-defined property from the selected method.

Reinherit When you modify a method or property of an object in an instance of a user-defined class, any subsequent changes in the original class will not change the instance, even if you remove the modifications you made (see Chapter 6 for details on user-defined class inheritance). However, you can use this button to reverse the changes and reinherit all the properties and methods of the original class.

User Properties Edit Mode (Prop Edit Mode)

You enter the User Properties Edit mode by selecting the User Properties menu item from the View menu (in either Design mode or Form Designer mode). You define new properties and methods in this mode. These user-defined properties and methods can then be dragged onto an object's property sheet. This is discussed more fully at the end of Chapters 7 and 8. Figure 3-16 shows the menu bar and toolbar when adding or editing user properties.

The File menu is identical to the one in the Form Designer mode, although several items are grayed out. The Edit, Window, and Help menus all remain the same as the ones in Design mode. A new Property menu appears, and the View menu changes. These two menus are described below.

Property Menu

The Property menu, shown here, contains two items, which are used to delete or sort user-defined properties.

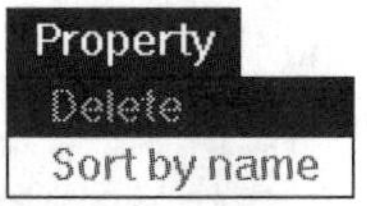

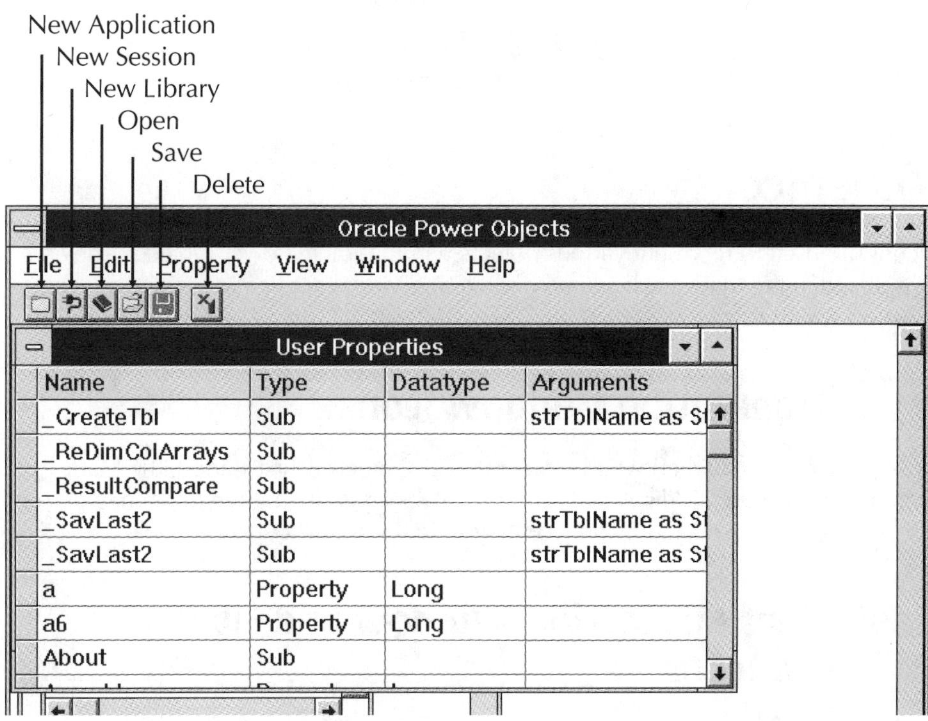

FIGURE 3-16. *Prop Edit mode menus and toolbar*

Delete This item is used to delete the selected user-defined property. You must be very sure when deleting a property that it is not used in any application's methods.

Sort by Name Because you add new properties to the end of the user property list, this menu item resorts the property list and places newly created properties in proper alphabetical order.

View Menu

This menu, shown in the following illustration, is very similar to the Design mode View menu but is lacking the Refresh menu item. Each of these items were described earlier in the chapter in the "View Menu" section under the Design mode.

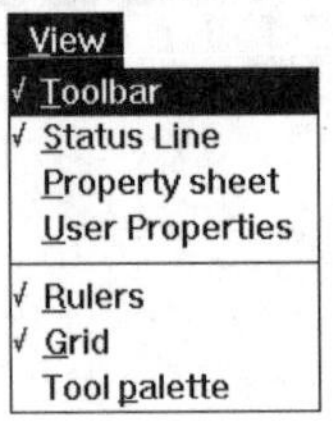

Other Icons

Icons are used to represent various objects within Oracle Power Objects. They are displayed in the Main application window, individual application windows, and session windows.

Main Application Window Icons

As we mentioned earlier, when Oracle Power Objects is first started, the Main application window is displayed. This window can contain three different types of objects, each represented by an icon. These icons are described in Table 3-1.

Individual Application Window and Library Window Icons

When an application is opened, it can contain five different icons representing forms, classes, reports, bitmaps, and OLE objects. These are described in Table 3-2.

Icon	Name	Description
TUB	Session	This icon represents a session, which connects to a database. Double-click on this icon to connect to the database to view the tables, views, sequences, etc., defined in the database.
TUBAPP	Individual Application	Double-click on this icon to open the application to be edited or run.
TUBLIB	Library	Double-clicking this icon opens a window displaying the contents of the library from which you can access the objects.

TABLE 3-1. *Object Icons in the Main Application Window*

Icon	Name	Description
Form12	Form	All forms within the application are represented by a copy of this icon with the form's name as its label. Double-click on this icon to edit or run the individual form.
Class11	Class	All classes within the application are represented by a copy of this icon with the class's name as its label. Double-click on this icon to edit or run the individual form.
Report13	Report	Double-click on this icon to edit or run the individual report.
HONEY	Bitmap	This icon takes the name of the bitmap imported into the application. Double-click on the icon to see the bitmap displayed.
OLE10	OLE	This icon takes the name of the OLE object imported into the application by using the Insert Object or Paste Special menu item. Click and drag the icon onto an open form to add the object to the form.

TABLE 3-2. *Individual Application Window and Library Window Icons*

Session Window Icons

When a session is opened, Oracle Power Objects connects it to the database named in the Run Design property. Upon connection, Oracle Power Objects retrieves every table, synonym, index, sequence, and view defined in the database for the defined user. It places an icon representing each object in the session window. Each object's name is placed below the icon. The icons are described in Table 3-3.

Icon	Name	Description
TUB	Connect	This icon shows whether the session is attached to the database. If it is not attached, the little plug on the left is not attached to the cylinder. If it is attached, then it appears as shown.
CUSTS	Table	This icon represents a table. Double-click on a table icon to display the fields and their properties defined for the table.
EMPLOYEE	Synonym	This icon represents a synonym for another database object such as a table or view.
PK_CITIES	Index	This icon represents an index placed on a table, as discussed in Chapters 2 and 6. You cannot modify an index from a session window.
123 CUSTIDSEQ	Sequence	This icon represents a sequence-unique number generator.
CUSTAMT	View	This icon represents a view, which is like a table but is composed of fields from one or more tables combined into one pseudotable.

TABLE 3-3. *Session Window Icons*

Conclusion

This chapter has briefly described every menu item, toolbar button, and icon that Oracle Power Objects uses. Its purpose was to give you an overall picture of what is available for your use while developing applications. The following chapters go into much more detail on how to create sessions, applications, libraries, etc., by using these menus and toolbars.

CHAPTER 4

Getting Started with Oracle Power Objects' Database Sessions

The power of Oracle Power Objects lies in the manner in which you create forms and reports and the ease with which these forms are tied to databases. Oracle Power Objects Designer provides the tools to create Blaze databases and to modify local databases or remote databases. In Chapter 1, we introduced the concept of object-oriented programming and Oracle Power Objects; in Chapter 2, we provided an overview of fundamentals of relational database design; and in Chapter 3, we covered the menus and toolbars that make up the Oracle Power Objects Designer user interface. In this chapter, we introduce you to starting Oracle Power Objects Designer and using database sessions. You will also learn how to use database session objects, such as tables and indexes, and relating the data stored in tables with views. While property sheets are introduced here, a more complete explanation of using the power of properties and methods is handled in Chapters 8 and 9.

Starting Oracle Power Objects Designer

To start Oracle Power Objects on both the Windows and Macintosh operating systems:

1. Open the Oracle Power Objects group in the Program Manager in Windows or the Oracle Power Objects folder on the Macintosh (see Figure 4-1).
2. Double-click the Oracle Power Objects Designer icon (Windows) or the pwrobjx icon (Macintosh) to start Oracle Power Objects Designer.

Opening Oracle Power Objects Designer displays the Desktop Manager window and all of the icons of any database sessions, libraries, and applications that have been opened and saved in the window (see Figure 4-2). The first time you open Oracle Power Objects, the Main window may be blank until you create new or open existing sessions, applications, or libraries.

Database Sessions

In Oracle Power Objects you can create applications, sessions, and libraries. Applications act as a front end to data stored in either a local Blaze database or a remote Oracle7 or SQL Server database. A session is an Oracle Power Objects object that stores the necessary information to activate a database. Once you create a session, multiple applications can then connect to the database by means of the session. You can activate a database using the session object to view the database objects and data. You can also declare a session as the default session of an application. When you run the application, it calls the specified session which activates the database. Neither sessions or applications store data. In Chapter 5, we will explain how you specify the database session(s) to be activated when an application is run.

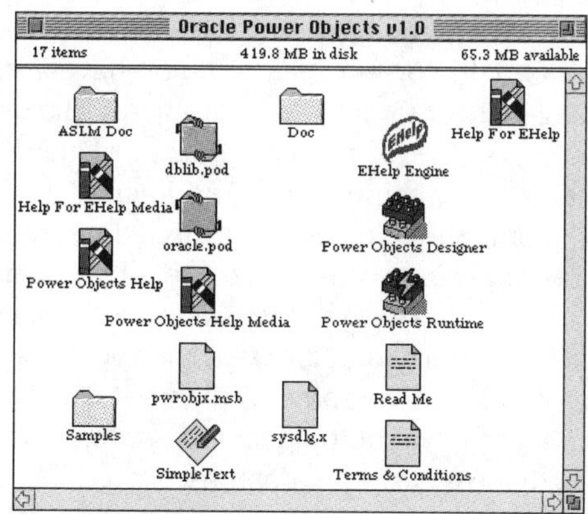

FIGURE 4-1. *On the Macintosh, the Oracle Power Objects folder contains the Power Objects Designer, Power Objects Runtime, and the EHelp application and its files*

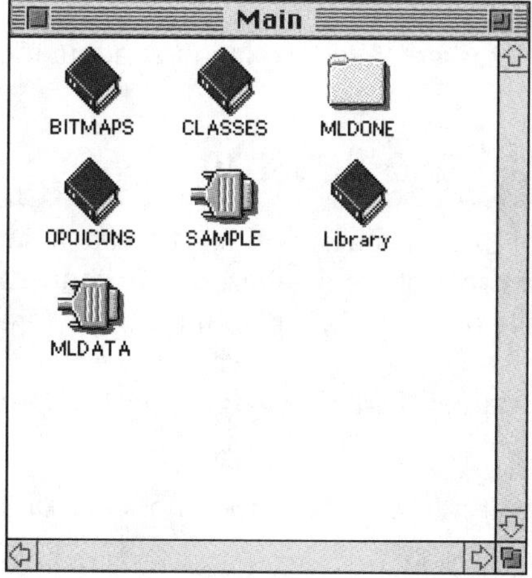

FIGURE 4-2. *Open Main window*

There are many types of database connections that you can establish in a session depending on whether you are using the stand-alone edition or the client/server edition of Oracle Power Objects. If you have a stand-alone edition, you can only create sessions for Oracle Power Objects' Blaze database. However, with the client/server edition, you can access Blaze or Personal Oracle7 databases running locally on the same machine on which Oracle Power Objects is running, a remote Oracle7 Workgroup Server database accessed through a network, a DB2 database, SQL Server database, a Sybase database, or an open database connectivity (ODBC) database. Through the use of sessions, you can develop an unlimited number of connections to databases. Each of these sessions may be used by different end users to activate the same or different databases. Oracle Power Objects also allows users to have multiple sessions open at the same time. For example, you could activate a customer database stored in a Blaze database and then activate an order entry database stored in a remote database.

Besides storing the information necessary to connect applications to a database, the session acts as a container for all of the database objects that are accessed when it is active. The session stores information as to how the database session is to become active, whether or not the selected database is to be selected as the default session, the connect string (which contains the information needed to activate a database), the name of the session, and methods that can be used to determine how data will be updated in the database.

When you perform a database query or select the next record, the database session passes the message through the Record Manager to the database, which analyzes the message and passes back the desired information through the session to the application. Modifications, additions, or queries on a database are sent through the Record Manager to the database, and the results are returned to the recordset (see Chapter 5 for a detailed explanation about the Record Manager and the recordset).

Creating a Database Session

Before you can connect to a database, you must create a database session and define the location and name of the database in the connection string. Each session is saved as a separate file on the disk, and in the case of Oracle Power Objects for Windows, the file has the .POS extension. The following example creates a new Blaze database session named Tub.POS that connects to a previously created Blaze database.

1. Select New Session from the File menu or click on the New Session icon on the toolbar.

This displays the Create Database Session wizard dialog box, shown in Figure 4-3. This dialog box shows a default name in the Database window and a field for entering the session's connect string.

2. Select Blaze as the database type from the Database drop-down list, and type in a connection string using the syntax ***username/password@filepath:database name*** in the Connect String text box (see Figure 4-3). Press ENTER or click OK.

If you make a mistake typing in the connection string, Oracle Power Objects will display an error window. The Session wizard creates a connection string that describes the database type (Oracle7, Blaze, etc.), user name, and the network address. If you were creating a session named Tub for a remote Oracle7 Server database, you would select Oracle from the drop-down list and type in a connect string using syntax like ***username/password@t:servername:database name.*** Note that you can change the connect string in the DesignConnect property field in the Session property sheet.

3. Oracle Power Objects displays a Create As dialog box for naming and saving the session file. Name the file, select the destination directory (or folder), and click Save.

The screen will now look similar to Figure 4-4. The new session is displayed in the Main Application window as a computer cable connector, the session window itself is displayed with the session icon, and the property sheet for the session is shown.

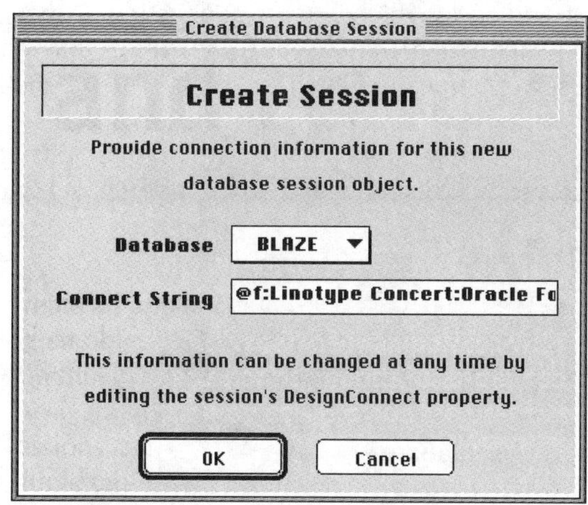

FIGURE 4-3. *The Create Database Session dialog box with a sample session name and connect string*

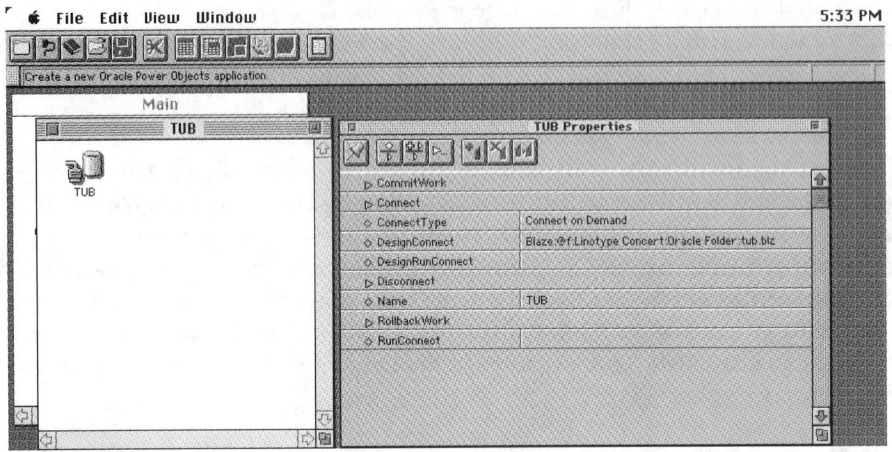

FIGURE 4-4. *The new Session window (Tub) with its property sheet (notice the connection string in the DesignConnect property)*

The Connection String

The information necessary to establish a connection with a database is stored in one or more of three properties. The default property is the DesignConnect property for the session. All connection strings contain the type of database (Oracle, Blaze, SQL Server) to which you are connecting. Depending on the type of database to which you are connecting, the connection string may include the user name, the server name, and the name of the database to which you are connecting.

The three types of databases use a connect string to establish the link to a database. Its format is shown below with a description of each part following.

```
database_type:[username/password][@database_address][;connect_options]
```

database_type This is the type of database, such as Blaze or Oracle, to which your application will connect. The three valid database types are

Database Type	Database
blaze	Blaze
oracle	Oracle7 Server
dblib	SQL Server

username/password This is the name of the *schema* (a group of database objects owned by a user account) to which you are connecting (or the path to the database to which you are connecting). The schema contains the user name and password for a user of the database. These must be set by the database administrator before the application can attach to the database. It can be used to make sure the user is authorized to access the database by having the user enter the appropriate user name and password upon startup.

@database_address This is the location of the database, whether it's a filename for the Blaze database or a network address. If the database is running on your local machine, then you do not need to enter the address. The database_address requires a prefix for certain types of database connections and an instance following the database_address. For example, you insert **t:** before the name of an Oracle7 Server using SQL*Net V1 and **:[instance]** after the database address to specify an instance of the database to which you are connecting. (An instance is the background processes and the system global area that interface with the data stored in a database.) An explanation of setting up a client-server relationship between Oracle Power Objects and a database using TCP/IP protocol is provided in Appendix A. The following is a table of the various prefixes needed to properly identify different databases:

Address Prefix	Database Address Type
f:	Blaze database
t:	Oracle7 Server using SQL*Net V2
x:	Oracle7 Server on Netware
none	Oracle7 Server using SQL*Net V1
none	Personal Oracle7

connect_options These are options used as startup settings for the Blaze database. S is for single user and R is for read only.

For example, connecting to a database named db1 that uses the username/password marble/rock is shown below on different machines, databases, and networks:

Example Connect Strings	Database Parameters
blaze:marble/rock@data/db1.xdb	Blaze database on Windows
blaze:marble/rock@Hard Disk:Data:db1:R	Blaze database on Macintosh (read-only)
blaze:dba/dba@Hard Disk:Data:db1	Blaze "DBA" account on a Macintosh
oracle:marble/rock	Personal Oracle7 on Windows
oracle:marble/rock@t:snowbird:db	Oracle7 Server on TCP/IP network
oracle:marble/rock@x:db_server	Oracle7 Server on Netware SPX network
dblib:marble/rock@Sql_Server1:db1	SQL Server database

Manually Activating Sessions

Manually activating a database session establishes the connection to the database specified in the connection string and allows you to work directly with its database objects. Oracle Power Objects provides an impressive number of tools to manipulate the database. For example, you can create and manipulate tables, views, sequences, indexes, and synonyms. You can also view data in tables and view and edit data stored within tables. The following examples assume that each session and its connection string has already been created. Note that when you run an application or form, Oracle Power Objects automatically activates any sessions used by the form or application.

Activating a Blaze Database Session To manually activate a Blaze database session and view its database objects:

1. Double-click on the session icon. This opens the session window (but not the session) and displays the inactive connect icon, shown here:

2. Double-click on the connect icon.

The database connect icon changes to an active connect icon (the plug is plugged in) and displays all of the selected database's tables, views, sequences, and indexes in the session window. Also, new icons appear on the toolbar to create new tables, views, indexes, and sequences, as shown in Figure 4-5. Once you have

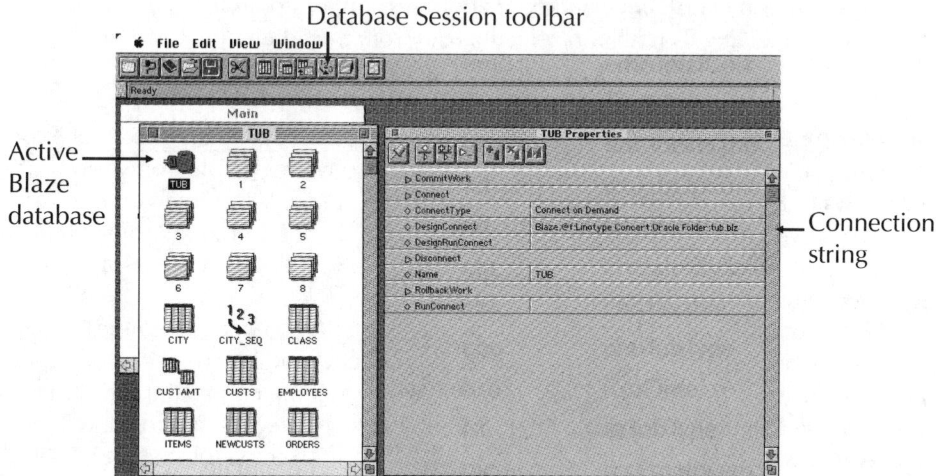

FIGURE 4-5. *An active Blaze session window, with all of its database objects and the Database Session toolbar. Note the connection string in the property sheet*

activated a session, it will remain active until you manually deactivate the session or quit Oracle Power Objects.

Note that the Main window does not show every application, session, or library that is available. For example, if you copy an application between computers, the application is not automatically shown in the Main window. After you open an application, session, or library in the Main window, it will be displayed every time you open Oracle Power Objects.

If the MLDATA session icon does not appear in the Main window, click the Open icon from the toolbar or select Open from the File menu. Select MLDATA from the Open dialog box, shown here, then click on the Open button.

Samples
Linotype Co...
Library
MLBUILD.DMP
MLBUILD.SQL
MLDATA
mldata.blz
MLDATA2
MLDEMO
Eject
Desktop
Cancel
Open

Note that you can *remove* an application, session, or library from the Main window by selecting its icon and selecting Cut from the Edit menu. This merely removes the object from the window, but it does not delete the object.

Activating a Remote Database Session Before activating a remote database session, you need to have the appropriate network software installed on your Windows or Macintosh and have SQL*Net V1 or SQL*Net V2 running on the Oracle7 server. You must have both SQL*Net and TCP/IP set up on your machine to be able to connect to the Oracle7 server. For help setting up the necessary network software, see Appendix A.

Once you have all of the necessary software installed, to open a remote database and examine its database objects, double-click on the connect icon. Figure 4-6 shows an active MLDATA session window. If the connection fails, make sure that the database to which you are attempting to connect is running and that the server's SQL*Net is running (see Appendix A for an example of starting up the Oracle database). If the remote database and server are set up correctly, check that your computer's TCP driver is set up properly and running, that the SQL*Net host file contains the server's IP address, and that there are no typing errors in the connection string.

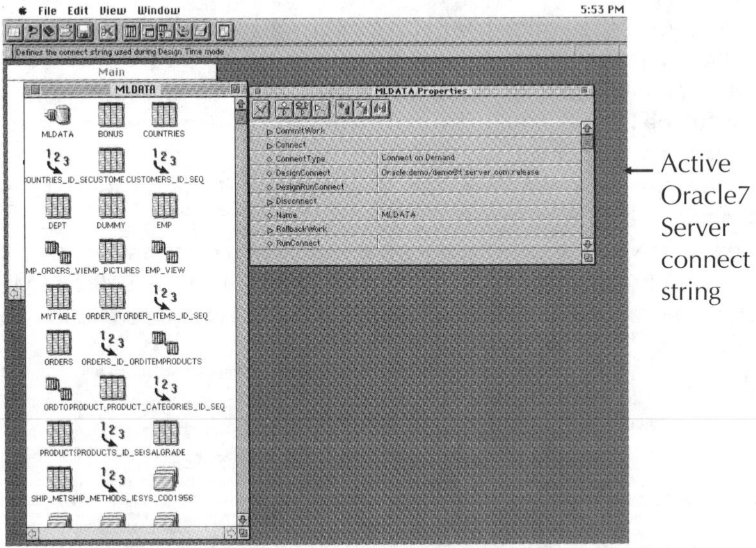

FIGURE 4-6. *The active MLDATA session window running on an Oracle7 Server with all of its database objects and the Database Session toolbar. Note the connection string in the property sheet*

Manually Deactivating a Session

To deactivate an active session means to disconnect from the associated database. Sessions are deactivated by exiting an Oracle Power Objects application, double-clicking on the connect icon, or quitting Oracle Power Objects. When the session has been deactivated, the session window is blank except for the inactive connect icon. The only time you need to manually deactivate a session is when you have been designing or manipulating database objects in the session window and are finished working with them.

Changing the Connection String

The only time you need to change the connection string is if you make a typing error when creating a session or if the database's location or schema has been altered. For example, as a company grows, the company may move the database from a Blaze database to an Oracle7 server. To change the connection string:

1. Double-click the session icon to activate the session.
2. Click on the Open Property Sheet icon on the toolbar.
3. Make any necessary changes to the session. For example, to change a session that accesses the MLDATA database in a Blaze database to a local Personal Oracle7 database, change it from blaze:mldata to oracle:mldata.

Creating a Blaze Database

Blaze databases are compact and efficient databases that are created and maintained by Oracle Power Objects. All other types of databases (except Oracle7 database objects) need to be created and maintained using the tools that come with the database. Blaze databases will be used both by developers of personal or small company databases and by developers who want to create and test corporate databases without the hassle of having to connect with remote databases or the inconvenience their work would have on corporate database users. Note that while Blaze databases are often termed databases, they should not be mistaken as single-user databases. You can access a Blaze database as a multiuser database with simultaneous sessions by placing it on a Novell or TCP/IP server.

Blaze databases contain all of the basic types of database objects: tables, views, indexes, and sequences. These objects are organized into schemas. (Recall from earlier that a schema is a collection of database objects and user rights that are organized into a user account.) You access data stored in Blaze databases using Oracle Basic and SQL.

You create a new Blaze database by generating a Blaze database file. To create a new Blaze database named tub.blz:

1. Select New Blaze Database from the File menu.
2. Enter the name of the database in the Create Database dialog box and click the Save button. In Windows, a .blz file extension is automatically appended to the file's name.
3. A dialog box reminds you that the database has been created, and gives its name and the directory location of the file.
4. Click the OK button in the dialog box.

Naming Blaze Database Objects

When naming Blaze database objects, such as tables and columns, there are several rules that you need to keep in mind. Following these rules will make it easier to refer to these objects with SQL and Oracle Basic.

- Names need to be from 1 to 30 characters in length.
- Names should contain only alphanumeric characters and _, $, and #. However, Oracle suggests that the $ and # characters be avoided.
- Names need to begin with an alphanumeric character.
- A name must be unique across its namespace, meaning that you cannot have two tables in a session with the same name or two columns in the same table with the same name. Also, a user cannot have two database objects, like a table and a sequence, with the same name.
- Names are not case-sensitive. Therefore, if you name a column with all caps in the table, you can reference it in SQL or Oracle Basic in lowercase.
- You cannot use an Oracle reserved word to name an object (see Appendix C).
- It is recommended that you do not use any Oracle SQL keywords (see Appendix C). SQL keywords are not reserved, but using them will make referencing an object confusing when using SQL.
- You should not use DUAL as either a part of or all of the name of any database object.
- Names cannot contain quote marks.
- You can enclose a database name inside double quotes. Names enclosed in double quotes can contain any type of characters and avoid the concerns of using reserved words or SQL words.

If you are working with a database other than Blaze, you should check its documentation to ensure you follow the appropriate rules for that database. For those using Personal Oracle7 or Oracle7 Server, see "Naming Objects and Parts" in the *Oracle7 SQL Language Reference Manual.*

Tables

A table is where data is physically stored in a database. A table consists of a group of columns containing related pieces of information. Information stored for a single item, such as employee, is stored in a record. A database may consist of many tables, which store information about the same object.

There are two views of every table. When you initially open a table, it appears in the Table Editor window, where the structure of the table is displayed. In the Table Editor window, you create and define columns and edit the definition of existing columns. Selecting the Table Browser button runs the table, and displays the data stored within the table. In the Table Browser window, you add, delete, or modify the information stored in the table.

Opening the Table Editor Window

You define or edit table fields (columns) and their structure in the Table Editor window. Opening a table or creating a new table in the session window displays the table in the Table Editor window.

For example, to open the Products table in the MLDATA session:

1. If the MLDATA session is not active, double-click on its icon to open the window and then double-click on the connect icon to activate the session.
2. Double-click the Products icon in the MLDATA session window to open it in the Table Editor window (see Figure 4-7).

Parts of the Table Editor Window

The Table Editor window looks like a spreadsheet. The rows of the Table Editor contain the fields that define the columns that make up the table. Each row includes information that define the table's column, such as the column name, datatype, and size. The following is an overview of the parts of the Table Editor window.

Primary Key Tool The primary key tool appears as a key in the upper-left corner of the window. The key field uniquely identifies each record in a table, such as a customer id number, an order number, or a part number. This is called the primary key for the table.

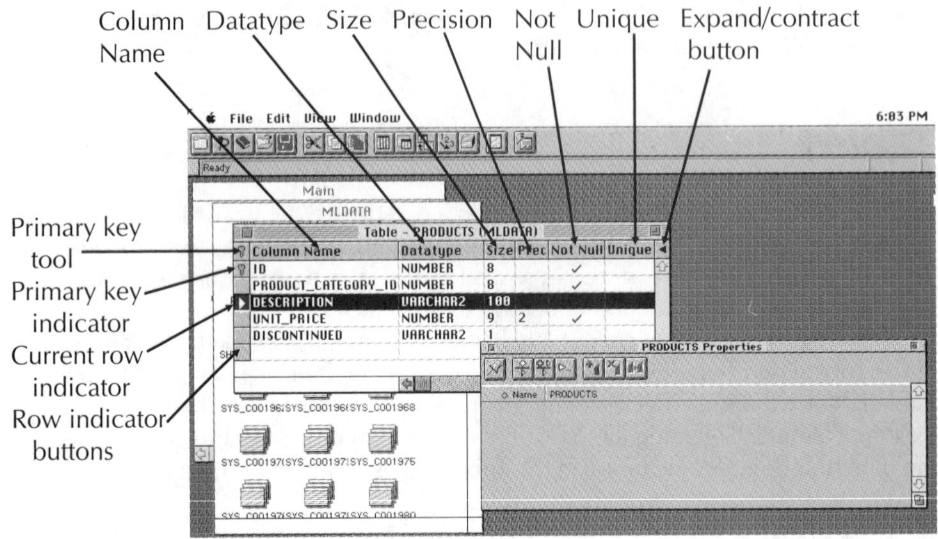

FIGURE 4-7. *The Products table shown in the Table Editor mode with its table structure*

Primary Key Indicator Setting a column as the primary key field, places a key in the row indicator button next to the column.

Current Row Indicator An arrow appears just to the left of the column name in the row indicator button to indicate which column is being edited.

Column Name The name of the column or field.

Datatype The datatypes displayed depend on the database specified in the database session. For example, Oracle7 and Blaze use different names for these datatypes. Table 4-1 lists datatypes used by Blaze, Table 4-2 lists those datatypes used by Oracle7, and Table 4-3 explains the datatypes used by SQL Server.

Size The maximum size of values in the column. For example, for most small companies a column that will contain employee salaries probably needs

Blaze Datatype	Type	Comments
CHAR(*n*)	string	This is a fixed character string up to 32,000 characters.
VARCHAR(*n*)	string	It is the same as VARCHAR2.
VARCHAR2(*n*)	string	VARCHAR2 is a variable length field up to 32,000 characters.
NUMBER(*p*)	integer	This datatype is expressed as positive and negative decimal numbers or in scientific notation. It can contain integers between $2^{31}-1$ to $-2^{31}-1$ (4 bytes). Blaze ignores precision.
NUMBER(*p,s*)	float	This datatype is expressed as positive and negative decimal numbers or in scientific notation. +/–1.79763134862315e308. Blaze ignores precision (p) and scale (s) for NUMBER datatype.
NUMBER	float	This datatype is expressed as positive and negative decimal numbers or in scientific notation. +/–1.79763134862315e308.
INTEGER	integer	INTEGER is a signed long integer and can contain integers between $2^{31}-1$ to $-2^{31}-1$ (4 bytes).
LONG	string	This is a variable-length string data up to 4GB characters in length. Any number of LONG/LONG RAW columns are allowed for a table.
DATE	date	DATE stores date and time information between Jan. 1, 100 A.D. to Dec 31, 9999 A.D.
RAW(*n*)	binary	RAW is a binary data up to 32,000 characters.

TABLE 4-1. *Datatypes Supported by Blaze Database Engine*

Blaze Datatype	Type	Comments
LONG RAW	binary	This is the same as RAW, but it can contain binary data up to 4GB in length. In Blaze this is used to store bitmaps. Any number of LONG/LONG RAW columns are allowed for a table.
ROWID	string	ROWID stores a hexadecimal string value that uniquely identifies a row in a table.
MLLABEL	N/A	It is for Oracle's security use only.

TABLE 4-1. *Datatypes Supported by Blaze Database Engine* (continued)

Oracle7 Datatype	Type	Comments
CHAR(*n*)	string	This is a fixed character data up to 255 characters.
VARCHAR(*n*)	string	It is the same as VARCHAR2, but it may change in a future release of Oracle7.
VARCHAR2(*n*)	string	VARCHAR2 is a variable length field up to 2,000 characters.
NUMBER(*p*)	integer	This datatype is expressed as positive and negative decimal numbers or in scientific notation. It can contain integers between 1 to 9e125 and –1 to –9e125. Precision (p) identifies the total number of digits (1-38).
NUMBER(*p,s*)	fixed-point	This datatype is expressed as positive and negative decimal numbers or in scientific notation between 1e130 to 9.99...9e125, 0, and –1e–130 to –9.99...9e125. Precision (p), same as above. Scale (s) is the number of digits to the right of the decimal point.
NUMBER	float	This datatype is expressed as positive and negative decimal numbers or in scientific notation between 1e130 to 9.99...9e125, 0, and –1e–130 to –9.99...9e125.

TABLE 4-2. *Datatypes Supported by the Oracle7 Servers*

Oracle7 Datatype	Type	Comments
LONG	string	This is a variable length data string up to 2GB characters in length. Only one LONG/LONG RAW column is allowed for a table.
DATE	date	DATE stores date and time information between Jan 1, 5712 B.C. to Dec 31, 4712 A.D.
RAW	binary	RAW is a binary data up to 255 bytes.
LONG RAW	binary	This is the same as RAW, but can contain binary data up to 2GB in length. Only one LONG/LONG RAW column is allowed for a table.
ROWID	string	ROWID stores a hexadecimal string value that uniquely identifies a row in a table.
MLLABEL	N/A	It is for Oracle's security use only.

TABLE 4-2. *Datatypes Supported by the Oracle7 Servers* (continued)

SQL Server Datatype	Type	Comments
CHAR(*n*)	string	This is a fixed character string up to 255 characters.
VARCHAR(*n*)	string	This is a variable character string up to 255 characters.
TEXT	string	TEXT is a string of values up to 2^{31}–1 characters.
FLOAT	float	This datatype is expressed as positive and negative decimal numbers or in scientific notation. 1.7e–308 to 1.7e308, 0, –1.7e–138 to –1.7e308 (8 bytes).
REAL	float	This datatype is expressed as positive and negative decimal numbers or in scientific notation. 3.4e–38 to 3.4e38, 0, –3.4e–38 to –3.4e38 (4 bytes).

TABLE 4-3. *Datatypes Supported by SQL Server Databases*

SQL Server Datatype	Type	Comments
MONEY	fixed-point	+922,337,203,685,477.5807 to –922,337,203,685,477.5807 (8 bytes).
SMALLMONEY	fixed-point	+214,748.3647 to –214,748.3647 (4 bytes).
INT	integer	INT is a signed long integer and can contain integers between 2^{31}–1 to –2^{31}–1 (4 bytes).
SMALLINT	integer	SMALLINT is a signed integer and can contain integers between 2^{15}–1 to –2^{15}–1 (2 bytes).
TINYINT	integer	TINYINT is a signed integer and can contain integers up to 255 (1 byte).
DATETIME	date	DATE stores date and time information between Jan. 1, 1753 A.D. to Dec 31, 9999 A.D.
SMALLDATETIME	date	Stores date and time information between Jan. 1, 1900 A.D. to June 6, 2079 A.D.
BINARY(*n*)	binary	BINARY contains binary data up to 255 bytes.
VARBINARY(*n*)	binary	It contains variable-length binary data up to 255 bytes.
IMAGE	binary	1 to 2,147,483,647 bytes.
BIT	binary	1 bit.
TIMESTAMP	—	It is a value equal to the VARBINARY(8) that's used to track currency.
SYSNAME	—	—
user-defined	any	Can contain any range or size of data depending on the underlying system datatype.

TABLE 4-3. *Datatypes Supported by SQL Server Databases* (continued)

to be no larger than five or six digits. You are only required to set the size for string datatypes, as all other datatypes can use the default size.

Precision Precision sets the numeric precision of FLOAT datatype columns.

Not Null Clicking on the Not Null field places a check mark in the field and ensures that data is entered in this field before committing the record.

Unique Clicking on the Unique field places a check mark in the field and ensures that the values entered into this field are unique before committing the record.

Expand/Contract Button The expand/contract button displays an abbreviated or expanded view of the table structure. To abbreviate the information displayed about each column, click on the small triangle in the upper-right corner of the window next to the Unique field.

Creating Tables

When you create a table, it contains no information or structure. You should therefore take a piece of paper and lay out all of the information that needs to be stored, what tables will need to be created, the type of data to be stored in each column, and make certain that you have properly related all of the tables together by using primary and foreign keys.

For example, to create a table to store sales order information in the database:

1. Open and activate the session by double-clicking on the connect icon.
2. Click on the New Table button on the toolbar. A blank Table Editor window and its property sheet is opened.
3. Scroll down the Name property in the Table property sheet and change the name of the table from Table1 to a name that specifies the purpose of the table (Orders).

Defining Columns

Once you have created a table, you need to begin defining its columns. Remember, a table should contain information that logically fits together into a single category, that contains foreign keys to the necessary associated tables, and that properly defines the column's datatype. For example, the Orders table will contain columns pertaining to the company with the specific types of information that identify a specific order.

To store sales orders, you need to store data in more than one table for the orders. Information related to sales orders is stored in a Custs table for customer data, an Employees table for the sales representative who made the sale, an Orders table to store information about each order, an Order_Items table for each product associated with the order, and a Products table for all of the products sold. There actually may be more tables needed to avoid any duplication of information in the database (shipment method, method of payment, etc.).

The following illustrates how to create primary key, foreign key, and other columns in a table for entering orders.

To create a primary key column in a table:

1. Click in the first Column Name field and type the name of the primary key (**Id**) to create the table's primary key. This is the field used to uniquely identify each order.
2. Press the TAB key to move to the Datatype field. Select Integer from the pop-up list. The Id column of an Orders table should have a sequence that automatically inserts a sequential number as new orders are entered into the Orders table (see Chapter 5 on how to attach a sequence to a column).
3. Click on the Primary Key icon in the upper-left corner of the Table Editor window to set the field as the primary key field for the table.

To create foreign key columns in a table that establish links to other tables:

1. Move the cursor to the next row and type in the name of a foreign key field, such as **Customer_Id** to create a relationship to the table containing customer data. The Custs table needs to have a primary field associated to the foreign field created in the Orders table.
2. Press TAB to move to the Datatype column and select Integer from the pop-up list.
3. Repeat steps 1 and 2 to create foreign key columns for all other related tables.

To add the other columns to the Orders table, enter columns for Orderdate, Promisedate, etc. and select the appropriate column parameters for each, as shown in Figure 4-8.

Saving Changes to a Table's Structure

To save a new table or modifications to the table definition, click on the Save button on the toolbar. The Save button is grayed out (unavailable) until you have

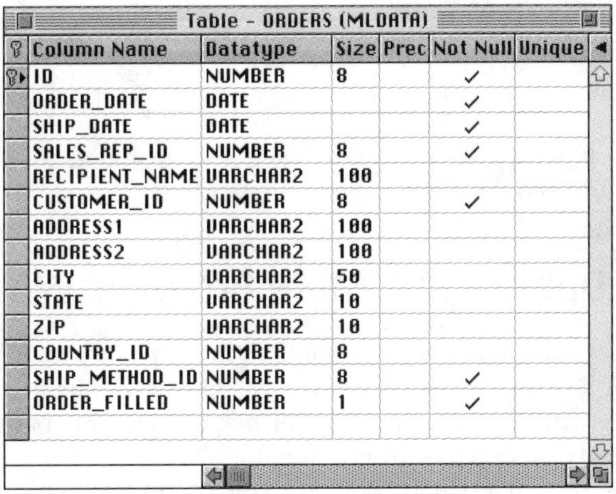

Table - ORDERS (MLDATA)

Column Name	Datatype	Size	Prec	Not Null	Unique
ID	NUMBER	8		✓	
ORDER_DATE	DATE			✓	
SHIP_DATE	DATE			✓	
SALES_REP_ID	NUMBER	8		✓	
RECIPIENT_NAME	VARCHAR2	100			
CUSTOMER_ID	NUMBER	8		✓	
ADDRESS1	VARCHAR2	100			
ADDRESS2	VARCHAR2	100			
CITY	VARCHAR2	50			
STATE	VARCHAR2	10			
ZIP	VARCHAR2	10			
COUNTRY_ID	NUMBER	8			
SHIP_METHOD_ID	NUMBER	8		✓	
ORDER_FILLED	NUMBER	1		✓	

FIGURE 4-8. *The completed Orders table with a primary key for the Id column, columns for the information about the order, and the necessary foreign keys*

actually made a change to the table's structure. When you save changes to the Table Editor window, Oracle Power Objects creates a SQL statement based on the new structure of the table and redefines the table in the database.

Moving and Copying Tables Between Sessions

One of the exciting capabilities of Oracle Power Objects is its ability to establish multiple sessions. With multiple sessions open, you can move or copy tables between the open sessions using Oracle Power Objects. This allows you to copy database tables (and other session objects like sequences) into new databases that are similar to a previously developed database. After copying similar tables to the new session, you can then make the necessary modifications to the table's structure in Oracle Power Objects. It can also be used to move or copy a database developed in a Blaze database to a company server database like Oracle7 Server. In this example, we will copy the Orders table from the MLDATA session window to the TUB session window.

To move or copy a table between database sessions:

1. Open and activate both sessions.
2. Select the table (Orders) to be moved by clicking on it, and then drag and drop the table onto the other session.

3. To copy a table to a different session, select the table and then hold the ALT key (Windows) or OPTION key (Macintosh) while dragging the table to the other session.

Copying or moving a table from one database session to another moves both the table structure and the data stored in the table.

Viewing Data in the Table Browser Window

To quickly view, add, or delete data stored in the table, you use the Table Browser window. The Table Browser window displays the stored data in a window similar to a spreadsheet with the column names displayed at the top of the window and with each record displayed as a row across the window.

To view the data in the Ship_Methods table of the MLDATA sample database in the Table Browser:

1. Open the Ship_Methods table by opening the MLDATA session and then double-clicking on the table's icon.
2. With the table open, click on the Run button on the toolbar (see Figure 4-9).

The records (rows) appear in the table in the order in which they have been entered. The first record is selected by default, as can be seen by the active row indicator (a green triangle on Windows and a black triangle for the Macintosh) on the left side of the record. Clicking inside another record places a black padlock in the row indicator. When you click anywhere in a row, Oracle Power Objects automatically locks that row in the table. If two individuals are using the same table at the same time, the first person to select a row gains control of the record (locks the record) so that no one else can make any changes or delete the row.

If you cannot see all of the data in a column, you can change the column's size by moving the mouse to the right side of the column heading. The cursor changes to a black two-headed arrow. When the cursor changes, click and drag on the column header divider to either increase or decrease the width of the column.

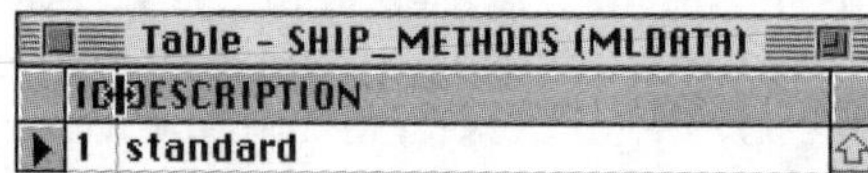

Adding Records to a Table

Although you normally add records to a table in the database using an application, you can add records directly in the Table Browser window. You are most apt to add records to small tables in the Table Browser window, such as a table

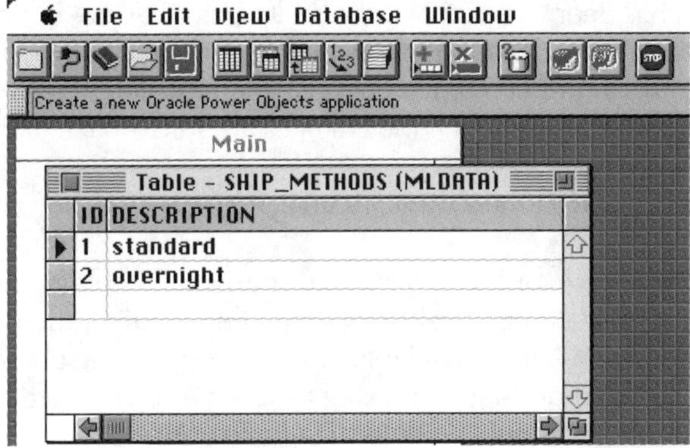

FIGURE 4-9. *The Table Browser window with its accompanying toolbar to insert and delete records and to commit or roll back changes made to the table*

containing the shipment method or method of payment. These contain only a couple of columns and a small number of entries. It is, therefore, much simpler to enter the information in the Table Browser window than to create an application form to enter this data.

For example, to add a new shipment method to the Ship_Methods table in the MLDATA database:

1. Open the Ship_Methods table and click the Run button on the toolbar.
2. Click on the Insert Row button on the toolbar or click in any field of the empty row at the bottom of the table.
3. In the table's primary key column, Id, type in the next sequential number (**3**). The Id column is the primary key for the table and is used to link the Ship_Methods table to the Orders table.
4. In the Description column, type **ground**, as shown here:

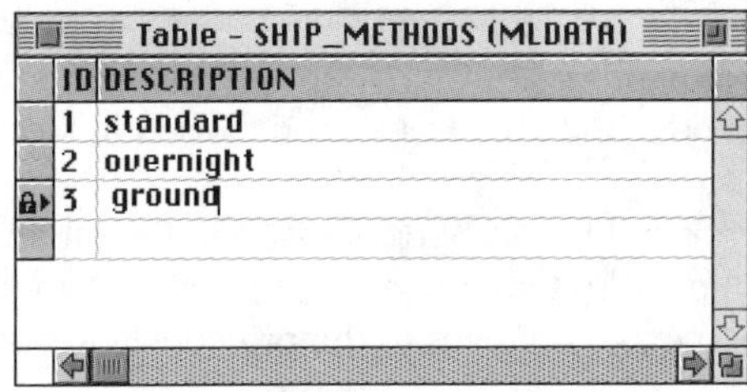

A new record has been entered into the table, but it has not been saved. The row displays a black padlock in the row indicator next to the row until changes made to the table are either commited (saved) or rolled back (restored to the last committed condition of the table). If the changes are rolled back, any changes to the table will be undone.

Editing a Row

To edit information in a record, you need to first open the table in the Table Browser and select the data in the table record to be modified, then start typing. You can select the data by either clicking and dragging the cursor over the characters to be changed or double-clicking to select a single word.

Any time a row(s) has been edited, Oracle Power Objects displays a black padlock in the row indicator(s) until you either commit or roll back the changes made to the table.

Deleting a Row

When you no longer need the information stored in a row, you can delete the row from the table. To delete a record from a table:

1. Click the row indicator button on the left side of the record to be deleted.
2. Click the Delete Row button on the toolbar.

The record disappears from the Table Browser window. Remember the record isn't deleted from the table until you commit the table.

Committing and Rolling Back Changes Made to a Table

As you add a row, delete a row, or modify existing data in a table, two things happen. First, the rows that have been affected are locked so that no one else can make changes to modified rows. (You can imagine the havoc that would take place if multiple users could edit the same rows in a table at the same time. Whoever saved the changes last would win.) Second, as you make changes to the data, only you can see the changes made to the rows. All changes to the database are held by the Record Manager, awaiting you to either commit or roll back all changes that have been made to a table.

To save changes made to a table, you select the Commit Work button on the toolbar. Once you commit changes to the table, you cannot undo those changes. To undo all changes made since the last commit, you click on the Rollback Work button on the toolbar.

Once you commit or roll back changes made to the table, all of the record locks are released in the table. Other users will see the changes made to the table, and they will be able to make changes to the previously locked records.

Closing the Table Browser Window

To close the Table Browser window and return to the Table Editor window, you just click on the Exit button on the Table Browser window or select Close from the File menu. If there are transactions pending (changes to a record(s) that have not been saved), you will be asked to either commit or roll back the edits before leaving the Table Browser window.

Views

A *view* is a means of querying multiple tables and displaying that information in a single spreadsheet-like view window. Views do not store data but only query other views and tables and display the results of the query. Views are similar to tables in that you use a View Editor window to create the view and a View Browser window to view the queried data. You can create views with either the View Editor window or you can create a form with a button control that has a SQL script to create the view in its Click( ) method.

Besides using views as a means of displaying related data, you can use views to simplify many database operations in Oracle Power Objects. You can use a view for either of the following purposes:

- To display data stored in multiple tables on a form, a report, or a repeater display from a single data source. This eliminates the hassle involved in having to specify all of the relationships between columns stored in different tables when creating forms in applications. For example, the items of an order only contain a reference (foreign key) to the name, description, and unit cost of products being sold. By creating a view that relates the order items to the product name and description, you could place the necessary view columns in a form displaying the order items and see all of the desired information without having to specify their relationship on the form.
- To display a subset of data stored in a table or in multiple tables. In views, you can specify data ranges (data constraints) for columns to be viewed, or you can store Oracle Basic Exec SQL expressions in the view for querying purposes. For example, you can create views with a data constraint on the Order_Date column of an Orders table that selected only those orders between January, 1995 to March, 1995.

Creating a New View

As an example, we will create a view that will relate the information stored in a Products table to the order line items stored in an Order_Items table. To create a new view in the database session:

1. Open and activate the database session.
2. Click on the New View button in the toolbar.

The View Editor window and its properties window are opened. You use the View Editor window to create or edit the definition of a database view. Whenever you create a new view or open an existing view, the View Editor window is displayed.

3. Change the name of the view in the Name property of the View property sheet to an appropriate name (**Orditemproducts**).

The View Editor Window

You create or edit the structure of a view in the View Editor window. The View Editor window consists of a Table List area, where all tables to include in the view are placed, and a Column List area, for specifying the specific columns to place in the view.

Placing Tables in the Table List Area You place all of the base tables that will be used in the view in the Table List area. For this example, we will again use an Order_Items table and a Products table. To place the tables in the Table List area:

1. Activate the database session window.
2. Hold down the SHIFT key and click on each of the base table's icons (Order_Items and Products) and drag them to the Table List area (see Figure 4-10).

The tables are shown in a rectangle with the table title at the top of the box and all of the table's columns in a scrolling list below. If you drag tables over one at a time, try to place the tables to be related in proximity to each other, to make it easy to create relationships between the tables.

Removing Base Tables from a View If you accidentally place a table in the Table List area, you can delete it from the Table List area. To remove a base table from a view:

1. Select the table in the Table List area by clicking on it.
2. Delete the base table by selecting the lower-right corner of the base table window and dragging it to the upper-left corner.

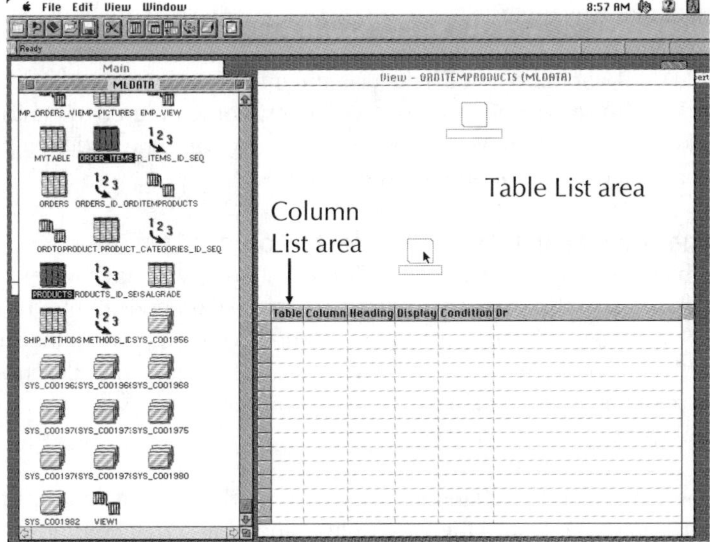

FIGURE 4-10. *The outlines of the Order_Items and Products tables being dragged from the session window to the OrdItemProducts view's Table List area*

Joining Base Tables Once you've placed all of the tables in the Table List area, you need to physically relate the tables. In this example, the two columns used to relate the tables are the Product_Id column (foreign key) in the Order_Items table and the Id column (primary key) in the Products table. The primary field is usually the primary key field of a table and the secondary field is the foreign key field on another table.

To relate the Order_Items and Products tables:

1. Click on the Product_Id column in the Order_Items table. It is a foreign key to the Products table.
2. Drag the selected column to the Id column in the Products table (the primary field to which it is associated) and release the mouse. A line is drawn between the two tables and visually establishes their relationship, as shown here:

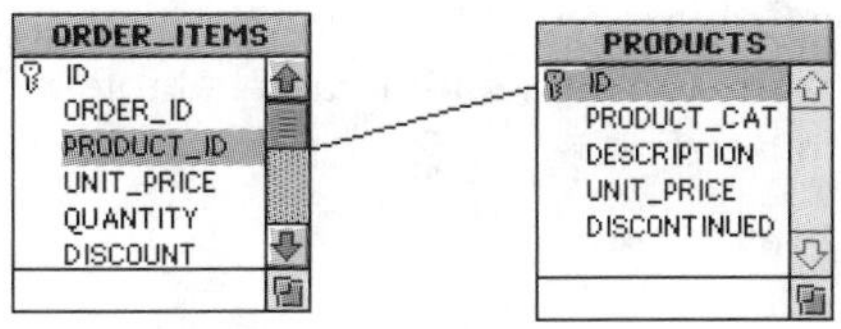

Drawing a line between two tables to join them generates the SQL code used to query the data. If you are acquainted with SQL, the join line corresponds to WHERE table1.col=table2.col in a select statement.

If you make a mistake when joining two tables, you can remove the join line and rejoin the tables. To remove a join line, select the join line and then press the DELETE key or click on the Cut button on the toolbar.

Defining the View Structure in the View's Column List Area

Once the tables have been related in the Table List area, you have to select the columns to be used in the view and define the view's data constraints. To define the structure of a view, click and drag the columns from the table to the Column List area. In this example, we want to be able to display the name, description, and price of a product associated to an order line item.

To complete the view definition:

1. Drag the Order_Id, Quantity, Product_Id, and Discount columns from the Order_Items table and the Description and Unit_Price columns from the Products table into the Column List area.
2. This view will also include an expression in a column to total cost of the line item by multiplying the Unit_Price by Quantity. Click in an empty row and type in the Column field **=UNIT_PRICE * QUANTITY** and type **Total** in the Heading field. (The view will be used to simplify the creation of a form in Chapter 6.)

When a column is placed in the Column List area the Table and Column fields are filled in with the appropriate information and set the Display field to TRUE (see Figure 4-11).

You can set the following parameters for each column in the Column List area:

Table This is the base table for the selected column.

Column This is the table column that will be used to display data in the view. This column can contain an expression for displaying derived values.

Heading You can type in a name to be displayed in the View Browser window that is different than the Column name from which the data will be retrieved. The heading can include spaces so you could rename a table column, e.g. Fname, to First Name for a column heading.

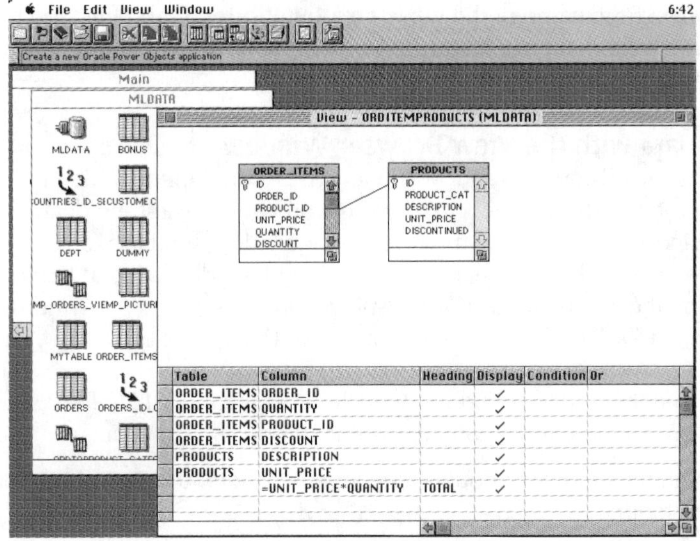

FIGURE 4-11. *The completed view*

Display To use a column in a view but not display its values, you click on the Display field to turn it off. You might want to include a field for use in an expression in another column but not want to display that value when running the view.

Condition The Condition field is used to place restrictions on the values that will appear in the view. You can use the >, <, and = signs to place restrictions on the values to be displayed in the view. For example, you could set the condition for the SALARY column to >50000 to display only those employees with a salary greater than $50,000.

Or This is used to set an additional condition on the view.

Saving a View

After you have named and defined the view you need to save it in the database session. To save a view:

1. Click on the Save button on the toolbar or select Save from the File menu. Oracle Power Objects displays a standard Open dialog box.

2. Type in the name of the view, **OrdItemProducts**, and click on the Save button. Saving a view executes a SQL CREATE VIEW statement in the database.

Viewing Data with the View Browser Window

You use the View Browser window to view data stored in the table. If the view is set in the property sheet to be a read-write, you can also edit the data. The View Browser window displays the stored data in a window similar to a spreadsheet. The columns' names (or heading name if you set one) are displayed at the top of the window and the related records are displayed in rows across the window. To view the data in the OrdItemProducts view of the MLDATA session in the View Editor:

1. Open the OrdItemProducts view by opening the MLDATA session and then double-clicking on the OrdItemProducts view icon.
2. With the OrdItemProducts view open, click on the Run button on the toolbar.

The view displays the queried information in the view and displays the Order_Id, Quantity, Product_Id, Discount, Description, Unit_Price, and Total.

Closing the View Browser Window

To close the View Browser window and return to the View Editor window, just click on the Exit button on the View Browser window or select Close from the File menu. If the view is a read-write view and there are transactions pending (there are changes that have been made to a record(s) that have not been saved), you will be asked to either commit or roll back the edits before leaving the View Browser window.

Sequences

A *sequence* is a database object that provides a means of assigning unique sequential integers to each row of a table. Sequences are used to create the integers used in primary key columns. Some sequences may be used to number all primary keys that begin with the number one, such as employee, each customer, each order a company makes, and each line item for each order. Sequences for customer orders usually start at a higher number than one, thus avoiding the anxiety felt by a customer who receives an order form with the number one on it.

To create a sequence object that will number customer orders beginning at 1001:

1. Open a session and then double-click on the connect icon to open the session.
2. Click on the New Sequence button, or select New Sequence item from the Edit menu, which displays the Create Sequence window.
3. Type in a sequence name that identifies the sequence object's purpose, like **Orders_OrderId_Seq**.

Because a sequence is frequently used with a specific column and table, it is common to name the sequence so it is easily recognized with the table and column to which it will be associated. However, you may want to create a sequence that can be used by many different columns. For instance, columns such as EmpId and LineItems may both be configured the same and could therefore be used with both columns.

4. Set the Starting value to **1001**. The first order will start with the number 1001 instead of 1.
5. Set the Increment By value to the amount to be incremented to the current highest value.
6. Press the Create button to create the new sequence.

In Chapter 5, we explain how you apply a sequence object to a column on a form and how to use the other property sheet properties and method for creating and configuring sequences.

You can create a sequence object by using Exec SQL by attaching this script, **create sequence ORDERID increment by 1 start with 10001**, in the Click( ) method of a button located on a form.

Indexes

Indexes are database objects that provide a means of quickly locating stored data. A database index is similar to an index in a book—it acts like a lookup table to a value in a column. An index contains a listing of keywords associated with the keyword's location. You should create indexes for key information that you will need to query or sort on a frequent basis in large tables. Your database administrator needs to provide you with the necessary permissions to create or drop an index.

You should consider creating indexes for the following types of columns:

- **Primary key columns** Because primary keys are frequently used to search or sort, an index will speed either querying or sorting the data in a table.

For example, an order primary key number should be indexed as it will be used frequently to search for a specific order or to sort orders.

- **Foreign key columns** Because foreign keys are used to join tables in a master-detail relationship, indexes on a foreign key will speed displaying related data.
- **Sorted columns** Any column that will be set to sort a table's data. You may frequently sort clients by their first and last name or sort them by their state for reporting purposes.

To create an index:

1. Click on the New Index icon on the toolbar, which displays the Create Index dialog box, shown here:

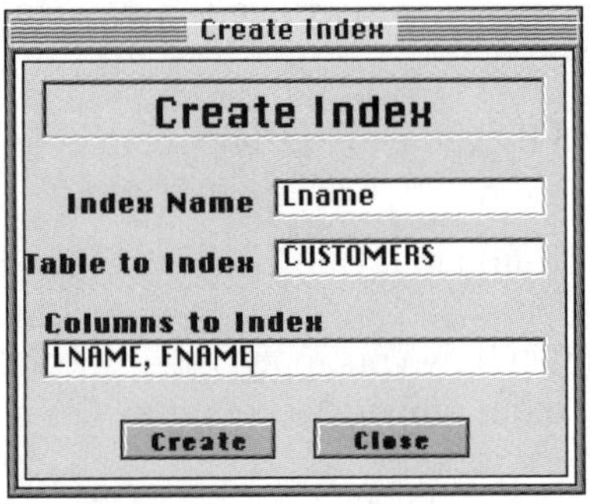

2. Type in the name of the index to identify the information to be indexed (such as Lname).
3. Set the table to be indexed.
4. Type the name of the column to be indexed in the Columns to Index field. If there are multiple fields to index, enter the fields in the order of sort priority and separate them with a comma.
5. Click on the Create button to create the index. In the illustration shown above, the index Lname sorts the table first by Lname and then by Fname, so the table displays the customers sorted by their last name and their first name.

You can also create an index for an Oracle7 database with the following SQL command:

```
CREATE INDEX[schema] index ON [schema.] table (column)
```

To create an index named i_emp_Lname on the Lname column in the Emp table:

```
CREATE INDEX i_emp_Lname ON emp (Lname)
```

Note that while indexes greatly improve query speed, they also increase the size of your database and should only be used with tables containing over 20 rows.

Synonyms

A *synonym* is a database object that acts as an alias to another database object, such as a table, view, or sequence. Synonyms provide database security and convenience in referencing database objects. Creating a synonym allows you to:

- Hide the location of the database object being referenced.
- Hide the owner of the database object.
- Provides a simpler means of referencing database objects in another user's schema when using Oracle Basic or Exec SQL.
- Manipulate a database object with DDL (data definition language) and DML (data manipulation language) operations by referring to the object's synonym.

To create a synonym with Oracle Power Objects:

1. Click on the New Synonym button on the toolbar, which displays the Create Synonym window, shown here:

2. Type in the synonym name.

3. Type in the name of the object referenced by the synonym.
4. Press the Create button to create the new synonym.

You can also create synonyms with the SQL command create synonym:

```
CREATE [PUBLIC] SYNONYM [user.] FOR [user.] object [@db_link]
```

To create a synonym employee for the Emp table in the schema scott:

```
CREATE SYNONYM employee FOR scott.emp
```

Your database administrator needs to provide you with the necessary permissions to create or drop a synonym. To drop a synonym with SQL:

```
DROP [PUBLIC] SYNONYM [user.] synonym
```

In this version of Oracle Power Objects, you cannot create or view synonyms in the database session, but you can refer to synonyms with SQL statements.

Conclusion

In this chapter, we have explained how to use Oracle Power Objects' tools to set up and use all of the database objects (tables, views, sequences, indexes, and synonyms). Chapter 5 builds on the information found in this chapter and explains how to create applications and how to use forms. In Chapter 5 you will learn how to connect application objects like forms and reports to the database objects discussed here.

CHAPTER 5

Creating Applications and Forms

When you create an application in Oracle Power Objects, you are developing an object (which can be manipulated with Oracle Basic code) that can contain other objects (forms, reports, user-defined classes, bitmaps, and OLE objects). These application objects provide the user interface to data stored in database sessions. Several application objects (forms, reports, and classes) can be linked to multiple tables and to multiple database sessions, and they are equivalent to projects in Microsoft's Visual Basic.

Oracle Power Objects applications can contain all of the normal objects (dialog boxes, scroll bars, menu bars, toolbars, etc.) found in normal Windows and Macintosh programs. You can also call Windows' DLLs and embed OLE objects and OCX controls. Oracle Power Objects will also create applications that are not connected to a database session. For example, the Launch sample application delivered with Oracle Power Objects is a Windows application that acts as a launch pad for starting other applications.

The first section of this chapter will cover applications, an overview of all the applications objects, how to tie (bind) application containers to database objects, referencing object containers, working with applications, and common application object properties. The next section will cover manipulating forms in both Design mode and Run-time mode. Advanced uses of certain application objects are discussed in Chapters 6 and 11. Chapter 6 goes into greater detail on how to create complex forms with master-detail relations, classes, and reports that include information stored in multiple tables. Chapter 11 discusses advanced reporting techniques and the use of OLE application objects and OCX controls.

Applications

An *application* is an Oracle Power Objects object that contains forms, classes, reports, bitmaps, and OLE objects. Normally, Oracle Power Objects applications act as the front end or user interface to the data stored in one or more databases. Applications present data in a meaningful manner, allowing the grouping of related pieces of information from multiple tables on a single form, related forms, or in reports. Oracle Power Objects provides tools that simplify creating the application's user interface for adding, editing, deleting, and querying data stored in a database. However, it is you, the application developer, who decides on the final user interface to the data being stored in the database.

An application is stored on disk as a single file, and in Windows the filename has the .POA extension automatically appended to it. For example, if you create an application named TUBS, the application would be saved to disk as TUBS on a Macintosh and as TUBS.POA in Windows. This system file contains all of the information containing the application's forms, reports, classes, OLE objects, and bitmaps.

Application Object Types

When you open an existing application or create a new application, Oracle Power Objects opens the application in a window similar to the Main window. The application window can contain forms, classes, reports, bitmaps, and OLE objects as icons (see Figure 5-1). Some of these objects act as containers for other application objects, such as controls and static objects.

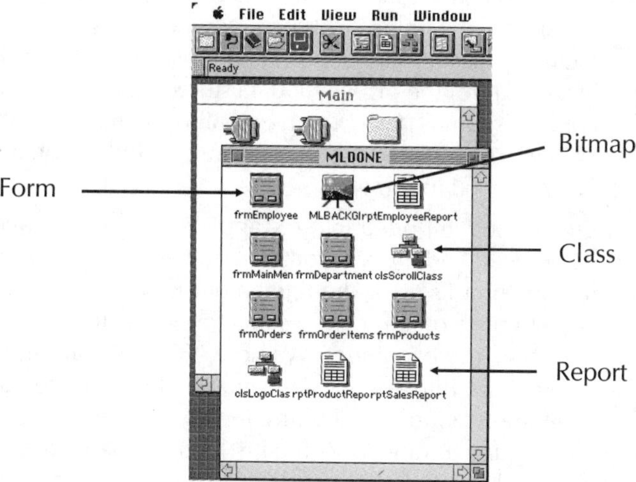

FIGURE 5-1. *An application window with a variety of forms, classes, reports, and bitmaps*

There are six major application object types: containers, static objects, controls, bitmaps, OLE objects, and classes. Some of the object types like the rectangle and oval objects can act as either static objects or as containers. The following table provides a brief description of the application object types:

Application Object	Description
Containers	Containers are application objects that can contain other objects. For example, forms and reports can contain static text, bitmaps, controls, etc. Forms, embedded forms, reports, classes, and repeater displays are all containers. You can also use rectangles and ovals as containers.
Static Objects	Static objects are objects placed onto containers to make the displayed information easier to understand. Static text explains the type of data displayed on a form or in a field. Rectangles, ovals, or lines help divide information on a container into logical areas.

Controls	Controls regulate the user interface and the display of data in a container. Text fields, list boxes, combo boxes, pop-up lists, picture objects, radio buttons and radio frames, and check boxes control the display of data stored in a database. Other controls such as push buttons, scroll bars, and current row pointers dictate how the user interacts with the container and the displayed information.
Bitmaps	Bitmaps are imported into the application window and can then be dragged and dropped onto containers or added to push button controls using the Bitmap property or by using method code to push button controls to add interest to the user interface. You can import Windows' BMP bitmaps into an application. Bitmaps are static graphic files used to add interest to an application object (form, report, or control), such as a background graphic or company logo. Bitmaps should not be confused with picture objects (which display bitmaps stored in a database record).
OLE Objects	Imported OLE (object linking and embedding) objects provide a means of viewing and editing the OLE object data with the interface of another application. For example, a Microsoft Word document could be imported as an OLE object. To edit the object, you double-click the object and Microsoft Word's user interface appears for editing the document. OLE objects are only available on the Windows version. Using OLE objects is discussed in more detail in Chapter 11.
Classes	User-defined classes are reusable application objects. Classes are objects that, once they have been created, you can reuse on any form or report in your application. A class that is placed on a form or a report is called a *subclass.* Subclasses inherit all of the behaviors and actions of the master class. For example, you can create a class containing a company logo with the company address information or a set of buttons to commit or roll back changes made to the database. Once you create a class, it can be placed in a number of forms or reports. For more information on using classes, see Chapter 6.

Object Naming Conventions

To make it easier to identify the type of object that is being referenced in Oracle Basic (and help prevent the accidental use of a reserved word), Oracle recommends that you incorporate the naming rules for application objects listed in Table 5-1 (Object naming conventions are specified in the Oracle Power Objects Coding Standards document.)

Object	Type	Prefix	Example
Containers	embedded form	emb	embTotalCost
	form	frm	frmTub
Static Objects	lines	lin	linClockHand
	rectangles	rct	rctTubOptions
	static text	txt	txtTubEntry
Controls	chart	cht	chtSalesBySalesman
	check box	chk	chkTaxable
	combo box	cbo	cboTubType
	horizontal scroll bar	hsb	hsbOrders
	list box	lst	lstTubType
	picture box	pic	picEmployees
	pop-up list	pop	popTubType
	push buttons	btn	btnClose
	radio buttons	rad	radPrestigeElite
	radio button frames	rbf	rbfTubTypes
	text box	fld	fldNotes
	vertical scroll bar	vsb	vsbOrderItems
Bitmaps	bitmaps	bmp	bmpLogo
OLE Objects	OLE object	ole	oleChart
Classes	class	cls	clsAddress
Databases	session	ses	sesTubs

TABLE 5-1. *Naming Conventions for Application Objects*

Application Containers and Database Objects

In Chapter 4, we discussed how database sessions work as a container for database objects when the session is connected. The concepts discussed there become more important as you develop applications that associate data stored in a database to the application objects. Therefore, it is important to understand how Oracle Power Objects performs transaction processing and how Oracle Power Objects controls the flow of data between an application and the database.

The Record Manager and Recordset Objects

In an application, when you perform actions like querying a database, modifying a record, or creating a new record, the Oracle Power Objects Record Manager passes the information through the database session to the database. The database then analyzes the message and passes back the desired information through the session and the Record Manager to the application. All insertions, deletions, or modifications to a record (row) or queries on a table are sent through the Record Manager to the database, and the results are returned to the Record Manager (see Figure 5-2).

The Record Manager keeps track of all the application's transactions by maintaining recordset objects. A recordset object is an invisible Oracle Power Objects object that contains data queried from a RecordSource and modifications made to the data by an application object. Each recordset object is related to a specific container, such as a form, report, or embedded form. The Record Manager holds in memory the recordset object for each *bound container* (an application object that is associated, or bound, to a table or view in a database). While the recordset object is usually associated with a bound container (a form, a class, a repeater display, or a report), it is possible to define a recordset object independent of a bound container. For example, you could create an application for performing amortizations whose results are not stored in a database.

Bindable Containers

A *bindable container* is an application object (such as a form, repeater display, frame, etc.) that has a RecordSource property (a table or a view) and a RecSrcSession property (a session). A container that has its RecordSource and RecSrcSession set is a bound container. The recordset object populates the bound

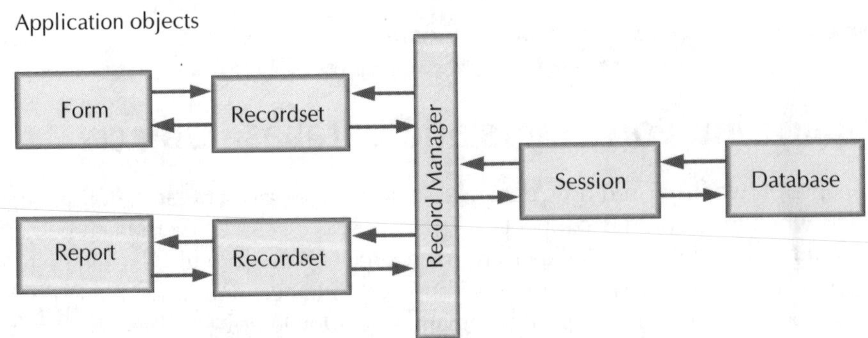

FIGURE 5-2. *The information displayed and modified on a form is passed down and back to the database through the Record Manager and the database session*

container from the results of a query to the table or view to which the container is associated. When you commit or roll back the changes to the recordset, the Record Manager updates the database and creates a new recordset by requerying the database.

When you open an application's bound form, the application queries the associated database object (table or view) and holds the results of the queried data in memory in a recordset object. This is an important concept, as any changes to the recordset (adding, deleting, or modifying records) only modifies the recordset and not the actual database object. So if you accidentally delete a thousand records using an application and then discover that you didn't really want to do that, you can roll back the pending transactions without modifying the database object.

In the case of a bound form that contains a master-detail relationship, there are multiple recordsets associated with the form. Each bound container (form, any embedded forms, or repeater displays) has its own recordset that populates the bound container.

Bindable Controls

A *bindable control* is a control object (such as a field, radio button frame, etc.) with a DataSource property. A control whose DataSource property is set to a column in a table or view is called a bound control. The DataSource must be set to a column located in the table or view specified in the containerRecordSource. It is this ability to bind a control to a table column that allows you to read from or write to a column in a table in the database.

When you drag and drop a column from a table or view in an open database session onto an unbound form, it sets the RecordSource and RecSrcSession of the container. Oracle Power Objects then adds a text field control and a static text control to the form and sets the text field control's DataSource. You can also drag and drop a column onto an existing control on a form to set its DataSource.

Object Containment Hierarchy

Although Oracle Power Objects automates many operations that normally have to be programmed in other programs, the examples throughout this book use small scripts of Oracle Basic code to perform common tasks needed by an application. To accomplish these tasks, you may need to refer to other objects to retrieve or set their value. Therefore, you need to understand the manner in which Oracle Power Objects identifies objects. Oracle Power Objects identifies an object by its name (set in the Name property) and by each of its container's names.

The following rules govern the object containment hierarchy:

- The *top-level object* is the file object (i.e. session, application, or library).

- A next level is the *parent* or *container* (i.e. form, embedded form, report, class, or other object used to contain other objects).
- All objects contained in a container are referred to as the container's *children.*
- All objects contained in a container are referred to as *siblings* to each other.
- A method or property of an object is referenced immediately after the object.

When you reference an object in Oracle Basic, you reference the object by separating each part of the hierarchy with a period. For example, to activate the HasScrollBar property of a text control (fldNote) on a form (frmOrders), you type:

```
frmOrders.fldNote.HasScrollBar = TRUE
```

Oracle Power Objects allows you to identify an object, its value, and its containers in a generic manner by using the keywords described in the following section.

Object References

You can refer in Oracle Basic code to objects in this object hierarchy using the keywords **value**, **self**, **GetContainer**, **GetTopContainer**, and **inherited**. We suggest that you use the object references, GetContainer, GetTopContainer, and self, as often as possible to take full advantage of the object-oriented nature of Oracle Power Objects. This allows you to easily reuse buttons, classes, etc., as you don't have to change Oracle Basic code in the object's methods when placing them onto new containers.

Value The Value property refers to the current value held in an object. For example, you could reference the value currently displayed in a field control:

```
frmOrder.fldFirstName.value
```

Self The Self property refers to the object in which the method code is being executed. Even if you change the name of the object containing the Oracle Basic code, the code will work. To set the value of the object containing the Oracle Basic code to NULL:

```
self.value=NULL
```

The Self property works differently with an instance of a class object than with other types of objects. When you use the Self property of an instance of a class, the self refers to the class's container and not itself. Therefore, using the Oracle Basic script self.value=NULL given above with a class object sets the value of its container to NULL and does not affect its own value.

GetContainer and GetTopContainer The GetContainer and GetTopContainer methods allow you to refer to an object's parent or its top container, without specifying its name. This allows you to reuse the object in multiple containers, without having to rewrite references to objects. For example, instead of referring to the value using the fldFirstName field as shown in this value property example:

```
frmOrder.fldFirstName.value
```

you could replace it with:

```
GetContainer.fldFirstName.value
```

If you change the order of the reference to fldFirstName.container, the reference would refer to the form, frmOrder, instead of the field, fldFirstName. You could also refer to the value of the fldFirstName field with GetContainer.self.value.

Inherited.Method_Name( ) Anytime you write Oracle Basic code in a method, it replaces the default process of the method. You can execute a standard method's process with the inherited.method_name statement. Using inherited.method_name allows you to control when the standard method code will be processed within your own code. For example, to process the standard actions of the PostChange( ) method, you would type:

```
Inherited.PostChange()
```

Opening Existing Applications

Applications (as well as sessions and libraries) are displayed as icons in the Oracle Power Objects Main window. To open and view the objects stored in an application, double-click on the application's icon in the Main window. This opens the application window and displays all of the objects associated with the application.

Note that not all of the applications stored on your hard drive will be presented in the Main window. An application may not be displayed if you move the application to a different directory or folder (or if you have manually removed the icon from the Main window). Also, if you copy an application to the hard drive, Oracle Power Objects will not automatically display the application in the Main window. Once you open an application, session, or library in the Main window, it will be displayed every time you open Oracle Power Objects.

If the application's icon is not displayed in the Main window:

1. Select Open Application from the File menu. The Open Application dialog box appears.

2. Navigate (if necessary) to the directory or folder where the application is located, select the application's name, and click OK. The application window is opened and the application's icon is placed in the Oracle Power Objects' Main window.

Creating New Applications

Although Oracle Power Objects comes with several good sample applications, you will probably want to create your own applications to meet your specific needs.

To create an application:

1. Open the Oracle Power Objects Main window.
2. Select New Application from the File menu or press the New Application button on the Form Designer toolbar. A New Application dialog box, shown here, is displayed.

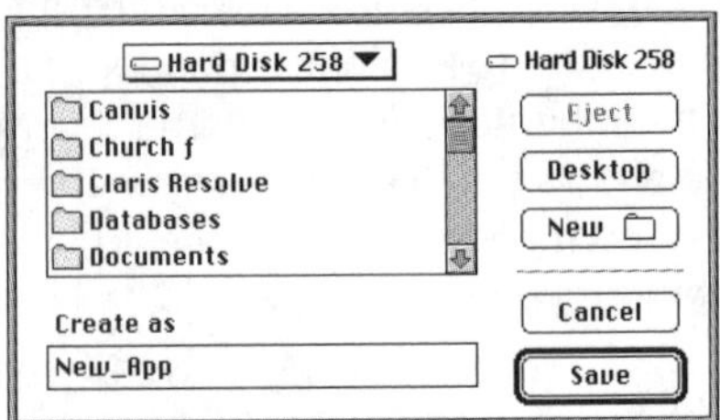

3. In the New Application dialog box, type the name of the new application, select the directory or folder where you want to place the application, and click Save. Remember, if you're creating an application on a Macintosh that will also be used in Windows, the application name needs to conform to MS-DOS naming conventions.

A window for the application appears with its accompanying property sheet. The Name property for the application is set to the name given in the New Application dialog box and the application's icon appears in the Main window. If you create an application in Windows, Oracle Power Objects appends a .POA extension to the application's name.

Removing Applications from the Main Window

Once you have opened an application, the application's icon will appear in the Main window. Sometimes you will want to remove an application's icon from the

Main window. For example, if you have been reviewing another developer's application and are now finished looking at it, you can easily remove it from the Main window.

To remove an application:

1. Select the application in the Oracle Power Objects Main window.
2. Select the Cut menu item from the Edit menu or click on the Cut button on the toolbar.

The application is removed from the Main window, but it is not deleted from the disk. To delete an application, you must use the Windows File Manager or the Macintosh trash can to delete the application.

NOTE
Anytime you delete an application or move it to a new location, Oracle Power Objects will inform you that it cannot find the application and will remove the application's icon from the Main window.

Property Sheets

Property sheets control the connection of fields and forms to database objects, the display of the data, the user interface of the form and controls, and actions that will take place based upon mouse clicks or tabbing through fields. Chapters 8 and 9 give a detailed explanation of each of the available properties and methods, but this section provides a quick overview of some the most commonly used properties and methods that will be needed for setting up simple forms.

Naming Properties

Each object has a Name and a Label property, which may or may not be the same. The Name property is the object name used in SQL and Oracle Basic scripts, and must be a single word, such as OrderForm. The Label property is the name displayed in conjunction with the object. In the case of a form, the Label property is the name that appears at the top of the form window. The label attached to a pop-up list or radio button group is the name that appears in connection to the list or radio button group. Often, the Name and Label property will contain the same name, but they will differ if it is more appropriate to use a multiword label, such as Tub Color.

Internal Value Properties

Some properties control the values displayed in controls. Many of these properties are automatically set by dragging table columns from a database to a form. These properties establish the database session, table, and column bound to the different form controls. Dragging columns onto forms also specifies the DataSize and DataType. If you manually create a text field control or another control like a pop-up list, you have to manually set these properties. Other properties used in association with controls establish value options such as the default value, a list of values to be displayed in the control using the DefaultValue, Translation, ValueList, and ValueOn properties. These latter properties will be explained in more detail in the "Providing Data Accuracy" section.

Physical Appearance Properties

Many of the properties are used to define the appearance of the application forms. These properties set such characteristics as the font properties, tabbing order between fields, whether objects have borders or scroll bars, if objects will be filled with a color, or the form's window style.

Forms

You use forms to control the display of data and provide an attractive user interface to the data stored in tables, or to control the application's user interface. With Oracle Power Objects, you create forms that perform one or more of the following interface tasks:

- **Display data** A form can be set to display data queried from the database or data resulting from a calculation (called a *derived value*). For example, the MoonLight Demo-DONE application has a form that displays the sales tax for the selected item.
- **Manipulate data** Most forms allow you to manipulate (add, delete, and edit) data stored in a database.
- **Navigate to other forms** You can place buttons on a form that open or close other forms or reports.
- **Create links to other applications** In the Windows version of Oracle Power Objects, you can create links to other applications with either OLE objects or by calls to procedures defined in Dynamic Link Libraries (DLLs).

- **Set properties** You can create forms that act as normal Macintosh or Windows dialog boxes in which the user can change the properties of an application, a form, or another application object. For example, you could create a window that lets a user change the background color of a form.

A form is comprised of a window in which you place control objects that determine the manner in which you display and manipulate data. Controls consist of objects such as static text for descriptive text, text fields for entering and editing data, buttons to perform actions like closing the form window, repeater displays to display multiple records in a table or related records from multiple tables on a form, or embedded forms (covered in more detail in Chapter 6) to display data from another table. You can place objects like check boxes and radio buttons, which provide easy ways to enter selections on a form. You can also place on forms other special types of forms such as an instance of a class (which can contain any object that can be placed on a form) or embedded forms (on which you can place controls to show data from another table). Bitmaps can be placed as backgrounds for both forms and controls to add interest to a form.

Every bound form has a RecordSource property set to a default table or view (explained in "Binding Columns and Containers to Database Objects" later in the chapter). You can use forms to display data from one record at a time or multiple records at a time from a table specified in the RecordSource property. Specific controls like an embedded form or a repeater can specify a different record source than the form's record source (to display related data from another table). You can also create forms to act as dialog boxes to prompt the user to make choices or give directions.

Creating a New Form

You create forms in an application window. To create a new (standard) form, click on the application window (if it is not already active), and then click on the New Form button.

The new form appears as an empty window with its property sheet and the Object palette, and is assigned a default name (default form names are form1, form2, etc.), as shown in Figure 5-3

1. Scroll in the property sheet to the form's Label property and click on the default label name and type in a new one. The Label property is the text that is displayed at the top of the form in the title bar.
2. Scroll in the property sheet to the form's Name property and click on the default form name and type in the new name. The Name property is the name used to reference the form object in Oracle Basic code. To help

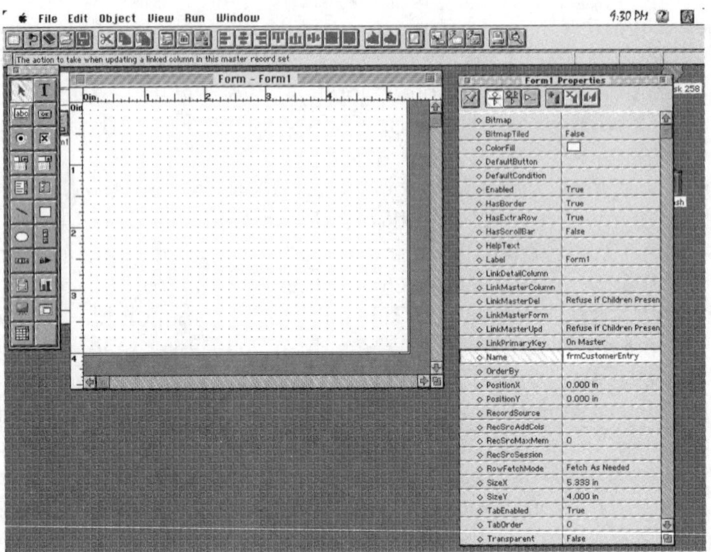

FIGURE 5-3. *The New Form window with the Form Designer toolbar, the Object palette, and the property sheet*

distinguish the form object, the Oracle Power Objects Coding Standards suggest using the "frm" prefix before the form name (e.g., frmCustomerEntry).

3. Click on the Save button on the toolbar to save the new form.

Opening and Deleting Existing Forms

To open an existing form, double-click the icon of the form in the application window. The form is opened in the Form Designer window with its property sheet.

If a form is no longer needed, or if you accidentally create a form with the New Form button, you can permanently delete a form. To do so:

1. Activate the application window and select the form.
2. Click on the Cut button on the toolbar or select Cut from the Edit menu.
3. Click OK on the warning dialog box reminding you that deleting a form is irreversible.

Copying or Moving a Form Between Application Windows

To move or copy a form to another application:

1. Select the form in the application window.
2. To move a form, drag and drop the form onto the open application window. To copy a form, hold down the CTRL key (COMMAND key on the Macintosh) and drag and drop the form onto an open application window.

NOTE
You can also copy (or cut) the form from an open application window and paste it into another open application window.

Form Designer, Form Run-time, and Application Run-time Modes

Forms can be viewed in either the Form Designer, Form Run-time, or Application Run-time modes. The Form Designer mode is where you develop the form. The Form Run-time and Application Run-time modes provide a quick and easy method of ensuring that a form or application works as you intended it to work without having to compile the application.

Form Designer Mode

Form Designer mode is where you, the designer, create, review, and edit the form layout. In this mode, you add controls and graphic objects to a form and position them. You can also set the property sheets associated with the form and its control objects to control the user interface's appearance, and define SQL and Oracle Basic code to control the behavior of the form and its controls.

Form Run-time Mode

You can test your form at any time by clicking on the Run Form button on the Form Designer toolbar. In this mode your form runs as if the form were compiled. The form queries the database and displays all associated data (an example of which is shown in Figure 5-4). This mode allows you to quickly check how the form will look and its basic functionality. However, if the form has references to other forms or reports or relies on declarations (such as global variables) made in the application's property sheet, it will give you an error when you attempt to run the form.

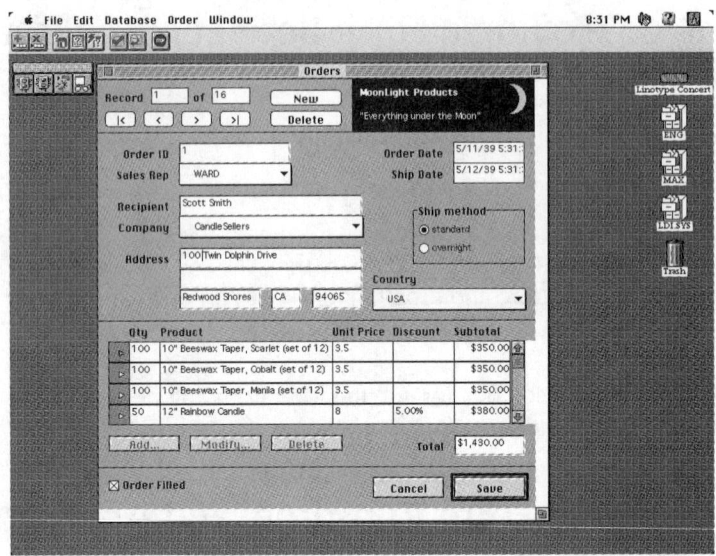

FIGURE 5-4. *Running the fmOrders form located in the MoonLight Demo-DONE application in Form Run-time mode*

Application Run-time Mode

You can test your application at any time by clicking on the Run button on the Form Designer toolbar to get into Application Run-time mode. In this mode, your application runs as if the entire application were compiled (an example of which is shown in Figure 5-5). The application queries the database and displays all associated data. This mode allows you to quickly check how the application and all of its features will look. The application can resolve all references to other forms or reports and opens just as if you were opening the compiled application. However, running the application in the Application Run-time mode might force you to navigate to the form you need to test, slows your test time as it runs the entire application, and introduces other application objects that might be bound to a database (making it more difficult to resolve bugs in a single form).

Working with Forms in Designer Mode

As mentioned earlier, forms are bindable containers and can contain any of the items that can be created with the Object palette, bitmaps, or classes. You design forms in Designer mode. In this section, we cover how to bind forms and controls

FIGURE 5-5. *Running the MoonLight Demo-DONE application in Application Run-time mode*

to database session objects and how to add application objects to forms and set their properties.

Binding Columns and Containers to Database Objects

One of the most impressive features of Oracle Power Objects is the ease with which you bind an application object (containers or controls) to a database session object (table or view). Once an application object like a form is bound to a database session object, all of its bound controls display the desired information at run time. A container must have its RecordSource and RecSrcSession properties set to bind it to the appropriate database object, and all controls must have their DataSource, DataType, and DataSize properties set to the appropriate table or view column.

There are several ways in which you can bind containers or controls to a database session object. You can graphically connect the application object either with drag and drop, manually connect the object using its property sheet, or derive a single value with the Translation property or with SQLLookup (see Chapter 10 on how to use SQL).

Automatically Binding Containers to Tables or Views

The quickest and easiest method of binding controls and containers is to drag and drop a database object (table, view, or a column) from an open database session onto a container or control. Dragging and dropping tables or views onto a container sets the RecordSource and RecSrcSession properties of the container. Also, dragging and dropping a column onto a control sets the DataSource, DataType, DataSize, Name, and ScrollWithRow properties of the control. The following example shows how to bind a frmCustomerEntry form (to enter and modify customer data) to the Customers table in the MoonLight Data session.

To bind a container to a table or view:

1. Open the container to be bound (frmCustomerEntry form) in the Designer window.
2. Open the database session window (MoonLight Data) containing the table or view that will be connected to the form.
3. Double-click the connect icon in the session window to activate the database session, if the session is not already active.
4. Select the database table's icon (Customers) and drag it onto the container window (see Figure 5-6). Note that you can open a table or view and select only the necessary columns by holding down the CTRL key (COMMAND key on the Macintosh) and clicking on the desired columns.

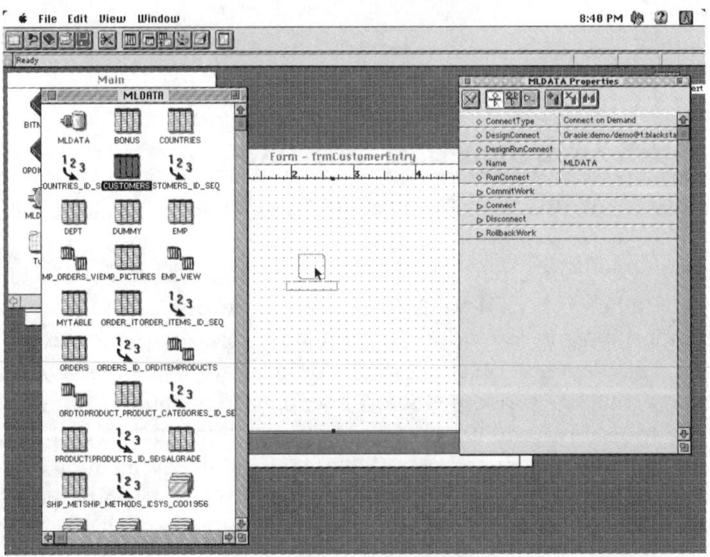

FIGURE 5-6. *The frmCustomerEntry form and the Tubs session with the tblCustomers table selected*

This creates and places text field controls for all of the columns in the table and their accompanying static text labels, places the controls and static text labels onto the form, and sets the control's name and label to the column's name (see Figure 5-7). If there is not enough room on the form for all of the controls and text labels, Oracle Power Objects only places the text field controls on the form. The form is also bound to the tblCustomer table, and the text controls are all bound to the appropriate column in the table. You can manually set the RecordSource and RecSrcSession properties to bind a container to a table or view.

Binding a Column to an Existing Control

If you have to manually place a control onto a container, you can use drag and drop to bind the control to the column. To bind a column to an existing control:

1. Open the container with the control to be bound (frmCustomerEntry form) in the Designer window.
2. Open the database session window containing the table or view that will be connected to the form.
3. Double-click the connect icon to activate the database session, if the session is not already active.

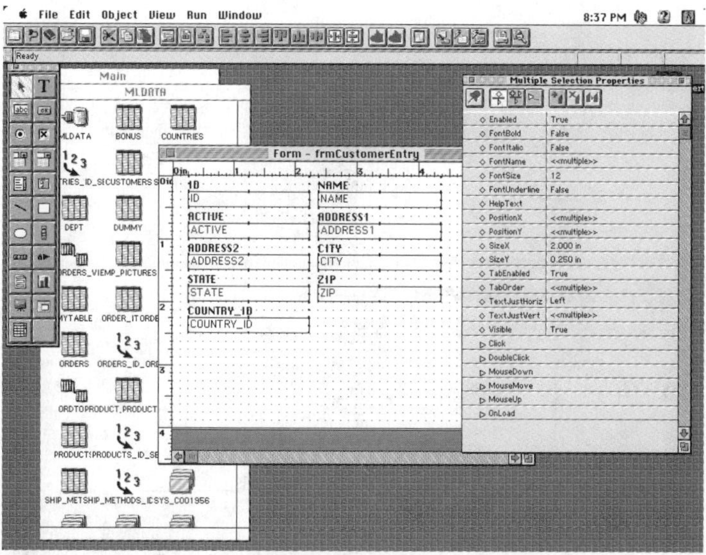

FIGURE 5-7. *The text field controls and static text labels placed on the form after dragging and dropping the tblCustomer columns onto the form*

4. Double-click on the table's icon to open the table in the Table Browser mode.
5. Click on the desired column and drag and drop it onto the control (see Figure 5-8).

Dragging and dropping a column onto the control sets the DataSource, DataType, DataSize, Name, and ScrollWithRow properties of the control. You can manually set all of these properties to bind a column to a control.

Modifying a Text Control

You can change the appearance of all of the text in a text field using the control's property sheet. Common properties that you will change are the FontName, FontSize, alignment (vertical and horizontal), FormatMask, and DrawStyle (allows you to create 3-D looking fields). Chapter 8 covers all of the text control properties.

Changing Multiple Selection Properties to Controls

Another nice feature of Oracle Power Objects alluded to in earlier chapters is the ability to change the properties and methods of several objects at the same time. Selecting multiple objects is done in two ways. The first is performed by clicking in

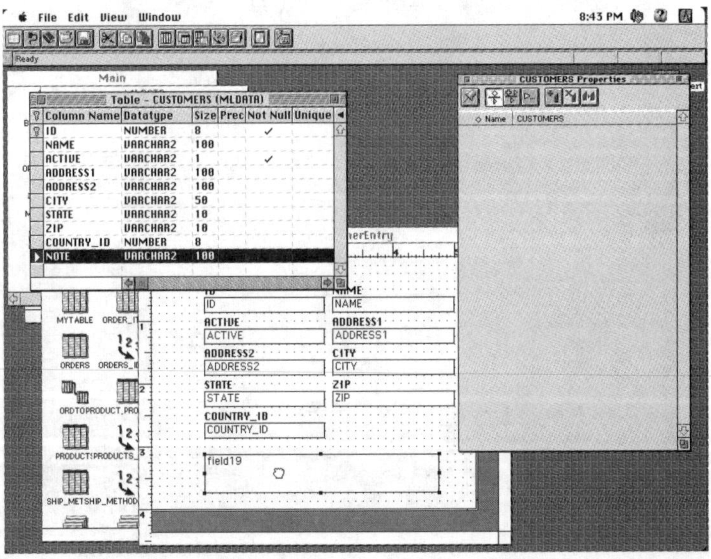

FIGURE 5-8. *Dragging and dropping a new Note column in the Customer table onto a text control field on the frmCustomerEntry form*

the container outside of any specific object within the container and dragging a rectangle, shown by a rubber band box, around all the objects whose properties you want to change. The second way is to click on the first object and then select other objects to be added to the selection list in the same container by pressing the SHIFT key while clicking on the other objects. When one object is selected, its border has eight black squares, bisected by the border outline, one on each corner and one in the middle of each side.

When multiple objects are selected, only the inside half of the black boxes on the border around each object is displayed, and the property sheet's header (if one is displayed) shows "Multiple Selection Properties." A very common use for this feature is to change the text justification or font for all of the static and control text fields in a form at the same time. You could also set all text field controls to have a 3-D appearance or apply the same bitmap property to several buttons at the same time. You will find that applying multiple selection properties to similar controls is a great time-saver in developing forms and reports.

Derived Value Calculation Fields

When you place a text control onto a form, you have to set its DataSource property in order for it to display a value queried from the database. In order to eliminate storing values that are easily calculated, you can enter a derived value in the control's DataSource property. A derived value is not stored in a column in a table but is simply calculated when the form is run. Derived values can consist of Oracle Basic expressions that perform simple mathematical operations, aggregate functions, or text concatenation and that start with the equal sign (=).

Mathematical expressions consist of arithmetic calculations such as addition or multiplication. A common use of a mathematical expression is to calculate in a field (fldUNITTOTAL) the total amount of a product on an invoice by multiplying the unit cost of a product (fldUNITPRICE) by the quantity (fldQTY) of the product being sold. The formula =fldUNITPRICE*fldQTY would be placed in the fldUNITTOTAL DataSource property.

Derived values can also be used to perform aggregate functions. *Aggregate functions* perform calculations (minimum, maximum, sum, etc.) and are based upon all of the values of a column in the container's recordset. If all of the line items of an order are displayed in a repeater display, you could calculate the sum of the fldUNITTOTAL field with =SUM(repeater1.fldUNITTOTAL). This aggregate function sums all of the values stored in the fldUNITTOTAL field on a repeater display named repeater1.

You can also use a derived value field to concatenate text. A simple example of using this is to combine the first and last names of clients printing their name on mailing labels. Type the following in the DataSource property: **=fldTitle &" "& fldFName &" "& fldLName**. The ampersand (&) symbol translates both columns to the string datatype and joins the fields together. Quotation marks contain any text to be placed in the field, which in this case places a space between the customer's name. You could also use this to place a customer's city, state, and ZIP code data into one string. Note that the & character is also used in Oracle Basic to continue a line of code to the next line (see Chapter 7 for more information on using the & symbol).

Setting the Tab Order of Text Controls

Setting the tab order of a group of text controls means establishing the order in which the *focus* (a control that is selected and ready to receive input) is moved from control to control when you press the TAB key. If you drag and drop a table or view onto a container, Oracle Power Objects automatically sets the tab order to move from left to right and then top to bottom.

You may later add other controls (such as a derived field) or rearrange the existing fields and may need to modify the tab order. Also, in some cases, such as on an invoice form, you may wish to tab vertically down the "Bill To:" set of controls and then tab to the "Ship To:" set of text controls.

To change the tab order of a control, you select the control and change its TabOrder property to be one greater than the value in the previous control. If the controls are not sequentially numbered, the focus is moved to the next highest number.

Using Scroll Bars

You can use scroll bars to view more data in a text field, a list, or repeater display; browse records in a container's recordset; or browse records queried from a database using the ScrollPos property (described in Chapter 8). Oracle Power Objects provides both vertical and horizontal scroll bar controls.

Using the Scroll Bar to Browse Records

Placing a scroll bar onto a bound container (form or class) sets the ScrollObj property of the scroll bar to its container. The scroll bar allows you to scroll through records in the recordset of the container set in the ScrollObj property.

To create a scroll bar for browsing records on a bound form:

1. Select the Horizontal Scroll Bar control on the Object palette and click on the bound container wherever you want the scroll bar. This sets the ScrollObj to the name of its container (see Figure 5-9).
2. Resize the scroll bar with one of the six black squares on the edges of the scroll bar.

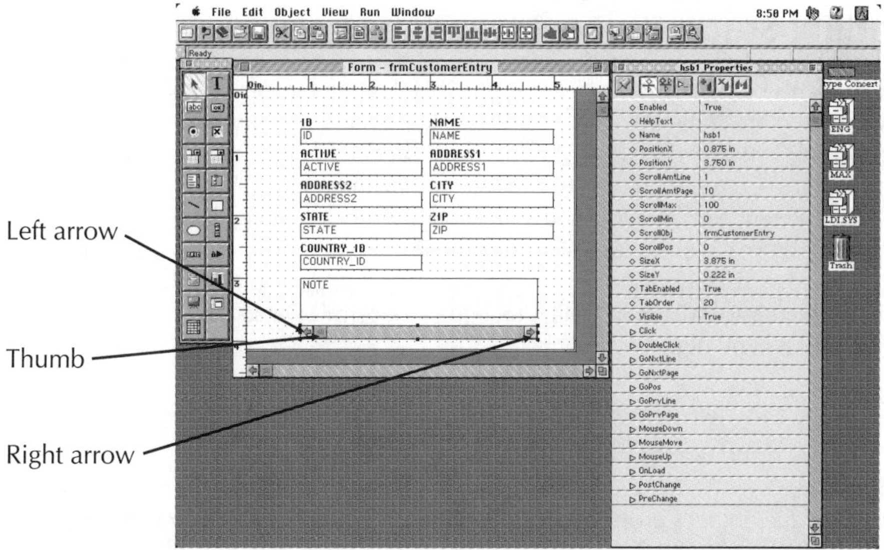

FIGURE 5-9. *Scroll bar placed onto a form with its ScrollObj property set*

To test a scroll bar in Form Run-time mode:

1. Click on the Run Form button on the Designer toolbar.
2. Click on the right arrow to move to the next record in the recordset. Click on the left arrow to move to the previous record.
3. You can use the scroll bar thumb to move to different locations in the recordset. Dragging the thumb all the way to the left moves to the first record in the recordset and dragging it all the way to the right moves to the last record in the recordset.

Scroll Bars on Other Controls

Scroll bars can appear as a part of most application objects, such as the text field control (which will contain multiple lines of text) or a repeater display (which has more records than it can display). This type of scroll bar is not a control but is only a property of the object. You display the scroll bar as part of a form or a control with the HasScrollbar property of the application object. To add a scroll bar to a multiline text field or to a container, you simply click on the application object's HasScrollbar property to set the property to TRUE. Note that you need to set the MultiLine property of a text field controls to TRUE to display or enter multiple lines of text.

Adding Static Objects to a Form

Static objects consist of static text, lines, ovals, and rectangles. All of these help to organize and make the information displayed on the container easier to understand. *Static text* is commonly used to label text fields or to label areas of a form, such as "Customer Information" or "Shopping Information." The *line* objects often separate different parts of a form, such as separating the company logo and address information from the client information on an invoice form. *Ovals* and rectangles can also be used to visually group data into a logical grouping or as an embedded form for binding controls to a different DataSource than the form's DataSource.

To add a static object to a form:

1. Select a static object control on the Object palette.
2. Click and drag to define the limits of the object.

Any of the object's properties can be modified using its property sheet. For example, the properties that you will want to change for text are ColorText, FontName, FontBold, FontSize, etc. See Chapter 6 for a detailed explanation of using object properties.

Adding Bitmaps to a Container or to a Control Object

You can add bitmaps (BMP files) to a form or a control to add interest to the object. Before you can attach a bitmap to either a form or a control, you have to import a copy of the bitmap into the application.

To add a bitmap to an application:

1. Activate the application window into which the bitmap will be imported.
2. Select Import BMP from the Edit menu.
3. Select the BMP file from the Open dialog box, shown here:

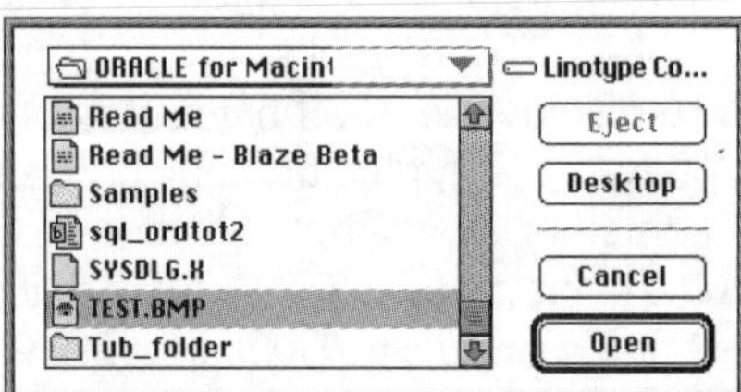

4. Name the BMP object with a legal Oracle Basic name (e.g., bmpTest) in the New Object Name dialog box.

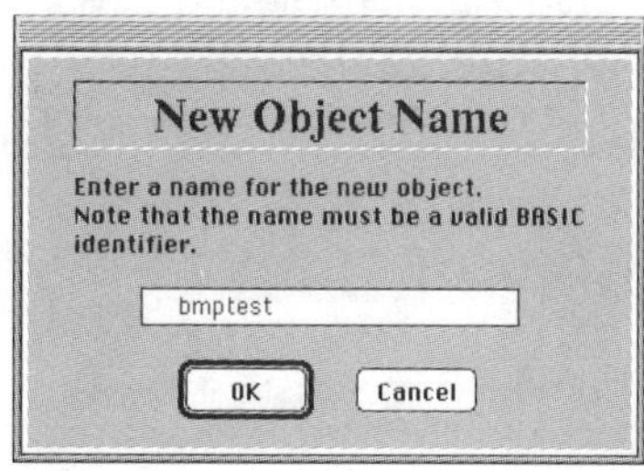

The imported bitmap object's icon is placed in the application window. To view the bitmap, double-click on the bitmap's icon in the application window.

To place a bitmap onto a form:

1. Open the form into which the bitmap will be imported and select the bitmap's icon in the application window.
2. Drag and drop the bitmap's icon onto the form (see Figure 5-10).

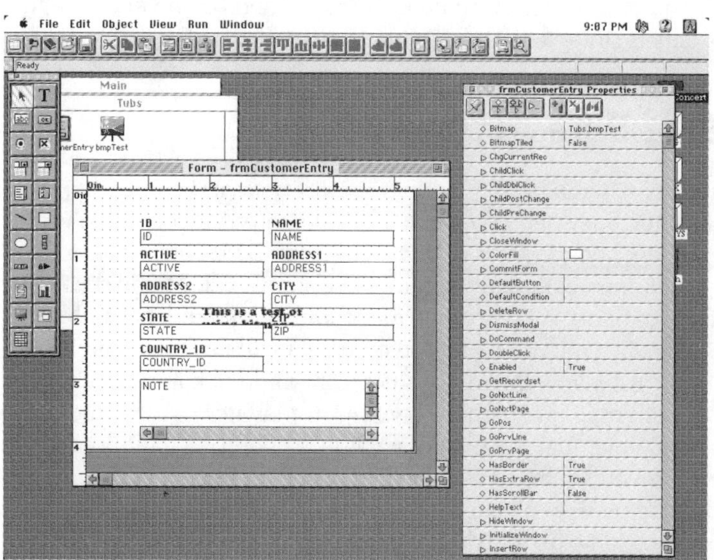

FIGURE 5-10. *The bitmap snaps to the center of the form and sets the Bitmap property for the form*

Oracle Power Objects places the bitmap in the center of the form. With the bitmap imported onto the form, you can change the form's properties controlling the bitmap object. Using the set BitmapTile property of the container you can have the bitmap repeated multiple times on the object. Both the Bitmap and BitmapTile properties can be changed at run time with Oracle Basic.

Sorting the Display of Data

You can define the order in which records are displayed by using a container's or a control's OrderBy property. When the OrderBy property is set to a database column(s), Oracle Power Objects queries the database session and sorts the resulting recordset by the selected column(s). You could use this to order all of your clients by state and then by the client's last name and first name. To do this, you type in the column names in the order in which you want the records sorted and separated by commas. For this example, you would type the following column names:

```
state, lname, fname
```

The OrderBy property can be set for container objects such as forms or repeater displays and controls such as list boxes or combo boxes. The OrderBy property changes the order in which the data is displayed and has no effect on the order in which the data is stored in the database.

Providing Data Accuracy

Use of check box, radio button, pop-up list, list box, and combo box controls helps to ensure the accuracy and consistency of data entry. Anyone involved in data entry knows how common it is for the same item to be entered in many different ways. For a column containing Yes and No options, values could be entered as Y, N, Yes, yes, No, or no. A company name could be entered as Smith's Incorporated, Smith's, Smith's Inc., etc. Use of these controls regulates how data is presented and selected. They also allow the use of easy point-and-click methods to select items from lists of options. Some of these controls display items from other tables or from values that you enter into the control's Value property.

There are several items to consider regarding these controls. Some of these controls provide no easy means for selecting an item that doesn't appear in the list of options. Also, some people do not enjoy using a mouse and prefer using the keyboard instead of a mouse for data entry.

Check Boxes

Check boxes allow users to select multiple items with simple mouse clicks. Any number of items can be turned on or off with the check box options. Check box values are set using the Value On, Value Off, and Default Value properties. If the Value Off property is left blank, it defaults to a NULL value. The column to which the check box is connected can only contain two values (Value On and Value Off). Therefore, if you want to use checkmarks, there must be a column in the table associated with each check box. You set the value to which a check mark will set when a new record is created using the Default Value.

An example of using check marks is for a company selling items with multiple options. You could use a check box to specify if a purchase order item is tax-related. To create a tax-related check box:

1. Select the Check Box tool on the Object palette and click where you want to place the check box.
2. Type **Tax Related** to change the check boxlabel to Tax Related.
3. Activate the associated database session and open the table containing the tax-related column (this example assumes that a tax-related column already exists).
4. Drag and drop the table column on the check box to bind the check box to the proper column. This sets the check box DataSource, DataType, DataSize, and other properties.
5. Set the DefaultValue, ValueOn, and ValueOff values. Remember that the DefaultValue must be identical to either the ValueOn or the ValueOff value.

Radio Buttons and Radio Group Frames

Unlike check boxes, radio buttons are mutually exclusive within their own radio button frame. The radio button frame ties the radio button group together and binds their values to one table column. Thus, multiple items can be placed together, and the user can select the item from the list. Unlike check marks, which require you to specify the data source for each check mark, you only set the data source for the radio group *frame*. Because radio buttons are tied to a radio group frame, you can use multiple radio button groups on the same form.

When creating a radio button group, you need to first create the radio button group frame and then place the radio buttons on it. The radio button group frame has at least three properties that need to be set: Label, Name, and most importantly DataSource. The data source specifies the column where the selected radio button data will be stored. You can automatically set the DataSource properties by dragging and dropping a column from a table or view. Then all you need to do is set the radio button Name property and the Value On property for each radio button.

To create a radio button group frame:

1. To create an area for placing the group of radio buttons, select the Radio Button control from the Object palette and click on the form. You can move the frame by selecting its border with the mouse and moving it, and you can resize the frame by selecting the black boxes on the border and pulling them to the needed size.
2. Drag and drop the column associated to the values in the radio button group frame onto the radio button group frame (the column is normally a primary key for the table). It sets the DataSource property for the radio button group frame to the table column that will store the selected radio button items, sets the Datatype property to the appropriate datatype, and sets the DataSize property.
3. Set the Name and Label properties for the frame (if desired).
4. Press the Save button on the toolbar to save your work. Figure 5-11 shows a completed radio button group frame with all of its radio button options.

You can optionally set a DefaultValue for each radio button. Be sure to set the DefaultValue property to the exact value specified in one of the radio button's ValueOn property.

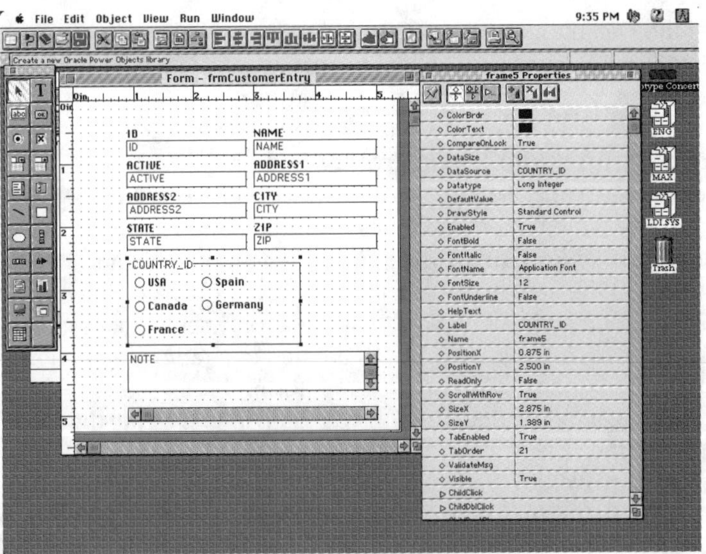

FIGURE 5-11. *The completed radio button group frame and its options*

To set the radio buttons and their values:

1. Select the Radio Button control from the Object palette and click in the radio button group frame. This attaches the radio button to the frame and its data source.
2. Set the control's Label property to the name you want displayed at run time and set the Name property to a legal Oracle Basic name (in case you need to refer to it with Oracle Basic code).
3. Set the ValueOn property to the value to be stored in the table column when the radio button is selected.
4. Repeat steps 1 to 3 for all of the other items to be placed in the radio button frame group.

In this example, we set the ValueOn property for each item to match the primary key value assigned to each radio button in the associated Countries table. Selecting USA sets the value in the Customer column to 1, which is the primary key value for USA in the Countries table.

Pop-Up Lists and List Boxes

Both list boxes and pop-up lists are bindable controls that display a static list of items from which the user can select values. Through the use of the Translation property, you look up values from another table and display those values in the list (populate the list). With the Translation property you store a different internal value for the control than the value displayed in the list, because the control stores the foreign key value in the control's internal value instead of the control's displayed value.

For example, the company pop-up list's Translation property is set to =customers.name=id and its DataSource is set to customer_id. The translation property displays the values stored in the Name column in the Customers table and stores the value in the Id column in the Customers table in the customer_id in the Orders table. For example, selecting "Allison Gifts" as the company on the Orders form in MoonLight Demo-DONE stores the value "4" in the customer_id column.

There are a couple of advantages to using the Translation property to populate a list box or pop-up list. First, you save disk space by storing an integer number instead of a data string. Second, you can modify the foreign table's string column and not affect the value stored in the internal value of the control.

The only functional difference between a list box and a pop-up list is that the user has to click on the pop-up list to view the list of values, while the list box is a box from which the user scrolls to view items not displayed in the box. Therefore, when developing a complicated form with a limited amount of space available, you should use a pop-up list to save screen real estate.

To populate a list box or pop-up list:

1. Select either the List Box or Pop-up List control from the Object palette and click on the form where you want to position the control.

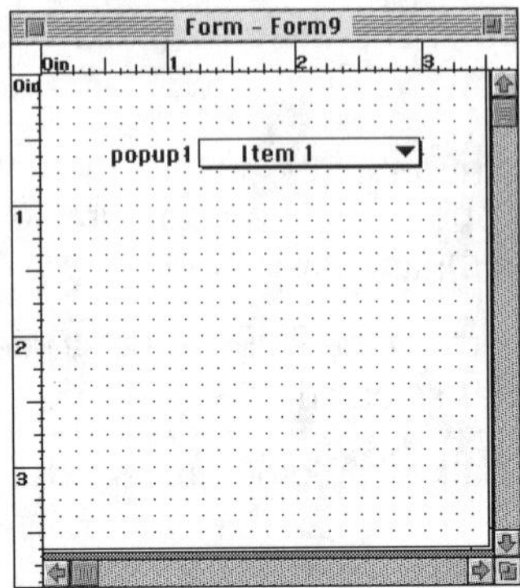

2. Set the DataSource property to store the internal value by dragging and dropping the column onto the control.
3. Set the DataType and DataSize properties to match the internal value to be stored. The DataType will usually be an integer if you are storing a value from a foreign key field.
4. Set the Translation property to select the foreign key field value and display another field. The syntax for populating a pop-up list from a column in a foreign table is

```
=SELECT column_name[the column name from which data will be displayed, column
[foreign key column value to be stored] from table
```

For example, to populate a list box from a TubColor table with a column Color, you enter the following in the ValueList property (see Chapter 7 for more details on using Oracle Basic to select values):

```
=SELECT Color, ColorId from TubColor or
=TubColor.Color=ColorId
```

This stores the ColorId value in the internal value of the pop-up list and displays in the pop-up list the Color column value in the control.

Combo Boxes

Combo boxes are used to display a set of values in a pull-down menu. Combo boxes differ from pop-up lists and list boxes because they contain a field in which you can enter your own value instead of having to select a value from the list, which must be linked to a data source, which contains a string datatype. The value of the combo box is either the selected list item or the entered value. You populate a combo box list by entering values or an expression in its ValueList property that selects the values.

To create a combo box:

1. Select the combo box control and click on the form where you wish to place the control.
2. Drag and drop a table column onto the combo box to set its Name, Datatype, DataSize, and DataSource properties.
3. Enter an expression in its ValueList property to how the combo box will be populated.

There are three different ways to set the populate a combo box with the ValueList property. The following explains the different methods for entering those values. For each of these methods, we are using a list of tub colors.

- **Hard-coded value list** The simplest way to populate a combo box is with a list of values entered into the ValueList property. Each value is separated by a hard return at the end of the value. For example,

  Granite
  Onyx
  Marble

- **Table column mapping** The syntax for mapping a combo box from a column in a foreign table is =[AT Session] table.column. For example, to populate a combo box from a TubColor table with a column Color, you enter in the ValueList property:

  =TubColor.Color
  or
  =AT Blaze TubColor.Color

- **Queried values** The most flexible way to populate a combo box is with a query. The syntax for querying a value from the record source is =[AT session] SELECT column FROM table WHERE condition ORDER BY column. To populate and sort the values in a combo box:

  =SELECT Color FROM TubColor BY Color
  or
  = AT Tubs SELECT Color FROM TubColor BY Color

Now when you run the form, the combo box will display the selected values in its pull-down menu.

Updating a ValueList Source Combo boxes do not use the concept of foreign keys to populate the control as used in the Translation method by pop-up lists and list boxes. Therefore, while it is easy to populate a combo box using a foreign table in the ValueList, it is more complicated to save an entered value into a column in the source table for the ValueList and display the new value in the combo box list.

The following example gets the recordset object for the combo box, selects the new value entered into the combo box, enters the new value into the recordset for the combo box, and then updates the list of values displayed in a pop-up list.

Type the following code in the PostChange method, where combo1 is the name of the pop-up list.

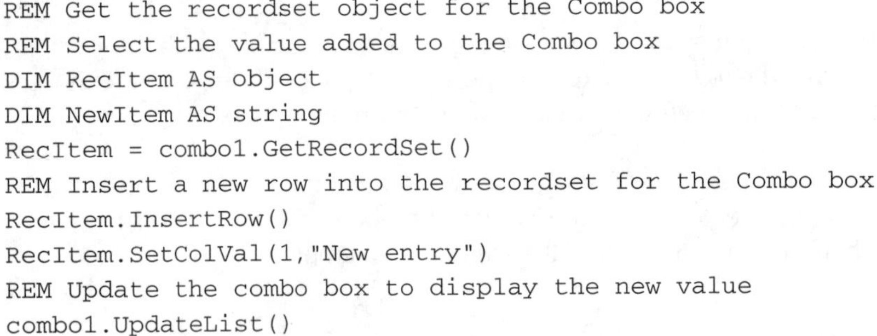

```
REM Get the recordset object for the Combo box
REM Select the value added to the Combo box
DIM RecItem AS object
DIM NewItem AS string
RecItem = combo1.GetRecordSet()
REM Insert a new row into the recordset for the Combo box
RecItem.InsertRow()
RecItem.SetColVal(1,"New entry")
REM Update the combo box to display the new value
combo1.UpdateList()
```

Push Buttons

A push button control simulates a real push button like a on/off button on a computer or TV. Pressing the button causes some action to take place. Opening other forms, okaying changes to a form, or canceling changes made to the form are common uses of push buttons.

You define the action to be executed when a user clicks the push button in the push buttonClick( ) method. The push buttonClick( ) method has no default action associated with it, except in a certain scenario with modal forms.

Specifying a Push Button as the Default Button

If you want to specify one push button on a form to be the default button, you set its DefaultButton property. The default button performs the safest action (you wouldn't want a push button that deletes the selected recordset as a default button) or the action most commonly chosen. Setting the DefaultButton property to TRUE places a thicker border around the button and allows the user at run time to press the ENTER (Windows) or RETURN (Macintosh) key to select the push button to select the push button.

Push Buttons and Modal Dialog Boxes

In the specific case of a push button on a modal form, selecting the button can hide the form without adding any Oracle Basic code to the Click( ) method. This does not close the window (unload the form from memory), but instead hides the form and keeps it in memory. This is useful if you have the user set some preferences that you need to keep in memory, but you want to hide the form to unclutter the screen.

To hide a modal form:

1. Set the push button's IsDismissBtn property to **TRUE**.
2. Open the form with the OpenModal( ) method. To close the modal form (i.e., to unload it from memory), you must use the CloseWindow( ) method.

Adding Graphics to Push Buttons

You add a bitmap to a button by using the push button's Bitmap property. By modifying the push button's Bitmap property with Oracle Basic code, you can change the bitmap associated with the push button at run time.

To add a BMP file to a push button:

1. Open the form containing the push button.
2. Select the BMP file to be added to the button in the application window and drag and drop it onto the button.

Using Picture Controls

You can create picture controls that can store and display BMP files (Windows native bitmap format) or PICT files (Macintosh native bitmap format) in a Long Raw column in a database. You might want to save a picture of each employee in the employee table or a picture of each product that you produce in the product table.

To create a picture control:

1. Select the picture control and click and drag the control to the desired size.

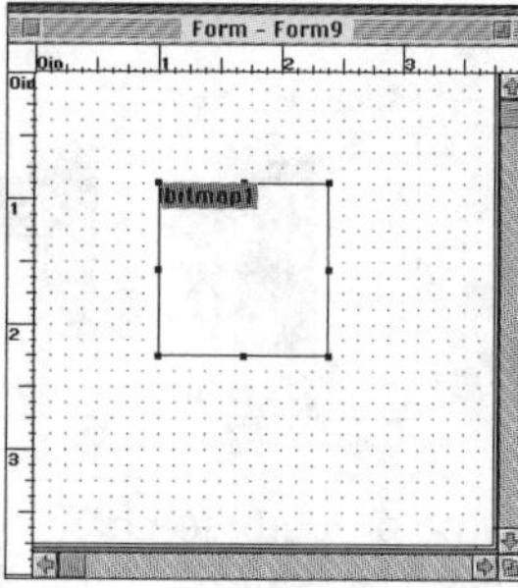

2. Activate the database session and open the table in which the picture data will be stored.
3. Select the picture column from the table and drag and drop it onto the picture control to bind the control to the column.

To add a picture object to the control when you are running the application:

1. Copy the bitmap in the application that created it.
2. Select the picture control and click the Paste button to paste the bitmap image into the control.

Using Chart Controls

Chart controls are used to create charts or graphs based upon the data queried from a table. A chart can be bound to multiple columns in a table to display multiple information.

The following example shows how to create a chart control that graphs the sales of each employee for each department. To accomplish this, the employee name, ENAME, and the employee's salary, SAL, both located in the Emp table, are linked to the Dept table in the MoonLight Data database session.

To create the sample chart:

1. Click on the New Form button to create a new form.
2. Drag and drop the DNAME column from the Dept table onto the form.
3. Select the Vertical Scroll Bar control from the Object palette and drop it on the right side of the form. This allows you to scroll between the different departments and view the salaries for each department.
4. Select the Chart control from the Object palette and place the chart control on the form. This displays the chart with sample data.

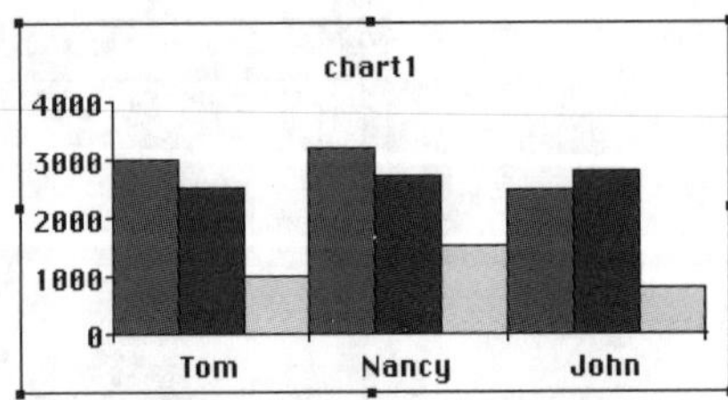

5. Set the chart's Name property to **chtSalaries** and its Label property to **Salaries**. The chart now displays "Salaries" at the top of the chart (see Figure 5-12).

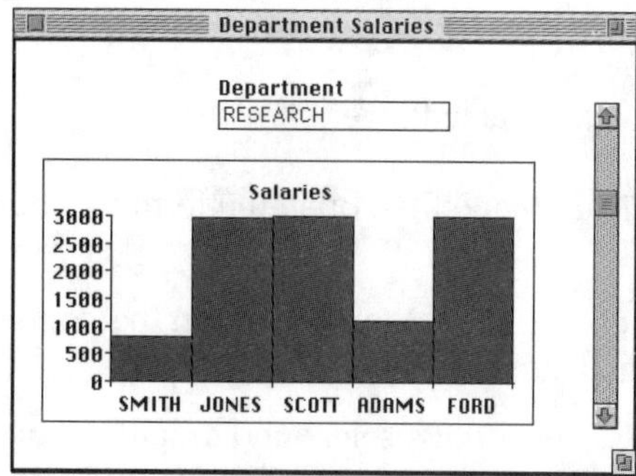

FIGURE 5-12. *Completed chart control in Run-time mode*

6. Set the XChartCol property to the **ENAME** column in the Emp table to display the name of the employees across the X axis at the bottom of the chart.
7. Set the YChartCol property to the **Sal** column (which contains each employee's salary) in the Emp table.
8. Set the RecordSource property of the form to the **Emp** table.
9. Set the LinkMasterColumn and LinkDetailColumn properties of the chtSalaries chart to **DEPTNO**. This links the employees to their department.
10. Set the LinkMasterForm to **frmSalaries** to link the chart to the selected department.
11. Set the RowFetchMode property of the chart to **Fetch All Immediately**. Failure to set this property may cause some data to not be charted.

You can set other properties, such as changing the chart style, changing the width between bars, adding a legend, etc. (see Chapter 9 for an explanation of all of the chart control's properties).

Assigning Sequences to a Field

In Chapter 4, we discuss how to create sequences as a means of assigning unique sequential integers to each row in a table. Sequences are used to create the integers used in primary key columns and they are assigned to columns on a form level. For example, you need to have a unique number identifying each employee, each customer, each order a company makes, and each line item for each order. You apply a sequence to a field on a form by dragging the icon of the sequence from an open session onto the field.

To use a sequence with Oracle Power Objects:

1. Open the application and then open the form by double-clicking on their icons.
2. Open the session and then double-click on the connect icon (if the session is not already activated).
3. In the open session window, select and drag the icon of the desired sequence onto the field on the open form (see Figure 5-13).

You can sometimes use a single sequence in conjunction with several different fields and forms. For example, create a sequence with a beginning number of 1 and an increment number of 1. You could then apply this sequence to the primary key columns of both the EMP table and the Customers table.

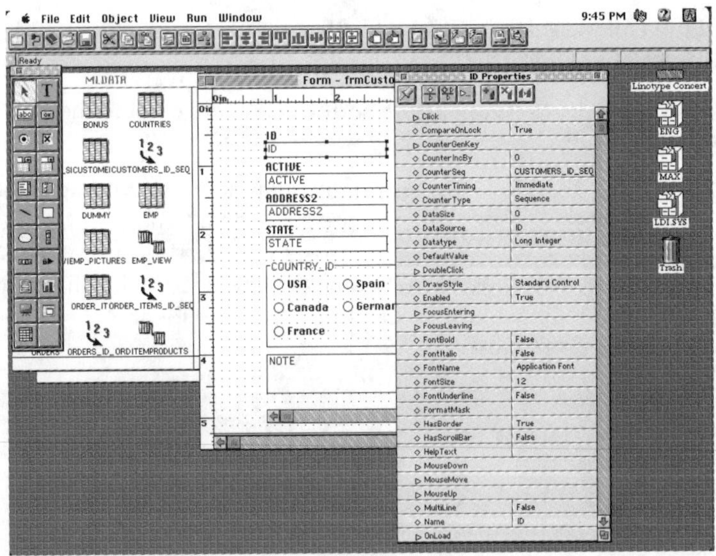

FIGURE 5-13. *The open database session with the CUSTOMERS_ID_SEQ sequence and a text field control set to the CUSTOMERS_ID_SEQ sequence*

Setting the Default Form to Open When an Application Is Run

When you create an application, you will always need to set the default window (form) that will open when the application is run and is set in the OnLoad( ) method. This default window may be the main form to be used or a main menu from which the user can select other forms. The OnLoad( ) method is, therefore, one of the most common methods that you will set in the application property sheet. The OnLoad( ) method opens a default form when the application is run.

To have a form called MasterForm open when the application is run, you type **MasterForm.OpenWindow( )** in the OnLoad method. More information is given on the OnLoad( ) method in Chapter 8.

Driving the Values Displayed in Other Fields

You can set up a control so that it will drive the values displayed into other controls. For example, the MoonLight Demo-DONE application uses the following expression in the Validate property of the Company pop-up list on the order form to extract the customer's address values from the Customers table and insert those values in the associated order fields.

```
DIM a, b, c, d, e, f as long
DIM myNewValue as long
myNewValue = newVal
exec sql select address1, address2, state, zip, country, country_id &
into :a, :b, :c, :d, :e, :f from customers where id = :myNewValue
address1.value = a
address2.value = b
city.value = c
state.value = d
zip.value = e
country.value = f
Validate = TRUE
```

Using Format Mask

To control the way in which text strings, numbers, and dates are displayed in a text field or a combo box, you create character strings in the FormatMask property of the text control. The format mask is set for one control at a time and affects the display of the data but not how the data is entered or stored. For example, to display the date as March 16, 1996, you select the Long Date FormatMask property. However, you still enter the date **3/16/96** into the text control, and the date is stored as 3/16/96 in the database.

Custom Format Masks In addition to the predefined formats, you can use custom formats by using the #, @, and & symbols to represent where digits are to be placed. For example, to display a ten-digit telephone number in a normal telephone format, you place the following string in the FormatMask entry field: (@@@) @@@-@@@@. With this format mask, a phone number is entered (and saved in the database) as "8002345678", but it is displayed as (800) 234-5678. You use the & character the same as @ to act as placeholders for text character data, or the # symbol to act as a placeholder for numeric data. The entire set of characters that can be used in the FormatMask property fields and in Oracle Basic code are listed in Appendix B.

Specifying Column Datatypes Every bound control (text field, pop-up list, list, etc.) must have its Datatype property set to an appropriate datatype. Because Oracle Power Objects can connect to many different types of databases (each with its own set of database datatypes), Oracle Power Objects converts all of these different datatypes to one of four datatypes: Long Integer, Date, Double, or String. These are a subset of the Oracle Basic datatypes used to declare variables.

If a control is bound to a column in the database by using drag and drop, Oracle Power Objects automatically converts the column's datatype to one of these four datatypes. However, if you manually bind a control to a column, you will have to set the control's datatype property to an appropriate datatype.

Table 5-2 explains each of Oracle Power Objects property datatypes and how Oracle7 databases are converted to the associated datatype property.

Note that the Oracle7 datatype Long Raw is used to store bitmaps in the database, but there is no datatype associated with the picture control.

Testing Forms in Form Run-time Mode

As you are developing an application, you can test the form at any time by pressing the Run Form button. When you run a form or the application, the form queries the database and returns the queried data to the form's recordset. When testing a bound form, you need to verify that it is working properly, which includes the ability to add, delete, or modify data using a form and the ability to query the recordset of the form. The following sections explain how to manipulate data and query data.

Property Datatype	Oracle7 Datatypes	Explanation
Long Integer	NUMBER	A Long Integer datatype contains whole numbers between –2,147,483,648 and 2,147,483,647. Note that all integers are stored as long.
Date	DATE	A Date datatype stores both date and time data. The date can contain any date between 1/1/100 A.D. to 12/31/9999 A.D. and has a default format of DD-MON-YY. Every value stored in the column consists of both a time and a date component. The time has a one-second precision with a range spanning 00:00:00 to 23:59:59. You can access either the time, the date, or both the time and date using SQL or Oracle Basic, then display the appropriate information in a text field control using the FormatMask property.
Double	NUMBER(*p*,*s*)	A Double datatype stores numeric data that is either fixed-length or floating-point decimal value. A Double datatype can store a floating point number between 1.40129E–45 and 3.402823E38, negative values between –3.402823E38 and –1.401298E–45, and 0.
String	CHAR, VARCHAR2, LONG	A String datatype stores any combination of alpha, numeric, spaces, punctuation marks, and other special symbols up to 32,726 characters long. The String datatype is used to store any data except that which will solely contain numeric or date and time information.

TABLE 5-2. *Oracle Power Objects Property Datatypes and Associated Oracle7 Datatypes*

Entering and Deleting Data in a Form

When you run a form or application, the toolbar changes to the Form Run-time toolbar that has buttons for inserting and deleting rows in the recordset and buttons to commit or roll back changes to the recordset.

To insert a row in the recordset, click on the Insert Row button in the Form Run-time toolbar. You are presented with an empty form that is ready for inputting a new record in the recordset.

To delete a row in the recordset:

1. Move the record that you want to delete.
2. Click on the Delete row button in the Form Run-time toolbar.

To commit all of the changes made to the recordset and save them to the database, click on the Commit button. This process is irreversible, and all of the modifications that have been made to the recordset are sent to the database and the database is requeried.

Using Query By Form

Anyone working frequently with databases needs quick and easy methods for locating specific information. For example, locating aging invoices that are overdue 60 days and unpaid or perhaps reviewing all of the purchase orders by a specific client. Most other database applications require you to either develop SQL expressions or select the tables and columns to be searched in a separate query window and then enter the values to be matched and any special filters. With Oracle Power Objects, you can also create a special report to retrieve this data or use SQL or various Oracle Power Objects form query methods to search for a specific record or set of records. However, the simplest way to search for record(s) in the Run-time mode is to use the Query By Form.

Query By Form makes it easy to perform impromptu queries while looking at data in a form. With Query By Form, you can query for data in multiple fields, use wildcard characters, and place filters on the data such as greater than, less than, is not null, or between two values. You can also use check boxes, radio buttons, combo boxes, pop-up lists, and list boxes to specify values.

For this example, we will use the Query By Form to locate all of the sales for a salesperson named Smith between January 1, 1995 to March 31, 1995 in the Orders form in the MoonLight Demo-DONE application. To perform a Query By Form:

1. Click on the Query By Form button or select Query By Form from the Database menu. This displays a blank copy of the form on top of the form to be queried with "Find What" in the title bar (see Figure 5-14).
2. Enter **Ward** in the Sales Rep field. This translates to a SQL select command to select all the orders with Ward as the sales representative.
3. To refine the query to only include those sales made by Ward between January 1, 1995 to March 31, 1995, type **>= 1/1/95 and <=3/31/95** in the Order Date field.

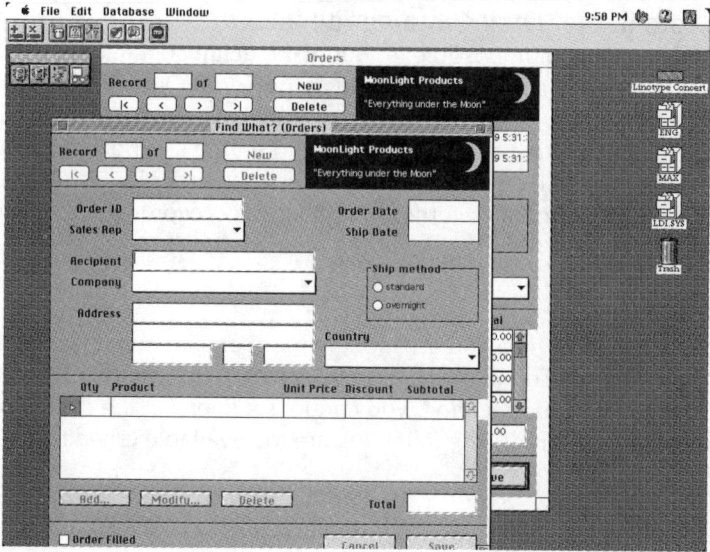

FIGURE 5-14. *The blank Query By Form window used to query the Orders form*

4. Apply the query by selecting Apply Form Query from the Database menu or by clicking on the Apply Form Query button. (Refer back to Figure 5-4 to see the Order form showing the results of the query.)

To review the results of the query, close the Enter Query form and scroll through the selected recordset.

Clearing the Enter Query Form Window

The Enter Query form window does not disappear after you apply the query. Therefore, if you have made a mistake, you can simply change the values that need changing and then select the Apply Form Query button again. To clear the Enter Query form, you can delete all of the text on the form or (if the query is not too large) you can select the Apply Form Query button. This will clear the form but not close the Enter Query form.

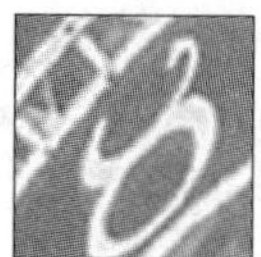

NOTE

The Query By Form window is related to that portion of the form containing the focus. Therefore, if the cursor is in an embedded form or a repeater display, the Query By Form will only display that portion of the window for performing the query.

Querying Data in the Detail Container on a Form

It is more difficult, but not impossible, to query the detail container of a master-detail relation on a form with the Query By Form. Querying the detail container of the form returns all master records that have detail records that match the criteria. To perform such a query, you need to set the LinkPrimaryKey property of the detail container to Here(on detail). Querying the order item's detail container on an order form for a product returns all of the master records of the order form for the selected product.

Query Criteria

In order to select just the data you are looking for, there are numerous types of criteria that can be entered in fields or combo boxes (while radio buttons, list boxes, etc. can be used for querying, you cannot set filters on the data contained in their accompanying column). The following are the available criteria types:

Type of Criteria	**Definition**
simple expression	Selecting a simple text value will query for the selected value. For example, if you select "Ground" from a Shipment Method pop-up list, the query will retrieve all orders shipped by Ground.
% Wildcard	A wildcard character for multiple characters. For example, T%r could select Tyler.
_ (underline)	A wildcard character for a single character. For example, T_r could select Tar.
single date	Queries the column for the specified date. For example, 6/1/95 retrieves all the records with the specified date in a record.
>	Selects values greater than its value. For example, >2300 retrieves all records with numbers greater than 2,300 in the column.
<	Selects values less than its value. For example, <2300 retrieves all records with numbers less than 2,300 in the column.
=	Equal to
>=	Greater than or equal to
<=	Less than or equal to
!=	Is not equal to
^=	Is not equal to
< >	Is not equal to

Type of Criteria	Definition
like	Selects values like the entered value. For example, name like ('%ill%') selects Jill, Bill, William, etc.
not like	Selects values that are not like the entered value. For example, name not like ('%ill%') selects everyone but Jill, Bill, William, etc.
between	Selects all values between the two entered values. For example, between 2,500 and 10,000
not between	Selects all values that are not between the selected values. For example, not between 2,500 and 10,000
compound criteria	An expression with multiple criteria, such as >2500 AND <10000
in	Queries the column for one of the values. For example, IN (Johnson, Smith, Baldwin) would select only those records with one of these names
is null	Selects all records where the value is NULL (not set). For example, Paid is NULL selects all records where the Paid column is NULL
is not null	Usually used to check that the column has a valid value (including 0)

Conclusion

This chapter presented an overview of applications, all of the application objects, how to bind application containers to database objects, referencing object containers, and how to populate various controls. Chapters 6 covers creating reusable application objects called classes, establishing master-detail relations, using repeater displays, and creating reports. Chapter 11 provides examples of advanced reports and the use of two other application objects, OLE objects and OCX controls.

CHAPTER 6

Classes, Subforms, Repeater Displays, and Reports

Chapters 4 and 5 covered the basics of getting started with Oracle Power Objects. In this chapter, you will expand upon that by learning to use classes, subforms, repeater displays, and reports. The first three objects greatly increase your ability to add functionality to the applications to be developed. You use classes to build reusable, stand-alone objects as building blocks for more complex reusable objects. Because a form can access only one table, subforms add the ability to an application to access any number of tables. Repeater displays provide a convenient method to display several records at the same time.

Reports are essential for any business and many household applications. The Oracle Power Objects report object allows you to use subforms, user-defined classes, repeater displays, and tools from the Object palette to easily create simple to complex reports on the data from a database.

The description of classes, how they are created, the effects of modifying classes, and the use of classes are first discussed in this chapter. You will learn the basics of how to access information from the database using subforms, classes, and repeater displays that are added to forms that will be used by the application being developed. The creation of a sample report that lists each sales representative's customers with the total amount of their purchases will be described. Finally, the three different forms and the report that you create will be combined together in a single application that can be compiled and run as a stand-alone program. As in Chapters 4 and 5, some new properties will be introduced, but all properties and methods are described fully in Chapters 8 and 9.

As you create classes, you'll want to place them where they can be accessed and reused by as many applications as possible. The last part of this chapter describes libraries, and how you can use them to store reusable objects.

Classes

Oracle Power Objects classes incorporate the reusability, inheritance, and encapsulation that are the main characteristics of an OOP environment. Virtually every object in Oracle Power Objects is a class, either predefined or user-defined. When a form is opened, it is actually an instance of the form class predefined by Oracle Power Objects, and it inherits all of the default functionality built into the form class. You can change this instance of the form by adding new user-defined properties and methods or by overriding the default values inherited from the form class.

User-defined classes are those that you create to solve the needs of the particular application under construction. They have all of the same default functionality of forms, inherited from the Oracle Power Objects definition, plus all the new functionality needed, which is added by the user. Generally, user-defined classes serve two main purposes. The first is to meet the common needs of several different applications. These classes are placed in a library where many applications can access them. An example of this type of class would be an Exit button.

The second purpose of user-defined classes is to simplify the development of features of an application, where several features have different functionality but share some common properties. This is done by putting all of the common properties into what Oracle Power Objects calls a master class (many programmers call this a base class). This master class is then used as the foundation for other user-defined classes, referred to as subclasses. The different functions needed by the application are created by adding new features to the separate subclasses. Using classes in this way greatly reduces the repetition of effort and the size of applications that would occur if the common features for several functions were duplicated in each separate function.

Creating a Master Class

To illustrate some of the principles of object-oriented programming, inheritance, reusability, and encapsulation, we will create a new application, BUTTON, and then build a simple master class called Button. We'll then build two subclasses, Exit and OK, from that Button master class. Once they are created, you will modify different properties in the different classes to see the effects on each.

The master class you will construct simply consists of a small form with a single button labeled "Button" that is centered in a small colored field.

1. After Oracle Power Objects is started, open a new application by selecting either the New Application toolbar button or the New Application item from the File menu.
2. Set the Name property of the application to **BUTTON**.
3. Press the New Class button on the toolbar. This opens up a class editor window (called, by default, Class-Class1), which includes the underlying form in which you add other objects. It also opens the Class1 properties sheet. Both of these are shown in Figure 6-1.

   To add an object to the class:
4. On the Object palette, click on the Push Button tool, which turns red. As you move the cursor into the form in the class editor window, it changes to a small plus sign (+) with an image of the button control attached to it. Click again to drop the button on the class form.
5. Drag the corner of the form in the class editor window so that it becomes a small box, about one inch by one and a half inches around the button. You may need to enlarge the class editor window by dragging an edge or corner of the window so that the form inside the window is completely visible.
6. Place the button in the center of the form by pressing the Horizontally Center in Container and Vertically Center in Container toolbar buttons.

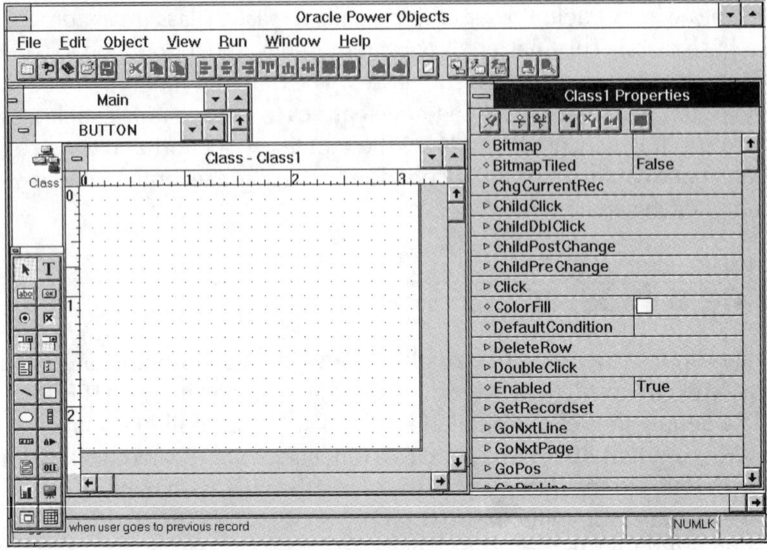

FIGURE 6-1. *Empty class editor window with its associated property sheet*

To set the object properties:

7. Click on the button you've just created (if it is not already highlighted) to display its property sheet, and change the Name and Label properties to **Button** as shown in Figure 6-2.

NOTE
The Name property value is used by Oracle Power Objects to reference the object internally, and the Label property value is displayed, if appropriate, when the object is on screen.

Now let's establish the standard look of the class by setting the class properties:

8. Click outside of the button so that the class itself is highlighted and the class property sheet is displayed.
9. Change the new class' Name property to **ButtonClass** and Label property to **Button Class** in the class property sheet. (Even though the name of the class is ButtonClass, we'll refer to it generally as the "Button class.")
10. Click on a color in the ColorFill property in the property sheet, and the area around the button changes to the selected color. (In our example, we chose white.)

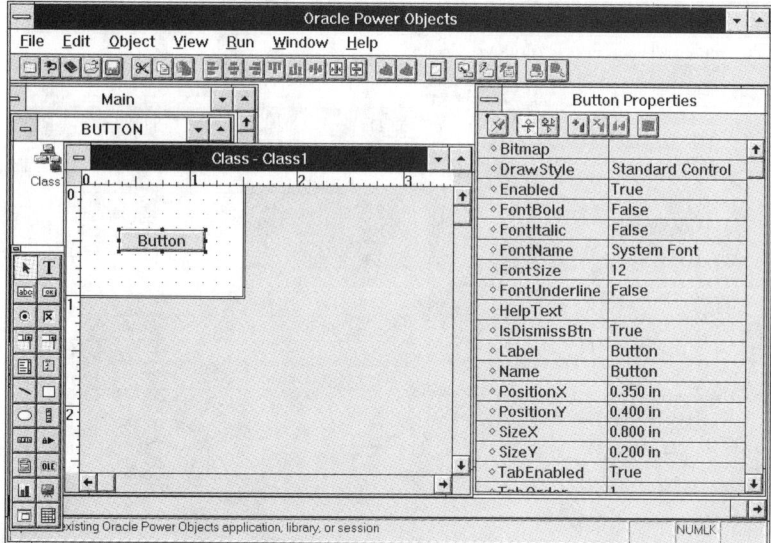

FIGURE 6-2. *Class editor window with an object (button) and the button's property sheet*

11. Click on the Button object and add the statement **MSGBOX "Master Class button"** to the Click( ) method.
12. Save and close the newly created Button class by selecting the Close item in the File menu or, on the Macintosh, by pressing the Close button on the upper-left corner of the window. The Oracle Power Objects windows now look similar to Figure 6-3.

Creating Subclasses

You are now ready to build subclasses based on the Button class. As described earlier, a subclass uses a master class as a start and then increases the functionality by either adding more objects or overwriting the properties inherited from the master class. To create the Exit subclass, complete the following steps.

1. Click on the ButtonClass icon in the BUTTON application window to highlight it (don't open it, just select it), and then select Create Subclass from the Edit menu. A new class editor window is displayed, containing a button (defined by the Button class just created) and a property sheet for the new class.

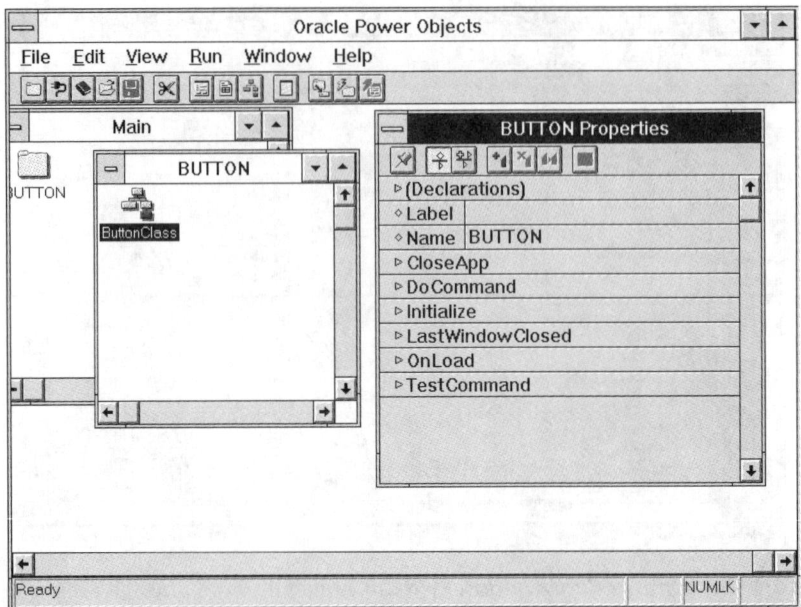

FIGURE 6-3. *The Main application window with the BUTTON application, the BUTTON application window with the Button class defined, and the BUTTON application property sheet*

2. On the new class property sheet, change the Name property of the class to **ExitClass** and the Label property to **Exit Class**. (We'll refer to it generally as the Exit subclass from now on.)
3. Click on the button to display its property sheet, and change its Name property to **ExitButton** and its Label property to **Exit**.
4. Click on the Click( ) method in the property sheet to open its text entry field and enter the Oracle Basic phrase **GetContainer.GetContainter.CloseWindow( )** in the method's work area.

Note the misspelled name "GetContainter" in the code. This is to demonstrate a small part of Oracle Power Objects' debug facility later in this section, so be sure to type it in as shown. You use the Oracle Power Objects keyword **GetContainer** twice, to first retrieve the reference to the class form containing the button, and then to the reference to the form containing the ExitButton class. Thus when the button is clicked in Run-time mode, the form containing the Exit class button will close. The Oracle Power Objects windows should now look similar to that shown in Figure 6-4.

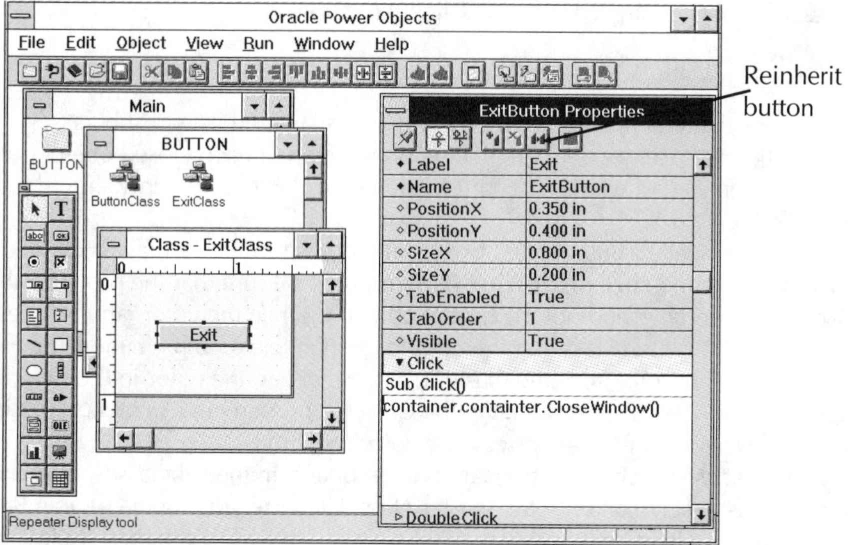

FIGURE 6-4. *The Exit subclass' object property sheet with the Click( ) method open*

Note the black triangles before the Name and Label properties. When the triangle is black, it indicates that the property in the instance of the class has overridden the property or method of the master class. If you need to have the property revert back to inheriting the master class values, click on the property name, then select the Reinherit button on the property sheet toolbar (see Figure 6-4). When this button is pressed, any data in the selected property or method will be deleted and the property or method will inherit its values from the master class.

Now save your work by clicking on the Save toolbar button and close the Exit (sub)class by selecting Close from the File menu. The BUTTON application window now contains two classes: the master class Button and the subclass Exit. To create another subclass called OK, follow the steps above with the following differences.

- Change the class Name property to **OKClass** and the class Label property to **OK Class**.
- Change the class ColorFill property to another color (black in our example).
- Select the object (button) in the class and change its Name property to **OKButton** and its Label property to **OK**.

- Do not add any code to the Click( ) method.
- Save the new OK subclass.

To view the relationship between the master class and its two subclasses, open all three classes by double-clicking on the icon of each closed object in the BUTTON application window. Your Oracle Power Objects window should look similar to Figure 6-5.

Select the opened Button class by clicking on its form to display its class property sheet, and click on the ColorFill property. Be sure that the property sheet is for the Button *class* and not the button object. Change the color, and you see that the color of the Button class and the color of the Exit class both change. The Exit class inherited its color from the master class. However, the color in the OK class stays the same, because by changing the ColorFill property in its class properties sheet, it has overwritten the master class color property.

Note that as you changed the name of the button in the subclasses, only the subclass was affected and not the master class. Likewise, adding the Oracle Basic function in the Click( ) method of the Exit class did not affect the master class or the OK class. The Button master class' action, assigned in the Click( ) method, will

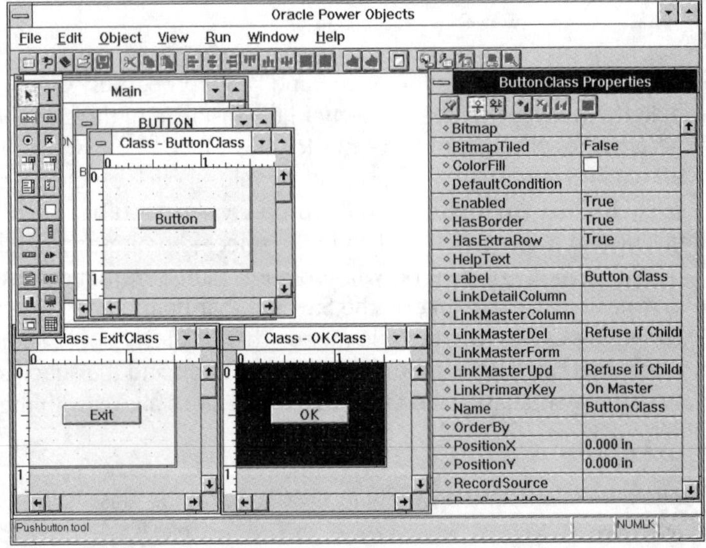

FIGURE 6-5. *All three classes open with the master class, ButtonClass, property sheet*

happen when the OK button is pressed, while the Exit button will execute its own action.

Adding Subclasses to a Form

Both the Exit and OK subclasses can be added to another form and have their respective actions used by that form. In this case, clicking on the Exit button closes the window and clicking on the OK button displays the "Master Class Button" message. To see just how this works, click on the New Form button, then click and drag the OK class icon and the Exit class icon onto the new form. Note that the second class covers the first when added to the form. Select the Exit class and move it (the cursor looks like a hand) to the side of the OK class. Your screen should now look similar to Figure 6-6.

Now click on the Run Form button on the toolbar, and Oracle Power Objects goes into Run-time mode and displays the newly created form with the two button classes.

Recall the misspelled word "GetContainter" in the Exit button's Click( ) method. Click on the Exit button, and Oracle Power Objects displays an error message that

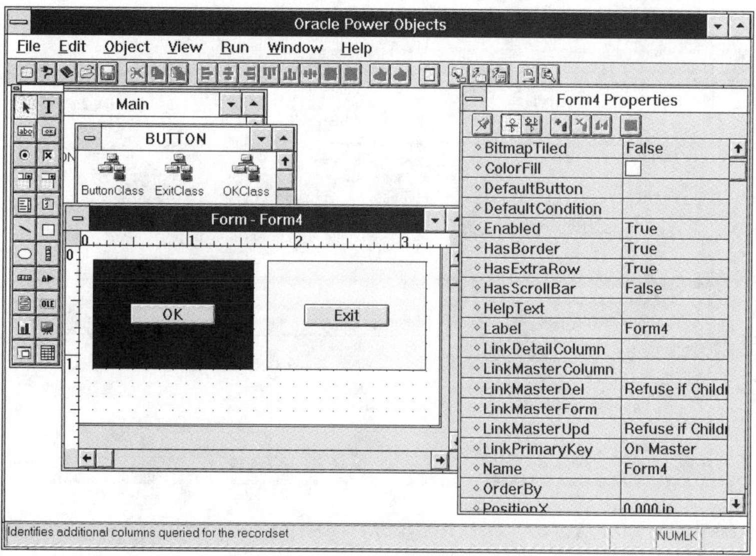

FIGURE 6-6. *Exit and OK subclasses on a new form*

a property name was expected. More importantly, the Exit button class is opened with its associated property sheet, and the Click( ) method is opened so that you can see exactly where the problem is in the code, as shown in Figure 6-7. Note the error code BAS-00302 shown in the figure. You can use this number to look up more information about the error in the online documentation on the Oracle Power Objects error codes.

Correct the misspelling and save your changes. Note that you make the change in the Exit class' button, not the Exit button in the ExitClass instance in the form. Now run the form again by selecting the Run Form button from the toolbar. If you press OK, the message box with the statement "Master Class Button" will be displayed. The OK subclass inherited the code placed in the master class' button's Click( ) method. Press on the Exit button. Oracle Power Objects closes the running form, leaving you in Form Designer mode again. The code in the Exit class' button's Click( ) method overwrote the code in the master class.

This has been a very simple example of the power of classes and the relation between master classes and subclasses. While the Exit class is actually quite useful, it does not really need to be built from a master class that does nothing. This was done just to show a simple example of OOP inheritance and how to build classes

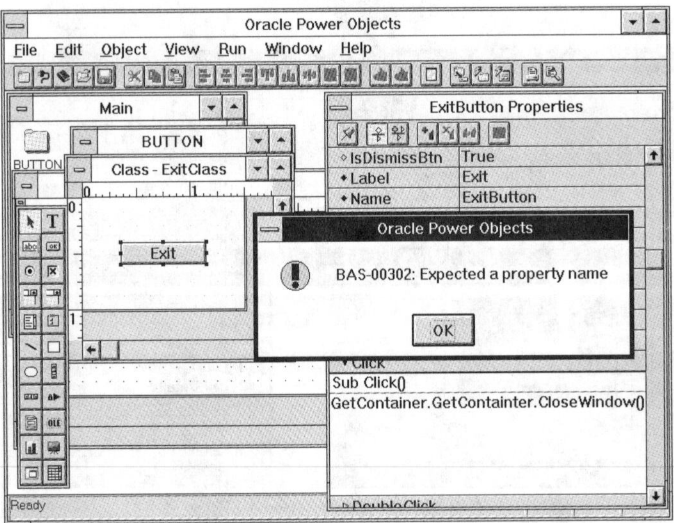

FIGURE 6-7. *Exit class error showing the opened property sheet and method where the error occurs*

and subclasses. A class can be very complex and can contain any number of embedded forms, fields, buttons, other classes, etc., each of which may contain complex Oracle Basic functions in their methods. They may be built using a hierarchy of subclasses. For example, the OK button could be used as a master class for an Accept button, which does something just a little different than the OK button but uses some or all of the attributes of the OK class and its underlying master class.

An example of a more complex class used in different applications is a class that looks up addresses. When assigned to different applications, the class will need its RecordSource property changed to reflect the source of the data to be retrieved (the containing form, a different table, etc.), but the class would retain all its functionality to collect and display the data for an address.

Subforms (Embedded Forms)

Forms can contain one or more different kinds of objects, but the form itself (and by implication, the objects attached to the form) can reference only one table in a database. This restriction is overcome by the use of repeater displays or embedded forms (subforms), in which various objects (list boxes, text fields, etc.) can access data from a different table. The primary key of the table accessed by the outer form is generally associated with a foreign key column in the table accessed by the embedded form. The embedded form can retrieve from its table the detail data that is related to the record displayed in the outer form by using the relationship between the foreign key in the detail form and the primary key in the outer form. The embedded form then displays the detail data. Using embedded forms, primary keys, and foreign keys is Oracle Power Objects' way of relating data from different tables.

For instance, in the whirlpool company database example we used in Chapter 2, the address of each customer contains just the id to a city rather than the city itself. This is in keeping with the relational database constraints in two ways: (1) the full city name is not duplicated every time you add a customer who lives in the city, and (2) the data entry clerk does not need to worry about possible misspellings for the same city, he or she just chooses from a list of cities contained in the Cities table. If necessary, a new city can be added by filling in the proper forms used to add cities to the database. In addition to the Cities table is a States table. The Cities table contains a State column, which uses the two-letter state identification as a foreign key to the primary key in the States table. Thus, the key is either used directly as the state value in the address or used to access the full name of the state. (The Tub database for the whirlpool company discussed in Chapter 2 is used for all further examples in this chapter.)

Class with Embedded Forms

For this example of using subforms, two separate embedded forms will be used to develop an Address class. The Address class can be used later on all reports or forms that need to use customer address information. The steps to create this class are as follows:

1. Open a new application window and set its Name property to **TUBAPP**. This application will be used for the rest of the examples in this chapter.
2. Click on the New Class button. This opens up the blank class editor window, as you saw in the preceding section.
3. Change the Name and Label properties of this class to **AddressClass** and **Address Class**.
4. Open the Tub session (created in Chapter 4) by clicking on the Tub icon. Connect to the database by clicking on the Connect icon, and then open the Custs table by clicking on its icon. This will open the Custs table editor.
5. While holding the CTRL key (in Windows, or the Option key on the Macintosh), select the ADDRESS, ZIP, PHONE, and FAXNO fields in the Custs table, by clicking on the select box to the right of the column name, and drag them onto the Address class form. Oracle Power Objects adds a text field and static field for each column and automatically updates the RecordSource property of the class and the DataSource, DataType, and DataSize properties of the text fields. The static field contains the name of the column in its Label property. Arrange the fields in a nice way, but leave space to the left of the ZIP field for the embedded forms that will be added later. Click on the ZIP static object and delete it by either clicking on the Cut button on the toolbar or pressing the DELETE key on the keyboard.
6. Select all the text fields and static fields at once by pressing the mouse button with the cursor in the containing form (but outside any field) and dragging the rectangle to cover all the fields. This changes the property sheet to the multiple-object property sheet. This is a very nice feature of Oracle Power Objects, because you can change the same property for many objects at the same time.
7. Change the HasBorder property to **False** and the TextJustVert property to **Center** by clicking on those properties and selecting the appropriate value. This action deletes the default border around the field at run time and centers the text within the field.

8. To avoid confusion of duplicate names of objects, click on the Address text field and change its Name property to **Addfld**.
9. Change the FAXNO static field's Label property to **Fax #**.

You have now added text fields to display the customer address and phone number data from the Custs table, although the city and state information is still missing. Oracle Power Objects' Desktop Manager in Windows should look similar to Figure 6-8. To add city and state data to the Address class, you must use embedded forms, because the city and state data are in contained in different tables.

10. Click on the Embedded Form tool on the Object palette and click on the empty space in the class form just above the PHONE static field.
11. Adjust the size of the embedded form by stretching the right edge of the newly added form to the left edge of the Zip text field and the left edge of the new form to the left edge of the class form. Adjust the height of the form appropriately. When stretching any object, place the cursor on the small box in the center of the appropriate edge (the cursor changes to a double horizontal arrow), press the mouse button, and drag the edge to the desired location.

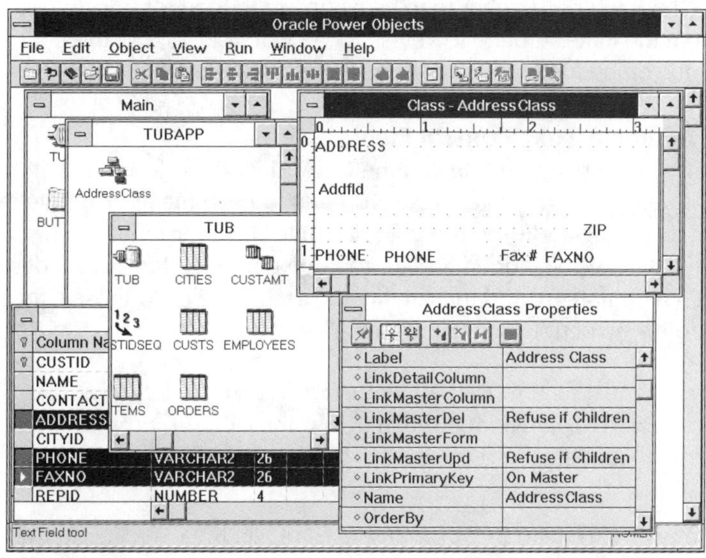

FIGURE 6-8. *Oracle Power Objects' Desktop Manager, after completing the first steps of creating the Address class*

12. Change the Name property of this subform to **City** (it's not required, but it helps to identify the purpose of the form).
13. Open the Cities table in the Tub session window, select the CNAME field, and drag it onto the City embedded form.
14. Stretch the right edge of the CNAME text field to near the end of the City form, leaving enough room for a two-letter state abbreviation, and its left edge to the left edge of the main form. Change its Name property to **Cityfld**.
15. Add an embedded form to the City subform (make sure it is inside the City form and not just in the Address class container) just to the right of the Cityfld text field, adjust its size to contain two letters, and change its Name property to **State**.
16. Open the States table in the Tub session and select and drag the STATEID field into this new form. Adjust the size of the text field to fit into the State embedded form.
17. Change the HasBorder and TextJustVert properties of both the State and City control fields to **False** and **Center**, respectively. Again, to make the field names more understandable, change the STATEID text field to **ST**.
18. Select the City and State embedded forms and change HasBorder to **False**.

In this case, we could have simply used the Cities table's STATEID column in a text form to show the state rather than using an embedded form to retrieve the STATEID from the States table. However, if you wanted to show the entire state name, then the embedded form would be necessary.

Manually Adding a Text Control Field

In the steps above, when you selected the CNAME column from the Cities table or the STATEID field from the States table, you had to have the appropriate tables opened and then drag and drop the columns onto the appropriate forms. Alternatively, after you've added the appropriate embedded forms (as described earlier), you can *manually* add the Cityfld and Stateid fields to those City and State embedded forms by performing the following steps.

1. To add a text field to the City embedded form, click on the Text Fields tool on the Object palette and then click in the City subform. You must now manually update the properties of the text field that describe the data it is to contain.
2. Change the DataSource property to **CNAME**, the DataSize to the same as the size defined in the database (in this case, **30**), and the DataType to **String**. Finally change the Name property of the text field to **CITYFLD**.

3. You must also tell Oracle Power Objects where the embedded form, City, is to retrieve the data for its control fields. This is done automatically for you when a field from a table is dropped into a form. But when you manually add fields, you must tell Oracle Power Objects where the data for the fields is to be retrieved. This is done by setting the RecordSource and RecSrcSession properties. To display the City subforms property sheet, click outside the City form and then click on the City form (you need to move outside the City form because the CITYFLD and ST embedded forms use up all the area inside the form where you could click). Set the RecordSource property to **CITIES** and the RecSrcSession to **Tub**.
4. Add an embedded form to the City form and add a text field to it just as you did for the City form. Set the subform's Name property to **State**.
5. Set the text field's Name property to **ST**, the DataSource property to **STATEID**, the DataSize to **2**, and the DataType to **String**.
6. Set the State embedded form's RecordSource property to **STATES** and the RecSrcSession to **Tub**.

The Class Designer window is now similar to that shown in Figure 6-9.

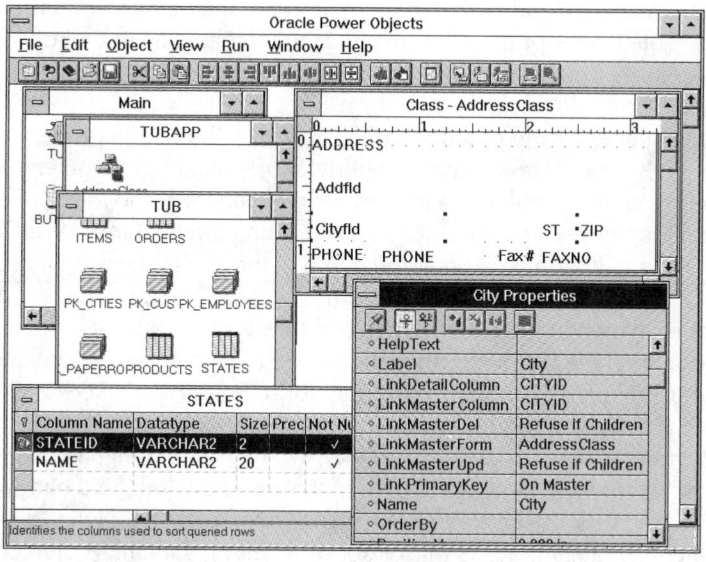

FIGURE 6-9. *Address class with the City and State embedded form and the City embedded form's property sheet*

Linking the Embedded Forms to Their Containers

At this stage, all the required fields have been placed in the class, but they are each independent of each other. In order to make the parts work together, the different forms' tables must be linked together through the use of the foreign and primary keys in the separate tables. To do this, Oracle Power Objects includes three linking properties for all container objects (forms, embedded forms, repeater displays, and user-defined classes). These properties are LinkDetailColumn, LinkMasterColumn, and LinkMasterForm.

In this kind of relation, one form controls which data a second form displays. The controlling container is called the *master form*, and the controlled, or driven, container is called the *detail form*. The link properties are set in the detail form. Its RecordSource table generally, but not always, has the foreign key that references the primary key of the table attached to the controlling or master form. In this example, these link properties are set in the property sheets of the City and State embedded forms. The Address class controls the City embedded form, and the City embedded form controls the State embedded form.

In this type of relationship, the master form first accesses the data it requires. Then the detail form retrieves its rows in one of two ways (depending on which form contains the foreign key). If the detail form's table contains the foreign key, it retrieves all rows from its table whose foreign key matches the primary key of the row the master form just retrieved. In a one-to-one relation where the master form contains the foreign key (rather than the detail form), the detail form retrieves the row from its table whose primary key matches the foreign key in the row retrieved by the master form. This second method is the case for the address-to-city relation in our example.

You set the names of the primary and foreign keys in the link properties of the detail form. In the LinkDetailColumn property of the detail form, you enter the name of the key in the detail form's record source (generally the foreign key) that matches the primary key in the master's record source. In the LinkMasterColumn property of the detail form, you enter the name of the key in the master record source that matches the key in the detail form's record source. The name of the master form is entered in the detail form's LinkMasterForm property.

In our example, the City subform is linked to the Address class container, and the State embedded form is linked to the City form. Set City's LinkDetailColumn property to **CITYID**, which is its record source's (Cities table) primary key, and set City's LinkMasterColumn property to **CITYID**, which is the foreign key in the Address class' record source (Custs table). In this case, the link field names in the City table and the Custs table are the same, CITYID. Finally, you tell Oracle Power Objects which container is City's master form by setting the LinkMasterForm property to **Address**. Similarly, link the State embedded form to the City form by setting State's LinkDetailColumn and LinkMasterColumn to **STATEID** and the LinkMasterForm to **City**. Now when the Address class is used, it will use CITYID to cause the City embedded form to retrieve the correct city name. The City embedded form will use STATEID to cause the State embedded form to retrieve the correct state abbreviation.

Adding a Class to a Form

The previous section discussed adding embedded forms to a master form. In this section, we will expand upon the meaning of embedded forms by adding the AddressClass just created to a form. In essence, the AddressClass can be considered a glorified embedded form.

To illustrate this example, a new form is needed, and it will use the Address class constructed in the previous section. This form will show the customer name with a scroll bar and the Address class. As the user scrolls through the customer names, the address of each will be displayed. The steps to do this are listed below.

1. Select the New Form button in the toolbar (assuming the TUBAPP application is still open; if not, open it by double-clicking on the Tubapp session icon in the Main application window) and set the Name and Label properties in the property sheet of the new form to **CustomerNames** and **Customer Names** respectively. (Remember, the Label is displayed as the title of the form in Run-time mode.)
2. Click and drag the CNAME field from the Custs table and drop it onto the CustomerNames form.
3. Enlarge the form slightly by dragging the lower-right corner of the form further to the right. This is necessary because the Address class is just a little larger than the default size of the form. You cannot drop an object into a form that is the same size or smaller than the added object.
4. Adding the class to the form is extremely simple: just click and drag the Address class icon in the TUBAPP application window onto the CustomerNames form.
5. Click in the middle of the Address class (the cursor should be a small hand) and move it just below the CustomerNames text field (Oracle Power Objects automatically places objects dropped into a form in the upper-left corner).
6. Select the CNAME text field and stretch it to be the same length as the Address class. Stretch the CNAME static field to be large enough to contain the label Customer Name and change its Label property to **Customer Name**.

7. Click on the Vertical Scroll Bar tool in the Object palette and then click in the CustomerNames form at the right edge. Adjust the position of the scroll bar to fit flush against the Address field and extend it from the top of the CustomerNames form to the bottom of the Address class. Note that when the scroll bar is added to the form, it automatically associates itself with the container form. However, if you need a scroll bar to step through data in an object that references a different table or is an embedded form, you need to change the ScrollObj property in the scroll bar's property sheet to the name of the object to be scrolled. For instance, if you wanted to scroll through the address, you could associate the scroll bar with the Address class, rather than the CustomerNames form, by typing in the statement **GetContainer.AddressClass** in the ScrollObj property's text field. However, the customer names would not change because the CustomerNames form is not tied to the AddressClass.
8. Shrink the CustomerNames form to fit snugly against the objects within it by clicking on the lower-right corner of the form (the cursor changes to a diagonal double arrow) and drag the form up against the lower-right edge of the scroll bar.
9. In order to link the Address class to the CustomerNames form, the link properties that describe where the data for the Address class is to be retrieved must be filled in, just as was done for the embedded forms in the Address class. Even though the class and the form use the same table, these properties must be filled in as if they didn't. In this example, the CustomerNames form is the master and the Address class is the detail of the master-detail relation. Figure 6-10 shows the completed CustomerNames form and the property sheet for the Address class in the CustomerNames form after filling in its link properties.

Because the Address class and the CustomerNames form both use the same table in the Tub session, it is more efficient to have the Address class refer to CustomerNames as the source for its data. This is done by changing the RecordSource property of the Address class instance in the CustomerNames form, not in the Address class itself, to **=CustomerNames**. This tells Oracle Power Objects to have the Address class access the same table the CustomerNames form accesses.

Running a Completed Form

You can now test run this form by pressing the Run Form button or by setting the TUBAPP application to run the form when the application is run. The difference is that the Run Form button runs only the active form. Therefore, if the active form is

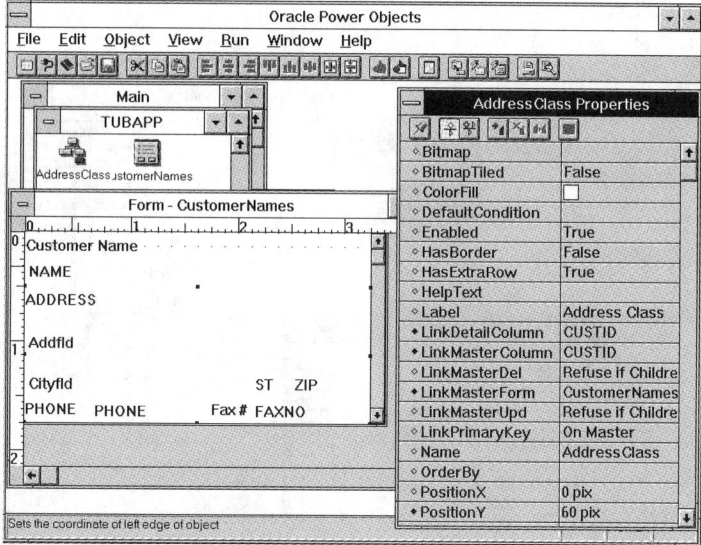

FIGURE 6-10. *The completed CustomerNames form and the filled-in link properties for the Address class*

set to open another auxiliary form (for example, by having the Click( ) method of a button on the active form open a new separate form), it will fail to run. The Run button enables all top-level (stand-alone) forms to be run if they are opened. If you use the Run button, the OnLoad( ) method of the application must have code entered in its text field specifying which form(s) to open when the application begins. This is done by selecting the TUBAPP application and entering the Oracle Basic statement **CustomerNames.OpenWindow( )** in the OnLoad( ) method for the TUBAPP property sheet, as shown in Figure 6-11.

Now when the Run button is pressed, the CustomerNames form is executed. The running form is shown in the following illustration. As you click on a scroll bar button, the form displays each customer's name and address.

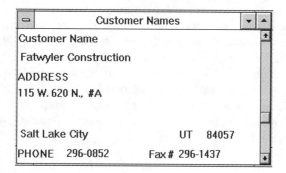

Customer Names
Customer Name
Fatwyler Construction
ADDRESS
115 W. 620 N., #A
Salt Lake City UT 84057
PHONE 296-0852 Fax # 296-1437

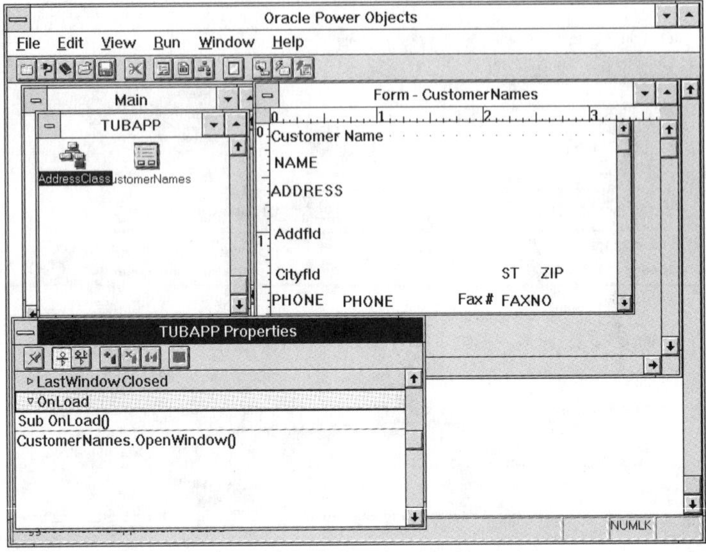

FIGURE 6-11. *The OpenWindow function for the OnLoad( ) method*

In this section, we have shown a simple use of embedded forms to access related data from different tables. It included the explicit use of embedded forms to access the Cities and States tables for the Address class and the implicit use of an embedded form by using the Address class as the detail and CustomerNames as the master of a master-detail relationship.

Repeater Displays and Master-Detail Relationships

A very important common use of database applications is to display detailed information about a selected item in the database. The detail information can simply be additional data associated with a selected item, or it can be a list of many records containing data that are related to the selected item. This association of detailed information with a single more generic item is called the *master-detail relationship.* The previous sections on embedded forms and the AddressClass are actually master-detail relationships with a one-to-one relation. To illustrate the display of a one-to-many master-detail relation, we will demonstrate the use of a repeater display object.

A repeater display consists of a set of panels, each of which contains the same controls. It can be used as a stand-alone form or in a master-detail form. Repeater displays are most often used in master-detail relationships in which several rows (the detail) from one table or view are associated with a single row (record) from another table or view (the master). When used as the detail part of the relationship, it is essentially an embedded table that displays a set of records. These records are retrieved from the table(s) associated with the controls that have been placed in the primary repeater display panel. Figure 6-12 shows a repeater display with its four parts labeled. The primary panel can contain any of the controls and static objects from the Object palette, and the controls are repeated in each secondary panel. You stretch the frame of the repeater display to increase or decrease the number of rows to be displayed at the same time.

To demonstrate the use of repeater displays, a new form will be created to show sales reps and their associated customers. First, a repeater display will be added to the form to show all the customer names in the database as a stand-alone object. Then additional controls will be added to make the repeater display the detail of a master-detail relationship, by having it display all the customers of a given sales rep.

Stand-Alone Repeater Display

The steps to create a stand-alone form that displays several rows of data at a time using a repeater display are as follows.

1. Open the TUBAPP application (if it is not already open) by double-clicking on its icon in the Main application window.
2. Select the New Form button and change its Name and Label properties to **SalesReps**.
3. Set the ColorFill property to light gray (this is done to show contrast between the form and the repeater display).
4. Click on the Repeater Display tool on the Object palette and then click inside the newly opened form. The Form Designer window now looks similar to Figure 6-12.

Control and static objects are placed in the white primary panel at the top of the repeater display. The gray secondary panels simply show how many times the primary panel will be displayed at a time, each panel with a different row of data. Oracle Power Objects automatically retrieves enough data to fill at least ten panels even if less than ten panels are to be displayed. It retrieves enough data to fill all the panels if more than ten are to be displayed. The properties and methods for the

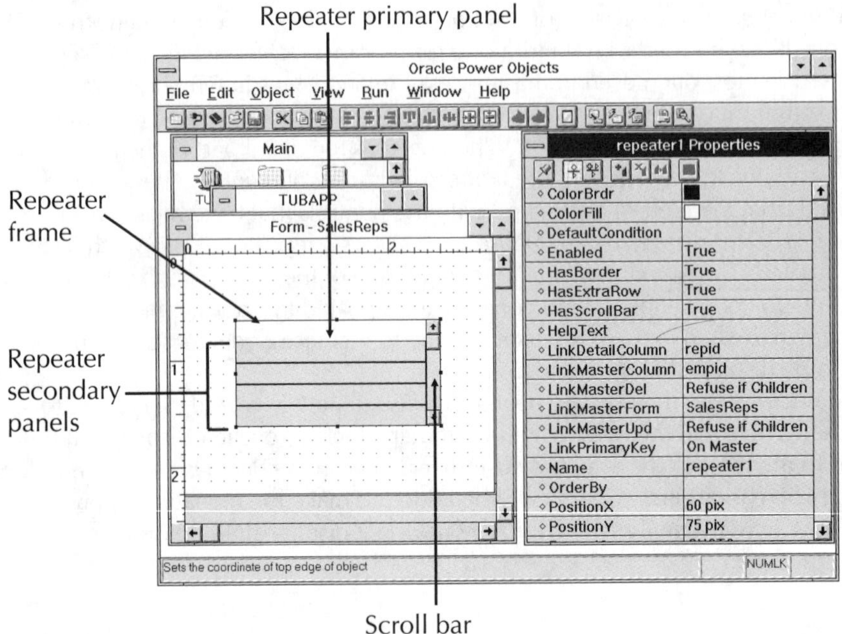

FIGURE 6-12. *The four parts of a repeater display*

panel are displayed when you click on the repeater display, which selects the frame that surrounds the repeater display panel. The properties and methods apply to both the frame and the primary panel. The scroll bar is added to the repeater display by default but can be removed by setting the property HasScrollBar to False.

Sizing the Repeater Display

You can position the repeater display in the form by selecting and moving the entire repeater display (the cursor looks like a closed fist) or size the repeater by dragging an edge of the frame (the cursor changes to a double arrow head when placed over an edge of the repeater display) to the desired location. Note that the repeater display panels are not attached to the frame and do not expand as the frame changes.

To make the repeater display panels fill the frame, select the white primary panel and then drag the edge of the panel to the edge of the frame. The gray secondary panels adjust their sizes to match the size of the white primary panel. Oracle Power Objects increases or decreases the number of secondary panels to fit the frame with complete panels. It leaves space between the frame and the panels if there is not enough room to insert a complete panel. You can leave space between the repeater frame and the repeater panels to put in static text fields for legends or other static information that is not to be repeated.

Adding Controls to the Repeater Display Primary Panel

To add controls to the repeater display primary panel, complete the following steps.

1. Position the repeater display a little below the top of the SalesReps form.
2. Add a static text field for a heading by clicking on the Static Text tool in the Object palette and then clicking in the SalesReps form above the repeater display.
3. Change the Label property of the static object to **Customers**, center the object by clicking on the Horizontally Center in Container button, and change the TextJustVert property to **Center** to center the text vertically in the text field.
4. Open the Tub session, if not already open, and open the Custs table.
5. Select the NAME field (by clicking on the gray button on the left side) and drag it onto the white primary repeater display panel. Be sure the primary panel is selected (its border displays eight black squares) and not the repeater frame, or it will not work.
6. Adjust the size of the NAME text field to fill the repeater display, and set the TextJustVert property to **Center**. Change the Name field to **CustName**.

The repeater display on the SalesReps forms needs a mechanism to show which name was selected. This is done with the Pointer Arrow tool.

7. Click on the repeater display twice to select the primary repeater panel and move the CustName text field over about a quarter inch to allow room for the cursor arrow.
8. Click on the Pointer Arrow tool on the Object palette and then click on the space between the edge of the SalesReps form and the CustName field.

The RecordSource property for the repeater display is automatically set to the Custs table and the RecSrcSession property to the Tub session when the NAME column was dropped in the primary panel. The form can now be tested by selecting the Run Form button. The completed SalesReps form looks similar to this:

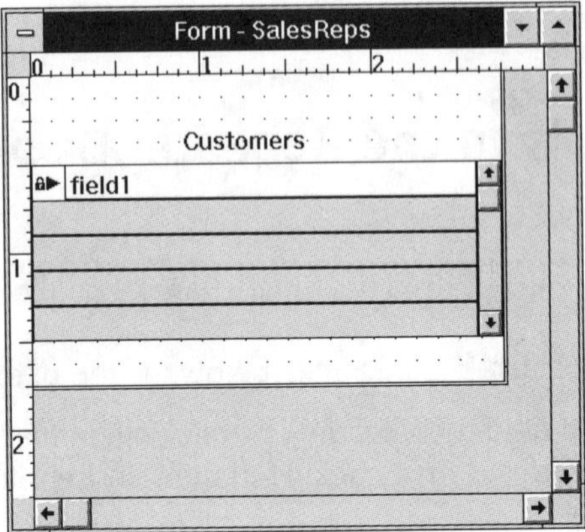

The Repeater Display in a Master-Detail Relationship

To complete our example of a master-detail relationship, we will add objects to the form containing the repeater to create a master-detail relationship that lists every customer for each sales rep. This is accomplished by adding a control field that accesses the Employee table in the Tub session. To do this, follow these steps:

1. Enlarge the SalesReps form by dragging the lower-right corner down a half-inch or so and move both the Customer Name static field and the repeater display object down to the bottom of the form. This is done to create enough room for the master controls that will be added.
2. Open the Employee table in the Tub session, select the NAME field, and drag it onto the SalesReps form above the repeater display. This automatically sets the SalesReps form's RecordSource property to the Employee table. This text field is then the master control for the repeater display.
3. Change the Label property of the static field to **Sales Representative** and the TextJustVert property of both the static and control fields to **Center**.
4. Adjust the two fields so that the NAME text field extends across the form and the NAME static field is large enough to hold the Sales Representative label.

5. Add a vertical scroll bar to the right edge of the NAME text field by clicking on the Vertical Scroll Bar tool and then clicking to the right of the NAME text field. Oracle Power Objects automatically fills in the ScrollObj property of the scroll bar to be the SalesReps form. This scroll bar allows the end user to scroll through all the employee names in the Employee table.
6. Polish the appearance of the form by adjusting the position of the various control fields and the repeater display.
7. Now link the repeater display to the master control (the NAME text field). Set the link properties (LinkDetailColumn, LinkMasterColumn, and LinkMasterForm) of the repeater display to **REPID**, **EMPID**, and **SalesReps**, respectively. Remember that when linking a master-detail relation, you set the *detail object's* link properties, not the master's properties. Thus, when a user scrolls through the employee names, Oracle Power Objects selects all records in the Custs table whose foreign key, REPID, matches the primary key, EMPID, of the currently displayed employee name from the Employee table. These records are then displayed in the repeater display. The completed SalesReps form, using a repeater display in a master-detail relationship, is shown in Figure 6-13 (along with the property sheet for the repeater).

Running the Repeater Display Master-Detail Form

Now that the SalesReps form is completed, you can test run it by using either the Run Form button or the Run button. For this example, we will use the Run Form button.

To test run the SalesReps form, click on the Run Form button. When the form is run, the user can step through all the employees in the database and view all the customers that the sales representative services. If there are more customers than the repeater has panels, the remainder of the customers can be viewed by using the scroll bar that is automatically added to the repeater display. The SalesReps form, as generated by pressing the Run Form button, is shown here:

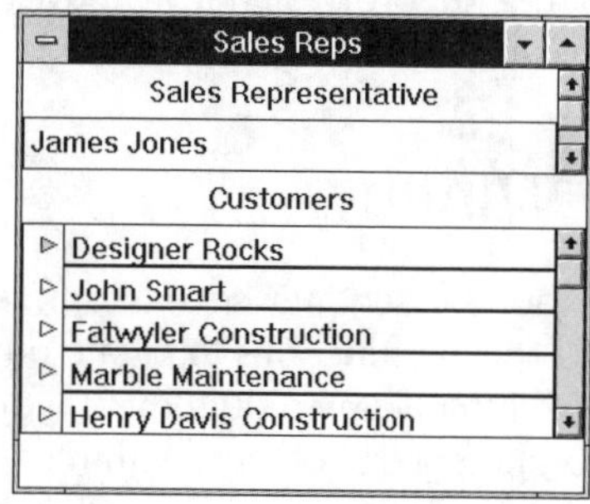

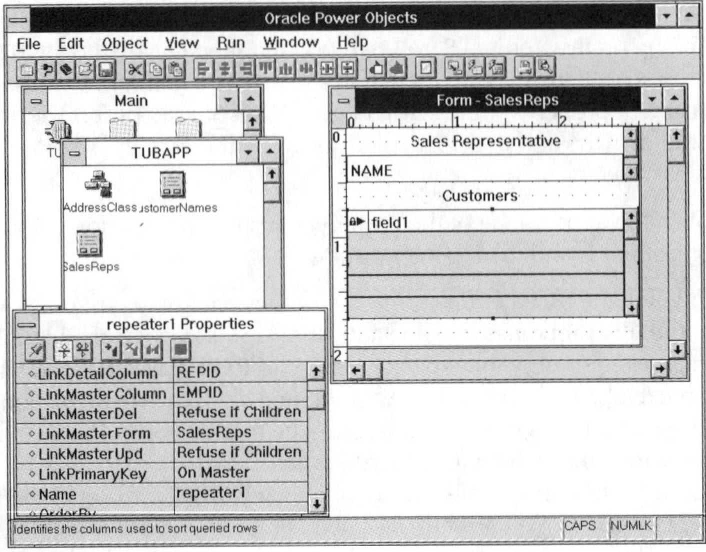

FIGURE 6-13. *The completed SalesReps form with link properties shown*

This is a relatively simple use of the repeater display in a master-detail relationship. The repeater display panel can contain very complex sets of objects, including embedded forms and classes. Each panel displays subsequent records of the data retrieved associated with the objects in the primary repeater display panel.

Reports

The report-building capability of Oracle Power Objects is very substantial. It allows you to use embedded forms, user-defined classes, text fields, static fields, and various graphical objects to create the exact format in which to show the desired data. Reports are built using the Report Designer window. This section describes the Report Designer window and explains how to use it to create a simple report.

Report Designer Window

This Oracle Power Objects tool is essentially several different forms (or panels) in one form, each of which has special functions to create different parts of a report. To customize your report for virtually any requirement, you can place any kind and any number of static objects and control objects within each part of the Report

Designer window. The Report Designer window creates a report object, which is added to the open application. It is shown in the Main application window with the Report icon and labeled with the report's name, as described in Chapter 3. Once the report is created, it can be run in three ways:

- Open it (by double-clicking on its icon) and press the Run Form button or the Print Preview button.
- Enter the Oracle Basic statement **report_name.PrintPreview( )** in the OnLoad( ) method of the application.
- Enter the Oracle Basic statement **report_name.PrintPreview( )** in a method, such as the Click( ) method, of another object. For example, you could place reports in a report menu or you could have a Print Report button on an invoice form.

The Report Designer window is displayed by clicking on the New Report button on the toolbar when an application is open. The window is separated into five or more subwindows, depending on whether the Group Heading feature (described later) is added. Each subwindow's label, or name, is above it on a separator field. Figure 6-14 shows a Report Designer window that has one Group Header added (you can add more than one group header to create nested groups in a report).

Each part of the Report Designer window is a form in which you can insert Oracle Power Objects control and static objects. Each subwindow of the Report Designer window has its own property sheet, which is displayed by clicking on the name of the subwindow. These properties are used to customize each part of the report. One of the properties of each of these subwindows is the Enabled property, which tells Oracle Power Objects whether or not to include that part of the report in the final copy when it is printed. A full description of Report Designer window properties is found in Chapter 8.

Following is a description of each subwindow of the Report Designer.

Report Header You include in this subwindow all of the information that you want printed once at the beginning of the report. You could include your company name and address, or a report title and the author name, along with a text field to print the current date. You can make the size of this window equal to one full page, so that all the information is printed on a separate page, or just as a header on the first page of the report. (See the discussion on resizing the subwindows in the "Resizing Report Designer Panels" section.)

Page Header You can place items to be printed at the top of every page, such as page number and report title, in this panel. If you do not use a group header,

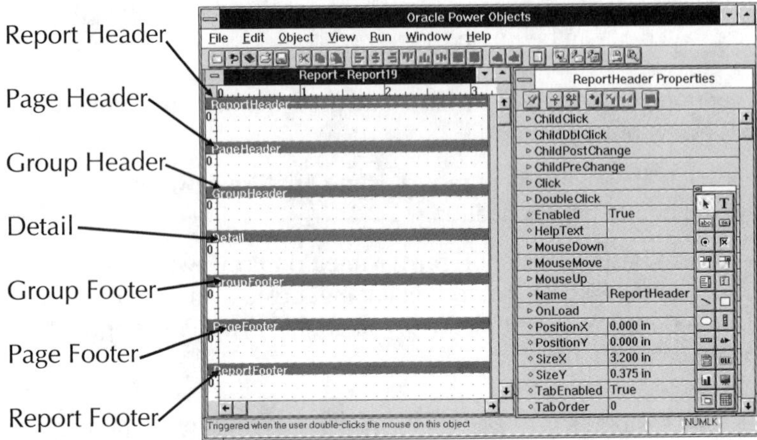

FIGURE 6-14. *The initial Report Designer window including the Group Header feature*

you can include static fields as heads of columns in the detail part of the report. You set the FirstPghdr property to True, if you want this information on the first page of the report, or to False, if you want just the Report Header data to be on the first page. The Page Header data is placed in the top margin above the Report Header information.

Group Header This is one of the most powerful features of the Report Designer window. Often you need reports that require similar data be grouped together. An example of such a report is one that lists all employees by department. This part of the Report Designer window allows you to enter headers at the start of each grouping of data. For example, you could place a text control field in an embedded form in this Group Header subwindow to display the department name. Then the printed report displays the department name, followed by the names of all employees in that department, for each department. This subwindow is not automatically included when you first select the New Report button. You must explicitly add groupings to an open Report Designer window as described later in this chapter in "Adding Group Headers and Footers." When you add a group header to a report, it adds a Group Header and Group Footer window area to the Report Designer window.

Detail This is where the meat of the report is placed. Include all of the text controls, classes, embedded forms, etc. that are necessary to retrieve and present the data needed for the report. Every row that is retrieved to fill the control objects is printed in the final report. Any static objects, such as Lines or Static Text, will be repeated for each row retrieved from the database. If detail information needs to be retrieved from multiple tables, it is suggested that you create a view (as explained in Chapter 4) containing the information to be used in the report. This will save you the trouble of adding embedded forms and linking them with each other to synchronize the records to be retrieved.

Group Footer As each grouping of data is completed, your report may require a printed summation, such as the total salary for the department or total sales for each salesperson. Add the objects needed to display that information in this subwindow. This subwindow is only displayed when the Group Heading control is added to the Report Designer window.

Page Footer In addition to having a page header, you may want to have information printed at the bottom of the page. Include the static and control fields needed to retrieve or create the data to be printed at the bottom of each page in the report in this subwindow.

Report Footer Your report might require a final summation to be placed at the end of the printed report. Place the objects needed to retrieve or construct the data to be printed at the end of the report in this subwindow. For example, you could have a summation of the total sales of all sales representatives.

Adding Group Headers and Footers

As mentioned earlier, the Group Header and Group Footer features are not automatically included in the Report Designer window. You add this functionality by clicking on the Report Group tool on the Object palette and then clicking on the report in which group heading/footers are required. By adding two or more group headers to the report, the Group By feature can be nested so that you can have subgroups within a group. For example, your report could be a list of sales personnel grouped by department and the company's customers grouped according to their sales representative. This would be done by adding two group headers to the Report Designer window. The GroupCol property in the property sheet for the Group Header is used to designate which column in the table is to be used for the Group By function. This will be explained in more detail in the "Building a Report" section below.

Resizing Report Designer Panels

You resize the various subwindows by clicking on the window's title and separator bar and then dragging the cursor (double arrow shape) up or down to the desired position. You change the size of the subwindows to add or reduce space around the objects you place into them. For example, if you place one static text field as a title in the Report Header subwindow and then size the window to fit snugly against the title, the amount of space for the title in the printed report will be just enough to print the title. You could, however, open up the window enough to take an entire page. You could then vertically center the desired objects to create a front page for your report. Similarly, if you place a text field in the Detail subwindow and fit the window snugly against the object, then there will be no space between printed rows in the main part of the report. However, if you leave a little space below the text field, then there will be that amount of space between each row in the printed report.

Building a Report

With the brief introduction to the Report Designer window above, you can now begin designing a simple report. The requirements for this report are that each salesperson in the company be listed, followed by the list of all of his/her customers and the total amount of each customer's purchases. The total dollar amount of sales for the salesperson is to be printed following the list of customers. The printed report must have a title page and a closing page, the latter including the total of all sales for the company.

Printing the total amount for each customer's purchases could be the most difficult problem to solve in this example. However, there are two or three ways to accomplish this task. The first is to create a view that contains the customer id and name, the sales rep's id, and a column that sums the AMOUNT column in the Orders table for a given customer. To create the view in Oracle's sqldba program, or other relational databases, you would use a SQL statement similar to the one shown below. You could add any additional fields required for other uses of the view.

```
CREATE VIEW CUSTAMT (CUSTID, CUSTNAME, REPID, TOTAL) AS
   SELECT ORDERS.CUSTID CUSTID, NAME CUSTNAME, REPID REPID,
   SUM(AMOUNT) TOTAL FROM CUSTS, ORDERS WHERE CUSTS.CUSTID = ORDERS.CUSTID
   GROUP BY ORDERS.CUSTID, NAME, REPID;
```

However, for this example we will use the Oracle Basic function SQLLookup. This method may cause the report to take a little longer to load because it must do its own query, while a report based on a view has the work done inside the database server. However, if there is not a need for other applications to access the view, it saves database resources. Also, this method requires that you know a little SQL, while using a view is just like using a table. Thus, if the system administrator creates the view, the application developer does not need to be proficient in SQL. But to use Oracle Power Objects to its full power, it is best to know SQL (see Chapter 10), and this is a good example of how to use one of the more powerful functions in Oracle Basic.

Now let's begin building the report. First, open the TUBAPP application window (if it is not already open) and for convenience, open the Tub session (so that the text control fields do not have to be filled in manually). Click on the New Report toolbar button, to have Oracle Power Objects open a blank Report Designer window and automatically load the report into the application. Change the Name and Label properties of the report to **SalesbyCust** and **Sales by Customer**, respectively (again, this is not required, but is good design practice). You may want to enlarge the Report Designer window to the width of the paper on which the report will be printed so that it is easier to correctly place the control objects.

The requirements of the report, as stated above, dictate the steps in creating it. The requirement to group the customers together according to their sales representative necessitates the use of the Group By function for the Report Designer window. Click on the Report Group tool on the Object palette and then click anywhere on the Report Designer window. The Group Header and Group Footer windows are now present, and you are ready to begin creating the report. As you add static and text control fields, change all of their TextJustVert properties to Center and the static field's TextJustHoriz properties to Center.

Build the report header by following these steps:

1. Place a static field in the ReportHeader subwindow, enlarge it to about six inches by one-half inch. If the requirement is a single page for the report title, then enlarge the window to be page size and place the static field appropriately. In this example, we will leave it to be just a part of the first page.

2. Enter the text **Customer Sales** by **Sales Representative** in the Label property of the static field and set the FontBold property to **True** and the FontSize property to **18**.

3. Center the static field by pressing the Horizontally Center in Container button on the toolbar.

4. Drag the GroupHeader title bar and separator field up next to the PageHeader title bar and separator field to conserve space in the work area. (We won't be using a page header in this example.)

This completes the report header part of the report. The meat of the report is the list of the customers and the total purchase amount of each customer. The controls to provide this information are placed in the Detail part of the Report Designer window.

5. Open the Custs table, click on NAME and CUSTID and drag them onto the Detail area. This will automatically set the RecordSource and RecSrcSession properties of the report to CUSTS and TUB respectively. The static fields NAME and CUSTID, which Oracle Power Objects automatically added when the table names were dropped on the report, are not needed for this report. Select them by clicking on them one at a time (or select both by clicking on one and SHIFT-clicking on the other) and delete them by either pressing the DELETE key on the keyboard or the Cut button in the toolbar. The CUSTID field is necessary only so that we can access the Custid value in the SQL statement needed for the TOTAL field (added next). Therefore, set its Visible property to **False**.
6. Change the Name property of the NAME field to **CUSTNAME** just to make it a little more specific.
7. Add another text control field to the right of the CUSTS field and name it **TOTAL** and change its DataType property to **Double**, the TextJustHoriz property to **Right** and its FormatMask property to **Currency**.
8. Now the important part: Enter the following statement **=SQLLookup("SELECT SUM(AMOUNT) FROM ORDERS WHERE CUSTID = " + CUSTID)** in the DataSource property of the TOTAL text control field. This statement will sum all of the amounts in the Orders table for each given customer based on the customer's id in the CUSTID field, and store that value in the TOTAL field.
9. Enlarge the CUSTNAME text field to about three inches long and the TOTAL field to about one inch long and place them both on the same line at the top of the Detail area.

This completes the Detail part of the report, but the grouping of the customers and the heading for each group must now be implemented. This is all done in the GroupHeader part of the Report Designer window. The sales representative's name and the headers for the customer names and the totals are placed here.

To set up the Group By feature, click on the GroupHeader title to display its property sheet. Now set the GroupCol property to REPID. This tells Oracle Power Objects by which field the retrieved records in the Detail part of the report are grouped; in this example, all records with the same REPID will be grouped together.

The requirement of having the customer's names listed after the name of their sales representative lends itself to creating a master-detail relationship. Usually, the part of the relationship that contains the most information and the foreign key to the other table is the detail. However, in this case, the grouped customers are the master part of the report and the sales representative's name is the detail, which seems backwards. But if you consider the grouped names as a single entity and that as this entity is displayed, Oracle Power Objects looks up additional detail information in the form of the sales representative's name that is associated with the entity, then the master-detail relationship is easier to see. The objects needed to display the required information at the start of each group of customers are created by the following steps.

1. For the sales representative's names, add an embedded form to the GroupHeader area, enlarge it to about three inches by one-half inch and change its Label and Name properties to **Employee**.
2. Open the Employees table and select and drag the NAME field onto this embedded form. Again, this automatically sets the RecordSource and RecSrcSession properties of the Employee embedded form appropriately.
3. Delete the NAME static text field (added by Oracle Power Objects), enlarge the NAME text field, and change its name to **EmpName**.
4. Place a static field above the embedded form in the GroupHeader area, enlarge it, set its Label property to **SalesRep**, set the FontBold property to **True** and set the FontSize to **18**.
5. Center this title and the embedded form in the Group Heading form by selecting both of them and then pressing the Horizontally Center in Container toolbar button.
6. To finish the heading for each group of customers, place two static text control fields below the embedded form in the GroupHeader area and change their Label properties to **Customer Name** and **Sales**, respectively.
7. Adjust them so they will be over the CustName text field and the Total text field in the Detail area.
8. Just for decoration, click on the Lines tool on theObject palette and add a line underneath the Customer Name and Sales static fields.

The static part of the heading for each group is now completed, but the connection between the Employee embedded form and the underlying report needs to be created. The base table for the report is the Custs table. Each customer record has a key (REPID) to the sales employee that services their account. This is the key by which the report groups the customers in the Detail area and selects the salesperson associated with that group.

By using the values set in the link properties, Oracle Power Objects informs the Employee embedded form which records to retrieve. The Employee embedded form is linked to the Group Header form by setting its link properties as listed here:

1. Set the LinkDetailColumn to **EMPID**.
2. Set the LinkMasterColumn to **REPID**.
3. Set the LinkMasterForm to **GroupHeader**. (This is an example of object inheritance, in that the Group Heading form has inherited the record source, Custs, of the underlying report, SalesbyCust.)

Remember that the detail column in an embedded form is what links the embedded form to the master form. The detail column is from the table that has been entered as the embedded form's RecordSource property. The master column (derived from the table that has been entered as the master form's RecordSource property) is where the master form and the detail column are linked.

The title, the group heading, and the detail part of the report are now completed. Your Report Designer window should look similar to Figure 6-15. The link properties for the Employee embedded form are also displayed. You can preview the report made so far by pressing the Print Preview button.

To finish fulfilling the requirements for the report, you need to show the total sales for each sales representative and the grand total sales. To do this:

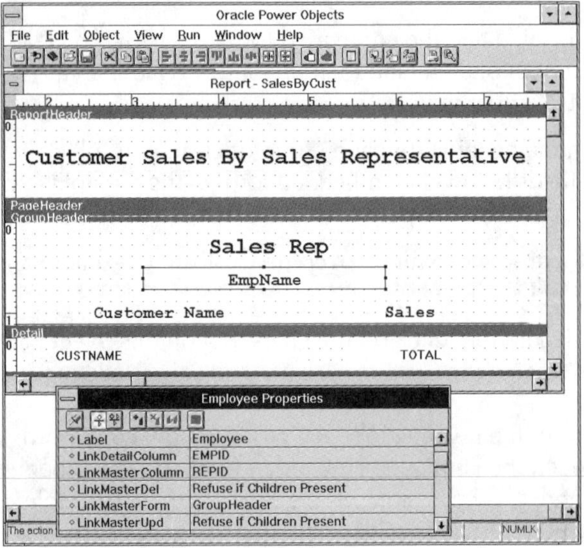

FIGURE 6-15. *Preliminary setup of the SalesByCust report*

1. Add a static field to the Group Footer area, change its Label property to **Sales Rep's Total Sales**, and change its text justification properties appropriately.
2. Add a text field to the right of the static field and adjust the text field so that it is the same size as, and aligned with, the Total text field in the Detail area.
3. Set its DataType to **double**, the FormatMask to **currency**, and the Name property to **Stotal**.
4. Use the Oracle Basic sum function to show the total for the group by typing in **=SUM(TOTAL)** in the DataSource property of the Stotal text field.
5. Again, just for looks, place a line along the top of the Group Footer area to separate the different groups.

The object to show the grand total of all sales is placed in the Report Footer area. To create the final summation, repeat the steps above, except do them in the Report Footer area with the following differences.

- Set the static field's Label to **Total Sales**, the text field's DataSource to **=SUM(Stotal)**, and the Name property to **Gtotal**.
- Add two lines just below the top of the Report Footer window area.

This completes entering all the objects and setting properties for the report. However, to make it look nicer, place a margin on the right side of the report by moving every object in the Report Designer window one inch to the right. The Report Designer window should now look similar to Figure 6-16.

To view the report, press the Print Preview button on the toolbar or press the Run Form button (Print Preview shows the report as it will be printed). The full and close-up views of the report are shown in Figure 6-17.

Putting It All Together

So far, we have created individual forms, reports, and classes loosely aggregated in one application, but they are not unified in one application that is easily used. In this section, the different objects that have been created will be combined so that they can be run from one window.

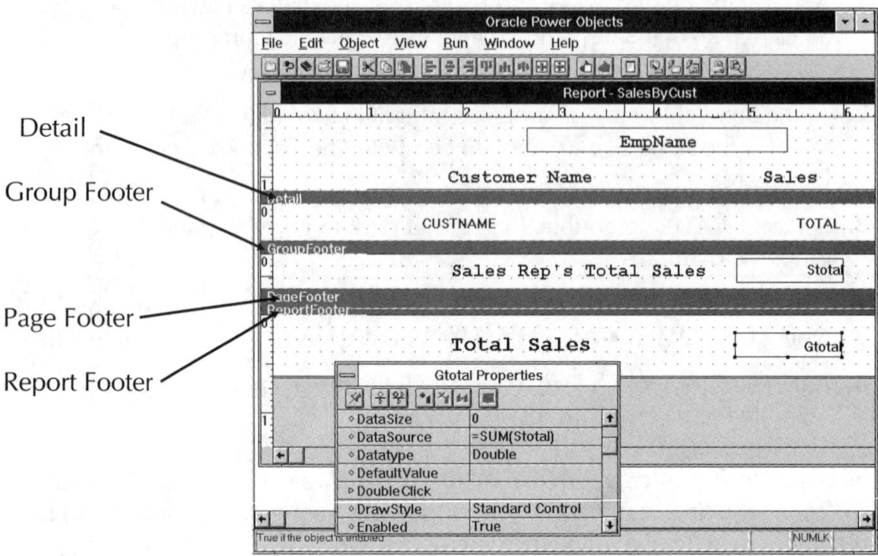

FIGURE 6-16. *The final setup of the SalesByCust report with an Oracle Basic expression in the Gtotal DataSource property*

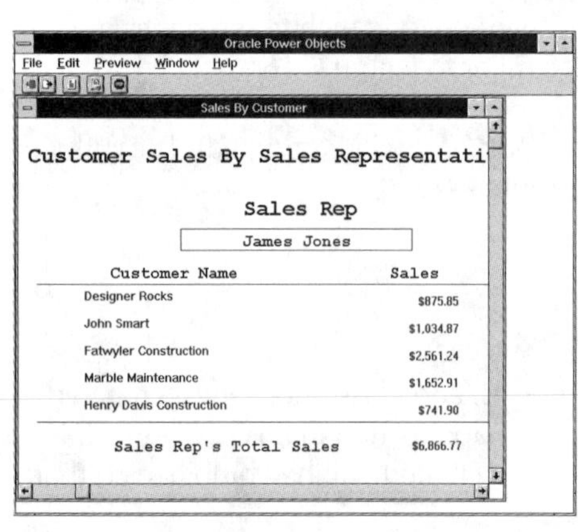

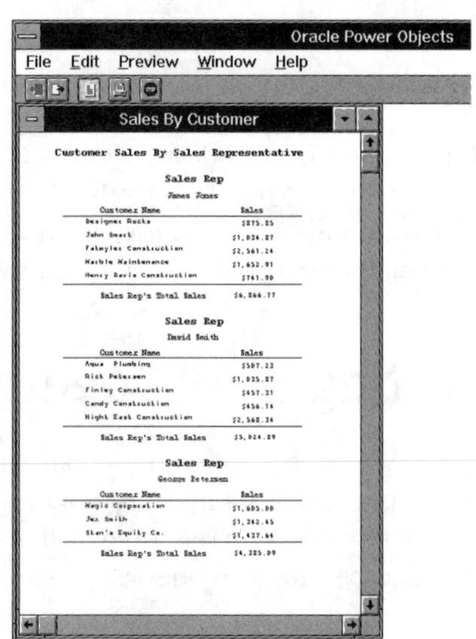

FIGURE 6-17. *The final report in full-page and close-up display*

Combining Two Forms to Display Related Data

Often, it is necessary or useful to have one form on which most of the work is done, but occasionally, on demand, you need to have another form displayed to augment the work. This is done by giving the main form the ability to open the second form by the end user. In this example, the SalesReps form is the *controlling form* and the CustomerNames form is the *secondary form*.

But before we start, we'll create a simple ExitBtnClass class to be used to close different windows after they are opened. This is just a button with no background, with the Exit button's Click( ) method set to GetContainer.GetContainer.CloseWindow( ), similar to what was done at the start of this chapter. (As was explained then, the creation of the Exit class based on the Button class was overkill, so this will correct that excessive behavior.)

1. Open the Tubapp application form if it is not already opened.
2. Click on the New Class button on the toolbar. Change the Label to **Exit Class** and the Name to **ExitBtnClass**.
3. Click on the Push Button icon in the Object palette and then click in the ExitBtnClass form.
4. Change the Label to **Exit** and the Name to **ExitBtn**.
5. Add the line **GetContainer.GetContainer.CloseWindow( )** to the Exit button's Click( ) method.
6. Shrink the class form up snug against the button so that there is no space around the button.
7. Save and close the class.

Now we will join the SalesReps and CustomerNames into one subapplication. You will start by adding the ExitBtnClass to the SalesReps form so that it can be closed when it is running, and you'll add another button to open a window to display the address of the customer selected in the SalesReps form when the button is pressed. The following steps are done to accomplish this task.

1. Open the SalesReps form and make the form a little taller by moving the bottom of the form down a little, allowing room for the Exit button and an Address button.
2. Drag the ExitBtnClass onto the SalesReps form and then move it to the bottom of the form (Remember that Oracle Power Objects always places an object dropped into a form at the upper-left corner of the container).

3. Place a new button on the SalesReps form by clicking on the Push Button tool on the Object palette and then clicking at the bottom of the SalesReps form.
4. Vertically align the two buttons and adjust their positions so that they look nice on the form.
5. Click on the new button and change its Label property to **Address**, its Name property to **AddressBtn**, and set its Click( ) method to **CustomerNames.OpenWindow** as shown in Figure 6-18. This causes Oracle Power Objects to open the CustomerNames form and display the selected person's address when the Address button is clicked.

The final SalesReps form is shown in Figure 6-18. Note the properties of the Address button.

At this point, the SalesReps form knows about the CustomerNames form by way of the Address button, but the CustomerNames form knows nothing about the SalesReps form. The CustomerNames form must now be modified so that it knows where to access its information related to the SalesReps form that it needs to load into its form. This is accomplished by changing the link properties of the CustomerNames form. Because the purpose of the form is to display just one

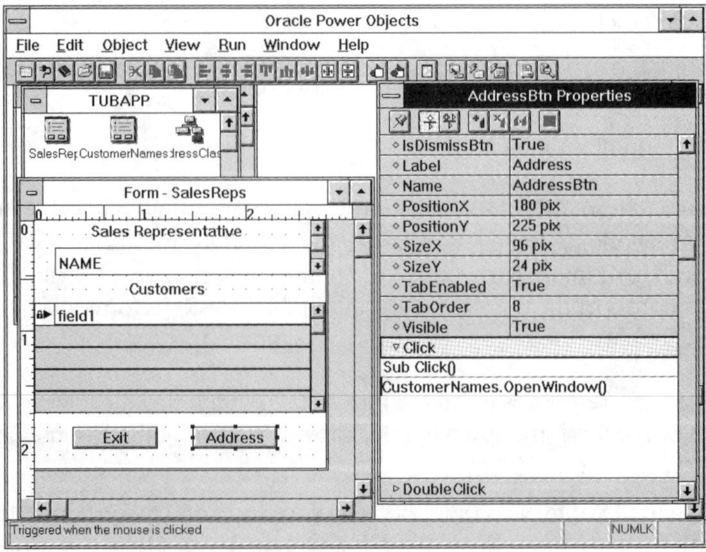

FIGURE 6-18. *SalesReps form showing new additions and the Address button properties*

person's address (instead of scrolling through all customers), the scroll bar can be deleted. These procedures are done in the following steps.

1. Open the CustomerNames form. Select and delete the scroll bar that is no longer needed, as only one address is to be displayed at a time.
2. Drag the bottom of the form down a little to provide room for the Exit button and then drag and drop the ExitBtnClass icon onto the form.
3. Move the Exit button to the bottom and center it in the container by pressing on the Horizontally Center in Container button on the toolbar.
4. Click on the form itself to display the CustomerNames property sheet, and set the LinkDetailColumn property to **CUSTID**, the LinkMasterColumn property to **CUSTID**, and the LinkMasterForm to **SalesReps.repeater1**.

An important aspect of Oracle Power Objects is shown in this example. A master form for a detail object does not have to contain the detail object or even be in the same container as the detail object. However, the master and detail objects do have to be in the same application. The modified CustomerNames form and its link properties are shown in Figure 6-19.

Now, when the Address button is pressed in the SalesReps form, the name and address of the selected customer are displayed in a separate window. Oracle Power Objects accomplishes this by having the SalesReps form's repeater send the selected

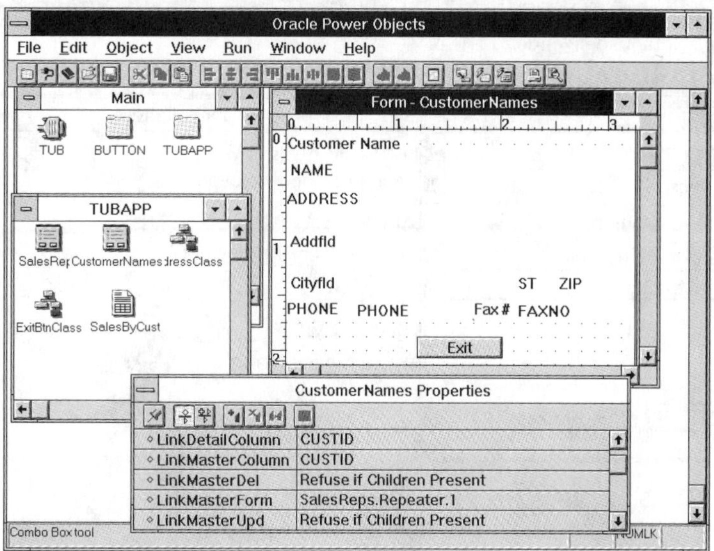

FIGURE 6-19. *Modified CustomerNames form showing link properties*

customer's CUSTID to the CustomerNames form. The CustomerNames form is then opened and uses the CUSTID received from the SalesReps form to display the selected customer's address. Once the form is opened, each time you click on a customer in the SalesReps repeater, the Address form displays the currently selected person's address. You do not need to press the Address button again unless you exit the Address form.

When building this combination of SalesReps and CustomerNames, it is important to note that you cannot test the functionality of the Address button in the SalesReps form in Run Form mode. If the SalesReps form is in Run Form mode and you press the Address button, you will get the error "Must have an object property" and the Click( ) method of the Address button's property sheet will be highlighted. This is because only one form at a time can be run in Run Form mode. To run the combination of the two forms, you must use the Run toolbar button and set the OnLoad( ) method of the TUBAPP application to **SalesReps.OpenWindow( )**.

With the TUBAPP OnLoad( ) method set, the combination of the two forms can be run by clicking on the Run button. The SalesReps form is displayed in its running form. Press on the Address button, and the address of the currently selected person is shown in the CustomerNames form. The default selection when the SalesReps form is first displayed is shown by a gray arrow cursor. When you select another person, the cursor arrow is black. Unselected cursor arrows are white. The running combination of the two forms is shown in Figure 6-20.

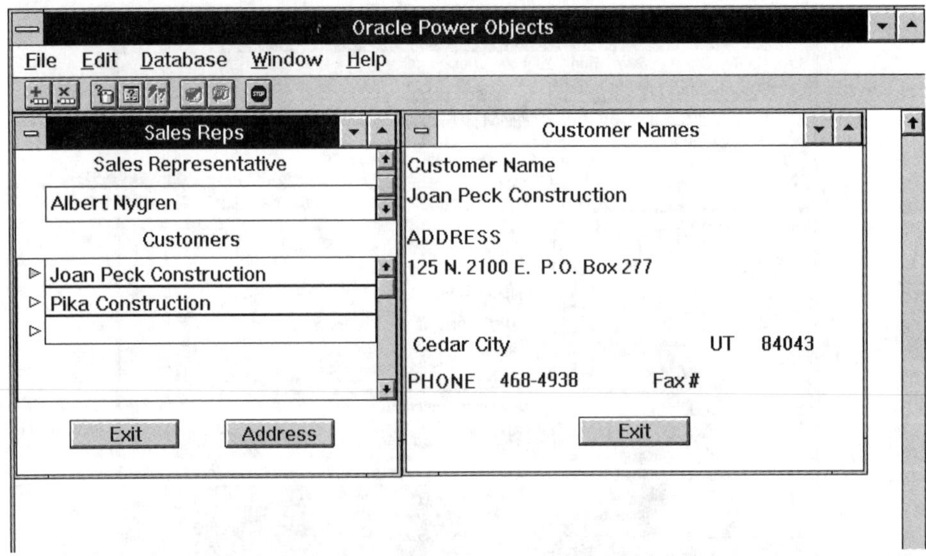

FIGURE 6-20. *Combination of the SalesReps and CustomerNames forms running together*

Combining All Forms and Reports

This last section of this chapter shows how to combine all of the functional objects created into one form to be run when the application is loaded. This application can then be compiled and run by an end user. To do this, a new form with just a title and three buttons is created that ties all of the forms and reports created in the TUBAPP application together. This application provides the end user with a control window that has a button to create a sales report, a button to list all salespersons, and an Exit button. This is done in the following steps.

1. Open the TUBAPP application window if it is not already open.
2. Open a new form and change its Name property to **Compforms**.
3. Drag the ExitBtnClass onto the form and center it at the bottom.
4. Place a static field at the top of the form and enlarge it to about three inches by one-half inch and change its Label property to **MODERN TUB COMPANY FORMS**.
5. Set the FontBold property to **True** and the FontSize property to **18**.
6. Click on the Push Button tool on the Object palette and click on the right side of the form, and do it again on the left side.
7. Change one button's Label property to **Sales Report** and its Name to **Sales Report**.
8. Change the other button's Label property to **Customers** and its Name to **CustBtn**.
9. Change the Sales Report button's Click( ) method to read **SalesbyCust.PrintPreview( )**. When the Sales Report button is pressed, the report will run in Print Preview mode. The report can be sent directly to the printer by setting the method to **SalesbyCust.Print( )**. But the user would not be given the opportunity to review it before it is printed.
10. Change the Customers button's Click( ) method to **SalesReps.OpenWindow( )**. The final Compform should now look as shown in Figure 6-21.
11. The final step is to select the TUBAPP application, open its property sheet, and change the TUBAPP OnLoad( ) method to **Compforms.OpenWindow( )**.

Now, test the program by clicking on the Run button. Click on the Sales Report button, and the sales report is displayed. A word of caution: pressing the Exit button on the toolbar will end the entire application, not just the sales report. To exit the sales report and leave the Compform running, select the Close item from the File

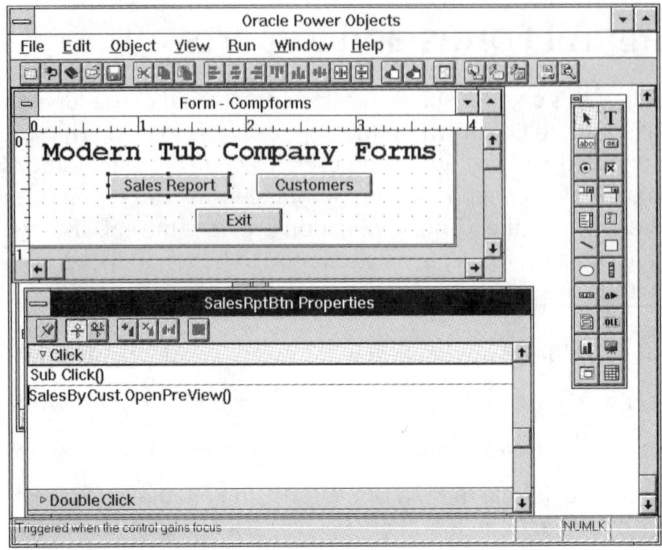

FIGURE 6-21. *Final Compform with the Sales Report button's properties displayed*

menu. Click on the Customers button to display the list of customers by sales representative. Click on a customer's name and the Address button to show the address of the customer. You can click on the Exit button in either form and only the subwindows will close, not the whole application. Figure 6-22 shows all three parts of the application running when started from the Main application window.

Compiling and Running an Application

Now that the application has been developed, it can be compiled so end users can easily access it. You have two choices: the application can be a stand-alone executable program or a module to be run by a run-time version of Oracle Power Objects. The former method will create a large memory-intensive program for every application developed, while the latter method creates several smaller modules run by a master run-time program.

To compile the completed application into a module to be run by Oracle Power Objects' run-time program or into a stand-alone executable, you first select the program to be compiled by clicking on its icon (for this example, the TUBAPP

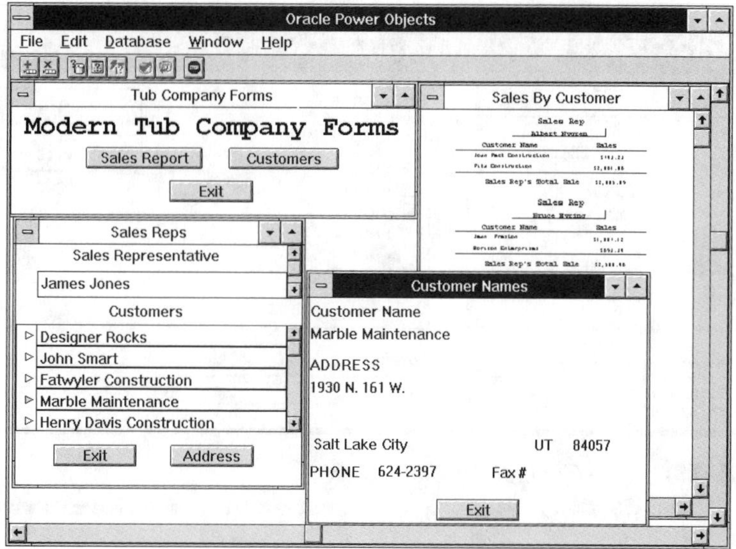

FIGURE 6-22. *A sales report, list of customers, and a customer's address are all displayed*

icon) in the Main application window. Next, you click on the Compile Application button in the toolbar. Oracle Power Objects displays a dialog box, shown in the following illustration, where you select the type of program to be compiled.

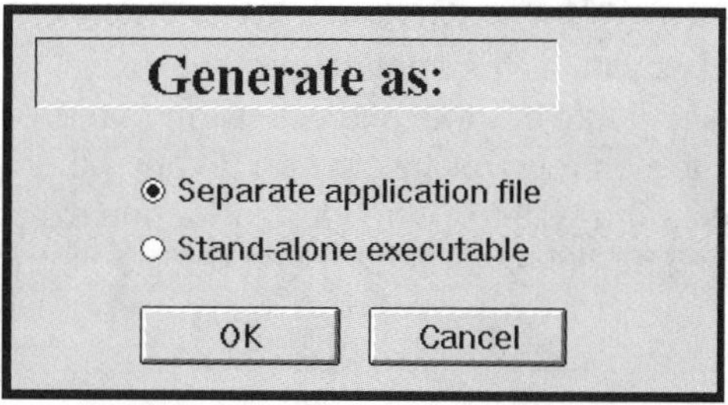

In this example, the TUBAPP program is to be compiled into a run-time module. After you select the type of program to be compiled, Oracle Power Objects opens the Generate as dialog box where you name the compiled application and select the directory in which it is to be saved. Figure 6-23 shows this dialog box with the name of the module to be tubapp.po located in the c:\orawin\opodir1.

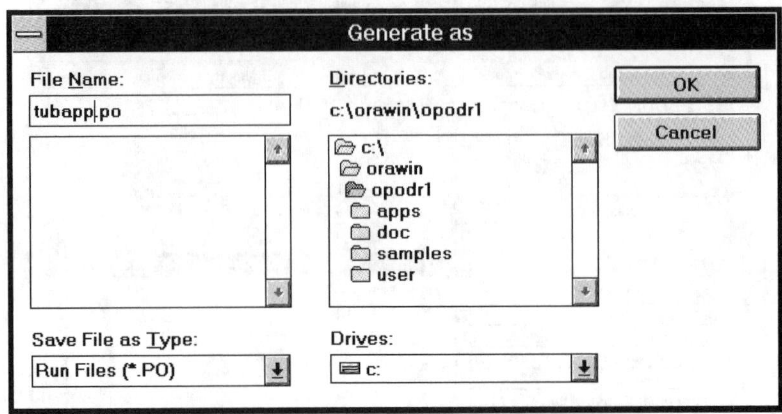

FIGURE 6-23. *The Generate as dialog box*

Once the application is compiled, it can be run from the Oracle Power Objects run-time program. To do this, start the run-time program in Windows by clicking on its icon in the Oracle Power Objects group window. Figure 6-24 shows the run-time window open and a selection window with the newly compiled TUBAPP application as one of the modules that can be selected to run.

By selecting tubapp.po, the application will be opened and run, just as was described above and shown in Figure 6-22. When you click on Exit in the last form displayed in Oracle Power Objects' window, Oracle Power Objects' run-time window will be closed as well as the application.

The stand-alone executable has the .exe extension in the Windows environment. You run these programs just as you do any other executable program in your computer's operating system. When a stand-alone executable runs, it looks just like a run-time module after it has been selected from the run-time selection window.

Libraries

Libraries are used to store classes and bitmaps that you wish to reuse in different applications without having to duplicate them.

You create libraries much as you do applications. Click on the New Library button or select the New Library option from the File menu. This will open a Create as dialog box (which is very similar to the Generate as dialog box shown in Figure

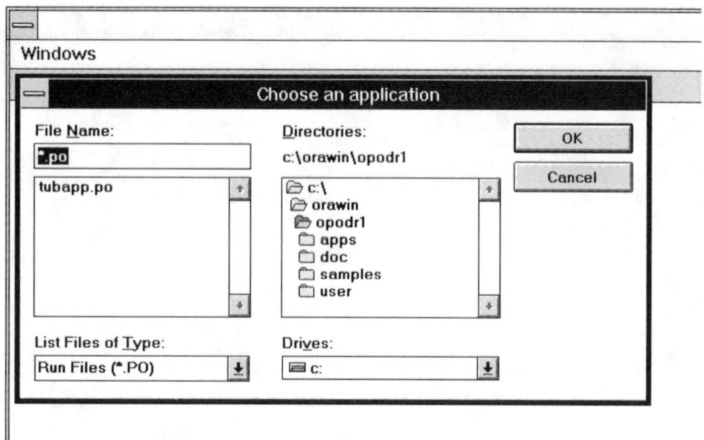

FIGURE 6-24. *The Oracle Power Objects run-time program with the selection window open*

6-23) in which you enter the name of the library and select the directory in which it is to reside.

After clicking on the OK button, Oracle Power Objects will create an empty library form and place its icon and name in the Main application window. Figure 6-25 shows an empty library window with its property sheet.

Once the library form is open, you add classes and bitmaps to it just as you do a regular application. These objects should be those that can be used in various applications, otherwise, it is a waste of resources to place a once-used class or bitmap in a library rather in the application that requires it. The ExitBtnClass and AddressClass are examples of objects that can be reused in other applications and are good candidates to be placed in a library. You should also place commonly used bitmaps, such as the bitmap of the company logo, in a library so that you can add it easily to the different applications used by the company. To add a class or bitmap to a form from the library, simply drag and drop the selected bitmap or class onto the open form. A class or bitmap added to a form in this way will act just as if it were created in the application to which the form belongs. For a bitmap, you can simply type in the bitmap name, prefixed to the library name, in the Bitmap property of an object that uses bitmaps, for example, mylib.complogo.

When you open a form that contains library objects, the library must be present in the Main window or you will get an error dialog box stating that the object is missing. The dialog box displays the application and the libraries currently in the Main window. You can either select a library that contains a similar object or close the dialog box and retrieve the necessary library. An existing library is loaded into

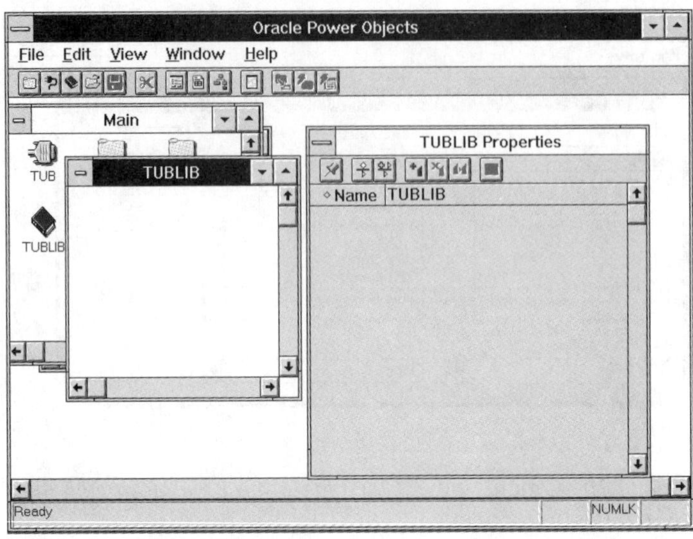

FIGURE 6-25. *Empty library with its property sheet*

the Main window by selecting Open from the File menu or the Open button on the toolbar. This will bring up the Open dialog box from which you select the library to be added to the Main window. When the necessary library is in the Main window, reopen the form and it will automatically load the object from the library. However, if you desire to select a different object, choose the library containing the object in the Select Object dialog box, shown in the following illustration, and Oracle Power Objects will list the objects contained in that library. The object you select will replace the one that was missing when the Oracle Power Objects first attempted to open the form.

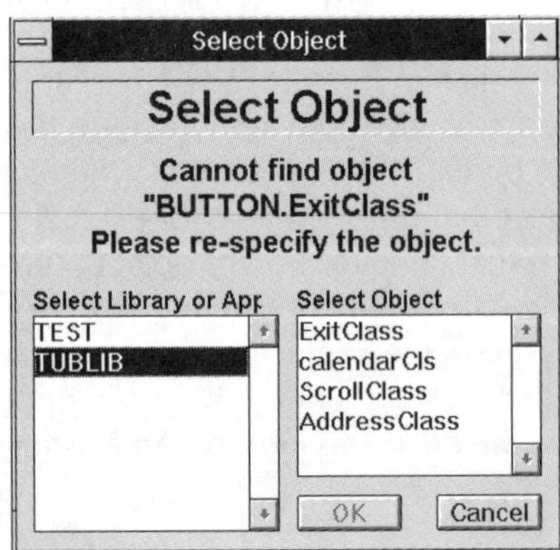

Libraries are a very powerful tool in Oracle Power Objects and should be used extensively to reduce the amount of duplicate coding in your applications.

Conclusion

This chapter introduced the use of classes, embedded forms, repeater displays, reports, and libraries. Chapter 11 describes more advanced reports and forms that include modifying the menu bar, toolbar, and status line of the application at run time. The next chapter reviews Oracle Basic code, which is used extensively in Chapters 8 and 9.

CHAPTER 7

Getting Started with Oracle Basic

In the following chapters, we will present numerous examples of using Oracle Basic, especially in conjunction with Oracle Power Object's properties and methods. In this chapter, we will introduce you to the important concepts in BASIC. Specifically, we will cover coding standards and the essential language components. You will also be introduced to using user-defined functions, decision structures, loops, and the Oracle Basic debugger.

Introduction to Oracle Basic

When personal computers were first introduced, BASIC (beginners' all-purpose symbolic instruction code) was one of the first major programming languages. BASIC was slow and awkward, and it has since been superseded by other languages, such as Pascal, C, and C++. While these programming languages are fast and provide compact code, they are difficult to learn and implement for untrained programmers. In recent years, Microsoft has used an object-oriented form of BASIC called Visual Basic for Applications (VBA). Most of Microsoft's products share a similar form of Visual Basic, which provides an easy-to-learn and consistent way to write code for all of their applications. Oracle Power Objects uses Oracle Basic, which is very similar to Microsoft's Visual Basic. Those acquainted with Visual Basic will be able to quickly learn and use Oracle Basic.

It needs to be stressed that Oracle Basic, like Visual Basic, is an object-oriented, event-driven programming language. Oracle Basic code is attached to an Oracle Power Objects object. All of these objects have specific default actions that they perform in response to an event, such as entering or leaving a field, clicking or double-clicking a button, or holding down certain keys and clicking on an object. For example, if you create a button on a form and then run the form, the button by default recognizes a mouse click and responds to the click by changing its appearance. To alter the default action of an object, you attach Oracle Basic code to that object. Most code consists of small pieces of code attached to the properties and methods of Oracle Power Objects' objects. An event, such as clicking a button, activates these small pieces of code, called *event procedures,* and causes Oracle Power Objects to perform an action.

However, one of the main differences between Oracle Basic and Visual Basic is that Oracle Basic can only be attached to the properties and methods of objects. Visual Basic can be exported into a single file and treated much more like a traditional programming language.

Statements in Oracle Basic

A *statement* is a single line of instructions, constants, or variables that the Oracle Power Objects compiler understands. There are three different types of statements in Oracle Basic: remarks, assignments, and commands. A *remark,* or comment, is a statement that explains the following coding or the statement to the left of the remark. An *assignment* consists of assigning a value to a variable or object property. A *command* is simply any syntactically valid use of any of the Oracle Basic commands or functions. A statement is normally placed on one line; however, you can use special characters to break long statements into multiple lines or place multiple statements on one line for easier reading.

Breaking Long Statements

You can break a statement with an ampersand (&) when a statement becomes so long that the entire line cannot be viewed in the property sheet or when breaking it will make it more readable. Consider the following statement:

```
EXEC sql SELECT upper(user) &
    INTO :username &
FROM dual
```

In this example, the EXEC sql statement is broken into three lines to increase its readability. If the ampersand isn't the last character of the line (including spaces), it is assumed to be an operator in the statement. Therefore, you cannot place comments to the right of a line break. You cannot use an ampersand in a literal text string to break a long line, as the ampersand is seen as a part of the text string. Also, when you use an ampersand to concatenate (join together) two separate text strings into a single text string, you must break the line at the ampersand. The statement is broken with two ampersands (&&), the first ampersand to concatenate the text and the second to break the line.

Placing Multiple Statements on One Line

To place multiple lines of Oracle Basic code on a single line, you separate the statements with a colon (:). The statements are executed from left to right, just as if they were on successive lines. For example, the following mulitple statements

```
IF ans = 6 THEN
    Inherited.PostChange()
ELSE
    self.value = NULL
END IF
```

could be put on a single line, as shown here:

```
IF ans = 6 THEN : Inherited.PostChange() : ELSE : self.value = NULL : END IF
```

Remark (REM) Statements

Remarks (REM), also known as comments, are added to programs to explain the purpose of the code. Remarks can be preceded by either REM or a single quotation mark ('). Remarks are useful to developers to remind them of what they are trying to accomplish with a piece of code, and more importantly, they provide great assistance to other developers attempting to modify the code without the original developer's help. The compiler ignores everything to the right of a quotation mark or REM.

There are a few general rules that you should follow when commenting code:

- Place comments at the beginning of the code with a description of what the method code will accomplish.
- Comment all variables to explain their purpose.
- Place "header" comments before all logical sections of code. You should also place a blank line before all section header comments.
- If a comment is extremely long, place it just prior to the statement it is explaining, unless the statement is preceded by a session comment header.
- Capitalize the first letter of a comment.
- All method names should be followed by parentheses, e.g., HasBorder( ).

The following code is based on the Validate( ) method of the Company pop-up list control on the frmOrders form in the MLDONE application. The code has been modified to follow proper commenting rules.

```
REM This code in the Validate() method drives the values located
REM in address1, address2, city, state, zip, and country_id fields
DIM vNewValue AS Long
REM Sets the variable's value to the control's value
vNewValue = newVal

REM Performs a SQL query of the following columns based
REM on the value of the vNewValue variable
EXEC SQL AT mldata SELECT address1, address2, city, state, zip, country_id &
    INTO :vAddr1, :vAddr2, :vCity, :vState, :vZip, :vCountry FROM customers &
WHERE id = :vNewValue
address1.Value = vAddr1
address2.Value = vAddr2
city.Value = vCity
state.Value = vState
zip.Value = vZip
country.Value = vCountry
Validate = TRUE
```

Assignment Statements

An assignment statement assigns a value to a variable or to a property of an object. An assignment statement has two parts separated by an equal sign (=). On the right side of the equal sign is a value or expression that creates a value. On the left side of the equal sign is the variable or property to which the value is being assigned.

```
variableName = value
```

Assigning Literals to a Variable

A *literal* is a fixed numeric, text, or date value. The following sections explain how to assign the different types of literals to variables.

Numeric Literals

Numeric literals can include any integer, floating point number, or scientific notation values. If you do not specify the literal's datatype, the appropriate datatype of the numeric literal is assigned by Oracle Basic. Therefore, a small whole number between -32,768 and 32,767 will be assigned an integer datatype, a number larger than 32,767 or less than -32,768 will be assigned as a long, etc. The following examples assign a literal numeric value to a variable.

```
x = 1
vinterest = 8.75            'assigns the value of 8.75 to a variable
```

Text Literals

A text literal is a string of text that can include any variety of characters, including the tab character. You identify a value as a text literal by surrounding the text string with double quotes. To assign a string of text to the value of a text control, place .value = at the end of the control name.

```
MyHelpText.value = "Enter the company's name to receive the shipment."
fldSalesman.value = "John Dow"
```

If you need to include double quotes in the text string, you have to separate the text string into multiple parts, concatenate the strings together, and use the CHR (character) function to generate the double quote character.

```
vError = "Error 23" & CHR(34) & "Only dates can be entered here." & CHR(34)
```

Date and Time Literals

Just as text strings must be surrounded with double quotes, date and time literals have to be surrounded by the pound symbol (#). The following example shows how you can assign a date or time value:

```
vBeginDate = #1/31/95#
```

Assigning Values to Properties

You can set the value of an object's property. The first example assigns the color of the ColorText( ) property of the fldSalesName field, while the second changes the label of a button.

```
fldSalesName.ColorText = 3

btnOpen.Label = Cancel      'assigns the text on the button to Cancel
```

Assigning Function Values to a Variable

You can also assign a function's value to a variable. In the following examples, the first statement assigns the current date to a variable named CurDate and the second statement assigns the recordset of the custamounts table to the recobj variable.

```
vCurDate = now()            'assigns the current date to a variable

recobj = custamounts.getrecordset()
```

Capitalization Standards for Oracle Basic Code

Earlier in this chapter, we explained the rules for writing effective comments in Oracle Basic code. Following capitalization rules also adds consistency to your code, making the code easier to understand and read. The following capitalization rules come from the Oracle Power Objects Coding Standards.

- All Oracle Basic commands and functions are written in all caps. For example: DIM, OPEN, INPUTBOX.
- Constants are also written in all caps. For example: CONST, FALSE, NULL.
- All Oracle Basic standard properties and methods follow the capitalization displayed in the property sheet, or if one does not appear on the property

sheet, it follows the capitalization used in the Oracle Power Objects online help. For example: DataSize, OpenWindow( ), Bitmap.

- All datatypes use initial caps. For example: String, Long, Double, Object.

Constants

A *symbolic constant* is a placeholder for set values. They are called constants because their value cannot be modified by Oracle Basic code. You set the value of a constant when you declare it. To declare a constant, you precede the constant with a CONST statement and type the constant name in uppercase. For example:

```
CONST OVERTHIRTY = 30
```

To specify the datatype of a constant, you have to place the datatype suffix at the end of the constant's name. If you do not declare the variable, Oracle Basic assigns the variable the simplest datatype possible to the constant. Thus, in the example above, the datatype would be set to Integer.

If you need to declare a constant as a *global constant* (a constant available throughout the entire application), you can place it in the Declaration section of the application or place the **global** keyword before the constant.

Predefined Oracle Basic Constants

There are many predefined constants in Oracle Basic. You can call these predefined constants for either Boolean operations or for declaring the value of a property. The constants for properties take the form of property_setting, where property is the name of the property and setting is the manner in which it is set. Therefore, to set the window style of a form to the standard_document option:

```
Form1.windowstyle = windowstyle_standard document
```

or you can use the integer value assigned to the property's constant name:

```
Form1.windowstyle = 0
```

Table 7-1 shows the assigned property type, followed by the constant's name and assigned value.

Property Type	Constant Name	Value
Boolean operators	FALSE	0
	TRUE	1
CounterType	countertype_none	1
	countertype_sequence	2
	countertype_table_max_counterincby	3
	countertype_user_generated	4
CounterTiming	countertiming_immediate	0
	countertiming_deferred	1
DataType	datatype_integer	0
	datatype_long_integer	0
	datatype_float	1
	datatype_double	1
	datatype_string	2
	datatype_date	3
Direction	direction_upper_left_to_lower_right	0
	direction_lower_left_to_upper_right	1
LinkMasterDel	linkmasterdel_refuse	0
	linkmasterdel_cascade	1
	linkmasterdel_orphan	2
LinkMasterUpd	linkmasterupd_refuse	0
	linkmasterupd_cascade	1
	linkmasterupd_orphan	2
PrimaryKey	primarykey_on_master	0
	primarykey_here	1
TextJustHoriz	textjusthoriz_left	0
	textjusthoriz_center	1
	textjusthoriz_right	2
TextJustVert	textjustvert_top	0
	textjustvert_center	1
	textjustvert_bottom	2

TABLE 7-1. *Oracle Basic's Constant Reserved Words and Values*

Property Type	Constant Name	Value
WindowStyle	windowstyle_standard_document	0
	windowstyle_fixed	1
	windowstyle_document_without_ maximize	2
	windowstyle_standard_dialog	3
	windowstyle_plain_dialog	4
	windowstyle_alternate_dialog	5
	windowstyle_movable_dialog	6
	windowstyle_palette	7
	windowstyle_palette_with_close_box	8

TABLE 7-1. *Oracle Basic's Constant Reserved Words and Values* (continued)

Variables

Variables are temporary placeholders for values. They are called variables, because the values they hold can vary or be modified by Oracle Basic code. When you define a variable, you need to name the variable and specify the type of data (datatype) to be stored in the variable. There are two types of variables: local and global. A local variable exists only as long as the Oracle Basic code that declares it is running. However, once a global variable is created, it is available to all parts of the application.

Variable-Naming Conventions

Variable names must begin with a letter and can be up to 39 alphanumeric characters in length. Variables cannot contain spaces or any other punctuation except the underscore (_) and cannot contain the arithmetic operators *, +, -, /, &, %, $, and @. You cannot use any reserved Oracle words or Oracle Basic keywords for variable names. (See Appendix C for a list of all reserved words.) Variables are not case-sensitive, so you only need to remember how to spell the variable. The following is an example of valid and invalid variable names:

1A_Variable	Invalid (begins with a number)
A_Variable	Valid
A.Variable	Invalid (contains a period)
A Variable	Invalid (contains a space)

When you name a variable, you should try to make its name meaningful and present it in an easy-to-read manner. The Oracle Power Objects Coding Standards suggests capitalizing the first letter of every significant part of the variable name (SignificantNames) to help ease reading variable names. Therefore, a variable used to contain the total sales for a salesperson could be given a name like vTotal_Sales, TotalSales, or Total_Sales. And to specify that the variable holding the total sales of a salesperson is of a double datatype, you could name it dbl_Total_Sales.

Declaring Variables

When declaring a variable, you should specify the datatype of a variable so that it will match the datatype of the information you are manipulating in the recordset and set the variable's value. You can either implicitly declare a variable with the value assigned to the variable, or explicitly, by declaring the datatype of the variable in a DIM, GLOBAL, STATIC, or REDIM statement and later assigning a value to the variable.

Scope and Duration of Variables

All variables have the properties of scope and duration. The *scope* of a variable determines its visibility. A variable becomes visible at the time it is declared and remains visible based upon the scope you assign to it. While a variable is visible, values can be assigned to the variable, modified, and used by expression. When the scope of the variable becomes invisible, the variable's value is reinitialized and becomes inaccessible to the application.

The second property of a variable is its duration. The *duration* of a variable is the time period in which a variable is available to the application. This time period depends upon the way in which it is declared. For instance, a local variable (declared with the DIM statement) becomes visible for the length of time that the method code in which it is declared is executed, whereas a variable declared with the GLOBAL statement is initialized at the time the application is executed, and it is available to the entire application as long as the application is executed.

Implicit Variables

You can assign a value to a variable with a simple statement like x = 1 without declaring its datatype. It is common to implicitly declare variables like this for use in loops. Any implicit variable is assigned the Variant datatype (a datatype that can contain numbers, dates, or string values and performs the appropriate conversion to the type of value stored in the variable). You can also implicitly create a variable and specify its datatype with a type suffix (a symbol attached to the end of the variable that specifies its datatype).

The following are the Oracle Basic type suffixes:

Datatype	Suffix	Example
Double	#	vTotal_Sales#
Integer	%	vInv_No%
Long integer	&	vProd_Id&
Single	!	vInterest!
String	$	vErr_Text$

Therefore, you could implicitly set the value and datatype of a variable to hold an interest rate as a single with the following statement:

```
vInterest! = 8.75    Implicitly declares vinterest as a single datatype
```

Declaring Local Variables with DIM

To declare a local variable, you use the DIM statement. Variables declared with the DIM statement become undefined as soon as the method (subroutine or function) in which it is declared finishes its execution. The statement declares the variable, its type, and, if you are declaring an array, its dimensions. The syntax of the DIM statement is DIM VariableName AS DataType. You can either use the AS clause or use a type suffix to explicitly declare a variable, but you cannot use both! Once you have declared the variable, you then need to assign the variable a value. For example:

```
DIM vInterest AS Single    ' DIM vInterest! could also be used here
vInterest = 8.75
```

If you fail to set the datatype of the variable, in either a DIM statement or by using a suffix character, Oracle Basic will automatically set the type to Variant.

Declaring Variables with GLOBAL

A global variable is a variable that can be modified by a method (subroutine or function) called by any of the application's objects (forms, controls, buttons, etc.). If you want to make a variable visible to any method in an application, you have to declare it with the GLOBAL statement in the Declarations property of the form or application. The syntax of the GLOBAL statement is GLOBAL VariableName AS DataType. For example:

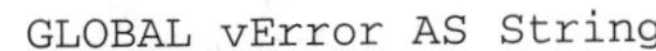

```
GLOBAL vError AS String
```

Declaring Variables with STATIC

A STATIC variable is a local variable that stores its value and remains visible during the entire duration of the application's execution (unlike a variable declared with a DIM statement, which becomes undefined when the method finishes its execution). The scope of a STATIC variable is based upon where it is declared. If you want the value of a STATIC statement available to all methods and functions of the application, you need to place the statement in the Declaration section of the Application.

A STATIC variable is held in the computer's memory during the entire time the application is executed, therefore, you should avoid using too many STATIC variables. Also, you must use the STATIC statement to declare a fixed-size array (arrays are discussed in the "Arrays" section later in the chapter).

Using the REDIM Statement

The REDIM statement declares either a local variable or an array and specifies the array's size. You can also declare dynamic arrays with the REDIM statement and specify the size of the array with up to eight subscripts (using subscripts in arrays will be discussed in the "Arrays" section later in the chapter). Once you create a dynamic array, with either DIM or REDIM statements, you can use other REDIM statements to redimension the array and declare the number of dimensions in the array and the size for each dimension.

Values and Datatypes

When defining an Oracle Basic variable, you specify its datatype to match the datatype of the information you are manipulating in the recordset. You can use the VARTYPE function to determine the datatype of any variable. The VARTYPE function returns a long integer value that identifies the variable's datatype. Table 7-2 lists the nine variable types with their VARTYPE value and a description of the data they can hold.

If you do not declare the type of a variable, Oracle Basic does a best guess at its datatype and assigns a type for the variable. This is much slower than manually declaring the variable, as Oracle Basic has to perform conversions every time the variable is used.

Arrays

An *array variable* is a variable that can contain multiple values, which are called *elements* of the array. You specify the number of elements that can be stored in the array (or the *size* of the array) with a subscript. The subscript value is placed in parentheses. To declare a simple array, you can use the DIM vVarName (subscript)

Datatype	VARTYPE Value	Description
Null	1	Null represents a variable without any value.
Integer	3	An integer is a positive or negative number without decimal places. An integer variable contains 16-bit signed integer values between -32,768 and 32,767.
Long Integer	3	A value that holds 32-bit signed integers between -2,147,483,648 and 2,147,483,647.
Single	5	Single variables hold 4-byte single precision floating-point numbers between $\pm 1.401298E^{-45}$ to $3.402823E^{30}$ and zero.
Double	5	An 8-byte double-precision floating-point value between $\pm 4.94066^{-308}$ to $1.79763134862315E^{308}$ and zero.
Date	7	A value storing date and time information between Jan. 1, 100 A.D. to Dec 31, 9999 A.D.
String	8	A value storing a string of text from 1 to 32,767 characters.
Object	9	A reference to an object, such as a control or container.
Variant		A variant variable can store any variable type value and therefore has no VARTYPE value associated with it.

TABLE 7-2. *Oracle Basic Datatype's Vartype Values*

AS datatype statement. For example, to create an array that will contain the names of the six tubs sold by a tub manufacturer:

```
DIM vTubNames (5) AS String     'this reserves 6 elements
```

Notice that you place "5" in the subscript to hold six elements in the array. This is because the array holds values from 0 to 5 (which holds six elements). You can also declare a *range* of values (such as 0 to 5) for an array in a subscript. You would write the preceding example as:

```
DIM vTubNames (0 to 5) AS String 'this also reserves 6 elements
```

If you needed to store in an array some information for a range of invoice numbers between 11234 to 12345, you could specify the range of the array, for example:

```
DIM vInvoices (11234 to 12345) AS Long
```

You can also declare a dimension to an array. The *dimension* is the number of different values that will be associated with an element of the array. For example, to store data in an array from both the tub's name and price columns, you have to declare a multidimensional array. When you declare the array, you separate the dimensions of the array with commas, as shown in the following example:

```
DIM vTubNames (5, 5) AS String '6 elements for name and price
```

You can create a *dynamic array* (an array whose size can be changed) with either the DIM or REDIM statements, but you can only declare a *static array* (an array whose size cannot be changed and has a duration the length of the application's execution) with a STATIC statement.

Dynamic arrays are extremely useful when you are unsure of how many elements will have to be placed in the array. Once an array has been declared by either a DIM or REDIM statement, you can enlarge (but you can't reduce) the array with a REDIM statement. In the following example, we will create an array with only one element, find the number of elements in the recordset, and redimension the array to be large enough to hold all of the records in the recordset.

```
DIM NumRows AS Long
DIM vTubs() AS String
NumRows = GetContainer.GetRowCount()
REDIM vTubs (NumRows)
```

Note that the above example is actually one element larger than it needs to be, because the array begins with zero.

Referring to Objects or Containers

Every object in Oracle Power Objects has a name by which you refer to it and properties that can contain a value. When you add Oracle Basic code to a method, you can refer to or set an objects' value. To refer to the value of an object, you have to specify the form or container in which it is contained. In its simplest form, a value contained in a field on a form is referenced by form1.field1.value. The value of a field, Grand_Total, contained in an embedded form, Invoice_Total, on a form, Invoice, is referenced as Invoice.Invoice_Total.Total.

You can also set a property of an object in the same manner. For example, if you have a button that opens another form, you could set the name of a button Open to Close when opening the form. Clicking on the same button, now named Close, could then close the same form. You would refer to the button object as Form.Open_Button.name.

Operators in Oracle Basic

Operators are words or symbols used in expressions that perform an operation on one or two values to achieve a new value. There are six different types of operators: math, string, comparison, logical, date, and object. Each will be discussed in more detail in subsequent sections in this chapter.

Operator Precedence

When you create a complicated expression, it is critical for you to understand the order in which Oracle Basic evaluates the operators. For instance, 8+2*12 either returns 120 or 32 depending on how Oracle Basic analyzes the expression. Each category of operators is given in their order of precedence. Therefore, 8+2*12 results in 32, because the multiplication symbol has a higher precedence than addition.

You can alter the order of precedence by placing parentheses around those operations that need to be evaluated first. By rewriting the above expression, (8+2)*12 results in 120, because Oracle Basic first adds the 8 to the 2 and then multiplies it by 12.

Note that several operators have equal precedence, such as the + and - operators and the * and / operators. Oracle Basic evaluates equal operations from left to right. Here is a more complicated example:

```
8*2+12/2-2*2+2^2
```

In this example, Oracle Basic first analyzes the exponent at the end of the operation:

```
8*2+12/2-2*2+4
```

Next, Oracle Basic performs the multiplication and division operations from left to right:

```
16+6-4+4
```

Finally, it performs the addition and subtraction from left to right:

22

Math Operators

A math operator is a symbol placed between two numeric operands, and it returns a numeric value. The following table lists all of the math operators, their names, examples, and results of the examples.

Operator	Name	Example	Result	Description
^	Exponentiation	2^4	16	
–	Negation	–(3+8)	–11	
*, /	Multiplication, division	12/3*2	8	
\	Integer division	13.5667\4	3	Returns an integer and disregards the remainder
Mod	Modulo arithmetic	13 mod 4	1	Returns the remainder as an integer
+,–	Addition, subtraction	7–3+25	29	

String Operators

String operators are used to concatenate text strings. The ampersand (&) operator translates the datatype of both operands to a string and returns the result as a string. The plus (+) operator doesn't translate the datatype of the operands, so attempting to concatenate a string to any other datatype will produce unexpected results. The following table shows several examples of using the ampersand and plus string operators.

Operator	Name	Examples
&	ampersand	"John" & " " & "Smith" = "John Smith" "John" + " " +"Smith" + 1 = "John Smith1" vNewFile = vAppName & ".txt"
+	plus	"John" + " " +"Smith" = "John Smith" "John" + " " +"Smith" + 1 = error

Comparison Operators

Comparison operators evaluate two values and return the result as a Boolean value with a long integer datatype. A returned value of -1 or any nonzero number is TRUE, and a returned value of zero is FALSE. Note that you never use comparison operators with object datatypes. The following table lists all comparison operators, the datatypes they can be used with, examples of the operator, and the result of the example.

Operator	Description	Datatype	Example	Result
=	Equal to	All	(2*5 = 21/2)	FALSE
< >	Not equal to	All	(2*5 < > 21/2)	TRUE
<	Less than	Dates, strings, numerics	12/1/94 < 2/5/95	TRUE
>	Greater than	Dates, strings, numerics	"s" > "cb"	TRUE
<=	Less than or equal to	Dates, strings, numerics	59/3 <= 35	FALSE
>=	Greater than or equal to	Dates, strings, numerics	200/2>=100	TRUE

Logical Operators

Logical operators evaluate numeric operands and return the result as a Boolean value with a long integer datatype. NOT returns the opposite of what the expression returns. The NOT expression therefore returns TRUE when the expression is false. AND returns TRUE if both conditions are true, and the OR operator returns TRUE if either condition is true. The XOR is an exclusive where one or the other of the components of the expression can be true, but not both. XOR returns FALSE if they both return FALSE or both return TRUE. EQV checks to see if both of the expressions return equivalent results. IMP returns FALSE only if the first is true and the second expression is false. A returned value of -1 or any nonzero number is TRUE and a returned value of zero is FALSE. The following table lists each of the logical operators, their functions, examples, and the results of the examples.

Operator	Name	Example	Result
NOT	Logical negation, is the opposite	NOT(1=2)	= TRUE (-1, nonzero)
AND	Logical conjunction	(2=18/9) AND (1=2)	= FALSE
OR	Logical disjunction	(2=18/9) OR (1=2)	= TRUE (-1, nonzero)
XOR	Exclusive disjunction	(2=18/9) XOR (7=7)	= FALSE
EQV	Logical equivalence	(6<2) EQV (2<3)	= FALSE
IMP	Logical implication	(6<2) IMP (2<3)	= TRUE(-1, nonzero)

Date Operators

Date operators allow you to subtract dates to find out the number of days between two dates or to add or subtract a number of days from a date to return a different date. If the dates contain a time component, the results of the expression will take in consideration the time component. For example, 9/13/95 7:00 AM - 9/13/95 7:00 PM yields 0.5 (12 hours, or half a day).

Operator	Description	Example	Result
date-date	Subtracts two dates and returns the number of days	9/11/95 7:00 PM - 9/3/95 1:00 PM	8.25
date - number	Subtracts a number of days from a date	9/30/95 - 20	9/10/95
date + number	Adds a number of days to a date	9/11/95 + 15	9/26/95

Object Operators

The object operator NEW allows the dynamic creation of objects (i.e. recordset, menu bar, menu, toolbar, or status line) at run time. Objects that you create with NEW act the same as objects (like buttons or text fields) that are created statically. An object created with NEW has no Name property associated with it and must therefore be referred to by a variable name.

To create an object with NEW, you first declare the object as an object variable and then assign the object type to the variable:

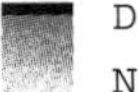

```
Dim NewObject as Object
NewObject = new [Object] 'Object is replaced by RecordSet, MenuBar, etc.
```

The following table shows how to assign the different objects:

Object	Description
new DbRecordSet(session)	Creates a database recordset for the specified session
new RecordSet	Creates a local database recordset that holds values and is unrelated to a database session
new MenuBar	Creates a menu bar
new Toolbar	Creates a toolbar
new StatusLine	Creates a status line

Once an object is created with the NEW operator, you need to remember to delete the object when it is no longer needed. Failure to delete the object will keep active menus, status lines, or other objects in memory and visible long after they are applicable. To delete an object, type the following:

```
delete [object] 'Object is replaced by the Object's variable name
```

To delete multiple objects at the same time, you list the objects and separate them with commas.

The syntax for creating both bound and unbound recordsets is slightly different from the syntax for creating other types of in-memory objects, such as MenuBars or StatusLines. The syntax for creating a bound recordset is

```
Dim vRecSet AS Object
vRecSet = NEW DBRecordSet(session, deferred, optimistic, inMemory, maxMem)
```

The following parameters are available

- **Session** This parameter specifies the session object to which the recordset will be attached.
- **Deferred** (optional) The deferred parameter sets whether changes made to the recordset are committed when the recordset is committed (TRUE) or when the current row changes (FALSE). The default value is FALSE.
- **Optimistic** (optional) This specifies that the row locking is optimistic (TRUE), which is best for a single-user database. Setting this value to FALSE (the default) sets it to pessimistic. Setting it to pessimistic prevents one user from overwriting another user's changes when the recordset is committed.
- **InMemory** (optional) Setting this parameter to TRUE specifies that the recordset will be held in memory and will not be swapped to disk. Setting

InMemory to FALSE allows the recordset to be swapped to disk when the recordset exceeds the maximum cache size.

- **MaxMemory** (optional) MaxMemory specifies the maximum cache size in kilobytes that is available for holding the recordset. Once the recordset exceeds the MaxMemory parameter, the recordset is swapped to disk and the InMemory parameter is set to FALSE. The default value is 4K.

The syntax for creating an unbound recordset is

```
Dim vRecSet AS Object
vRecSet = NEW RecordSet(inMemory, maxMem)
```

The following parameters are available

- **InMemory** (optional) Setting this parameter to TRUE specifies that the recordset will be held in memory and not swapped to disk. Setting InMemory to FALSE allows the recordset to be swapped to disk when the recordset exceeds the maximum cache size.
- **MaxMemory** (optional) MaxMemory specifies the maximum cache size in kilobytes that is available for holding the recordset. Once the recordset exceeds the MaxMemory parameter, the recordset is swapped to disk and the InMemory parameter is set to FALSE. The default value is 4K.

Functions

A *function* performs a calculation that returns a result. Oracle Basic contains many predefined functions, and you can also create your own functions. Functions can be used to parse text files, check user input, check which keys on the keyboard are being pressed by the user, perform financial functions, convert datatypes, perform aggregate calculations, etc. Some examples of Oracle Basic predefined functions are NOW (the present time and date), AVG (the mean average of the selected values), and PMT (the payment in a financial expression).

You can also add user-defined functions to a form, class, or report. In the MoonLight Demo-DONE application, there is a CalculateTax function that is declared in the User Properties window. The CalculateTax function is then called in the Click( ) method of the bthCalculateTax button of the frmProducts form. For a detailed explanation of using user-defined functions, see "User-Defined Properties" in Chapter 8.

Commands

An Oracle Basic *command* is a keyword that performs an operation (but, unlike a function, does not return a value). You are already acquainted with many Oracle Basic commands, such as REM for commenting code. You call a command by placing the command at the beginning of the line and passing arguments to the command (often inside parentheses). The following section covers how to use commands for conditional statements and for repetitive operations.

Conditional Statements

Conditional statements test to find out if a condition is TRUE or FALSE. Conditional statements all begin with the IF command and use the comparison operators to compare data. Based upon the result of the condition (TRUE or FALSE), the Oracle Basic code moves to a different line of code.

The IF...THEN...END IF Structure

A conditional statement can involve just a simple TRUE or FALSE condition. If the condition is TRUE, then Oracle Basic performs the action(s) specified before the END IF statement; otherwise, it skips to any code below the END IF. For example:

```
IF vUserText = "Hello" THEN
   MsgBox "How are you doing today"
END IF
```

The IF...THEN...ELSE Structure

The IF...THEN...ELSE conditional statement can be placed on one line, which states "*If* the condition is true *then* do this, *else* do something different," and it doesn't require an END IF statement. A simple example of this type of statement could be created to pay an employee a bonus based on the individual total sales:

```
IF vTotalSales > 20000 THEN vCommission = 1000 ELSE vCommission = 0
```

You can use multiple operators with conditional statements. For example, a bonus could be based on both the total number of sales and on the total sales amount:

```
IF vTotalSales > 20000 AND vNumSales > 12 THEN vCommision = 1000 ELSE Commission = 0
```

The IF...THEN...ELSE...END IF Structure

You can create conditional statements that involve multiple decisions that need to be analyzed. In the following example, the condition is used to set the text color property of employees' name in the SalesPName text control to a color depending on the department in which they work.

```
IF  deptid.value < 20 THEN
  SalesPName.ColorText = 3
ELSE IF deptid.value >= 20 and deptid.value < 30 THEN
  SalesPName.ColorText = 5
ELSE
  SalesPName.ColorText = 8
END IF
```

The SELECT CASE...END SELECT Structure

If there are many alternatives that need to be analyzed, it is better to use the SELECT CASE structure than using a series of IF...THEN...ELSE IF statements. SELECT CASE works faster because it goes directly from the condition statement to its corresponding statements, whereas the IF...THEN...ELSE IF structure has to evaluate each condition until the condition is TRUE. Also, long, nested IF statements can be confusing to read and maintain. The following is the syntax of the SELECT CASE structure.

```
SELECT CASE selector
   CASE case_expr_list
   [ statements ]
   [ CASE case_expr_list
   [ statements ] ]
   [ CASE ELSE ]
END SELECT
```

In the following example, the condition vDeptId determines the department in which the employee works. The SELECT CASE then sets the text color property of the employee's name in the NAME text field control to a different color depending on the employee's department.

```
SELECT CASE vDeptId
   CASE 10
        Name.ColorText = 3 'accounting department employee
   CASE 20
        Name.ColorText = 5 'research department employee
   CASE 30
        Name.ColorText = 8  'sales department employee
```

```
   CASE 40
        NAME.ColorText = 10 'operations department employee
END SELECT
```

Repetitive Operations (Looping with FOR and DO)

Looping repeats an operation until a specified condition is met, and then the loop is exited. For example, you may want to perform an operation on every row in a table or perform an operation to every element in an array; when all of the specified conditions are met, Oracle Basic exits the loop and continues with the remainder of the code.

The FOR...NEXT Statement

The FOR...NEXT statement repeats an operation or set of operations for a specified number of times. The following is the format of the FOR...NEXT statement:

```
FOR Counter = StartNumber to EndNumber [Increment]
    Statements to be executed
    [Optional Exit For to exit the loop]
Next [Counter]
```

You can specify the starting number and ending number of the loop and optionally declare the value it will be incremented by. If you don't specify the amount it is incremented by, it will always be incremented by one.

In the following example, we create an array, vTubNames, and redimension the size of the array to the number of rows in the recordset. The FOR loop selects the row "x" in the recordset and the array element according to the loop variable x. Then each element of the array is assigned to the value stored in the TName column.

```
DIM NumRows AS Long
DIM vTubNames() AS String
DIM TubObject AS Object
GetContainer.FetchAll
TubObject = GetContainer.GetRecordSet()
NumRows = TubObject.GetRowCount()
REDIM vTubNames (1 to NumRows)
For x = 1 TO NumRows
    TubObject.SetCurRow(x)
    vTubNames(x) = TubObject.GetColVal("TName")
NEXT x
```

The DO...LOOP Statement

DO...LOOP has four different ways in which it can perform loops. You can perform loops either while a condition is TRUE or until a condition has been met. The WHILE or UNTIL arguments can be placed at either the beginning or end of the loop.

The DO...WHILE...LOOP Statement The DO...WHILE loop continues to repeat the statements while a condition is TRUE. With this type of a loop, you can either place the WHILE condition at the top or the end of the loop. Placing the WHILE at the bottom of the loop will cause the body of the loop to be performed at least one time, because the specified actions are performed prior to testing a condition. When the WHILE condition is placed at the top of the loop, the body of the loop may never be performed if the condition is FALSE. Placing the WHILE condition at the bottom of the loop causes the loop to be executed one more time than if it is placed at the top of the loop.

```
DO [ WHILE condition ]
          [ statements ]
          [ EXIT DO ]
          [ statements ]
LOOP
```

The following example causes the computer to beep and repeats the BEEP command, while the variable *x* is less than or equal to 20. The variable is initialized to 1 and incremented by one every time through the loop.

```
x = 1
DO WHILE (x  < 20)
    x  =  x + 1
    BEEP
LOOP
```

The DO...UNTIL...LOOP Statement The DO...UNTIL loop continues to repeat the statements *until* a condition is TRUE. With this type of loop, you can either place the UNTIL condition at the top or the end of the loop. When the UNTIL condition is placed at the top of the loop, the body of the loop may never be performed if the condition is TRUE. Therefore, placing UNTIL at the bottom of the loop will cause the body of the loop to be performed at least one time. Placing the UNTIL condition at the bottom of the loop causes the loop to be executed one more time than if it is placed at the top of the loop.

```
DO [ UNTIL condition ]
        [ statements ]
        [ EXIT DO ]
        [ statements ]
LOOP
```

In the following example, we sequentially assign a RepNo to each customer in the Custs table (to a new column called RepId). The Oracle Basic code gets the number of sales reps and the number of customers and creates two arrays that hold their primary key values. The DO...UNTIL loop cycles for the number of customers and sequentially assigns a sales rep to the customer.

```
DIM vRepId(), vCustId(), vNumReps, vNumCusts AS Long
DIM vIndex AS Integer
EXEC SQL SELECT COUNT(*) into :vNumReps FROM Emp where deptno = 30
EXEC SQL SELECT COUNT(*) into :vNumCusts FROM Custs
REDIM vRepId (0 to vNumReps - 1)
REDIM vCustId (0 to vNumCusts - 1)
EXEC SQL SELECT EmpNo into :vRepId FROM Emp where deptno = 30
EXEC SQL SELECT Id into :vCustId FROM Custs
x = 0
DO UNTIL (x  >= vNumCusts)
   REM Sequentially sets the vIndex to the next RepId, cycles from
   REM 0 to the 1 less than the number of sales reps
   vIndex = (x mod vNumReps)
   EXEC SQL INSERT into Customers (REP_ID) VALUES (:vRepId(vIndex))&
   where Id=:vCustId(x)
 x  =  x + 1
LOOP
```

The WHILE...WEND Statement

The WHILE...WEND statement repeats an operation as long as the condition it evaluates is TRUE. When the WEND statement is encountered, the program returns to the WHILE statement and checks the WHILE condition. A FALSE result causes execution to skip to the program statement immediately after the WEND statement.

The following is the format of the WHILE...WEND statement:

```
WHILE condition is TRUE
   Statements to be executed
WEND
```

The syntax for using the WHILE...WEND loop is identical to the DO...WHILE loop, except the loop has no equivalent to the EXIT DO. It is suggested that you use the DO...WHILE loop instead of WHILE...WEND.

The following example causes the computer to beep and repeats the BEEP command, while the variable *x* is less than or equal to 20. The variable is initialized to 1 and incremented by one every time through the loop.

```
x = 1
WHILE (x  < 20)
   x  =  x + 1
   BEEP
WEND
```

Using the Debugger

Because most developers make either typing or logic mistakes when creating method code, Oracle Power Objects has a debugger to assist in the testing of the application's methods. With the debugger turned on, whenever you run a form, report, or application, the Debugger palette is displayed in the upper-left corner of the window and pops up the debugger window whenever a problem arises. You can also use the debugger to examine and change object properties and Oracle Basic variables or to execute an Oracle Basic method, step through a method one line at a time, or set a breakpoint in a method.

The debugger system has three different windows: the Debugger palette for invoking the other two windows, the debugger window, which displays all of the properties and methods of the selected application, form, or report (whether you are running the application or form), and the expression window, where you can evaluate Oracle Basic expressions.

You activate the debugger by selecting the Use Debugger item on the Run menu. If you want to debug the application's startup scripts, you need to select the Debug Startup Code item on the Run menu.

The Run-Time Debugger Palette

Whenever you run an application, form, or report and the Use Debugger option is selected, the Debugger palette is available in the upper-left corner of the screen. The Debugger palette has four icons, described in the following table.

Button	Name	Action
	Resume	Resumes the program's execution. For example, you use this button after the program execution is stopped by a breakpoint in Oracle Basic code.
	Stop	Exits the Run-time mode and returns to the Designer window.
	Start Debugger	Opens the debugger window, where you can examine the application's properties and methods, step through code, and set a breakpoint or watchpoint in the code.
	Expression Window	Opens the expression window to evaluate Oracle Basic expressions.

The Debugger Window

When you open the debugger window, all of the properties and methods of all objects loaded in memory can be viewed. There are four major areas of the debugger window: the object list, the property/method list, the Debugger toolbar, and the code window (see Figure 7-1).

The Object List

When the debugger window is first activated, it lists the current application and container in the upper-left corner of the window. To view the controls or containers of the current container, you click on the small black triangles next to the container in the list. Clicking on any container in the list displays all of the objects it contains. Selecting an object from this list displays all of the properties and methods associated with the object in the upper-right corner of the window.

The Property/Method List

When you select an object in the object list, all of the object's properties (standard and user-defined) and those methods to which you have attached code appear in the upper-right corner of the debugger window. Property values are displayed next to the property in the list, but because methods can contain multiple lines of code, the method code is displayed in the code window at the bottom of the debugger window.

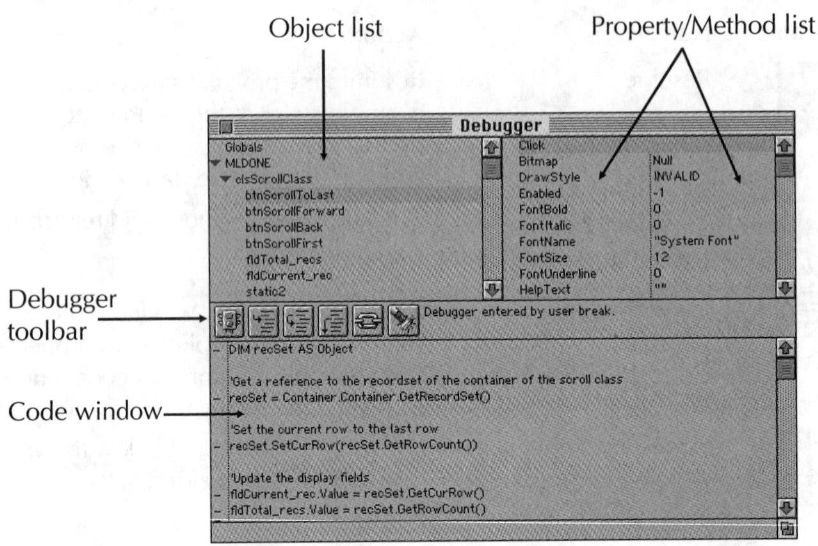

FIGURE 7-1. *The debugger window*

You can edit a property in the list by selecting the property in the list and typing in a new, valid value. Remember that many of the properties contain Boolean values and are set to either TRUE (–1) or FALSE (0).

As mentioned before, you can view the code attached to a method by selecting the method in the property/method list. Selecting the method displays the method's code in the code window at the bottom. Once a method is selected, you can edit the method code, step through the code, or set a breakpoint in the code.

The Debugger Toolbar

The Debugger toolbar is used to step through the selected Oracle Basic method code. The Debugger toolbar is described in the following table.

Button	Name	Action
	Resume	Continues the normal execution of the program.
	Step Into	Executes the current line and then moves to the next line of code.
	Step Over	Acts the same as the Step Into button, except it steps over any calls to other methods. Otherwise, the debugger would leave the current method and move into the called method.
	Step to End	Executes all of the code to the end of the method and stops at the end of the code.
	Call Chain	Pops up a window displaying the methods in the call chain. Because one method can call another method, which in turn calls another method, the Call Chain button allows you to view the method call heiarchy.
	Clear All Breakpoints	Clears all breakpoints.

Setting a Breakpoint

A *breakpoint* is the line of code at which you want the code's execution to pause. You normally use this if you have encountered an error in your code and want to pause the code at a line previous to where the error is occurring. At this point, you can analyze the status of the code and then step through the code.

To set a breakpoint:

1. Open the debugger window by selecting the Start Debugger button on the Debugger palette.
2. Select the application object.
3. Select the method for the object that you want to debug.

4. The method's code will appear in the code window of the debugger window. Click just to the left of the line of code to be set as the breakpoint. Setting a breakpoint places a red circle to the left of the breakpoint line (see Figure 7-2).
5. Press the Resume button in the Debugger palette to execute the selected code up to the breakpoint.

Stepping Through Code

At this point, you can open the Watcher window and interrogate the current values of variables in the method's code. You can then step through each line of the code with the Step Into, Step Over, and Step to End buttons on the Debugger toolbar and check values of variables or expression as needed in the Watcher window.

You can also move the execution of code to any point in the method, by dragging the highlight (a blue-green bar) from the current line to any line (below or above) that you want processed next.

The Watcher Window

You can interrogate the values assigned to a variable or property or evaluate the result of an expression in the Watcher window. The Watcher window opens

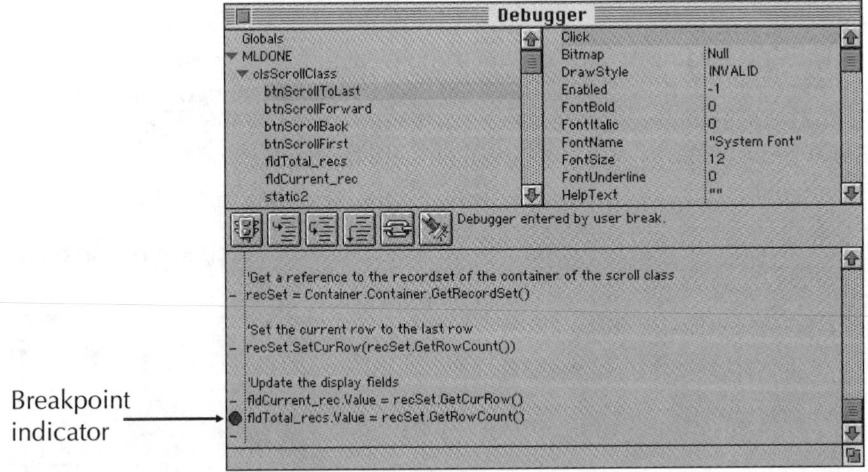

FIGURE 7-2. *A breakpoint is set in the Click( ) method of the btnScrollToLast button*

automatically when a breakpoint has been reached or it can be opened with the Debugger palette.

Interrogating Values with the Debugger

You can type in any expression, property, or variable name to interrogate the associated object's value. An expression can include any Oracle Basic operators and functions (except for the EXEC SQL command). For example, you could check to see if a button's Visible property is set to True or False. The next sections provide examples of how to check the values of the following types of objects.

Property Values To check the property of an object (button, recordset, etc.), you type the object's name followed by a period (.) and the property name in the Watcher window. To get the RowCount of a recordset in conjunction with the MLDONE sample application, for example, you would type **recSet.GetRowCount( )** and press ENTER on a PC or RETURN on the Mac. The result of the expression appears in the result area to the right of the expression (see Figure 7-3).

Variable Values To interrogate the value of a defined variable, you type the variable's name and press RETURN. For example, to check the value stored in the variable vInterest that contains the current interest rate, type **vInterest** and press

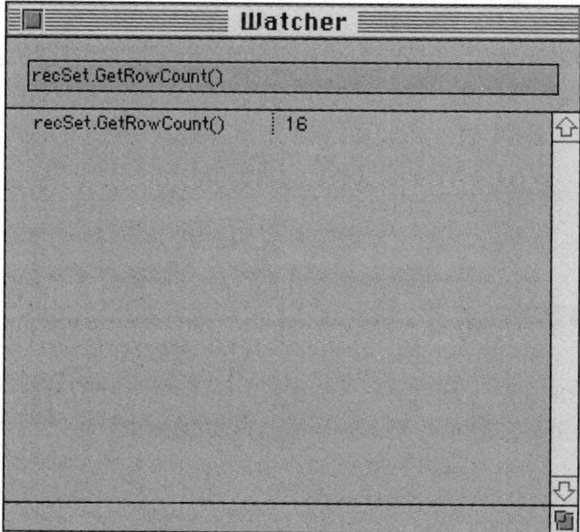

FIGURE 7-3. *The number of rows in the recordset are shown to the right of the property*

ENTER on a PC or RETURN on the Mac. The current interest rate is then displayed to the right.

Control Values To query the value stored in a control (text field, pop-up list, etc.), type the control's name and press RETURN. For example, to check the value stored in the text control field fldLastName, type **fldLastName.value** and press ENTER on a PC or RETURN on the Mac. The result of the expression appears in the result area to the right of the expression.

Setting a Watchpoint

A *watchpoint* is a variable or expression whose value is updated and displayed every time a breakpoint or a watchpoint is encountered and the program's execution is paused. To set a watchpoint:

1. Open both the debugger window and the Watcher window.
2. Select an object and then the desired method in the debugger window.
3. Click in the expression field in the Watcher window, and enter the expression(s) to be interrogated when the watchpoint or breakpoint is encountered.
4. Press the ENTER key on the PC or RETURN on the Mac.
5. Click to the left of the expression in the Watcher window. A yellow triangle appears to the left of the expression, as shown in Figure 7-4, indicating that the expression is a watchpoint. The current value of the watchpoint(s) will be displayed at every breakpoint.

As the value assigned to the property or variable changes, the Watcher window continues to display the new values.

Conclusion

This chapter provided you with a basic overview of how to use Oracle Basic. We've explained Oracle Basic statements, using constants to assign values to

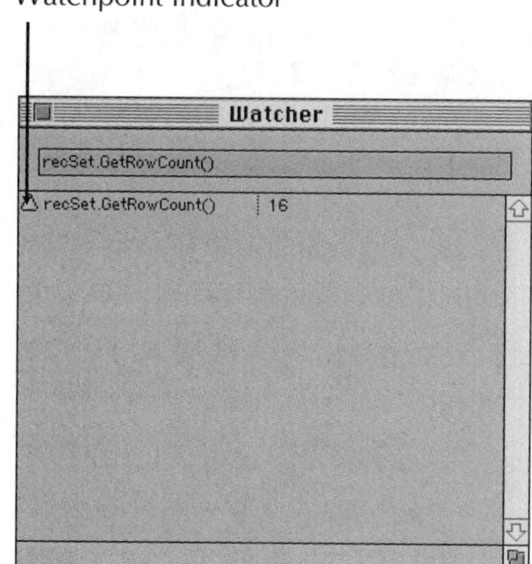

FIGURE 7-4. *The Watcher window with a set watchpoint*

variables, using operators in expressions, decision structures (what if and loops), manipulating Oracle Power Objects properties and methods, and using debugging tools. Chapters 8 and 9 will cover the various properties and methods available in Oracle Power Objects, with numerous examples of using Oracle Basic to manipulate their values. Using SQL in Oracle Basic code with EXEC SQL is covered in detail in Chapter 10.

Properties

A very important part of using Oracle Power Objects is determining the traits and attributes assigned to each object as well as the actions an object takes upon certain events. Properties, as briefly discussed in Chapter 2 and other previous chapters, are those attributes of an object that help describe and control the object when it is in Run-time mode. Methods are actions that the object takes when certain events that affect the object occur. This chapter covers all properties of the many Oracle Power Objects' objects and describes how to create and use user-defined properties that allow you to add new attributes to an object. Chapter 9 covers the methods of all Oracle Power Objects' objects.

The knowledge of Oracle Basic gained in Chapter 7 is needed to more fully understand the examples given in this chapter and in Chapter 9. There are comments in the examples to explain what the code is doing. Appendix B is a reference for Oracle Basic if you need additional information to further understand some of the examples. In addition, you should know the fundamentals of SQL, such as using the select statement. The basics of SQL are described in Chapter 10.

Property Sheet

Each object in the Oracle Power Objects' environment has properties and methods assigned to it, and they are displayed in the object's property sheet. A property sheet for an application is shown here:

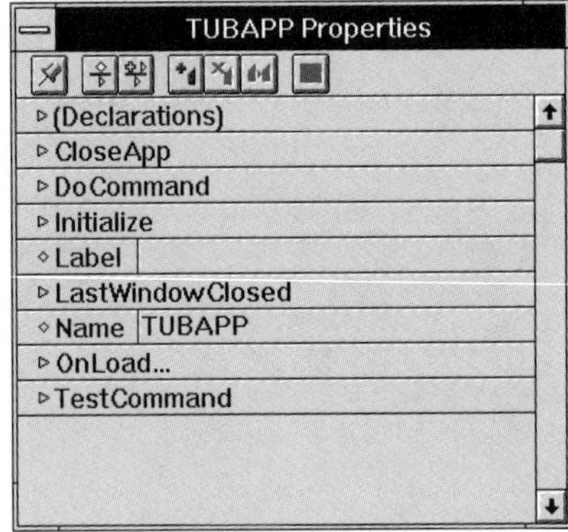

The properties are indictated by a small diamond to the left of the property name, and methods are indicated by a small arrowhead pointing to the method name. A property that has not been set has a blank gray field to the right of the name; otherwise, the value for the property is displayed in the property entry field. To change a property's value, click in the entry area and type in the required data, or click on the property name and select from the pop-up list of choices for that property. As we mentioned in Chapter 5, you can select several objects at the same time to display their common properties and change them all at the same time.

By now you may have noticed that as you build different entities with Oracle Power Objects, the property sheet changes when you focus on a different object (by clicking on it or by creating a new instance of an object). However, there may be times when you want to view the property sheet of two or more objects at the same time. When you need the property sheet for a given object to remain on the screen, you can press the Push Pin button on the property sheet toolbar. Now, as you select different objects, the property sheet that was "pinned" will not change. To view the properties of a different object while a property sheet is pinned, select the object of interest from the opened form, report, or user-defined class, and press the Open Property Sheet button in the toolbar.

Alternatively, you can select Property Sheet from the View menu, and the property sheet for the currently selected object will be displayed. However, it will not display two property sheets for the same object. You can have as many property sheets displayed as you need, but they sure do clutter up the screen fast if you have more than two shown at the same time. This function of Oracle Power Objects is especially useful when you need to compare the properties of two objects or when you need to use a pinned property sheet as a template of properties for other objects you create.

You cannot copy an entire property sheet onto another. However, you can copy the object whose property sheet you want to duplicate by first selecting the object in the open container, or the entire form in the application, and then pressing the Copy button in the toolbar. Move the cursor onto the form or application on which you want the new object, and then press the Paste button. You then simply change the properties and methods as needed for the new object.

When using a property sheet as a template, you can copy the code from a method or property from one property sheet and paste it into another (or a different area in the same sheet) by using the keystroke sequence CTRL-C to copy the code and CTRL-V to paste the code in the Windows environment, and Command-C and Command-v on a Macintosh. The process is to highlight the code or property to be copied by pressing the left mouse button at the beginning of the text to be copied, dragging the cursor to the end of the desired text, and releasing the button. Press the copy key combination and then paste the copied code into another method's or property's text field by placing the cursor in the text field and pressing the paste key combination. Do not use the Cut, Copy, or Paste buttons in the toolbar or menu items to copy text, because these functions only work with selected objects.

There are many system properties and methods defined by Oracle Power Objects, some of which have been introduced in earlier chapters. In this chapter, each property is described in detail (methods are described in Chapter 9). Table 8-1 shows all of the system properties and the Oracle Power Objects' objects associated with them. This table is a handy reference if you don't remember the names of all the properties and which objects are associated with them. It can help you recall specific properties that you may dimly remember using before, or it can give you ideas on which objects to use to accomplish certain tasks by using the properties associated with that object.

Oracle Power Objects Properties

The properties that have common purposes or similar attributes are grouped together in this chapter in much the same way that Oracle Power Objects' online help has grouped them. Not only is it a logical way to introduce each set of properties, but it also maintains consistency between this book and the Oracle Power Objects help feature.

	Bitmap	Chart	Check Box	Combo Box	Current Row Control	Forms	Horizontal Scrollbar	Line	List Box	OLE Object	Oval	Pop-up List	Push Button	Radio Button	Report	Rectangle	Repeater Display	Repeater Display Panel	Report Area	Static Text	Text Field	Frame	Property Datatype	Writeable at Run Time
Naming Properties																								
Label		X				X						X	X	X	X					X		X	S	Y
Name	X	X	X	X	X	X	X	X	X	X	X	X	X	X	X	X	X	X	X	X	X	X	S	N
Control Behavior Properties																								
DefaultButton						X																	S	Y
Enabled	X	X	X	X	X	X	X	X	X		X	X	X	X	X	X	X	X	X	X	X		L	Y
HasExtraRow		X				X									X		X						L	Y
HasScrollBar						X											X				X		L	Y
IsDismissBtn													X										L	Y
MultiLine																					X		L	Y
ScrollAmtLine							X																L	Y
ScrollAmtPage							X																L	Y
ScrollMax							X																L	Y
ScrollMin							X																L	Y
ScrollObj							X																L	Y
ScrollPos							X																L	Y
TabEnabled	X	X	X	X	X	X	X	X	X	X	X	X	X	X	X	X	X	X	X	X	X	X	L	N
TabOrder	X	X	X	X	X	X	X	X	X	X	X	X	X	X	X	X	X	X	X	X	X	X	L	N
Counter Generation Properties																								
CounterIncBy																					X		L	N
CounterSeq																					X		S	N
CounterTiming																					X		L	N
CounterType																					X		L	N
Internal Value Properties																								
DataSize			X	X					X			X		X							X	X	L	N

TABLE 8-1. *Predefined Properties for All Objects in Oracle Power Objects. Datatypes are S=String, L=Long, B=Boolean, O=Object, and V=Variant (either Long or String)*

	Bitmap	Chart	Check Box	Combo Box	Current Row Control	Forms	Horizontal Scrollbar	Line	List Box	OLE Object	Oval	Pop-up List	Push Button	Radio Button	Report	Rectangle	Repeater Display	Repeater Display Panel	Report Area	Static Text	Text Field	Frame	Property Datatype	Writeable at Run Time
DataType			X	X					X			X		X							X	X	L	N
DefaultValue			X	X					X			X		X							X	X	S	N
ReadOnly	X		X	X					X			X		X							X	X	L	Y
Translation									X			X											S	Y
ValueList				X																			S	Y
ValueOff			X											X									V	Y
ValueOn			X											X									V	Y
Miscellaneous Properties																								
DefaultSession	This property applies only to an application object. It is on the property sheet.																						S	N
HelpText	X	X	X	X	X	X	X	X	X	X	X	X	X	X	X	X	X	X	X	X	X	X	S	Y
HelpTextVisible	This property applies only to a status line object. It is not on any property sheet.																						B	Y
ValidateMsg			X	X					X			X		X							X	X	S	Y
ValidateRowMsg		X				X									X		X						S	Y
WindowStyle						X																	L	Y
Object Appearance Properties																								
Bitmap						X							X										S	Y
BitmapTiled						X																	L	Y
ColorBrdr	X		X					X			X			X		X	X	X					L	Y
ColorFill			X			X					X			X	X	X	X	X					L	Y
Direction								X															S	Y
FormatMask				X																	X		L	Y
HasBorder						X									X		X	X			X		L	Y
PositionX	X	X	X	X	X	X	X	X	X	X	X	X	X	X	X	X	X	X	X	X	X	X	L	Y

TABLE 8-1. *Predefined Properties for All Objects in Oracle Power Objects. Datatypes are S=String, L=Long, B=Boolean, O=Object, and V=Variant (either Long or String)* (continued)

	Bitmap	Chart	Check Box	Combo Box	Current Row Control	Forms	Horizontal Scrollbar	Line	List Box	OLE Object	Oval	Pop-up List	Push Button	Radio Button	Report	Rectangle	Repeater Display	Repeater Display Panel	Report Area	Static Text	Text Field	Frame	Property Datatype	Writeable at Run Time
PositionY	X	X	X	X	X	X	X	X	X	X	X	X	X	X	X	X	X	X	X	X	X	X	L	Y
SizeX	X	X	X	X	X	X		X	X	X	X	X	X	X	X	X	X	X	X	X	X	X	L	Y
SizeY	X	X	X	X	X	X		X	X	X	X	X	X	X	X	X	X	X	X	X	X	X	L	Y
Transparent						X					X					X	X	X					B	Y
Visible	X	X	X	X	X	X		X	X	X	X	X	X	X	X	X	X	X	X	X	X	X	L	Y
WindowInitPos						X																	L	N
WinPositionX						X																	L	Y
WinPositionY						X																	L	Y
WinSizeX						X																	L	Y
WinSizeY						X																	L	Y
Internal Object Properties																								
Container																							O	N
ControlType																							L	N
FirstChild																							O	N
ObjectType																							L	N
Self																							O	N
TopContainer																							O	N
Value																							V	Y
Recordset-Related Properties																								
CompareOnLock	X					X									X		X							
DataSource	X		X	X					X			X		X							X	X	S	N
DefaultCondition		X				X									X		X						S	Y
LinkDetailColumn		X				X											X						S	N
LinkMasterColumn		X				X											X						S	N

TABLE 8-1. *Predefined Properties for All Objects in Oracle Power Objects. Datatypes are S=String, L=Long, B=Boolean, O=Object, and V=Variant (either Long or String)* (continued)

	Bitmap	Chart	Check Box	Combo Box	Current Row Control	Forms	Horizontal Scrollbar	Line	List Box	OLE Object	Oval	Pop-up List	Push Button	Radio Button	Report	Rectangle	Repeater Display	Repeater Display Panel	Report Area	Static Text	Text Field	Frame	Property Datatype	Writeable at Run Time
LinkMasterForm		X				X											X						S	N
LinkMasterDel		X				X											X						L	N
LinkMasterUpd		X				X											X						L	N
LinkPrimaryKey		X				X											X						L	N
OrderBy		X				X											X						S	Y
RecordSource		X				X											X						S	N
RecSrcAddCols		X				X											X						S	Y
RecSrcMaxMem		X				X											X						L	Y
RecordSrcSession		X				X											X						S	N
RowFetchMode		X													X		X						L	Y
ScrollWithRow	X		X	X					X			X		X							X	X	L	N
Report Properties																								
FirstPgFtr																			X				L	N
FirstPgHdr																			X				L	N
GroupCol																			X				L	N
LastPgFtr																			X				S	N
PageOnBreak																			X				L	N
Session Properties																								
ConnectType																							L	N
DesignConnect																							S	N
DesignRunConnect																							S	N
RunConnect																							S	N
Text Properties																								
ColorText			X											X						X			L	Y
FontBold		X	X	X					X			X	X	X						X	X	X	L	Y
FontItalic		X	X	X					X			X	X	X						X	X	X	L	Y

TABLE 8-1. *Predefined Properties for All Objects in Oracle Power Objects. Datatypes are S=String, L=Long, B=Boolean, O=Object, and V=Variant (either Long or String)* (continued)

	Bitmap	Chart	Check Box	Combo Box	Current Row Control	Forms	Horizontal Scrollbar	Line	List Box	OLE Object	Oval	Pop-up List	Push Button	Radio Button	Report	Rectangle	Repeater Display	Repeater Display Panel	Report Area	Static Text	Text Field	Frame	Property Datatype	Writeable at Run Time
FontName		X	X	X					X			X	X	X						X	X	X	S	Y
FontSize		X	X	X					X			X	X	X						X	X	X	L	Y
FontUnderline		X	X	X					X			X	X	X						X	X	X	L	Y
TextJustHoriz																				X	X		L	Y
TextJustVert																				X	X		L	Y
Chart Properties																								
ChartAutoFormat		X																					B	N
ChartGap		X																					L	N
ChartLabelStyle		X																					L	N
ChartLegendHAlign ChartLegendVAlign		X																					L	N
ChartLineStyle		X																					L	N
ChartMaxVal ChartMinVal		X																					L	N
ChartOverlap		X																					L	N
ChartPieCircle		X																					B	N
ChartRowCount		X																					L	N
ChartShowGrid		X																					L	N
ChartShowLegend		X																					B	N
ChartStacked		X																					B	N
ChartStyle		X																					L	N
ChartXCol ChartYCol		X																					S	N

TABLE 8-1. *Predefined Properties for All Objects in Oracle Power Objects. Datatypes are S=String, L=Long, B=Boolean, O=Object, and V=Variant (either Long or String)* (continued)

There are two main categories of properties: attributes and controls. *Attribute properties* describe how an object is to be displayed, such as its color, whether it has a border, its size, whether it is visible, etc. The *control properties* are used to tell the object where to retrieve the data for its internal fields, the forms to which the object is linked, etc. As each property is described, it is evident whether it is a control or attribute property. In addition to the system properties described in this chapter, you may create your own properties as needed and attach them to objects that require the new property. This subject is covered in more detail in "User-Defined Properties" at the end of this chapter.

Each property has an attribute called Value (discussed in more detail later), which is one of the following types of data: text, the value TRUE or FALSE (or another on/off type of value), numeric, date, or a value selected from a list. Data entered in a property's text entry field can be of the following types:

- Constants, such as Cname in the property DataSource, which is the name of a column in the Customers table, or 30 as the size of the data in the DataSize property.
- Modified SQL statements, such as salary > 13000 in the QueryWhere property or =SQLLookup("select amount from orders where id = "&orderid) in the DataSource property.
- Text, such as The total Sales, added to the Help property of a text control field.
- Expressions, such as field1.value * field2.value in the DataSource property.

When no value has been assigned to a property, it has the NULL value. A NULL value is not zero; it means simply that the property has no value. Oracle Basic includes the function ISNULL to check for NULL values, so that you can verify that the property has a usable value before acting on it. As each property is described in the following sections, examples of valid entries or the type of data to be entered are given.

Naming Properties

These properties are used to name the object externally (the name that will be displayed during run time) and internally (the name used by other objects to reference the object).

Label

The Label property determines the external name of the object. This is the text that is displayed during run time in a static text field, on a button, adjacent to radio buttons, check boxes, and combo lists, and in the title bar of forms, user-defined classes, and reports.

You can set the Label property in one of two ways. The first is to simply open the property sheet and type in the desired text in the Label property entry field. The second method is to select the object in which the label is displayed. If the label is highlighted, then just type in a new label or edit the existing label. If it is not highlighted (which will be the case for buttons), place the cursor on the label and double-click. The label will now be highlighted, and you can edit it. Labels should represent what the object is, such as "Exit" for a button that dismisses a window.

Name

Every object in Oracle Power Objects has a Name property. It is by this name that objects refer to each other (in properties, and Oracle Basic code in methods) in the application. Object names are not case-sensitive, cannot exceed 39 characters in length, and must not be a reserved word in Oracle Basic, such as While or If (for a complete list, see Appendix C), or the name Container or Self (see the descriptions for these properties below). Names cannot include spaces, periods, or parentheses. In addition, you must observe the following rules:

- For forms, reports, and classes, the name must be unique within the application.
- For tables, sequences, indexes, and views, the name must be unique within the database.
- For objects placed within containers, the name must be unique within that container. However, the name can be repeated for an object within nested containers (e.g., an embedded form may contain an object with the same name as an object in the embedded form's container).
- For applications, libraries, and sessions, the Name property matches its filename (minus the extension in Windows). For example, the Name property of an application stored in the file TUBAPP.POA is TUBBAPP.

As with labels, the name should represent what the object is, to help the developer remember the purpose of the text fields, embedded forms, etc. that are placed on the form. Then, as other objects need to reference those objects, it is easier to remember their names. Naming the exit button class "ExitBtnClass," for example, is better than calling it "Button3." You can set a variable to the value of the Name property of an object by using the Oracle Basic statement objname=obj.name. However, you cannot change the object name at run time.

Control Behavior Properties

These properties are all of the control type. They are used by the object to determine what accessories are to be displayed, how data is to be entered, how many records to scroll at a time, etc.

DefaultButton

The name of the default button for the form or class is entered into this property's text field. It tells the form (or class) which button on the form is to be automatically activated by an accept action, such as a return, when no button on the form has been explicitly selected. The default button is displayed with a thick border. If no value is entered in this property, there will be no default action if no object is currently selected and the ENTER key is pressed. Often, the name of an OK button is given as the DefaultButton property.

Enabled

A control object uses this property to determine whether or not it can accept input from the user during run time. It is set to TRUE by default. During run time, its value can be changed to reflect changing states in the application. For example, if a field depends on data in other currently empty fields, a method can set its Enabled property to FALSE to prevent data being entered until the other fields contain data. Text in a disabled field is grayed out. The following code is added to the PostChange( ) method of a text control field to activate a button. This code is used in conjunction with the example for the WriteColToFile( ) method in Chapter 9.

```
IF len(self.value) THEN
   WriteBtn.Enabled=TRUE
    Inherited.PostChange()
ELSE
    MSGBOX "Cannot have 0 length column name"
END IF
```

HasExtraRow

Normally, when a form displays records from the database with scroll bars or a repeater, there is a blank row at the bottom of the display in which the user can enter new data. However, if the application is to be read only, such as one displaying purchases during the previous year, the HasExtraRow should be set to FALSE so that the user cannot enter a new record.

HasScrollBar

By default, a repeater display will have a scroll bar on the right side. This property can be set to tell the object to not use a scroll bar, which would probably necessitate other controls (such as push buttons) to navigate through the records in the repeater. A text field with the MultiLine property set to TRUE has the scroll bar set to FALSE by default. If the text to be displayed contains several lines, this property should be set to TRUE.

IsDismissBtn

This property applies to push buttons in a *modal form* (one which must be dismissed before any further work is done), which is usually a dialog box or user-defined class. It simply means that when the button whose name is entered in this property is pressed, the window will be hidden (not closed; see OpenModal( ) in Chapter 9), generally triggering some kind of processing, such as loading a selected filename into the application.

MultiLine

The need for text fields with several lines of text is common, such as entering a multiline title over a column of values. By setting this property to TRUE (default is FALSE), this ability is realized. When MultiLine is set to TRUE, the HasScrollBar property should be set to TRUE as well, so that the user can scroll through the displayed text if the object containing the text is not large enough to display all lines at once.

ScrollAmtLine

Usually, a scroll bar is set to move one record at a time through the retrieved data by pressing on the arrow buttons on either end of the scroll bar. However, if you have a need to move more than one record at a time, set this property to the desired number of records to be incremented/decremented when the arrow buttons are pressed. For example, if the number 5 is entered in this property's text field, the form will display every fifth record as the scroll buttons are pressed.

ScrollAmtPage

By clicking in the space between the slider (thumb) on the scroll bar and the end arrow button, the object will scroll through the number of records set in this property. The default number is set to ten records.

ScrollMax

When attached to a bound container, the ScrollMax property is automatically set to the number of records retrieved. However, if the scroll bar is attached to a derived field, then you may want to set the maximum number to that which the scroll bar can increment. For example, a scroll bar used with a text field that selects an hour in the day would have the ScrollMax property set to 24. The default value is 100.

ScrollMin

ScrollMin is similar to the ScrollMax property but sets the lower limit of the scroll bar. For example, a scroll bar attached to a field that selects the degrees of an angle between -180 and 180 degrees would have the ScrollMin property set to -180. The default value is 0.

ScrollObj

This property's value is used to tell the scroll bar the name of the object to which it is attached. Oracle Power Objects automatically sets the scroll bar's ScrollObj property when the scroll bar is dropped into a container with bound controls, so you usually do not need to set it. The scroll bar allows the user to view each record retrieved by the query formed by the container. If the container is not bound, you must manually set the ScrollObj property to the name of the object whose data is to be scrolled. Another use for a scroll bar is to generate values for data entry or values needed for a calculation; an example is the scroll bar mentioned in the ScrollMin property that generates the degrees of an angle from -180 to 180. When a scroll bar is used in this way, the ScrollObj property is left blank.

ScrollPos

This is the current position of the slider in the scroll bar. In a bound field, it represents the position (or a range of records in a repeater display) of the displayed record in the list of records being displayed. For a derived field, it represents the current position between the minimum and the maximum value. Figure 8-1a shows a simple form with a field that changes from 0 to 24 as the arrow buttons are clicked or the slider is moved. Notice that the DataSource property for field1 and the ScrollObj property for hsb1 are left blank. The key to making this work is the setting of the scroll bar's PostChange( ) method to assign field1's value to the scroll bar's position. As the scroll bar buttons are pressed or the scroll slider is moved, the value in field1 changes accordingly. The form in Run-time mode is shown in Figure 8-1b after the scroll slider was moved to position 4.

It may seem that it would be easier to simply set field1's DataSource property to hsb1's ScrollPos property, but the DataSource property, or any property for that matter, cannot determine the internal value of another property. In other words, field1's DataSource property cannot recognize the scroll bar's current position during run time in order to set field1's value. Thus, it must be done by having the scroll bar's PostChange( ) method set field1's value as the scroll bar's value changes.

Another primary use of the ScrollPos property is to synchronize the scrolling of two (or more) related fields (with one-to-one relationships) in different forms. For example, if one form shows specifications for a tub and another shows the tub

a)

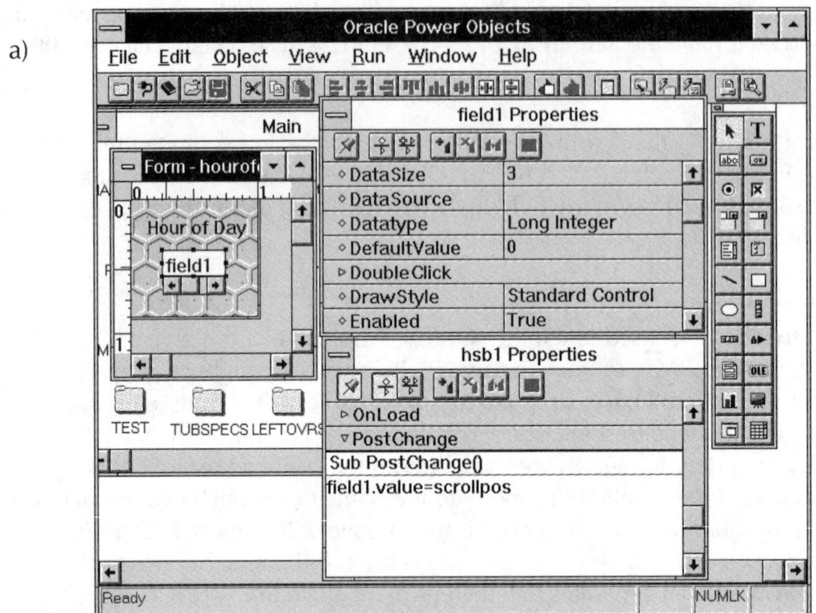

b)

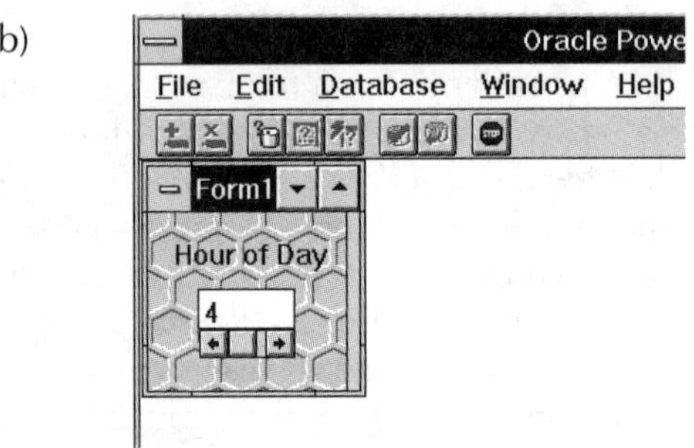

FIGURE 8-1. *(a)The PostChange( ) method of scroll bar using ScrollPos to set the field1 value, and (b)The same form in Run-time mode showing the ScrollPos value in the text field*

name, then two scroll bars can be used to synchronize the display. This is done by entering Oracle Basic code in the TubName scroll bar's PostChange( ) method to move the TubSpecs scroll bar's ScrollPos to the same position, using TubSpecs scroll bar's GoPos( ) method. The TubSpecs scroll bar's Visible property is set FALSE, so the end-user can use only the Tub Name scroll bar to scroll though the tub specification data. Figure 8-2a shows the two forms in Form Designer mode.

Notice that HideWindow is on top of the scroll bar in the TubSpec form. When the application is run, the scroll bar in TubSpec is invisible, as shown in Figure 8-2b.

a)

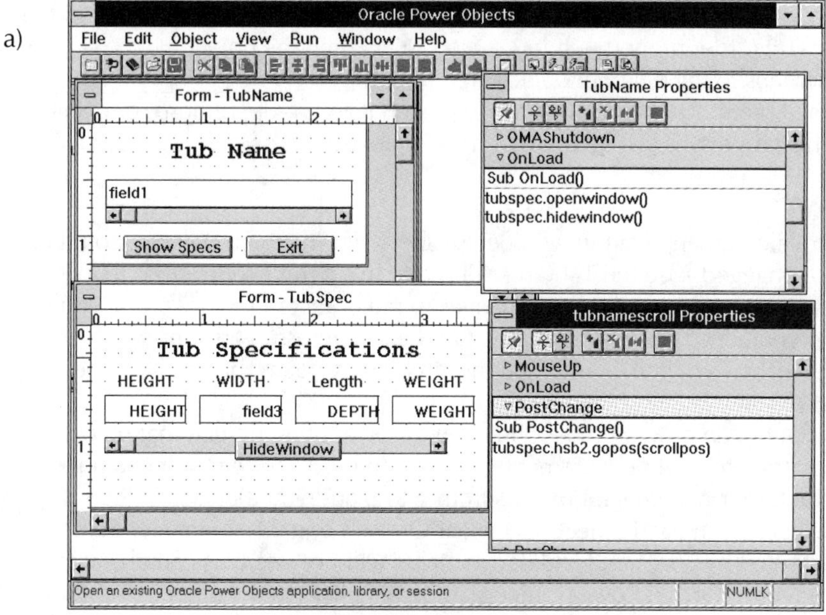

b)

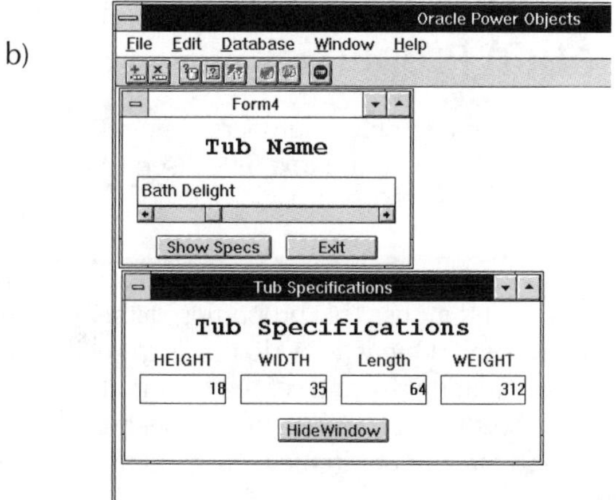

FIGURE 8-2. *(a)The TubName and TubSpec forms plus TubName's container and scroll bar property sheets. (b)The forms in Run-time mode. Notice the scroll bar in TubSpec is invisible*

TabEnabled

This property simply determines whether the object (field, repeater, button, etc.) is in the tab order in the form. Being in the tab order means that as the user presses the TAB key, Oracle Power Objects' focus changes to the next object listed in the tab order (TabOrder property). If it is set to FALSE, then the object will be skipped as the user tabs to the different objects in the form.

On the Macintosh, you cannot tab to push buttons, radio buttons, or check boxes. This property is just ignored for these objects.

TabOrder

As you develop an application, you decide the order in which objects should be viewed or changed. Use the TabOrder property to set this sequence so that as the user presses the TAB key, the focus changes to the object in the order that you have set in each object's TabOrder property. On the Macintosh, you can set the TabOrder for push buttons, radio buttons, and check boxes, but they will be skipped.

If you put in an order number already used by another object, that object's TabOrder property will be incremented by one in the TabOrder. For example, if you set TabOrder numbers for objects from 1 to 8 and you then set Field9's TabOrder to 3, then each object whose TabOrder is equal to or greater than 3 will be incremented by one, i.e., Field7's TabOrder will now be 8. As an object is added to a form, Oracle Power Objects automatically sets the object's TabOrder value by the order in which it is added to the form.

Counter Generation Properties

These properties are used to generate unique numbers, generally used in key fields, for different tables. They apply only to bound text fields (see Chapters 3 and 5).

CounterIncBy

There are times when you may want to have unique id numbers for a product, department, etc., that are not contiguous. This property sets the amount by which the numbers are to be incremented. One way to do this is to set the CounterType property to Table, MAX( ) + CounterIncBy and set the CounterIncBy property to the increment amount. Oracle Power Objects will then retrieve the maximum number of the current column and add the amount in the CounterIncBy property to generate the next id number.

CounterSeq

When the CounterType property is set to Sequence, you enter the name of the database sequence from which the id number is to be retrieved in the CounterSeq text field. The sequence must be in the same database session as the table to which the field is bound. For example, a form used to enter new customers could have its CounterSeq property set to CustomerSeq, which is the name of a sequence generator defined in the database.

CounterTiming

To avoid excessive database access time, you may not want Oracle Power Objects to update the counter field until you commit all the work you have done. In this case, set the CounterTiming property to Deferred. However, you generally want to see the id of the new record you are entering displayed as you enter new rows, or you want to use it while testing master-detail relationships. In this case, set the property to Immediate.

CounterType

Every table in a relational database must have a unique identifier. In addition, there may be other fields that must be unique for each record. Oracle Power Objects helps you to generate these unique numbers by the use of this property. It designates the type of number sequence generator used to automatically give a unique number to a record newly added to a table in the database. There are four possible values for this property.

Counter Type	Description
None	The field is not a counter field (default).
Sequence	The new value is retrieved from a sequence number generator defined in the database specified in the CounterSeq property.
Table, MAX( ) +CounterIncBy	The new value is determined by taking the maximum current value in the column and adding the value of the CounterIncBy property.
User-Generated	The new value is calculated using Oracle Basic code entered in the CounterGenKey method.

Some databases do not support sequence objects, and the last two options shown in the table above must be chosen to generate unique numbers. The Sequence technique is the best solution to generate unique numbers for databases that do support sequence objects.

Internal Value Properties

These properties describe what the internal value of an object is, how it is derived, and whether it can be changed.

DataSize

In Chapter 4, the concept of the size of string data was introduced. For example, city names can be entered in a field in a table with a defined size of 30 characters. When a new text control field is added to a form, the default value is set to zero, unless a field from a table is dragged and dropped onto the text field. The DataSize property is then set automatically to the size defined in the database for that field. It must be set manually when the DataSource property is set manually. If you set the size too large, Oracle Power Objects will display error messages informing you of that fact. This property is ignored by integer, double, and date fields.

DataType

The datatype of an object describes how the data is to be stored in the database and dictates how the value can be used in Oracle Basic code in the various methods. This is a fundamental property, and if it is not set correctly, the value of the object will be displayed incorrectly or other methods will not correctly set the object's value. While most databases have several different datatypes, including Oracle, there are only four types of data recognized by this property: string, long integer, double, and date. Oracle Power Objects will automatically convert other datatypes in the database to one of these four types. (The Table Editor window, described in Chapter 4, uses all the datatypes defined by Oracle.)

Datatype	Description
Long Integer	A whole number between -2,147,483,648 and 2,147,483,647. Note that all integers are stored as longs.
Double	Double-precision floating point number between +/- 1.79763134862315 E308.
String	Text string up to 32,767 (32K) characters long. The Oracle datatype long raw is converted to this type.
Date	Dates have a date component and a time component. The date component spans 1/1/100 A.D. to 12/31/9999. The time component has one-second precision, spanning 00:00:00 to 23:59:59. When you specify a time without a date, the first day of the current month is used by default. When you specify a date without a time, 00:00:00 (midnight) is used by default.

You select the datatype from a list in the property's entry field. The DataType property value is an integer representing one of the datatypes listed above. The table below lists the integers and their associated datatypes. You can access an object's datatype by using the Oracle Basic statement objdatatype=obj.datatype.

Datatype	Datatype Property Value
Long Integer	2
Double (floating point)	5
String	8
Date	7

DefaultValue

A field can contain a value that is displayed when the application is first run or when a new record is added but that particular field is not filled in. This default value is set in this property. The default value is overwritten if the query finds data in the column associated with the field. It can also be overwritten by the user if the Enabled property is set to TRUE. If the DefaultValue property is not set and it is not filled in by a query or by the user, the object's value will be NULL (see the explanation of NULL in the "Oracle Power Objects Properties" section earlier in this chapter). Therefore, it is generally a good idea to set this property to a valid value.

ReadOnly

This property is similar to the Enabled property in that it allows or disallows the user to change a control's value though the current value remains visible. However, the text in a field with Enabled set to FALSE is grayed out, while in a field with ReadOnly set to TRUE, it appears normal. A read-only control cannot have the focus, thus it will be skipped over when the user tabs from field to field. The value of a read-only control can be changed by Oracle Basic code in methods or, in the case of bound controls (see the DataSource property described in the "RecordSet-Related Properties" section later in this chapter), by changing the display to another record.

Translation

This is the property of list boxes and pop-up lists (described in Chapter 5) that is used to set the translation between what is displayed in the list and what Oracle Power Objects sets as the list's internal value. It must be set, or no values will be displayed in the list. The end user selects the desired item displayed in the list by clicking on it. At the same time, Oracle Power Objects sets the internal value of the list to the value corresponding to the selected item.

The Translation property is set in one of three ways: hard coded, two columns from a table, or by a SQL select statement (see Chapter 10 for examples of using SQL). A hard-coded list is explicitly defined by the developer by entering each item to be displayed and its associated internal value in the Translation entry field. An example is a list from which the end user selects a color for a product. In this example, the Translation property is set to hard-coded color values.

```
Red = 1
Blue = 2
Green = 3
```

The first item is displayed in the list, and the second is the value assigned to the internal value of the list object when the user selects a color. For example, when the user selects Green from the list, the value of the list is set to 3. If other methods need to know the value of the list object, they will receive the value 3.

Probably the most common way to set the values in the Translation property is by mapping it directly to two fields in a table. In other words, you define the table and columns from which the display values (the first column) and the internal values (the second column) are to be retrieved. The full syntax for this method is

=AT session_name table_name.column1 = column2

If the table is in the database session that is referenced by the container, the AT session_name part is left out. For example, you would map customer names to the customer id by entering code similar to that shown below in the text entry area of the Translation property.

```
=Custs.name = custid
```

Generally, a list is used to allow the user to select one of several values from a table different from that used by the list object's container. If the list is from the same table as its container's table, then you do not need to use the table name in the code. In the example above, the list will display the customer names and use the customer id numbers as the associated internal values for the list object.

The third method of setting this property is to use a direct query of the database. In this technique, you query values from two columns in the table that describe the same characteristic of a record (such as custid and name for a customer) by writing the SQL select statement yourself. The list box uses the first column specified in the Select statement as the display column and the second column as the values used by Oracle Power Objects to set the internal value of the list object. The select statement uses the following syntax:

=SELECT display_column, corresponding_column FROM table WHERE condition ORDER BY column

In this syntax, the where and order by clauses are optional. This option for the Translation property has the advantage over the table column mapping method in that you can add where and order by statements to the translation. For example, the following will retrieve the names of all sales personnel except those in department 10 and order the list by their department id.

```
SELECT name, empid FROM employees WHERE deptno != 10 ORDER BY deptno
```

ValueList

This property is associated only with combo boxes. As explained in Chapter 5, combo boxes are very similar to pop-up lists, except the end users can enter their own value in the combo box's text field if none of the items in the list meets their current needs. The ValueList property is very similar to the Translation property described above, except that the second column is not used and the selected item is used as the internal value of the combo box object.

The values for the combo box ValueList property are derived using the same three methods used to set the Translation property values as explained above, except that the second column or value is left off. Therefore, the "hard-coded" values for a combo box that lists colors is simply Red, Blue, Green, etc., each on a separate line.

The syntax for the table assignment method (as explained in the Translation property section) is simply

=AT session_name Table_name.column_name

The table assignment method to list the customer names is =custs.name. The table assignment method will retrieve the values from the database in the order that they are entered in the database. Thus, customer names may not be in alphabetical order.

The direct query syntax is

=SELECT display_column FROM table WHERE condition ORDER BY column

The example to list all employees except those in department 10 and ordered by their department is as shown below.

```
SELECT name FROM employees WHERE deptno != 10 ORDER BY deptno
```

Remember, the chief reason for using the select statement is to add order to the list and to add filters (the where clause) on which values are retrieved from the database to be displayed.

ValueOff/ValueOn

These properties are used by radio buttons and check boxes. Depending on the datatype of the object, you enter what the value is to be for the object, depending on whether the button or box is checked or not. When the object is first displayed in run time, it will have a NULL value unless the DefaultValue property is set or the object is a bound control. Therefore, in the case that the object is not a bound control and the DefaultValue has not been set, the user must click on the button or box before the object will have a value. For example, a check box with a datatype of string could have the value Do Not Print in the ValueOff property and the value of Print OK in the ValueOn property.

Miscellaneous Properties

These properties just don't seem to fit in any other category. (Isn't miscellaneous a wonderful term?)

DefaultSession

If the RecSrcSession property is not set for a container, the application will automatically use the default session for the application as designated by the DefaultSession property of the application. Only one session can be the default session for an application. If this value is not set, and there is more than one session in the application, Oracle Power Objects will inform you that it does not know which session to use when a form's RecordSource property is left blank.

Generally, your application uses one session most of the time, so set the Default Session to this session's name. Now you need to set the RecSrcSession only for those containers using the less-used sessions. The SQL functions EXE SQL and SQLLookup will use this session if not directed to use another session with the AT clause.

```
count = cint(SQLLookup(MlData, "Select inventory from Products where id = 1"))
```

```
EXEC SQL AT MlData select inventory into :count from products where id = 1
```

HelpText

In Figure 3-1 of Chapter 3, the status bar is shown at the bottom of the Desktop Manager window for Windows. This area is used to display a brief help message about the object on which the cursor is resting. The HelpText property is used to set this message for the objects you create. Because the space in the status bar is limited, it is best to limit the message to 60 characters. If you use more than 60 characters, the trailing characters will not be displayed.

HelpTextVisible

This property specifies whether the first panel in the Status Line (status bar) should display the help message associated with the object, menu, toolbar button, etc., that the mouse cursor is currently over. If it is an object that you have added to an application, the help message is the one stored in the HelpText property described above. Set this property to TRUE (default value) to display the message and to FALSE to not display the message. Oracle Basic code in a method can set this property.

ValidateMsg

When the Validate( ) method is used, it determines whether the data entered in a control is valid. If the data is not valid, Oracle Power Objects will display the message entered in the ValidateMsg property in a message box with a warning icon. For example, a form that is used to give employees a raise has a text control field in which the raise percentage is entered. The text control field's ValidateMsg property is set to: Salary Increase must be less than 10%. The Validate( ) method contains Oracle Basic code to verify that the newly entered value is less than ten. If a user tries to give a salary increase greater than or equal to 10 percent, the following message box is displayed.

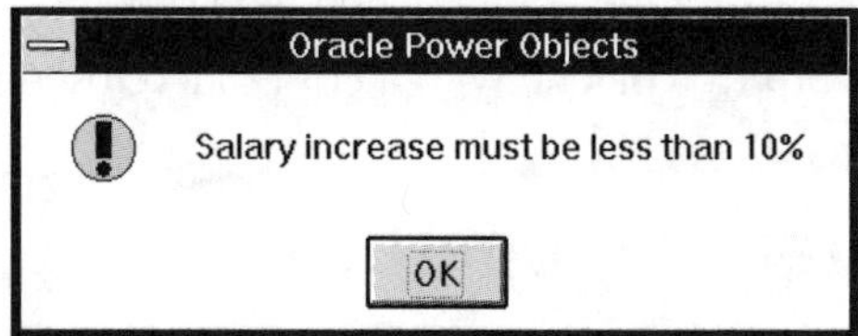

ValidateRowMsg

This property is similar to ValidateMsg, except it applies to the ValidateRow( ) method, which, when set with Oracle Basic code, verifies that newly entered data is valid for a row in the database. If the data is not valid, the data is not entered in the database and the message in the ValidateRowMsg property text field is displayed in a window with a warning icon. See the example given for the ValidateRow( ) method in Chapter 9.

WindowStyle

This property places limits on how the end user can move and resize a form's window in Run-time mode. In addition, it tells the form's window whether it is a dialog window or not. A dialog window captures the focus and disables all other Oracle Power Objects windows from receiving the focus until the dialog window is dismissed. Choices for the WindowStyle property include the following:

Window Style	Description
Standard Document	A standard window, both moveable and resizable. This is the default.

Window Style	Description
Document without Maximize	A standard moveable, resizable window without the maximize button.
Fixed-Size Document	A moveable window of fixed size.
Standard Dialog	A nonresizable, unmoveable dialog box, with no title bar and smaller borders in Windows. On the Macintosh, a thick border surrounds the dialog box.
Alternate Dialog	Similar to a standard dialog box except that, on the Macintosh, the dialog box appears with a shadow beneath it.
Moveable Dialog	A moveable, nonresizable dialog window with a title bar.
Plain Dialog	On the Macintosh, a dialog box with no border.
Palette	A moveable dialog type specific to the Macintosh.
Palette with Close Box	A palette with a control to close the window.

Object Appearance Properties

All of these properties influence the appearance or placement of the various objects to which they apply. Oracle Power Objects automatically sets the values of many of these properties when they are placed in a form and when moved or resized by use of the sizing controls on the objects. You can set the values during run time to cause the object to move, grow, become invisible, etc.

Bitmap

Oracle Power Objects allows you to use bitmaps (BMP format only) in various ways to add color, decoration, or symbols to your application. They can be added to buttons to visually indicate the button's use, or they can be added to forms, either top level or embedded, to provide an interesting background. You enter the name of the bitmap to be used in the Bitmap property of the object that is to display the bitmap. The bitmap file must be loaded into the application window by selecting the Import BMP menu item in the File menu for the application form. Once the bitmap is loaded into the application, you no longer need to keep a copy of it on the computer.

An alternative to manually setting the Bitmap property is to drag and drop the bitmap icon from the application window onto the form. Oracle Power Objects will automatically enter the name of the bitmap in the Bitmap property entry field. You can create your own bitmap files by using the various bitmap editors available on PCs and Macintoshes. A standard bitmap editor in windows is PaintBrush (pbrush.exe). A common shareware package that can convert various graphic files to a bitmap file on PC is Paint Shop Pro (psp.exe), which can also be used to change resolution, crop the picture, adjust the colors, and capture a full or partial picture of the current screen. One very useful shareware program that converts graphic files and allows you to edit graphic files on the Macintosh is the Graphic Converter program. The example of the ScrollPos property above in Figure 8-1 (a and b) uses the Windows Honey bitmap.

BitmapTiled

If a bitmap placed on a form is not large enough to fill the form, it will be placed in the center of the form. If it is too large, only the upper-left corner of the bitmap will be displayed as the background. To allow the use of small bitmaps, use the BitmapTiled property to tell Oracle Power Objects to display the bitmap repeatedly until the entire window is filled.

ColorBrdr

This property is used to set the color of lines, rectangles, and ovals. It is also used to set the border color for radio buttons and check boxes, exclusive of the label. You select the color desired from the palette in the ColorBrdr property. The color can be changed when methods containing Oracle Basic code to do so are activated. For example, a list box can be created with a list of colors from which the end user selects a color. Oracle Basic code entered in the PostChange( ) method of the list box would then set the color of named objects with code similar to that shown below.

```
LineObject.ColorBrdr.value = Self.value
```

Self refers to the listbox itself and its value is the currently selected color id number (see the Translation property in the "Internal Value Properties" section earlier in this chapter).

ColorFill

You choose a color from the color palette displayed when the ColorFill property is selected to fill the interior of rectangles, ovals, radio boxes, and check boxes. The ColorFill property designates the color to fill in the entire background of forms, repeater displays, and user-defined classes.

Direction

You set the direction of line objects from upper-left to lower-right or lower-left to upper-right by selecting one of these two choices from the Direction property. This seems to be kind of a useless property, because it is easier to just drag the line to the desired position. However, this property is changeable at run time, so there may be times when you would want the direction of the line in a form to change.

For example, you could make a small box with one line running from the upper-left to the lower-right. In a method with Oracle Basic code that cycles many times through a loop, you could add this Basic statement: line_name.direction = (x mod 2). This causes the line to change direction each time through the loop to indicate to the end user that the program is still running and is not hung. This code uses the modulo operator, which simply returns the remainder of the division of two into the loop counter x. Thus, the value will cycle continually from 1 to 0 and back to 1.

FormatMask

Though there are only four datatypes used in Oracle Power Objects, the manner in which the numbers and dates are displayed can be set in several different ways by selecting one of the format masks in the FormatMask property. The list of formats is shown in Table 8-2.

In addition to the predefined formats, you can use custom formats by using the number symbol (#) to represent where the digits of a number are to be placed. For example, if you want a ten-digit number to be shown in telephone-number format, place the following string in the FormatMask entry field: (###) ###-####. Use the @ or & characters as placeholders for character data. The entire set of characters that can be used in the FormatMask property and in Oracle Basic code is listed in Appendix B under the FORMAT statement.

If FormatMask is not used, the format set for the column when added to the table will be used for bound controls. Chapter 4 describes how to use this type of formatting.

HasBorder

This property applies to embedded forms, repeater displays, panels in a repeater display, user-defined classes, and text fields. If you desire the object to have a border around it (default) during run time, set this property to TRUE; otherwise, set it to FALSE.

The following four properties all use units of measurement that can be in inches, cm, or pixels. The nonpixel units are scaled appropriately on different platforms, but the pixel measurements are not. Oracle Power Objects has made the entry of data in this property very flexible. You can type in fractions, which are converted to decimal, type in a unit designator to change the units of the property (for example, typing cm to change 96 pixels to 2.54 cm in Windows), or type in a number to simply take the unit of measurement currently stored in the property. The default unit of measurement is the default unit specified by the operating system. The international value is stored as pixels.

Name	Applies To	Example	Notes
General Number	integer, double	100000.	
Currency	integer, double	$100,000.00	Enforces two decimal places and rounds appropriately for the display value (e.g., if the value in the table is 99999.999, the value displayed is $100,000.00).
Fixed	integer, double	100000.00	
Percent	integer, double	32.00%	The decimal point moves two places to the right when displayed and the percent sign is added
Scientific	integer, double	1.E+5	
Yes/No	integer, double	Yes	0 = No; any nonzero value = Yes
TRUE/FALSE	integer, double	TRUE	0 = FALSE; any nonzero value = TRUE
On/Off	integer, double	On	0 = Off; any nonzero value = On
All Caps	string	HELLO	
Init Cap	string	Hello	
All Lowercase	string	hello	
General Date	date	10/8/95 11:11:11	
Long Date	date	October 8, 1995	
Medium Date	date	10/8/95	
Short Date	date	8-Oct-95	
Long Time	date	11:11:11 AM	
Medium Time	date	11:11 AM	
Short Time	date	11:11	

TABLE 8-2. *Available Predefined Format Masks for the Given Datatype*

PositionX

This property sets the horizontal position of the left edge of an object from the left edge of its run-time form or report window. It can be changed during run time with Oracle Basic code entered in various methods. Thus, you can be fancy and move an object across its container's window or just rearrange objects to meet different run-time conditions. An example of using this property is shown in creating the Avery Label application in Chapter 5.

PositionY

Like PositionX, this property determines where an object is placed in its run-time form's or report's window. It sets the distance between the top of the object and the top of the form. It too can be changed during run time to change the position of the object, as shown in the Avery Label application example in Chapter 5.

SizeX

This property is used to set the width of an object. During development, the size is changed most easily by selecting the object, then dragging the right or left edge to the desired position. But it can be changed during run time to accommodate changes in the size of the data it is to contain, if necessary. The Avery Label application example in Chapter 5 uses this property to set the correct size of the repeater panel for the selected Avery label.

SizeY

This property is used to set the height of an object. During development, the size is changed most easily by selecting the object, then dragging the top or bottom edge to the desired position. It can be changed during run time to accommodate changes in size of the data it is to contain, if necessary. The Avery Label application example in Chapter 5 uses this property to set the correct size of the repeater panel for the selected Avery label.

Transparent

This is a Boolean property that applies to containers, ovals, and rectangles. When set TRUE, Oracle Power Objects draws the object without its fill color, which allows the underlying object to be visible.

Visible

There are times when an object's value is needed for derived fields or for synchronization of displaying data, but it is not needed to be seen. Use this property to hide objects that are not to be displayed by setting it to FALSE. It can be changed to TRUE during run time to display text fields, buttons, etc. that may need to be displayed as conditions change while running the application. Similarly, you may want to remove objects from the display as the user moves through different phases of the application. An example of a scroll bar that should be hidden is the one described in the ScrollBar property section. The scroll bar that moves through the list of tub names would be displayed, while the one that controls tub properties to be displayed would have its Visible property set to FALSE.

WindowInitPos

This property applies only to forms. It allows you to have Oracle Power Objects place the running form's window exactly where you want it on the computer screen. The property can have one of the values shown in Table 8-3.

WinPositionX

This property value is the distance in pixels between the left edge of the client area (desktop on the Macintosh) and the right edge of the window. The value changes as the user moves the window on the screen. If the WindowInitPos property is set to WinPositionX/Y, Oracle Power Objects uses the WinPositionX value to set the initial position of the window.

WinPositionY

This property value is the distance in pixels between the top edge of the client area (desktop on the Macintosh) and the top edge of the window. The value changes as the user moves the window on the screen. If the WindowInitPos property is set to

Value	Window Placement	Description
0	Automatic (Default)	Oracle Power Objects places the window where it best fits within the client area in Windows and on the desktop on the Macintosh.
1	WinPositionX/Y	Specify the exact coordinates for the upper-left corner of the window with the WinPositionX and WinPositionY properties.
2	Center	The form is centered within the client area in Windows and on the desktop on the Macintosh.
3	Dialog Position	The form appears one-third the vertical distance between the menu bar and the bottom of the client area in Windows or on the desktop on the Macintosh. It is horizontally centered.
4	Maximize	The form is maximized in Windows and expanded on the Macintosh.

TABLE 8-3. *Values and description for the WindowInitPos Property*

WinPositionX/Y, Oracle Power Objects uses the WinPositionX value to set the initial position of the window.

WinSizeX/WinSizeY

These two values set the initial size of the window that surrounds a form or report when it is opened. The window may be larger or smaller than the form it contains depending on the form's SizeX and SizeY properties. The values of these properties change as the user stretches or shrinks the window. The displayed value of these properties is in inches but the internal value is in pixels.

Internal Object Properties

None of these object properties are displayed in property sheets, but they are very useful when accessed by Oracle Basic in methods to determine the characteristics and current values of the object that triggered the method.

Container

Every object in Oracle Power Objects has this property set to the reference to the form, report, or repeater display in which the object resides. Top-level forms that are not contained by any other object have this property set to NULL. This value is an object value and can be used to access the methods and properties of that object. For example, a button placed in the form Myform has its Container property value set to Myform. Thus, the methods in the button object can access the methods of Myform by using this syntax: container.Method_name( ). The button's methods can access the properties of Myform in the same way. This is very handy, so that you do not have to remember the name of the form, report, or repeater display in which the object is placed when the object needs to access its parent's methods and properties.

This property is a very powerful feature that allows classes to be truly reusable. When a user-defined class (see Chapter 6) depends on its container for its RecordSource, use the class' Container property as the RecordSource rather than the explicit name of the form in which the class resides. In other words, enter the Oracle Basic statement =Container in the user class' RecordSource property. This allows the class to be placed in any appropriate container, and you do not have to explicitly set the RecordSource property to the name of the form in which the class is placed. It will use the record source of its parent.

ControlType

There are times when the application may need to know the type (just what the object is, e.g., text field, combo box, etc.) of an object contained within the application. Oracle Basic can determine what the type is by using the ControlType property of the named object. The list of object types is shown in Table 8-4.

For example, you may want the application to enable previously disabled text control fields upon certain situations—if a password must be entered before entries can be made in an Add Employee application, you would have Oracle Power Objects enable all of the entry fields after a valid password is entered. This can be done by using the FirstChild property (see next section) of the main form and the NextControl( ) method (see Chapter 9) of each child object to cycle through every object in a given container. As the application cycles through the objects in the form, it uses the ControlType property to determine if the control is a text field, and if so, enables it by setting the Enable property to TRUE. The Oracle Basic code to do this is entered in an appropriate method, such as the PassWord field's PostChange( ) method, and it is shown below.

```
DIM vCurObj AS Object
vCurObj = MainForm.FirstChild
Do WHILE (NOT(ISNULL(vCurObj)))
   IF vCurObj.ControlType = 2 THEN
      vCurObj.Enable=TRUE
   END IF
   vCurObj=vCurObj.NextControl()
LOOP
```

Description	Value	Description	Value
Static text	1	Rectangle	11
Text field	2	Oval	12
Push button	3	Vertical scroll bar	13
Radio button	4	Horizontal scroll bar	14
Check box	5	Repeater display	16
Combo box	6	Repeater display panel	17
Pop-up list	7	Line	19
List box	8	Icon	20
Radio button frame	9	Current row control	21
Form or embedded form	10	Report area	22

TABLE 8-4. *Control Types and Their Integer Representation*

FirstChild

The FirstChild property is an essential element of Oracle Power Objects for applications that must visit or access objects within a container. It is set to the last object added by the developer to a container. The value of FirstChild can change as an application is running, but that just means that the object at the head of the list of objects in a container changes. By using the NextControl( ) method, you cycle through all the sibling objects in a container, regardless of where you start in the list.

Oracle Power Objects has a hierarchy of objects, which means that each container object can have children objects, which can also contain children, and so on. The example above cycled through the "siblings" in a container. A more elaborate example of Oracle Basic is to cycle through every object in a top-level container by using the FirstChild property repeatedly to traverse the children, grandchildren, etc. of the container by repeatedly looking at the FirstChild of each child object in the chain. FirstChild returns NULL if the object has no children. The NextControl( ) method returns a NULL when it has completed the cycle through the list of direct children in the container. The following code, entered in the Click( ) method, will visit every object contained in the TopLevelForm.

```
DIM vCurObj AS Object
DIM vNextObject AS Object
DIM vNotTraversed AS Long Integer
DIM vSName AS String
vCurObj = Self.FirstChild
vNotTraversed = 1
DO WHILE NOT(ISNULL(vCurObj))
   REM For each object first go to the bottom of its hierarchy if
   REM it has not already been traversed.

   IF vNotTraversed AND NOT(ISNULL(vCurObj.FirstChild)) THEN
       vCurObj = vCurObj.FirstChild
   ELSE
   REM We are at a leaf in the hierarchy so process it
   REM In this example just print the name of the object.
   REM This is where you would include real code such as that described
   REM in the discussion of user-defined properties at the end of this chapter.
       vSName = vCurObj.name
       MSGBOX"This object's name is "&vSName
       REM at this level see if the object has any siblings
       vNextObject = vCurObj.NextControl()
     IF ISNULL(vNextObject)
        REM There are no more objects at this level, so go up one level
        vNextObject = vCurObj.GetContainer
```

```
            IF ISNULL(vNextObject) THEN
                REM at the top level again
                REM so just get the next sibling at the top level
                vCurObj=vCurObj.NextControl()
                vNotTraversed = 1
            ELSE
                REM set the current object to the containing object
                REM The nottraversed flag will keep Oracle Power Objects from
                REM traversing this branch again.

                vNotTraversed = 0
                vCurObj = vNextObject
            END IF
        ELSE
            REM there is a sibling so set curobj to the sibling and
            REM reset the nottraversed flag

            vCurObj = vNextObject
            vNotTraversed = 1
        END IF
    END IF
LOOP
```

ObjectType

This property lets you evaluate the current object for the general class of objects of which it is an instance at run time. You can then tailor the application to react appropriately to different object classes. For visible objects (ObjectType = 1), you can use the ControlType property to determine the type of control, static object, or container to further refine the actions the application should take. Table 8-5 lists the object types.

Self

This property is used to refer to the object that triggered the method in which the Oracle Basic code being processed is written.

TopContainer

Oracle Power Objects automatically sets the value of this property of every object to the form or report that forms the window in which the object resides. It is used much like the Container property described above, except it refers to the very top level container object rather than the object's immediate container. If the object is a TopLevel object, its TopContainer property is set to NULL.

Description	Value
Visible object	1
Recordset (not bound to a database)	2
Bitmap resource	3
Application	5
Session	7
Menu	9
Menu bar	10
Toolbar	11
Status bar	12

TABLE 8-5. *Object Class Values Associated with the ObjectType Property*

Value

For all objects that can take a value, such as text fields, radio buttons, list boxes, etc., the value is stored in this property. All other objects can access the value of each object by knowing the name of the object (or by obtaining a pointer to the object using the FirstChild or Container properties or the NextControl( ) method), and then using a statement such as that shown below to access the value.

```
myvariable = objectname.value
```

The Value property can be set by the end user or by Oracle Basic in methods in the following ways:

- **Within methods** You can change the values held in a control by using the following syntax:
  control_name.Value = new_value
- **User changes** The user can enter new values into the control.
- **Database browsing** The Value property will change as the end user browses through the records retrieved from the database. Each bound control will display the data from a column in a table or view (set in the DataSource property) from which the control reads values.
- **Derived value** A value can be calculated using a derived value, as set through the object's DataSource property. This value is read-only.

- **ValueOn and ValueOff** For radio buttons and check boxes, the Value property is set to the control's ValueOn property, ValueOff property, or NULL.
- **DefaultValue** If this property has been set, Oracle Power Objects assigns that value to the Value property when the application first begins. If the DefaultValue property is not set, the control's Value is NULL unless it is a bound container with data retrieved from the database or until the end user enters a value.
- **Radio button frames** For these objects, the Value property is the same as the ValueOn property of the currently selected radio button within the frame.

The Value property refers to the currently selected item in a list box or pop-up list. In the case of combo boxes, the Value property refers to the data in the data entry window for the control, whether or not it was selected from the combo box's drop-down list.

Recordset-Related Properties

In Oracle Power Objects, a *recordset* consists of the set of records retrieved from the database by the query created by Oracle Power Objects to populate the controls in a bindable container (form, embedded form, etc.). The records retrieved are defined by the DataSource property for bound controls and by the RecordSource and RecSrcSession properties of the bound control's container. The controls are bound to a column in the table (or view) defined in the RecordSource property of the container. The table or view must be in the database to which the associated session, listed in the container's RecSrcSession property, is connected.

The recordset can also consist of records used to populate a list, pop-up list, or combo box that is retrieved from a table (or view) using the Translation or ValueList property of the list. Each separate container can have its own recordset. Once a recordset is populated by Oracle Power Objects, it is controlled by the Record Manager methods, which are described in Chapter 9.

The properties listed in this section are all used to help define and constrain the set of records in a container's recordset.

CompareOnLock

Generally, when an application queries a database, the rows retrieved from the database are locked after the query is completed. Thus, when a query requires a lot of time and the network is slow, some records already retrieved may have been altered before the query is finished and the appropriate row locked. The CompareOnLock property tells Oracle Power Objects whether to review the records retrieved with the current records in the database just before it locks the row. If the property is set to TRUE and the record has been changed, the application will not lock the row, and the application can add code to handle the situation. If the property is set to FALSE, Oracle Power Objects will not check the records and lock the row. To check the status of the row returned, use the GetRowStat( ) method described in Chapter 9 to determine if the row is locked after the query is completed.

Verifying that the data is unchanged is only a concern if there are multiple users editing the same fields that contain large amounts of data (such as a long raw field that contains all the data needed to draw a map). For example, in an application in which maps are added to the database, Sue may retrieve a map just as Sam commits changes he has made to the map. Sue's map may be the original map, and any changes she makes will overwrite the changes made by Sam when she commits the edited map. This can happen if the map Sam edited is placed in the database and its lock released just after Sue's query retrieves the original map but before her application tries to lock the row. If CompareOnLock is set to FALSE, Sue's application will lock the row, and Sue will have no way of knowing that changes were made. If the CompareOnLock property is set to TRUE, she can verify that she has the lock and if not, requery the database to get the most recent version of the map.

DataSource

There are three choices for the DataSource property: unbound, bound, and derived. When a control is bound, it is connected to a column in a database table. Once you set the DataSource property, the control will read from and write to that column. You bind a control by setting its container's RecordSource property to the table that contains the column and its container's RecSrcSession property to the session that accesses the table, and by setting the control's DataSource to the name of the table. This is done automatically for you by Oracle Power Objects when you drag and drop a column from an open table editor onto a control.

When a control's content is derived, the data displayed in it is the result of a calculation or SQL statement. You define the calculation through the property sheet of the control by entering a valid Oracle Basic expression into the text field associated with the DataSource property. Derived values are always read-only, and the controls in which they appear cannot be bound.

Very important derived values are based on the Oracle Basic aggregate functions, which act upon controls that have repeated values, such as a repeater display. The aggregate functions, SUM, MAX, MIN, AVG, and COUNT, sum all the values, return the maximum or minimum value, average the values, or simply count the values in the repeater control referenced by the function. The syntax for an aggregate function entered in the DataSource property is shown here, where amount is a column displayed in a repeater display (see Chapter 6).

=SUM(amount)

Derived DataSource values can also be arithmetic calculations based either on values in records associated with the form or other data based on variables declared in the Declarations( ) method of the application. An example of an arithmetic-derived DataSource for a TotalCost text control field with a datatype of double is the calculation of a final price for a customer's order based on each individual's discount, as shown below.

```
=(NumPurchased * ItemPrice * PriceFactor)
```

The three names in the expression are names of text control fields in the current form. They may be bound to different tables (which implies a control is in an embedded form) as long as all the tables are in the same session. When control fields are used in this context, you do not use the Value property of the controls, just their names.

DefaultCondition

There are times when you as a developer know that only a restricted set of data should be retrieved when the Query( ) method of a form, repeater display, user-defined class, etc. is activated. Use this property to enter the conditions to be added to the where clause of the SQL statement created by the form when it queries the database. The condition placed in this property determines the default subset of data to be retrieved. An example is to create a customer form that returns only the customer names of the salesperson who is using the application, as shown below. This would be placed in the DefaultCondition property of the container that contains the text fields that displays the customers' names.

```
vRepid = gblSalesPersonEmpId
```

vRepid is a column in the Custs table, and gblSalesPersonEmpId is a global variable set to the user's employee id when the application is loaded into memory.

This property can be changed during run time to reflect the changing needs of the application. Using the QueryWhere( ) method overrides the DefaultCondition property.

LinkDetailColumn, LinkMasterColumn, LinkMasterForm

These properties are the three properties used to set up a master-detail relationship, as discussed in Chapter 6, and they apply to forms, embedded forms, and repeater displays. These properties are set in the detail object. The master object's Link properties are left blank. Generally, the detail object's LinkDetailColumn property is set to the name of the column (the foreign key) in the detail form's RecordSource (the table from which the data is retrieved) that corresponds to the primary key of the master form's RecordSource. The LinkMasterColumn property of the detail form is generally set to the primary key in the master form's RecordSource. The master form's name is entered in the detail object's LinkMasterForm property.

Usually, in a master-detail relationship, the master table contains the general or global attributes of the relationship and the detail table contains one or more records that are associated with one record in the master table. This is a one-to-many relationship, as described in Chapter 2. Commonly, there are no columns in the master table that refer to the detail table. Instead, each record in the detail table contains a foreign key that contains the value of the primary key of one record in the master table.

For example, if each customer is assigned to a salesperson, then the Custs table will contain a column called repid (a foreign key) that corresponds to the empid column (the primary key) in the Employees table. When a customer is added to the database, the customer's repid field is set to the employee number of the salesperson who handles the customer's account. There are no references to customers in the Employees table.

Consider a master form containing a text control field that displays the employee's name, a scroll bar that scrolls through all the employees, and a repeater display that shows all the customers of each salesperson. The LinkDetailColumn in the repeater display is set to repid (the foreign key in the Custs table), and the LinkMasterColumn of the repeater display is set to empid (the primary key in the Employee table). Finally, the master form's name is entered in the repeater display's LinkMasterForm property. This example is shown in Figure 8-3.

You can link different groups together by entering a list of columns or forms as appropriate in these three properties. Each property must have the same number of items in its list. The items are separated with semicolons. For example, you can create a form that contains a repeater display and an embedded form to display part names, manufacturers of parts (there can be several manufacturers of the same part), and a list of orders of parts. The main form displays the name and id of parts used to create a tub. The embedded form displays the name of a manufacturer of parts, and the repeater shows orders of parts. The Link properties are set in the repeater to show the orders with a specific part purchased from a given manufacturer. Figure 8-4 shows the form and the property sheet for the repeater display showing the list of part orders.

LinkMasterDel

This property sets a constraint to ensure data integrity so that you do not delete records that are referenced from other tables without explicitly telling Oracle Power Objects to do so. LinkMasterDel is a property of the container that holds detail records, not the container holding the master records. However, the constraint is placed on the master container in that the restrictions allow or

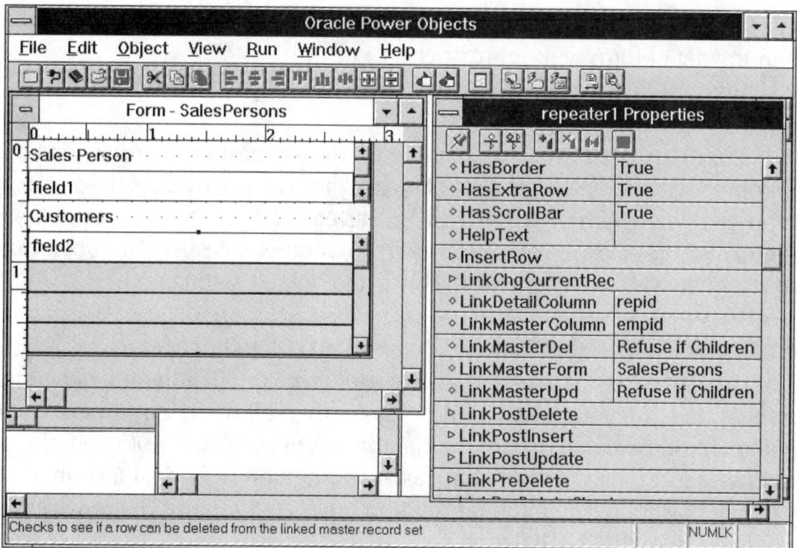

FIGURE 8-3. *The property sheet for the detail part (the repeater display) of a master-detail relationship*

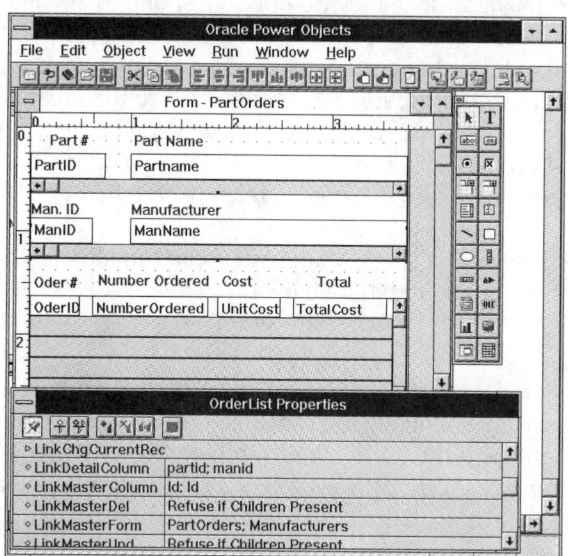

FIGURE 8-4. *Repeater Display property sheet showing double link of a detail form to two master forms*

disallow changes in records in the master container. You can change or delete records in the detail form without restriction.

The settings for LinkMasterDel include the following:

Refuse if children present You cannot delete a master record as long as there are detail records linked to it. This is the safe way to go. If a salesperson quits, before you can delete him or her using the master-detail form, you would first have to reassign all of the salesperson's customers to another salesperson. Once this is done, you can delete the salesperson. This is the default setting.

Delete cascade The application deletes all associated detail records when you delete their parent record. This can be very useful or very deadly. If LinkMasterDel is set to this value and you delete a salesperson, then all of the customers represented would be deleted from the database, which would not make the boss happy. However, if your company has just discontinued selling all tubs made from plastic, delete plastic from the tub fabrication table, and all tubs made with plastic will be deleted from the database as well.

Orphan details With LinkMasterDel set to this value, the application deletes the master record but leaves all associated detail records untouched. The detail records are now orphaned, since they do not correspond to any master record. For example, if a salesperson quits and is deleted from the database with this constraint, then all of his or her customers would no longer have a salesperson, but at least they are still in the database. You would have to then reassign each "orphaned" customer to another salesperson. However, you may miss one, so it is best to use the first option. This is the least restrictive constraint, because it forces no checks on whether the deleted record is referenced by other tables in the database.

This property takes only a single value and applies to all master forms when a list of columns/forms are entered in the Link properties.

LinkMasterUpd

LinkMasterUpd is similar to the LinkMasterDel property described above. It has the same three options with essentially the same effects. However, the Orphan details option could actually be quite useful. For example, if you leave the Empid the same, you could replace the employee data of a salesperson who has just quit with a new employee's data, and all the customers would automatically be assigned to the new salesperson.

The Update cascade option is less dangerous than the Delete cascade, because no data is deleted and is in fact quite time-saving. If a reorganization necessitates changing employee numbers, for example, then as you change each salesperson's empid, the repid in the Custs table would be updated as well.

This property is set in the form displaying the detail part of the master-detail relation, not the master form. It takes only a single value and applies to all master forms when a list of columns/forms are entered in the Link properties.

LinkPrimaryKey

The foreign key in a master-detail relationship is normally in the detail form's RecordSource's table. However, there are times, especially in one-to-one relationships, when the foreign key is in the master table. In this case, the LinkPrimaryKey is used to tell Oracle Power Objects that the master key is on the detail container so that the actions prescribed by LinkMasterUpd and LinkMasterDel will be taken correctly, i.e., the delete or update restrictions will be placed on the detail container, not the master container.

This property, set on the container holding the detail records, has two possible values:

- **Here (on detail)** The field holding the primary key values is associated with the detail recordset.
- **On Master** The field holding the primary key values is associated with the master recordset. This is the default setting.

An example of the detail side of the relationship containing the primary key is one in which you browse through the list of customers one at a time, and, at the same time, the name of the salesperson for that customer is displayed. In this case, the master is the list of customers and the detail is the form that displays the salesperson's name. Therefore, you would set the LinkPrimaryKey of the detail form (the one with the salesperson) to Here (on detail), because this form is the one using the primary key to the Employee table.

OrderBy

As Oracle Power Objects retrieves records from the database using the query set up by the controls in the container, you may want the records to be returned in a certain order. Or you may set up radio buttons to change the order of retrieved records at run time as the user selects different buttons. OrderBy is the property to use to set the columns Oracle Power Objects should use to order the records. You may enter one or more column names. The order by default is ascending, but you can add ASC or DESC after each column name to have the order ascending or descending, based on the column's lexigraphical or numerical value. You simply enter the column name, such as PurchaseDate, in the entry area of this property to have the data ordered by that column.

RecordSource

The RecordSource property defines one part of a recordset for a container. A recordset consists of the name of the table or view, from which the container retrieves data, entered in the RecordSource property, and the name of the session, in which the table can be found, entered in the RecSrcSession property. You can manually enter a table name into the RecordSource for a form, embedded form, repeater, or user-defined class by clicking on the property to open the text entry window and typing in the name of the table. You must then set the RecSrcSession property as well.

An efficient method to set these properties is to drag the table or view icon from the session window onto the container to create fields for every column in the table, or drag a column(s) from a Table Editor window and drop it onto the form. Both the RecordSource and RecSrcSession properties are automatically set by Oracle Power Objects. In addition, when you drag a column onto the form, Oracle Power Objects adds a text field and label field for each column dropped onto the form. The DataSource, DataSize, and DataType properties for each text field are all set automatically as well.

RecSrcAddCols

There may be times when you want to access and modify or evaluate data in more columns than you want to display on a form. Use RecSrcAddCols to enter the names of these extra columns. You may then use the Record Manager methods (see Chapter 9) to modify, tabulate, evaluate, etc., these extra columns. The user cannot see or directly modify these added columns. An example is to add the custid column to this property in a form that is used to view customer data but does not display the customer id number. The application can access this column's value to be used as a filter in an SQL statement to retrieve additional data from other tables.

For example, the following Oracle Basic code could be placed in the PostChange( ) method of a text field to display the total number of orders a customer has made as the user scrolls through the customer names. Unfortunately, the value of the added column can be accessed only by use of the Recordset Manager methods. You cannot directly access the value of the custid column by use of the Custid.value syntax.

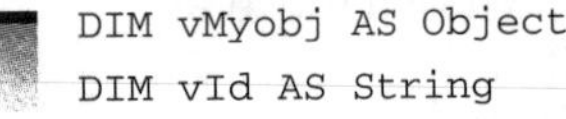

```
DIM vMyobj AS Object
DIM vId AS String

REM Get the pointer to the recordset
vMyobj = GetContainer.GetRecordSet()

REM Get the value of the Custid column added to the RecordSet by way
REM of entering its name in the RecSrcAddCols property of the container.
```

```
vId = vMyobj.GetColVal("CUSTID")

REM Set the value of the order total field to the total number of
REM orders made by the customer

fldTotal.value = &
SQLLookup("select count(*) from orders where custid = "CSTR(vId))
Inherited.PostChange()
```

This example uses the Oracle Basic function SQLLookup, which returns one value from the database based on the SQL statement inside the parentheses. The SQL statement in quotes is appended to the custid value, which is converted to a string using the CSTR Oracle Basic function. The ampersand (&) is Oracle Basic's string concatenation operator. Custid is the column name placed in the RecSrcAddCols property of the form used to traverse through the data in the Custs table. See Chapter 7 or Appendix B for more details on Oracle Basic functions. Figure 8-5a shows the property sheet for the Customers form with Custid added to the RecSrcAddCols property and the property sheet of the fldCName field showing the code added to the PostChange( ) method. Figure 8-5b shows the form in Run-time mode.

RecSrcMaxMem

Use the RecSrcMaxMem property to control memory allocation in an Oracle Power Objects application. When a container's recordset memory requirement exceeds the container's RecSrcMaxMem property, the application begins to cache records to disk. This allows you to query large amounts of data without exceeding the memory of the machine. However, the speed of the application is drastically reduced if the application has to continually fetch and store data to disk.

The default setting for RecSrcMaxMem is 0 (no caching occurs). If the retrieved recordset exceeds the amount of memory available, Oracle Power Objects will cancel the query and report that there is not enough memory.

RecSrcSession

As described at the start of this section, this is one of the two properties that define a recordset object in Oracle Power Objects. It is the name of the session (see "Session Properties" later in this chapter) to which the table entered in the RecordSource property belongs. It is automatically entered into the RecSrcSession property's text field when either a table (or view) icon is dragged and dropped onto a bindable form or when column names from an open Table Editor window are dragged and dropped onto a form. You can set it manually by entering the name of the session in the text field of this property.

a)

Oracle Power Objects

File Edit Object View Run Window Help

Form - frmTotalOrders

Customer Name

fldCName

Telephone Total Orders

PHONE fldTotal

frmTotalOrders Properties

PositionY	0.000 in
RecordSource	CUSTS
RecSrcAddCols	CUSTID
RecSrcMaxMem	0
RecSrcSession	TUB
RowFetchMode	Fetch As Needed

fldCName Properties

PostChange

```
Sub PostChange()
DIM vMyobj AS Object]
DIM vId AS String

REM Get the pointer to the recordset
vMyobj=GetContainer.GetRecordSet

REM Get the value of the CustId column added to the RecordSet by way
REM of entering its name in the RecSrcAddCols property of the container.

vId=Myobj.GetColVal("CUSTID")

REM Set the value of the order total field to the total number of orders
REM made by the customer
fldTotal.value=SQLLookup("select count(*) from orders where custid="&vId)
Inherited.PostChange()
```

b)

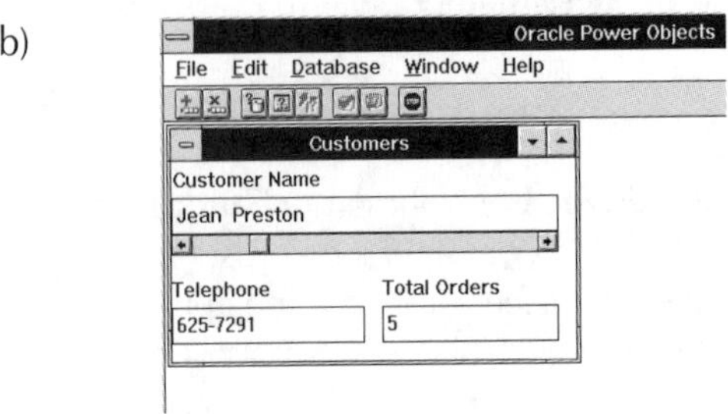

FIGURE 8-5. *(a)Property sheets showing the use of a column added to the RecSrdAddCol property. (b)The Customers form in Run-time mode*

RowFetchMode

This property tells the repeater display and report objects how many records to retrieve at a time when querying the database. There are three choices:

- Fetch as Needed (default)
- Fetch count First
- Fetch All Immediately

Fetch as Needed just retrieves enough records to fill the currently displayed fields and requeries the database if more data is needed as the user scrolls through the data. The problem with this value is that if a scroll bar is used, the scroll button moves erratically, because the scroll bar's range is reset each time a query is made.

Fetch count First solves the erratic scroll button problem by querying the database for the exact count of records available. It then sets the min and max values for the scroll bar appropriately. Next, it retrieves records only as needed, but the scroll button will move appropriately as more records are retrieved.

Fetch All Immediately forces Oracle Power Objects to fill the container's recordset with every record from the database that meets the requirements of the query. This can improve performance as long as there are only a few records to retrieve. However, if there are many records to retrieve, never use this value, as it will fill the computer's memory and freeze the machine. Even if it does not freeze the machine, it will drastically reduce the performance of Oracle Power Objects.

ScrollWithRow

Normally, for each record in the recordset there is a specific value for each control in the container, even though not all of the controls are bound. For example, the value of a derived text control field could be the product of the values of two bound control fields representing the cost of an ordered item and the quantity of items ordered. As the user scrolls through the orders, the unbound control will change according to the cost of the item ordered and the number of items ordered.

However, there are times when you want the value in a control to be unrelated to the rows in the recordset, and it should not change as the user scrolls through the records. For example, a control field can be on the form that represents the amount of discount during a sale. Though the field is not related to the recordset, by default, Oracle Power Objects will recalculate the discount field each time a new record is displayed. Any entered values in the field will be deleted and the discount field value will be set to NULL each time the user scrolls to the next record, forcing the user to reenter the value. However, by setting the discount field's ScrollWithRow property to FALSE, Oracle Power Objects will not recalculate the unbound control and the discount field's value will not change as the user scrolls through the data. The default value for ScrollWithRow is TRUE.

You could set the DefaultValue property for the discount field to a constant value, and the field will always show the default value as the user scrolls through the data if ScrollWithRow is set to TRUE. But this hardwires the value, and you may as well use a constant in any calculation rather than using a text control field. If the ScrollWithRow property is set to FALSE, the form will show the default value when the form is first displayed in Run-time mode, but if the user enters a new value, it will remain as the user scrolls through the records.

Report Properties

These properties are all specific to the different areas of a Report Designer window. Each part of the Report Designer window (see Chapter 6) has its own property sheet, and those specific to reports are described in this section.

FirstPgFtr

This property determines whether a page footer appears on the first page of a report. It is set to FALSE by default. Generally, the first page of a report is the report header, which does not require a first page footer or header.

FirstPgHdr

This property's default value is FALSE. Set this property to TRUE to display the page header on the first page of the report. Generally, the report header is sufficient for the first page.

GroupCol

A report can have data in the detail part of the report grouped according to the values in a specific column in the RecordSource table for the report. Enter the name of the column by which the data is to be grouped into the text entry field of the GroupCol property. This property is on the property sheet for the GroupHeader segment, which you must explicitly add (see Chapter 6) of the report. As an example, if you want all customers of a salesperson to be grouped together in a report, enter Repid in the GroupCol property. As the report retrieves the customer names, all the customers with the same repid will be displayed together in the report. You can add controls to the GroupHeader to display the salesperson's name associated with the group of customers (see Chapter 6). You can add ASC or DESC after the column name to have the column groups ordered in ascending or descending order.

LastPgFtr

This property determines whether the page footer will be displayed on the last page of the report. The default setting is FALSE, but it seems that the last page should have the page footer more often than not.

PageOnBreak

If a report groups data together, set this property to TRUE if you want each new group to start a new page in the report. The default setting is FALSE.

Session Properties

These properties are used to set up and describe the session to which bindable controls are attached. It is through a session object that an application gains access to the data in the database. In addition, through the session, the application can access other objects in the database, such as sequence number generators. As described in Chapter 3, each defined object in the database accessed by the session is shown in an opened session window as named icons. The properties in this section define how the session is to connect to the database, either at design or run time, and describe other attributes of the session.

Three of the connect properties use a connect string to make the connection to a database. The connect string format is shown below. For a more complete description of connect strings, see Chapter 4.

```
database_type:[username/userpassword][@database_address][:connect_options]
```

ConnectType

This property is used to instruct your application when to attach itself to the database through its session object. The three choices are

Connect on Startup	Activate the session as soon as the application begins execution (default)
Connect on Demand	Wait until the application first references the session to establish the database connection
Connect Manually	Manually activate the session by executing the Connect( ) method of the session (see Connect( ) in Chapter 9 for an example of using this property)

The first two values for the ConnectType property allow your application to establish the connection to the database through the session automatically as the program starts up or first needs data from the database. You may have an application with some functions that do not need to access the database, so you would save resources by connecting to the database only when needed.

Use the Connect Manually ConnectType property when you want to explicitly control the activation of a session. For example, you might want to customize your application based on individual users who have different access rights to the database. Thus, you would use the ConnectType property to tell the application to use the Connect( ) method to access the database rather than to connect automatically.

DesignConnect

The DesignConnect property sets the type and location of the database with which Oracle Power Objects will connect when the session connect icon (see Chapter 3, the "Session Window Icons" section) is double-clicked. The syntax for the connect string is described at the beginning of this section. This is the default connect string for the session and is used at all connect times if the DesignRunConnect and RunConnect properties are not set.

DesignRunConnect

There are times when running an application in Design mode that you may want to connect to a different database from the one you have used to add columns to forms. For example, you may use a database that simply has the tables defined but contains no data while designing the application. But to test run the application, you want it to connect to a database that actually contains data. To accomplish this, set the connect string to the desired database to which the application will connect when Run-time mode is activated by pressing the Run button. If this property is not set, the application will use the connect string in the DesignConnect property.

RunConnect

When an application is finished, it may need to use a completely different database or schema (i.e., a different user, such as production rather than development) in the database than the one used during development. In this case, set the connect string in the RunConnect property appropriately. If this property is not set, the application will use the connect string in the DesignConnect property. You can enter a question mark (?) in single quotes to have Oracle Power Objects query the user for a connect string at run time.

Text Properties

These properties are used to set the physical and other attributes of text used in the following objects: static text, text fields, radio buttons, radio button frames, check boxes, combo boxes, list boxes, and pop-up lists. Not all objects using text have all of these properties. All of these properties can be changed during run time by methods triggered by various actions. In the case of the various lists, the properties define the text in the control head label, not the text in the list itself.

ColorText

When you click on the ColorText property, a color palette will be displayed from which you select a color to set the text in static text fields and the labels in radio buttons and check boxes. This property is writable at run time by having a method set the ColorText property to another color (from 1-20, corresponding to the colors shown in the color palette). This is done by using an Oracle Basic expression such as the one shown here:

```
object-name.ColorText=8
```

This code could be put in a PostChange( ) method of a field that checks the new data, and if it meets certain criteria, it could indicate that user action is urgent by changing the color of the text in the label of a button from an initial color of green to red.

FontBold
Set this property to TRUE to have the text in any control that uses text to be displayed in a boldfaced font. This Boolean property can be changed during run time.

FontItalic
Set this property to TRUE to have the text in any control that uses text to be displayed in an italics font. This Boolean property can be changed during run time.

FontName
Any font loaded on the client machine (where Oracle Power Objects is running) can be used as the font for the text objects. Set the name of the font to be used in the text field of the FontName property. Two fonts, Application and System, are always available. Generally, System font is used by default if this property is not set or if the font named in the property is not loaded on the client machine. Thus, Oracle Power Objects handles portability concerns about naming fonts nicely.

FontSize
You set the point size of the font in this property. Any positive integer can be used, but if the font is not a TrueType font or a font handled by Adobe Type Manager, the size of font closest to the entered number will be used. The area for text in a control does not expand to fit text that increases in size because of a FontSize change. Oracle Power Objects will crop the text to fit the area in which the text is to be displayed, thus if the application changes the font during run time, be sure to add code to increase the size(s) of the container(s) as necessary.

FontUnderline
If this property is set to TRUE (default is FALSE), the text to be displayed in the control will be underlined.

TextJustHoriz
There are three choices to determine how the text is to be horizontally justified in static text and text field controls:

Left	The left edge of the text is placed flush against the left edge of the control.
Centered	The text is horizontally centered within the control.
Right	The right edge of the text is flush against the right edge of the control.

TextJustVert

There are three choices to determine how the text is to be vertically justified in static text and text field controls:

Top	The top edge of the text is placed flush against the top edge of the control.
Centered	The text is vertically centered within the control.
Bottom	The bottom edge of the text is flush against the bottom edge of the control.

Chart Properties

A very powerful feature of Oracle Power Objects is the chart control object, which can graphically display data in forms, reports, and user-defined classes. As described in Chapter 5, you can create pie, line, and bar charts in the chart control.

The properties described in this section set the various characteristics for the chart object. Not all properties apply to all chart object types. The type(s) of chart objects the property affects is listed in each separate property description. All charts must have one entry in the ChartXCol property. The line and bar charts can have one or more column names entered in the ChartYCols property. All columns must be contained in the RecordSource defined for the chart object.

For example, you can create a bar graph that shows the actual cost of a tub and the suggested retail price of the tub. Along the X axis, there are two bars, the cost and price, for each type of tub listed along the X axis. A form containing a chart object that shows this relationship is shown in Figure 8-6. When the form is run, Oracle Power Objects will display the chart as shown in Figure 8-7.

ChartAutoFormat

This is a Boolean property that applies to line, vertical bar, and horizontal bar graphs. When set to TRUE, it will automatically size the graph to fit the maximum and minimum values retrieved from the database for the Y axis. If you set this property to FALSE, you must enter the maximum and minimum values in the ChartMaxVal and ChartMinVal properties. The chart in Figure 8-6 has this property set to TRUE, so the min and max value properties are not used.

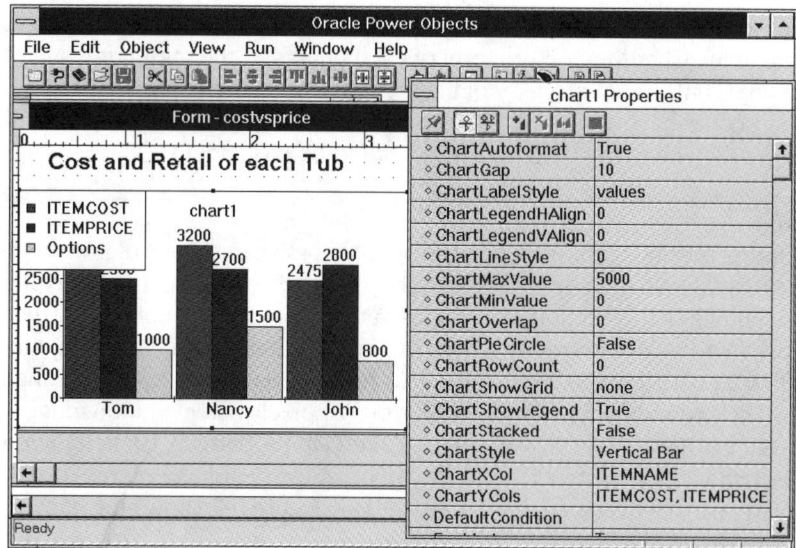

FIGURE 8-6. *The Cost vs Price form with its chart object and the chart's property sheet*

You would set ChartAutoFormat property to False when you use several different charts to display related data in which you want the scale for each chart to be the same. For example, you may want to create a report with a graph showing your company's income by month for five years, using a separate graph for each year. In order for the graphs to accurately reflect the changes between years, each

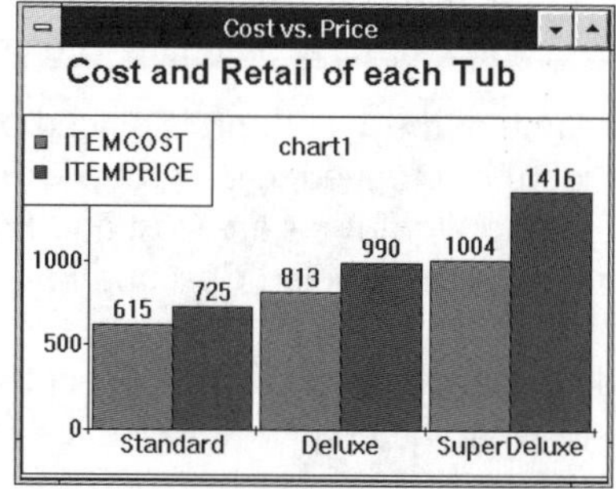

FIGURE 8-7. *The form in Run-time mode*

graph must have the same scale. This is done by setting the maximum value for the five years in the ChartMaxVal property of each chart and the minimum value for all years in the ChartMinVal property of each chart. If you set the property to TRUE, each chart could have a different scale depending on the retrieved max and min values for each chart, and the visual effect could be misleading.

ChartGap

This property sets the number of pixels displayed between groups of bars in the horizontal and vertical bar graphs. It is not used in other chart styles. As explained at the beginning of this section, bar graphs can take multiple Y columns. The chart object displays the Y columns as groups of bars (one bar for each column entered in the ChartYCols property) along the X axis for each value retrieved from the X column. This property does not set the number of pixels between individual bars but between groups of bars. If you set the ChartGap property to 10, as shown in Figure 8-6, the cost vs price example described at the beginning of this section will display ten pixels between each tub's set of bars. Figure 8-7 shows the gaps between the groups of bars.

ChartLabelStyle

A bar chart can have labels for the bars in a vertical or horizontal bar chart. You use this method to set the type of label for the bars. Following are the choices for the bar labels:

- **None** There will be no label over the bar(s).
- **Values** The value of the Y column is placed over the bar(s).
- **Names** The name of the value from the X column is placed over the bar(s). If there is more than one bar for each X value, each bar in the group will have the X value name over it. For example, if the value of the X column is Standard Tub, then each bar in the group above the Standard Tub position in the graph will have Standard Tub as its name.
- **Categories** The name of the Y column is placed over the bar(s). If there is more than one Y column retrieved, each group will have the same named bars. For example, if the Y columns are Cost and Price, each group along the X axis will have two bars labeled Cost and Price, respectively.

When you select the different values, the chart object template in the form will adjust to show a mock-up of what the chart will look like. Figure 8-6 shows values over the bars in the chart template.

ChartLegendHAlign, ChartLegendVAlign

When the ChartShowLegend property is set to TRUE, you use these properties to position the legend box. You cannot arbitrarily place the legend for the graph. Oracle Power Objects places the legend in one of the four corners of the graph, depending on the values of ChartLegendHAlign and ChartLegendVAlign properties. You may use the legend in bar and line graphs.

If the ChartLegendHAlign is greater than zero, the legend is placed on the right side of the chart. If the value is less than or equal to zero, Oracle Power Objects places the legend on the left side of the chart.

If the ChartLegendVAlign is greater than zero, the legend is placed on the bottom of the chart. If the value is less than or equal to zero, Oracle Power Objects places the legend on the top of the chart.

ChartLineStyle

You use this property to set the style of the line in line graphs. It is not used for other chart styles. The choices are solid, dashed, etc.

ChartMaxVal, ChartMinVal

If you set the ChartAutoFormat property to FALSE for line or bar graphs, you must set these values to reflect the minimum value and maximum value you want displayed along the Y axis of the graph. As explained in the beginning of this section, you must use these properties to keep the scale the same for several charts showing related data. Oracle Power Objects ignores these properties when ChartAutoFormat is set to TRUE.

ChartOverlap

Setting this property to a value greater than zero will cause the bars in a group to overlap by the given number of pixels. You should use care with this property when ChartLabelStyle is set to other than None, because the labels may overlap, resulting in the display of an unsightly graph. Its main use is to better accentuate groups of bars when you do not use the ChartGap property. As you can tell, this property applies only to bar graphs.

ChartPieCircle

You have two choices for a pie chart: either a circle or an oblique oblong. Set this property to TRUE to view the pie chart as a circle (as if looking straight down on a pie setting on the floor). When set to FALSE, the chart is displayed as an oblique oblong (as if looking at a pie on the floor a few feet in front of you). Again, it is obvious that this property is ignored by all chart styles except the Pie style.

ChartRowCount

If you want to limit the number of records displayed in the chart, set the number you want displayed in this property. Oracle Power Objects will display the lesser of the number of records retrieved in the query and the number set in the ChartRowCount property. Set this property to 0 (the default value) to display all records queried. This property applies to all styles of charts.

ChartShowGrid

Use this property to have Oracle Power Objects display a grid on line and bar scatter plots. The choices for this property are

None	Display no grid lines on the chart.
Horizontal	Display only horizontal grid lines. The grid lines begin on the tick marks on the Y axis.
Vertical	Display only vertical grid lines. The grid lines begin on the tick marks on the X axis. Vertical grid lines help separate groups of bars on vertical bar graphs.
Both	Display both horizontal and vertical grid lines on the graph.

ChartShowLegend

When set to TRUE, Oracle Power Objects displays a legend that places the name of the column adjacent to a colored box, line, or pie slice that corresponds to the bars, lines, or pie slices representing that column on the chart.

ChartStacked

In some cases, the values retrieved for the Y columns are shown more effectively by stacking the values on top of each other rather than creating a separate bar for each value retrieved. Set the ChartStacked property to TRUE to create a bar graph of this type. For example, if you want to show the total compensation received by a salesperson and, at the same time, show the relative amounts of salary and commission, set this property to TRUE. The ChartXCol property is set to the Name of the salesperson, and the ChartYCols property is set to Sal and Comm. (Most likely you would have to create a view that shows the salesperson's name, salary, and commission. This is because the commission would be a column of values calculated from the total sales the person made, which would be in a separate table. Charts can retrieve values from only one table or view.) This property applies only to bar charts.

ChartStyle

This property is used to set the type of chart to be displayed. By clicking on the property name in the property sheet, Oracle Power Objects displays the following options. The list shows the associated internal values as well.

Vertical Bar	1
Horizontal Bar	2
Line	3
Pie	4

ChartXCol, ChartYCols

These two properties define which columns of data from the RecordSource of the chart object Oracle Power Objects is to display in the chart. ChartXCol defines the X coordinates for the chart, and ChartYCols defines the Y coordinates for the chart. You must designate columns for each property (even for pie charts, though it ignores the ChartYCols property), or Oracle Power Objects will display an error when you try to load a form containing a chart object. ChartYCols is not used for pie charts and takes one or more column values for line and bar charts. When more than one column is used for line graphs, Oracle Power Objects will display a line for each column entered in the ChartYCols property. For bar charts, Oracle Power Objects will display a bar for each Y column at each X position on the X axis. See Figure 8-7 for an example of a chart with two Y columns.

User-Defined Properties

Oracle Power Objects includes a rich set of properties for each of its many objects. However, they cannot meet every need that arises when developing new applications. Thus Oracle Power Objects supplies the capability for the developer to create new user properties and add them to the property sheet of selected objects as you develop the application.

To illustrate the use of this feature, we will add a user property to store the previous value of a constant control object (non-bound text field, radio button, etc). This is to provide an "Undo" feature for non-bound controls. Bound controls have the rollback feature to correct mistakes made when entering data in them.

First, open an application and a form within the application by clicking on the appropriate icons. Click on the Add User Property button in the property sheet toolbar of any currently opened object (the user-properties are global for all applications loaded in the Main window of Oracle Power Objects). This will display the User Properties table as shown in Figure 8-8 (the new property is also shown).

1. If necessary, scroll to the bottom of the table and click in the Name column of the empty row at the bottom of the table and type in the name **OldValue**.
2. Click in the Type column and select **Property** from the pop-up list.
3. Click in the DataType column and select **String** from the pop-up list. We need to make it a string because we want the value to be general. The individual controls will have to convert the string value to the appropriate datatype when resetting the current value to the old value. Alternatively, you could create an OldValue property for each of the datatypes.

Once you close and reopen the user property sheet, the newly added property is listed in the sheet in alphabetical order.

For this example, add the fields and buttons shown in Figure 8-9 to the open form. Now to add the new property to the fldlRate property sheet, simply click and drag the small button at the left of the new property's row and drop it on the opened property sheet. The new property will be inserted into the property sheet in

User Properties

Name	Type	Datatype	Arguments
noteid	Property	Long	
notetype	Property	String	
ntype	Property	String	
OldValue	Property	String	
oppid	Property	Long	
orient	Property	Long	
orientation	Property	String	
owner	Property	Object	
owner	Property	String	
parentFrm	Property	Object	
parobj	Property	Object	
port	Property	Long	
postDoChart	Sub		

FIGURE 8-8. *The User-defined properties and methods table with the new OldValue property*

alphabetical order. User-defined properties have a thick "+" added to the name in the property sheet as shown in the fldIRate text field's property sheet in Figure 8-9.

Now add the Oracle Basic statement

```
self.OldValue=CSTR(self.value)
```

to the Validate( ) method of the control in addition to the validation code as shown in the property sheet for the fldIRate text field in Figure 8-9.

Now place the following code in the Revert button's click method. When pressed, the value of the interest rate field will be changed back to the previous value and the total interest will be recalculated.

```
IF NOT ISNULL(frmCalcInterest.fldIRate.OldValue) THEN
  frmCalcInterest.fldIRate.value = fldIRATE.OldValue
   frmCalcInterest.btnCalculate.Click()
END IF
```

Another very useful user-defined property is used in the calendar class in the notebook example provided with Oracle Power Objects. This is the ReturnObj property in the calendarCls. It enables you to have a control in one form set the

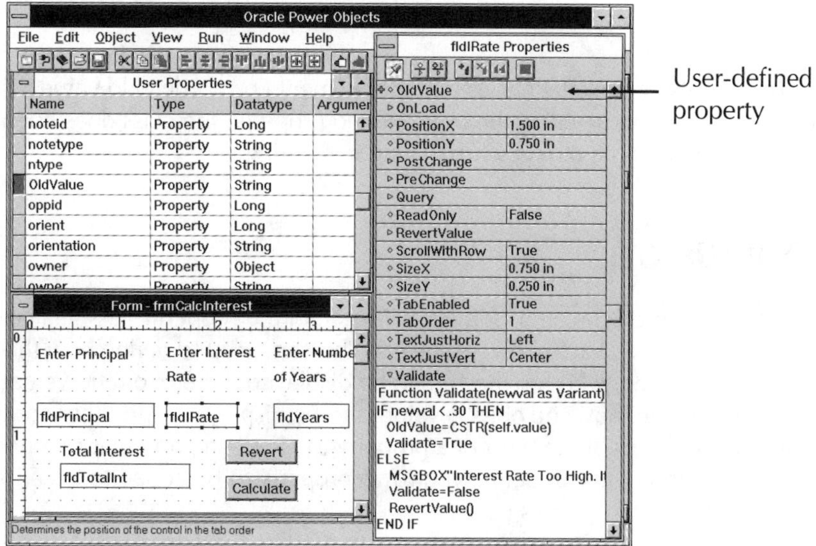

FIGURE 8-9. *User-defined property in the user property table and in a text control's property sheet. Note the code in the Validate method to set the OldValue*

value for a control in a different form without having to know the names of objects. The form in which the control to receive the value resides sets the returnObj property of the second form to the control's reference. Then, when the second form has a value to transfer to the first form, it simply sets the returnObj.value. The code in the first form could be placed in the Click( ) method of a button that opens the second form. It would take the following two lines. This sets the returnObj property to the dateFld object itself, not its value.

```
FormB.calenderCls.returnObj.value = FormA.dateFld
FormB.OpenWindow()
```

The code in FormB to set the dateFld in FormA is placed in the Select button of the calendarCls object and consists of the three lines of code below. The currDate is another user-defined property that stores the currently highlighted date in the calendar in FormB.

```
IF NOT ISNULL(calendarCls.returnObj) THEN
   REM if the returnObj property has a value, then set that
   REM object's value to the
   REM current date stored in the currDate property of the class
   calendarCls.returnObj.Value = currDate.value
END IF
FormB.CloseWindow()
```

This has the same effect as using the statement FormA.dateFld.value = currDate.value, but by using the user-defined property, the class does not need to know the name of the object whose value it is setting.

Conclusion

This chapter has discussed in some detail each of the properties associated with all objects defined by Oracle Power Objects. They are used to define how the objects are to be displayed, whether they are to be displayed, where to retrieve data to set the object's value, how the objects value is to be displayed, and other controlling or display attributes. If there is not a property to handle a particular requirement for your application, you can define your own property to be added to the appropriate objects.

While this chapter has described how to modify and control objects, Chapter 9 will discuss how the objects in Oracle Power Objects react to different events that are triggered by the user, Oracle Power Objects itself, or by Oracle Basic code. The reactions are controlled by functions and subroutines called methods, and every method defined by Oracle Power Objects will be described in Chapter 9.

CHAPTER 9

Methods

In Chapter 8, we discussed how each object defined by Oracle Power Objects, such as a form, repeater display, line, application, etc., possesses properties and methods. Together, these two attributes completely define each Oracle Power Objects object. Methods are the actions take by Oracle Power Objects when triggered by various events. A user clicking on a button, Oracle Power Objects' internal application calls, and an Oracle Basic statement calling one method from another method are all events that can trigger a method. As with properties, the property sheet lists all methods associated with each object.

This chapter describes each method in Oracle Power Objects and, in most cases, gives an example of how to accomplish various tasks using that method. Again, we assume that you are familiar with a programming language, hopefully a dialect of BASIC. We have included comments in the examples that explain what is being done. However, if you need further information to understand the code, Chapter 7 discusses the use of Oracle Basic, and Appendix B is a reference to the syntax of Oracle Basic commands and functions. Chapter 10 is an introduction to the SQL language and can serve as a reference for the SQL statements in the examples.

In general, we use the naming conventions suggested by Oracle, as described in Chapter 7. However, when a text control field or static text label is automatically named by Oracle Power Objects to the name of the column to which it is bound, we do not bother to go back and append the "fld" or "txt" prefix to the text control's name as suggested. (We get lazy at times and use whatever time-saving devices are available.) In addition, the loop counters with a single character as a name do not have the "v" prefix.

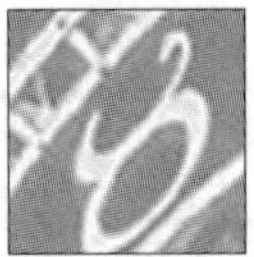

NOTE

GetColVal( ) is a method used frequently in the examples in this chapter. It returns the value of the given column in the recordset as a string. Thus, for numeric or date variables being set to the return value of the GetColVal function, you must use one of the Oracle Basic conversion functions. You will notice that in all the examples, GetColVal is always used in conjunction with a conversion routine unless the column's datatype is String.

Oracle Power Objects Methods

Some methods discussed in previous chapters have had simple Oracle Basic code added to them to open a window on load, to change a property during run time, etc. This section describes the methods in detail and gives some more complicated examples on how to use the methods to perform different functions required in your application.

Most methods have a default action defined by Oracle Power Objects. These default actions are replaced by actions you define when you add Oracle Basic to a method, and thus the default action is not executed when the method is triggered. For example, if you add code to the Connect method, the application will perform your code but will not connect to the database unless your code tells the application how to do it. However, Oracle Power Objects provides a very handy function in Oracle Basic that allows you to call the default code to be executed with your code. This is the Inherited.Method_Name( ) statement discussed in earlier chapters. Simply enter this code in the method in the desired sequence that you want your code and the default code to be processed. Be sure to include any arguments that are passed into the method as arguments in the Inherited.Method_Name( ) Oracle Basic statement. For example, if you add code to a form's PreUpdateCheck( ) method, you must add the statement Inherited.PreUpdateCheck(rownum) to your code, or Oracle Power Objects will raise an error saying Property Unknown.

Explanations of what the code is doing are given for the more complicated examples, but generally the comments in the code and the code itself let you know what is being done. However, if you do have questions about some of the code, see Chapters 7, 10, or Appendix B for detailed explanations of functions, etc., that you may not understand here.

To add code to a method, you must first open its text entry field. To open a method's text entry field, click anywhere on the gray bar containing the method's name. When you open the text entry field, three items are displayed in the first line of the text entry field, namely the name of the method, its declared type if it is a function (discussed later in the chapter in "User-Defined Methods"), and any arguments passed to that method when triggered. The illustration below is a partial property sheet showing a few methods as they are normally displayed and two lines of Oracle Basic code entered in the text entry field of the opened ChgCurrentRec( ) method.

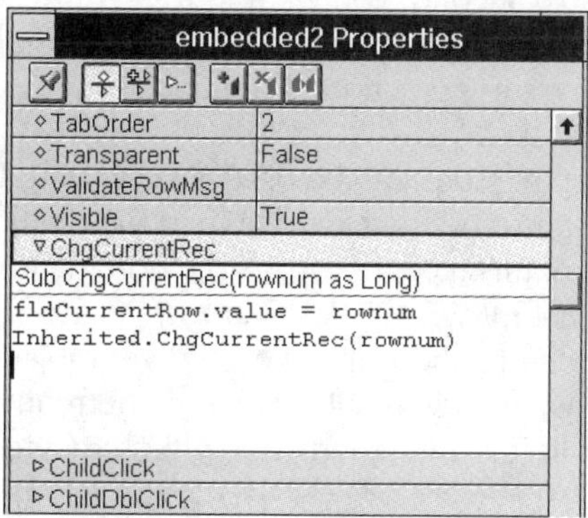

To close the window, simply click on the method name. Oracle Power Objects will automatically close the entry window when you change the focus to another object or close the form containing the object. To identify which methods have Oracle Basic code added to them, Oracle Power Objects adds an ellipsis (...) to the end of the method name on the property sheet. This is shown in the following illustration that shows a few properties and methods of a button. Oracle Power Objects has added the ellipsis to the name of the Click( ) method to which code was added.

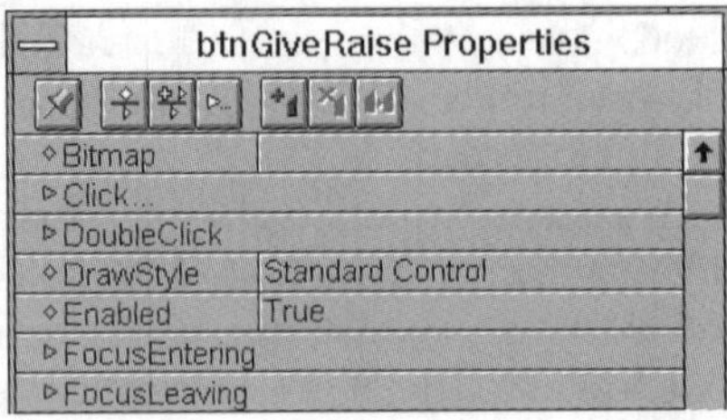

The next several sections of this chapter describe the various groupings of methods, according to their commonality, and describe each method in that group. In most cases, there is an example of the use of the method.

There are generally two ways that methods can be used. The first way is to simply have one method trigger another method by including an Oracle Basic statement similar to frmMyForm.Click( ) in the first method. This code simply tells Oracle Power Objects to trigger the frmMyForm's Click( ) method. You want to call a method from within a separate method for two reasons. First, you want to complete the same action as is done in the other method, to avoid duplicating code in different methods. Second, you want to trigger the default action of the other method, such as retrieving a calculated value or completing some required action, before completing the execution of the code in the current method. Not all methods can be called in this.

The second way that methods can be used is by adding Oracle Basic code to a method to accomplish a user-defined action when the method is triggered. Most of the examples given are of this type, because you won't learn much from an example that simply says frmMyForm.PostChange( ).

Table 9-1 lists all of the methods in Oracle Power Objects. It shows which methods apply to objects, the arguments each method requires (if any), the datatype of the method (if it is a function), and which methods can be called from Oracle Basic code.

Application Methods

The following methods all deal directly with the application itself. Each method must have the word "Application" prepended to the method name. You do not use the application name.

CloseApp( )

This method is used to notify an application that it is going to be closed. The syntax to close the application using Oracle Basic code in a method within the application is different from that of invoking the other methods. The syntax is always the same:

```
Application.CloseApp( )
```

Oracle Power Objects invokes this method when the user selects the Close or Exit menu item from the File menu in Run-time mode.

	Application	Bitmap	Chart	Check Box	Combo Box	Current Row Control	Forms	Frame	Scrollbar	Line	List Box	MB, TB, SL Objects	OLE Object	Oval	Pop-up List	Push Button	Radio Button	Record Set	Rectangle	Repeater Display	Report	Session	Static Text	Text Field	Method Return Type	Call With Oracle Basic	Method Arguments
Application Methods																											
CloseApp	X																								N	Y	
GetFirstForm*	X																								O	Y	
GetFocus*	X																								O	Y	
GetNextForm*	X																								O	Y	CurObject
GetFormByName*	X																								O	Y	FrmName
Initialize	X																								N	Y	
LastWindowClosed	X																								N	N	
SetCursor*	X																								N	Y	CursType
Recordset Methods																											
ChgCurrentRec			X				X													X	X				N	Y	Rownum
FetchAllRows*																		X							N	Y	
FetchToRow*																		X							N	Y	RowNum
GetRecordset			X		X		X				X				X					X	X				O	Y	
GetRowCountAdvice*																		X							L	Y	
GetRowStat*																		X							L	Y	
Record Manager Object Methods																											
AddColumn*																		X							N	Y	ColName, ColType
CopyColFrom*																		X							B	Y	DestCol, SrcObj, SrcCol
DeleteRow			X				X											X		X	X				N	Y	
GetBindColumn*				X	X						X				X		X							X	L	Y	
GetColCount*																		X							L	Y	
GetColName*																		X							S	Y	Column _number
GetColNum*																		X							L	Y	Column_ name

TABLE 9-1. *Predefined Methods for all of the Objects in Oracle Power Objects. (Keys to the return values are B=Boolean, L=Long, O=Object, S=String, 0/F-0 is success anything else is failure, 0/C-0 executed Click( ) once otherwise twice, N=None. An * means that the method is not on a property sheet*

	Application	Bitmap	Chart	Check Box	Combo Box	Current Row Control	Forms	Frame	Scrollbar	Line	List Box	MB, TB, SL Objects	OLE Object	Oval	Pop-up List	Push Button	Radio Button	Record Set	Rectangle	Repeater Display	Report	Session	Static Text	Text Field	Method Return Type	Call With Oracle Basic	Method Arguments
GetColVal*																		X							V	Y	Colname or Colnumber
GetCurRow*																		X							L	Y	
GetRowCount*																		X							L	Y	
InsertRow			X				X											X		X	X				N	Y	
SetColVal*																		X							B	Y	Colnum or Colname, newv
SetCurRow*																		X							L	Y	Rownum
I/O Methods																											
CanPasteFrom Clipboard*		X	X																						B	Y	
CopyToClipboard*		X	X																						B	Y	
PasteFromClipboard*		X	X																						B	Y	
ReadColFromFile*																		X							B	Y	ColNum or ColName, File#
ReadFromFile*		X	X																						B	Y	File#
WriteColToFile*																		X							B	Y	ColNum or ColName, File#
WriteToFile*		X	X																						B	Y	File#
Database Navigation Methods																											
GoNxtLine							X		X											X	X				N	Y	
GoNxtPage							X		X											X	X				N	Y	
GoPos							X		X											X	X				N	Y	Position
GoPrevLine							X		X											X	X				N	Y	
GoPrevPage							X		X											X	X				N	Y	

TABLE 9-1. *Predefined Methods for all of the Objects in Oracle Power Objects. (Keys to the return values are B=Boolean, L=Long, O=Object, S=String, 0/F-0 is success anything else is failure, 0/C-0 executed Click( ) once otherwise twice, N=None. An * means that the method is not on a property sheet* (continued)

	Application	Bitmap	Chart	Check Box	Combo Box	Current Row Control	Forms	Frame	Scrollbar	Line	List Box	MB, TB, SL Objects	OLE Object	Oval	Pop-up List	Push Button	Radio Button	Record Set	Rectangle	Repeater Display	Report	Session	Static Text	Text Field	Method Return Type	Call With Oracle Basic	Method Arguments
Database Link Methods																											
LinkChgCurrentRec			X				X													X					N	Y	Rec, Rownum
LinkPostDelete			X				X													X					N	Y	Rec, Rownum
LinkPostInsert			X				X													X					N	Y	Rec, Rownum
LinkPostUpdate			X				X													X					N	Y	Rec, Rownum, Colnum
LinkPreDelete			X				X													X					N	Y	Rec, Rownum
LinkPreInsert			X				X													X					N	Y	Rec
LinkPreUpdate			X				X													X					N	Y	Rec, Rownum
LinkPreDeleteCheck			X				X													X					N	Y	Rec, Rownum
LinkPreInsertCheck			X				X													X					N	Y	Rec
LinkPreUpdateCheck			X				X													X					N	Y	Rec, Rownum
Database Change Methods																											
LockRow																		X							B	Y	
PostDelete			X				X													X	X				L	N	Rownum
PostInsert			X				X											X		X	X				L	N	Rownum
PostUpdate			X				X											X		X	X				L	Y	Rownum, Colnum
PreDelete			X				X											X		X	X				L	Y	Rownum
PreInsert			X				X											X		X	X				L	Y	Rownum
PreUpdate			X				X											X		X	X				L	Y	Rownum

TABLE 9-1. *Predefined Methods for all of the Objects in Oracle Power Objects. (Keys to the return values are B=Boolean, L=Long, O=Object, S=String, 0/F-0 is success anything else is failure, 0/C-0 executed Click( ) once otherwise twice, N=None. An * means that the method is not on a property sheet* (continued)

	Application	Bitmap	Chart	Check Box	Combo Box	Current Row Control	Forms	Frame	Scrollbar	Line	List Box	MB, TB, SL Objects	OLE Object	Oval	Pop-up List	Push Button	Radio Button	Record Set	Rectangle	Repeater Display	Report	Session	Static Text	Text Field	Method Return Type	Call With Oracle Basic	Method Arguments
PreDeleteCheck			X				X											X		X	X				L	Y	Rownum
PreInsertCheck			X				X											X		X	X				L	Y	
PreUpdateCheck			X				X											X		X	X				L	Y	Rownum
Query Methods																											
OnQuery			X				X													X	X				N	Y	
Query		X	X	X	X		X	X			X		X		X		X			X	X			X	N	Y	
QueryWhere			X				X													X	X				N	Y	Condition String
QueryMasters			X				X													X	X				N	Y	
ReQuery																		X							N	Y	
SetQuery																		X							N	Y	QueryString, UpdateFlag
Session Methods																											
CommitWork																						X			0/F	Y	
Connect																						X			N	Y	
Disconnect																						X			N	Y	
GetSession*																		X							O	Y	
IsConnected*																						X			B	Y	
IsWorkPending*																						X			B	Y	
RollbackWork																						X			0/F	Y	
User Action Methods																											
ChildClick							X													X	X				N	N	ChildObj
ChildDbleClick							X													X	X				N	N	ChildObj
ChildPostChange							X													X	X				N	N	ChildObj
Click		X	X	X	X	X	X	X	X	X	X		X	X	X	X	X		X	X	X		X	X	N	Y	
DoubleClick		X	X	X	X	X	X	X	X	X	X		X	X	X	X	X		X	X	X		X	X	0/C	Y	
FocusEntering		X	X	X	X			X			X		X		X	X	X							X	N	Y	

TABLE 9-1. *Predefined Methods for all of the Objects in Oracle Power Objects. (Keys to the return values are B=Boolean, L=Long, O=Object, S=String, 0/F-0 is success anything else is failure, 0/C-0 executed Click( ) once otherwise twice, N=None. An * means that the method is not on a property sheet* (continued)

	Application	Bitmap	Chart	Check Box	Combo Box	Current Row Control	Forms	Frame	Scrollbar	Line	List Box	MB, TB, SL Objects	OLE Object	Oval	Pop-up List	Push Button	Radio Button	Record Set	Rectangle	Repeater Display	Report	Session	Static Text	Text Field	Method Return Type	Call With Oracle Basic	Method Arguments
FocusLeaving		X	X	X	X			X			X		X		X	X	X							X	N	Y	
MouseDown		X	X	X	X	X	X	X	X	X	X		X	X	X	X	X		X	X	X		X	X	N	N	Xpos, Ypos, Keyflag
MouseMove		X	X	X	X	X	X	X	X	X	X		X	X	X	X	X		X	X	X		X	X	N	N	Xpos, Ypos, Keyflag
MouseUp		X	X	X	X	X	X	X	X	X	X		X	X	X	X	X		X	X	X		X	X	N	N	Xpos, Ypos, Keyflag
PostChange		X		X	X	X	X	X	X		X		X		X		X			X	X			X	N	N	
PreChange		X		X	X	X	X	X	X		X		X		X		X			X	X			X	N	N	
SetFocus		X		X	X						X		X		X		X							X	N	Y	
Constraint/Business Rule Methods																											
RevertValue				X	X			X			X				X		X							X	N	Y	
RevertRow							X													X	X				N	Y	
Validate			X	X	X			X			X				X		X							X	B	Y	Newval
ValidateRow							X													X	X				B	Y	Rownum
Container Methods																											
CloseWindow							X																		N	Y	
CommitForm							X															X			N	Y	
DismissModal							X																		O	Y	Btn
ForceUpdate							X																		N	Y	
GetContainer*		X	X	X	X	X	X	X	X	X	X	X	X	X	X	X	X	X	X	X			X	X	O	Y	
GetTopContainer*		X	X	X	X	X	X	X	X	X	X	X	X	X	X	X	X	X	X	X			X	X	O	Y	
HideWindow							X																		N	Y	
NextControl	Used only by an instance of a Control object. See FirstChild property.																								N	Y	
OpenModal							X																		O	Y	True or False
OpenWindow							X																		N	Y	
RollbackForm							X															X			N	Y	
ShowWindow							X																		N	Y	

TABLE 9-1. *Predefined Methods for all of the Objects in Oracle Power Objects. (Keys to the return values are B=Boolean, L=Long, O=Object, S=String, 0/F-0 is success anything else is failure, 0/C-0 executed Click( ) once otherwise twice, N=None. An * means that the method is not on a property sheet* (continued)

	Application	Bitmap	Chart	Check Box	Combo Box	Current Row Control	Forms	Frame	Scrollbar	Line	List Box	MB, TB, SL Objects	OLE Object	Oval	Pop-up List	Push Button	Radio Button	Record Set	Rectangle	Repeater Display	Report	Session	Static Text	Text Field	Method Return Type	Call With Oracle Basic	Method Arguments
Printing Methods																											
OpenPreview							X														X				N	Y	
OpenPrint							X														X				N	Y	
Miscellaneous Methods																											
CounterGenKey																								X	S	Y	
OMAMsgRecvd							X																				
OMAShutdown							X																				
OLEInsertObject*													X														
OnLoad	X	X	X	X	X	X	X	X	X	X	X		X	X	X	X	X		X	X	X		X	X	N	Y	
UpdateList					X						X				X										N	Y	
Menu and Toolbar Methods																											
DefaultMenu|ToolBar*							X																		N	Y	Menu|ToolbarObj
DoCommand	X						X																		B	Y	CmdCode
GetMenu|Toolbar*							X																		O	Y	
GetStatusLine*							X																		O	Y	
InitializeWindow							X																		N	Y	
SetMenu|Toolbar*							X																		N	Y	Menu|ToolbarObj
SetStatusLine*							X																		N	Y	StatLineObj
TestCommand	X						X																		B	Y	CmdCode
Customize Menus, TB Buttons and Status Line Methods	These methods all work with an object created with the NEW Oracle Basic function. They are not on any property sheet.																										
GetMenuCount												X													L	Y	
GetItemCount												X													L	Y	
GetTBGetCount												X													L	Y	
GetStatCount												X													L	Y	

TABLE 9-1. *Predefined Methods for all of the Objects in Oracle Power Objects. (Keys to the return values are B=Boolean, L=Long, O=Object, S=String, 0/F-0 is success anything else is failure, 0/C-0 executed Click( ) once otherwise twice, N=None. An * means that the method is not on a property sheet* (continued)

	Application	Bitmap	Chart	Check Box	Combo Box	Current Row Control	Forms	Frame	Scrollbar	Line	List Box	MB, TB, SL Objects	OLE Object	Oval	Pop-up List	Push Button	Radio Button	Record Set	Rectangle	Repeater Display	Report	Session	Static Text	Text Field	Method Return Type	Call With Oracle Basic	Method Arguments
GetMenu												X													O	Y	MenuPos
GetMenuItem												X													O	Y	MenuPos, What
TBGetButton												X													O	Y	BtnPos, What
GetStatPanel												X													O	Y	PanelPos, What
ClearMenuBar												X													N	Y	
DeleteAllMenus												X													N	Y	
ClearToolbar												X													N	Y	
ClearStatusLine												X													N	Y	
AppendMenu												X													N	Y	MenuObj
AppendMenuItem												X													N	Y	Label, CmdCode, HelpIndx, AccelStr
TBAppendButton												X													N	Y	CmdCode, Bitmap, Style, HelpIndx
InsertMenu												X													N	Y	MenuPos, MenuObj
InsertMenuItem												X													N	Y	ItemPos, Label, CmdCode, HelpIndx, AccelStr
TBInsertButton												X													N	Y	BtnPos, CmdCode, Bitmap, Style, HelpIndx
InsertStatusPanel												X													N	Y	PanelPos, Width, MaxMsgLen

TABLE 9-1. *Predefined Methods for all of the Objects in Oracle Power Objects. (Keys to the return values are B=Boolean, L=Long, O=Object, S=String, 0/F-0 is success anything else is failure, 0/C-0 executed Click( ) once otherwise twice, N=None. An * means that the method is not on a property sheet* (continued)

	Application	Bitmap	Chart	Check Box	Combo Box	Current Row Control	Forms	Frame	Scrollbar	Line	List Box	MB, TB, SL Objects	OLE Object	Oval	Pop-up List	Push Button	Radio Button	Record Set	Rectangle	Repeater Display	Report	Session	Static Text	Text Field	Method Return Type	Call With Oracle Basic	**Method Arguments**
DeleteMenuItem												X													N	Y	ItemPos
TBDeleteButton												X													N	Y	BtnPos
DeleteStatusPanel												X													N	Y	PanelPos
RemoveMenu												X													N	Y	MenuPos
SysDefaultMenuBar												X													N	Y	
SysDefaultStatusLine												X													N	Y	
SetMenuItem												X													N	Y	ItemPos, What, Value
TBSetButton												X													N	Y	BtnPos, What Value
SetStatDisplayList												X													N	Y	PanelPos, CmdCode, enblStr, disStr, chkdStr, disChkcStr
SetStatusPanelMsg												X													N	Y	PanelPos, MsgStr

TABLE 9-1. *Predefined Methods for all of the Objects in Oracle Power Objects. (Keys to the return values are B=Boolean, L=Long, O=Object, S=String, 0/F-0 is success anything else is failure, 0/C-0 executed Click( ) once otherwise twice, N=None. An * means that the method is not on a property sheet* (continued)

Code added to this method is generally used to clean up before closing the application. The example in the IsWorkPending( ) method illustrates the need to check if there is pending work. If so, the user is requested to save or cancel the work. This way, the user's wish is executed rather than arbitrarily canceling the work by closing the application without asking for confirmation. You could enter the code in the example given in the DisConnect( ) method to log the usage of the application in the CloseApp( ) method. You cannot stop the application from being closed by entering code in this method.

GetFirstForm( )

This method returns the reference to a randomly selected form or report in the application. You use this method in conjunction with the GetNextForm( ) method (described below) to cycle through all forms and reports in an application. For example, if you want every form and report in an application to be opened when the application is started, enter the following code in the applications OnLoad( ) method.

```
DIM vCurObj AS Object
vCurObj = Application.GetFirstForm( )
WHILE NOT ISNULL(vCurObj)
     vCurObj.OpenWindow( )
     vCurObj = Application.GetNextForm(vCurObj)
WEND
```

GetFocus( )

This is strictly an application method. It returns the reference to the control object in the application that currently has the focus or NULL if no object has the focus. Its syntax is

Application.GetFocus( )

You must use the word Application and not the name of the application.

You use this method when you need to know which control has the focus. For example, you could have a user-defined method (in a form serving as a library, which contains several user-defined methods) that is called by various controls. This method could use the GetFocus method to determine which control called it and then act accordingly. The following code is a skeleton of such a method.

```
DIM vCallingObj AS Object
vCallingObj = Application.GetFocus( )
IF ISNULL(vCallingObj) THEN
     statements to handle NULL condition
     EXIT SUB
END IF
SELECT CASE vCallingObj.name
     CASE "fldName1"
           statements to process fldName1
```

```
     CASE "fldName2"
          statements to process fldName2
     CASE ELSE
          statements to handle unknown control
END SELECT
```

GetNextForm( )

You use this method to traverse all forms and reports in an application in conjunction with the GetFirstForm( ) method. This method takes as an argument a reference to a form or report object contained in an application. You retrieve the first object reference to a form or report with the GetFirstForm( ) method discussed above. When the last form or report has been retrieved, GetNextForm( ) returns a NULL. The syntax for the GetNextForm( ) method is

Application.GetNextForm(cur_obj)

See the example in the section on GetFirstForm( ) on how to use this method.

GetFormByName( )

If you know the name of the form to which you want a reference, use this method. The syntax for this method is

Application.GetFormByName(form_name)

For example, if you have a selection of forms in a pop-up list from which the user selects a form to open, the following code will open the form selected. This code would be placed in the PostChange( ) method of the pop-up list.

```
DIM vFrmObj AS Object
SELECT CASE Self.Value
     CASE 1
          vFrmObj = Application.GetFormByName("Form_1")
     CASE 2
          vFrmObj = Application.GetFormByName("Form_2")
     CASE 3
          vFrmObj = Application.GetFormByName("Form_3")
END SELECT
vFrmObj.OpenWindow( )
```

Initialize( )

This method applies only to applications and is called when an application is started. However, Oracle Power Objects triggers it when you run individual forms or reports in Form Run-time mode. This allows the use of global variables by the forms and reports in the application even when the full application is not run during testing. Thus, you should place any code needed by all forms in this method and place code needed only when you run the full application in the OnLoad( ) method.

For example, if you have global variables that must be initialized, you would add the code to this method rather than the OnLoad( ) method. During testing, the forms and reports in the application will have access to the initialized variables rather than just the declaration of the variables.

You can call this method during run time. This can be useful if you need to reset the initial value of global variables.

LastWindowClosed( )

This method is called when the last window in an application is closed but before Oracle Power Objects triggers the CloseApp( ) method. This method calls the CloseApp( ) method by default. Thus, you can keep the application alive by having the LastWindowClosed( ) method reopen a default beginning window or toolbar after all other windows are closed.

If you are using modal dialog boxes, which are not closed but hidden when dismissed, you must close all of those windows before this method can be called. If you close a modal dialog box at the same time it is dismissed, Oracle Power Objects will hang. Therefore, you must close those windows sometime after they are dismissed rather than during the time they are dismissed. This can be done by forcing the closure of any modal windows when the window in which the modal windows were invoked is closed.

An example of code that can be used to ask if the user really wants the application to be closed is shown below.

```
DIM vAns AS Long

REM This example will display a Yes and No button
REM with a "?" icon.
vAns = MSGBOX("Really close the Application?",36)
IF vAns = 1 THEN
   REM Use the default code to close the application
   Inherited.LastWindowClosed( )
ELSE
   REM else simply reopen the beginning window.
   ToolForm.OpenWindow( )
END IF
```

SetCursor( )

This is another application-specific method, and you must use the word "Application" itself, not the application name. This method changes the appearance of the cursor to the type specified by the value given as the argument. The acceptable values are described in Table 9-2. These familiar cursor shapes allow you to change the cursor as needed to clue the user as to what is happening in the system.

```
Application.SetCursor(cursor_type)
```

If you pass any other value (including NULL) to SetCursor( ), the cursor appears as a normal arrow. As an example, the following code changes the cursor to the hourglass or watch until the processing in the code is completed.

```
Application.SetCursor(1)
FOR x = 1 TO 2000
    statements
NEXT x
Application.SetCursor(0)
```

Recordset Methods

Recordset methods are used to work with and obtain a recordset from a query developed by the currently active form. Once Oracle Power Objects loads a recordset, you use various methods to manipulate the records, particularly the

Value	Cursor Appearance
0	Normal arrow cursor
1	The busy cursor (hourglass on Windows, watch on Mac)
2	Text-editing cursor (an I-beam)
3	Open hand
4	Closed hand
5	Up/down arrow
6	Left/right arrow
7	Upper-right/lower-left diagonal arrow
8	Lower-right/upper-left diagonal arrow

TABLE 9-2. *Values Associated with Various Cursor Shapes*

Record Manager object methods. As implied by the name of the group to which these methods belong, these methods apply only to bound controls in forms, embedded forms, repeater displays, and user-defined classes. The recordset retrieved will contain all of the controls' values currently displayed in the form or report from which the recordset object is retrieved, whether or not the control is bound to a database. However, the container must be bound to the database through its RecordSource property. A control not bound to the database is called a "local" control and has no recordset name. A bound control's recordset name is the name of the database column to which the control is bound (not the name property entered in the property sheet). In addition to the bound and local controls, system columns are included in the recordset by the various database drivers to enable them to coordinate the retrieved recordset rows with the corresponding rows in the database. For example, system columns include the Rowid column added by the Oracle driver. You cannot update these columns, but you can get their names and values.

ChgCurrentRec( )

Generally, Oracle Power Objects invokes this method when the user scrolls through the data in the recordset using a scroll bar attached to a form, embedded form, repeater display, or user-defined class. According to the online help, the default action is to move the pointer in the recordset, display the new record, and if a new primary key is in the new record, tell the application about it. (The application needs to know about any change in the primary key to update master-detail relationships.) However, the pointer has already been moved when this method is called. The online help says you must include the Inherited.ChgCurrentRec( ) statement to the code, or the row pointer will not be moved and the new record will not be displayed. (Well, we left the statement out when moving the record with a scroll bar and it works fine; but just to be safe, the statement should be included.)

You use this method in two ways. The first is to have some other method force a form to display a new row in the form's recordset by invoking this method with the row number of the record you want displayed. You must include the inherited ChgCurrentRec in this case.

The second use of this method is to add code to do various preliminary actions before the row is displayed. For example, you could add the following code to change the color of the label of a text field as the user scrolls through the recordset. As the user scrolls through the list of chemicals, the color of the static field that labels the chemical name's text field will change appropriately to show different levels of toxicity based on the toxicity id number. There are two ways to retrieve the value of the toxicity id, which is used to decide which color to use. The first way is to add a text control field bound to the ToxId column in a Chemicals table and use its value for the decision. If you do not want the value of the fldToxId text field to be displayed, toggle the text field's Visible property to FALSE. The second way does not require placing the text control on the form. Instead, you add the ToxId column to the RecSrcAddCol property (see Chapter 8), which places the column in the recordset.

The fldToxId text field's DataSource is the ToxId column in the Chemicals table, and ChemicalName is the label over the Chemical name's text field. The code below will cause the txtChemicalName label to turn red for a toxicity id less than 20 (fatal), yellow for toxicity id between 20 and 30 (hazardous), and green for any toxicity id greater than or equal to 30 (harmless). As stated above, when ChgCurrentRec( ) is called, Oracle Power Objects had moved the pointer to the new position in the recordset, but has not updated the values in the fields. They still contain the values of the previous record. Thus, you must use the recordset object to get the values of the current fields. If you use the values in the fields at the time ChgCurrentRec( ) is called, they will be one record behind (or before) the current record. Remember to include the default method code by using the Inherited statement and pass the rownum argument to the system code.

```
DIM vCurobj AS Object
DIM vCurid AS Long Integer

vCurobj = GetRecordSet( )
vCurid = CINT(vCurobj.GetColVal("TOXID"))

REM invoke the default action for ChgCurrentRec, passing along the row number
Inherited.ChgCurrentRec(rownum)
REM Change the color of the ChemicalName label according to its ToxId value
IF  vCurid < 20 THEN
  txtChemicalName.ColorText = 3
ELSEIF vCurid >= 20 and vCurid < 30 THEN
  txtChemicalName.ColorText = 5
ELSE
  txtChemicalName.ColorText = 8
END IF
```

FetchAllRows( )

If you need all data retrieved at the same time, use this method with its associated recordset object. This method forces Oracle Power Objects to retrieve every record that meets the query requirements and makes them available for manipulation with the other recordset methods. This is a necessary call when you are cycling through all the records and not just those retrieved by default. The example given for the Go methods described in the "Database Navigation Methods" section uses this method. It is necessary to use in this case because only one record is retrieved at a time by default, thus the MoveTo text field will not work properly unless this method is used. You do not need to use this method if the RowFetchMode property is set to Fetch All Immediately.

FetchToRow( )

This method is very similar to FetchAllRows, except it gives you the flexibility to retrieve a limited number of rows. This is required when selecting data from a large table, because Oracle Power Objects could load so much data that it becomes bogged down. It then either quits working or becomes so slow you wish it would quit. Again, this method is not needed if the RowFetchMode property is set to Fetch All Immediately, which you should never use when retrieving from a large table.

As an example, the following code is an alteration of the example given for the Go methods.

```
DIM vPos, vMaxpos AS Long Integer
DIM vMyobj AS Object

REM  Get the current recordset and the row number to which we need to scroll
vMyobj = GetContainer.GetContainer.GetRecordSet( )
vPos = fldNewPosition.value

REM Get the number of rows retrieved and if the number is less than the
REM current number of records in the recordset, then fetch more records
REM (This assumes that the FetchToRow will not crash if asked to fetch
REM  to a row that exceeds the number of total rows to be fetched.)
vMaxpos = vMyobj.GetRowCount( )
IF vPos > vMaxpos
   vMyobj.FetchToRow(vPos+3)
END IF
vMaxpos = vMyobj.GetRowCount( )

REM  Now just make sure the number is within bounds and move to that record.
IF vPos <= 0 THEN
    vPos = 1
    fldNewPosition.value = 1
ELSEIF vPos > vMaxpos THEN
   vPos = vMaxpos
   fldNewPosition.value = vPos
END IF
GetContainer.GetContainer.GoPos(vPos)
```

GetRecordSet( )

This method is used to retrieve the recordset for the given bound container (form, repeater display, lists, etc.) based on the recordset properties (RecordSource and RecordSession or Translation and ValueList) described in Chapter 8. Oracle Power Objects assigns the recordset to a recordset object that can be scrolled through in Oracle Basic code to manipulate the data. In the following example, the invocation of several recordset methods gives employees in a given department a department-wide raise. This example consists of a form with a repeater that shows each employee and his or her salary grouped by department and a button that pops up a small "Give Raises" form. The GiveRaise form contains fields in which a percentage value (fldRaise) and the department id (fldDeptNo) are entered and a button to activate the raise. In the Click( ) method of the Apply button, you enter code to retrieve all of the employees in the entered department. Then you give each one in the department a raise based on the value in the fldRaise text field. This code is shown below and in Figure 9-1.

```
DIM vEmplRecs AS Object
DIM vNumRecs AS Long

REM Set the constraints on the employees form to retrieve only those in the
REM given department.
frmEmployeeList.repEmps.QueryWhere("DEPTID ="&fldDeptNo.value)

REM Get the recordset with the new query constraint and the number of records
vEmplRecs = frmEmployeeList.repEmps.GetRecordSet( )
vNumRecs = vEmplRecs.GetRowCount( )

REM for each employee in the given department set the Salary column value
REM to the salary plus calculated raise
FOR x = 1 TO vNumRecs
REM advance the recordset pointer to the current row number (x)
   vEmplRecs.SetCurRow(x)
   REM make sure there is a value in the salary (wage might be commission
   REM only)
   IF NOT (ISNULL (vEmplRecs.GetColVal("SALARY"))) THEN
       REM calculate the raise and set the salary column to the new value
       vEmplRecs.SetColVal(1, (CDBL(vEmplRecs.GetColVal(1))* &
(1 + fldRaise.value)))
   END IF
NEXT x

REM Set the current row back to one.
vEmplRecs.SetCurRow(1)
GetContainer.CloseWindow( )  'Close the window.
```

This example uses several methods that are discussed more fully below and are only briefly described here. The first two lines of the code declare two variables: the first is the pointer to the recordset object that is to be retrieved, and the second holds the number of records in the recordset. Before you retrieve the recordset, make sure it contains only the employees in the given department. To do this, activate the employee form's (frmEmpByDept) QueryWhere( ) method to set the entered department id as the constraint on the Employee form's query. The next two lines retrieve the recordset containing the employee names and the number of records in the recordset.

```
vEmplRecs = frmEmpsByDept.repEmps.GetRecordSet( )
vNumRecs = vEmplRecs.GetRowCount( )
```

The first line sets the object variable vEmplRecs to the value returned by the GetRecordSet( ) method belonging to the repeater in frmEmpsByDept (not frmEmpsByDept's GetRecordSet( ) method). Note you have to use the full chain of objects to call the correct method. The next line gets the number of records in the recordset by using the object variable Emplrec's own GetRowCount( ) method, not the repeater's method. Now loop through each record using the Oracle Basic FOR statement. The first line in the loop sets the row pointer in the recordset to the

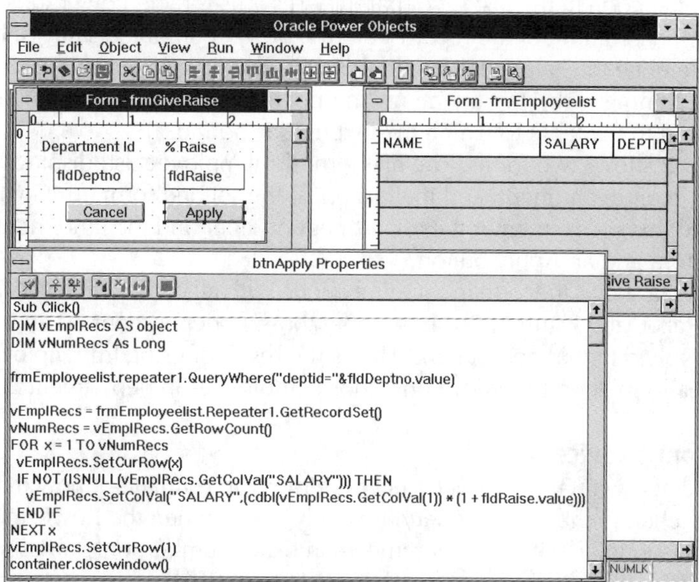

FIGURE 9-1. *Code in the Click( ) method for the Apply button to give all employees in a given department a raise*

current value of the loop counter, "x," by using the recordset's (pointed to by the variable vEmplRecs) SetCurRow( ) method.

Now set up the most important part of this example, which is to give everyone in the department a raise. First, make sure that there is a value in the database with which to work, by using Oracle Basic's ISNULL function. This is good practice, because the salary could be NULL (the salesperson works on commission alone). However, the code would still work, because any operation with a NULL value returns a NULL value, but good coding should not rely on such assumptions. The next line shown below does an awful lot and could be made simpler by using more variables, but it wasn't, to show the power and conciseness of nested function calls.

```
vEmplRecs.SetColVal(1, (CDBL(vEmplRecs.GetColVal(1))* (1 + fldRaise.value)))
```

Parentheses are used to keep things in order. To evaluate the code, start within the innermost parentheses and work from left to right to evaluate the expression within the parentheses. The first thing done is the retrieval of the value of the Salary field. (Note that the order of the columns in the recordset is the reverse of the order of entry, that is, the last field added to a form is column 1.) This value is retrieved using the GetColVal( ) method of the retrieved recordset vEmplRecs and then converting the returned string to a double using the CDBL Oracle Basic function. Next, the fldRaise value is added to 1 and then the two values are multiplied together.

Finally, the code in the last set of parentheses tells Oracle Power Objects to set the number one column of the recordset to the newly computed salary. Note that you can reference the Salary column in this recordset in two ways: the column number (beginning with 1) or the name (in uppercase letters and in double quotes) of the column in the table to which the text field is bound.

Figure 9-2 shows two forms. The first form (frmEmployeeList) displays all of the employees, their department, and their salaries; the second form (frmGiveRaise) displays two text fields to enter the department number and the amount of raise, a Cancel button, and an Apply button.

Figure 9-2a shows the form in Run-time mode with all of the employees displayed before the raise, and Figure 9-2b shows only those in department 20 after the raise has been applied to that department. This is the result of using frmEmployeeList's QueryWhere( ) method to retrieve only those employees in department 20.

GetRowCountAdvice( )

Use this method with a recordset object to retrieve an estimate of how many rows are to be fetched in the current query. It is only useful when the RowFetchMode is set to Fetch Count First. It does not retrieve an exact number, only an estimate. Once you know the approximate number of records retrieved, you can enter code to decide when more records will be required and handle the condition appropriately. For example, the user-defined scroll object described in the "Database Navigation

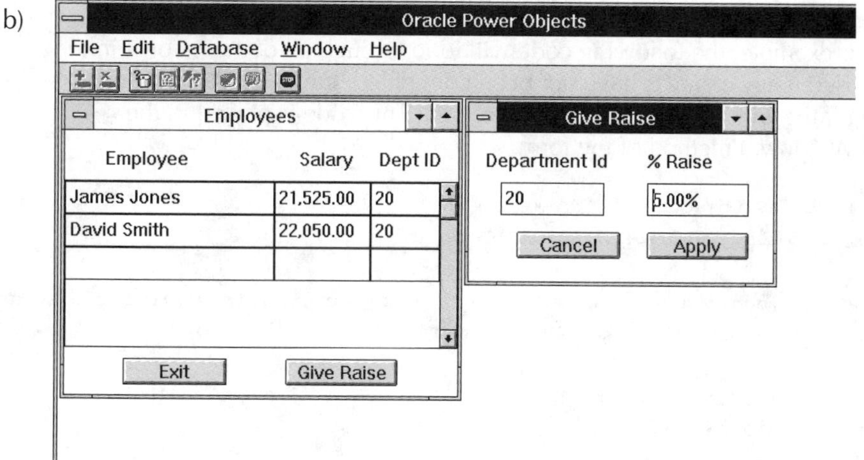

FIGURE 9-2. *(a) All employees listed; (b) Department 20 employees after giving them a raise*

Methods" section would need to know when to retrieve more records when it is used in conjunction with a form bound to a table with a large amount of data.

GetRowStat

This method returns the status of the current row in a given recordset. To use this method, you must have already set a variable to the object by using the GetRecordSet( ) method. You could use this method to check on the status of rows before you closed a window. Or use it to pop up a window to tell the user that a row has already been changed and ask for confirmation before allowing any further changes. This method is not shown on the property sheets because it is a method for the recordset, which does not have its own property sheet.

The integer values returned from GetRowStat( ) include the following:

Value	Meaning
0	The current row is unlocked.
1	The current row is newly inserted into the recordset, and the insertion has not been committed.
2	The current row is locked, but unchanged.
3	The current row is locked and has been changed.
4	Changes to the current row have been flushed to the database.

For example, the following code will loop through all of the records in the recordset; if any changes have not been committed, it will pop up a message box asking if the window should really be closed. This code is placed in the CloseWindow( ) method of the form.

```
DIM vMyObj AS Object
DIM x, vStatus, vNumRecs, vAns AS Integer

REM get the container recordset object, make sure all rows are included and
REM get the number of rows

vMyobj = Self.GetRecordSet( )
vMyObj.FetchAllRows( )
vNumRecs=vMyObj.GetRowCount( )
vAns = 1

REM Loop through the rows in the record set and check the status of
REM each row. If any have uncommitted changes, popup a message box and
REM ask if the window should close anyway. Then break out of the loop.
For x =1 to vNumRecs
   vMyObj.SetCurRow(x)
   vStatus = vMyObj.GetRowStat( )
   IF vStatus = 1 OR vStatus = 3 THEN
      vAns = MSGBOX("There are unsaved changes. Close the Window anyway?", &
           33, "Close Window?")
      EXIT FOR
   END IF
NEXT X

REM Now if the vAns variable still is = to 1, close the window.
IF vAns = 1 THEN
```

```
    Inherited.CloseWindow( )
END IF
```

Record Manager Object Methods

These methods are used to manipulate, update, and generally work with the records in a recordset object.

AddColumn( )

You use this method with a recordset created with Oracle Basic's NEW operator (see Chapter 7 and Appendix B) to add columns to the newly created recordset object. The recordset object must be a nonbound recordset (it does not retrieve its data from a database) and must be empty when this method is used. It takes two arguments: a string as the name of the column, and an integer representing its data type. Predefined integer constants for the datatype are

```
RecDty_String
RecDty_Integer
RecDty_Long
RecDty_Double
RecDty_Date
```

An example of the use of a nonbound recordset and associated methods is to precalculate various data based on a given recordset. For example, it may be advisable to do some time-consuming calculations at startup (when a user is more inclined to be patient) than each time the user scrolls to a new record. The code to do this is shown below, though in this example the calculation is a simple one and would not need to be done before scrolling to the new record. Nevertheless, it can be used as a template when you precalculate more complex data. The recordset object is declared in the declarations area of the application (GLOBAL vCalcObj AS Object). This makes it accessible to any form that needs to keep the nonbound recordset in sync with the bound recordset. The following statements placed in the PostChange( ) method belonging to the bound form's scroll bar will keep the bound form and the nonbound recordset in sync and display the correct result.

```
vCalcObj.SetCurRow(ScrollPos)
frmBndForm.fldResult.value=vCalcObj.GetColVal(1)
```

The following code is placed in the bound form's OnLoad( ) method or the OpenWindow( ) method, whichever is more appropriate.

```
DIM a, b, vResult AS Integer
DIM vCount, index, i AS Long Integer
DIM vBndobj AS Object

REM  Create the non-bound recordset and add one column to it
vCalcObj = NEW RecordSet
vCalcObj.AddColumn("Result", RecDty_Integer)

REM  Get the BoundForm's recordset and make sure all the rows are retrieved
vBndobj = BoundForm.GetRecordSet( )
vBndobj.FetchAllRows( )       'Assuming that the table is not too large.
vCount = vBndobj.GetRowCount( )

REM  Now cycle through every record in the BoundForm and calculate the value
REM  to place in the single column in the vCalcObj non-bound recordset.
FOR i = 1 TO vCount
    vBndobj.SetCurRow(i)
    vCalcObj.SetCurRow(i)
    vCalcObj.InsertRow( )
    a = vBndobj.GetColVal(2)
    b = vBndobj.GetColVal(3)
    vCalcObj.SetColVal(1, a + b)
next i
```

With this code, Oracle Power Objects creates a recordset with data that corresponds to each record in a bound form. It is used just as if the data had been retrieved from a database. You must remember to delete the vCalcObj using the Oracle Basic Delete command when the BoundForm is closed, or some other opportune time. For example, the following statement could be placed in the CloseWindow( ) method of BoundForm. The second statement is necessary only if the BoundForm will be opened again before the application is closed.

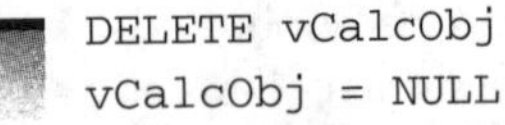

```
DELETE vCalcObj
vCalcObj = NULL
```

CopyColFrom( )

This method gives the developer the ability to allow the end user to copy one column from a recordset to a column in another recordset. For example, the application may create a temporary nonbound recordset in which the end user experiments with the values until they are as he or she desires. The end user then can click an Accept button and copy the experimental values into a bound recordset to preserve the data in the database. You use this method only with a recordset object. Its arguments are

- **dstCol** The destination column in this recordset, given as either the name of the column or an integer representing the position of the column in this recordset.
- **srcCol** The source column as either the name of the column or as an integer representing the position of the column in the source recordset.
- **srcRec** The source recordset for the data.

It returns TRUE on success and FALSE otherwise. Its full syntax is

```
vRecobj.CopyColFrom(dstCol, srcRecSet, srcCol)
```

DeleteRow( )

This is the method that deletes a row when the Delete Row menu item is selected. Other methods using Oracle Basic code can call an object's DeleteRow( ) method. You do not pass it an argument; it deletes the current row in the bound container. Its primary use is to perform some action before or after the deletion. You should always use the inherited function when code is added to this method, or the deletion will not occur. Use this method to verify that according to given rules Oracle Power Objects can delete the row. For example, you can enter code in the DeleteRow( )'s text entry area to check if a product is in a current order. If the product is in a current order, disallow the deletion. Enter the code to do this in the DeleteRow( ) method for the container from which the row is to be deleted. You cannot use field values in an SQL statement, so use temporary Oracle Basic variables to hold the necessary values as shown in the code below.

```
DIM vQuant AS Long
DIM vTemp AS Long

REM get the product id value from the text control field
vTemp = ID.value
REM find out how many of the products are in current orders
vQuant=CLNG(SQLLookup &
("select count(product_id) from order_items where product_id=" &vTemp))
REM if there are any of the products in current orders send an error message,
REM otherwise delete the row
If vQuant > 0 THEN
   frmErrMsg.OpenWindow( )
ELSE
   Inherited.DeleteRow( )
END IF
```

This code will select the number of items that are ordered from the Order_Item table based on the current id in the ID text field (to be realistic, you would normally use a filter on those not yet shipped). If there are no products with that id in the Order_Item table, the row may be deleted, otherwise the message window in Errmsg will be displayed. The Oracle Power Objects online help says the Oracle Basic function SQLLookup returns the datatype of the item it selects. However, according to the user's guide, the return value depends on the database interface driver. For the Oracle driver, its SQLLookup is set to return a string value. Therefore, you must use the CLNG Oracle Basic function to convert the string to a long value. Alternatively, you can use an EXEC SQL statement to accomplish the same task as the SQLLookup function, as shown in the next code example.

If you want to perform this action in a repeater display, note that the ID.value in a repeater display is a range. Therefore, to use a repeater to scroll through the products and select one row from the repeater to be deleted, additional code must be used to retrieve the id from the selected row. The following code performs the same action as the example above but deletes the row from a repeater display instead of the form.

```
DIM vQuant AS Long
DIM vTemp AS Long
DIM vRecobj AS Object
vRecobj = self.GetRecordSet( )
vTemp = CLNG(vRecobj.GetColVal("ID"))
EXEC SQL select count(product_id) into :vQuant from order_items where
product_id=:vTemp
IF vQuant > 0 THEN
   frmErrMsg.OpenWindow( )
ELSE
   Inherited.DeleteRow( )
END IF
```

The main difference between these two examples is the use of recordset methods to get the value from the currently selected row. Note the use of the special name self instead of the name of the repeater. This is one of the powerful features of Oracle Basic that makes reusable code feasible. You do not need to enter the name of the object, which may change if the object is stored in a library (see Chapter 6) and reused elsewhere.

GetBindColumn

This method is used to retrieve a control's position in a recordset that is bound to a database. It returns NULL if the recordset is not bound to a database or the control is not stored in a recordset (the control's container is not bound to the database).

The Record Manager methods, such as GetColVal( ) or SetColVal( ), can use the column number returned by GetBindColumn( ). The syntax is

vColNumber = control_name.GetBindColumn( )

This method is used in the example for the OnQuery( ) method discussed below.

GetColCount( )

This method only works on a recordset object retrieved with GetRecordSet( ) as described above. It simply returns the number of columns in the current record set. Normally, the number is the same as the number of controls (bound or not) in the container plus any system columns added by the appropriate database driver. However, data in additional columns can be retrieved by entering their names in the RecSrcAddCols property of the container. GetColCount( ) will return the number of all columns in the recordset, including the extra ones selected in the RecSrcAddCols property. Normally, you use RecSrcAddCols to add columns that you do not want displayed but from which you need to retrieve data to the recordset using RecSrcAddCols( ).

GetColName( )

There are times when you may know the column order in the recordset but not the name of the column in the database. Or you may just want to cycle through all of the controls in the recordset to retrieve the name of the DataSource for the bound controls. Use this method to retrieve the column's name by passing in the column number as the argument, e.g., GetColName(2). Note that the column order is the reverse of the order of entry.

GetColNum( )

This is the opposite of the GetColName( ) method and is used only on retrieved recordset objects. You pass the name (in all caps and in double quotes, e.g., GetColNum("NAME")) of the column from the database as the argument to the GetColNum( ) method to retrieve the position the column occupies in the retrieved recordset. A possible use of this method is to process only the last few columns in a form. Get the column number of the first column to be processed and then use a FOR loop to process all following columns, as shown in the code below. You could write this code in the Click( ) method of a form. The order of the columns is opposite to the order in which they are added to the form. If you drop an entire table on a form, the position order is the reverse of the order the columns are displayed in the Table Editor window.

```
DIM vRecobj AS Object
DIM vColNum, vCount, x AS Long Integer
```

```
vRecobj =GetContainer.GetRecordSet( )
vCount = vRecobj.GetColCount( )
vColNum = vRecobj.GetColNum("REPID")
FOR x = 1 TO vCount
     MSGBOX"COLUMN "&CSTR(X)&"=  "&vRecobj.GetColVal(x)
next x
```

This little bit of code simply retrieves the column number of the text control field bound to the column Repid. It then has Oracle Power Objects display the values of the Repid column and all of the columns that were placed in the form before the Repid column. Note the use of the Oracle Basic text concatenation operator & to make one sentence that will read something like

```
Column 5 = 378-9670
```

GetColVal( )

This is another of the methods that works only on a retrieved recordset and is not displayed in any property sheet. GetColVal( ) returns the value of the given column as a string and it must be converted to the correct datatype using one of the Oracle Basic conversion functions CDBL, CLNG, etc. It takes as an argument either the number of the column, beginning with 1, or the name of the column in all caps and double quotes, e.g., GetColVal("QUANTITY") or GetColVal(2). This method is used in the example for the GetRecordSet( ) method described above.

Note that this method returns the value in the recordset last retrieved. Thus if the user has modified the recordset after the original query but has not committed the change, the column value in the recordset may not correspond with the column value in the database.

GetCurRow( )

GetCurRow( ) returns the row in the recordset that is currently being displayed in the bound container's text fields or the currently selected row in a repeater display, list, pop-up list, or combo box. This method can be used to retrieve the row number to synchronize a control object in one bound container with the display in another bound container's repeater display. This works as long as the two containers retrieve data that are related, that is, for each row in one container, there is a matching row in the other container. The following code will get two recordsets, one from a repeater display showing the descriptions of products and the other from a separate form with just a single text field displaying the id of the product. They both access the same table Products. When the user presses the Show Id button in the Descriptions form, the ProdId form will pop up and display the id of the product whose description is displayed in the currently selected row in the repeater display. This code is entered in the btnShowid button's Click( ) method. Once the frmProdId form is opened, the id will change whenever the user clicks on a description in the repeater display. (Obviously this is a contrived example, but it does show how you can use the GetCurRow( ) method.)

```
DIM vTemp as LONG
DIM vReptrObj AS Object
DIM vFormObj AS Object

vReptrObj = repDescriptions.GetRecordSet( )
vFormObj = frmProdId.GetRecordSet( )
vTemp = vReptrObj.GetCurRow( )
vFormObj.SetCurRow(vTemp)
frmProdId.OpenWindow( )
```

GetRowCount( )

This method simply gets the number of rows in the recordset object retrieved with the GetRecordSet( ) method. One of its main uses is to obtain the number of the rows to be used as the limit for a loop that cycles through each record in the recordset. The example in GetRecordSet( ) method described above uses this method.

InsertRow( )

When the user presses the Insert Row icon, selects the Insert Row menu item, or enters data in the empty row at the end of the recordset displayed in controls in a container, this method is called. It inserts the data into the record above the current row and sets the recordset pointer to the new row. The newly entered data is not entered into the database until the Commit button is pressed, which calls either the CommitWork( ) or CommitForm( ) methods. If you add Oracle Basic code to this method, you must include the Inherited.InsertRow( ) statement, or the data will not be inserted into the recordset.

You may add Oracle Basic code to the InsertRow( ) method to process additional data either before or after the insertion takes place. The placement of the Inherited.InsertRow( ) statement determines when the additional processing takes place, that is, before insertion if the code is placed before the statement and after otherwise. For example, this method may pop up a new form in which the user enters additional required data each time an insertion is made. This just takes the following two lines of code placed in the InsertRow( ) method of the form in which data was entered.

```
Inherited.InsertRow( )
frmMoreData.OpenWindow( )
```

SetColVal( )

Use the SetColVal( ) method to update the data in the columns in the current recordset object, retrieved with the GetRecordSet( ) method. Any data entered in this manner is not added to the database until Oracle Power Objects triggers either the CommitWork( ) or CommitForm( ) method, generally by the user pressing the Commit icon in the toolbar (see "Session Methods" later in the chapter for more information on CommitWork( )).

The arguments for the method is the column (as either the column name in caps and double quotes or the column number in the recordset) and the value to be entered into the recordset, i.e., SetColVal("NAME", "George") or SetColVal(1, 45.78). This method is used in the example for the GetRecordSet( ) method described above. When changing a column that is not bound to the database, you must be careful that it is not a derived value or the data it displays may not correspond to the values from which it is derived. In addition, because the column is not bound to the database, you must use the column number, which can be retrieved with the control's GetBindColumn( ) method, in the SetColVal( ) method. If the row in the recordset is locked, SetColVal( ) returns FALSE to indicate that the change was not made otherwise it returns TRUE.

SetCurRow( )

When it is necessary to cycle through the records in a recordset object retrieved with the GetRecordSet( ) method, use SetCurRow( ) to move the pointer to each succeeding record. You give it the number of the row to which the pointer is to move. Record position numbers begin with 1. This method is used in the GetRecordSet( ) example given above. It simply moves the pointer to the next record and the "Give Raises" code then updates the Salary column in that record.

I/O Methods

These methods are used to copy OLE or bitmap objects from or to files or the Clipboard and writing or reading column data from a recordset to or from files. These methods are internal methods and are not on the property sheet of the object. For OLE and bitmap objects use the Object.Method_Name( ) syntax, and for the column methods use the RecordSet_obj.Method_Name( ) syntax in Oracle Basic code. The file used in these methods must be opened in binary mode with the appropriate read or write permission set. The methods can read or write from or to any point in the file, so take care to be sure the file pointer is in the correct location. When a file read/write method is finished, Oracle Power Objects positions the file pointer at the byte following the last byte of data read or written to the file. You can store other data in the file in any format you desire, but you need to keep track of where in the file the object data is located. They all return TRUE if the call is successful and FALSE if not.

CanPasteFromClipboard( )

This is a simple function that returns either TRUE or FALSE depending on the current data stored on the Clipboard. If you want to paste data from the Clipboard into an OLE object, use this method to verify that the data on the Clipboard is an OLE object. The following code uses this and other Clipboard methods. This method works the same for a bitmap object but checks to verify that the data on the Clipboard is in BMP format.

```
IF oleMyObj.CanPasteFromClipboard( ) THEN
    oleMyObj.PasteFromClipBoard( )
ELSE
    MSGBOX "Clipboard does not contain an OLE object"
END IF
```

CopyToClipboard( )

Copies the OLE or BMP data from the OLE or bitmap object to the Clipboard. It replaces any existing data on the clipboard and returns TRUE if the copy is successful, otherwise it returns FALSE. When it returns TRUE, a call to the PasteFromClipBoard( ) method should succeed.

PasteFromClipBoard( )

Use the CanPasteFromClipboard( ) method to verify (though verification is not required) that the data on the Clipboard is appropriate for the control, and then copy the object from the Clipboard into the OLE or bitmap control with this method (see the example for CanPasteFromClipboard( )above). For an OLE control, this is equivalent to selecting the Paste Special menu item in the Edit menu. For a bitmap control, it is equivalent to selecting the Paste item in the Edit menu.

ReadColFromFile( )

Use this method to retrieve data for a given column from a file in which data was written using the WriteColToFile( ) method. It is used only with a recordset object retrieved with the GetRecordSet( ) method or one created with the Oracle Basic command, NEW. The arguments for this method are the column (either an integer representing the position of the column in the recordset or the name of the database column in all caps and in double quotes) and the integer value returned when the file was opened. Examples of the syntax are vRecobj.ReadColFromFile("NAME", 2) or vRecobj.ReadColFromFile(3, 2). You can read any type of data from the file into appropriate columns. Oracle Power Objects automatically converts an integer column into a double column or a char column into a Varchar2 column as well as other appropriate conversions. This method can read Long and Long Raw data into appropriate columns, but the data for these two types must have been written from matching columns.

An example of using this method is to read a column of data (written from a separate database or table into the file) into the current database. The code to do this is shown below. It is entered in the Click( ) method of a button on a form in which the name of the file, the table, and the column name is entered before the button is activated. The code to activate the button is shown in the example for the Enabled property in Chapter 8 and is entered in the PostChange( ) method of the ColFld text control field.

```
DIM vFName, vTName, vCName, vSelectStr AS String
DIM vColObj AS Object
DIM vCount, vStart, x, vFileNum AS Long Integer

REM retrieve the names of the file from which to read the data. (it
REM must have been written by WriteColToFile( )), the table, and the column
REM name.
vFName = fldFileName.value
vTName = fldTable.value

REM The column name must be in caps for use as arguments to some methods
REM used below, so use the Oracle Basic function to change all letters to
REM uppercase.
vCName = UCASE(fldColumn.value)

REM make a command string (to be used in the SetQuery method.)
vSelectStr = "select "&vCName+" from "+vTName

REM now use the Oracle Basic NEW operator to make a new recordset
REM tied to the "tub" session.
vColObj = NEW DBRecordset(tub, TRUE)
IF NOT ISNULL(vColObj) THEN
   REM query the database for the given column and make the rows updatable
   vColObj.SetQuery(vSelectStr, TRUE)
   vColObj.ReQuery( )
   REM 'Oracle Basic function to get lowest available file number
   vFileNum = FREEFILE
   REM open the file previously written to by WriteColToFile( )
   OPEN vFName for Binary access read lock read as # vFileNum

   REM get the number of rows in the recordset to append the new
   REM data to the end, but before the automatic blank column.
   vCount = vColObj.GetRowCount( )
```

```
   IF vCount = 0 THEN
      vCount = 1
   END IF
   vStart = vCount
   REM set the current row to the end of the data and insert a new row
   vColObj.SetCurRow(vCount)
   vColObj.InsertRow( )

   REM Now while there is data in the file read it into the newly
   REM inserted row
   DO WHILE vColObj.ReadColFromFile(vCName, vFileNum)
      REM update the vCount and insert a new row.
      vCount = vCount + 1
      vColObj.SetCurRow(vCount)
      vColObj.InsertRow( )
   loop
   REM Now delete the row which was inserted but not filled by the
   REM ReadColFromFile method
   vColObj.DeleteRow( )

   REM disable the ReadBtn until a new column name is entered
   ReadBtn.Enabled = FALSE
   Inherited.Click( )

   REM now commit the recordset data to the database, close the file
   REM and delete the object
   vColObj.GetSession( ).CommitWork( )
   CLOSE # vFileNum
   DELETE vColObj
   vCount = vCount - vStart
   MSGBOX "Added "&vCount+" records and data to table " &
+vTName+" in column "+vCName
ELSE
   MSGBOX "could not create recordset"
END IF
```

ReadFromFile

When you have written an OLE or bitmap object to a file and want to retrieve it, use this method to read the object into the appropriate control from the given file. The ReadFromFile( ) method reads in OLE objects only from files written to by the WriteToFile( ) method. However, this method can read any bitmap file in BMP format into a bitmap (or picture) object.

WriteColToFile( )

There may be times when you need to store or send a single column of data to other sites or just for a selective or temporary backup. You use this method to write the data from the given column to a file, which can be read by another application using ReadColFromFile( ). The arguments for this method are the column (either an integer representing the position of the column in the recordset or the name of the database column in all caps and in double quotes) and the integer value returned when the file was opened. Examples of the syntax are myvRecobj.WriteColToFile("NAME", 2) or myvRecobj.WriteColToFile(3, 2). You can write to file any type of data, including Long and Long Raw. An example to write the values of a single column to a file is shown below. The code is entered in the Click( ) method of a form that first requires the name of the file, table, and column name before the Write Column button is active. See the code shown in the example for the Enabled property in Chapter 8 for an example of using the Enabled property.

```
DIM vFName, vTName, vCName, vSelectStr AS String
DIM vColObj AS Object
DIM vCount, x, vFileNum AS Long Integer

REM retrieve the names of the file from which to read the data. (it
REM must have been written by WriteColToFile( )), the table, and the column
REM name.
vFName = fldFileName.value
vTName = fldTable.value

REM The column name must be in caps for use as arguments to some methods
REM used below, so use the Oracle Basic function to change all letters to
REM uppercase.
vCName = UCASE(fldColumn.value)

REM make a command string (to be used in the SetQuery method.)
vSelectStr = "select "&vCName+" from "+vTName

REM now use the Oracle Basic NEW operator to make a new recordset
REM tied to the "MoonLight Data" session.
vColObj = NEW DBRecordset(mldata, TRUE)
IF NOT ISNULL(vColObj) THEN
   REM query the database for the given column and make the rows
   REM non-updatable by setting the update flag to FALSE. Retrieve all rows.
   vColObj.SetQuery(vSelectStr, FALSE)
   vColObj.ReQuery( )
   vColObj.FetchAllRows( )
```

```
    REM get the number of rows in the recordset to write to file.
    vCount = vColObj.GetRowCount( )

    REM if there are records then open the file
    IF vCount > 0 THEN
      REM 'Oracle Basic function to get lowest available file number
      vFileNum = FREEFILE

      REM open the file in Binary mode
      OPEN vFName for Binary access write lock write as # vFileNum

      REM Now for every record, write the column value to the opened file
      FOR x = 1 TO vCount
         vColObj.SetCurRow(x)
         vColObj.WriteColToFile(vCName, vFileNum)
      next x
      REM disable the ReadBtn until a new column name is entered
      ReadBtn.Enabled = FALSE
      Inherited.Click( )

      REM now close the file and delete the object
      CLOSE # vFileNum
      DELETE vColObj
ELSE
    MSGBOX "No records were retrieved"
END IF
ELSE
   MSGBOX "Could not make a new Recordset"
END IF
```

WriteToFile( )

Use this method to write an embedded OLE object or a bitmap (in BMP format) from the respective controls to the specified file (identified with the integer returned when the file was opened in write mode).

Database Navigation Methods

These methods are used inside of forms, embedded forms, user-defined classes, and repeater displays to move the pointer to the appropriate location in the recordset. You can enter Oracle Basic code to be processed before or after the action indicated by the method name takes place or to stop the default action altogether. In other words, if you want an action to take place before the user scrolls to a new record, place the Oracle Basic code before the Inherited.Method_Name( ) statement in the Go method. Place the code after the Inherited.Method_Name( ) if you want the code to be processed after the action takes place. To stop the action, leave the Inherited.Method_Name statement out of the Oracle Basic code. If you enter code in these methods to update a control on the form before the inherited statement, you will not see the change until you return to that row in the recordset. This is the result of Oracle Power Objects loading the data into the column in the current row of the recordset, not the row to which you are going. In other words, if you put the statements

```
field2.value = field3.value
Inherited.GoNxtLine( )
```

in the container's GoNxtLine( ) method, Field2 will be blank when you scroll forward one record after the form first comes up. This is because Field3's value in the first row is loaded into Field2's column in the first row. Oracle Power Objects then executes the inherited code and scrolls forward to the next record in the recordset, which, as yet, has no value for Field2 to display. When you scroll back to the first row, you will see the data in Field2.

To access these methods in Oracle Basic, you use the <container_name>.method( ) syntax and not the <recordset_object>.method( ) syntax.

A very common use for these methods is to create a user-defined class to scroll through the records of a bound container and use it on other forms instead of a scroll bar. An example of a scrolling class that uses all of these methods is given below. The completed class and a form to which it is added to scroll through order items from the Order_items table is shown in Figure 9-3.

To simplify the creation of the scroll class, add one button to the class form and add the code necessary to move to the desired location as shown in the btnBack Click( ) method in Figure 9-3. Adjust its size appropriately. Then copy and paste the button three times and align and space the buttons nicely. It is then a simple matter to change the code in the Click( ) method of each button to make them work as desired.

The text field fldMoveTo, which uses the GoPos( ) method, requires more code to check for boundary conditions before moving to the new row as shown in Figure 9-3 and the listing below.

```
DIM vRecobj AS Object
DIM vPos AS Long
DIM vMaxpos AS Long

REM Set the various variables. Remember, this is a class so the first container
REM is the class form, not the object containing the scroll class object.
vRecobj=GetContainer.GetContainer.GetRecordSet( )
```

```
vPos=self.value
vMaxpos = vRecobj.GetRowCount( )

REM make sure the user entered valid data
IF vPos <= 0 THEN
     vPos = 1
     Self.value = 1
END IF

REM  GoPos takes values starting with 0 for the positions, so subtract 1
IF vPos <= vMaxpos THEN
     GetContainer.GetContainer.GoPos(vPos - 1)
ELSE
     GetContainer.GetContainer.GoPos(vMaxpos -1)
     self.value = vMaxpos
END IF
Inherited.PostChange( )
```

This code is entered in the fldMoveTo text field's PostChange( ) method. The code simply retrieves the value entered in the field, verifies that it is valid, and then moves the pointer to the desired row in the recordset.

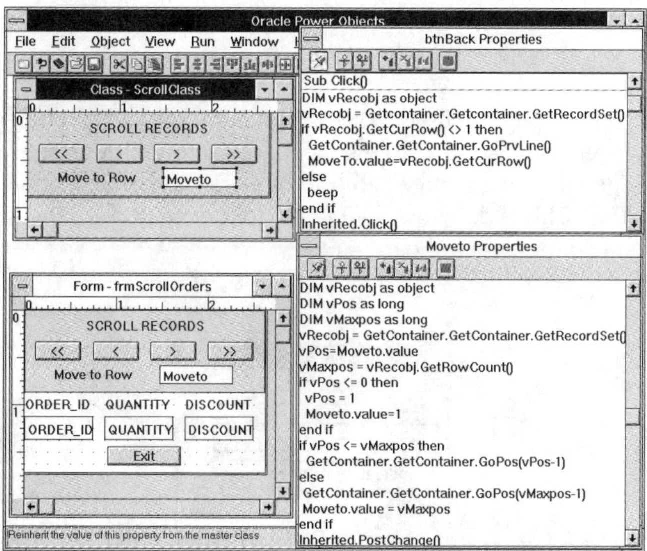

FIGURE 9-3. *User-defined class scrollclass and a new form to which it was added*

Note that for this class to work properly, it needs to have all the records retrieved immediately (the RowFetchMode property set to Fetch All Immediately). Otherwise, more code is needed to retrieve more rows as the user scrolls to the end of the data in the current recordset (see the example in the FetchToRow( ) method's description).

The final form in Run-time mode is shown in Figure 9-4.

GoNxtLine( )

Move to the next line or row in the records retrieved by the form unless it is the last record, in which case it does nothing.

GoNxtPage( )

This method moves the record pointer through a whole page (the number of records retrieved at a time) of records. This method is more useful for repeater displays than text control fields, because forms with bound text fields seem to retrieve just one record at a time, while a repeater display retrieves ten records by default and more if there are more than ten repeater fields to fill.

GoPos( )

You use this method to move the pointer in the form's recordset to the given position. Unlike most other methods that operate on rows in a recordset, the first row is 0 and not 1. Thus in our example above, you must subtract 1 from the position to make it work correctly. The syntax is

```
object_name.GoPos(NewPosition)
```

This method is commonly used to sync an outer form and an embedded form together. The outer form uses a visible scroll bar to scroll through the recordset, and the embedded form uses an invisible scroll bar. The visible scroll bar drives the invisible scroll bar. This is done by placing the following code in the PostChange( ) method of the main form's scroll bar.

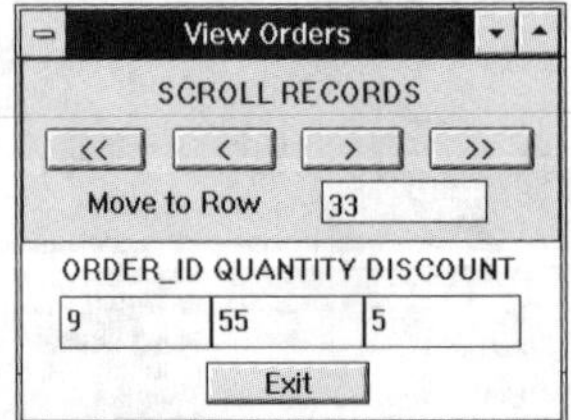

FIGURE 9-4. *The View orders form using scrollclass to move through the records*

```
embedded_form_scrollbar.GoPos(self.ScrollPos)
```

This statement first retrieves the scroll bar position of the outer form and then tells the embedded form's scroll bar to move to the same position. You can sync two separate forms with their own windows in the same way. (See the ScrollPos property in Chapter 8.)

GoPrvLine( )

This method is used to move the pointer to the record just before the current row if the current row is not the first record.

GoPrvPage( )

Similar to GoNxtPage( ) except displays the previous page if possible.

Database Link Methods

Oracle Power Objects uses the following methods to keep the data in master-detail relations in sync. They also provide the developer the opportunity to add code to methods that are triggered before or after a particular action, such as an insert or a delete, takes place. Any Oracle Basic code to modify the methods is entered in the detail container's methods, not the master container's methods. Most of these methods have as an argument the *rec* object, which is the object pointer to the recordset object of the master bound container. It can be used with the Record Manager methods, such as rec.SetCurRow( ) to modify or obtain values from the master recordset without having to call the GetRecordSet( ) method.

LinkChgCurrentRec( )

When the row changes in the master recordset (as controlled by a scroll bar or as directed by Oracle Basic), Oracle Power Objects uses this method to tell the detail records that they need to requery the database using the new values being displayed in the new master record as the foreign key. The syntax for this method is

```
Detail Form.LinkChgCurrentRec(rec, rownum)
```

The first parameter, rec, is the master container's recordset and the second, rownum, is the number of the newly displayed master record. You can access the recordset of the master form by using the object rec.

You use this method when you need to have the application perform some action each time the master row changes. For example, suppose you want the application to display the static text title (proddesc) over the products column of a repeater (detail) in different colors as different classes of products (master) are displayed. For example the colors could be red for flammable, yellow for toxic, etc., as the user scrolls through the different classes of products. (It would be nice if you could change the color of the text in the controls themselves, but this is not one of the properties available.) The code is written in the detail form's (generally a repeater) LinkChgCurrentRec( ) method, not the master's method. The code to do this is shown below.

```
Sub LinkChgCurrentRec(rec as Object, rownum as Long)
DIM vProdId AS Long
vProdId = CLNG(rec.GetColVal("ID")
IF vProdId = 3 THEN
   frmProdClass.txtProdDesc.ColorText=8
ELSEIF vProdId = 2 THEN
   frmProdClass.txtProdDesc.ColorText=8
ELSE
   frmProdClass.txtProdDesc.ColorText=8
END IF
Inherited.LinkChgCurrenRec(rec, rownum)
```

In this example, the title for the product description static field, txtProdDesc, is on the frmProdClass master form, just above the detail repeater display. As the user scrolls through the product classes, the txtProdDesc text will change color according to the id of the product class. The form is shown in Figure 9-5 with the property sheet for the repeater.

NOTE
If the id column is not displayed in the master container, then add it to the recordset for the master records by entering its name in the RecSrcAddCol property of the master container.

LinkPostDelete( )

This method is called after the records in both the master and detail bound containers are deleted when a master record is deleted. This is the result of setting the LinkMasterDel property to Delete Cascade in the detail bound container part of the master-detail relation. Because the deletion has already been done, you cannot stop the delete with this method. It is used to do postprocessing, such as closing a Delete Records window after the deletion, or to reset other windows.

LinkPostInsert( )

LinkPostInsert( ) is called after a record is inserted into the recordset of the bound container. You cannot stop the insertion with this method but can use it to accomplish postprocessing. For example, Oracle Basic code entered in this method can reset the current row pointer in the recordset or display a message indicating

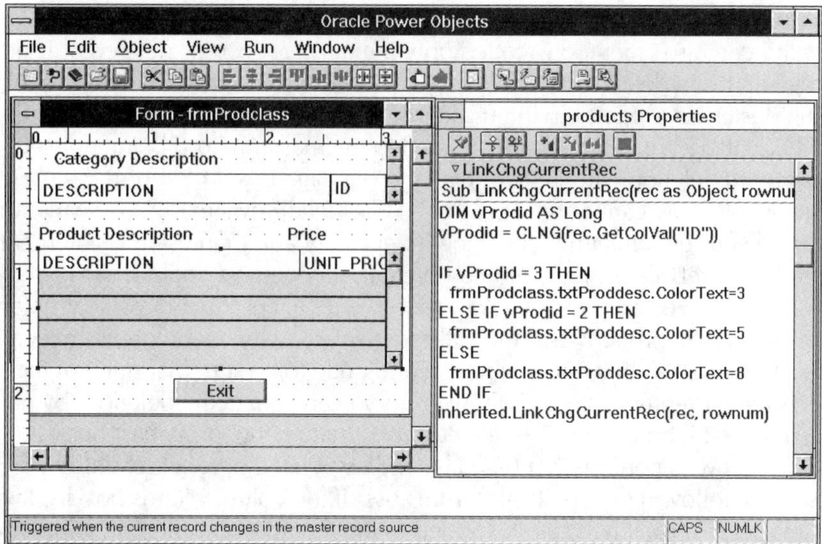

FIGURE 9-5. *Master-detail relationship with code to change the txtProdDesc static field*

that the insertion took place and should be committed to the database by pressing the Commit button.

LinkPostUpdate( )

Just like the other LinkPost methods described above, this method is used to process code after the indicated action has occurred. It cannot be used to stop the action. And like the LinkPostDelete( ) method, it is called after a master record has been updated and the foreign key in all associated detail records has been updated. This is dependent on LinkMasterUpd property set to Update Cascade in the detail container of the master-detail relationship. It can be used to have different forms requery the database to update their recordsets if they may have been changed by the data modified in the current bound container.

LinkPreDelete( ), LinkPreInsert( ), LinkPreUpdate( )

These three methods are called before the indicated action takes place. However, unlike the following three methods, you cannot stop the action with these methods. They are triggered in the bound container containing the detail records of a master-detail relationship. They really don't seem to be too useful in that any preaction processes should be added to the LinkPre<action>Check methods, and any postaction process should be added to the LinkPost<action> methods.

LinkPreDeleteCheck( )

This detail container method is called only if a master record is deleted. It is not called when just a detail record is deleted. It performs the integrity checks set by the LinkMasterDel property in the master container. If it is set to Refuse if Children Present and there are detail records related to the master record being deleted, the master record deletion will not take place. A message box will inform the user that the "Master row cannot be deleted because detail rows exist." You can add code to do your own integrity checking if necessary and then use the statement Inherited.LinkPreDeleteCheck( ) to complete the processing, including the default integrity checks. For example, if a user tries to delete a product classification and the LinkMasterDel property is set to Cascade Delete (which would automatically delete all products in that class), you can add code to be sure that none of the products are currently in stock. If there are, you can cancel the deletion (by not processing the Inherited.LinkPreDeleteCheck( ) statement), or at least open a Yes-No window to confirm that the class and associated products should be deleted. The following code illustrates this use. If the column "Id" is not displayed in the master record, it needs to be added to the recordset by entering it into the RecSrcAddCol property of the master container.

```
DIM vCount AS Long
DIM vId AS Long
id = CLNG(rec.GetColVal("ID")

REM Note the '&' at the end of the line. This is a line continuation
REM character to allow you to put multiple lines in an EXEC SQL statement.
EXEC SQL select sum(inventory) into :vCount from Products where     &
Product_Category_Id=:vid

REM Check for NULL which is returned from EXEC SQL if no Products
REM have the product_description being deleted.
IF ISNULL(vCount) THEN vCount = 0 END IF
IF vCount = 0 THEN
   Inherited.LinkPreDeleteCheck(rec, rownum)
   LinkPreDeleteCheck=TRUE
ELSE
   MSGBOX "Category has product in inventory. Cannot Delete"
   LinkPreDeleteCheck=FALSE
END IF
```

This code retrieves the id of the product and then issues a SQL statement to retrieve the number of products in the inventory table. If there are none, the deletion is allowed to proceed, otherwise an error box is displayed.

LinkPreInsertCheck( )

You can stop insertion of master rows if necessary by adding code to this method and setting LinkPreInsertCheck to FALSE. It is not triggered when rows are added to the detail recordset but when a row is added to the master recordset by using the Insert Row menu item in the Database menu. It can be used to complete the addition of data to the record being inserted if there are additional columns set in the RecSrcAddCol property in the master container. For example, if the id is not displayed but is included in the RecSrcAddCol property, query for the maximum id in the product_category_id table, increment it by one, and set the id of the row to be inserted to that value. Then add the Inherited.LinkPreInsertCheck( ) and LinkPreInsertCheck = TRUE statements to complete the insertion of the row.

LinkPreUpdateCheck( )

This method is called if the LinkMasterUpd property is set to Update Cascade in the detail bound container and a master record is updated. It can be used to see that other forms that are open are updated by displaying a message to the user stating that records have been updated and current displays may be out of date. If the work is committed, the other forms may need to issue the QueryForm( ) method or have the user press the Query button on the toolbar to update their displays. This method is not called if just a detail record is updated. It is triggered on the first character typed into the control. Subsequent characters after the first do not trigger the method.

Database Change Methods

These methods are used when altering the recordset of any form, embedded form, user-defined class, or repeater display. The work is not fully entered into the database until the CommitForm( ) or CommitWork( ) methods are either called by Oracle Basic or triggered by the user when the Commit or RollBack button is pressed. Most of these methods involve deleting, inserting, or updating the current row in the recordset. All of these methods have the rec parameter, which is the recordset object of the bound container triggering the method. This variable can be used to work with the recordset to retrieve values, change the current row, etc., such as rec.GetColVal("NAME").

LockRow( )

This method allows you to lock the current row in the recordset for whatever reason until any changes to the record are committed to the database or rolled back. It can be used to lock certain rows in the database (not just in the recordset) at all times by invoking the LockRow( ) method on a row in a recordset during the execution of the OnLoad( ) or the Commit( ) methods of its container. Thus the

LockRow( ) method will be called whenever the container is loaded into memory or the work on other rows in the recordset is committed. This can be applied to a row in a table that is the default row to which records in other tables refer if they have not had other explicit data bound to them. For example, the data in the first row in a table of aircraft types could be set blank. Then a table in the database that has a nonNULL field that points to an aircraft type can be set to the blank record when the aircraft type is unknown. This ensures that the data entry person at least tried to find an aircraft type rather than just forgot to enter it. You would want to keep this row locked at all times so that no one inadvertently deletes or modifies it.

Because you probably do not want the blank row displayed in a form just to keep it locked, you need to create a recordset not bound to a form. This is done using Oracle Basic's NEW DBRecordSet(session) statement. An example of locking the blank row using a database bound recordset and its methods is given below. The code is placed in the OnLoad( ) method of a form that updates aircraft information. Alternatively, it could be placed in the OnLoad( ) method of the application to be sure no other form in the application can access the blank row.

```
DIM vBndrec AS Object

REM Create the database bound recordset
vBndrec=NEW DBRecordSet(airsession)

REM Populate the recordset with the single blank row, set the row and lock it.
vBndrec.SetQuery("Select * from AirCraftType where id = 0", FALSE)
vBndrec.SetCurRow(1)
vBndrec.LockRow( )
```

When using an object created with the NEW operator, you must remember to delete the object when finished with it, or it will continue to use up RAM memory even if it is no longer used, as long as the application is running. Because of this, the vBndrec variable in the code above should be a global variable that can be deleted when the form is closed by entering the statement DELETE vBndrec in the CloseWindow( ) method of the aircraft update form.

PostDelete( ), PostInsert( ), PostUpdate( )

These three methods are invoked after the indicated action has taken place. You cannot stop the action by overwriting the default code. However, they can be used to notify the user that the change has taken place by popping up a message window, changing the color of a row indicator, etc. "Housekeeping" chores can also be invoked, such as causing other forms using the same recordset to update their displayed values by use of the form.Query( ) method. However, forms using a different recordset from the one just changed, but retrieving data from the same table, cannot see the change until the Commit button is pressed or the

CommitWork( ) or CommitForm( ) method is invoked to permanently make the changes in the database.

PreDelete( ), PreInsert( ), PreUpdate( )

Before a delete, insert, or update is performed, the appropriate method is called. However, when the method is called, it is assumed that the action has already been confirmed and the action cannot be stopped. These methods can be used to prepare the application for the change that is about to take place, especially if the preparation is required before the change is made. Otherwise it may be more appropriate to use Post<action> methods. An example of an action that would be appropriate for either post- or predelete or update is one that updates fields that depend on the changed data but are being displayed from a different recordset. For example, one form may have a field that displays a customer's total expenditure and another form that displays all orders. If an order amount changes or the order is deleted, then the form showing the total expenditure needs to be informed of the action in order to display the correct value. The example of code below updates the value of a field in a form that refers to data in the current row of a repeater display whenever the current row in that repeater display is deleted. This code is designed to handle a delete by changing the value of the field in the form to blank if the deleted record in the repeater display is the only one in the recordset. It sets the value to the record following a deleted row if the deleted row is not the last one in the recordset, or to the previous row if the record is the last one in the recordset. Very little modification is needed to make it fit an update or insertion.

```
DIM vTotal AS Long
DIM vRecobj AS Object

REM get the recordset and number of records in the repeater display
vRecobj=repProducts.GetRecordSet( )
vTotal=vRecobj.GetRowCount( )

REM rownum is the variable passed into the method designating the
REM row being deleted.
IF rownum = vTotal THEN
REM The only record in the recordset.
   IF vTotal = 1 THEN
      frmProdClass.field3.value =""
   ELSE
   REM The last record in the recordset. Get the previous row's
   REM value and set the field.
      vRecobj.SetCurRow(rownum-1)
      frmProdclass.field3.value =vRecobj.GetColVal("DESCRIPTION")
```

```
    END IF
    ELSE
    REM The deleted row has records following it. Get the next value and set
    REM the field.
    vRecobj.SetCurRow(rownum+1)
    frmProdClass.field3.value =vRecobj.GetColVal("DESCRIPTION")
END IF
```

Note that the current row in the recordset is the row to be deleted. The cursor will not be moved to the next or previous record until the PostDelete( ) method is processed.

PreDeleteCheck( ), PreInsertCheck( ), PreUpdateCheck( )

These methods are processed before the action has been completed. Thus you use these methods to verify that the action should or should not take place based on rules developed according to the requirements of the application. The rules may enhance database integrity checks or verify business rules, such as not deleting a product that is on order or other criteria. If the action is approved to proceed, you must include the Inherited.Pre<action>Check( ) statement in the additional code in order for the action to be processed properly by Oracle Power Objects.

These methods cannot be used to verify the newly entered data in a field because they are called before the new information is accepted. Thus when the methods are called, the value in the field being checked is the original value, not the newly entered value. These methods are best used to verify that other conditions are met before an update to a control is made. The following example has Oracle Power Objects check a customer's credit rating before allowing an order to be made on credit. Two conditions must be met before the update is allowed for a change. The charge box on the form must be checked and the customer's credit rating must be TRUE. As the sales rep begins to enter a value in the fldAmount control, Oracle Power Objects checks the two conditions. If OK, the update can proceed. Otherwise, it displays a message informing the sales rep that the customer has poor credit. If the customer is paying cash, the program allows the processing to continue.

```
DIM vRating AS Long
DIM vRecobj AS Object
DIM vCid AS Long

vRecobj = custamounts.GetRecordSet( )
vCid =CLNG( vRecobj.GetColVal("CUSTID"))

REM get the credit limit allowed for the customer.
```

```
EXEC SQL select CredRate into :vRating from custs where custid=:vCid

IF (vRating and chkCharge.value) or chkCharge.value=FALSE THEN
     Inherited.PreUpdateCheck(rownum)
     PreUpdateCheck = TRUE
ELSE
     MSGBOX "Customer has poor credit"
     PreUpdateCheck = FALSE
END IF
```

The Pre<action>Check( ) methods return a TRUE or FALSE, so you must set the method to the proper value in order for the calling process (either Oracle Power Objects or another method) to know whether to proceed with the update or not. These methods apply to the container that has the recordset, not to the container's individual text fields in which the changes are made.

Query Methods

The following methods are used to populate or repopulate recordsets in a bound container by causing the container to requery the database and thus refresh the data in its controls. This is required when the form is first opened and any other time a different form changes data that is used by the form. Some of these methods are called automatically by Oracle Power Objects under certain conditions (such as when the form is first loaded into memory to be displayed), and all can be called using Oracle Basic.

OnQuery( )

OnQuery( ) is automatically called whenever a form queries the database. It is this method that reloads the values in the bound controls and derived fields and updates the range of the scroll bar after the Query( ) method loads the recordset. Its purpose is to allow you to specify exactly how you want certain fields to be updated, whether to allow the update, or to trigger other actions after the form's recordset has been repopulated by the Query( ) method. An example of code that changes the format mask of a field depending on the maximum value of all rows in the fldTotals column is shown below.

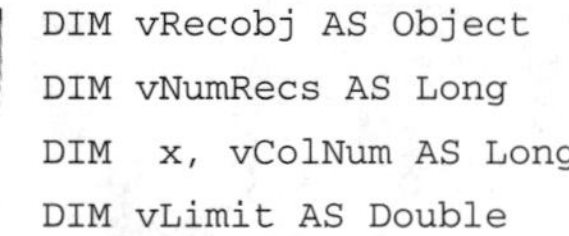

```
DIM vRecobj AS Object
DIM vNumRecs AS Long
DIM  x, vColNum AS Long
DIM vLimit AS Double

REM get the recordset for the form and make sure all rows are retrieved
```

```
vRecobj = self.GetRecordSet( )
vRecobj.FetchAllRows( )

REM get the record set column number of the non-bound container
vColNum=fldTotals.GetBindColumn( )

REM set the default format for the totals field to standard
fldTotals.FormatMask="Standard"

REM get the number of rows and begin cycling through the recordset
vNumRecs = vRecobj.GetRowCount( )
FOR x = 1 TO vNumRecs
    REM set the row and get the value of the Totals column using the vColNum
    vRecobj.SetCurRow(x)
    vLimit=vRecobj.GetColVal(vColNum)

    REM Now if the value is not NULL, compare it to the MAX size and if greater
    REM then set the formatmask of the Totals field to scientific and exit.
    IF NOT (ISNULL (vLimit)) THEN
        IF vLimit > 9999.0 THEN
            fldTotals.FormatMask="Scientific"
             EXIT FOR
        END IF
    END IF
NEXT x

REM set the row back to the beginning and finish the OnQuery method
vRecobj.SetCurRow(1)
Inherited.OnQuery( )
```

This code will cycle through every record in the container's recordset. It retrieves fldTotals' column number in the recordset to use to retrieve its value as Oracle Power Objects cycles through the recordset. If the value is greater than a predefined limit, the FormatMask for the fldTotals field is changed to Scientific so that the values are displayed in a format suitable for the size of the data. If it is not too large, then Oracle Power Objects will continue to display the values in standard format.

Query( )

This method is automatically called when a form is opened. Additionally, Oracle Power Objects runs the Query( ) method any other time the form queries records, including when Query( ) is called through Oracle Basic code. If any code is added to this method, the Inherited.Query( ) statement must be placed in the code, or the controls in the form will not be loaded with data from the database. When this method is called, Oracle Power Objects performs the following actions, the most significant is that any pending work will be committed.

- The Query( ) method flushes (commits) all changes to the database.
- Oracle Power Objects queries the table or view set in the recordset property, using the condition set through the DefaultCondition property.
- The values for all bound controls are refreshed.
- All derived values on the container are recalculated.
- Oracle Power Objects updates the range of any scroll bar used to scroll between records.
- Oracle Power Objects requeries the recordset object for the bound container or list control, if the record source is not shared.
- Query( ) sets the pointer to the first row in the recordset.

Query( ) is used whenever a form needs to update its recordset because the table from which it gathers data is changed. The data may be needed for bound controls or derived controls that use a query in the DataSource property. For example, if formA deletes a row from the Products table in the database and formB uses that table in a derived control, then formA would need to have formB requery the database to update the value in the derived control. The following Oracle Basic statement could be put in the ChildPostChange( ) method of formA.

```
formB.Query( )
```

Now any time a control in formA is changed by deletions, updates, or insertions, the controls in formB will be updated.

QueryWhere( )

There are times when you may need to populate a recordset based on a condition unknown at load time. You can use this method to accomplish this task. The syntax for its use is to simply enter the condition as a WHERE clause as the argument to the method. You do not use the **where** keyword, however. An example of its syntax when using Oracle Basic code to requery the recordset in another form, using a customer's id from a text field as a filter, is shown here:

```
Otherform.QueryWhere("CUSTID = "&fldCustid.value)
```

If the customer's id is 104, this will cause Otherform to requery the database using the WHERE clause "Where CUSTID = 104" and reset its controls appropriately.

The QueryWhere( ) method is described and used in the example for the GetRecordSet( ) method described earlier in this chapter.

QueryMasters( )

The QueryMasters( ) method is a shortcut to have all top-level containers in memory that hold master records be requeried. After QueryMasters( ) is triggered in an open form, Oracle Power Objects triggers the Query( ) method for the main form (the one that creates the window) and each embedded master form (that is, the embedded form is not linked to the main form) contained in the main form. The OnQuery( ) method is then called recursively on all subforms, setting the recordset row for each form back to the first record and refreshing all bound containers in both the detail and master forms. The purpose of QueryMasters( ) is to update top-level containers holding master records. This method is triggered when the form is loaded into memory and when the Query button on the toolbar is pressed. When the Query button on the toolbar is pressed, the QueryMasters( ) method is triggered in every open form in the application.

You can call QueryMasters( ) to initiate a query on master forms to update all detail forms contained in the master form. However, when you trigger the method in this way, the Query( ) method is triggered only in the embedded master forms contained in the master form in which the QueryMasters( ) method is triggered. It does not update other open forms in the application, as is the case when the Query Database button is pressed. To call the QueryMasters( ) method using Oracle Basic, use the following syntax:

```
master_form_name.QueryMasters( )
```

Requery( )

This method is used only with a recordset object. It is not on the property sheet, and you cannot use it with the GetContainer.requery( ) syntax. It must be used with an object retrieved with statements such as vRecobj = GetContainer.GetRecordSet( ) or vRecobj = new DBRecordSet( ). The GetContainer.Query( ) method is the easiest to use to requery the database for a bound form, but if the form's recordset object has been retrieved for other use, either method works. Requery( ) is most often used in conjunction with the SetQuery( ) method. The SetQuery( ) method loads the SQL statement to be used by the object to query the database. The Requery( ) method executes the statement and loads the object with the data retrieved. See the example for the ReadColFromFile( ) method.

SetQuery( )
This method is used with a recordset object not bound to a form but bound to a database. It is used only on an empty recordset created with the Oracle Basic statement vBndobj=NEW DBRecordSet(session). (See Appendix B for the full syntax for this function.) This method populates the empty bound recordset with values retrieved from the database using the SQL query contained in the string argument to the method. It takes an optional argument to state whether the data in the recordset is updatable (records can be changed). If the recordset is updatable, the query cannot use *. See the description of the LockRow( ) method for an example using SetQuery( ).

Session Methods

As described in Chapter 4, a session is composed of a database name and the connect string that is used to connect to the database. The methods in this section are all used to directly interface with or retrieve information about the database with which the session is associated. Several of these methods are invoked in Oracle Basic by using the name of the session as the prefix to the method. Others use a session object attached to the recordset. For example, if the session name is Marble, the method can be called with the following statement.

```
Marble.<method_name>( )
```

However, this hardwires the name of the session and makes the code difficult to reuse. Thus to make the code nondependent on a given session or if the session name is not known, use the session object retrieved with the GetRecordSet( ). GetSession( ) methods. For example, if all the work in the session referenced by FormA is to be saved to the database, the following code is used.

```
DIM vSessobj AS Object
vSessobj = FormA.GetRecordSet( ).GetSession( )
vSessobj.CommitWork( )
```

The three lines above can be combined into one Oracle Basic statement as shown below.

```
FormA.GetRecordSet( ).GetSession( ).CommitWork( )
```

Each of the methods associated with a session is described below.

CommitWork( )

The CommitWork( ) method is used only in Oracle Basic code to commit any pending changes that have been made by all forms using the same session. It is not listed on any property sheet. It first flushes any pending updates to the database and then issues the SQL command COMMIT. The CommitWork( ) method saves only the changes made for the given session. A form can have objects attached to two different sessions. In that case, only the changes in the given session's recordset will be made. You invoke this method as described at the beginning of this section.

Its most common use is to commit changes to the database at the will of the user. For example, enter Oracle Basic code in the Click( ) method of a Commit or Save button on a form to save any changes to the database by clicking on the button. See the example in the description of the IsWorkPending( ) method below. The CommitWork( ) method applies only to the top-level containers.

Connect( )

This method is called by Oracle Power Objects to connect a session to the database. You invoke this method when you double-click on the connect icon in the session window or when you call it with Oracle Basic using the syntax described at the beginning of this section. It gives you the opportunity to add code to be executed before the connection is made. For example, you can place code in this method to verify that the end user has the proper user name and password to connect to the database. Or you can have Oracle Power Objects retrieve needed global data for the application from the database after the connection is made. An example of not connecting until the user has entered a valid user name and password is given in the code below. First set the ConnectType property of the session to Connect Manually. Create a form in which the user enters a user name/password string with an OK button. Place the following code in the Click( ) method of the OK button. This code retrieves the connect string from the session and compares the value entered by the user. If they are the same, the Connect( ) method is called, otherwise, an error message is displayed.

```
DIM vConstr AS String
DIM vStr2 AS String

REM get the user/password string entered by the user
vConstr = fldUserName.value
REM get the connect string from the Session's RunConnect property
vStr2 = Tub.RunConnect

REM if the user/password string is in the connect string then go ahead and
REM connect. This is not a real secure method but it serves as an example. You
REM could add more checks such as start position and length of string, etc.
```

```
REM to make it more secure.
IF instr(vStr2,vConstr) > 0 THEN
    Tub.Connect( )
    REM Make sure it is connected then bring up the main menu
    IF Tub.IsConnected( ) THEN
        CompForms.OpenWindow( )
        GetContainer.CloseWindow( )
    ELSE
        MSGBOX"user/password OK but connection failed"
    END IF
ELSE
    REM the entered string is not valid.
    MSGBOX "Bad user/password: try again"
    IF Tub.IsConnected( ) THEN
        REM the session was already connected so disconnect it.
        Tub.Disconnect( )
    END IF
END IF
```

The form and the code in the OK button's Click method is shown in Figure 9-6.

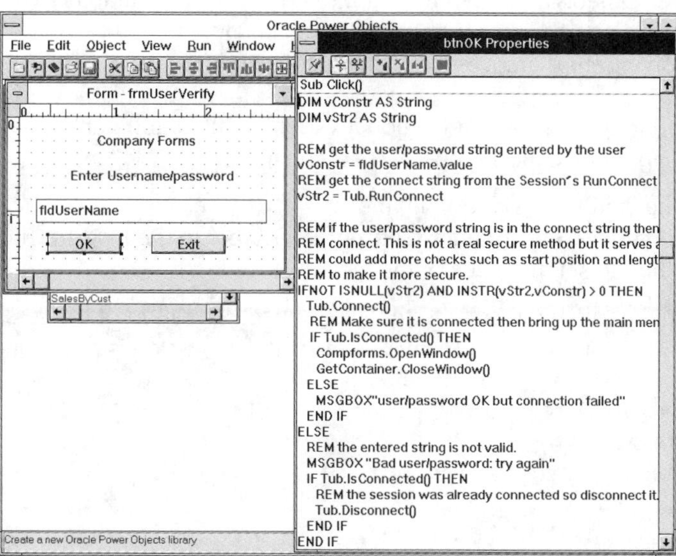

FIGURE 9-6. *The UserVerify form and the code entered in the OK button's Click( ) method*

DisConnect( )

This method is called when the session is disconnected from the database. It is called by double-clicking on the connected icon in the session window, or it is called automatically when Oracle Power Objects' Run-time programs are exited. This method is not called at Design time. Thus to test any Oracle Basic code placed in this method, you must compile the application and run it either as a stand-alone or as a run-time object to be executed using the Oracle Power Objects Run-time program. If you add no code to the method, any uncommitted changes to the database will be rolled back when the disconnection is completed. You can call this method with Oracle Basic statements as described at the beginning of this section.

A common use of this method is to check for uncommitted changes and query the end user if the work should be committed. Another example of using DisConnect( ) in a session is to log the user name, form name, and date every time a form is exited. You might want to do this to gather statistics on which forms are being used and by whom. This example gives the opportunity to show the use of global variables used between sessions and applications. (You could add the following code to the ExitBtnClass's Exit button's Click( ) method to accomplish the same task. This method would simplify the necessary code in that a global variable would not be needed.) To do this example, the database to which you are connected must contain the ProgramUsage table, which has the following fields: Handle (long integer), Username (string 30), Used_date (date), and Progname (string 30). You can create this table in Oracle Power Objects as shown in Chapter 4 or with your database's interface programs. You also need a sequence called Usageinc.

The following steps are needed to make this work.

1. In your application, add a global variable called gblPname as shown in the Tubapp application property sheet in Figure 9-7.
2. In the ExitBtnClass, add the line **gblPname=GetContainer.GetContainer.label** to the ExitBtn Click( ) method to set the value of the global variable.
3. Add the following code to the DisConnect( ) method of the session used by the application. The property sheet for the Tub session is shown in Figure 9-7.

```
DIM vUsername AS String
DIM vCurdate as Date
REM gblPname is global and set by the application which is disconnecting

vCurdate = NOW( )
REM - get login name of current oracle user
EXEC SQL select upper(user) into :vUsername from dual

REM The following SQL statement inserts the data into the database.
```

```
REM the '&'is Oracle Basic's line continuation character
EXEC SQL insert into ProgramUsage &
values(Usageinc.nextval, :vUsername, :vCurdate, :gblPname)

REM Because the data is being placed into the database directly,
REM you must explicitly commit the change
EXEC SQL commit

REM Now disconnect from the database
Inherited.Disconnect( )
```

An important note here is that you must commit the insertion of the usage data before you DisConnect, or by default, all uncommitted changes will be lost. To be more careful, add code, before the insertion of the usage data into the database, to ask the user if he or she wants to commit all changes. Then based on the user's response, either roll back or commit the changes and then insert the usage data and issue the commit statement.

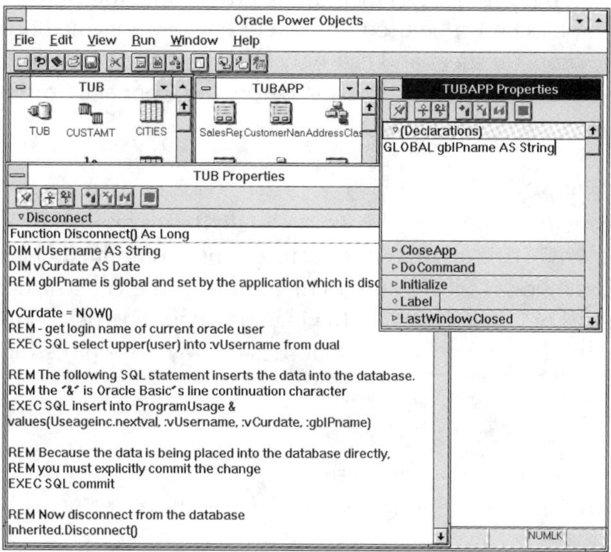

FIGURE 9-7. *Property sheets for the Tubapp application and the Tub session with the code needed to add an entry to the database every time the DisConnect( ) method is called*

There may be times when the application may need to close a session but continue to run. In this case, you would use one of the following the Oracle Basic expressions:

```
SessionName.Disconnect( )
```

or

```
TopLevelForm.GetRecordSet( ).GetSession( ).DisConnect( )
```

GetSession( )

Once a session is opened and a recordset object has been retrieved from an open form, use this method to acquire the session object associated with the recordset. By using the session object in Oracle Basic code in various methods, you can invoke several of the methods described in this section to manage the session. The beginning of the section describes the use of the session object.

IsConnected( )

If an application requires knowledge on whether the application is connected to the database or not, it can use this method to retrieve that information. The session name or session object must be used as the reference for this method. It is not included in any property sheet and can only be called using Oracle Basic. It is most often used to verify the state of the session before the Connect( ) or DisConnect( ) methods are called.

IsWorkPending( )

This is another method that is used only in Oracle Basic statements. When an application disconnects itself from a session, any noncommitted changes are rolled back. Thus this method is ideal to use in methods that are called when an application exits. For example, the following code could be placed in the CloseApp( ) method of an application that uses the MySession session.

```
DIM vAns AS Long

IF MySession.IsWorkPending = TRUE THEN
  vAns = MSGBOX("There are changes pending. Save them?",33, "Save Changes?")
  IF vAns = 1 THEN
     MySession.CommitWork( )
  END IF
END IF
Inherited.CloseApp( )
```

This code uses a hardwired session name because there is no direct way to obtain the session directly from an application object. You could put a global declaration of an object variable in the application and then have the first form that connects to the database obtain the session object and assign it to the global variable. The CloseApp( ) method could then use that session object rather than the hardwired session name.

The Oracle Basic function MSGBOX is very useful and up till now has been used to simply provide information to the user. The syntax used in this example for the MSGBOX function designates that a ? icon with an OK and a Cancel button be displayed with the message. The function returns the value of the button pressed. For more information on this handy function, see Chapter 7 and Appendix B.

RollbackWork( )

This method is the complement of the CommitWork( ) method described above. It is not found on any property sheet and is invoked only by the use of Oracle Basic. The RollbackWork method applies only to the top-level container. When called, it first flushes any pending changes to the database and then issues the SQL rollback statement. Oracle recommends that this method always be used rather than explicitly issuing the rollback statement using SQL. A very common use for this method is to first verify that currently uncommitted changes are to be undone when a Cancel button is pressed and then issue the RollbackWork( ) statement referenced with its session object as described at the beginning of this section. Another use is to verify that a user has the permissions to make changes to a particular table, such as a salary table. This is shown in the code below, which is placed in the Click( ) method of a Save button in a form from which salaries can be changed. This example is based on the application having an entry screen in which a user enters a unique user name and password. The unique name is stored in the global variable vUsername.

```
DIM vMsess AS Object
DIM vDeptno AS Long Integer

REM Get the session object for the recordset of the form
vMysess=GetContainer.GetRecordSet( ).GetSession( )

REM if there are any changes in the database then check the user
IF vMysess.IsWorkPending( ) THEN
    REM get the department number of the user.
    EXEC SQL select deptno into :vDeptno from employee where name = :vUsername
    REM if the user is not a manager rollback the changes otherwise commit them
```

```
    IF vDeptno <> 10 THEN
        MSGBOX"You must be a manager to change salaries"
        vMysess.RollbackWork( );
    ELSE
        vMysess.CommitWork( );
    END IF
END IF
```

This code simply finds the department in which the user works. If it is the manager department, then the work is committed, otherwise a message box is opened and the work is rolled back. If there are no changes pending, the Save button does nothing. As with many of the methods, this is only one of several methods, such as the form's OnLoad( ) method, with which you can verify user access. Additionally, you can keep the Save button grayed until changes are made in the data by using the button's Enabled property (see the example for the ReadColFromFile( ) method above).

User Action Methods

Many of the examples above use the Click( ) method. It is one of several that are directly invoked by end user actions. This section describes the methods that are invoked when a user clicks a mouse button over an object, adds text to a text field, moves the mouse cursor, or uses the TAB key to traverse objects in a form.

ChildClick( )

When a user clicks on an object in a container, Oracle Power Objects signals the container that the event occurred. Generally, any special processing will occur directly within the object where the click occurred, but the ChildClick( ) method gives the container the opportunity to process the action as well. The ChildClick( ) method is called automatically after the Click( ) method in the child object is processed. If there is any Oracle Basic code in the object's Click( ) method that does not include the Inherited.Click( ) statement, the ChildClick( ) method of the container is not called. If there is some general processing that must take place whenever an object is clicked, this method can be used to avoid duplicating the code in the Click( ) method of each child object. For example, if you wanted to audit which programs are being used by the end users from several that are opened using a set of buttons on a form, you could enter code similar to that below. Oracle Power Objects passes the pointer to the child object in which the Click( ) method was invoked to the ChildClick( ) method.

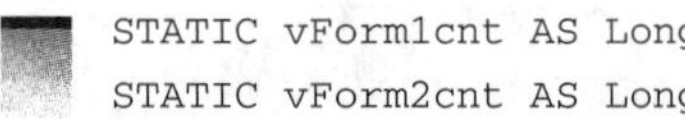

```
STATIC vForm1cnt AS Long
STATIC vForm2cnt AS Long
```

```
DIM vCName AS String

REM child is the object in which the Click occurred and is passed to
REM ChildClick( )
vCName = child.name
IF vCName = "Btn1" THEN
     vForm1cnt = vForm1cnt + 1
ELSEIF vCName = "Btn2" THEN
     vForm2cnt = vForm2cnt + 1
END IF
```

This code uses two static variables (variables that retain their values as long as the application is open) to keep track of every time either Btn1 or Btn2 is clicked. Any other objects clicked on in the form are ignored. If the static variables are declared globally, then a message box could be opened showing the counts when the application is closed or the data entered into the database as a permanent record of program usage.

ChildDbleClick( )

This method is very similar to the ChildClick( ) method described above, except it registers double-clicks rather than single clicks. What constitutes a double-click is determined by the system parameters you set up for either Windows or the Macintosh. Double-clicking on an object in a container causes Oracle Power Objects to activate the container's ChildDblClick( ) method. This method is called automatically unless Oracle Basic code is entered in the object's DoubleClick( ) method and the Inherited.DoubleClick( ) statement is not. The reference to the child on which the double-click occurred is passed as an argument to the ChildDblClick( ) method. It is used just as the ChildClick( ) method is used.

ChildPostChange( )

Whenever a user changes the internal value of a child object, whether directly, by typing in a value, or indirectly, by triggering a method that uses Oracle Basic to change an object's internal value, the change is first processed in the child object. The child object then calls its container's ChildPostChange( ) method as long as the Inherited.PostChange( ) statement is included in any method code added to the child's PostChange( ) method. The reference to the child object is the argument to this method. Just as with the child click methods described above, this method is most useful if some general processing must be done when one of the container's text fields changes. One possibility is to enable certain text fields after a user makes a selection from a list of options. An example of how this is done is shown below. This code enables text entry fields to be enabled or disabled based on which printer option, File Only, Printer Only, or Both, the user selects from the list box. The code is added to the ChildPostChange( ) method in the container's property sheet. (This code could just as well be placed in the PostChange( ) method of the list box by appending GetContainer to the text field's names, using Self.Value in the select clause and deleting the IF statement.)

```
IF child.name = "popFiledest" THEN
   SELECT CASE child.value
     CASE 1
       fldFilename.Enabled=TRUE
       fldPrintername.Enabled=FALSE
     CASE 2
       fldFilename.Enabled=FALSE
       fldPrintername.Enabled=TRUE
     CASE 3
       fldFilename.Enabled=TRUE
       fldPrintername.Enabled=TRUE
  END SELECT
END IF
```

Click( )

This method is probably one of the most often used and easily understood of all the methods. It is invoked whenever the left mouse button (if there is more than one button on the mouse) is pressed while the mouse cursor is inside the boundaries of the object. It applies to all of the Oracle Power Objects' application objects. It is generally used to process Oracle Basic code to perform an action related to the object, such as select an item, open a window, retrieve records from the database, and load various fields. Several of the examples above illustrate the use of the Click( ) method.

Oracle Basic code in methods in the same or other objects in the application can call any other object's Click( ) method. This can be very useful to avoid duplication of Oracle Basic code in several objects' that may invoke the same action in different ways. Take for example the related forms described in "Combining Two Forms to Display Related Data" in Chapter 6. The repeater in the SalesReps form could be enhanced to have its DoubleClick( ) method call the Address button's Click( ) method to display the selected customers address automatically.

When code is added to the Click( ) method, the Oracle Basic statement Inherited.Click( ) must be included to call the container's (if there is one) ChildClick( ) method.

DoubleClick( )

An object's DoubleClick( ) method is triggered when the user quickly clicks the left mouse button (if there is more than one button) twice in succession while the mouse cursor is within its boundaries. The computer's system environment sets the interval between clicks to qualify the action as a double-click and is generally less than one second. It is important to note that Oracle Power Objects will always call the Click( ) method for the object first and then the DoubleClick( ) method. This means that if there is code in both methods, Oracle Power Objects processes the Click( ) method code first and then the code in the DoubleClick( ) method if the second click is within the time parameter.

This method is generally used as a shortcut to trigger the accept or select action of a form. This is in keeping with the general use of the double-click, which is to open windows, restore icons, accept a selection in a list, etc. When an OLE object is double-clicked, Oracle Power Objects automatically loads the object into its server application.

Any code added to this method must include the Oracle Basic statement Inherited.DoubleClick( ) to trigger the call to the container's (if there is one) ChildDblClick( ) method.

FocusEntering( )

As discussed in Chapter 5, an object that has the focus is the currently active object in the application. For example, a user cannot enter data into a text field until it receives the focus. In Windows, text fields, buttons, the various list controls, and check boxes can all have the focus. On a Macintosh, only text fields and combo boxes can have the focus. An object receives the focus in one of two ways: the user clicks on the object or tabs to the object if it is in the TabOrder for the application. As explained in Chapter 8, Oracle Power Objects automatically adds an object that can have the focus to the TabOrder as it is added to the application. FocusEntering( ) can be called from Oracle Basic but it does not move the focus to the object whose FocusEntering( ) method is called, the focus stays in the calling object.

This method is used to activate various default routines to prepare the control for action by the user. It is often used to set the value of the object receiving the focus to a default value if necessary or to some other value, such as the current value in a list. Another use of this method is to update the value of a different object. For example, you may decide that the HelpText property that is used to give a very brief explanation of the purpose of the object that the cursor is over in the status line is inadequate. Thus you could make your own help panel in a form by adding a text control field named HelpPanel with its MultiLine and HasScrollbar properties set to TRUE. Each control in the form then sets the HelpPanel's value to its own help text as it receives the focus. This is done with just one line of Oracle Basic code in the FocusEntering( ) method for each control in the form. The line would be similar to that shown below.

```
MyHelpText.value= &
"Enter the name of the company to which the shipment is to be sent."
```

FocusLeaving( )

This method can be used to augment or substitute for the Validate( ) method. However, it cannot force the focus to remain in the object as the Validate( ) method can. As the focus leaves the control by either the user tabbing to the next object in the TabOrder (see FocusEntering( ) above or TabOrder in Chapter 8) or by clicking on another object, Oracle Power Objects triggers this method. Developers commonly use this method to validate the data in the control by comparing it with values retrieved from the database. Oracle Power Objects' online help on FocusLeaving( ) gives an excellent example of this use. Another use is to accomplish postprocessing that requires the data in the control. For example, a simple calculation of the length of time between a start and end time can be done as the focus leaves the EndTime text field. The form would contain three text fields, StartTime, EndTime, and Duration. As the EndTime text field loses the focus, the Oracle Basic code entered in its FocusLeaving( ) method first checks for data in the StartTime field. It verifies that there is data and that it is less than EndTime (this example assumes stopwatch time, not clock time, to avoid having to check for different days). The code to do this is shown below.

```
DIM vStart, vEnd, vDuration AS Double

vStart = StartTime.value
vEnd=self.value

IF ISNULL(vStart) THEN
   MSGBOX"A value must be entered in the StartTime field"
ELSEIF vStart > vEnd THEN
   MSGBOX"The end time must be less than the Start time."
ELSE
   Duration.value = vEnd-vStart
END IF
```

This code, with some revising, could be added to the StartTime field as well.

One reason you may want to use this method for this type of postprocessing rather than the Validate( ) method is to allow the focus to leave the field. For example, if the end user entered the correct end time after entering a wrong start time, Oracle Power Objects must be able to move the focus to the StartTime field. If the above code is placed in the Validate( ) method, the focus is forced to stay in the EndTime field.

MouseDown( ), MouseMove( ), MouseUp( )

These three methods are so closely related that they are grouped together in this discussion. Every time the user presses the left mouse button (if there is more than one button), Oracle Power Objects calls the MouseDown( ) method of the object currently beneath the mouse cursor. The MouseUp( ) method is called as soon as the user releases the button. While the button is down, Oracle Power Objects triggers the MouseMove( ) method each time the mouse cursor moves at least one pixel. There is no default action for these methods. These methods can be used to move objects within their containers, which is essential to create drag-and-drop applications.

Oracle Power Objects passes the mouse location in pixel coordinates and a key flag indicating what keys are pressed at the same time as the mouse button is pressed as arguments to the MouseDown( ) method. The values for the key flag in Windows and on a Macintosh are shown in the table below.

Windows	**Macintosh**
0 = none	0 = none
1 = Shift	1 = Shift
2 = Control	2 = Option
4 = Alt	4 = Command
	8 = Control

This key flag is especially useful to differentiate between a simple press of the mouse button or a combination of keys pressed at the same time the user presses the mouse button. This can dictate which actions to take depending on what other keys are pressed when the mouse button is pressed. For example, you may want to drag and drop when the mouse button and SHIFT key are pressed, but simply move the object when the mouse button and SHIFT and CTRL (COMMAND on the Mac) keys are all pressed at the same time. Oracle Power Objects assigns the sum of the values of each key pressed to the key flag. Thus when the SHIFT and CTRL keys are pressed, the key flag will equal 3.

When you want the application to simply recognize a click of the mouse button, you should use the Click( ) method rather than a combination of the MouseDown( ) and MouseUp( ) methods. The order in which these methods are called is shown below.

1. MouseDown( )
2. MouseMove( ) (if the cursor is moved while the mouse button is down)
3. MouseUp( )
4. Click( )
5. DoubleClick( ) (if two clicks are close enough together)

When you use these methods, you generally will want to keep track of the beginning point and possibly other information. Thus you should declare global

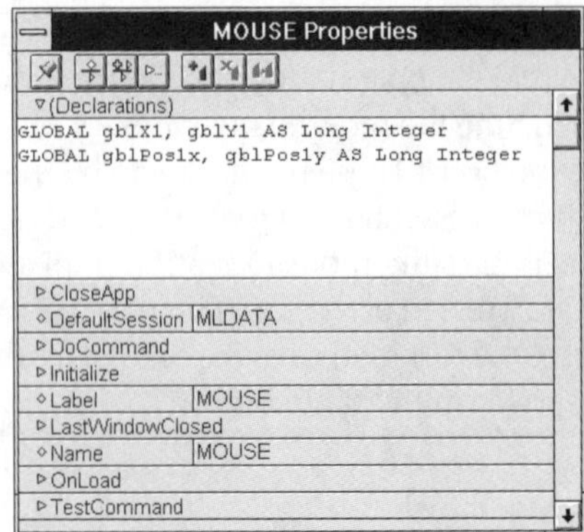

FIGURE 9-8. *The declaration of global values for the application*

variables in the application to contain the beginning and X-Y coordinates. You enter global variables in the declaration text entry area in the application's property sheet, as shown in Figure 9-8.

As the cursor is moved over other objects while the mouse button is pressed, their mouse methods are not invoked. Oracle Power Objects triggers only the mouse methods of the object that was beneath the cursor when the mouse button was pressed.

An example of using these methods is to give the end user the capability to move the objects in a form to redesign the layout to his or her own liking. The only restriction is that the object must remain in its own container—that is, the user cannot move a user-defined class in an embedded form to the outer form. The first step is to declare several global variables used to keep track of the original location of the object and the beginning X-Y coordinates as shown in Figure 9-8. Secondly, you set the global variables in the MouseDown( ) method of an embedded form as shown below.

```
MouseDown
Sub MouseDown(x as Integer, y as Integer, shift as Inte
if shift = 1 then
   gblX1 = x
   gblY1 = y
   gblPos1x = self.positionx
   gblPos1y= self.positiony
end if
```

The global variables gblX1 and gblY1 are set to the position of the mouse when the SHIFT key is pressed and the mouse button is first pressed. The original position of the embedded form is stored in the global variables gblPosx1 and gblPosy1.

The following code is entered in the MouseMove( ) method to move the embedded form within its container as the user moves the mouse cursor. While the user moves the mouse cursor, he or she must continually press the SHIFT key and the mouse button, or the embedded form will stop moving. The code checks to be sure that the object is not moved from its container.

```
DIM vCurx, vCury, vMaxx, vMaxy AS Long Integer

REM Make sure that the shift key is pressed, otherwise do nothing
IF shift = 1 THEN
   REM  set the position of the embedded form to the change in the mouse
   REM position plus the original position of the form.
   vCurx = x - gblX1 + gblPos1x
   vCury = y - gblY1 + gblPos1y

   REM  Calculate the maximum x and y position values which is simply the
   REM  difference in the size of the container and the object. Remember the
   REM  Position of an object is in relation to the upper left corner of its
   REM  container.
   vMaxx = GetContainer.Sizex - self.sizex
   vMaxy = GetContainer.Sizey - self.sizey
   REM  if the new position is less than zero, the form would be to the left of
   REM  its GetContainer, set it to 1
   IF vCurx <= 0 THEN
       vCurx = 1
   REM  if the new position is greater than Max, the form would extend past the
   REM  right side of the container
   ELSE IF vCurx > vMaxx  THEN
      vCurx = vMaxx
   END IF
   REM make the same checks for the y coordinate to keep the object in the
   REM container.
   IF vCury <= 0 THEN
      vCury = 1
   ELSE IF vCury > vMaxy THEN
      vCury = vMaxy
```

```
    END IF
    REM   Now reset the position of the moving object.
    self.PositionX=vCurx
    self.positionY=vCury
END IF
```

You place this code in the MouseDown( ) and MouseMove( ) methods of each object that you want to allow the user to move. The MouseUp( ) method can be used to reset variables to default values when the user releases the mouse button. Alternatively, if you do not want the object to move with the cursor, place the code to set the final position of the object in the MouseUp method, and the object will "jump" to the new position when the mouse button is released.

PostChange( )

This method is called after a user makes a change in a control object, i.e., after pressing a radio button or entering data in a text field. The PostChange( ) method is called after the object loses the focus and can be used much like the FocusLeaving( ) method. In order for the ChildPostChange( ) method of the container (if there is one) to be called, you must enter the Oracle Basic statement Inherited.PostChange( ) in the code. The change will take place even without this statement, even though the online help example seems to indicate that you can stop the change.

The following example simply verifies that the data entered is correct. If it is not, it will blank the text field but not process the change made by blanking the text field. In other words, when the data is not accepted, there are two changes to process: the first is the data the user entered, and the second is changing the field to NULL. Actually, there will be times when you do not want the value to be reset to NULL, particularly if the value is lengthy. In this case, you would want the data to remain in the field so that the user can simply correct the error. You cannot revert the value to the original data. Oracle Power Objects only does this in the Validate( ) method described below.

```
DIM vAns AS Long

REM Make sure the value is not NULL
IF !ISNULL(self.value) THEN
   REM  This MSGBOX will display a "?" icon with yes and no buttons.
   vAns = MSGBOX("Is the entered value "&self.value"&" correct?", 36, "Verify
Answer")
   IF vAns = 6 THEN
      Inherited.PostChange( )
   ELSE
       self.value=NULL
   END IF
END IF
```

The illustration below shows the message box that is displayed on each change in the field. See the description of the MSGBOX Oracle Basic function in Appendix B for the key code to display various buttons and icons in the message box.

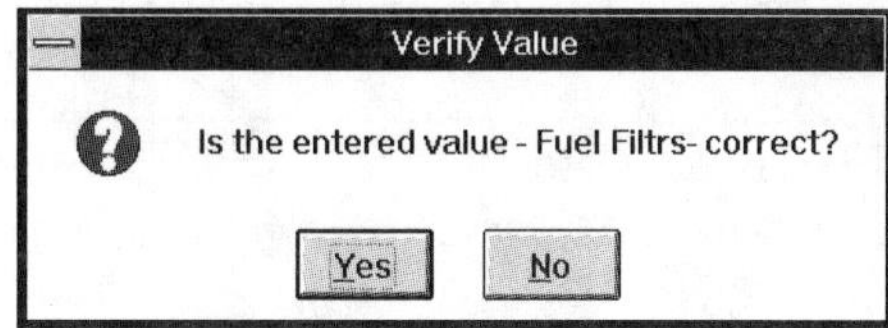

PreChange( )

This method is called after the FocusEntering( ) method is called and at the moment the user begins changing the value of the object. It can be used much like the FocusEntering( ) method to verify that preconditions for entering data in the field are met. The online help says it is also used to prevent any data being entered if preconditions are not met, but there is no way to stop the entering of the first character of the data. You can pop up a message telling the user that he or she cannot enter data and even set the enabled flag to FALSE to disable any further data entry, but the first letter typed in the field will still be used. PreChange( ) is called only on the first change. That is, the first letter typed in a text field triggers the PreChange( ) method, but any further data entry does not trigger the method. It is not called when the field's value is changed by Oracle Basic in another method. If code is entered in this method, the Oracle Basic statement Inherited.PreChange( ) must be included to trigger the ChildPreChange( ) method of the object's container, if there is one. We recommend that you use the FocusEntering( ) method rather than this method, because Oracle Power Objects will use the first data entered regardless of any other action when PreChange( ) is used.

SetFocus( )

There are times when you want the focus to go directly to a designated control. This method is used with the control's name to move the focus to it. The syntax is

```
control_object.SetFocus( )
```

For example, in the discussion on ChildPostChange( ), the code could be changed to move the focus directly to the enabled text control fields, as shown below.

```
IF child.name = "popFiledest" THEN
   SELECT CASE child.value
     CASE 1
       fldFilename.Enabled=TRUE
       fldPrintername.Enabled=FALSE
```

```
        fldFilename.SetFocus( )
      CASE 2
        fldFilename.Enabled=FALSE
        fldPrintername.Enabled=TRUE
        fldPrintername.SetFocus( )
      CASE 3
        fldFilename.Enabled=TRUE
        fldPrintername.Enabled=TRUE
        fldFilename.SetFocus( )
  END SELECT
END IF
```

Constraint/Business Rule Methods

These methods ensure that certain conditions are met after changes are made in text fields, radio button frames, combo boxes, etc. They can revert the values back to the original if the conditions are not met, though this is not always desirable, as explained below.

RevertValue( )

You use this method in conjunction with the Validate( ) method described below. It simply resets the value of an application object (text field, radio button, combo box, etc.) to the original value if the Validate( ) method returns FALSE after the value of the object is changed. When the object is a bound control, the RevertValue( ) method resets the value of the column. In addition, if the change in the column is the only change in the current row, then Oracle Power Objects resets the flag indicating a change in the database so there will be no pending changes in the database. It does not have any effect if it is called from methods other than the Validate( ) method. We tried it in the example of the PostChange( ) method to revert the field's value if the data entered was incorrect, but it did not work.

You can add code to this method to verify that the data is to be reset or to accomplish other cleanup activities upon reverting the value back to the previous value. See Validate( ) for an example of this method's use.

RevertRow( )

The RevertRow( ) method is similar to the RevertValue( ) method, except that it is associated with the ValidateRow( ) method and it resets all columns in the row rather than just the changed column. Unlike the RevertValue( ) method, RevertRow( ) applies only to bound containers (forms, embedded forms, etc.), while RevertValue( ) works for both bound and unbound controls. Its default actions depend on what has previously taken place in the current record in the container's recordset. The list of these actions is below.

1. Removes the row from the recordset if it was newly inserted.
2. Resets all edited columns in the row to their last committed values.
3. Sets the state of the row when queried from the database if no other edits had occurred.
4. Calls the OnQuery( ) method to reset the values of all affected controls.

As with the RevertValue( ) method, this method only works in conjunction with the ValidateRow( ) method, not with other methods.

You can add code to this method to verify that the data is to be reset or to accomplish other clean up activities upon reverting the record's values back to the previous values. See ValidateRow( ) for an example of this method's use.

Validate( )

You can use several methods to validate data entered in application controls, including FocusLeaving( ) and PostChange( ). However, Validate( ) is the preferred method to use to enforce various rules that the application requires. Some of its uses are to verify that a file whose name is entered in a text field exists, that the radio button pressed is applicable to the current state of an application, or that required data is in the database. If the validation fails and the ValidateMsg property has a value, Oracle Power Objects displays a warning message box to inform the user of the problem. This method is called right after the PostChange( ) method when a user tabs out of the control, clicks on a different object, presses the ENTER key for Windows or the RETURN key for the Mac when in a text field, or selects a new choice in a list or button. The new value for the object is passed as an argument to the Validate( ) method. It is not triggered when the data is changed programmatically.

If several control fields all have the same validation criteria, you can add the code to one control's Validate method and then simply call that Validate method from the other controls that use the same criteria. You would simply add the following line to the Validate method of the other controls.

```
Validate = MainForm.MainControl.Validate(newval)
```

The argument newval is passed into the Validate method by Oracle Power Objects.

Oracle Power Objects will not return the data displayed in the object to its original value unless the RevertValue( ) method described above is called, but the internal value of the object will revert back to the original. Thus it is possible to have a value displayed that is different from the TRUE value of the object. For example, suppose a user enters a Social Security number, such as 123-45-6789, into a field that originally contained the value 987-65-4321. Now if the new value fails the validation test and RevertValue( ) is not called, the internal value of the text field will be 987-65-4321 but the display will show 123-45-6789. The reason this is allowed is to let the user edit a field without having to retype the entire value. However, because the focus will not leave the control until the error is corrected, you do not need to worry about displayed values not equaling the true value.

As an example of the use of this method, suppose that a salesperson is entering the total amount of a customer's order. The validate method for that field could check the current amount the customer owes, add it to the newly entered amount, and compare it to a credit limit assigned to that customer. If the amount is too great, the salesperson is informed of the situation and the total amount field is reverted back to whatever was there previously. Otherwise, the amount is accepted and the order is made. Place the string "Not enough credit left for this purchase" in the Total field's ValidateMsg property and place the following code in the Validate( ) method.

```
DIM vCurval, vTotal AS Double
DIM vMyobj AS Object
DIM vClim AS Double
DIM vCid AS Long Integer

REM Get the recordset for the form, custid was placed in the
REM RecSrcAddCol property so must retrieve the value using the GetColVal method.
vMyobj = GetContainer.GetRecordSet( )
vCid = CLNG(vMyobj.GetColVal("CUSTID"))

REM  Now get the credit limit for the indicated customer.
EXEC SQL select cred_limit into :vClim from custs where custid = :vCid

REM Get the amount the customer currently owes
EXEC SQL select sum(total)into :vTotal from orders where custid = :vCid

REM  Calculate the total balance if this purchase is approved
vCurval = vTotal + newval

REM  If the new balance is greater than the credit limit then set validate to
REM  FALSE which will cause the error message in the ValidateMsg property to be
REM  displayed. Also revert the value in the field to whatever was there
REM  previously. Otherwise set validate to TRUE.
IF vCurval > vClim THEN
   RevertVal( )
   validate = FALSE
ELSE
   validate = TRUE
END IF
```

ValidateRow( )

This method is similar to the Validate( ) method in that it is used to verify that entered data fits defined rules for the application. It differs in that it applies only to bound container forms, such as embedded forms and repeaters, and that it applies to the entire current record in the recordset rather than one column. This method is triggered when the user tries to commit the changes in the current row or by navigating to a new row in the recordset. The row number of the newly inserted, updated, or deleted row is passed as an argument to the ValidateRow( ) method.

To verify that the newly entered data in a row is consistent with application rules is the main use of the ValidateRow( ) method. Some of these rules might enforce that begin dates are less than end dates, that the user has authority to modify the data, and that the user has entered data in all required fields. If the verification fails and if an error message is entered in the ValidateRowMsg property, Oracle Power Objects displays the error message. The displayed data will not be changed back to the controls' original value if the validation fails unless the RevertRow( ) method is called. If the RevertRow( ) method is called the changes for the entire row will be reversed (see RevertRow( ) above). You may not want to revert the changes to allow the user the opportunity to simply correct a mistyped date rather than being forced to retype all changes.

As an example of the ValidateRow( ) method, consider a salesperson entering an order for a customer. When all the data is typed in, the Commit button is pressed, which triggers the ValidateRow( ) method. Inside the method is code to verify that the ordered item is in stock. If it is not, then a message in the ValidateRowMsg will be displayed or the message can be left blank and a message box can be displayed, which allows the sales rep to order the items if the customer wants to wait. Enter the code shown below into the ValidateRow( ) method to do this.

```
DIM vMyobj AS Object
DIM vNumLeft AS Long Integer
DIM vProd AS Long Integer
DIM vAnsw, vDoIt AS Long Integer

REM  Get the recordset for the container, it contains the ProdId column
REM  that is not shown in the form but is added in the RecSrcAddCol property

vMyobj = self.GetRecordSet( )
vProd = vMyobj.GetColVal("PRODID")

REM  this flag is used to set the return value for ValidateRow
vDoIt = TRUE

REM   find out if there is any of the product on hand
```

```
EXEC SQL select onhand into :vNumLeft from products where ProdId = :vProd
IF vNumLeft = 0 THEN
    REM There are none on hand, ask if to order, if so update the Numordered
    REM column otherwise revert the values to the original and set the doit
    REM flag to FALSE.
    vAnsw = MSGBOX("Product out of Stock, Do you want to Order it?", 36,&
"Order Item")
    IF vAnsw = 6 THEN
        EXEC SQL update products set numordered = numordered+1 where ProdId = &
:vProd
   ELSE
      RevertRow( )
      vDoIt = FALSE
   END IF
ELSE
   REM decrement the onhand column in Products table
   EXEC SQL update products set onhand = onhand - 1 where ProdId = :vProd
END IF
REM  Now just set the ValidateRow method to the return value.
ValidateRow = doit
```

Container Methods

Container methods apply to forms, user-defined classes, repeaters, and reports. Some of the methods apply only to top-level forms that have a window associated with them; others apply to all types of containers.

Several of the methods in this section refer to modal windows. The term *modal* has been briefly used in this and earlier chapters but has not been defined. There are two types of modal windows: system and application. A system modal window is a dialog box that requires a response from the user before any further work can be done in any application, whether it is an Oracle Power Objects application or not. An application modal window is a dialog box that requires a user response before any further processing is done in Oracle Power Objects. These dialog boxes are generally used to warn the user of a problem or to gather required information before further work is done.

There are essentially three types of methods in this section: window management, database management, and control navigation.

CloseWindow( )

The CloseWindow( ) method closes the form and removes it from both the screen and memory. However, if another form has accessed its recordset, the recordset remains in memory and the other form can manipulate it. This method is triggered only when the form is being closed by either selecting Close or by Oracle Basic code such as that used in the ExitBtnClass described in Chapter 6. If Oracle Basic code is added to this method, you must include the statement Inherited.CloseWindow( ) or Oracle Power Objects will not close the window. Thus, you can use this method to perform a final data check to enforce application rules that may have been missed by other validation methods.

An example of using Oracle Basic code to verify that the form can be closed is one that checks if any database changes are pending. If so, you can disallow closing the window until either the data is rolled back or committed. Place the code shown below in the CloseWindow( ) method of the top-level form. This assumes only one session is used by the form.

```
DIM vAns AS Long
DIM vMysess AS Object

vMysess = self.GetRecordSet.GetSession( )
IF vMysess.IsWorkPending THEN
REM If a string is too long to be read easily in the
REM text entry field, break it into two parts and
REM use the Oracle Basic string concatenation operator &.
  MSGBOX"There are uncommitted changes in the form. Either commit or rollback &
before closing this form."
ELSE
  Inherited.CloseWindow( )
END IF
```

CommitForm( )

This method is called when the Commit button is pressed or when called from Oracle Basic code in a method. CommitForm( ) applies only to top-level containers. It will perform what is called a two-phase commit. This ensures that if there is more than one session used in the form, all the transactions in all sessions will be committed or none will be committed. In other words, Oracle Power Objects does not commit the transactions in one session, which makes the changes permanent, and then commit the transactions in the next session. If the transaction in the second session cannot be committed, there could be serious data integrity problems, since the first session's transactions were committed. Therefore, if Oracle Power Objects finds that any session cannot have its transactions committed, Oracle Power Objects will roll back the transactions in all the sessions. Otherwise, Oracle Power Objects commits the transactions in all the sessions, thus keeping the data in all the sessions in sync.

The most common use of this method is to verify that changes are to be saved before actually committing them to the database. You can do this by adding code to the CommitForm( ) method of the container itself or by having some other method verify that the data is ready for saving and calling the container's CommitForm( ) method. An example of the CommitForm( ) method being called from a separate method is shown below. You enter the code in the Click( ) method of a Save button. The code first verifies that all the data is present by traversing every control in the toplevel form, checking if it is a text field and if so, verifying that it contains data. If not, it sets the vGoAhead flag to FALSE and exits the loop. If the vGoAhead flag is still TRUE when all controls have been traversed, call the top-level container's CommitForm( ) method, otherwise display an error message. The message includes the name of the control that failed verification.

```
DIM vTopCont AS Object
DIM vCurobj, vNextChild AS Object
DIM vNotProcessed AS Long Integer
DIM vSname AS String
DIM vGoAhead AS Long Integer

REM  First find the top level form by using the GetTopContainer method
vTopCont = GetTopContainer( )

REM this code is from the description of the FirstChild property in Chapter 8
REM It traverses every object in a toplevel form.
vCurobj = vTopCont.FirstChild
vNotProcessed = 1
vGoAhead = TRUE

REM while there is a valid object check if it is a container and if so
REM see if it has any children. Do this until you reach a non-container
REM object and process it. Then work backup processing each object as you go.
DO WHILE NOT(ISNULL(vCurobj))
  IF vNotProcessed and NOT(ISNULL(vCurobj.FirstChild)) THEN
     REM  this is a container so check its children
     vCurobj = vCurobj.FirstChild
  ELSE
     REM  A control is found, make sure it is a text field and then check its
```

```
        REM  values
        vSname = vCurobj.name
        IF vCurobj.ControlType=2 AND (ISNULL(vSname.value) OR &
           LEN(vSname.value) = 0) THEN
           REM the field is empty, set the vGoAhead flag and exit the do loop
           vGoAhead = FALSE
           EXIT DO
        END IF
        REM check the next child in this container
        vNextChild = vCurobj.NextControl( )
        IF ISNULL(vNextChild) THEN
           REM there are no more children so go back to the parent
           vNextChild = vCurobj.container
           IF ISNULL(vNextChild) THEN
              REM there is no container which means you are at the top level
              REM get the next control in the top level and
              REM flag the object so it will be checked for children
              vCurobj=vCurobj.NextControl( )
              vNotProcessed = 1
           ELSE
              REM this is a top level object that has already been checked for
              REM children
              vNotProcessed = 0
              vCurobj = vNextChild
           END IF
        ELSE
           REM process the next child
           vCurobj = vNextChild
           vNotProcessed = 1
        END IF
     END IF
  LOOP
  IF vGoAhead THEN
     REM All fields have data so commit the work done in this session
     vTopCont.CommitWork( )
  ELSE
     MSGBOX("The text field "&vSname&" must be filled in")
  END IF
```

This example is fairly complex. Usually, only a couple of known fields would need to be verified before committing the work, or maybe just a simple Yes-No confirmation message box is all that would be used. However, this is a fairly generic example that can be used to test every object in the window.

DismissModal( )

This method is used to dismiss a modal window that you opened with the OpenModal( ) method. Dismissing a window simply removes it from the screen but not from memory. This allows the application to continue referencing any data stored in its controls. The DismissModal( ) method is called when a button with its IsDismissBtn property set to TRUE is pressed or if called from Oracle Basic code in a method. This method is passed the reference to the button that triggered the DismissModal( ) method as an argument. This allows you to determine which button closed the window. The online help states that you can determine if the window was closed with a system or Oracle Power Objects button. However, the Windows version of an Oracle Power Objects modal window does not contain the Close option in the Control menu (accessed by the button with the bar in the upper-left corner of the title bar), so you cannot dismiss the modal window with the Control menu.

An example of using this method is to have a modal window pop up to request a user name and password for an application. The dialog box includes fields in which the end user enters the user name and the associated password. When the DismissModal( ) method is called, it verifies that the user name/password is valid and then dismisses the window. The application can then continue to reference the user name and/or password as needed. For example, the application may need to use the user name and password to retrieve data from a secure database. (The user name and password could be assigned to global variables instead and save the overhead of keeping the window in memory, but for this example the modal window is used). This is done in the code below.

```
DIM vUname, vPassWrd AS String
DIM vHasName AS Long Integer

REM  must use variables rather than the control values because the
REM  EXEC SQL statement cannot use the control values.
vUname = fldName.value
vPassWrd = fldPassword.value

REM  First check that the user is in the database and then that the
REM  Password is correct. If both are good then dismiss the window.
REM  The application still has access to the username and password.
EXEC SQL select count(username) into :vHasName from users where username =
 :vUname
IF vHasName = 0 THEN
  MSGBOX"Unknown user, Try again"
ELSE
  EXEC SQL select count(password) into :vHasName from users where &
```

```
                    username = :vUname and password = :vPassWrd
   IF vHasName = 0 THEN
      MSGBOX"Unknown user, Try again"
   ELSE
      Inherited.DismissModal(btn)
   END IF
END IF
```

Do not use DismissModal( ) to close system modal dialog boxes. This is because if a system modal dialog box is hidden, not closed, the system will hang because there is no longer a way to close the window. Remember that a system modal dialog box requires that it be closed before any further work is done on the machine, not just the application. If the modal window is no longer displayed, you cannot close it and no other window will respond to user input. Thus you cannot redisplay the hidden window in any way. Always use the CloseWindow( ) method rather than the DismissModal( ) method to close a system modal dialog box.

You can get into trouble in other ways as well when the window is opened in system modal mode. If the Switch menu item is inadvertently selected, the Switch Window dialog box comes up. If the Switch Window dialog box covers the system modal window, you can no longer access the system modal window to close it, and the system hangs. Be very careful when using a system modal dialog box.

ForceUpdate( )

There are times when you may want to force Oracle Power Objects to redraw the form before it would normally do so. Usually, Oracle Power Objects will redraw the form only when a method making changes to the form is completed or during idle time. However, if you want to animate the shrinking of a control, you would use the following code. If you did not include the ForceUpdate( ) method, the change in size would simply jump from the large to the small.

```
DIM vIncrx, vIncry AS Integer

REM shrink the form to one half of its original size in 100 steps
vIncrx = (frmGrow.sizex - (frmGrow.sizex/2))/100
vIncry = (frmGrow.sizey - (frmGrow.sizey/2))/100

FOR x = 1 to 100
    REM You must convert the double values to integer or you
    REM will get the error "Error setting system property value"
    frmGrow.Sizex = cint(frmGrow.Sizex - vIncrx)
    frmGrow.Sizey = cint(frmGrow.Sizey - vIncry)
    frmTopLevel.ForceUpdate( )
NEXT x
```

GetContainer( )

You have seen this method used in several examples throughout this book. It simply returns the reference to the container object in which the application object is placed. It is often necessary to refer to the container for a number of reasons, such as to close the window, to access other controls in the container, etc.

GetTopContainer( )

When you need the reference to the top-level form of an application object, use this method to retrieve the reference to the top container object. (This is the object that opens the window that contains all the form's objects.) If you need to traverse every object in a top-level container, use this method to retrieve the reference to the top-level container and then the FirstChild and other properties to complete the traversal. The example for CommitForm described earlier in this section is an example of container traversal. It does not use the GetTopContainer( ) method.

HideWindow( )

This method is similar to the DismissModal( ) method described earlier, but it applies to regular windows rather than modal windows. Its main use is to hide a window; that is, remove it from the screen, but keep it in memory to allow continued processing of the recordset attached to the window's form. This saves the overhead of repeatedly requerying the database every time an often-used window is needed to display values for a short time. Some windows can take a considerable amount of time to query the database and load the values in its controls. A hidden window is redisplayed by another object using Oracle Basic to call the hidden window's ShowWindow( ) method.

For example, a salesperson may need to view the complete selection of tub options fairly often while setting up a customer's order, but may not need it to be displayed continually. Because the option window contains many controls and possibly some complicated queries, it takes several seconds to load the first time. Thus the application is written so that the user can hide the window with a Hide button when it is not needed and redisplay it with a Show button when it is needed. The code needed to do this is the simple Oracle Basic statement shown below and is added to the Hide button's and Show button's Click( ) methods, respectively.

```
TubOptions.Hidewindow( ) and  TubOptions.ShowWindow( )
```

NextControl( )

This method is used to find the next control in a container. You must first obtain the reference to an object in the container by using the FirstChild property of the container. After processing the first object in the container, you cycle through the rest of the objects in the container by repeatedly using the current object's NextControl( ) method to get the next control object. The method returns only the siblings to the first object and does not traverse the hierarchy of objects. For example, if a top-level container contains four text control fields and one embedded form, which also contains four text control fields, NextControl( ) will find only the top-level four control fields and the one embedded form. It will not find the text control fields in the embedded form. The NextControl( ) method returns NULL when it has reached the end of the list of controls in the container. This was explained in some detail in Chapter 8 in the description of the FirstChild property. The descriptions of the FirstChild property in Chapter 8 and the CommitForm( ) method above contain examples that use this method.

OpenModal( )

This method is used when a dialog box is required, i.e., no further work is to be processed until either the user enters the required data in the dialog box or acknowledges the warning message in the modal dialog box. As explained in the beginning of this section, there are two types of modal windows, application and system. You open application modal windows by using the OpenModal( ) method with an argument equal to 0 or FALSE. A system modal window is opened with an argument not equal to zero or TRUE. System modal windows should only be used when a drastic error or a possibly disastrous condition is detected. Hopefully, the dialog box displayed will give the user an idea of how to avoid the disaster, such as closing other applications if memory is running low. You use application modal windows to inform the user of errors that require acknowledgment before work continues, or to require the user to enter necessary data before the work continues. An example of an application modal window is one in which the user enters a user name and a password to gain access to the application.

Generally, an application modal dialog box is opened using Oracle Basic code in the Click( ) method of a button or by error detection code in other validation methods. The Inherited.OpenModal(sys_exclusive) Oracle Basic statement must be included in any code entered in the OpenModal( ) method or Oracle Power Objects will not open the window. You would enter in the Click( ) method of an Open button an Oracle Basic statement similar to that shown below to open an application modal dialog box.

```
CheckValue.OpenModal(0)
```

Use the CloseWindow( ) method to remove the window from the screen and memory. You must use this method to close a system modal window or you will hang the system. You can dismiss an application modal window from the screen but not from memory by using the DismissModal( ) method described above. This method is called when any button in the form whose IsDismissBtn property is set TRUE (default) is clicked. If you use the DismissModal( ) method, be sure to close the window when you exit the application.

OpenWindow( )

Before any form or report can be used, Oracle Power Objects must load it into memory and attach it to a window. This method is used to accomplish this task. Generally, a main menu or form palette is opened first, from which end users access other forms and reports. The main menu is opened by placing an Oracle Basic code statement similar to MainMenu.OpenWindow( ) in the OnLoad( ) method of the application. The example in Chapter 6 illustrates this use where the OnLoad( ) method of the Tubapp application opens the main menu CompForm. Other forms or reports are then opened by calling the appropriate form's OpenWindow( ) method from the Click( ) method of designated buttons.

Oracle Basic code entered in a form's OpenWindow( ) method is commonly used to prepare the form for display. For example, you can disable certain fields when the form is first displayed. Then as the user enters required data, you can have Oracle Power Objects enable the appropriate fields. The following code disables tub specification fields. After the tub type is entered, method code in the PostChange( ) method of the tub type field enables the specification fields.

```
self.Colorspec.Enabled = FALSE
self.materialspec.Enabled = FALSE
Inherited.OpenWindow( )
```

As illustrated in the code, the Oracle Basic statement Inherited.OpenWindow( ) must be included in the code in the OpenWindow( ) method or the window will not be opened.

NOTE
The IsDismissBtn property for buttons in a form opened with this method is ignored.

RollbackForm( )

This method is the opposite of the CommitForm( ) method described above, and applies only to top-level containers. It is included on all container property sheets but mainly applies to forms and user-defined classes. As mentioned in the CommitForm( ) description, this method applies to all transactions in the form, even if the form uses more than one session. To roll back the work in just one session, use the CommitWork( ) form for the session.

When the transactions are rolled back, Oracle Power Objects removes any newly inserted rows from the recordset and replaces deleted rows. Any value changed in the columns in the recordset is reverted to the value at the last-committed transaction or the original query from the database.

This method is invoked from the Rollback button on the main toolbar or invoked from code added to other methods, such as the Click( ) method of a

Cancel button. The main use of this method is to include a message box to confirm that the rollback is to take place, as shown in the sample code below.

```
DIM vAnsw AS Long Integer
vAns = MSGBOX("Cancel all changes?", 33, "Cancel...")
IF vAnsw = 1 THEN
   Inherited.RollbackForm( )
END IF
```

ShowWindow( )

This is the complement to the HideWindow( ) method described above. It simply redisplays a window that has been removed from the screen but not from memory. It cannot be used to open a window. An example of the use of the ShowWindow( ) method is to redisplay a tub specification window. In addition, the window can have the data updated to represent a particular tub type before it is redisplayed. Keeping the window in memory decreases the amount of setup time needed to query the database and display the window, but it does use up your RAM. In this example, the TubSpec form contains data showing the specifications for various hot tubs, each of which have different specifications. While filling out an order form, the salesperson selects the tub type in the TubType list box and then presses the ShowSpecs button to display the TubSpec form. The TubSpec form contains a Dismiss button that hides the TubSpec form. The following code illustrates how this is done and is placed in the Click( ) method of the ShowSpecs button. When Oracle Power Objects first opens the application, it sets the global variable called TubSpecOpen to FALSE.

```
DIM vTType AS Long Integer

vTType = TubType.value
IF TubSpecOpen = TRUE THEN
  REM  Use the QueryWhere method to load the form with the correct specs
  TubSpec.QueryWhere("type = "&vTType)
  TubSpec.ShowWindow
ELSE
  REM  open the window, load it with the correct specs and set the global
  REM  variable
  TubSpec.OpenWindow( )
  TubSpec.QueryWhere("type = vTType")
  TubSpecOpen = TRUE
END IF
```

An alternative to a global value to check if the form is open is to insert the statement TubSpec.OnLoad( ) in the application's OnLoad( ) method. This will load the form into memory but will not display it, as explained below in the discussion of the OnLoad( ) method. Thus you need only use the ShowWindow( ) method and not check to see if it is open.

Printing Methods

The following two methods are generally used for reports but can be used for forms. The first method simply opens a window in which the user can see what the report or form will look like on the printed page. The second method sends the form or report directly to the printer.

OpenPreview( )

Often, an end user will want to see what a report looks like before it is printed. This is accomplished by calling the OpenPreview( ) method from Oracle Basic code in the Click( ) method of a button on a master menu, such as the CompForm application described in Chapter 6. Alternatively, it can be called from the OnLoad( ) method of an application that consists of just the report. The syntax for the call is ReportName.OpenPreview( ).

This method also applies to a top-level form. When a form is printed, Oracle Power Objects prints a view of the complete form for each row in the recordset. Thus, printing forms that create invoices prints a copy of each invoice in the recordset. It is also useful to allow the user to see how the form will look on a printed page to be used as an illustration in a manual. Obviously, there are situations when printing a form is excessive and a report would be much more efficient. It depends on the purpose of the application.

When a report or form is opened in Print Preview mode, the usual run-time toolbar is replaced with the Print Preview toolbar, as described in Chapter 3. This toolbar provides the user the means to page forward and backward through the report, to view an entire or magnified portion of a page of the report, and to send the report to the printer.

OpenPrint( )

You generally enter code in the Click( ) method of a Print button to call this method. It opens the system's common Print dialog box, from which the user selects the print options and then sends the report or form to the printer (or cancels the print job). You can add Oracle Basic code to the OpenPrint( ) method of the object. The code can be used to verify that the database is available by making a connection or to verify that the user has the appropriate authority to print the report. As usual, the Oracle Basic statement Inherited.OpenPrint( ) must be included in the code, or Oracle Power Objects will not open the system Print dialog box.

As explained in the OpenPreview( ) method, printing a form will print a page with the entire form on it for every record in the form's recordset.

Miscellaneous Methods

The following is a collection of methods that don't fit into any broad classification. These methods include ways to generate unique primary key values, create wireless applications, insert OLE objects, and specify which form(s) to open when loading an application.

CounterGenKey( )

This method, which applies to text control fields only, is used to generate a value that is generally used as either a primary key for a row in a table or a value for other columns with the unique constraint. It returns the new key as a string. Thus the key can be either a number or a unique combination of alphanumeric characters. The method of key generation depends on the key generation properties CounterType, CounterSeq, and CounterIncBy, as described in Chapter 8. If the CounterType property's value is User, the method returns a NULL. Usually you enter code in this method to generate a sequential number when the database being accessed does not support sequences. The online help example for the CounterGenKey( ) method is an excellent example of how to generate unique numbers in sequence.

OMAMsgRecvd( )

This method and the following method are used in conjunction with the Oracle Mobile Agents (OMA) program which is an API used to write "wireless" applications. Normally, you connect to the database over a LAN and connections happen immediately. With wireless applications, there may be a couple of seconds between each command. The use of the OMA program is beyond the scope of this book. For further information, see the documentation for Oracle Mobile Agents.

Oracle Power Objects triggers this method when an Oracle Mobile Agents message is received by a form, report, or user-defined class. It is applicable to Windows only and corresponds to the Windows message for message received. You can trigger this method with the usual GetContainer.OMAMsgRecvd( ) Oracle Basic statement, but it is intended for use by the Oracle Mobile Agents program.

OMAShutdown( )

When Oracle Mobile Agents shuts down, Oracle Power Objects triggers this method. It is applicable to Windows only and corresponds to the Windows message for message manager shutdown. Its syntax is the usual GetContainer.OMAShutdown( ) Oracle Basic statement. For further information, see the documentation for Oracle Mobile Agents.

OLEInsertObject( )

This method allows you to programmatically trigger the Insert Object menu item in the Edit menu. Oracle Power Objects will display the Insert Object dialog when this method is called. OLEInsertObject( ) returns TRUE if successful and FALSE if it fails or if the user presses the Cancel button in the dialog box. See Chapter 11 for more information on using OLE objects.

OnLoad( )

We have mentioned this method several times in this chapter as the method used to open a specific form when an application is loaded. This is the most common use of this method. But some other important uses are to check for needed data in files before the application is opened, to check that the user has the necessary clearance to use the application, or to do other types of preliminary processing. The default action for the OnLoad( ) method when an application is opened is to randomly open one of the forms in the application. Thus it is generally necessary to add a statement similar to MainForm.OpenWindow( ) in the OnLoad( ) method of an application.

When Oracle Power Objects first opens a form, it triggers a sequence of methods. Oracle Power Objects triggers the OnLoad( ) method after it executes the Query( ), OnQuery( ), and OpenWindow( ) methods. This means that Oracle Power Objects loads all the controls in the form with the retrieved data and displays the window. It then calls the OnLoad( ) method. Thus if the OnLoad( ) method changes any values in the newly loaded bound containers, Oracle Power Objects will see the change as a change in the recordset. This will activate the database Commit and Rollback buttons, and the user will need to accept the changes made by the OnLoad( ) method or roll them back.

This method also applies to all other application objects but has no default action. It is triggered when the object is loaded into memory. You can call a form's OnLoad( ) method from another method even if the form is not yet opened. When this happens, Oracle Power Objects loads the object into memory but the object remains hidden. This allows you to load some forms that may take quite a while to load on startup when the user is more inclined to be patient. You then open the forms with their ShowWindow( ) methods as discussed in the ShowWindow( ) method section above.

If you add code to the OnLoad( ) method for other than forms or applications, you do not need to add the inherited statement. Just as with code entered in the application's OnLoad( ) method, code entered in form's and other container's OnLoad( ) method is used to accomplish preliminary actions before Oracle Power Objects loads the object into memory.

UpdateList( )

This method applies to lists, pop-up lists, and combo boxes. When the user or Oracle Power Objects changes the data referenced by a list control, the list will not be updated until you have Oracle Power Objects call this method. For example, if the program deletes a row from a list, the method that deleted the row should also call the list's UpdateList( ) method to refresh the list. You can add code to the UpdateList( ) method to inform the user that the list has changed or to cycle through the changed list and update other records that reference the list.

An example of code in the UpdateList( ) method to update a different control that depends on the values in the list is shown below. When the list's UpdateList( ) method is called, the code compares the value of the dependent control to the values in the list. If the value is found, the code simply updates the list, otherwise, the user is informed of the change and the dependent object's value is set to NULL.

```
DIM vMyobj AS Object
DIM vFound, x, vNumRecs AS Long

REM  update the list values
Inherited.UpdateList( )

REM get the list's record set and number of records
vMyobj = self.GetRecordSet( )
vNumRecs = vMyobj.GetRowCount( )
vFound = FALSE

REM  for each record compare it to the fields value, if Found break out of the
REM  loop
FOR x = 1 TO vNumRecs
   REM advance to the current row counter
   vMyobj.SetCurRow(x)
   IF Dependent.value = vMyobj.GetColVal(1) THEN
      vFound = TRUE
      EXIT FOR
   END IF
NEXT x

REM if the value was not found, set the fields value to NULL and inform the user
IF NOT vFound THEN
    Dependent.value = NULL
    MSGBOX"The value for the Dependent Field has been set to NULL"
END IF
```

Form's Menu and Toolbar Methods

When you need to update your application's menu bars, toolbars, and status lines, use these methods. Of the methods listed in this section, only the Create<object_name>, DoCommand( ), and TestCommand( ) methods are on the form property sheet, but all use the GetContainer.method_name( ) Oracle Basic syntax when called. Chapter 11 gives examples of the use of these methods.

DefaultMenuBar( ), DefaultToolbar( )

These two methods are used to fill the menu bar or toolbar object, passed in as the argument to the method, with the system and application default menus or toolbar buttons appropriate for the form or report. You call these methods with Oracle Basic code any time you need to populate a new menu bar or toolbar object with the default menus or buttons. These methods first delete any existing menus or toolbars in the menu bar or toolbar. These methods do not add the toolbar or menu bar to the screen, they just populate the objects with the appropriate menu and toolbar button objects. The menus added to the menu bar object by Oracle Power Objects are true objects and can be manipulated just as if you created them with the NEW Menu Oracle Basic function. The following code illustrates how to create the objects and then populate them with these default methods. This code would be placed in the form's InitializeWindow( ) method.

```
DIM vMenuBarObj, vToolbarObj AS Object
vMenuBarObj = NEW MenuBar
vToolbarObj = NEW Toolbar
GetContainer.DefaultMenuBar(vMenuBarObj)
GetContainer.DefaultToolbar(vToolBarObj)
```

DoCommand( )

You enter Oracle Basic code to handle the execution of a selected menu item or toolbar button in this method on the appropriate form or report. These methods are on the property sheets for applications, forms, and reports. When the user selects a menu item or toolbar button, Oracle Power Objects reads the command code (an integer representing a command) from the selected menu item or toolbar button. Oracle Power Objects then checks the main, top-level form that created the active window to see if that object is to handle the selection. This is done by triggering that object's DoCommand( ) method with the command code read from the menu item or button as the argument.

If the top-level form's DoCommand( ) method inherits the system default code (no code is placed in the method), Oracle Power Objects checks the DoCommand( ) method of the application to which the active window belongs. If the request is still not handled, Oracle Power Objects then checks the system menu and toolbar handlers back at the form level to see if they handle the command. If this test fails, Oracle Power Objects finally checks the system handlers at the application level. If this final check fails, it simply reports that the command is not recognized.

The default action for the DoCommand( ) method is to return FALSE, indicating to Oracle Power Objects that it should look further down the chain for an entity to process the request. This chain of processing the command code from the selected menu or button allows you to set up your own global command processing code by entering the code at the application level. Thus every form that is opened in an application will use the same command processor. This allows you better control of what is going on in your application by having a central "application manager" that knows who is doing what to whom.

The system uses the predefined command codes listed in Table 9-3.

When you create menu items and add toolbar buttons, you should use code numbers for your commands that are greater than or equal to the constant Cmd_FirstUserCommand. For example, you can declare several known global menu and toolbar command codes at the application level in the declaration area on the application's property sheet. You then use these command codes in the various menus or toolbars for the forms and reports in the application. The following code shows how this is done.

```
GLOBAL gblNewMenuCmd1, gblNewTbBtn1, gblNewMenuCmd2, gblNewTbBtn2 AS Long
GLOBAL gblNumNewCmds AS Long
gblNewMenuCmd1 = Cmd_FirstUserCommand
gblNewMenuCmd2 = Cmd_FirstUserCommand + 1
gblNewTbBtn1 = Cmd_FirstUserCommand + 2
gblNewTbBtn2 = Cmd_FirstUserCommand + 3
gblNumNewCmds = 4
```

Then as you add menu items and toolbar buttons associated with command scripts, you can use these predefined command code variables. If you need to create other menu items or toolbar buttons that trigger a command, use code similar to that shown below.

```
vEvenNewerCmd = Cmd_FirstUserCommand + gblNumNewCmds
gblNumNewCmds = gblNumNewCmds + 1
```

Chapter 11 describes how this method is used in detail.

GetMenuBar( ), GetToolbar( ), GetStatusLine( )

In order to manipulate existing menus, toolbars, or status lines, you must have a reference to the object. You use these methods to retrieve the reference to the appropriate object in the existing form or report. Once you have the reference to the object, you use it with other methods to add, delete, or change objects contained

Cmd_New	Cmd_Copy	Cmd_QBF
Cmd_Open	Cmd_Clear	Cmd_QFFRun
Cmd_Close	Cmd_Paste	Cmd_Commit
Cmd_Save	Cmd_PasteSpecial	Cmd_Rollback
Cmd_SaveAs	Cmd_InsertObject	Cmd_NextPage
Cmd_Print	Cmd_Help	Cmd_PrevPage
Cmd_PrintSetup	Cmd_HelpOnHelp	Cmd_FullPage
Cmd_PrintPreview	Cmd_About	Cmd_Print
Cmd_Quit	Cmd_InsertRow	Cmd_RunStop
Cmd_Undo	Cmd_DeleteRow	Cmd_Cut
Cmd_Redo	Cmd_AppQuery	Cmd_FirstUserCommand

TABLE 9-3. *Oracle Power Objects Command Codes*

in the menu, toolbar, or status line. The following code illustrates using this code to retrieve a menu bar object. You use the other methods similarly.

```
DIM vMBar AS Object
vMBar = GetContainer.GetMenuBar( )
```

InitializeWindow( )

When you customize a window, using Oracle Basic to create your own menus, toolbars, and status lines, enter the code to do so in this method. This is the method Oracle Power Objects calls when an application opens a new form. This method takes no arguments and returns no value. By default, it loads the default menu bar, menus, and toolbar appropriate for the container. There is no default status line in run-time forms.

If you add code to this method, Oracle Power Objects will process your code to add to the form the objects your code creates. Oracle Power Objects requires that there be a menu bar and toolbar for each form. However, the method is smart enough to create and add the default menu bar to the form if you do not create and add your own menu bar to the form. The same applies to the toolbar, but the status line is optional. Thus, you can create a form that has the default menus but a customized toolbar by creating and adding only a toolbar in Oracle Basic code placed in this method. Use the methods described in the "Menu, Toolbar Button, and Status Line Customization Methods" section below to build and modify your own customized menu bars, menus, toolbar, and status line. For an example using this method, see Chapter 11.

SetMenuBar( ), SetToolbar( ), SetStatusLine( )

After you finish updating an existing object retrieved with the Get<object_name> method or created with the Oracle Basic NEW command, you replace the form's current menu bar, toolbar, or status line with these methods. These methods all take a reference to the new object as the only argument, i.e., GetContainer.SetMenuBar(myMenuBar). These methods do not delete the old objects. Therefore, if you need to delete the replaced object, by retrieving the old object with the appropriate Get<object_name> method before using the Set<object_name> method.

After replacing the old object, you use the DELETE Oracle Basic command to delete the replaced object, which must have been created by the NEW command, not created by default upon startup. This requires that you remember which objects you created and which objects the system created for you.

These methods can be used any time you need to change the menus in a form dependent on different conditions being met. For example, you may want to add a menu to select different printers after a Send to Printer button is pressed. The code to do this is shown below and assumes the printer menu, gblPrintMenu, has been created previously.

```
DIM vCurMenuBar AS Object
vCurMenuBar = GetContainer.GetMenuBar( )
vCurMenuBar.AppendMenu(gblPrintMenu)
GetContainer.SetMenuBar(vCurMenuBar)
```

TestCommand( )

Oracle Power Objects uses this method to check which menu items are to be enabled, checked, disabled, or disabled and checked when a user pulls down a menu. Oracle Power Objects then grays out a menu or toolbar item (disabled), adds a check by it, or enables the item depending on the return value of the method. In this way, your code can keep the menus updated as to what options are available to the user. It works in much the same way as DoCommand( ) does, in that Oracle Power Objects follows the same processing chain, and if no form or report handles the command, TestCommand( ) returns FALSE. There are four predefined constants used to indicate the status of a menu item:

TestCommand_Enabled	Command is enabled.
TestCommand_Checked	Command is enabled and checked.
TestCommand_Disabled	Command is disabled.
TestCommand_Disabled_Checked	Command is disabled and checked.

See Chapter 11 for an example of this method's use. Oracle Power Objects will call the DoCommand( ) method only if a menu or toolbar item is enabled and selected by the end user.

Menu, Toolbar Button, and Status Line Customization Methods

When you create an application that requires menus, toolbars, and status lines different from the ones the system creates, use these methods to accomplish that task. These methods work with objects created with the Oracle Basic NEW function and are not on the property sheet. There are four objects that are used: MenuBar, Menu, Toolbar, and StatusLine. These objects are created using the syntax vNewobj = NEW <object_name>. Creating these objects and their management currently is done in Oracle Basic scripts only. There will be graphical interfaces to work with these objects in future releases of Oracle Power Objects.

The purpose of these objects is to allow you to customize the run-time menu bars, toolbars, and status lines of your applications. See Chapter 11 for an example of using these objects and the associated methods. Because Chapter 11 covers the use of these methods in more detail, no examples are given here. Methods with like purposes are described together because the actions are the same but affect different objects.

GetMenuCount( ), GetItemCount( ), TBGetCount( ), GetStatCount( )

These methods simply return the number of items in the object. The syntax is

```
vCount = vMyobj.Get<object_name>Count.
```

This count is necessary if you need to cycle through the items in the object.

GetMenu( ), GetMenuItem( ), TBGetButton( ), GetStatPanel( )

These methods return a reference to the object requested that is contained in the object making the call (MenuBar, Menu, Toolbar, or StatusLine object). The first argument in each of these methods is an integer representing the position that the desired object occupies in the container. All but GetMenu( ) take a second argument, an integer, that describes what information the method is to return. The predefined constants for each type of data that can be returned are listed below.

- Data returned by GetMenuItem( ) using the following predefined integer constants:

MenuPart_Label	Returns a string with the item's label
MenuPart_Command	Returns the integer command code
MenuPart_Help	Returns an integer with the help context ID (or NULL if there's no help context)
MenuPart_Accel	Returns a string with the accelerator key (or NULL if there's no accelerator)

- Data returned by TBGetButton( ) using the following predefined integer constants:

ToolbarPart_Command	Button's command code
ToolbarPart_Bitmap	Bitmap object associated with the button
ToolbarPart_Help	Help context id of the button
ToolbarPart_Style	Item's style code

- Data returned by GetStatPanel( ) using the following predefined integer constants:

StatusLinePart_Text	Returns a string with the text currently displayed in the panel
StatusLinePart_Width	Returns the width in pixels of the panel
StatusLinePart_Command	Returns the panel's command code (an integer)
StatusLinePart_Msg_Enabled	Returns the "enabled" message string
StatusLinePart_Msg_Disabled	Returns the "disabled" message string
StatusLinePart_Msg_Checked	Returns the "checked" message string
StatusLinePart_Msg_Disabled_Checked	Returns the disabled-checked message string

The syntax for the use of these methods, except GetMenu( ), which does not use the What argument, is shown below. Simply delete the What argument for the GetMenu syntax.

```
vRtnValue = vMyobj.Get<object_type>(position, What)
```

where What is one of predefined constants appropriate for the object_type described above. The vMyobj variable must have been created with the NEW Oracle Basic command or retrieved with one of the Get<Menubar|Toolbar|StatusLine> methods described in the previous section.

ClearMenuBar( )

This method simply clears all menus from the calling MenuBar object. It does not delete them. If you need to delete the individual menus, first retrieve a reference to the menu with vMyMenuBar.GetMenu(menu_position), remove it from the MenuBar with RemoveMenu(menu_position), and finally delete it with the Oracle Basic command DELETE. If you are going to delete all the menu objects, then use DeleteAllMenus( ).

DeleteAllMenus( ), ClearToolbar( ), ClearStatusLine( )

These methods delete all objects contained in the respective container object. The syntax is

```
vMyobj.Method_name( )
```

You cannot delete the first panel in a StatusLine.

AppendMenu( ), AppendMenuItem( ),TBAppendButton( )

These methods enable you to add the named object to the end of the current list of items in the container. In Windows, the Window and Help menus will always be at the end of the MenuBar—in other words, AppendMenu( ) will insert the new menu before these two menus but after other existing menus. The syntax for each method is given below.

AppendMenu( ) The syntax is

```
MyMenubar.AppendMenu(vNewMenu)
```

where vNewMenu is first created with the Oracle Basic NEW command.

AppendMenuItem( ) The syntax is

```
MyMenu.AppendMenuItem(itemLabel cmdCode, helpContext, accelerator)
```

where

- itemLabel is the label of the menu item to be displayed in the menu.
- cmdCode is an integer greater than Cmd_FirstUserCommand (see DoCommand( ) above).
- helpContext is an integer that Oracle Power Objects passes to the system when the online help is triggered (such as F1 in Windows) to select previously created help files.
- The accelerator string is a keyboard shortcut to trigger the menu item. To create an accelerator (or keyboard equivalent) for the item, you specify a string containing the accelerator. The string uses the following syntax:

  ```
  [^] [+] {char | Fkey}
  ```

Element	Description
^	The system command key (the CTRL key on Windows, the COMMAND key on Macintosh) is part of the accelerator.
+	The SHIFT key is part of the accelerator (available only in Windows).
char	Specifies a standard alphabetic or numeric key equivalent in the range "A" to "Z" (either upper- or lowercase; the case of the character does not matter).
fkey	Specifies a function key in the range "F1" to "F12" (available only in Windows).

An alphabetic key equivalent always includes the system command key even if you do not specify it. For example, the accelerators "A" and "^A" are identical.

You can also choose a letter of the menu item label to act as a menu shortcut in Windows. The letter you identify is marked with an underscore when displayed. The user can select the menu using the keyboard by typing the ALT key, then the letter you specify. To mark a letter of the label as a menu shortcut, prefix the letter with an ampersand (&).

TBAppendButton( ) The syntax is

```
MyTB.AppendButton(cmdCode, design, style, helpcontext)
```

where

- cmdCode is an integer greater than Cmd_FirstUserCommand (see DoCommand( ) above).
- design is a bitmap (BMP format) object.
- style is a style of button using one of the following constants:

ToolbarStyle_PushBtn	A standard pushbutton
ToolbarStyle_Toggle	An on/off toggle button
ToolbarStyle_Separator	A space between buttons

- helpcontext is the help context ID number.

InsertMenu( ), InsertMenuItem( ), TBInsertButton( ), InsertStatusPanel( )
These methods are nearly the same as the Append methods described above except that you also give the position to insert the object in its container. The first position in each container is 1. In Windows, the Window and Help menus will

always be at the end of the MenuBar. The syntax for the first three methods is exactly the same as described in the Append<object> methods above except the first argument is an integer representing the position the object is to take in the container. The syntax for the StatusLine is

```
MyStatLine.InsertStatusPanel(panelPos, width, maxMsgLength)
```

where

- panelPos is the position in the status line the panel is to take.
- width is the width of the panel in pixels.
- maxMsgLength is the maximum length of the message string, in bytes, that can be displayed. Longer strings will be truncated. There is always at least one panel, and if it is the only one, it takes up the entire status line.

DeleteMenuItem( ), TBDeleteButton( ), DeleteStatusPanel( )

These methods delete the named object at the given position in the container. The syntax for these methods is

```
vMyobj.Delete<object_name>(objPosition)
```

The first panel in a status line cannot be deleted.

RemoveMenu( )

This method simply removes the menu at the given position from the MenuBar. It does not delete it. If it is to be deleted, retrieve the pointer to the object with vMyMenuBar.GetMenu( ), remove it from the MenuBar, and then delete it with the Oracle Basic command DELETE. The syntax for this method is

```
vMyMenuBar.RemoveMenu(menuPos)
```

SysDefaultMenuBar( ), SysDefaultStatusLine( )

These methods populate the object with the system, not application, default menus and panels. They clear out any existing menus or panels in the container and then fill the container with menus or status panels appropriate for the system. For example, invoking the SysDefaultStatusLine( ) method in Windows will fill the status line with the main message panel, and the keyboard indicator panels (Caps Lock, Num Lock, Scroll Lock). The menus and panels for systems may change with different releases of operating systems, so your scripts should not depend upon certain menus or panels always being there.

The menus created for the MenuBar are exactly as if you had created them yourself using Oracle Basic commands. Thus, you can remove them, modify them, or delete them as required by your application.

SetMenuItem( ), TBSetButton( )

Once a menu item or button is added to its container, use these methods to designate what is displayed in the menu item or toolbar button and what is invoked by selecting it. The syntax for these two methods is

```
vMyobj.Set<object_name>(objPosition, what, value)
```

where objPosition is the object to be updated, what is one of the constants described above in Get<object_name> methods, and value is the information to be set corresponding to the what argument. Thus to create one menu item, you must call this method four times to set the menu item's name, command code, help text, and accelerator string.

SetStatDispList( )

This method allows you to have Oracle Power Objects automatically display one of four strings at different times in the given panel. Oracle Power Objects uses the TestCommand( ) method (described in the "Form's Menu and Toolbar Methods" section above) to ascertain which string to display. When you call this method, you tell it which panel to use, what command id to use (the one TestCommand will be looking for), and the four strings to be displayed corresponding to the four values that TestCommand( ) can return (TestCommand_Enabled, TestCommand_Checked, TestCommand_Disabled, TestCommand_Disabled_Checked). The complete syntax for the method is

```
MyStatLine.SetStatDispList(panelPos, cmdCode, "enabled string",
                "checked string", "disabled string",
                "checkedDisabled string").
```

SetStatusPanelMsg( )

When you need to display your various status messages at different times, use this method. It simply places the given string in the given panel. Its syntax is shown below.

```
MyStatLine.SetStatusPanelMsg(panelPos, Message)
```

User-Defined Methods

Just as the developer can define additional properties to further refine the definition of the various objects in Oracle Power Objects, methods can be defined as well. When you define a method, you use the User Property Sheet, as described in Chapter 8 in the "User-Defined Properties" section. A user-defined method can only be declared as either a function or subroutine.

Basically, a function is a method that returns a value to the method that called it. The value returned can be a simple integer, a Boolean value (TRUE or FALSE), a string, or any other valid datatype in Oracle Power Objects. The value can be calculated within the function, retrieved from the database, or be simply a TRUE or FALSE to tell the calling method if the function succeeded performing the duties asked of it. A function can take arguments that are needed for the calculation or action to succeed. For example, a method may be defined to return the phone number of a customer whose id number is passed into the function. The customer id is the argument to the function, and the phone number is the value returned by the function.

A subroutine is a method that performs some action but does not return a value. Use a subroutine type of method when the calling routine does not need a value returned or does not need to know if the operation performed by the subroutine succeeded or not. Just like a function, a subroutine can take arguments (though it does not have to), which the method uses to complete its job. An example of a subroutine method is one that is called by a method to simply display the values passed in as arguments.

When you define a method, you define any arguments to be passed to the method when it is called by Oracle Basic code. You cannot predefine Oracle Basic code to be the default action for the newly defined method. Each individual object to which the user-defined method is added must have method code entered in the method, or it is simply ignored. The user-defined method is invoked only by Oracle Basic code in other methods. The syntax for triggering a user-defined method is the usual object name and method name, such as ObjectName.UserMethod( ). If any arguments were declared for the method, they must be included in the call, or the error message "Unknown Property" will be displayed when Oracle Power Objects executes the code calling the user-defined method.

You add the newly defined method to an object just as you add a user-defined property to an object. Select the box on the left of the method and then drag and drop the method onto the property sheet of the object that needs the new method. The next step is to add the method code to be processed when the method is triggered.

An example of a user-defined method is one that checks for SQL errors after the use of the EXEC SQL statement in other methods. To do this, open the User Properties editor by clicking on the User Properties icon on any property sheet toolbar. Page to the bottom of the editor and type in the name of the method, **SQLErrCheck**, in the first blank column. Set the type of the newly entered item to be a function (remember, a function returns a value after running the Oracle Basic code; subroutines do not return a value), set the return value to Long, and ignore the argument fields, as no arguments are needed for this example

Now open an object in which the EXEC SQL statement is used in one or more methods. Add the SQLErrCheck( ) method to the object's property sheet as explained above. Select the new method (its location on the property sheet is dependent upon which property sheet toolbar buttons are activated—see Chapter 3—and will have a large + in front of it) and add the following code to the method.

```
DIM vErrStr AS String
DIM vRtnVal AS Long Integer

vRtnVal = FALSE
REM See if there was an error in the EXEC SQL call. If so
REM retrieve the error
REM text and display it.
IF SQLERRCLASS( ) <> 0 THEN
  vErrStr = SQLERRTEXT( )
  MSGBOX "Query failed:" & vErrStr
  vRtnVal = TRUE
END IF
sqlerrcheck=vRtnVal
```

Now place the Oracle Basic statement err=self.sqlerrcheck( ) after the call to the EXEC SQL statement in all the other methods that use this function. Any error conditions encountered by the EXEC SQL function can now be handled appropriately by one method rather than having to have the error-catching code in every method that uses the EXEC SQL statement.

There is no clean way currently to add a user-defined method with predefined actions. The online help suggests making a separate Methods form within the application and add all of the user-defined methods to this form's property sheet. If the user-defined method needs to know which object triggered it, you can include as an argument to the method the reference to the object that called the method. Within the Methods form, add the code needed for each user-defined method. Now when another object requires the user-defined method, add an Oracle Basic statement similar to Methods.User_Method(self) to the method code in the object calling the new method. See the discussion on enabling the menu items under "Creating the Menu" in Chapter 11 for an example of a FileExists user-defined method used this way.

User-defined methods are a very powerful feature of Oracle Power Objects that can give you the ability to customize objects to fit virtually any requirement. As described above, you can use them to handle error conditions, to do specialized calculations that do not logically belong in the other methods of the object, or to do nearly anything else a creative mind can devise. This feature, along with the user-defined properties, makes Oracle Power Objects a truly powerful development tool.

Conclusion

This chapter's purpose is to acquaint you with every method provided by Oracle Power Objects and show how you can create your own methods. Hopefully, some of the examples given will help you in your application development process or at least trigger ideas to create solutions to meet your individual project's requirements.

CHAPTER 10

Using SQL with Oracle Power Objects

In many of the examples in previous chapters, we include SQL statements in either the EXEC SQL Oracle Basic statement or the SQLLookup( ) function. This chapter will help familiarize you with the SQL language, enough so that you can create simple queries and updates. The following topics will be covered in this chapter:

- General, basic description of SQL
- Review of some database concepts
- Operators and functions used in SQL

- Various SQL commands
- Using variables in SQL
- Using EXEC SQL and SQLLookup to execute SQL statements
- Short overview of the procedural language PL/SQL

The basic use of the main SQL statements is given in this chapter, but if you need more information on the exact syntax for a SQL command or you are interested in a detailed study of the SQL language, refer to your database manuals or any of the many published books on SQL. PL/SQL is an option for the Oracle server to provide procedural capabilities to SQL. This language adds more flexibility to SQL, providing methods to control the flow of the execution of SQL statements and create and call procedures. Other relational databases usually include their own extensions to SQL to provide this capability. You can use any such language in conjunction with both the EXEC SQL and SQLLookup functions described in this chapter.

Introduction

SQL was developed by IBM to provide an interface to the relational database they were developing in their San Jose research laboratory in the middle to late '70s. Since then, SQL has become the standard language to access most relational databases. Because of this, scripts of SQL statements are more or less portable between operating systems and different relational databases.

SQL is more than a query language, not withstanding its name. Within the SQL language, there are two major components: DDL (data definition language) and DML (data manipulation language) statements. The DDL statements are those used to define the database and include the CREATE, ALTER, and DROP statements. The DML statements are those used to manipulate and retrieve the data within the database, such as the INSERT, UPDATE, and SELECT statements. In addition, SQL includes statements that are used for administrative purposes, such as adding users and assigning tablespaces to users.

SQL is a programming language but it is not a procedural language. It does not contain process control statements (WHILE loops, IF statements, etc.), variables, or subroutines. Generally, SQL works on sets of data (tables) restricted by constraints included in the statement. A single SQL statement can retrieve a single item or thousands of items from the database depending on what the user requests in the SQL statement.

Though the formal SQL language does not use variables as such, Oracle Power Objects' version of SQL can use the same variables defined in the Oracle Basic code containing the SQL statement. These variables are called *bind variables.* Most often, variables are used when the SQL statements are "embedded" within a regular programming language such as C or Oracle Basic. Most of the SQL statements used in methods described in the examples in previous chapters are embedded SQL statements in Oracle Basic code. You can use most SQL statements as embedded statements with some variations. The SELECT...INTO statement is an example of an embedded SQL statement altered from the original SELECT statement. The INTO clause allows you to have the SELECT statement load values from the database into variables. Some SQL statements are embedded in Oracle Basic code without modification, such as the COMMIT and ROLLBACK statements.

Designing SQL Statements

Chapters 2 and 4 discuss the concepts behind database creation. By understanding how a database is created, you can more easily design SQL statements to accomplish the desired actions. You can run into trouble by not properly setting up the constraints in your query to the database. An example of this is joining two tables and retrieving much more data than anticipated. A *join* is the combining of two or more tables based on common fields in the different tables. This is done by requesting data from two or more tables and joining the tables with conditional statements in the WHERE clause of the SELECT command. The most common type of join, the *equi join,* is one that combines two or more rows of different tables based on common fields with equal values.

For example, a customer table and an employee table may both have a city field. These two tables can be joined to combine customers with employees in the same city. This may cause a large number of records to be retrieved, because if two employees are in the same city, then the retrieved recordset will have twice as many rows as there are customers that live in the city. In other words, every customer in the city is matched with each employee that lives in the city. This is called *fan out,* and you must be careful in your SQL statements to avoid unplanned fan out that can overwhelm your system.

Other joins are called *inequality joins,* which simply join two tables together when the data in a specified field in one table (A) is greater than or less than the value in a specified field in another table (B). This too can create a large fan out—every row in table A will join with every row in table B that meets the criteria. The only way to prevent large, unwanted fan outs is to carefully plan your database and construct your SQL statements to adequately restrict the query. This is done by normalizing the tables (see Chapter 2) in the database and using appropriate filters in the WHERE clause and modifiers in your SELECT statement. For example, you can use the DISTINCT modifier in a SQL statement to tell the database engine to retrieve no duplicates.

SQL and Oracle Power Objects

There are four ways in which Oracle Power Objects uses SQL to interface with your database. The first is completely hidden from you in that any time you run a form or report with bound controls or use the Table or View Editor, Oracle Power Objects automatically creates the appropriate SQL statements to accomplish the required task.

The second method is also done automatically by Oracle Power Objects but uses bits and pieces of SQL that you have included in the various property values. For example, in the QueryWhere( ) method, you add just a fragment of a SQL statement to the method, not a full statement, i.e., CNAME = 'Henry Jones'. Oracle Power Objects collects the necessary fragments of SQL, combines them with other necessary parts of the statement based on what is in the form, and then sends a complete SQL statement to the database for processing.

This work is done in Oracle Power Objects Record Manager. When working with the data retrieved by forms, reports, etc. using the methods associated with the object, you are working with the Record Manager. The Record Manager operates on the recordset object that is created by the query defined with the various properties of the object. It is the Record Manager that creates and executes the SQL statements necessary to accomplish the necessary actions upon the recordset object. One major difference of working with the Record Manager and SQL is that the Record Manager works with one row at a time, while SQL works with sets of data. You should not use SQL directly when working with a recordset but rather use the recordset methods associated with that object (see Chapter 9).

The last two ways in which Oracle Power Objects uses SQL to interface with your database involve the use of complete SQL statements you create. You use SQL when you need to accomplish tasks not normally or easily done using just the predefined methods in the Oracle Power Objects objects or when you need more direct control of data retrieval from the database. These tasks include database administration, loading derived controls (using SQLLookup in the DataSource property), or loading a list. Using complete SQL statements bypasses the Record Manager, thus Oracle Power Objects' methods to access the data retrieved by direct SQL cannot be used. You use Oracle Basic code, PL/SQL, or more SQL statements to utilize this data. You issue the SQL statements that you create with the EXEC SQL statement and the Oracle Basic function SQLLookup( ). These two methods are discussed in detail in the "Issuing SQL Commands" section later in this chapter.

SQL Overview

In this section, we will very briefly cover the operators, functions, and commands used in the SQL language. Only those items that are most commonly used will be discussed in any detail. SQL is case-insensitive, and all commands, table names (unless in double quotes), column names (unless in double quotes), etc. can be in either or mixed case. In this chapter, all SQL commands and reserved words are in all caps and the database names are in lowercase. SQL reserved words are listed in Appendix C.

SQL Operators

As with any programming language, there is a set of operators used by SQL to accomplish various actions. The different types of operators are grouped together according to their functionality.

Arithmetic Operators

You use arithmetic operators to modify numeric operands within the SQL statement. For example, the statement below increments the salary of employee #1234 by 5 percent using the =, +, and * operators.

```
EXEC SQL UPDATE employee SET sal = sal + sal * .05 WHERE vEmpId = 1234
```

Note the use of the = as both an assignment operator and as a comparison operator. The +, -, and / operators are also used in date arithmetic. Descriptions of each of the SQL arithmetic operators are given in the following table.

Operator	Description
+ (unary)	Makes operand positive
- (unary)	Negates operand
/	Division (numbers and dates)
*	Multiplication
+	Addition (numbers and dates)
–	Subtraction (numbers and dates)
=	Assignment operator. Sets the operand on the left to the expression on the right.

Comparison Operators

You use comparison operators to compare the values of one expression with another. An expression can be a literal, variable, function, or a combination of all. The result of a comparison is TRUE, FALSE, or NULL. The following table lists the comparison operators and definitions used by SQL. If any operand is NULL, the comparison returns NULL except for the IS [NOT] NULL operator, which returns TRUE or FALSE.

Operator	Description
=	Resolves to TRUE if both values are equal.
!=, ^=, ¬=, < >	Four versions of the inequality test, all mean not equal. Use the one you are used to.
>	The value on the left is greater than the value on the right.
<	The value on the left is less than the value on the right.
>=	The value on the left is greater than or equal to the value on the right.
<=	The value on the left is less than or equal to the value on the right.
IN	Resolves to TRUE if the operand value on the left is equal to any value in the following list of values.
NOT IN	Is TRUE if the left operand is not equal to any of the values in the following list.
ANY, SOME	Similar to IN but allows the use of the other comparison operators; =, !=, >, <, <=, or >=. These operators precede ANY or SOME.
ALL	Similar to ANY but the left value must meet the comparison operators condition for all values in the list. ALL must be preceded by =, !=, >, <, <=, or >=.
[NOT] BETWEEN x and y	[Not] greater than or equal to x and less than or equal to y.
x [NOT] LIKE y [ESCAPE z]	TRUE if x does [not] match the pattern y. Within y, the special character % matches any string of zero or more characters except null. The special character _ matches any single character.
EXISTS	Resolves to TRUE if a subquery returns at least one record.
IS [NOT] NULL	Checks the value to see if is [not] NULL. This is the only operator to use to check for NULLs.

Logical Operators

Very often you need to set up conditions that involve the logical combination of the results of expression (expressions resolve to TRUE, FALSE, or NULL). Use these operators to accomplish this task.

Operator	Description
NOT	Returns TRUE if the result is FALSE, otherwise it returns FALSE
AND	Returns TRUE if both conditions are TRUE, otherwise returns FALSE
OR	Returns TRUE if either condition is TRUE, otherwise returns FALSE

Set Operators

There are times when you need the filtered results of two queries. These operators allow you to choose which rows obtained by two queries are to be loaded into the recordset. For example, if you want to compare the customer table from two departments in the company, you could use these operators to select the common customers, the different customers, or only those customers in one table but not the other. You would have to make sure that the queries selected the same columns from the two tables. The following code could be placed in the Click( ) method of a Compare button on a form that also has two text fields. The user enters the names of two tables and then presses the Compare button to extract the names of those customers in the first table but not in the second. This example is fairly basic in that it hardwires the columns to select. The example could be expanded to allow the user to enter column names as well.

```
DIM vDiffs AS Object
DIM vTab1, vTab2 AS String
DIM x, i AS Integer

REM set two variables to store the table names.
vTab1 = TABLE1.value
vTab2 = TABLE2.value

REM create a new object to contain the records to be retrieved
vDiffs = NEW DBRecordset(TUB)

REM set the query to select the differences between table1 and table 2
REM this assumes that table1 contains the extra customers.
vDiffs.SetQuery(
     "SELECT custid, name FROM "+vTab1+" MINUS SELECT custid, name FROM "+vTab2, FALSE)

REM now query the database and make sure all rows are fetched
```

```
vDiffs.ReQuery()
vDiffs.FetchAllRows()

REM get the number of rows retrieved and then cycle through the data set and
REM display each different record.
x =vDiffs.GetRowCount()
IF x > 0 THEN
    FOR i = 1 TO x
        vDiffs.SetCurRow(i)
         MSGBOX("different customers "+CSTR(vDiffs.GetColVal("CUSTID"))+"; "&
+vDiffs.GetColVal("NAME"))
    NEXT i
ELSE
    MSGBOX("retrieved no differences")
END IF
REM now delete the recordset that was created.
DELETE vDiffs
```

The following table describes each set operator.

Operator	Description
UNION	Returns all distinct rows selected by either query
UNION ALL	Returns all rows selected by either query, including all duplicates
INTERSECT	Returns all distinct rows selected by both queries
MINUS	Returns all distinct rows selected by the first query but not the second

Other Operators

There are two more operators used by Oracle SQL, the || concatenation operator and the + operator. (Note that these are SQL operators, not Oracle Basic operators.) The || operator concatenates two string operands into one string. The + operator indicates that the preceding column is the outer join column in a join. Other databases may have more operators, such as bitwise operators, that you can use in the SQL statements you create to be processed by your particular database engine.

SQL Functions

Just as in other programming languages, there are many functions you can use to return desired values. The following tables list the SQL functions and a brief description of each. For detailed information on the use of the functions (most are fairly self-explanatory), see your database documentation.

Number Functions

These functions all return a numerical value. The following table shows the list of mathematical functions used in SQL.

Function	Description
ABS(n)	Returns the absolute value of n.
CEIL(n)	Returns the smallest integer value greater than or equal to n.
COS(n)	Returns the cosine of n.
COSH(n)	Returns the hyperbolic cosine of n.
EXP(n)	Returns e raised to the nth power.
FLOOR(n)	Returns the largest integer value less than or equal to n.
LN(n)	Returns the natural logarithm of n where n is greater than 0.
LOG(m, n)	Returns the logarithm to the base m of n. m must be any positive number not equal to 1 or 0, and n can be any positive number.
MOD(m, n)	Returns the integer remainder of m divided by n. Returns m if n = 0.
POWER(m, n)	Returns m raised to the n power. If m is negative, n must be an integer. Otherwise m and n can be any number.
ROUND(n, [m])	Returns the number n rounded to the number of decimal units given by the integer m. If m is omitted, it rounds to 0 places.
ROUND(d, [fmt])	Rounds the given date according to the fmt given.
SIGN(n)	Returns the sign of n as -1, 0, or 1 where n is < 0, = 0, or > 0 respectively.
SIN(n)	Returns the sine of n.
SINH(n)	Returns the hyperbolic sine of n.
SQRT(n)	Returns the square root of n. n must be positive.
TAN(n)	Returns the tangent of n.
TANH(n)	Returns the hyperbolic tangent of n.
TRUNC(n, [m])	Truncates any decimal part of a decimal fraction to the m number of decimals. If m is left out, it truncates to 0 decimal positions.

TRUNC(d, [fmt])	Truncates the given date according to the given format.

Character Functions

Most of these functions operate on character strings and return either a character or a string. The following table lists the string functions used by SQL.

Function	Description
CHR(n)	Returns the ASCII character equal to the binary value of n.
CONCAT(string1, string2)	Returns the string value of string1 and string2 concatenated together. Equivalent to the II operator.
INITCAP(string)	Returns the string with the first character of each word capitalized and all other letters in lowercase. The words are delimited by white space and nonalphanumeric characters.
LOWER(string)	Returns string with all letters in lowercase.
LPAD(string1, n, [string2])	Returns a string padded on the left with n characters from string2. If string2 is omitted, it pads with the space character. If string1 is longer than n, it returns the truncated string of length n.
LTRIM(string1, [string2])	Returns string1 with all characters in string2 removed from the left of string1 up to the first character not in string2. If string2 is omitted, it trims the space character, from the left of string1.
NLS_INITCAP(string1 [,nsl_param])	Same as INITCAP except it uses a NLS sort parameter. If omitted, it uses the systems default sort parameter.
NLS_LOWER(string1 [,nsl_param])	Same as LOWER except it uses a NLS sort parameter. If omitted, it uses the systems default sort parameter.

NLSSORT(string [, 'nls_parms'])	Returns the string of bytes used to sort string. If nls_parms is set to 'NLS_SORT=BINARY', NLSSORT returns string.
NLS_UPPER(string1 [,nsl_param])	Same as UPPER except it uses a NLS sort parameter. If omitted, it uses the systems default sort parameter.
REPLACE(string, search_string [,replace_string])	Returns a string with all occurrences in string that match the search_string with the value in replace_string. If replace_string is omitted, it returns string with all matches with search_string removed. If search_string is NULL, string is returned.
RPAD(string1, n, [string2])	Returns a string padded on the right to length n with characters from string2. If string2 is omitted, it pads with the space character. If string1 is longer than n, it returns the truncated string of length n.
RTRIM(string1, [string2])	Returns string1 with all characters in string2 removed from the right of string1 up to the first character not in string2. If string2 is omitted, it trims the space character, from the right of string1.
SOUNDEX(string1)	Returns a string with the phonetic representation of string1. It allows you to compare strings that are spelled differently but sound the same. It is useful in searches when you do not know the exact spelling of a word but you know what it sounds like.
SUBSTR(string1, m [,n])	Returns a string from string1 beginning with the letter at position m and is n characters long or the remainder of the string if less than n. If m is negative, it returns the string up to the character at position m counted towards the beginning of the string from the end of the string. m must not equal 0 and n must be greater than 1. If n is omitted, all remaining characters are returned.

SUBSTRB(string1, m [,n])	Same as SUBSTR but m and n are bytes. This is used for two-byte characters. For single byte languages, it is identical to SUBSTR.
TRANSLATE(string, from_str, to_str)	Returns the string in which all characters in the from_str are replaced by the corresponding character in the to_str. If there are more characters in the from_str than in the to_str, the remaining characters in from_str are removed from string.
UPPER(string)	Returns the string with all characters in string converted to uppercase.

Character Functions Returning Number Values

These functions return a number that you can use in Oracle Basic code to work with and validate character data. For example, the LENGTH function is commonly used to retrieve the length of character strings to validate data entry. The INSTR function is especially useful to verify that a required string is in a response received from the end user. The following table lists the string functions that return a numeric value.

Function	Description
ASCII(string)	Returns the decimal representation of the first character in string.
INSTR(string1, string2 [, n [, m]])	This function returns the character position of the mth occurrence of string2 starting with the nth position in string1. If n is negative, Oracle Power Objects searches from the end of the string. The returned position is always relative to the beginning of string1. If string2 is not in string1, it returns 0. If omitted, n and m equal 1.
INSTRB(string)	Same as INSTR except n and m represent bytes. In single byte languages, INSTR and INSTRB are identical.
LENGTH(string)	Returns the length of the string.
LENGTHB(string)	Returns the number of bytes in the string. For single byte languages, it is the same as LENGTH.

Date Functions

All of the functions listed in this table return a date.

Function	Description
ADD_MONTHS(d, n)	This function will return the date d plus the number of months n. If the day part of d is the last day of the month, the function will return the last day of the added month even if the resultant month has fewer days.
LAST_DAY(d)	Returns the last day of the month contained in d.
MONTHS_BETWEEN(d1, d2)	Returns the fractional number of months between the two dates, including the time fraction. If the day components are the same or are the last day of their respective months, the result is an integer number of months.
NEW_TIME(d, z1, z2)	Returns the time in z2 based on the date d in time zone z1. The time zone arguments are the standard three letter designations such as MDT (Mountain daylight time) or GMT (Greenwich mean time).
NEXT_DAY(d, string)	Returns the date with corresponding time of the first day of the week that matches the day's name in string that is later than the day in d.
SYSDATE( )	Returns your system's current date and time.

Conversion Functions

Very often, it is necessary to convert one datatype to another. Most often, it is necessary to convert a number to a string representation to be displayed in a message box. The SQLLookup function and the GetColVal method always return a string, thus the conversion functions, listed in the following table, are required to convert the string back to the original datatype (see Chapter 4 for details on datatypes).

Function	Description
CHARTOROWID(string)	Returns the database rowid represented by string, which must be of VARCHAR2 datatype.

CONVERT(string, dest_char_set [,source_char_set])	Converts the string from the source_char_set to a string using the dest_char_set. The default for source_char_set is the database's character set.
HEXTORAW(string)	Converts the string containing hexadecimal digits to a Raw datatype.
RAWTOHEX(string)	Converts the raw string to a string containing its hexadecimal equivalent.
ROWIDTOCHAR(rowid)	Converts a rowid datatype to a string of VARCHAR2 datatype that is always 18 characters long.
TO_CHAR(n | d [, fmt [,nls_param]])	Returns a string of VARCHAR2 datatype that represents the given number or date. The optional fmt string can be any of those described in Chapter 4. The nsl_param allows you to designate the language to which the date or number is to be converted. Its format is 'NLS_LANGUAGE=language'.
TO_DATE(string [, fmt [,nls_param]])	Convert the VARCHAR2 string to a date based on the given date format. If fmt is omitted, then string must be in the default date format. If fmt = J for the Julian format, string must be a number. The nls_param designates which language the string is in.
TO_MULTI_BYTE(string)	Converts all single byte characters to their multibyte representation. This function is useful only if the characters set contains both single and multibyte character representation.
TO_NUMBER(string [,fmt [,nls_param]])	Converts the VARCHAR2 string to a number according to the optional format string fmt. The nls_param designates the language.
TO_SINGLE_BYTE(string)	The opposite of TO_MULTI_BYTE. It does not convert multibyte characters that have no corresponding single byte character.

Group Functions

This is a very important set of functions. They provide the means to quickly gather various types of statistics from a table. They are very often used in conjunction with the GROUP BY clause in SQL to show the various statistics grouped by a given column. For example, the SUM function on the AMOUNT column in the orders table can give the total sales for each salesperson as shown in the SalesByCust example in Chapter 6. In that example, the GROUP BY clause is created automatically by Oracle Power Objects, but the SUM function is used in the DataSource property for the TOTAL field in the detail part of the report. When these functions are used, all items in the SELECT statement must also be a group function or included in the GROUP BY clause at the end of the statement. An example of a valid SQL statement with group functions is shown below.

```
SELECT repid, MAX(amount), MIN(amount), SUM(amount) FROM orders GROUP BY
repid;
```

The column REPID is not in a group function so it must be included in the GROUP BY clause. This statement will retrieve the largest and smallest sales and the total sales of each sales representative.

In several of these group functions, shown in the following table, you have the choice of telling the database engine to choose only the distinct values in the column (distinct) or all of the values. By default, all values are retrieved.

Function	**Description**
AVG([distinct | all]column)	Returns the average of all values in the given column.
COUNT({* | [distinct | all]column})	Returns a count of rows in a table. If you use *, it returns a count of all rows in the table including NULLs and duplicates. If you designate a column, it does not count NULLs and will count either all or distinct values in the column.
MAX([distinct | all]column)	Returns the maximum value in the column. Distinct seems a little redundant here.
MIN([distinct | all]column)	Returns the minimum value in the column.
STDDEV([distinct | all]column)	Calculates the standard deviation of the numbers in the column. The column must of datatype NUMBER.
SUM([distinct | all]column)	Returns the sum of all or the distinct values in a column.
VARIANCE([distinct | all]column)	Returns the variance of the numbers in column. Column must be of NUMBER datatype.

Miscellaneous Functions

In the following table are the usual nonclassifiable functions that just don't fit in the other categories. Some of these functions are rather esoteric, and we recommend that you review your database documentation and online help for more details and examples of their use.

Function	Description
DUMP(expr [,rtn_fmt [,start_pos [, length]]])	Returns a VARCHAR2 string containing the datatype code, length in bytes, and the internal representation of expr.
GREATEST(expr [,expr] ...)	Returns a VARCHAR2 string containing the expression with the greatest value. The datatypes of all expressions in the list are converted to the datatype of the first expression.
LEAST(expr [, expr] ...)	Opposite of GREATEST.
NVL(expr1, expr2)	If expr1 is NULL, it returns expr2, otherwise it returns expr1. Returns the datatype of expr1 or VARCHAR2 if expr1 is character data. This function is most useful to be sure a default value is returned if expr1 may be NULL.
UID( )	Returns an integer that uniquely defines the current user.
USER( )	Returns the current user in a VARCHAR2 string.
USERENV(option)	Returns information based on the option value about the current session in a VARCHAR2 string. The information can be the terminal type, session id, etc. See online help for more detail.
VSIZE(expr)	Returns the number of bytes containing the internal representation of expr.

SQL Commands

Because Oracle Power Objects does most of the work for you, you do not often need to use most of the SQL commands. For example, the Table and View Editors are much easier to use than the CREATE TABLE and CREATE VIEW commands. Similarly, it is much easier to type in the required data in an opened table rather than use the INSERT command. This section will simply list the various commands and their main use. If you need more information on using these commands, refer to your database documentation, online help, or a good SQL reference manual. The "Data Retrieval and Manipulation" section later in the chapter describes in more detail the commands of most use to Oracle Power Objects users.

As stated at the beginning of this chapter, there are three general groupings of SQL commands: DDL (data definition language), DML (data manipulation language), and other commands used to control transactions and system administration. The system administration commands are not described here, as they are beyond the scope of this book.

Data Definition Commands

These commands are used to create, modify, and delete the various objects in the database. Most of these commands are never needed by Oracle Power Objects users, because the work is done using graphical interfaces rather than by SQL code entered in the various methods. There are only three commands, but each command is used differently with different objects. The descriptions below show each command, the objects to which it can be applied separated by the | character, and a brief description of its use.

ALTER INDEX | SEQUENCE | TABLE | VIEW This command is used to modify an existing object. You use it to add or modify columns in a table, re-create a view (you cannot add or modify columns in a view), change the next number generated by a sequence, change the storage parameters for the objects, and accomplish various other tasks. You cannot delete a column from a table in Oracle. Most of these tasks are done by the various editors provided by Oracle Power Objects. The main use for this command is to alter the storage parameters for the object, because Oracle Power Objects does not have a built-in object to do this.

CREATE INDEX | SEQUENCE | TABLE | VIEW This command simply creates the designated object. All of these actions are done nicely by using the Oracle Power Objects editors. However, there are times you may need to use the CREATE TABLE and CREATE VIEW commands. For example, you may need to explicitly set the storage parameters for the object as you create it. The CREATE TABLE command can be very useful to create a table that is a subset of another table by using the AS clause. An example of this syntax is shown here:

```
EXEC SQL CREATE TABLE paris_custs AS SELECT custid, name, address, city FROM
Custs WHERE city = 'PARIS';
```

This statement will create a table with the customer id, name, and address of all customers who live in Paris. It does not need to use all the columns in the Custs table. If you want a table with all the columns, then use the * character rather than individual column names in the select statement.

DROP INDEX | SEQUENCE | TABLE | VIEW This command is very straightforward—it simply deletes the named object from the database. The simplest way to delete the object is to open the session in which the object resides, highlight it by clicking on it, and then select the Cut button on the toolbar. However, if you have created a temporary table in a method, you would use this command to delete it after the work using the temporary table was completed.

Data Manipulation Commands

These commands are used to modify, add, or otherwise manipulate the data within the database. These commands all act on tables (or indirectly on base tables through a view). Again, most of the time Oracle Power Objects has the facilities to accomplish these tasks without your needing to explicitly use SQL to invoke these commands. You can delete, update, and insert new data in a table using the Table Browser window. Every time you run a form that has controls bound to the database, Oracle Power Objects is using the SELECT command. The SELECT command is probably the most used SQL command in Oracle Basic code. The use of this command will be demonstrated in detail in the "Data Retrieval and Manipulation" section later in the chapter.

DELETE Deletes rows from the given table or view's base table. It can include the WHERE clause to filter the rows to be deleted. To delete a given employee from the Emp table, you would use the following command:

```
DELETE FROM Emp WHERE Empno = 104
```

INSERT Inserts a row into the given table or view's base table. You can designate the columns in which data is to be added and or a list of the values to be inserted in the columns in the table. Often, you will use a subquery using the SELECT statement to retrieve data to be inserted into the table. An example of inserting one row of data into the Bonus table is

```
INSERT INTO Bonus (Ename, Job, Sal, Comm)
              VALUES ('Jane Henry', 'Sales Rep', 35000, 0.10)
```

A more detailed description of the INSERT command is in the "Using the INSERT and UPDATE Commands" section later in the chapter.

LOCK TABLE Locks one or more designated tables in the lock mode specified. The lock mode includes EXCLUSIVE lock, which allows only you to update the table while others can query the table, and ROW SHARE mode, which allows others concurrent use of the table. Its main use is to override the automatic locking when a form is accessing a table. LOCK TABLE locks an entire table in the given mode. If you need to lock just a few rows, use the SELECT FOR UPDATE command discussed later in the chapter in "Using the SELECT Statement."

SELECT This command retrieves data from the designated columns in the given table or view. It is used as both a stand-alone command and as a subcommand within another commands. This command can become very complex, involving several tables, columns, conditions, and grouping parameters to retrieve the exact data required. For more complicated selects, you need a strong knowledge of relational algebra and database design, but for most needs, the command is relatively simple. This command is discussed in more detail in the "Data Retrieval and Manipulation" section.

UPDATE If you need to modify existing data in the database, use this command. You designate the table and rows to be updated and the new data with which the database replaces the old value. The WHERE clause allows you to specify the exact conditions to meet before the data is updated. A more detailed description of the UPDATE command is in the "Using the INSERT and UPDATE Commands" later in the chapter.

Transaction Commands

A transaction is a set of changes to related data. A transaction begins when you make the first change in the data in a form and ends when you either commit or rollback the changes. Generally, Oracle Power Objects handles these commands for you. They are invoked when you press the Commit or Rollback buttons on the toolbar or when you call the CommitWork( ), RollbackWork( ), CommitForm( ), or RollbackForm( ) methods. Oracle recommends that you use these methods rather than explicitly issuing the COMMIT or ROLLBACK SQL commands when working with a form's recordset. If you have made changes directly to the database using SQL (bypassing Oracle Power Objects normal interface to the database), then you must explicitly call ROLLBACK or COMMIT to remove or store the changes.

Oracle Power Objects simply uses the default TRANSACTION parameters. Thus, there may be times when you need to explicitly direct how Oracle Power Objects handles the transaction in which you are working. In these cases (for example, assigning a large rollback segment to the transaction), you must explicitly use the SET TRANSACTION SQL command. You could place it in the OnLoad( ) method of the application or form that updates large amounts of data at once. Following are brief descriptions of the transaction commands.

COMMIT Saves the work you have been doing by writing any stored information to the database. Once committed, the work cannot be removed with the ROLLBACK statement. Its syntax is simply the command COMMIT.

ROLLBACK If you decide that the work completed so far is wrong or not needed, you issue this command to flush the data from the buffers storing the changes. It does not allow the data to be written to the database. The syntax for the ROLLBACK statement is simply the command ROLLBACK.

SAVEPOINT This command sets a point in the transaction at which a rollback will stop. Since Oracle Power Objects does this automatically, you probably will not need to use this command.

SET TRANSACTION This command is used to set the read-write parameters and assign a specific rollback segment to your current transaction. Obviously, you need detailed knowledge of your database server to set the rollback segment (you cannot set the rollback segment in the Blaze database). You can either set the read-write parameter or the rollback segment at one time. You cannot do both with one command. By default, Oracle Power Objects uses a randomly assigned rollback segment and sets the transaction to read-write. There may be times when you know that the work involves a large amount of data. In this case, you use the SET TRANSACTION command to assign a large rollback segment to your transaction. Enter the code to do so in the OnLoad( ) method of the application or form that requires the large rollback segment. The statement below tells the database server to use Rollback Segment Rlarge and is placed in the form's OnLoad( ) method.

```
EXEC SQL SET TRANSACTION USE ROLLBACK SEGMENT Rlarge
```

Data Retrieval and Manipulation

In this section, the use of the SELECT statement, bind variables, and potential pitfalls are discussed. Normally, Oracle Power Objects retrieves data using the Record Manager to populate the controls in the various forms, reports, etc. that make up the application you are designing. However, there are times when you need to retrieve or modify data directly from the database, bypassing the Record Manager. As stated earlier, the SELECT SQL statement is the command that retrieves data, while the INSERT and UPDATE commands modify data. An important part of all these commands is the set of conditions used to restrict the action performed by the command to only certain records that meet all the restrictions.

Using the SELECT Statement

The SELECT statement has a very complex syntax, but we will illustrate only a part of the power of the SELECT statement in this section. If you need more information, see a good SQL reference manual or your database documentation. The abbreviated syntax for the embedded SELECT statement is shown here, followed by an explanation of the various parts.

```
EXEC SQL [AT {db_name | :host_variable} ]
    SELECT select_list INTO :host_variable [, :host_variable] ...
    FROM table_list [WHERE condition ] [GROUP BY expr [, expr] ... [HAVING condition]]
    [{UNION | UNION ALL | INTERSECT | MINUS} SELECT command ]
    [ORDER BY {expr|position} [, {expr|position}] ...]
    [FOR UPDATE]
```

The first option in this command, AT, allows you to select the session from which the data is to be retrieved. Note that it can take the explicit name of the session or an Oracle Basic variable that contains the name of the session.

The select_list is composed of either the * character or a list of column names, group functions, or sequence.{curval | nextval}. The * is shorthand for every column in the table(s) from which data is to be extracted. The group functions were described in the "SQL Functions" section earlier. The sequence.{curval | nextval} retrieves the appropriate value from the given sequence.

The values retrieved are inserted into host variables (bind variables), the number of which must match the number of columns retrieved. The variables may be arrays or simple variables, depending on the need. They are always prefixed with a colon (:). See the section "Bind Variables" later in the chapter for more detail.

The table list is simply the list of tables or views, and an optional alias for each, from which the SELECT statement is to retrieve data. If you are requesting columns with the same name in two tables, you must prefix the name of the column with either the name of the table or its alias.

A special table called DUAL is a dummy table automatically created with the database. It is used when you need to select values returned by functions, calculated values that are not in a table, or sequence values. For example, to retrieve the next value from a sequence, you would use the following statement.

```
EXEC SQL SELECT myseq.nextval INTO :nextnum FROM DUAL.
```

To retrieve the current date you would use

```
EXEC SQL SELECT sysdate INTO :curdate FROM DUAL.
```

The WHERE clause can be quite complex depending on the conditions that filter the data to be retrieved. It can be a simple equality check, such as retrieving all records from the customer table where the repid equals the given employee id. Or it can very complex with a series of logical operators and operands and even subqueries to retrieve additional information. For example, the following statement retrieves names of sales reps who have had sales greater than $2,000 and live in Salt Lake City. This statement uses all of the options except the AT option. Note the series of AND conditions it takes to link the sales rep to the orders. This is necessary because Orders does not include the sales rep's id. Thus the query first finds all customers who are serviced by the given sales rep and then sums the amounts in the orders for that customer.

This query could possibly be optimized by rearranging the conditions, but it serves its purpose in showing how complex select queries can become. Obviously it can become more complex by asking for the data between certain dates or on orders of specific items, etc. Note the alias "emp" for the Employee table. Because both the Custs table and the Employee table contains a column named Name, you have to tell the database which name column to retrieve by prefixing the column name with the table's name or its alias, in this case, "emp".

```
SELECT emp.name, SUM(amount) INTO :names, :totals FROM employees emp, orders, Custs
WHERE emp.cityid IN (SELECT cityid FROM cities WHERE cname = 'SALT LAKE CITY') AND
orders.custid = Custs.custid AND Custs.repid = emp.EmpId
GROUP BY emp.name HAVING sum(amount) > 2000 ORDER BY emp.name;
```

The GROUP BY clause is described in the "Group Functions" section earlier in the chapter. It simply tells the database engine the column by which the retrieved items are grouped. In this example, it groups the data according to the employee name.

The HAVING clause allows you to further restrict the information returned by setting conditions based on the value the group function returns. In this case, only those sales reps with summed sales greater than $2,000 are included in the retrieved data.

The set operators UNION, INTERSECT, etc. are discussed in the "Set Operators" section earlier in the chapter, which includes an example of their use.

The ORDER BY clause simply tells the database engine to return the data sorted on the given column(s). In the example above, the data will be sorted by the employee names.

The final clause, FOR UPDATE, simply locks the selected rows and disallows anyone else from modifying them.

Many of the examples in Chapter 7 make use of this command. In addition, some of the properties described in Chapter 8 use this command when issued by the SQLLookup function.

Using the INSERT and UPDATE Commands

Generally, you will not need to use these commands explicitly, because the insertion and updating of data in the database is done by the Record Manager. The only time you would need to use these commands is when you are inserting and updating data into a table that is not bound to a form or report. The example of auditing the use of programs in Chapter 7 inserts data into a programs-used table explicitly whenever an application is closed. The UPDATE command could be used to update the count of times used for a program rather than inserting a new record. The simplified syntax for both of these commands is given below.

```
EXEC SQL [AT {db_name | :host_variable} ]
   UPDATE {table | view} SET
       { (column [, column] ...) = (subquery)
       |  column = {expr | (subquery) } } ...
       [WHERE condition]
```

```
EXEC SQL [AT {db_name | :host_variable} ]
  INSERT INTO {table | view}
     [ (column [, column] ...) ]
     {VALUES (expr [, expr] ...) | subquery}
```

When you use a subquery, which is a SELECT statement, the number of values and the datatypes of the values returned from the subquery must match the number of columns and the datatypes of the columns in the column list. This applies to both the UPDATE and INSERT commands.

One example of the use of the UPDATE command is to update the salaries of all employees in a given department. This is shown below.

```
EXEC SQL UPDATE employees SET sal = (sal + sal * :raise) WHERE deptno = 30
```

The INSERT command is used whenever new data is inserted into a table. As mentioned above, an example of this command is to load the name of the user and program name when an application is closed. This code would be entered in the CloseApp( ) method of the application. It depends on two global variables, userid and progname, being set when the application is opened.

```
EXEC SQL INSERT INTO progusage (user, pname) values (:userid, :progname)
```

These examples and most other examples use variables that are declared in the Oracle Basic code that calls the EXEC SQL statement or the SQLLookup( ) function. The following section describes bind variables in detail.

Bind Variables

Bind variables are simply Oracle Basic variables used in a SQL statement executed with the EXEC SQL statement. The variable must be declared before use when used as an input variable, but it can be implicitly declared when used as an output variable. See Chapter 7 or Appendix B on how to declare variables for use in Oracle Basic code.

Restrictions on Bind Variables

Bind variables cannot be used in a string literal (as explained in the "SQLLookup" section later). To use the value of a variable in SQLLookup, it must be concatenated into the string using the CSTR( ) function when necessary and the Oracle Basic string concatenation operators + and &.

You cannot use the value property of an object as a bind variable. You must first assign the value of the object to a variable and use that variable in the SQL statement.

Another restriction on bound variables is that they cannot represent the name of a column or table in the database. In other words, the following code is *invalid* because it is using a variable containing the name of the table from which data is selected. The only exception to this is that the AT clause can take a variable containing the session name.

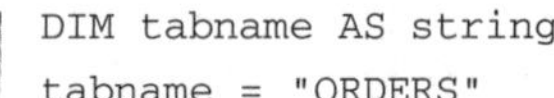

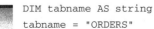

```
DIM tabname AS string
tabname = "ORDERS"
REM invalid use of a bind variable used as the table_list in the select
REM statement
EXEC SQL SELECT SUM(amount) FROM :tabname
```

Using Bind Variables

Now that we have covered the invalid uses of a bind variable, let's see just where they can be used. The following list shows the most common places a bind variable is used in SQL statements.

- With the INTO clause, which loads retrieved data into the given variables
- With the VALUES clause, which loads data into a row that is inserted into a table

- With the "column =" SET clause in the UPDATE command, which updates the value in that column
- With the "column <comparison operator>" clause in the WHERE clause where it is used in comparisons

Of course, output variables can have their values assigned to Oracle Power Objects control object's values once the SQL statement has loaded the variables. An example of each of the above conditions is given below.

```
DIM vEname AS String
DIM vMaxSal, vRaise AS Float
DIM vDeptNum AS Integer

REM set the vDeptNum variable because the EXEC SQL statement cannot take
REM the value of the deptno control object directly.
vDeptNum = myform.deptno.value

REM use output bind variables to store the retrieved data and an input
REM variable to designate the department number. This will retrieve only one
REM value because the variables are not arrays.
EXEC SQL SELECT name, MAX(sal) INTO :vEname, :vMaxSal FROM employees &
WHERE deptno = :vDeptNum GROUP BY name

REM use the values retrieved to load values into the Highest_Paid table
EXEC SQL INSERT INTO highest_paid COLUMNS (name, sal) VALUES(:vEname, :vMaxSal)

REM Again assign object values to variables
vDeptNum = myform.vRaise_dept
vRaise = myform.vRaise_val

REM use the variables to update the Employee table
EXEC SQL UPDATE employees SET sal = sal + (sal *:vRaise)WHERE deptno = :vDeptNum
```

In addition to *scalar variables* (holding one value), you can use arrays. They are most useful when used in the SELECT statement and in loops when updating or inserting data into the database. Again, you declare the array variable in the Oracle Basic code and then use it appropriately in the SQL statements. The array will be automatically filled when used as output variables, but you can use only one element at a time when they are used as an input variable. For example, the following code loads all of the employee names and ids into two arrays in one statement. However, when the variables are used as data in the VALUES clause of an INSERT statement, they have to be accessed one element at a time using temporary variables, because you cannot use an array, or even a subscripted array, as input variables. This example transfers employees from one department to another company.

```
REM arrays have to be declared as STATIC, not DIM
STATIC vEname(20) AS String
STATIC vEmpId(20) AS Integer
DIM vTmpEname AS String
DIM vTmpId, vDNo, vNumRows, i AS Integer

REM Get the department number for the employee transfer
vDNo = ChangeForm.deptno
REM select all of the names and employee id's INTO the two arrays at one time
EXEC SQL SELECT name, EmpId INTO :vEname, :vEmpId FROM employee        &
WHERE deptno = :vDNo

REM Get the number of rows selected and decrement by one because the array
REM starts with zero.
vNumRows = SqlRowCount() - 1

REM Now for each row, insert the employees into the new table. Note that you
REM cannot use an array inside the VALUES clause so you must set the
REM temporary scalar variables and use them.
FOR i = 0 TO vNumRows
   vTmpId = vEmpId(i)
   vTmpEname = vEname(i)
   INSERT INTO newcomp COLUMNS(name, EmpId, deptno) VALUES(:vTmpEname, & :vTmpId, :vDNo))
NEXT i
REM Because this is not using the Record Manager you must explicitly commit
REM the changes.
EXEC SQL commit
```

The examples that have been used up to now have all used Oracle Basic code to give structure and control to the scripts. See the "Brief Overview of PL/SQL" section later in the chapter for examples of using this SQL language extension to give process control to your SQL statements.

Issuing SQL Commands

Now that we have covered the basics of SQL, we can describe the two main ways to have Oracle Power Objects send the SQL statements to the database engine for processing. These are the EXEC SQL statement and the SQLLookup( ) function.

EXEC SQL

This is a very powerful function in Oracle Basic. It allows you to send your own SQL statements to accomplish tasks not done by Oracle Power Objects. You can use the EXEC SQL function in any of the system or user-defined objects' methods to send SQL statements to the database for processing. It gives you maximum control of the database (providing you have the necessary privileges). A very important characterization of this function is that Oracle Power Objects does not preprocess the command. It sends the statement exactly as written to the database with the exception of handling bind variables and identifying the session to which the statement is to be sent. This means that you use the SQL flavor that comes with your database. Each relational database generally has some unique additions to the SQL language that only that database understands. Thus, you can use Oracle Power Objects to send queries and receive data from database servers other than Oracle.

The syntax for using EXEC SQL is extremely simple, as shown here:

EXEC SQL [AT {session object name | :session_name_variable}] {SQL statement | :sql_stment_variable}

The information in the [ ] is optional and simply tells the function which session to use. If left blank, Oracle Power Objects will use the default session defined in the Main application window. Thus, if there is more than one session defined in the Main window, it is advisable to explicitly set which session the SQL statement is to use, because the default session may be changed as the application is developed and evolves. This can cause maintainability problems if the current default session is not correct for a SQL statement using the default session. The | indicates that you use an explicit statement or a variable, but not both. This means you can use either an explicit SQL statement with variables or a string variable that contains a valid SQL statement. (Bind variables must be prefixed by a colon.) However, you cannot use variables inside a SQL statement variable because Oracle Power Objects will send the string contained in the variable directly to the database and will not preprocess any variables in the command string. Obviously, the database would not handle variable names in the string properly. The following code is invalid because of this.

```
DIM sql_var AS String
sql_var = "SELECT name INTO :cname FROM Custs WHERE custid = :custno"
EXEC SQL :sql_var
```

The database accessed by the default session would not know what to do with :cname or :custno. The way to get around this limitation is to concatenate the necessary information into a single string. This is described later in this chapter in the "SQLLookup" section.

Normally, Oracle databases use single quotes as delimiters around string literals and ignore the double quote. However, if you have a database with column or table names that contain spaces or other reserved characters, use the double quote to force Oracle to use the entire string as the name of the object. For example, the following statement is legal if the database contains the quoted column name.

```
EXEC SQL SELECT "Customer Name" INTO :cname FROM Custs
```

Unlike SQL, Oracle Basic uses the double quote to delimit strings. This allows you to set a command variable that contains single quotes as shown in the code fragment below. The single quotes are required in the SQL statement to denote the string literal George Hill.

```
DIM cmd_stment AS String
cmd_stment = "UPDATE employees SET sal = sal + sal * .05 WHERE name = &
 'George Hill'"
EXEC SQL :cmd_stment
```

If the SQL statement is too long for the text entry field or you want to format the statement in an easily read manner, you can break the statement into parts by using the & character at the end of each break. (You cannot break a string literal, however.) This is especially useful when using PL/SQL or some other SQL extension that requires several lines of code. The following is an example of using the & character.

```
EXEC SQL                                                        &
    SELECT name, sum(amount) FROM Custs, orders                 &
       WHERE Custs.custid = orders.custid                       &
       ORDER BY name
```

Each time you use the EXEC SQL statement, it returns several result variables that can be accessed by Oracle Basic functions. You use these results to handle error conditions or, upon success, data control. These functions and their use are explained in the following sections. The last description in this section covers the use of the WHENEVER clause, which causes Oracle Power Objects to handle error or end-of-data conditions in different ways.

SQLRowCount( )

When the most recent EXEC SQL statement succeeds, Oracle Power Objects sets a rowcount variable that is accessed by the SQLRowCount( ) function. This variable contains the number of rows the query affected, i.e., the number of rows updated, retrieved, etc. If there is an error or the information is not available because the database driver does not set it, this function will return zero. On a query, the value returned by this function can be used to set a limit on an Oracle Basic or PL/SQL loop control structure.

SQLErrClass( )

This function returns an integer representing the success or type of failure of the SQL statement most recently processed. The table below shows the integer value and the classification associated with each integer. This classification code is independent of the database being accessed.

Value	Classification
0	Operation successful
1	General failure (no specific information available)
2	Unable to acquire resource lock
3	Referential integrity violation
4	Unable to acquire resource (disk full, etc.)
5	Syntax error in SQL statement
6	Table not found
7	Column not found
8	User/schema not found
9	Object not found
10	Value error (out of range, etc.)
11	Invalid/incorrect datatype
12	Invalid date value
13	Invalid format mask

While Oracle Power Objects does not have a premade object to accept SQL statements typed in directly from the end user, it is easy to create a form that allows the user to do so. This function would then be essential to let the end user know exactly what was wrong with a SQL statement that fails. For the developer, this function and the following functions are most useful for debugging the application under development. See the example given in the "User-Defined Methods" section in Chapter 9.

SQLErrCode( )

All databases sometimes have a very long list of error codes designed to help the user understand any mistakes made. This Oracle Basic function returns the error code provided by the database regardless of what database is being used. Upon receiving one of these error codes, the end user can refer to the documentation provided with the database to ascertain the remedy to the problem.

SQLErrText( )

Associated with the error codes provided by the database is a character string that gives a brief description of the problem. This Oracle Basic function returns this string. For more detailed information about the error and possible remedies, the user would use the error code returned by the SQLErrCode function to look up the error in the database's documentation.

WHENEVER Clause

Oracle Power Objects does not automatically inform you of any errors in a SQL statement sent to the database with EXEC SQL. However, by using the WHENEVER clause, you can direct Oracle Power Objects to raise an error message box or perform other actions when an error occurs. The syntax for the WHENEVER clause is

```
EXEC SQL WHENEVER {NOT FOUND | SQLERROR | SQLWARNING}
        {CONTINUE | GOTO label_name | STOP | DO routine_call | RAISE}
```

The NOT FOUND and SQLWARNING options and the GOTO, STOP, and DO actions are not available for the Blaze database. The RAISE option is not available for the Oracle Server.

The options are more or less self-explanatory: when a given condition happens during an EXEC SQL execution, the assigned action is to take place. The CONTINUE option is the default action for both the Blaze and Oracle database. This action simply allows the application to proceed to the next statement in the Oracle Basic code (or return from the method). The GOTO action causes the application to begin executing code beginning at the given label defined in the Oracle Basic code within the method in which the SQL statement was issued. The STOP action does just what it says—it tells Oracle Power Objects to stop running the application when an error occurs.

The DO action is probably the most useful in that it executes the given method. This can be a user-defined method designed to handle errors. If the error is not serious, the handler can simply return and let the calling method continue. Otherwise it can take appropriate action from stopping the application to correcting the error and allowing the application to continue.

The RAISE action simply causes Oracle Power Objects to display an error message window. If there is an error handler defined for the method (see ON ERROR in the online help) that called the EXEC SQL function, that handler is called when the error window is dismissed. Otherwise, the application will stop.

SQLLookup

This function is of most use in properties that can accept a derived value or where the application needs to access the database directly to derive a single value (see the SalesByCust example in Chapter 6). You use this function to return a single value from the database. If the query returns more than one value, only the first value is returned by the function. If the query retrieves no rows, SQLLookup( ) returns a NULL.

The *Oracle Power Objects User's Guide* states that the type of data returned depends on the datatype chosen by the database driver. The Oracle driver for Oracle Power Objects has SQLLookup( ) always return the queried value as a string. Therefore, you generally need to use one of the Oracle Basic conversion routines to convert the returned string value to the proper datatype.

This function sends a complete query to the database and uses only the SELECT command. You cannot use bind variables as output variables in SQLLookup. In other words, you cannot use the embedded SELECT...INTO: variable syntax. The application can use input variables only by concatenating them into the command string sent to the database by the SQLLookup( ) function. The syntax for SQLLookup is

SQLLookup([session name,] sql_statement)

The session name is optional and, like the EXEC SQL function, if the session name is left out, the SQLLookup( ) will use the default session. The sql_statement must be a valid SELECT statement delimited by double quotes. You can concatenate several different strings and variables together to form the single sql_statement string required by the function.

There are two Oracle Basic operators you can use to concatenate strings and variables together to create the sql_statement string. They are the & and the + characters. The difference between the two operators is that the & ignores a NULL if the value it is concatenating to the string is a NULL, leaving the first string intact (which may not be desired). The + operator will cause the entire string to be NULL if either side of the + operator is NULL. Thus, if your query depends on both sides of the concatenation operator to be not NULL, then use the + operator, because SQLLookup will then just return a NULL. The function will not send the query when the sql_statement is NULL. An example of the use of the + is given below. In this case, if the & is used and vMaxSal was NULL, the select statement would be invalid and cause a database error. With the + operator, if vMaxSal is NULL, the entire string is NULL and SQLLookup simply returns a NULL.

```
vMyStringVar = SQLLookup("SELECT name FROM employees WHERE SAL > " +
CSTR(:vMaxSal))
```

In addition to concatenating the value of Oracle Basic variables to the sql_statement string, you can concatenate the value of the form's text control fields to the string. For example, the SalesByCusts report example in Chapter 6 uses the SQLLookup( ) function as the DataSource for the TOTAL text field. To retrieve the correct data, the SQL statement must include the value of the text field CUSTID defined in the report. This statement is shown here:

```
=SQLLookup("SELECT sum(amount) FROM orders WHERE custid = " +
CSTR(CUSTID.VALUE))
```

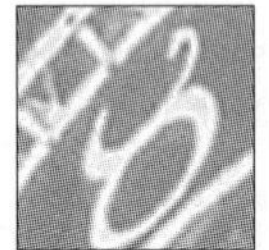

NOTE
The & concatenation operator will convert the numeric value in the text control CUSTID to a string automatically, but the + operator requires you to use the CSTR( ) Oracle Basic conversion function.

Brief Overview of PL/SQL

This extension to SQL created by Oracle is a separate product and is not supported by Blaze. If you have not purchased it for your Oracle server, any use of PL/SQL will fail. While this discussion is about PL/SQL, other databases have similar extensions, and this basic discussion applies to the use of them in a general way as well. This discussion is very limited and its purpose is just to acquaint you with the possibilities of PL/SQL and how to use it in Oracle Power Objects.

As described earlier, SQL itself is not a procedural language and has no process control commands. PL/SQL provides these missing ingredients to make SQL a full-fledged programming language. It is beyond the scope of this book to cover the language in any detail, and you will need to refer to your database documentation to make full use of this powerful language. However, a few constructs and examples are given in this section to acquaint you with the potential that PL/SQL has to solve the problems that Oracle Power Objects and SQL may have difficulty handling. The examples here are not complex and could be handled by Oracle Power Objects and SQL, but they will give you an idea about how the language can be used.

PL/SQL is executed in Oracle Power Objects by using the EXEC SQL procedure. EXEC SQL issues just one line of code to be processed by the database engine. However, that one line of code can contain many individual SQL or PL/SQL statements. This is done by using the line continuation character, &, at the end of each separate line in the PL/SQL block or series of SQL statements. A PL/SQL block can be as many lines long as necessary by using the & to concatenate the lines into one line of code for the EXEC SQL statement.

The syntax for using PL/SQL is

```
EXEC SQL                          &
[DECLARE                          &
  declaration statement]          &
BEGINs                            &
  PL/SQL or SQL statement         &
END
```

After the EXEC SQL command, a PL/SQL block must begin with either the DECLARE or BEGIN statement. If the DECLARE statement is used, BEGIN must follow the declaration statement. All subsequent lines must be either PL/SQL or SQL statements and the final statement must be END. Once inside the PL/SQL block, you do not use the EXEC SQL statement with the SQL statements.

You can create and store procedures made up of PL/SQL and SQL code in the database. You can call these procedures from any subsequent PL/SQL code in the current application or any other application that uses the database and knows about the procedure. Most likely, you would create the procedure outside of Oracle Power Objects and then just call it from the application that can use it. In addition to user-defined procedures, there are many system procedures that were created when the database was built or that can be added to the database by invoking the appropriate SQL scripts provided with the Oracle database. See your Oracle documentation for a list of these procedures.

The best way to see how PL/SQL works is through an example of a PL/SQL block of code. In the following example, you, as database administrator, use a form that contains fields bound to an empty BigTables table that contains columns to hold table names and sizes. The form also contains a button in which the following code is entered to check the sizes of all tables in the user's table space. If a table's size is greater than a given size specified in a SIZE text field, the procedure will insert the table name and size into the BigTables table. It then requeries the database so that other text fields in the form bound to the BigTables table can display the large tables found, if any. This is necessary because the form does not know the database has been changed, since the changes were made using SQL and PL/SQL rather than using Oracle Power Objects' predefined methods.

Note that variables declared inside the PL/SQL block cannot be used outside the block. If you need the information stored by these PL/SQL variables outside of the block, then you should declare the variable in the Oracle Basic code instead. You do not preface variables defined inside the PL/SQL block with a colon (:). This example uses a very powerful feature of PL/SQL—the cursor. A *cursor* is simply a pointer that keeps track of the current position in a set of records retrieved by the cursor definition. It can be used in iterative loops to retrieve data from the recordset, one record at a time. Instead of the assignment operator, which is := in

PL/SQL, you use the FETCH operator as shown in this example to assign values to a variable. When you declare a cursor, you define it with the SQL statement necessary to retrieve the data required.

This example uses the system-created table User_Tables, which stores information about all the tables the current user owns. However, the fields that contain the size information are filled only by running the ANALYZE command. Thus, for this example to work, the ANALYZE command must have been previously run for each table owned by the user. It is assumed in this example that this has been done before this code is executed. Note that each complete PL/SQL statement must end with a semicolon (;).

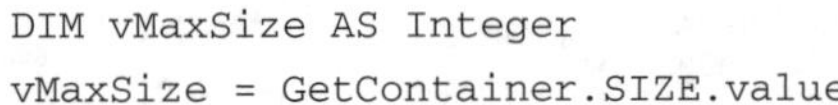

```
DIM vMaxSize AS Integer
vMaxSize = GetContainer.SIZE.value

REM You cannot use a bind variable in the cursor declaration but
REM you can use a variable declared in the PL/SQL block. Therefore set the
REM PL/SQL variable to the bind variable before you open the cursor.

EXEC SQL                                                                    &
DECLARE                                                                     &
   k  Integer;                                                              &
   c1 AS CURSOR                                                             &
      SELECT table_name,  blocks FROM user_tables WHERE blocks > k;         &
BEGIN                                                                       &
   k := :vMaxSize;                                                          &
   open c1;                                                                 &
      FOR c1rec in C1 LOOP                                                  &
         INSERT INTO BigTable values (c1rec.table_name, c1rec.blocks);      &
      END LOOP;                                                             &
END;
REM now have the form ReQuery the database to load the recordset with the
REM newly inserted data.
GetContainer.Query()
```

This example simply declares a cursor to retrieve all table names and their size if their size is greater than the value entered in the SIZE text field in the form. It then cycles through the cursor and inserts the table name and size in the BigTable. Note that you access the values of the cursor by prefixing the name of the column retrieved with the name of the cursor. You can fetch all of the values retrieved into bind arrays in one FETCH statement if desired. This is a relatively simple PL/SQL sample and just gives you a hint of the power of PL/SQL.

The PL/SQL language incorporates several process control constructs, including those listed below. In the loop constructs you can use the EXIT command to break out of the loop.

```
IF condition THEN
.......
END IF
```

Note that END IF is two words.

```
IF condition THEN
.......
ELSE
......
END IF
```

```
IF condition THEN
.......
ELSE IF condition THEN
........
END IF
```

```
LOOP
......
END LOOP
```

```
WHILE condition LOOP
.......
END LOOP
```

```
FOR counter in lbound .. ubound LOOP
......
END LOOP
```

There are many other powerful features of PL/SQL not covered in this very brief overview. The example presented in this section demonstrates how to execute a PL/SQL block of code in Oracle Power Objects. It gives you an idea of the power of PL/SQL and its potential to help you accomplish requirements for an application that cannot be done easily with Oracle Power Objects alone.

Conclusion

This chapter was an introduction to the SQL language. For real power SQL programming, refer to your database manuals or any of the many SQL manuals available. However, for most applications, the information in this chapter will suffice to help you write the SQL statements you need to meet your application's requirements. With the knowledge gained in this chapter, you can write fairly complex SELECT statements, add, modify, or delete data from the database, and control, in a minor way, the operation of the database. But the real power of Oracle Power Objects is that for many applications you will not need SQL at all.

Advanced Oracle Power Objects Features

In this chapter, we will cover a variety of Oracle Power Objects advanced features. The first section will explain how to create a cross-tab (cross-tabulation) report using values selected by a user on another form. A second advanced application will demonstrate the functionality of Oracle Power Objects in writing addresses onto Avery labels. We will then cover how to import and use OLE objects and OCX custom controls and use DLLs in Windows applications. The last section will explain how to modify the user interface by adding a custom menu and status line to an application.

Creating a Cross-Tab Report

One of the less obvious reports that you can create with Oracle Power Objects is a cross-tab report. A *cross-tab report* is a summary report that presents the desired data with headings across the top and the left side like a spreadsheet, with the data in the middle of the table with totals across the bottom and right side. Cross-tab is short for cross-tabulation, and it refers to the manner in which totals are provided at the right side and bottom. Common uses of cross-tab reports are for creating summary reports of sales by employees by quarter, sales by office by month, etc. Figure 11-1 shows a typical cross-tab report.

In Oracle Power Objects, there is no predefined cross-tab report object. Therefore, this example explains how to develop a cross-tab report similar to the rptSalesReport report included in the Oracle Power Objects sample MoonLight Demo–DONE application. The rptSalesReport is an aggregate report that lists each employee and lists below the employee those countries in which the employee has made a sale. This cross-tab report example lists the countries at the top of the report with the employees down the left side of the report. The report includes the sales by employee to different countries with the total sales for each employee on the right side of the report. The report also includes the total sales to each country along the bottom of the report, with the company's total sales in the lower-right side of the report.

MoonLight Products
"Everything under the Moo

Sales By Country

Saturday, JULY 08, 1995

Sales Rep	USA	Canada	France	Spain	Germany	Total Sales
ALLEN	$6,480.00	$0.00	$0.00	$0.00	$7,125.00	$13,605.00
WARD	$380.00	$2,362.00	$0.00	$0.00	$0.00	$2,742.00
MARTIN	$6,536.25	$0.00	$0.00	$0.00	$0.00	$6,536.25
BLAKE	$0.00	$0.00	$0.00	$0.00	$0.00	$0.00
TURNER	$371.25	$0.00	$0.00	$0.00	$0.00	$371.25
JAMES	$0.00	$0.00	$0.00	$0.00	$0.00	$0.00
Sales Totals	$13,767.50	$2,362.00	$0.00	$0.00	$7,125.00	$23,254.50

FIGURE 11-1. *Cross-tab report showing sales by country for each sales rep*

Creating a New Form (frmSBC)

We will first create a form, frmSBC. The form has five pop-up list controls to select the countries that will be used on the report, an Exit button to close the form, and a Create Report button to open the report in Print Preview mode.

To create the new form:

1. Click on the New Form button on the toolbar.
2. Set the ColorFill property to a light gray, the Name property to **frmSBC**, and the Label property to **Select Countries**.
3. Select the Static Text tool on the Object palette, click near the top of the form, and type **Sales By Country**. Set the FontName and other related properties to create the header.
4. Select the Pop-up List Box tool on the Object palette and click on the form to create a pop-up list.
5. Change the Name property to **cntry1** and the Label property to **Country1**.
6. Type in the Translation property, **=countries.name=id**, of the Cntry1 control.

This displays the names of the countries located in the Countries table in the pop-up list and sets the value of the Cntry1 pop-up list to the id of the selected country.

7. Select the Cntry1 pop-up list and click on the Copy icon on the toolbar and then click on the Paste icon four times.

The duplicate pop-up lists will be automatically labeled Country2, Country3, Country4, and Country5. The Name property will be automatically changed to cntry2, cntry3, cntry4, and cntry5. The rptSaleByCountry selects the country information from these pop-up lists to create the report.

You next place two buttons on the form, one to close the form and the other to open the rptSalesByCountry report in Print Preview mode.

8. Select the Push Button tool on the Object palette and click near the bottom of the form. Type **Exit** to set the label of the button.
9. Type **GetContainer.CloseWindow( )** in the Click( ) property.

Clicking on the Exit button in Run-time mode will close the frmSBC form.

10. Select the Exit button and copy and paste to create a new button. Type **Create Report** to set the button's Label property.

11. Type **rptSalesByCountry.OpenPreview( )** in the Click( ) property.

Clicking on the Create Report button on the frmSBC form in Run-time mode will open the rptSalesByCountry report in Print Preview mode.

Now change the OnLoad property of the MoonLight Demo–DONE application to automatically open the frmSBC form when the application is running. To change the OnLoad property:

12. Activate the MoonLight Demo–DONE application window.
13. Type **frmSBC.OpenWindow** in the OnLoad method of the MoonLight Demo–DONE application.

Creating a New View (OrderTotal)

To ease the development of the report, we have created a new view that relates the Emp, Orders, Order_Items, Products, and Countries tables. The view includes columns for each employee's name and id, the country's id, and most importantly a column that calculates the total for each order in the Orders table. Relating these fields in a view provides an easy means of accessing the country, sales employees, and order's total information. Because there is a country related to each order, the view provides an order total related to the specified country.

To create the view in Oracle Power Objects:

1. Double-click the MoonLight Data session icon to activate the session.
2. Click on the New View icon to create a new view.
3. Change the view's Name property to **OrdTot**.
4. Drag and drop the icons of the Emp, Orders, Order_Items, and Countries tables to the Table List area.
5. Create join lines to relate the tables by selecting the EMPNO column in the Emp table and drag it to the SALES_REP_ID column in the Orders table, select the ID column in the Orders table and drag it to the ORDER_ID column in the Order_Items table, and select the ID column in the Countries table and drag it to the COUNTRY_ID column in the Orders table. Finally, select the PRODUCT_ID in the Order_Items table and drag it to the ID column in the Products table. This creates relationships between the Orders, Order_Items, Products, Countries, and Employees tables.
6. Select the EMPNO column in the Emp table and drag it to the Column List area. Type **REP_ID** in the Heading field.
7. Select the NAME column in the Countries table and drag it to the Column List area. Type COUNTRY in the heading column.

8. Select the ID column in the Countries table and drag it to the Column List area. Type **CO_ID** in the Heading field.
9. Create an expression in the Column List area by typing **ORD_TOT** in the Name field. Type **SUM(UNIT_PRICE*QUANTITY*(1-DISCOUNT))** in the COLUMN field.

This column will calculate the total cost for each order (see Figure 11-2).

Using SQL to Create the OrdTot View

You can also create the view with the following SQL code:

```
create view OrdTot (repid, country, co_id, ord_tot) as
select emp.empno repid, countries.name country, countries.id  c o_id,
sum(unit_price*quantity*(1-discount)) ord_tot from
emp, orders, order_items, countries, products
where empno=sales_rep_id and orders.id=order_id and
country_id=countries.id and product_id=products.id
group by empno, countries.id, countries.name
```

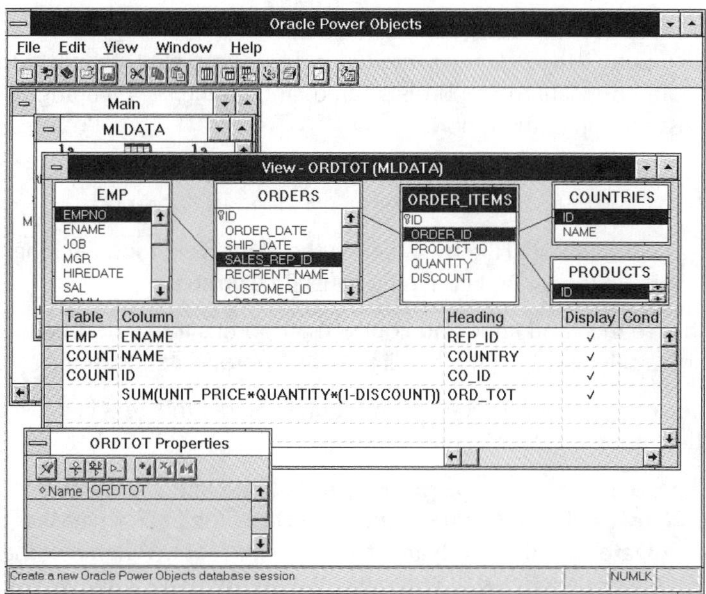

FIGURE 11-2. *New view to join employees with their total sales in different countries*

Creating the rptSalesByCountry Report

You next create a new report (rptSalesByCountry) in the MoonLight Demo-DONE application using the Report Header, PageHeader, Detail, and Report Footer areas of the report.

Create a New Report

Create a new report, change its name and label properties, and set the report to be 7 1/2 inches wide.

1. Open the MoonLight Demo–DONE application, if it is not already open.
2. Click on the New Report button on the toolbar.
3. Change the report's name to **rptSalesByCountry** on the property sheet.
4. Change the report's label to **Sales By Country** on the property sheet.
5. Set the DefaultCondition property of the report to **DEPTNO=30**. This restricts the report to include only those employees from the Sales Department (whose DEPTNO equals 30).
6. Set the Report's SizeX property to **7.5 in**. This provides a report with a half-inch margin on both sides (see Figure 11-3).

Set Up the Report Header Section

Place the company's logo class on the Report Header, create static text for the Report Title and the date the report is printed, and create the Headings that will appear across the top of the report.

1. Drag and drop from the MoonLight Demo–DONE window the clsLOGOCLASS to add the company's logo to the report.
2. Create the Report Title by selecting the Static Text tool, clicking in the Report Header area, and typing **Sales By Country**.
3. Change the FontName and FontSize properties to the desired font and size for the title and drag the heading to an appropriate location.
4. Create a text field to hold the print date. Select the Text Fields tool and click in the Report Heading area.
5. Change the field's Name property to **TodaysDate**, the DataSource property to **=Now( )**, the DataType property to **Date**, the SetFormatMask property to **Long Date**, and the FontName to the desired font. Whenever the report is printing or previewed, it will place the present date at the top of the report.
6. Select the Static Text tool to create the Sales Rep and Total Sales static text fields to appear at the top of the cross-tab report columns, click in the

Report Header area, and type **Sales Rep**. Set the FontBold property to **True** and the FontName to the desired font.

7. Copy the text and press the Paste icon. The previous text has already been formatted just like you want it, so copying and pasting the static text creates another static text object, which you can reposition and change its text.
8. Click on the duplicate static text object and change its Name and Label property to **Total Sales**.
9. Select the Text Fields control and click in the Report Header area to create the Country heading fields.
10. Change the text field's Name property to **Heading1**, toggle the HasBorder property to **False**, the DataType property to **String**, DataSize property to **30**, the FontBold property to **True**, and set the FontName property to the desired font.
11. Set the DataSource property to **=SQLLookup("SELECT NAME from COUNTRIES where ID="& cstr(frmSBC.Cntry1.value))**.

This will display the country selected in the Cntry1 pop-up list on the frmSBC form.

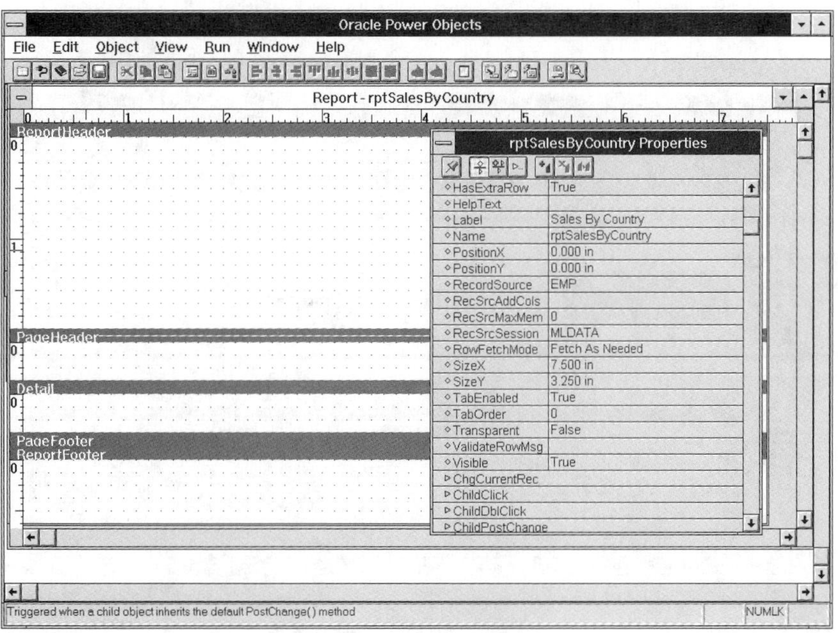

FIGURE 11-3. *The new report and its property sheet*

12. Click the Copy icon to copy the Heading1 text field and press the Paste icon four times. This copies all of the text field's attributes and automatically names the duplicate copies Heading2, Heading3, Heading4, and Heading5.
13. Select the Heading2 field and change its DataSource property's SQLLookup code to include frmSBC.cntry2.value in place of the frmSBC.cntry2.value. This selects the name of the country in the cntry2 pop-up list. Select Heading3 and change its SQLLookup to **cntry3**, and change in the same manner the SQLLookup for the Heading4 and Heading5 text fields.

Once you have positioned the headings approximately where you want them, you can select all of the text and click on the Align Top button on the toolbar to vertically align the headings (see Figure 11-4).

14. Click the Lines tool and draw a horizontal line below the heading text to separate the headings from the detail area.

Set Up the PageHeader Area

In the page header, replicate the heading fields from the Report Header area to be displayed on the second and all subsequent pages. This is done very easily.

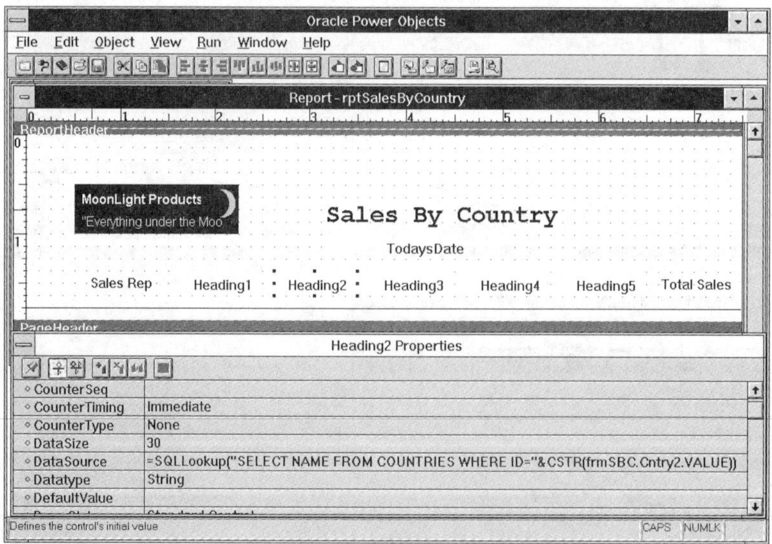

FIGURE 11-4. *The report with the completed report header*

1. Select all of the heading fields in the ReportHeader area by dragging the select box over them and then pressing the Copy button.
2. Move the cursor to the PageHeader area and press the Paste button. Oracle Power Objects will copy all the headings into the PageHeader area and automatically change the names of the text field controls by appropriately incrementing the number at the ends of their names, i.e., heading1 becomes heading6.
3. Open the PageHeader property sheet by selecting the PageHeader title bar. Change the FirstPgHdr to **False** so that the header will not be displayed on the first page.

Set Up the Detail Area

The detail area will have the employee's name listed on the left side of the report with the total sales per country across the center of the report and the employee's total sales at the far right side of the report. To set up the detail area:

1. Open the MoonLight Data session, if it is not already open.
2. Double-click on the Emp table to open it and drag and drop the EMPNAME column onto the detail area.
3. Select the Text Fields tool on the Object palette and click in the Detail area below the USA heading.
4. Change the Name property to **Country1**, the DataType property to **Double**, the FontName to the desired font, the FormatMask property to **Currency**, and the TextJustHoriz property to **Right** (to align the numbers).
5. In the DataSource, type in the following SQLLookup **=nvl(SQLLookup("SELECT sum(ORD_TOT) from ORDTOT where CO_ID=" +cstr(frmsbc.cntry1.value)+" and REPID="&cstr(EMPNO.VALUE)),0.0)**.

The SQLLookup selects the total sales of the employee for the same country as is selected in the Heading1 field. Note that using the nval function places 0.0 in the field's value if the result of the SQLLookup is NULL.

6. Now that the Country1 field is completely formatted and set up, copy the field and paste the field five times. This retains the formatting performed to the field, and, most importantly, Oracle Power Objects automatically changes the duplicate field's name property to be Country2, Country3, etc.
7. Select the Country2 field and change its DataSource property's SQLLookup code to include cntry2 in place of cntry1. This selects the order totals for the employee for the selected country. Select Country3 and change its

SQLLookup to select the total orders for the country selected in cntry3, and change in the same manner the SQLLookup for the Country4, Country5, and Country6 fields.

8. Change the Name property of Country6 to **TotSales** and change its DataSource property to **=Country1 + Country2 + Country3 + Country4 + Country5**.

This adds the sales in each country for each employee and performs the horizontal cross-tabulation of the cross-tab report.

9. Center the fields below their respective headings (see Figure 11-5).

Set Up the Report Footer Area

The Page Footer area is not used, so move the Report Footer bar up against the Page Footer bar. The Report Footer area will include the total sales for each country and the combined totals of all of the sales. We'll copy and reformat existing text and text fields to simplify formatting the fields for the Report Footer.

1. Select the Sales Rep static text in the Report Header area and copy and paste the static text. Change the Static Text Name property to **Sales Totals** and place the text in the Report Footer just below the ENAME field located in the Detail area.
2. Select Country1 in the Detail area and copy and paste the field.
3. Change the duplicate field's Name property to **Total1** and move the field to the Report Footer area just below the Country1 field.
4. Change the Total1 field's DataSource property to **SUM(Country1)**. This sums all of the values in the Country1 field and gives a total sales of the specified country.
5. Copy the Total1 field and paste it five times. This automatically renames the fields Total2, Total3, Total4, Total5, and Total6. These fields are the downward cross-tabulation of the cross-tab report.
6. Place the Total2, Total3, Total4, and Total5 fields under the appropriate country.
7. Change the DataSource property of the Total2 field to **SUM(Country2)**, the Total3 field to **SUM(Country3)**, etc. This creates fields to total the sales for each country.
8. Place the Total6 field in the Report Footer area directly below the TotSales field. Change the Name property of the Total6 field to **TotalSales** and the DataSource property to **=SUM(TotSales)**.

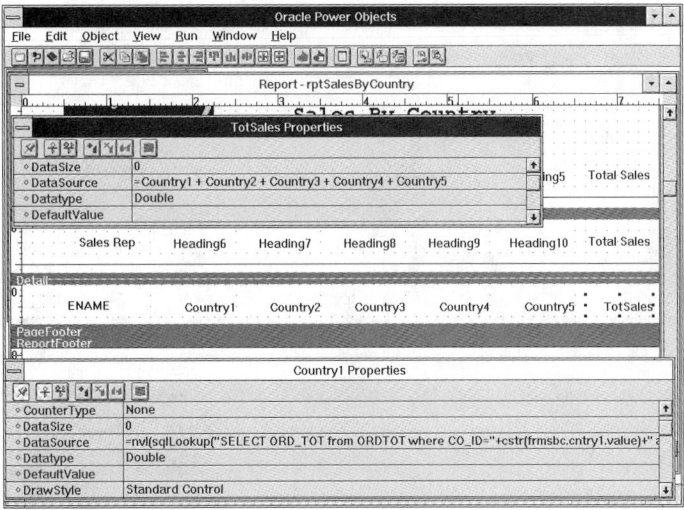

FIGURE 11-5. *The report with the completed PageHeader and Detail areas*

This creates a field that provides the total sales for all of the employees for all of the countries. The DataSource property could also be set to =SUM(TotSales) to achieve the same results.

9. Place a line above the fields in the Report Footer area to separate the total fields from the Detail area (see Figure 11-6).

To run the report, click on the Run button on the toolbar. Select the countries in the five list boxes and the select the Create Report button. The report will look like the one that was shown in Figure 11-1.

Repeater Fields and Multipage Forms

You can create forms to handle data that will continue for multiple pages by using repeater displays containing data continuing for multiple pages. This feature is normally used when creating an invoice that has so many line items it extends for multiple pages or when creating Avery address labels for your customer database. For an explanation of how to use repeater displays for creating master-detail relationships, see Chapter 6. In this example, we create a standard Avery label 5160. You can create mailing labels by using a display repeater on a form.

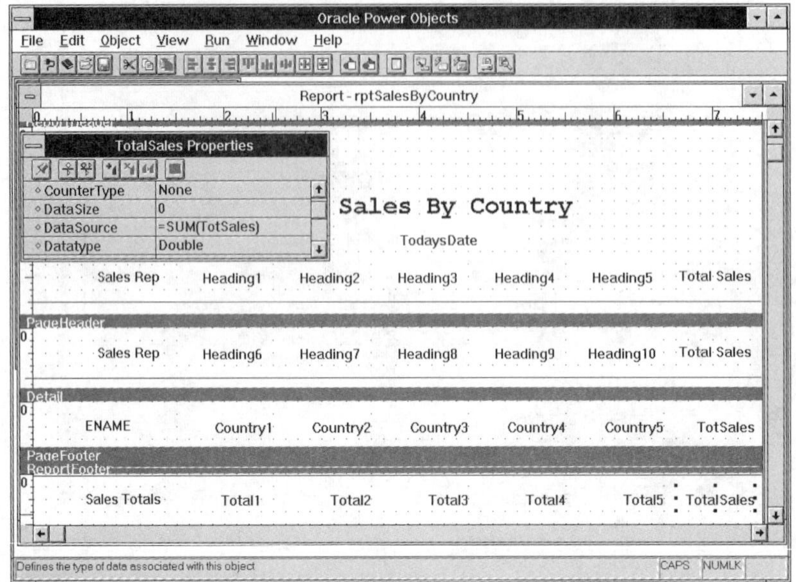

FIGURE 11-6. *The completed report*

1. Create a new form by clicking on the New Form button on the toolbar.
2. For the form, set the following properties:

   - Change the Name to **AveryLabel5160**.
   - Set SizeX of the form to **8.5** inches and the SizeY property to **11** inches. This creates a form the size of a sheet of paper.
   - Set HasBorder to **False** by clicking on the HasBorder property.

Place a repeater display on the form and set its properties. The repeater display's size needs to match the exact printable area of the label sheet, and the primary panel area needs to match the size of the individual labels.

3. Drag and drop a repeater display onto the form.
4. Set the PositionX to **0.25** inch and set the PositionY to **0.5** inch. This places the upper-left corner of the repeater a quarter-inch from the left edge and a half-inch down from the top of the page.
5. Set the HasBorder to **False** by clicking on the HasBorder property. All you want to print is the customer address information, not a box around each part of the address.

6. Set the HasScrollBar to **False** by clicking on the property. There is no need for the scroll bar, as this form is intended for printing purposes.
7. Set the SizeX property to **8** inches and set the SizeY property to **10** inches. The repeater panel is now a quarter-inch from both the left and the right side of the page and a half-inch from the top and bottom of the page.

Figure 11-7 shows the Avery label form and repeater with their property sheets. Set the properties of the repeater primary panel. Each Avery label is 1 inch high and 2 5/8 inches wide.

8. Click on the repeater panel in the repeater display.
9. Set the SizeX to **2.625** and the SizeY to **1**. Place the address fields from the Customers table onto the repeater panel.
10. Double-click on the MoonLight Data session icon to activate the session.
11. Open the Customers table or view and drag it onto the repeater panel in the repeater display.

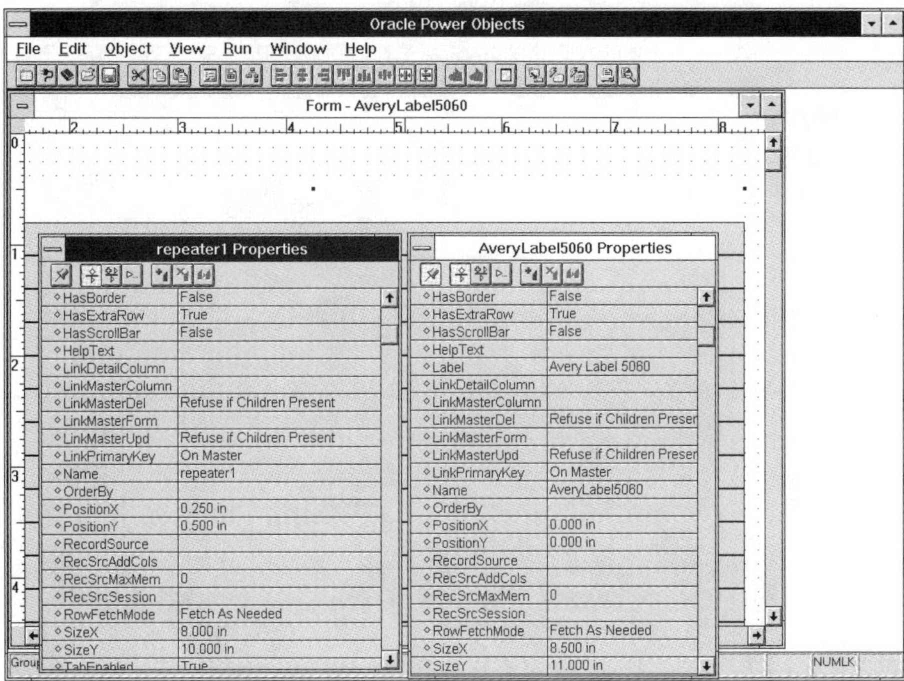

FIGURE 11-7. *The Avery label form and repeater with their property sheets*

12. Position the fields (NAME, ADDRESS1, CITY, STATE, and ZIP) on the repeater panel so they will fit comfortably in the center of the label (repeater panel) as shown in Figure 11-8.

13. To sort the order in which the addresses will appear on the form, set the OrderBy property for the repeater panel to sort the addresses by name, city, or state. To sort the addresses first by state and then by city, type **STATE, CITY** in the OrderBy property.

14. Run the form by clicking on the Run Form button on the toolbar. The form contains all of the customer addresses for the customer table, as shown in Figure 11-9.

15. To view the next page of a multipage document, click on the right arrow on the toolbar.

16. To print the labels, click on the Print button on the toolbar or select Print from the File menu.

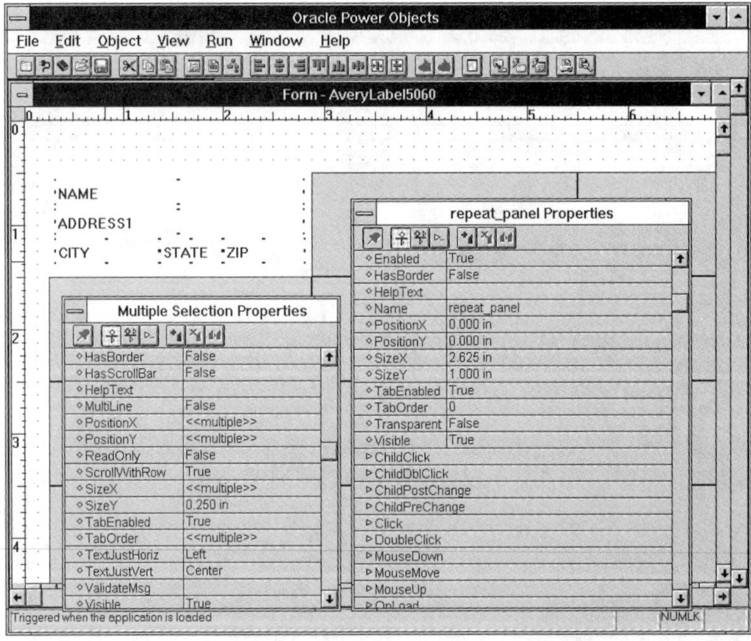

FIGURE 11-8. *The Avery label form with the repeater panel's size set and the address fields placed in the repeater panel, including the property sheets*

Avery Label 5060

Deuce Hardware	Illuminati, Inc.	The Lantern Company
Office 115	211 West Fifth Street	170 Hawley Blvd.
Beaverton OR 97005	Cincinnati OH 45202	Irvine CA 92714
Le Cadeau	CandleSellers	Allisons Gifts
3000 Laurier Blvd.	100 Twin Dolphin Drive	1102 Drummers Lane
Quebec	Redwood Shores CA 94065	Wayne PA 19087
Les Choses De La Lunette	Geschenk des Lichtes	The Lamp Store
14, Esplanade Charles de Gaulle	Leopoldstrasse 191	Princesa 33

FIGURE 11-9. *The Avery label form in Form Run-time mode*

Concatenating Text

Usually, when you design a table like a customers table, you create separate columns for the customer's address for street address, city, state, and ZIP. This is useful for performing sorts on the table, but it may not print data correctly in reports. To display that information in one field so it looks correct, you place a large text control field on top of the text field controls. Note that you need to keep the fields on the repeater so that you can access their data. You then concatenate the text and place it in a single text string. To concatenate text for a table named Customers with NAME, ADDRESS1, CITY, STATE, and ZIP fields:

1. Move all of the text field controls to the center of the display panel (on top of each other) and drag a text field control onto the repeater panel and stretch it to near the size of the panel.
2. Change the Name property of the text field control to an appropriate name, like **Address**.
3. Set the RecordSession property (if it has not already been set) to the appropriate session.
4. Set the Datatype property to **String**.
5. Set the DataSize property to a size large enough to contain all of the data that will be placed in it from the various columns.
6. Set the MultiLine property to **True** and HasBorder to **False**.

7. Type the following in the DataSource property **=fldNAME & CHR$(13) & address1 & CHR$(13) & city & ", " & state & " " & zip**.

Note that we had to change the name of the NAME text field control to fldNAME, because NAME is an Oracle Power Objects property, and trying to access NAME confuses the program. The ampersand (&) symbol joins the fields together and CHR$(13) places a carriage return to separate the address into multiple lines. Quotation marks contain any text to be placed in the field, which in this case places a space between the customer's name.

Changing the Properties of Multiple Controls

SHIFT-select all of the fields. With all of the fields selected, set the following properties: HasBorder to **False**, the FontName to **Times New Roman**, and the FontSize to **10** points.

OLE 2 Controls

Program development is tending to retreat from the huge, do-everything programs such as Word or WordPerfect to several small modules, each of which accomplishes one general task. These small modules are combined to form one program that does exactly what is required and no more. This means that as a programmer you can create a base module meeting your specific needs that no other applications meet. You then add other existing objects to your base program to accomplish the other required tasks to complete your total program. These other required tasks could include word processing or spreadsheet capabilities, which are done exceedingly well with Word or Excel. You don't have to write your own limited version of a word processor or spreadsheet to meet the requirements of your program.

The main technology to accomplish this task is OLE 2, developed by Microsoft. OLE is the acronym for the *object linking and embedding* technology. Any program that is OLE-compliant can be added to another program that can use OLE objects. Oracle Power Objects is OLE-compliant, and the application developer can add OLE objects to base Oracle Power Objects applications. However, this applies to the PC version of Oracle Power Objects only. The Macintosh version will support OpenDoc in future releases.

Overview of OLE 2

The use of an OLE object involves two distinct parts. In OLE terminology, these parts are called *client* and *server*. However, these terms are not analogous to the database term *client-server*. A database client is a stand-alone program that occasionally requires data from the database. It creates a query and sends it to the database server to process, which then returns the requested data to the client. In OLE, the client resides in the application and contains specific information that can only be processed and/or displayed by the server program. The server program must be installed on the same machine as the OLE client or be available over the network.

For example, consider an Oracle Power Objects form with a Microsoft PaintBrush OLE object. This form contains the information about what the picture should look like (it may be a reference to an existing bitmap file on the hard disk), but it cannot display or edit that information on its own. When the user needs to edit or view the PaintBrush information, he or she invokes the server (in this case, the PaintBrush program) through Oracle Power Objects to process the data contained in the Oracle Power Objects application.

There are two methods in which the client data is stored in the application: embedded and linked. An *embedded* client is one in which all of the data required for the server program to process is stored within the application. When the application is loaded into RAM memory during run time, the OLE data is loaded as well. Thus, the user can display and modify the data with the OLE-compliant server program, but it affects only that data stored in RAM. As soon as the user exits the program, any changes made in the OLE data is lost. At the next invocation of the program, the original OLE data is once again loaded into RAM. Oracle Power Objects cannot save OLE data that has been changed in RAM. The advantage of an embedded OLE object is that the data is always there when needed.

The other method of storing client data is accomplished by *linking* the data to the application. In this case, a file on the disk contains the required data for the server program. The Oracle Power Objects application stores the reference to the OLE data file. When the user requires the data to be processed, the application invokes the OLE-compliant server and passes the file reference to the server, which then loads the data from the file. The user can edit and modify this data in the server and save it back to the file. Thus, the information is saved from one invocation to another. The disadvantage of linking OLE data to the application is that the program is more difficult to move from one machine to another, because the linked files need to be moved as well. It is also possible that someone may move or delete the file containing the OLE object data, thus making it impossible for the application to find the data to process.

The method you choose to store the client data is dependent upon the ultimate purpose of the OLE object. Either you want to have the program initialized with static data that can be changed during run time but not saved, or you want to have the ability to change and save the client data. For example, if you have your company logo drawn by PaintBrush, an embedded OLE object would serve your purposes well because the data will not change. However, if you are using Word to write up the next day's job list, you would want to link the data to the application because the data must be changed every day.

There is one exception to an embedded OLE object being unable to save changed data. If you bind an embedded OLE object in an Oracle Power Objects application to a table in the database, Oracle Power Objects can save any changed data by writing it to the database. The OLE object must be an embedded object to be bound to the database.

The OLE object has the DataSource property that can be set only to a column of datatype Long Raw. When the application is running, it can send the information contained in the Long Raw column to the server to be processed when the OLE object is activated. After the user modifies the data, he or she can save the data, and the server will send the data back to Oracle Power Objects to store in the table. Thus, you have a compromise between the linked and embedded types of data storage, because the embedded object can save modified data, but the application is not linked to a specific file on the disk. You still need an extra file (the entire database) for the linked aspect of this OLE form, but the worry that someone may delete or move your linked file is much less. (At least it should be. Unauthorized people should not be able to delete data from the columns in the database).

Another advantage of a bound embedded OLE object is that the containing application may be more portable. If the application is a client to a database server on a network (rather than a stand-alone program), the application can be moved to any machine on the network that can communicate with the database server without having to worry if the bound data is still accessible. Of course the OLE server program must also be available either over the network or installed on the same machine as the Oracle Power Objects application.

In addition to having the data stored in two different ways in the form (embedded or linked), there are two different methods of displaying the OLE object on the form (both in Run-time and Designer modes). The default method is for Oracle Power Objects to add a window to the form in which the data information is displayed at all times (both in Designer mode and Run-time mode). When adding the OLE object using the Insert Object menu item in the Edit menu, you have the option of having the server represented by an icon on the form. Then during either Designer or Run-time modes, you double-click on the icon to activate the server to see and edit the data associated with the OLE object. These two display methods are discussed in more detail in the "Adding OLE to an Application Window" section later in the chapter.

Oracle Power Objects and OLE 2

Oracle Power Objects has made it very easy to add OLE objects to your applications. There are four methods by which you add OLE objects to your application. The first is by adding it to either the application window from which several forms can access the OLE object or to the form by using the Insert Object menu item in the Edit menu. The second is by adding an OLE object directly to a form, class, or report using the OLE Object tool from the Designer palette. The third method is by creating an object directly in the server program, such as PaintBrush, and then cutting the object and placing it on the system Clipboard. You can add the OLE object on the system Clipboard to either the application or an open form by selecting the Paste Special menu option in the Edit menu. These three methods are all done at design time. The fourth method allows the end user to add OLE objects to a form while in Run-time mode. This is done by using the OLE methods PasteFromClipboard( ) and OLEInsertObject( ). You call these methods from another method, such as Click( ), to add an OLE object to the application when the user activates the Click( ) method, perhaps by pressing a button.

Each of these techniques to add OLE objects to the application is discussed further in the following sections.

Adding OLE to an Application Window

When an OLE object is to be used by several different forms, reports, or classes in an application, it is best to add the object to the application window itself. The OLE object added to the application can be either linked or embedded. You add the object to the forms that require it by dragging and dropping the object onto the form. Thus, several forms can access the same OLE object. During run time, each form can modify the contents of its embedded form without affecting the other forms using the object. However, any changes made will be lost when the application closes. Those forms using a linked OLE object from the application can change the data and save it to the file. Thus every form using the same linked OLE object will reflect the changes (providing the form updates the display if it was open at the time the file was changed), because each has a copy of the OLE object that is linked to the same file.

There are two methods by which OLE objects are added to an application window. The first is by selecting the Insert Object menu item from the Edit menu, and the second is by pasting it into the application after placing the object on the system Clipboard.

Using the Insert Object Menu Item When using the Insert Object menu item to insert an object, the application window must be open and have the focus (its header bar is dark blue). When you select the Insert Object menu item, the dialog box shown in Figure 11-10 is opened. Figure 11-10 also shows the Change Icon dialog box, which is opened by clicking the Change Icon button.

Each of the selections possible in the dialog boxes is described below.

- **Create New** This is the default choice. It adds an embedded OLE object to the opened application window.
- **Create from File** Selecting this option gives you a choice of either adding an embedded object or a linked object to the open application. The window associated with this selection is shown here:

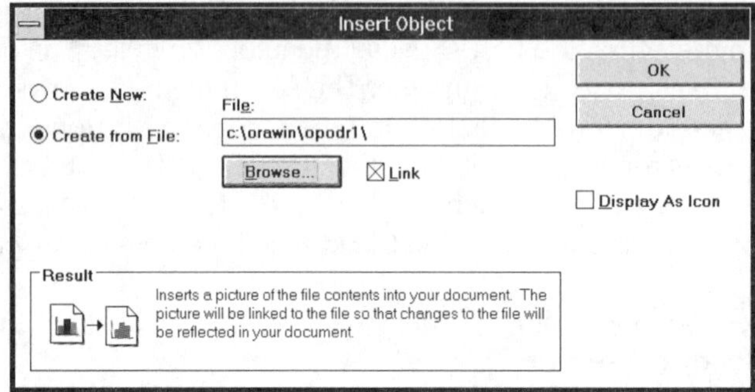

Most of the box remains the same as the previous Insert Object window, but with the following additions that replace the Object Type list.

File	This textbox shows the name of the file from which the OLE object is to be derived.
Browse	This button opens a dialog box to select a file from which an OLE object can be derived. For example, if you select a bitmap file (.BMP extension), Oracle Power Objects will insert a PaintBrush object into your application.
Link	You check this box if you want the server data to be obtained from the selected file. Otherwise, Oracle Power Objects will load the data from the file and store it as an embedded form.

- **Object Type** This is a list of OLE-compliant programs available on your system. Click on the object you wish to insert into your application.
- **Result** This is an information panel describing what the object is and how it will be displayed when inserted in the application.
- **Display As Icon** You have the choice to have the inserted object displayed continuously in a window or as an icon, which you as a developer or as a user must double-click to invoke the server to display the

embedded data. When this box is selected, Oracle Power Objects adds a picture of the icon for the selected object and the Change Icon button to the form. Pressing this button opens the Change Icon dialog box.

- **Change Icon** The options available in this dialog box, also shown in Figure 11-10, are

Current	This selects the icon the system is currently using for the server program.
Default	This selects the icon that is the default icon for the server program.
From File	This selects an icon from the current executable file. The text field shows which file is being currently read (by default, the server program), and the display box shows the icons available from that file.
Browse	Press this button to open a dialog box from which you select an executable file that contains icons.
Label	You may enter your own label for the icon when it is placed in your application.

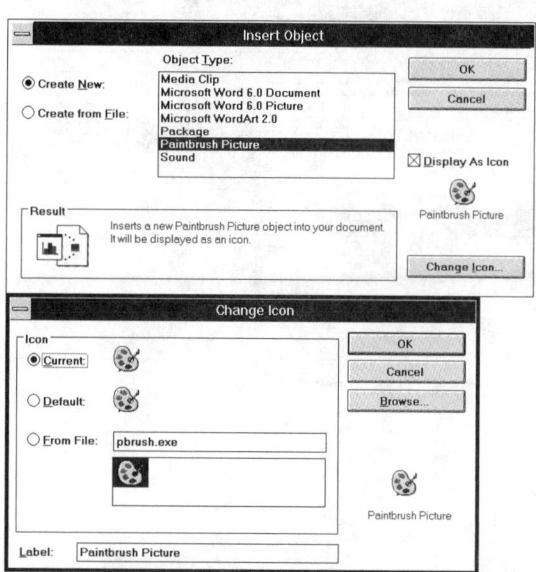

FIGURE 11-10. *The Insert Object dialog box and the Change Icon dialog box*

After you select an appropriate object and decide how you want the object to be displayed (icon or open frame), select OK. Oracle Power Objects will invoke the server to open the object and give you the opportunity to edit the data immediately if you chose to display as an icon. If you did not choose this option, Oracle Power Objects opens a frame in the OLE form in which you can modify the embedded data directly in your Oracle Power Objects form. After you have edited the data, select the Update (or similar) menu item from the OLE Server File menu and then the Exit and Return to Ole1 (or similar) menu item. This will return you to Oracle Power Objects.

As an example, a WordArt OLE object is added to a form. The newly inserted WordArt object to be displayed as an icon is in a form of its own with an associated property sheet, as shown in Figure 11-11.

The icon is deformed, because Oracle Power Objects has automatically created a frame in which the icon is displayed in the form, but the frame is too small. If you had not checked the Display As Icon box, the data would be displayed in a window in the form instead of the icon. Name the OLE object appropriately using the property sheet and close the object's form. The new object is now displayed in the application window as an OLE icon, as shown in Figure 11-11. You select this icon and drag and drop it onto forms that require the capabilities of the object.

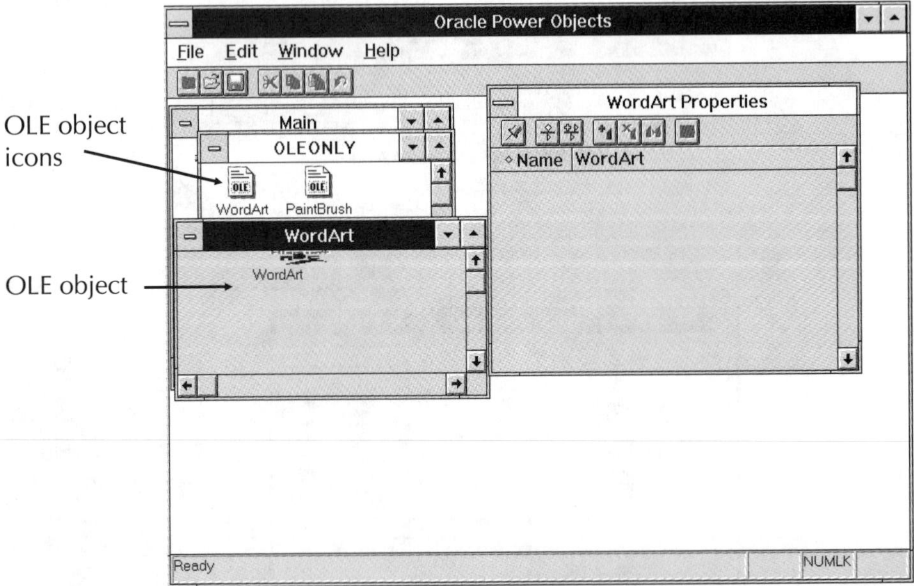

FIGURE 11-11. *Oracle Power Objects screen with the newly created OLE object in its own form and its property sheet*

Using the Paste Special Menu Item In order to use the Paste Special menu item, you must first open an OLE-compliant program and create an object. For example, let's say you draw a picture in PaintBrush or write a document in Word. You then cut or copy the object in the server program onto the system Clipboard. The next step is to open the application and select the Paste Special menu item in the Edit menu. This menu item is grayed out unless there is an OLE object on the system Clipboard. When the menu item is selected, the Paste Special dialog box is opened. The Paste Special dialog box is shown here, with the Display As Icon box selected.

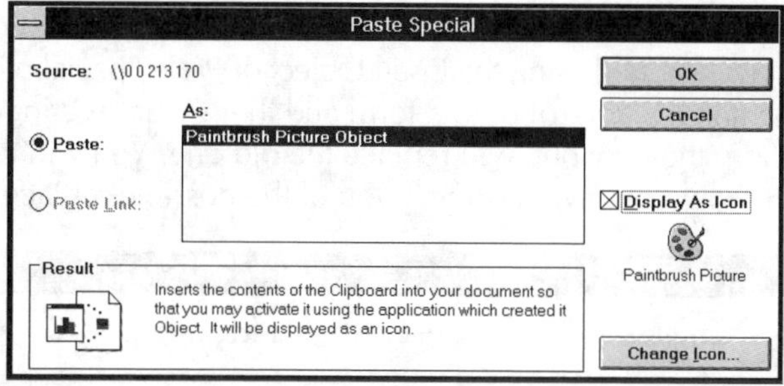

The dialog box displays what the OLE object is in the As text box. The Paste Link option is grayed out in this box, because the OLE object on the Clipboard had not been saved to a file. The Change Icon button is the same as described in the section on the Insert Object dialog box above. When you accept the object, the Paste Special dialog box is dismissed. If you chose the OLE object to be displayed as an icon, the server program is activated to give you a chance to modify the data copied from the Clipboard and embedded in the program. If the OLE object is displayed in its own frame, the object is displayed in the form. If you double-click in the frame, the server is activated and you can modify the data. After you select Update and Exit, Oracle Power Objects displays the finished OLE object in its own form just as if it were created with the Insert Object option described above.

Adding an OLE Object to an Opened Form, Class, or Report

There are four methods by which you directly add OLE objects to a form, class, or report. Whenever the term "form" is used in this discussion from this point on, you can substitute class or report. There is one method of adding an OLE object to a form during run time. These techniques are described in the following sections.

Adding an OLE Object During Application Development The first two methods of directly adding an OLE object to a form are identical to those used to add objects to an application window. But the results are different. The first difference is rather obvious in that the OLE object is placed directly in the open form, not in its own form as when added to an application window. The second difference is that the property sheet for an object placed in an application contains only the Name property while the property sheet of an OLE object in a form contains several properties and methods. Finally, when an OLE object is placed in a form, it is loaded in an OLE control within the form and has properties similar to the other controls that are placed in forms. (See the tables in Chapters 8 and 9 for the properties and methods associated with OLE controls.)

The third method of directly adding OLE to an opened form was referred to in the "Adding OLE to an Application Window" section earlier. It is done by simply dragging and dropping an OLE object from the application window onto the open form. The OLE object then has all the properties and methods associated with OLE controls just as if it were added using the Insert Object or Paste Special menu items. If you drag and drop an OLE control onto a form and there is an existing OLE object in that same position, the new one will replace the old one. You will receive a warning message, shown below, informing you of the possible replacement.

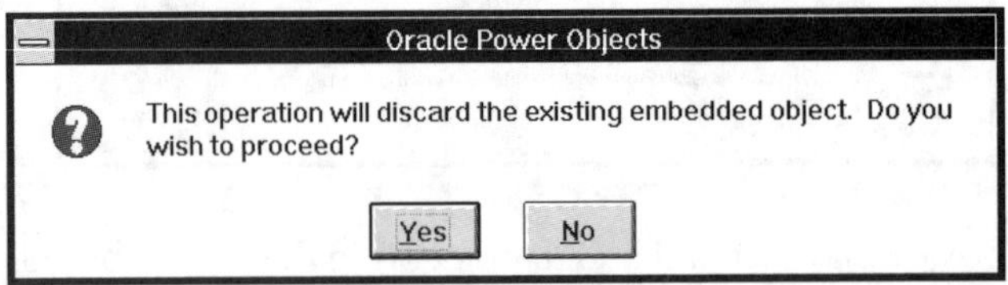

If you do not want the OLE object to replace an existing OLE object, simply move one or the other to a different spot on the form.

The fourth method to directly add an OLE object to a form is to select the OLE Object tool on the Designer palette and then click on the open form at the position you want Oracle Power Objects to place the OLE control. The Insert Object dialog box is then displayed. However, if you do not want to add the actual object to the control at this time (see "Adding an OLE Object During Run Time"), select Cancel in the dialog box, and an empty OLE control box will be left on the form. If you do want to fill the OLE control, use the same procedures described in "Adding OLE to an Application Window" on using the Insert Object dialog box.

Adding an OLE Object During Run Time As mentioned at the beginning of this chapter, you have the option to allow the end user to add his or her own OLE objects to a form while in Run-time mode. This is accomplished by placing an empty OLE control in a form and entering appropriate Oracle Basic code in a method, such as Click( ), which the end user can invoke. One series of steps that can make this work is listed below.

1. Load an empty OLE control in an opened form by clicking on the OLE Object tool in the Designer palette and then clicking in the form. Press the Cancel button in the Insert Object dialog box.
2. Name the control appropriately in the OLE control's property sheet. Resize the OLE control frame so that it is large enough to accommodate the object the end user will insert into the control. If necessary, you can add code to methods to enlarge or contract the control using its Size X/Y properties.
3. Place a button in the form or some other control (such as a custom menu item, as described in the "Customizing the Form Menu, Toolbar, and Status Line" section) to give the user a place to trigger the method that uses code to insert the OLE object.
4. In the appropriate method, add an Oracle Basic statement like **MyOle.InsertObject( )** to insert an OLE object into the empty control at run time. Note that the object entered in the control will be lost when the application is closed.
5. Alternatively, you can have Oracle Power Objects retrieve an OLE object from the system Clipboard. To do this, add the following code to the method used to trigger the adding of an OLE object to the form.

```
REM Make sure there is an OLE object on the clipboard, if so
REM paste it into the control.
IF MyOle.CanPasteFromClipboard() THEN
   MyOle.PasteFromClipboard()
ELSE
   REM Tell the user there is no OLE object on the clipboard.
   MSGBOX"There is no OLE object on the clipboard
END IF
```

When the form is run and the end user presses the button (or whatever) to activate the OLE control, the Insert Object dialog window is opened (if step 4 is used; otherwise, the object is inserted directly into the form), and the end user can choose the appropriate program to create the OLE object. The object that is created or pasted, whether it's a picture from PaintBrush or a document in Word, is displayed in the OLE control frame.

You can add other Oracle Basic code to the form to write the newly created object to a file, which can then be read in at later invocations of the program. Thus, the user has the choice of saving an object and using it again or creating a new one. An example of this can be found in the "Customizing the Form Menu, Toolbar, and Status Line" section later in this chapter.

Bound OLE Controls Normally, the data for an embedded OLE object is static from one invocation to another. It may be changed while in Run mode, but any changes are lost when the application closes. The exception to this is when the embedded form (you cannot bind a linked OLE object) is bound to a Long Raw column in a table. Oracle Power Objects then uses the data in the table to provide the data for the OLE server to process. When the server saves changes, Oracle Power Objects writes the data to the column in the database. You bind an OLE control to the database by simply setting the DataSource property of the control to the name of the Long Raw column in the table that is the RecordSource for the OLE control's container. This is a very powerful and useful feature of Oracle Power Objects.

As an example, suppose that in a database of authors and books is one table that contains information on each book. It contains the usual bookid, title, subject, etc. fields. In addition, it contains an OLE control with a Word object. This control is bound to the Abstract column of datatype Long Raw in the Books table. Now, when the end user enters a book into the database, he or she can also invoke the Word object in the form, write an abstract (or review, or whatever) of the book and save it. Oracle Power Objects will take the newly created Word document and place it in the Abstract column. The steps to create this BookEntry form are shown below.

1. Open a new form and add the bookid, title, and copyright fields from the Books table by opening that table and selecting and dragging the appropriate fields onto the form. Change the form's Name property to **BookEntry** and its Label property to **Book Entry**. Change the static text control's labels appropriately and set the TextJustVert property of all text fields to **Center**.
2. Add two list controls to the form, one from which the user selects the appropriate book subject and the other the appropriate publisher. These two lists access the Subjects and Publishers tables with the appropriate Select statement in the Translation property (see Figure 11-12).
3. Add a horizontal scroll bar below the text control fields.
4. Add a button and change its Name and Label to **Abstract**. Enter the Oracle Basic statement **BookAbstract.DoubleClick( )** in the Abstract button's Click( ) method.
5. Add another button, change its name and label to **Exit** and enter the Oracle Basic statement **GetContainer.CloseWindow( )**.
6. Add an OLE control to the form by clicking on the OLE Object icon in the Object palette and click on the form.

7. In the Insert Object dialog, select Word as the server. Because the form is not designed to display the abstract information at all times, check the Display As Icon box. Click OK.
8. When the Word program comes up (it is invoked automatically when Display As Icon is set), enter any default text you want (such as **No abstract yet**), then close the Word server. The default text is used if the Abstract column contains no data.
9. Now set the following properties in the OLE objects property sheet. DataSource: **Abstract**; Name: **BookAbstract**; Visible: **False**. There is no need to have the OLE object's icon displayed at run time.

It is assumed that there is a master form that controls all parts of the application that works with the library information. This master form contains a button or menu item to open this BookEntry form. The construction of the master form is beyond the scope of this example. Figure 11-12 shows this rudimentary book entry form with the property sheets for the Subject listbox and OLE control. There is much more that can be done with OLE objects (see the Oracle Power Objects user's guide) but this section should help you get started using OLE objects in Oracle Power Objects applications.

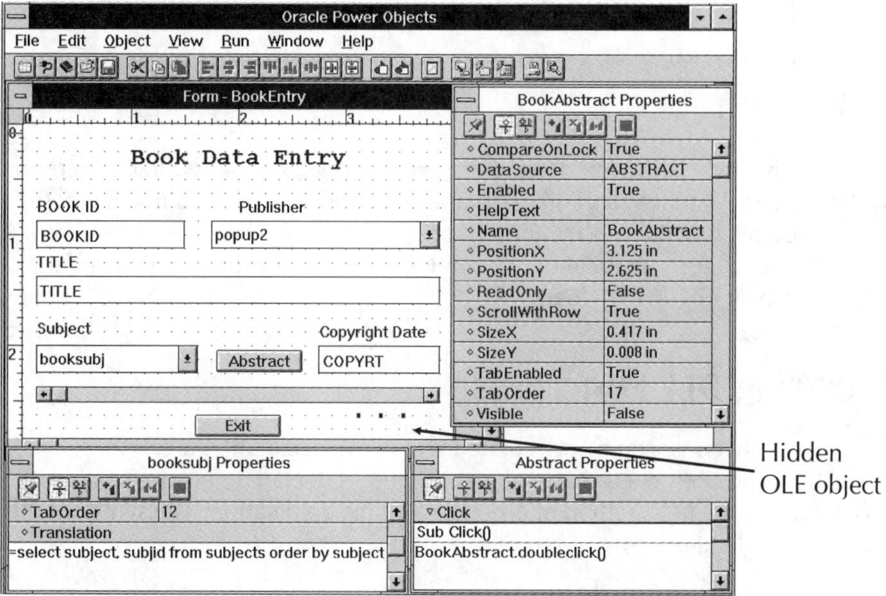

FIGURE 11-12. *The BookEntry form showing the property sheets of the Subjects list box and the Abstract OLE object*

Using Dynamic Link Libraries in Windows

One of the powerful features of Oracle Power Objects in a Windows environment is the ability to use functions defined by others and stored in a dynamic link library (DLL). Similar to an OLE object, you can call these functions from an Oracle Power Objects application. Unlike an OLE object, there is no preserved data for the function to process. There is no OLE style of client-server relationship between an Oracle Power Objects application and a DLL function. However, DLL functions can be of great use to developers to add flexibility and more power to their applications without having to write additional code to accomplish the same tasks. A DLL is simply a way to allow multiple programs access to the same functions so that the code is not repeated in every program that needs the capabilities provided by the DLL function. These functions can be simple to very complex.

There are two kinds of DLLs: those you create with your own C compiler and those provided by Microsoft and other third-party DLL vendors. Windows provides several DLLs to handle various programming needs in its API (application programmers interface), which you can use to accomplish a wide variety of tasks, from allocating memory to creating windows. The major libraries provided by Microsoft are

- GDI
- KERNEL
- MMSYSTEM
- USER

There are many Microsoft documents and third-party books written describing the API functions in these and other libraries. We recommend you review these books if you need to do some serious Windows API programming inside of your Oracle Power Objects application. If you desire to create your own DLL, refer to your C compiler documentation.

Declaring DLL Functions

To use DLL functions, you must declare them in the declaration area of the application's property sheet. Once the procedure is declared, it can be called by Oracle Basic code in a method of any object in the application. The syntax of the procedure declaration is

```
DECLARE {SUB | FUNCTION} localProcname LIB "libname" [ALIAS realProcname]
(arguments) AS {return_type | CSTRING}
```

You must declare the DLL procedure as either a subroutine or a function. When you declare a procedure as a function, you must declare its return datatype as well, using the AS return_type clause. You do not declare the return type for a subroutine. The AS clause takes as an argument either the datatype to be returned or the CSTRING constant, which converts a returned C-style string to an Oracle Basic string.

The localProcname is the name of the procedure as it will be used in the Oracle Basic application. If the name is not the same as the name in the DLL, you must use the ALIAS clause and list the name of the procedure as it is defined in the DLL. This aliasing of the procedure name is useful if a procedure you need in a DLL has the same name as an Oracle Power Objects or a user-defined method that you use in your application. By aliasing the DLL function name, you can call the functions by using the alias name of the DLL procedure and the actual name of the method.

The library name, libname, must be in quotes. The library must either reside in the same directory as the application or its directory must be in the PATH environment variable. You can enter the entire pathname of the library if you wish.

If there are arguments required for the function, you must declare them in the declaration of the DLL procedure. The syntax for the arguments is

([BYVAL] argn AS {ANY | datatype} [,...])

The optional BYVAL keyword tells the function that only the argument's value is passed to procedure. This means that the argument's data cannot be altered by the procedure. By default, the argument is passed by reference, which means a pointer to the argument's value is passed to the procedure, thus the data can be altered by the procedure. The ANY keyword designates an argument of any datatype.

The following is an example of the declaration of the function WinExec in the KERN386.EXE lib with the alias RunProg that returns an integer value that is the completion status of the call. WinExec is a function that executes the given program name. (See the Launch example in the Oracle Power Objects Samples directory.)

```
DECLARE FUNCTION RunProg LIB "KRNL386.EXE" ALIAS WinExec &
(ByVal ProgName AS string, ByVal flag as Integer)AS Long
```

The syntax for calling the procedure is simply the procedure's name and the appropriate arguments. If the procedure is a function, you need to either capture the return value in a variable or object value, or use it as the argument in a conditional statement (for example, IF funcname(arg1) THEN ...). The above function would be called with the following syntax:

rtnval=RunProg("pbrush", 1)

Using Windows' or third-party DLLs can greatly increase the capabilities of your application without the overhead of writing thousands of lines of code.

This section is simply an introduction to the use of DLLs. If you need to use them extensively, you may need to refer to the documentation associated with the library you intend to use. The Windows Software Developers Kit has help for all functions in the DLL's supplied by Microsoft.

OLE Custom Controls

OLE custom controls (OCXs) are a unique kind of OLE miniserver (an OLE server that does not run stand-alone). OCXs provide a means of extending the functionality of Oracle Power Objects. For example, Microsoft includes a calendar OCX with the Access Developer's Kit that can be used to place a calendar object onto a form. As time goes by, you will be able to purchase a large assortment of controls from third-party developers for Oracle Power Objects to fill in present gaps in the product. You should also be able to purchase OCXs developed for other products such as Visual Basic 4.0 that can be imported into Oracle Power Objects. Unfortunately, OCX controls are only available for Windows.

For those acquainted with Visual Basic, OCX controls are comparable to Visual BasicVBXs, but unlike VBXs, OCX controls are object-oriented controls that are embedded into object frames (like an OLE object). Unlike OLE objects, OCXs cannot be bound to a database object and do not link to a full server application. Any changes made to an OCX in an application will be disregarded when you quit the application.

When an OCX is imported into Oracle Power Objects, a new button is placed in the Object palette, which you can use just the same as any of Oracle Power Object's normal palette controls. OCXs have properties and methods associated with them, the same as all Oracle Power Objects objects. If the name of an OCX feature or component has the same name as an Oracle Power Objects property or method, the OCX's property sheet displays the component as a standard property or method. All other OCX components are designated as OCX-specific properties with a small OCX to the left of the property or method's name. You can override the default processing of an OCX specific method with Oracle Basic method code. You can also use the Inherited.method_name( ) statement to call the method default processing.

Importing an OCX

As OCXs are a special type of OLE object, you import the control in the same manner as an OLE object. To use OCXs, you need to install the OLE DLLs included with the Windows version of Oracle Power Objects. To import an OCX object into Oracle Power Objects:

1. Activate a form, report, or class container and select the Load OLE Control menu item from the File menu.
2. In the Open File window, select the custom control.
3. Click the OK button to import the selected control.

Oracle Power Objects adds the OCX to the Object palette and is immediately available to use with the selected container.

Placing an OCX onto a Container

You add an OCX to a container the same as any other designer object. To add an OCX to a container:

1. Select the OCX control on the Object palette.
2. Click on the container at the location where you want to place the container (clicking instead of clicking and dragging places the control using its default size).

Creating OCXs

Microsoft has developed the API for OCXs. To create an OCX, you need to follow Microsoft's guidelines and develop the OCX in C. The OCX guidelines allow you to designate components of the control to be recognized as either properties or methods.

Customizing the Form Menu, Toolbar, and Status Line

In keeping with being a very extensible program, Oracle Power Objects allows you to create your own custom menus, toolbars, and status lines. All the methods to create and modify menus, toolbars, and status lines are discussed in Chapter 9. To illustrate the creation of custom menu bars and the implementation of the action associated with the custom menu items, we will build a small stand-alone program with its own menus. This is a simple program in which the user selects a menu item to create or read in an OLE object that is displayed at the top of the form. It could be a picture or saying or whatever the user wants, depending on what OLE-compliant programs are loaded on the system. This will be done by using an empty OLE control object that is filled by selecting different menu items. The creation of custom toolbars is done similarly and is not covered in this book. A custom status line will be added to the bottom of the form.

Creating a Custom Menu

In order to illustrate creating a custom menu, a simple form to use the menu is first created. After the form is built, we will create a new menu, Add Object, with three menu items, Create New, Save to File, and Read from File. The menu items will allow the end user to select a server to create a new object, to save the created object to a file, and to fill the control by reading in a file containing an OLE object.

After a form is created, there are three separate areas that must be addressed in order for a new menu to work. The first is to create and add the menu to the menu bar. This is done in the InitializeWindow( ) method of the form. The second is to set up the criteria that must be met for the menu items to be enabled. This is done in the form's TestCommand( ) method. Finally, you must write code to perform the action requested by a selected menu item. This is done in the DoCommand( ) method of the form.

As a suggestion, if there are several actions that can be triggered by custom menu items and each action takes considerable code, it may be wise to create a user-defined method (see Chapter 9) to handle each action. DoCommand( ) then calls the appropriate method for the action selected. This keeps the code in the DoCommand( ) method easier to maintain because it is made up of many fewer lines and it is easier to see what the DoCommand is doing. This is because there is only one function or subroutine call for each option in the DoCommand select list. If the methods are named properly, it is much easier to see what the action is requesting by reading just the method name than by reading all the code and trying to figure out what the code is doing. DoCommand( )'s main purpose is to select the different actions to take. Separate methods are then called to actually perform the action. However, in our example, the code is simple enough for all the code for each action to be placed in the DoCommand( ) method.

Create the Container for the New Menu

Before the menu can be constructed, we must build a form in which to put the menu. The form is to contain an empty control object and a text field in which the user enters the name of the file from/to which the OLE object is read/written. The form could be made more sophisticated by adding a form to search for files from which an OLE object is read, but that is beyond the scope of this example.

Here are the steps to create this form:

1. Open an application and a new form. Change the form's Name property to **frmTestMenu** (or whatever name you like) and its Label property to **Test OLE Menu**.

2. Click on the OLE Object tool in the Object palette and click in the form.
3. Do not select a server in the Insert Object dialog box when it opens. Simply click on Cancel. This will leave an empty OLE control frame in the form.
4. Enlarge the OLE control frame to about three by three inches (or whatever you want) and change the OLE control's Name property to **OLEcontrol**.
5. Add a text control field and a static text field to the form. Name the text control field **fldFname** and the static control **Filename**. Set their Label properties similarly. Set the text control's DataType property to **String** and its DataLength property to **50**.
6. Add a button to the form, label it **Exit**, and add the code **GetContainer.CloseWindow( )** to the button's Click( ) method.

Creating the Menu

The steps to create a new menu in the menu bar are to create the new menu, add the menu items to the menu, create a menu bar, add the default menus to the menu bar if desired, add the new menu to the menu bar, and finally add the menu bar to the form's window. Each of these steps is described in detail below.

Creating and Populating the New Menu A menu is an object just like everything else in Oracle Power Objects. You create a new menu object with the following Oracle Basic code:

```
REM create a variable to be the olemenu object
DIM vOleMenu AS Object

REM Create the menu object with the Oracle Basic NEW command.
vOleMenu = NEW MENU
REM Now set the menu's label to ADD Object. This is the label
REM that will be displayed in the menu bar.
vOleMenu.label="Add Object"
```

Now with the menu object created, we can add menu items to the menu. Use the Oracle Basic statement AppendMenuItem to do this. The syntax for this statement is

AppendMenuItem(Label, cmdCode, HelpTxt, Accelerator)

The Label is a string that is displayed in the menu item. The cmdCode is the identifying number that the TestCommand and DoCommand methods will use to select the action to take. In this example, the HelpTxt and Accelerator are not used (see Chapter 9 for details on this command) and are set to NULL.

The cmdCode variables are declared in the application's declaration area. They are declared as Global so that the command codes can be seen by the three different methods that use them. The values of the three command variables are set in the application's Initialize( ) method. Remember that the Application's Initialize( ) method is called even if only the form is run in Run-time mode, thus the variables are always initialized properly. The Oracle Basic code to declare these variables in the application's declarations area is shown below.

```
GLOBAL gblNewObj, gblWrtFile, gblReadFile AS Integer
```

Now you need to assign values to the command codes before they are used. As explained in Chapter 7, Oracle Power Objects reserves certain command codes for the default menus. Therefore, to be safe, always set your command codes relative to the predefined constant Cmd_FirstUserCommand as done in this example. This code is entered in the Initialize method of the application.

```
gblNewObj   = Cmd_FirstUserCommand + 1
gblWrtFile  = Cmd_FirstUserCommand + 2
gblReadFile = Cmd_FirstUserCommand + 3
```

The code to add menu items to the new menu object is shown below and is entered in the form's InitializeWindow( ) method. AppendMenuItem is a menu object method, thus the syntax is the usual object.method( ) format.

```
REM Add three menu items with the appropriate label and cmdCode
OleMenu.AppendMenuItem("Create New", gblNewObj,NULL, NULL)
OleMenu.AppendMenuItem("Read Object", gblReadFile, NULL,NULL)
OleMenu.AppendMenuItem("Write Object", gblWrtFile,NULL,NULL)
```

Adding the Menu to the Form Even though the menu is created and populated, it is not yet visible to the form. To actually add the new menu to the form, you must first create a new menu bar. When you add code to the InitializeWindow( ) method of a form, Oracle Power Objects checks to see that you have created both a menu bar and a toolbar. If not, it will automatically create one for you. In this case, we want to create our own menu but use the default toolbar. Thus, the first step is to make a new menu bar and then populate it with menus. Oracle Power Objects will create the toolbar for us. To create the menu bar, you use the same syntax as used to create the menu. First declare the menu bar variable and then assign a new menu bar object to that variable as shown below.

```
DIM vMBar AS Object
vMBar=NEW MENUBAR
```

To populate the new menu bar and tell Oracle Power Objects the new menu bar is to be used by the TestMenu form, enter the following code in the TestMenu form's InitializeWindow( ) method.

```
REM Populate the new menubar with the default menus appropriate
REM for the TestMenu form
TestMenu.DefaultMenuBar(vMBar)
REM Append the newly created OleMenu to the menus in the menubar.
vMBar.AppendMenu(OleMenu)
REM tell Oracle Power Objects to use the new menubar, vMbar.
TestMenu.SetMenuBar(vMBar)
```

So far, we have shown fragments of the code entered in the form's InitializeWindow( ). All the code fragments necessary to make the new menu are combined below. This is the actual code you enter in the InitializeWindow( ) method.

```
REM declare variables to be the olemenu object and a new menu bar.
DIM vOleMenu AS Object
DIM vMBar AS Object

REM Create the menu object with the Oracle Basic NEW command.
vOleMenu = NEW MENU
REM Now set the menu's label to "ADD Object".
REM Oracle Power Objects will display this label in the menu bar.
vOleMenu.label="Add Object"
REM Add three menu items with the
REM appropriate label and cmdCode to the new Menu. The cmdCode
REM variables are declared in the Application's Declaration's
REM area and are assigned values in the Application's
REM Initialize() method.
vOleMenu.AppendMenuItem("Create New", gblNewObj,NULL, NULL)
vOleMenu.AppendMenuItem("Read Object", gblReadFile, NULL,NULL)
vOleMenu.AppendMenuItem("Write Object", gblWrtFile,NULL,NULL)

REM Create the menubar object
vMBar=NEW MENUBAR

REM Populate the new menubar with the default menus appropriate
REM for the TestMenu form
frmTestMenu.DefaultMenuBar(MBar)
```

```
REM Append the newly created OleMenu to the default menus in the
REM menubar.
vMBar.AppendMenu(vOleMenu)
REM tell Oracle Power Objects to use the new menubar Mbar as its
REM menu bar. Because we did not add a toolbar, Oracle Power
REM Objects will add the default toolbar automatically.
frmTestMenu.setmenubar(vMBar)
```

Don't forget to declare the command code variables globally in the declaration area of the application containing TestMenu and set them in the application's Initialize( ) method as discussed above.

Enabling the Menu Items

Just because a menu exists in the menu bar, Oracle Power Objects does not automatically enable the menu items in that menu. When the menu is selected, Oracle Power Objects checks the form's TestCommand( ) method and then the Application's TestCommand( ) method if necessary to see if the menu items should be enabled (see DoCommand and TestCommand in Chapter 9). Thus, you must add code to TestMenu's TestCommand( ) method. Because there are no restrictions on when the user can create and insert an object in the OLE control, the Create New menu item is always enabled. There must be an OLE object in the OLE control for the Write To File menu item to be enabled, and the file named in the Fname text control field must exist before the Read From File menu is enabled. You enter the code to check these conditions in TestMenu's TestCommand method. The following is the code listing to enable the menu items appropriately.

```
REM by default disable the menu item
TestCommand=TestCommand_Disabled

SELECT CASE cmdCode
    CASE gblNewObj
        REM always enable the Create New menu item
        TestCommand=TestCommand_Enabled
    CASE  gblWrtFile
        REM Use the global variable to see if there is an object
        REM in the OLE control. madeOLE is declared globally in
        REM the Declarations of the application and set to False
        REM in the application's Initialize() method. It is set
        REM to True in the DoCommand() method when the Create New
        REM menu item is selected. If the Create New or Read From
        REM File menu items were selected then enable.
        IF madeOLE THEN
```

```
            TestCommand=TestCommand_Enabled
        END IF
    CASE gblReadFile
        REM use the user-defined method FileExists to see if the
        REM file exists. Note: this does not ensure that there is
        REM an object in the file. The FileExists function is
        REM described below. If the file exists then enable the
        REM Read From File menu item.
        IF usermethods.FileExists(nvl(vFname.value,
        "olecntrl.bin")) THEN
           TestCommand=TestCommand_Enabled
        END IF
END SELECT
```

This code uses a user-defined function FileExists in the frmUserMethods, which is never displayed in the application. Its only purpose is to contain user-defined methods. Thus, you add the code only once to the FileExists method instead of each time you add the method to the property sheet of an object that needs to use the FileExists method. This method returns TRUE if the file exists, otherwise, FALSE. It simply tries to open a file in input mode. If the file does not exist, an error is raised that the error handler captures and then sets the OpenErr flag. The function then continues executing after the open statement and returns a value depending on the OpenErr flag. This is kind of a kluge but there is no nice way in Oracle Basic to check for the existence of a file. Note that this will not work in Form Run-time mode because the frmUserMethods is not initialized unless the application is run. Thus, if you want to test just the form with the OLE control, you need to open TestMenu in the application's OnLoad( ) method and then press the Run button. The following is the code entered in the user-defined FileExists method.

```
REM Declare the filenumber and the error code
DIM vFnum, vOpenErr AS Integer

REM Set the openerr flag to False (means there is no error
REM opening the file)
vOpenErr = FALSE

REM get the first available file number
vFnum = FREEFILE()

REM enable the error handler
ON ERROR GOTO 999

REM Try to open the file, if it succeeds then return True and
```

```
REM close the file
OPEN vFname FOR INPUT ACCESS READ AS vFnum
IF vOpenErr THEN
   FileExists = FALSE
ELSE
   FileExists = TRUE
   CLOSE vFnum
END IF

REM exit the function before the error code is executed
EXIT FUNCTION

999   'the label for the Error handler
REM received an error on open so set the openerr flag and go back
REM to the statement following the open statement
vOpenErr = TRUE
RESUME NEXT
```

Executing the Menu Item Action

The final step in creating your new menu is to assign actions to the menu items. This code simply uses the Select Oracle Basic statement, and depending on which cmdCode it receives, it performs the required action. This code is placed in the DoCommand( ) method of the TestMenu form.

```
REM Declare the filename and filenum variables
DIM vFilename AS String
DIM vFilenum AS Integer

REM Set the Filename and Filenum variables. The filename uses the
REM value in fname.value if there is one, otherwise it uses the
REM default filename "olecntrl.bin"
vFileNum = FREEFILE()
vFileName=nvl(vFname.value, "olecntrl.bin")
REM Now depending on the cmdCode received, do the appropriate
REM action using the OLEcontrol's various methods to insert an
REM object, write the object to a file or read the object from a
REM file. Set the madeOLE variable true if an OLE object is placed
REM in the OLE control so that the Write To File menu item can be
REM enabled.
SELECT CASE cmdCode
    CASE gblNewObj
       OLEcontrol.OLEInsertObject()
```

```
        madeOLE = TRUE
    CASE gblWrtFile
        OPEN filename FOR BINARY ACCESS WRITE AS vFileNum
        OLEcontrol.WriteToFile(vFileNum)
        CLOSE vFileNum
        madeOLE = TRUE
    CASE gblReadFile
        OPEN FileName FOR BINARY ACCESS READ AS vFileNum
        OLEcontrol.ReadFromFile(vFileNum)
        CLOSE vFileNum
END SELECT
```

This code is fairly simple, but it does show two things. It shows how to use various OLE object methods and how to set up the code in the DoCommand( ) method to process actions requested by the user selecting a menu item.

This section described the three main processes that must be completed to create and use custom menus. First, create the menu, menu items, and menu bar and add it to the form. Next, enable the menu items in the TestCommand( ) method of the form using the new menu, and finally, add Oracle Basic code to the DoCommand( ) method to process the actions requested by the selected menu items. You use these same steps to create custom toolbars (but use differently named methods in creating the toolbar). The creation of a custom status line is similar, but it does not use the DoCommand( ) method and the actions are triggered in the TestCommand( ) method.

Creating a Custom Status Line

The status line is the information bar at the bottom of the screen in Windows and below the toolbar on the Macintosh. By default, it is not created for forms or reports. Its main use is to display a small help message when the cursor is over various parts of your application and to display the time and other information you feel is useful to the end user. Depending on how you want the status line to behave, the code to create a status line is entered either in the InitializeWindow( ) method of each form or in the OnLoad method of the application. A global status line is easier to maintain, because the code to automatically update panels (if necessary) is placed only in the TestCommand( ) method of the application. If the status line is dependent on which form is currently active, then the code must be placed in the TestCommand( ) method of each form.

A status line is made up of panels, the first of which is always present and cannot be deleted. By default, this panel displays the help message associated with the various controls on the form. The rest of the status line is made up of default system panels (Caps Lock, Num Lock, and Scroll Lock in Windows and none on the Macintosh) and custom user-defined panels.

In order for the help summary panel to display data, you must enter a help message in the HelpText property of each control, or no message will be displayed when the cursor is over that control. You can disable the help summary feature by setting the status line's HelpTextVisible to FALSE. You can then use the panel just as you would a panel that you create. You just can't delete the panel.

There are two ways to set the message in a given status panel. The first is to simply call the SetStatusPanelMsg( ) method with the appropriate message. If the status line's name has been declared globally, then any method in the application can update the status line's panel messages as needed. The other method of setting the message is to have Oracle Power Objects automatically display one to four messages, depending on the result of testing in the TestCommand( ) method. You include a cmd_constant just as you did for the menu items and four message strings based on the four return values from Test command (TestCommand_Enabled, TestCommand_Disabled, TestCommand_Checked, TestCommand_Disabled_Checked). In the TestCommand method, you use a select statement to decide which value to return based on the condition upon which the status panel reports. A common panel that requires constant updating is one that displays the time.

To demonstrate how to create and use a status line, we will add a status line to the small OLE example above. First, add the following strings to the HelpText property of each control in the form. Do not use quotes around the string. This enables the summary panel to display the help message when the cursor is over the object.

- **OLEControl** OLE object is placed here
- **fname** Enter OLE object filename here
- **Exit** Exit the form

Now create a status line to display the summary help messages in the TestMenu controls. Add a panel to explain why the Read From File menu item in the Add Object menu is disabled or enabled and one to display the time. Include the system default panels. The following code accomplishes these tasks.

Add this global declaration of the StatusLine object and the gblCurTime variable in the declaration part of the application so that other methods can use the status line.

```
REM declare the status line object and a global time command variable

DIM gblSline AS Object
DIM gblCurTime AS Integer
```

Add the following line to the Initialize( ) method of the application.

```
gblCurTime = Cmd_FirstUserCommand + 4
```

Combine the following code with the menu customization code in the InitializeWindow( ) method of the TestMenu form.

```
REM Create the Status line object
gblSline=NEW StatusLine

REM Add the system default panels and add another panel next to
REM the help summary panel that is 300 pixels wide and
REM displays no more than 60 characters.
gblSline.SysDefaultStatusLine( )
gblSline.InsertStatusPanel(2,300,60)

REM Set just two messages to be displayed. Whether there is a
REM file to read in or not.
gblSline.SetStatDispList(2, readfile, "A File with OLE exists", &
"No known OLE file",NULL,NULL)

REM add a time panel. The gblCurTime variable is declared and set in
REM the application's declaration and initialization areas.
gblSline.InsertStatusPanel(3,75,9)

REM Set the panel to display the current time
gblSline.SetStatDispList(3, gblCurTime, TIME( ), NULL, NULL,NULL)

REM Now assign the status line to the form.

testMenu.setStatusLine(gblSline)
```

The final step is to add code to the TestCommand( ) method to display the correct messages in the panels. The first new panel needs no code, because the result is the same for the menu and the status line. The correct message will be displayed because it uses the same variable as the menu item. For the panel that displays the time, the following code is entered in the TestMenu's TestCommand( ) method.

```
SELECT CASE cmdCode
    CASE gblCurTime
        REM set the message in panel 3 to the current time.
        gblSline.SetStatusPanelMsg(3, TIME())
        TestCommand=TestCommand_Enabled
```

```
    CASE  ...
    CASE  ...
END SELECT
```

This is a simple use of the status line, but it illustrates the necessary steps to create a customized status line.

Conclusion

This chapter was designed to give you an idea of the power available in Oracle Power Objects to build virtually any application you may be required to create. Nearly all applications requiring an interface to various types of databases can be built with Oracle Power Objects—everything from a simple interface to retrieve recipes on a home database to sophisticated inventory control programs for a large company. Those tasks that may not be performed in Oracle Power Objects can be assigned to OCX controls, DLLs, OLE, and (in the future) to OpenDoc objects.

APPENDIX A

Setting Up Oracle Power Objects as a Client to a Database Server

This appendix describes how to use Oracle Power Objects with an Oracle7 database server on a UNIX or NetWare server. There are two Oracle products for networking: SQL*Net V1 and SQL*Net V2. These programs support several network protocol drivers. Some of the protocols supported are DECnet, LU6.2,

STARLAN, TCP/IP, SPX/IPX, and X.25. Each program and the protocols used may require different configuration files and setups. This appendix will show you how to set up the network using SQL*Net V1 on a UNIX and NetWare server using the TCP/IP protocol.

The steps needed to set up the connection between the client machine with Oracle Power Objects and the UNIX Oracle7 server using the other protocols is similar to that covered in this appendix. However, for the exact requirements, see your network and Oracle documentation. Oracle's manual, *Tools for UNIX Administrator's Reference Guide,* covers most of the information you need for setting up a UNIX server. Other information to set up SQL*Net V1 on the client and on the NetWare server is in the manuals in the SQL*Net documentation for Oracle7 found in the SQL*Net V1 Documentation Library.

There are three requirements to complete the client/server connection between a PC or Macintosh and an Oracle7 Server. First, a protocol like TCP/IP or NetBEUI (there are several; refer to the documentation) needs to be running on the client PC or Macintosh on which Oracle Power Objects is installed. Second, the client machine must be on the network with the server. Third, you must purchase and install Oracle's SQL*Net V1 program on both the client and server. Once these conditions are met, the actual configuration to set up the network connection using SQL*Net V1 and TCP/IP protocol is relatively easy.

For demonstration purposes, we will describe the steps needed to set up the client/server relationship using MacTCP on the Macintosh and Sun PC-NFS on the PC. There are many vendors that provide TCP/IP programs that are compatible with SQL*Net V1. These examples, while applicable to only the given product, serve as templates for what is required regardless of the software package purchased.

After the server and client are set up properly, Oracle Power Objects will access the remote database just as if it were on the same machine the end users will never need to know where the actual database resides.

Client Setup

In this section, the requirements to set up the client side of the network are reviewed. We have given examples only for Macintosh and Windows, because at the time this book was written, the OS/2 version had not been released.

Macintosh Setup

On the Macintosh client side, you need to install MacTCP and SQL*Net V1 (version 1.1.7 or higher) and set up the appropriate HOSTS files in the System folder and Oracle folder. Setting up the Macintosh as a client is not as daunting as you might think. MacTCP is now a part of System 7.5, and SQL*Net V1 comes on two disks with Oracle Power Objects. Where many people may stumble is in setting up the two HOSTS files—one in the Oracle folder and the other in the System folder.

Installing MacTCP

MacTCP is developed by Apple and provides the Macintosh a TCP/IP interface. It is recommended that you use the most current version of MacTCP (currently 2.0.6), which is available as part of System 7.5. The interesting thing about MacTCP is its ability to allow you to have multiple TCP/IP programs running at the same time. Therefore, a Macintosh can connect to an Oracle7 Server database, send and receive TCP-IP-based E-mail, and surf the Internet all at the same time.

To install and set up MacTCP:

1. If you own System 7.5, you use the custom install option with the System 7.5 install program to install MacTCP. You click the triangle next to the Networking Software Option, click on the square next to MacTCP, and then click the Install button. MacTCP will be installed in the Control Panel folder in the System folder and your computer will automatically be rebooted.
2. Once the computer reboots, you need to open the MacTCP control panel by selecting it from the control panels under the Apple menu (at the upper-left of the Macintosh screen).
3. When MacTCP first opens, it will have two icons in the upper half of the window: LocalTalk and Ethernet. Click on the Ethernet icon to direct MacTCP to the proper interface for talking to an Ethernet network.
4. Select the default numeric string in the IP Address field and type in your computer's IP address. If you don't know your address, talk to your network administrator to get the proper IP address.
5. Click the More button to go to a new screen. Select Manually in the Obtain Address section. The other options are used when connecting to Internet connections where the server provides you with a different IP address every time you connect.
6. In the upper-right corner, select the subnet mask specified by your system administrator. If no one knows what submask setting to use, select C and make sure the subnet mask reads 255.255.255.0.
7. Type in the gateway IP address for your network gateway to the Oracle7 Server.
8. Type in the domain server name, set its IP address, and select the Default button. If you use multiple domain servers and gateway addresses for

connecting to the database, you can get a freeware software package called MacTCP Switcher 1.0 by John Norstad (Academic Computing and Network Services, Northwestern University, j-norstad@nwu.edu). MacTCP Switcher allows you to save different MacTCP configurations as files. You double-click a file configuration to select a different MacTCP configuration. For instance, we use one configuration to connect to an Oracle7 Server database and another configuration to connect to the Internet.

9. Click OK to go back to the MacTCP window, close the MacTCP control panel window, and reboot your Macintosh. MacTCP is now fully configured, but you still need to open the System folder and then edit the HOSTS file.
10. The HOSTS file should include the network gateway, domain name server, your computer's network name, subnet mask type (A, B, C), and the IP address. For example:

```
computername.supp.com           A      205.290.247.5
gatewayname.supp.com            A      205.290.247.2
domainservername.supp.com       A      205.290.247.3
```

Installing SQL*Net V1

SQL*Net is necessary for Oracle Power Objects to communicate with the Oracle7 Server on a TCP/IP network. SQL*Net V1 is available from Oracle and comes on two disks. To install SQL*Net:

1. Insert the first disk and click on the Install icon.
2. Follow the onscreen directions.
3. Set up the HOSTS file to include the network gateway, domain name server, your computer's network name, subnet mask type (A, B, C), and the IP address, just as you did with the HOSTS file in the System folder.

PC Setup

These sections assume the TCP/IP program has been installed on the client machine. If it has not, refer to the documentation to install the program. This section first describes how to verify that a TCP/IP program is running and then how to install SQL*Net V1 on the PC client.

Checking the TCP/IP Program

The first step in setting up the client connection is to verify that the TCP/IP program is installed and running. In this case, we will verify that the Sun PC-NFS program is running on the PC client machine. You would take similar steps for other TCP/IP programs.

The list below shows some of the items required for the Sun PC-NFS program. If they are not there, you or the system administrator will need to refer to the Sun documentation and reinstall the TCP/IP program.

The autoexec.bat file should contain the following lines:

- <PC-NFS executables directory>\NET INIT
- < PC-NFS executables directory >\RTM
- < PC-NFS executables directory >\[RNMNIS|RNMFILE]
- NFSPATH=c:\pcnfs # or wherever you have installed the Sun PC-NFS files

The following lines need to be in the Windows system.ini file:

- [boot]
- network.drv=pcnfs.drv
- [386 Enhanced]
- device=pcnfs.386

The following DLL libraries must be in the \orawin\bin directory:

- mpcnfs4.dll
- mwinsock.dll (This is Microsoft's socket library, and most TCP/IP products use it.)

Many TCP/IP programs use the Dynamic Name Server to attach a hostname to an address. If it is not running on your machine, your TCP/IP program requires a HOSTS file, which resides in different directories depending on the vendor. For Sun PC-NFS, the HOSTS file is in the directory specified by the NFSPATH environment variable. If this variable is not set, SQL*Net V1 looks for the HOSTS file in the home directory for NFS. The HOSTS file must contain the Oracle7 Server's Internet address and name. An example of an entry in the HOSTS file is

```
127.127.127.11 OraServer
```

where OraServer is the name of the host server machine.

If all seems to be in order, you can check to verify that the network is up and running by executing the command:

```
c:\ ping oraserver
```

If you do not receive the response:

```
c:\ oraserver is alive
```

you must review the above checks and the vendor documentation to solve the problem.

Installing SQL*Net V1

The installation of SQL*Net V1 is done using the Install program that comes with Oracle products. You simply select the programs to be installed when queried. If you or your system administrator needs to install SQL*Net V1, refer to Oracle's installation documentation. While installing the programs, you should install the SQL*Net documentation. The documentation will be in the Oracle Group window and is called SQL*Net V1 Documentation Library.

Once you know the network is up and running, check to see that SQL*Net V1 with the TCP/IP driver is installed. When the SQL*Net V1 TCP/IP driver is installed, the following must be in the various system files.

DLL libraries in \orawin\bin:

- sqltcp.dll
- msocklb.dll
- ora7win.dll or ora71win.dll

.INI files in the \windows directory:

- vsl.ini
- oracle.ini

The following bulleted lists show the required entries in the files needed for the SQL*Net V1 program. These entries must be in the oracle.ini file:

- TCP_PORT=1525 (This is the default; specify a different port number if required.)
- TCP_VENDOR = <vendor_key>

where vendor key is one of the values found in the SQL*Net V1 documentation for the supported third-party software. For Sun PC-NFS, it must be one of the following, depending on the version of the software (4.0a, 5.0, or 5.1.5).

The following entries must be in the config.sys file:

- BUFFERS=16
- FILES=60
- BREAK=ON

Inside the win.ini file are the following entries:

- [ORACLE]
- ORA_CONFIG=C:\WINDOWS\ORACLE.INI

The autoexec.bat file requires the following entries:

- PATH=C:\ORAWIN\BIN;<other paths>

If your Windows Oracle home is not ORAWIN, substitute the appropriate name. These checks verify that SQL*Net TCP/IP for Windows is installed.

Server Verification or Setup

With SQL*Net TCP/IP and Oracle Power Objects installed on the client side, you need to verify that SQL*Net V1 on the server side is installed and running. This appendix assumes your server machine is on the network and the network is working properly. If not, contact the system administrator and have it installed according to Oracle7 documentation.

In this appendix, we will give just a brief overview to ensure that SQL*Net V1 is installed and that your client machine can communicate with the Oracle Server on a UNIX or NetWare server.

UNIX Server

The following must be done on the server in order for the client to communicate with the database on the server after the SQL*Net TCP/IP for UNIX is installed (use Oracle's Install program to install SQL*Net V1).

1. Make sure that the server knows about the client machine. Check the /etc/hosts file on the network server (it may not be the database server machine) on the UNIX side to be sure it includes the client's network address. It should have an entry such as the following:

   ```
   127.127.127.11 george        # Bruce Kolste's MAC
   ```

You can view the hosts available on the UNIX network by logging onto the network server and running the command YPCAT HOSTS. If the client machine is not listed on the UNIX network, have the UNIX system administrator add it to the network.

2. Be sure the socket number for the orasrv process is listed in the /etc/services file. You need an entry for orasrv similar to that shown below. Have the system administrator add this line to the services file if it is not present. You can change the socket number if it is already used by another service.

   ```
   orasrv 1525/tcp      # Enable network oracle
   ```

3. Add the appropriate database information in the /etc/oratab file in the directory. This file simply names the databases available and their home directory. It is used by most of the supported SQL*Net protocols. The general syntax for the entries in oratab is

   ```
   ORACLE_SID:ORACLE_HOME:[Y|N][:server]
   ```

   where ORACLE_SID is the name of the database; ORACLE_HOME is the home directory for that database; Y or N is an optional field to signal whether the system should start up the database automatically at startup time or not; and the optional :server designates which server to execute. The default for :server is oracle. The following are valid entries in the oratab file:

   - Dev:/home/oracle:Y
   - Rel:/home/oracle:N:Relserver

4. Make sure that the "orasrv" process is running on the server. It needs to run with setuid as root, so the system administrator will need to see that this program is running properly. This program is in the /$ORACLE_HOME/bin directory ($ORACLE_HOME is the environmental variable storing the name of the home directory for the Oracle programs). It is best if you have the UNIX system administrator include the starting of orasrv in the local

startup files on the Oracle7 Server. These files are different on the various UNIX systems, but a common startup file in UNIX is the /etc/rc or /etc/rc.xxx file. This program listens to the network for requests to connect to a database listed in the oratab file. If the database name is valid, this program will attach the requester to the database across the network.

If you have other UNIX machines on the network and the Oracle executables are available to those machines, you can test the SQL*Net connection by typing in the command below on a different UNIX machine than the server:

```
sqlplus scott/tiger@T:hostname:sid
```

where scott/tiger is the user/password, T indicates a TCP/IP connection, hostname is the name of the Oracle database server, and sid is the name of the database to which you want to connect. If it does not succeed, recheck the appropriate files to be sure the machines can see each other over the network. If everything seems OK, contact the system administrator or review the troubleshooting guides in your network and Oracle documentation.

Now you are ready to test the connection from Oracle Power Objects to the server by creating a new session (as explained in Chapter 4) and using the appropriate connect string. After creating the session, double-click on the session icon to see if it connects.

If it fails, you can have the system administrator restart the orasrv process in Debug mode. Kill the orasrv process on the server and then start it again from the command line with the following command:

```
orasrv debugon logon -O/usr/tmp/orasrv.log
```

This will cause orasrv to run in debug mode and send its output to the given file, in this case /usr/tmp/orasrv.log. Check the output file to see if the connection is being made or, if not, why the connection failed. If it is connecting correctly, messages similar to those below will be in the log file.

```
16-MAY-95 13:10:34 orasrv[  439]: DEBUG:  Waiting for connection request...
17-MAY-95 09:14:14 orasrv[  439]: DEBUG:  Connection from host george
17-MAY-95 09:14:14 orasrv[  439]: CONNECT request from george
```

If there are no messages in the output file when you try to connect from the client machine, then orasrv is not receiving a request to connect. This generally indicates that the TCP/IP files are not set up properly on the client machine and the request is not being made. Make sure that host files and addresses are correct as explained above.

NetWare Server

In this example, we will give brief instructions to set up and verify that SQL*Net TCP/IP for NetWare is installed and running on the network server. A separate TCP/IP network protocol driver must be running on the network, and the server must support both the SPX/IPX and TCP/IP protocols. The client on the network must also support SPX/IX. Obviously, Oracle Server for NetWare must also be installed.

Installing SQL*Net TCP/IP

Depending on whether your Oracle software is on a CD or on floppy disk, insert the proper media and then type in **orainnw**. Enter the requested data as it requests machine type, company name, file server, language, drive volume, and directory where you want SQL*Net TCP/IP for NetWare installed. The default directory is ORANW. The installer may then ask if it should make changes to the autoexec.bat file. Answer appropriately.

Once the installer is set up, you either insert the SQL*Net TCP/IP for NetWare floppy disk or immediately select the products from the product list to install if the product is on CD. Select the entry with the SQL*Net TCP/IP product, press TAB to select it, and then press ENTER. Two programs are installed: the listener, tcpsrv.nlm (orasrv), and the SQL*Net TCP/IP driver, sqltcp.nlm. Exit the installer and prepare to configure the server.

Configuring SQL*Net TCP/IP

Just as with a UNIX system, there are two required files on the NetWare system: sys:etc\hosts and sys:etc\services. The HOSTS file lists the Internet addresses and names for all hosts that are permitted to connect to the server. The syntax for the HOSTS file is

internet_address hostname [alias [alias ...]]

just as for the UNIX system. An example of a valid entry in the HOSTS file is shown below.

```
127.127.127.11   george             # Bruce Kolste's MAC
```

This HOSTS file is required on NetWare because Novell TCP transport does not use the Dynamic Name Server.

The SERVICES file contains port numbers and the associated program names. Port numbers indicate which socket the server and clients are to use to communicate with each other. Again, the syntax for entries in the SERVICES file is the same as for UNIX machines. It is

process_server_name port_number/protocol server_name

The port_number can be of your choosing, but Oracle recommends that 1525 be used if possible. The process_server_name for SQL*Net is orasrv. The recommended entry for the SERVICES file is

```
orasrv      1525/tcp      oracle
```

Once you install these programs and enter the required data in the system files, you should be able to run Oracle Power Objects on the client machine and connect to the NetWare Oracle7 Server.

Verifying the SQL*Net TCP/IP Setup

As a final check, confirm that SQL*Net TCP/IP has been installed by verifying that all the required files are present and the necessary programs are running on the network. To do this, you must have supervisor or similar privileges. If the SYS volume is mapped to the Q drive, type in the following to verify that the listener and driver programs are installed **dir q:oranw\nlm\tcpsrv.nlm** and **dir q:oranw\nlm\sqltcp.nlm**. If the files are not there, reinstall SQL*Net TCP/IP.

Now verify that the modules are loaded. From the server console type **:modules**. If orasrv is not loaded, then consult your documentation and correct the problems.

APPENDIX B

Oracle Basic Reference

This appendix describes all of the Oracle Basic commands and functions. There are no examples in this appendix; examples using Oracle Basic can be found throughout this book, and Chapter 7 provides an overview of Oracle Basic and how it is used. Thus, this appendix is a reference guide only to give a brief description and the syntax of each command and function. As with the rest of the book, the syntax description contains certain constructs to represent what is required and what is optional for each command. A list of items separated by a vertical line (|) indicates that one of the items is to be selected. A list of items enclosed in { } indicates that one item from the list must be chosen, and items in [ ] are optional. Required single items are simply named with no enclosing braces.

This appendix has two main sections: "Oracle Basic Commands" and "Oracle Basic Functions." Beneath each header, the commands and functions are grouped according to their common functionality.

Oracle Basic Commands

Oracle Basic commands define the language. They include commands to define variables, control the processing of Oracle Basic statements, direct the input and output of data from the program, define and call procedures, and other tasks needed to make a complete programming language.

Variable/Constant Definition and Control

All procedural programming languages use variables, and the variables usually must be declared as a specific datatype to store the given type of data. The datatype of variables in Oracle Basic is defined in three ways. The first is by declaring variable names at the beginning of the block of code with the variable or constant commands CONST, DIM, REDIM, GLOBAL, and STATIC. The second is by using specific suffixes that denote a variable of a given type. The following is a list of the suffixes and the datatype associated with it.

Suffix	Datatype
%	Integer (16-bit signed integer)
&	Long integer (32-bit signed integer: internally, all integers are long)
!	Single-precision (4 bytes) floating-point number
#	Double-precision (8 bytes) floating-point number: internally, all floating-point numbers are double-precision
$	String of characters

The third way is by implicitly declaring a variable to be of a specific type by assigning data to it. The first time this type of variable is assigned a value, it is given the datatype of that data and the variable retains that datatype while it is in use. Its datatype cannot be changed after the first assignment. This information is covered in more detail in Chapter 7.

In the syntax description of the declarative commands, there are several common features. The variable name is indicated by vname, subscripts are the dimensions of a variable array, and type indicates one of eight datatypes: Integer, Long, Single, Double, String, Date, Variant, and Object. The syntax for subscripts (up to 60 subscripts) is

[[lowerlimit TO] upperlimit] [, ...]

The array subscripts can be any number from -32,768 to +32,767. If lowerlimit TO is not entered here, Oracle Basic uses zero (0) as the lower limit. Thus, negative subscripts require using the phrase lowerlimit TO.

CONST

Declares the given variable as storage for constant data. A constant identifier cannot have its value changed in the program. Thus, the value must be assigned to it when declared. Using constants helps the readability and maintainability of your code by making the constants self-commenting and easy to change because they are changed in only one place. As with variables, you can append a suffix character to the identifier declared with CONST to establish its type. If you do not append a suffix, the identifier takes the type of the result of evaluating the expression. The syntax for CONST is

CONST cname = c_expression [, ...]

c_expression means any valid Oracle Basic expression using only constants.

DIM

Explicitly declares a variable. If it is an array, you declare the maximum size and optionally the minimum size of each of its dimensions. The AS clause explicitly types the variable. You cannot use a suffix datatype identifier and the AS clause together. The variable declared within a method is available for use only in that method. The exception is if a variable is declared using DIM in the declaration part of an application, it is available to all methods in the application. You cannot use DIM to declare an array in a subroutine or function—use REDIM or STATIC. You can declare a variable as a dynamic array by adding parentheses with no subscript. By default, this makes an array of size one. Other methods can resize the array with the REDIM command. The syntax for DIM is

DIM vname [(subscripts)] [AS type]
        [, vname [(subscripts)] [AS type]] ...

REDIM

You use REDIM to declare arrays and allocate the space needed to store the data assigned to the array. You can also declare scalar variables as well. You can use REDIM to resize the dimensions of an existing array without affecting the data stored in the original array. As with DIM, you can declare its data type with the AS clause. You cannot change the number of dimensions of an array previously declared. The syntax for REDIM is

REDIM [PRESERVE] Orig_vname [([subscripts])] [AS type] [, New_vname [(subscripts)] [AS type]] [...]

The optional key [PRESERVE] restricts the resizing of arrays to the last array dimension only. Contents of the original array are preserved.

Orig_vname is the name of an array previously declared as an array, for which you want to reallocate memory or reset the dimensions. New_name is another variable that you want to declare as either an array or scalar.

GLOBAL

A variable declared with the GLOBAL command is available to all procedures in all objects in the application. GLOBAL may be used only within the declaration section of the application's property sheet. The syntax for GLOBAL is

```
GLOBAL vname [ ( [subscripts] ) [ AS type] ] [, ... ]
```

STATIC

When a variable is declared in a method with DIM, as soon as the method is no longer being used, the value in that variable is lost. STATIC declares variables that retain their value as long as the application is being run. However, only that procedure can access the variable unless it is declared in the declaration part of the application. STATIC must be used to declare fixed-size arrays in a procedure. STATIC's syntax is

```
STATIC [ static_vname [ ( [subscripts] ) ] [ AS type ] ] [, ... ]
```

LET

A wordy way to assign a value to a variable. It really is a superfluous command. Its syntax is

```
[ LET ] vname = expression
```

DELETE

When you create an object with the NEW statement, the memory allocated to that object remains in use until the application finishes. The only way to reclaim the memory space for a no-longer-used object is to delete it with the DELETE command. Be sure you no longer need the variable before you delete it, because if you try to reference it again, unpredictable results will occur. The deleted variable is no longer available to Oracle Power Objects to be used. DELETE's syntax is

```
DELETE object_expr [, object_expr ] ...
```

MID

This command replaces all or part of the contents of a string variable with a value from a second string expression. The syntax for MID is

```
MID ( old_string, start_pos [, count ] ) = new_string
```

where old_string can be a variable or a property with datatype set to string, start_pos is the position in the character string from which the replacement occurs, start_pos can be an integer expression, count tells how many characters of the new_string to use in replacing the same number of characters in old_string (counting the character at start_pos as 1), and new_string is the string expression from which to take the characters to replace the characters in old_string.

ERASE

Deletes the elements of one or more static arrays or removes completely one or more dynamic arrays. It does this by reinitializing static arrays to the default values. ERASE releases the memory allocated for dynamic arrays (those defined with empty parentheses). You then must use REDIM to reuse the dynamic array. The syntax for ERASE is

```
ERASE vname [, ... ]
```

Execution Control

As Oracle Power Objects processes Oracle Basic code, it generally does so in a sequential manner, i.e., one statement after another. However, you may have parts of code you want executed only under certain conditions, or you may need more information calculated in a completely separate part of the application. These commands direct which part of the code is to be executed next. It ranges from calling a procedure to simple IF statements. Many commands use a condition to decide on which action to take. A condition is an expression that evaluates to either a nonzero and nonNULL value (TRUE) or to zero or NULL (FALSE). Any part of an expression that resolves to NULL will cause the entire condition to be NULL. Use the NVL function to check for NULLs if necessary. It returns TRUE or FALSE depending on whether the value is NULL or not.

CALL

This is another of the superfluous commands in Oracle Basic. It is used to invoke an Oracle Basic procedure (subroutine or function) along with the required arguments. However, you do not need to use this command to invoke the procedure—simply name the procedure with its arguments in parentheses. The syntax for CALL is as follows. The syntax to call a procedure without using CALL is exactly the same, except you leave the CALL command out.

```
CALL proc_name [ (arg_list) ]
proc_name [ (arg_list) ]
```

The arguments can be passed by reference (alterable by the called procedure) or by value (not permanently alterable). The default method is by reference, that is, by passing a pointer to the variable. Using this pointer makes the current value of the variable available to the called routine. If the called routine stores a new value in the variable, then code executed after the called routine exits, uses the new value.

The other method, by value, entails passing values directly instead of passing pointers. The called routine has no pointer to the variable itself, just a copy of the value. The called routine can alter the copy but not the original value You have two choices for using this method. One is to enclose the argument(s) inside parentheses when you call the procedure. Alternatively, you can establish pass-by-value for any or all the parameters when you first define the procedure. You do so by using the BYVAL keyword with the declaration of each parameter you want passed in this way. Then, in the call, you simply supply the value or variable as a parameter. (However, BYVAL cannot be used with objects or arrays, and using BYVAL with expressions is redundant because the expression is evaluated and passed by value in any case.)

To pass an array as a whole rather than a single element from the array, use its name alone, followed by no parentheses or parameters.

In Windows, you can call DLL procedures in your Oracle Basic code. (There is no direct operational equivalent on the Macintosh, though there are shared libraries that can be accessed through the Shared Library Manager.) Windows DLL procedures can be declared in the declaration section. (See DECLARE.) However, many such procedures do not support all of the Oracle Basic datatypes. For such procedures, there is an advantage to passing arguments by value so that Oracle Basic will attempt a conversion to a type that the receiving DLL can use. (BYVAL can also be used in the declaration of the DLL.)

DO

The DO command causes Oracle Power Objects to execute the code bounded by the DO and LOOP statements repeatedly, either until the condition is TRUE (UNTIL) or while the condition is TRUE (WHILE). It has two basic forms. Complete the execution of the code in the loop at least once (Form 1) or only if the condition is met at the beginning of the loop (Form 2). The option EXIT DO statement is used as a secondary check of conditions to break out of the loop. For example, you may want a loop to continue indefinitely by setting the condition to the constant value 1. You then set a separate IF statement inside the loop to check conditions. When the time is right, the IF statement allows Oracle Power Objects to execute the EXIT DO command to break out of the loop. The syntax for the two forms of the DO command are the following.

Form 1:

```
DO
   [ statements ]
   [ EXIT DO ]
   [ statements ]
LOOP [ ( WHILE | UNTIL ) condition ]
```

Form 2:

```
DO [ ( WHILE | UNTIL ) condition ]
  [ statements ]
  [ EXIT DO ]
```

```
  [ statements ]
LOOP
```

EXIT

Forces Oracle Power Objects to break out of the current loop or procedure it is processing. In loops, control passes to the statement following the **loop** keyword. When used in a called procedure, processing ends in that procedure when the EXIT statement is reached, and resumes in the calling procedure. You must designate which kind of loop or procedure is to be exited. The syntax for EXIT is

```
EXIT { DO | FOR | FUNCTION | SUB }
```

FOR

The FOR loop uses a counter to direct how many times the code between the FOR and NEXT statements is executed. Your counter is a number value (not necessarily, but usually an integer), which is incremented by one each time the loop is executed, unless the STEP clause sets the increment value to a different value (not necessarily an integer). The loop executes until the counter is greater than the last_val (not necessarily an integer). The NEXT statement increments the counter and any other variables named in the list each time the loop is processed. If you do not have any other variables to be incremented, you can leave the counter variable off the NEXT statement. The syntax for the FOR command is

```
FOR counter = first_val TO last_val [ STEP inc_val ]
[ statements ]
NEXT [ counter [, ... ] ]
```

GOSUB...RETURN

If you have a segment of code that needs to be executed repeatedly but at different places in the code, use the GOSUB command. It transfers execution to the given line number or label. That code is executed sequentially until it reaches the RETURN statement. Oracle Power Objects then returns processing control to the statement following the GOSUB command. It is recommended that you not use this command but create a user-defined method to accomplish the necessary task. The syntax for the GOSUB command is

```
GOSUB { line_num | label: }
```

The line number must meet the following criteria:

- First nonblank character on the line
- Unique per routine
- Ended with a space, not a colon
- Below 65,530 to be reported by the ERL function

The label must meet the following constraints:

- First nonblank character on the line
- Unique per routine
- Different from every Oracle Basic reserved word
- Fewer than 41 characters long, using only letters (a-z, A-Z), the digits 0 to 9, or the underscore character
- Ends with a colon, as shown in the syntax statement. Spaces after the colon are ignored.

GOTO

Similar to GOSUB, but the control does not return to the statement following the GOTO statement. As with GOSUB, it is recommended that you not use this command but use an IF statement instead. Its syntax is similar to the GOSUB command with the same restrictions on line_num and label.

GOTO { line_num | label: }

IF

The IF statement transfers control to a particular block of code based on testing a condition you specify within the IF statement. The IF statement can cause a block of code to be skipped, to execute alternative blocks of code, or process a condition and specify the action Oracle Power Objects is to take. The line_num identifier has the same restrictions as in GOSUB. The three forms of the IF statement are shown in the syntax descriptions below.

Form 1 (all on one line):

IF condition GOTO line_num[ELSE { line_num | statements }]

(For good coding practices, it is not recommended you use the line_num in the ELSE portion.)

Form 2 (all on one line):

IF condition THEN { line_num | statements } [ELSE { line_num | statements }]

(For good coding practices, it is not recommended you use the line_num in the ELSE portion.)

Form 3 (multiline):

```
IF condition_1 THEN
    [statements ]
[ELSEIF condition_2 THEN
    [statements ] ]
[ELSE
    [statements ] ]
END IF
```

The Form 3 IF statement must have the END IF statement following its executable code. Note that the END IF is two words.

ON

This function is not recommended. It can be hard to maintain. The command has two forms, both of which use an expression that resolves to an integer between 0 and 255 (or an error occurs). The integer value is then used to select the line number or label in the target list. The items in the list are comma-separated. If the integer expression resolves to 2, then transfer goes to the second item in the list. The difference between the two forms is whether the execution returns to the following line (GOSUB) or skips the code following the ON statement (GOTO). The syntax for the ON statement is

```
ON int_expr GOTO target_list
ON which_target GOSUB target_list
```

ON ERROR

Similar to ON, except the ERROR condition is set by Oracle Power Objects upon encountering run-time errors, such as divide-by-zero or accessing a NULL variable. This is actually a useful version of the ON command, because it allows you to set up code to handle system errors. If you do not include an error handler in the procedure, Oracle Power Objects will stop the application upon a run-time error.

The three choices you give Oracle Power Objects upon receipt of an error are transfer control to the given line or label, disable the error handler by setting GOTO 0, or continue with the next statement as if an error did not occur. When you disable the error handler, it simply means that Oracle Power Objects will not use the error handler and will simply stop the application upon the receipt of another error. Once you enter a block of code using the GOTO syntax, control remains in that code until the processing reaches a RESUME, EXIT SUB, or EXIT FUNCTION statement. If the execution reaches the end of the method before encountering one of the three statements above, an error occurs and the application is stopped. To determine the cause of the error, call the ERR function (see ERR/ERL, later in this chapter under "Array-Subscript Functions") that returns an integer representing an Oracle Basic error code. The syntax for the ON ERROR statement is

```
ON ERROR { GOTO { err_line_or_label | 0 } | RESUME NEXT }
```

RESUME

RESUME is one of the three statements that end an ERROR handler. It transfers the flow of the program according to the option selected. Selecting 0 returns control to the statement that caused the error, selecting NEXT transfers control to the statement following the error-causing statement, and giving a line number or label transfers control to that line or label. RESUME can only be used in an error handler. Its syntax is

```
RESUME { [0] | NEXT | restart_line }
```

RETURN

This simply causes the control of execution to return to the line following the GOSUB statement that called the subroutine containing the RETURN statement. Multiple RETURN statements can control program flow by issuing the RETURN statement on different conditions. Its syntax is

```
RETURN
```

SELECT CASE

Similar to a long IF...ELSE IF sequence of statements. It is used to transfer control to a designated block of code, the selection of which is determined by a selector. The selector is an expression that resolves to a numeric or string value. Oracle Power Objects evaluates the selector and then transfers the flow of control to the block of code that contains that exact value in the CASE clause of the statement. The expr_list in the CASE clause contains comma-separated values against which the selector is compared. It can contain a begin TO end clause, which means every sequential item between the begin and end values.

For example, a TO z includes every letter between a and z. For inequality comparisons, use the IS <comparison operator> clause, which simply means if the selector meets the comparison condition, that block of code is executed. Once execution begins in a block, it will process all statements to the next CASE or the END statement and then continue with the statements after the END SELECT statement. If the value of the selector does not match any in the expression lists, the code in the CASE ELSE block is executed. If there is no CASE ELSE, processing continues after the END SELECT statement. Its syntax is

```
SELECT CASE selector
        CASE expr_list
        [ statements ]
        [ CASE expr_list
        [ statements ] ]
        [ CASE ELSE ]
END SELECT
```

STOP

This statement is for debugging only. When processed, the execution stops and the debugger is invoked. You then use the Debugger menu to continue the program. Its syntax is

```
STOP
```

WHILE

Exactly like the DO WHILE loop with the condition at the start. If the condition is TRUE at the start, the code between the WHILE and WEND statements is executed until the condition is FALSE. Otherwise, control continues after the WEND statement.

```
WHILE condition
        [ statements ]
WEND
```

Procedure Definition

Procedures are functions or subroutines that are outside the scope of the current method. They can be user-defined methods or completely external procedures in Windows' Dynamic Link Libraries. Procedures allow the repeated use of code without having to repeatedly rewrite the code. And in Windows you can invoke procedures that may be beyond your ability to write.

The following statements declare, call, and otherwise enable you to use procedures. Several of these commands use an argument list. The argument list is a list containing each argument and its datatype separated by commas and enclosed in parentheses. The argument (if not an array) can be preceded by BYVAL, which means that Oracle Basic passes the argument's value to the procedure, otherwise it passes the argument's reference. The datatype of the argument can be declared using the AS clause, using datatype suffixes, or can be declared implicitly. When passing arrays to procedures, the syntax depends on whether the procedure is built-in or user-defined. You do not use parentheses appended to the array name when calling a built-in function, but you do add the parentheses when calling a user-defined procedure. The syntax for the argument list is

```
( [ [BYVAL] arg [AS type] ] [, ... ] ] )
```

DECLARE

In order to use external procedures written by others and stored in DLLs (Windows only), you must declare the procedure. The following statements declare functions or subroutines as available for use within the scope of the method. Procedures declared in the declaration part of the application are global to all objects in your application. The local name is the name of the procedure used in your application. The real_name is the name of the procedure in the library. If the local and real names are the same, the ALIAS clause is not needed. If you do not declare any arguments, then you may not pass arguments when you call it. A function can have its return datatype declared using the AS clause or with CSTRING, which means the function returns a NULL terminated string (a C language string). DECLARE's syntax is

```
DECLARE SUB local_name LIB lib_name [ALIAS "real_name"]
        [ argument _list]
```

```
DECLARE FUNCTION local_name LIB lib_name [ALIAS "real_name"]
        [ argument _list] [ AS type | CSTRING]
```

END

END signals the end of an IF or SELECT block of code and is required. It can also signal the completion of a function or subroutine but is not required. Its syntax is

```
END { FUNCTION | IF | SELECT | SUB }
```

FUNCTION

This definition is only for possible future versions of Oracle Basic, because you cannot explicitly use this command in this version of Oracle Power Objects. The only way to create functions or subroutines is by creating user-defined methods (see Chapter 9). However, in the future you may be able to create procedures in other ways, so we included it for future reference only.

This command defines a function, which is a procedure that returns a value. A function can have its return datatype declared using the AS clause or with CSTRING, which means the function returns a NULL terminated string (a C language string). Before the function is exited by either the END FUNCTION, the last statement in the function, or the EXIT FUNCTION statements, you must assign a value of the correct datatype to the function by using the assignment statement fname = return_val. Recursive functions (those that call themselves) are allowed. The syntax for the FUNCTION definition is

```
FUNCTION fname ( argument_list ) [ AS type | CSTRING ]
        [ statements ]
        [ fname = return_val1 ]
        [ EXIT FUNCTION ]
        [ statements ]
        [ fname = return_val2 ]
END FUNCTION
```

SUB

See the comments for the FUNCTION statement above. A subroutine performs some action but returns no value. Other than that, it is the same as a FUNCTION. SUB's syntax is

```
SUB sname [ ( argument_list ) ]
      [ statements ]
      EXIT SUB ]
      [ statements ]
END SUB
```

Input/Output

These commands allow you to read from and write to files on disk. Some of these commands require pathnames and volumes on your system. On a Windows machine, the volume is any single letter followed by a colon (:) up to the last drive volume designated in the config.sys file. The subdirectories are separated by the backslash character (\). A valid pathname in Windows is c:\orawin\opodr1\tubapp.poa. On a Macintosh, volumes are named just as the directories. Subdirectories are separated by a colon (:). A valid Macintosh pathname is main disk:oracle files:tubapp. Note that spaces are valid for Macintosh filenames.

CLOSE

After opening files for reading and writing, they should be closed when the action is completed. This frees up the number for use by other OPEN commands. It also frees up memory used by the open file descriptor. Once a file is closed, it must be reopened if it is needed again. If a file number is not given, it closes all open files. The file number must match the number of an opened file. Its syntax is

```
CLOSE [# file_num [, ... ] ]
```

GET

This command reads data from an opened file designated by the file_num into the variable vname. The exact data read depends on how the file was opened. If in Random mode, the rec_num means the record number, and if in Binary mode, it means the byte position. If rec_num is omitted (you still need two commas), it reads the next data in the file. See Chapter 7 for details on the amount of data read in. The syntax for GET is

```
GET [#]file_num, [ record_num ], vname
```

The # sign is optional.

INPUT

INPUT reads individual data items sequentially into the variables in the var_list. The datatype of the data item must match the datatype of the variable. It reads past end-of-line characters and continues to read data until all the variables are filled. The # sign is required in this command, the syntax of which is

```
INPUT #file_num, var_list
```

INPUTBOX

This is a nice little feature of Oracle Power Objects that allows you to easily query the user for input. It displays a modal dialog box with a message requesting input and a text box to receive the user's input. The input_title is simply the title of the input dialog box. The input_default allows the user to simply press the ENTER key to load the input box with the given default input. This is useful when the application has a good idea of what the input should be, such as a user's name, but checks to be sure. The horiz and vert arguments set the placement of the box from the left edge and top of the screen, respectively. If you use horiz and vert but no title or default input, you must include two commas between the input_message and the horiz and vert values. When the user presses the ENTER (or RETURN) key, INPUTBOX returns the string the user typed in. If Cancel or Escape is pressed, an empty string is returned. INPUTBOX syntax is

INPUTBOX(input_message [, [input_title] [, [input_default] [horiz, vert]]])

LINE INPUT #

LINE INPUT reads a single line of data into a string variable. It then skips over the end-of-line character. The # is required before the number of the opened file. The variable must be large enough to receive one full line of data. Its syntax is

LINE INPUT # file_num, vname

MSGBOX

This command can be either a function or a command. See MSGBOX in the "General Functions" section for a description of its use.

OPEN

Before you can access data from a file on disk, you must open it. This command opens the file for reading and/or writing and in different access modes. You must use a file number that is not currently being used. The function FREEFILE returns the lowest available number currently available. Use this function and store the number in a variable that other IO routines can use to access the opened file.

FOR mode designates the type of action to be performed on the file. They are Append, Input, Output, Binary, or Random. The first three modes indicate sequential data, such as strings and numbers. Binary and Random indicate binary data that are accessed in random positions in the file depending on the arguments of the commands that write or read data from the file.

The ACCESS method signifies whether the file is opened for Read, Write, or Read-Write mode. Lock_method designates the access others have to the file while your application has it opened. The file can be Shared, Lock Read, Lock Write, or Lock Read Write. The record length indicates the length of one record of data when the file is opened in RANDOM mode (128 bytes by default). You must include two extra bytes in the record length for storing strings of VARTYPE 2-5 (see the description of VARTYPE in the "General Functions" section) and four extra bytes for data of VARTYPE 8. When using the ACCESS clause, the share.exe program must be run on Windows and file sharing must be enabled on the Macintosh. The syntax for OPEN is

OPEN file [FOR mode] [ACCESS operations] [lock_method] AS [#]original_file_num [LEN=record_len]

PRINT

This command prints data in a formatted style to a sequential file. You must include the # character before the file number. The SPC or TAB keywords tell Oracle Basic how many spaces or tabs to print before it prints the next data item. The semicolon (;) tells Oracle Basic to print the next data item immediately following the last character written. The comma (,) tells Oracle Basic to print the next data item starting in the next print zone, which is every 14 characters. The syntax for PRINT is

PRINT #file_num, [[{ SPC(n) | TAB(n) }] data [{ ; | , }]] [, ...]

PUT

Writes data from a variable to a disk file opened in Binary or Random mode. The # character is optional before the required file number. In Random mode, the put_num is the record number at which the data in vname is to be written. In Binary mode, it is the byte position at which Oracle Basic will write the data. The length of the data PUT writes to the file is the value of LEN when the file was opened. If vname is shorter than LEN, then Oracle Basic pads the data. If put_num is left out, the new entry will be placed after the point in the file where the last access occurred. Also, when put_num is omitted, you must include two commas (put file_num, , vname). The syntax of the PUT command is

PUT [#]file_num, [put _num], vname

RESET

RESET flushes all opened file buffers to disk and then closes the files. Its syntax is

RESET

SEEK

You use this command to move the file pointer to the exact position in a file opened in Binary or Random mode for the next read or write. The # character is optional before the file identifier. The position is the record number or byte at which the next input/output operation is to begin. The syntax for SEEK is

SEEK [#]file_num , position

WIDTH

The default value of a line written to an OUTPUT file is 80 characters. Use this command to modify that length to the desired length. The # character is required before the file identifier. The line width can be 0, indicating no explicit limit, or 1-255, indicating the length in bytes of the output data to be written to the file. The syntax of WIDTH is

WIDTH # file_num , line_width

WRITE

Use WRITE to write string, numeric, or data into an open sequential file. The # sign is required before the opened file identifier. WRITE separates each entry with a comma and puts double quotes around strings. Its syntax is

```
WRITE #file_num [, expr ] [ ... ]
```

Directory/File Management

These commands allow you to change working directories, create directories, and manage files.

CHDIR

Use CHDIR to change your working directory to the one specified. Its syntax is

```
CHDIR directory_path_name
```

CHDRIVE

Use CHDRIVE to change to the given volume. The drive_name is a string and must be a letter between A and the last drive on a Windows machine, or the name of the volume on a Macintosh. The syntax of CHDRIVE is

```
CHDRIVE drive_name
```

KILL

KILL removes a file from the disk. Fname must be fully qualified (no wildcards). Its syntax is

```
KILL file_name_to_kill
```

LOCK

If you open a file in Random or Binary in Shared mode, you use this command to lock portions of the opened file. If you leave off the lock position clauses, it locks the entire file and no one can write to the file except your application. The # character is optional. You can lock a single record or a range of records or bytes by using the TO clause. The syntax for LOCK is

```
LOCK [#]file_num [, lock_position]
```

or

```
LOCK [#]file_num [, [lock_beg ] TO lock_end ]
```

MKDIR

Invoking MKDIR creates the specified directory on the current working volume or an explicitly specified volume. Its syntax is

```
MKDIR directory_path
```

NAME...AS

Use this command to move a file from one directory to another directory, change its name, or move it and change its name. Any named directories in the pathname must exist, or an error results. The pathname is a string expression. The syntax for NAME...AS is

```
NAME current_pathname AS new_pathname
```

RMDIR

Use RMDIR to delete the given directory from the current working volume or from a volume that you specify explicitly. The directory must be empty, or the command fails. Its syntax is

```
RMDIR path_name
```

Miscellaneous

It seems in any grouping of ideas, there are some that don't fit in a particular pigeon-hole (just like people). The following commands are of that "outsider" class.

BEEP

Use this command to signal the user's attention, whether it's an error or a dialog box that requires input. It sounds a tone through the speaker in the computer. The syntax is

```
BEEP
```

RANDOMIZE

Initializes the random number generator used by the RND function. If you do not use RANDOMIZE, RND will return the same number every time. It is best to use a numeric expression that resolves to a different number, such as the current time and date, every time the program is run, or you will generate the same sequence of random numbers each time. Its syntax is

```
RANDOMIZE [ numeric_expr ]
```

REM

Most code is more easily maintained when there is text explaining what the code is doing. REM allows you to enter text to be read. It is not processed by the machine. You can also use the apostrophe to signal a comment after an executable statement. The end of the comment is the end of the line. The syntax for REM and ' is

```
REM comments describing the code
oracle_basic_code statement 'comments describing the statement
```

Oracle Basic Functions

The following are Oracle Basic functions. Functions return a value that your Oracle Basic code can use to complete its task. The functions are grouped together according to functionality.

File Input/Output Functions

You use these functions to determine the application's current working environment and to work with files on the disk. Some of these functions require pathnames and volumes on your system. On a Windows machine, the volume is any single letter followed by a colon (:) up to the last drive volume designated in the config.sys file. The subdirectories are separated by the backslash character (\). A valid pathname in Windows is c:\orawin\opodr1\tubapp.poa. On a Macintosh, volumes are named just as the directories. Subdirectories are separated by a colon (:). A valid Macintosh pathname is main disk:oracle files:tubapp. Note that spaces are valid for Macintosh filenames.

CURDIR

CURDIR returns the current pathname for the specified or default volume as a string. The volume_id must be a literal string in double quotes or a string variable containing the name of an existing drive. By default, CURDIR returns the current default volume. Its syntax is

```
CURDIR [ [( ] volume_id [ )] ]
```

EOF

When reading a file, you need to know when you reach the end. This function is used to return TRUE or FALSE if the file pointer is at the end of the file. You give it the number of a currently opened file. Its syntax is

```
EOF(file_num)
```

FREEFILE

This function makes it easier for you to select a file identifier when opening a file. You do not need to keep track of all other opened files, because this function returns the lowest unused file number. Of course, you need to assign the numbers returned by FREEFILE to a variable rather than use it directly in the open statement, or you will have no idea what number to use when accessing the file. Its syntax is

```
FREEFILE
```

INPUT

Similar to the INPUT # command, it returns the specified number of characters, n, in a string from the designated sequential file. The file pointer moves to the position after the last character retrieved. It can be used on files opened in Input or Binary mode. It returns every character read, including the end-of-line character, which the command INPUT # ignores. The syntax for INPUT is

INPUT (n , file_number)

LOC

LOC returns the current numeric position of the file pointer in the designated open file. The value is the position modulo 128 for sequential files, the number of the last variable accessed in Random files, and the position of the last byte accessed in a Binary file. The first byte or number returned by LOC for a Binary or Random file is 0. The syntax for LOC is

LOC(file_number)

LOF

It can be very useful to know the exact length of the opened file so that you do not request more data than the file holds. This function returns the length (in bytes) of the designated open file. Its syntax is

LOF(file_number)

SEEK

SEEK returns the numeric position in the designated open file of the next value to be accessed. The value is the position modulo 128 for sequential files, the number of the next variable to be accessed in Random files, and the position of the next byte to be accessed in a Binary file. The first byte or number in a Binary or Random file is 1. (Note that LOC returns a 0 for the first byte.)

The command SEEK seems much more useful, because it moves the pointer to the designated position, while the SEEK function simply returns the position next to be accessed. The syntax for SEEK is

SEEK (file_number)

SPC

Use this function only in a PRINT # command to skip the number of given spaces before printing the next variable. It will print spaces to the position on the current or next line calculated by the following formula:

next_print_pos = current_pos + num_of_ spaces MOD length_of_line

If next_print_pos is less than current_pos, the function will print spaces to the calculated position on the next line. The syntax for the SPC function is (it is used only in a PRINT # command)

SPC(num_of_spaces)

General Functions

You use the following functions to access general data about your system and variables, or communicate with the end-user.

ENVIRON

This function applies only to Windows. It returns the string value of the environmental variable env_name that you supply. The env_name stands for such environment variables as PATH. On a Macintosh, ENVIRON returns NULL. If the env_name is not defined, an empty string is returned. The env_name is a string constant, and the name must be in double quotes and in all caps. The syntax is

ENVIRON(env_name)

MSGBOX

This is a very useful command and is used often in the examples found in this book. Its simplest form simply displays a dialog box containing msg_display and an OK button. By adding the msg_type argument to designate the symbol type and set of buttons to display, the MSGBOX can be used to accomplish a multiple number of tasks, from simple warnings to choosing among three options. The box_title is simply the name to display in the title bar of the dialog box. The msg_type is an integer derived by adding one number from each set of choices defining buttons, icons, defaults, and window type. The syntax for MSGBOS is

MSGBOX [(] msg_display [, msg_type] [, dialog_title] [)]

The ( ) are required if you check msg_type or dialog_title. The following table shows the four choice types and the numbers and associated options for each choice.

Button Choices	Button(s) Displayed
0	OK button only (default)
1	OK and Cancel
4	Yes and No
3	Yes, No, and Cancel
5	Retry and Cancel
2	Abort, Retry, and Ignore
Icon Choices	**Icon Displayed**
0	No icon (default)
16	Stop sign (Hand)
32	Question mark

48	Exclamation point
64	Information "I"
Default Button Definitions	**Default Button**
0	First button (default)
256	Second button
Modal Window Choices	**Type of Dialog Box**
0	Application (default)
4096	System

Values returned from MSGBOX when used as a function rather than a command signify which button the user pressed.

Value	Button Chosen
1	OK
2	Cancel (Esc)
3	Abort
6	Yes
7	No
4	Retry

SYSTEMNAME

SYSTEMNAME returns a string containing the name of the system (Macintosh or Windows) on which Oracle Power Objects is running. Its syntax is

SYSTEMNAME

VARTYPE

There are times when you may need to know the datatype of an expression in your Oracle code. For example, you may need to know if an expression resolves to NULL. This function returns an integer representing the datatype of the argument. The integer and associated datatype is shown in the table below.

Value	Datatype
1	NULL
3	INTEGER

3	LONG
5	SINGLE
5	DOUBLE
7	DATE
8	STRING
9	OBJECT

The syntax for VARTYPE is

```
VARTYPE(expr)
```

Array/Subscript Functions

These functions allow you to determine the upper or lower (or both) bounds of an array variable.

LBOUND, UBOUND

There are times when your application may need to know the bounds of an array, particularly if the array is dynamic and may have been redimensioned with REDIM. Use LBOUND and UBOUND to return the smallest/largest permissible defined value for the given array and given subscript dimension (which begins with 1 for a one-dimensional array). These are particularly useful in FOR LOOPs. The syntax for LBOUND or UBOUND is

```
LBOUND (array_name [, dimension_num ])
UBOUND (array_name [, dimension_num ])
```

Control and Test Functions

These control and test functions, in conjunction with the Execution Control Oracle Basic commands, allow you to control the flow of processing. Because the normal comparison operators can't distinguish between NULL and zero, the functions that test for NULL are especially useful.

CHOOSE

This function returns the value of the selected expression in the expression list. The selection is based on the value of the index that can be the result of an expression. The datatype of the value is the datatype of the evaluated expression. Expressions of any datatype can be in the list. The syntax for CHOOSE is

```
CHOOSE (index, expr1 [, expr2 ] ...)
```

ERR/ERL

These functions are best used in error handlers (see ON ERROR earlier). They return the error code and the line number of the statement that caused the error, respectively. The error codes are listed in the online help under the BAS errors. You should retrieve the error code immediately after entering the error handler, or the ERR/ERL may be reset by other procedure calls or even another error. The syntax for ERR or ERL is

```
ERR
ERL
```

IIF

IIF evaluates the given expression and then returns the resolved expression exprT if the expression is TRUE, otherwise returns the resolved expression exprF. It can be used to check for zeros where a zero value is inappropriate or do the same for NULLs in conjunction with the ISNULL function.

```
IIF(expr , exprT , exprF)
```

ISDATE

This function tests whether the given date, string, or numeric expr can be converted to a date. It returns TRUE if the expression can be converted, otherwise it returns FALSE. ISDATE's syntax is

```
ISDATE(n_d_s_expr)
```

ISNULL

This function allows you to identify an expression that resolves to NULL. If the expression does resolve to NULL, this function returns TRUE, otherwise it returns FALSE. The syntax for ISNULL is

```
ISNULL(any_expr)
```

ISNUMERIC

Identifies whether the argument could be converted to a number by returning TRUE if it can and FALSE if it can't. If the expression contains any numbers, it can be converted to a numeric value, so be careful using it. For example ISNUMERIC("ab2345hi") returns TRUE. ISNUMERIC's syntax is

```
ISNUMERIC(any_expr)
```

NVL

This is another very useful function that checks for NULL. It is particularly useful to ensure that variables are initialized to nonNULL values. If the first expression is NULL, NVL returns the second expression, which could be a default value for a variable. Otherwise, it returns the first expression. The syntax for NVL is

```
NVL(expr1,expr2)
```

SWITCH

Oracle Basic certainly supplies many ways to select alternative expressions. This one allows you to enter up to seven pairs of a conditional expression and a value expression. Oracle Basic starts on the left and evaluates the conditional expression of the first pair. If it evaluates to TRUE, it evaluates and returns the associated value expression. If the conditional expression is FALSE, Oracle Basic then moves to the next pair, and so on. If no conditional expression evaluates to TRUE, SWITCH returns NULL. Each value expression can be of different datatypes. Its syntax is

```
SWITCH(cond_expr1, value_expr1 [, cond_expr2, value_expr2 ...[,
cond_expr7, value_expr7 ]])
```

Mathematical and Trigonometric Functions

As in most languages, Oracle Basic has a rich complement of mathematical functions to help you meet all requirements of your design.

ABS

ABS returns the absolute value of the numeric expression you supply. It returns a positive number. The syntax for ABS is

```
ABS(num)
```

ATN

ATN returns the arctangent (in radians) of the given numeric expression. It returns a double-precision number. Its syntax is

```
ATN(num)
```

COS

COS returns the cosine of the given angle (in radians) as a double-precision number. Its syntax is

```
COS(angle)
```

EXP

EXP returns e (the base of natural logarithms, approximately 2.71828) to the power specified as num. The return value is double-precision. For single-precision values, num must be less than 88.0297, and for double-precision numbers, num must be less than 709.782712894. Its syntax is

```
EXP(num)
```

FIX

FIX truncates the fractional part of the given numeric expression to return the integer part of the number. Its syntax is

```
FIX(num)
```

INT

Similar to FIX, except it returns the largest integer less than or equal to the given numeric expression. The difference occurs only in negative numbers, where FIX(-4.8) returns -4 and INT(-4.8) returns -5. The syntax for INT is

```
INT(num)
```

LOG

LOG returns the natural logarithm of the given numeric expression as a double-precision number. Its syntax is

```
LOG(num)
```

MOD

This function is actually an operator. It returns the integer remainder after dividing the first operand by the second. Unlike most functions, the arguments are more like operands. The syntax for MOD is

```
num1 MOD num2
```

RND

RND returns a single-precision random number between 0 and 1. The control directs RND to return a random number according to the values in the table below.

ValueNumber	Returned
control <0	Always returns the same number for any given negative number
control =0	Returns the last number generated
control >0	Returns the next random number
control omitted	Returns the next random number

You should use the command RANDOMIZE to initialize the random number generator. Otherwise, every time the program is used, it will generate the same sequence of random numbers. The syntax for RND is

```
RND(control)
```

SGN

SGN returns -1, 0, 1 depending on if the given number is < 0, = 0, or > 0 respectively. The syntax for SGN is

```
SGN(num)
```

SIN

SIN returns the sine in double-precision of the given angle in radians. Its syntax is

```
SIN(angle)
```

SQR

SQR returns in double-precision the square root of a nonnegative numeric expression. The syntax for SQR is

```
SQR(num_expr)
```

TAN

TAN returns in double-precision the tangent of the given angle specified in radians. Its syntax is

```
TAN(angle)
```

SQL Functions

These Oracle Basic functions, SQLErrText, SQLErrCode, SQLErrClass, and SQLRowCount, which are used in conjunction with EXEC SQL, are discussed in detail in Chapter 10.

String Functions

These functions all return either a string value or information about the given string. Some are very similar to their COMMAND counterparts.

ASC

ASC returns the numeric ANSI code for the first character in the string you supply. It is the complement of CHR. If string is NULL, an error is raised. Its syntax is

```
ASC(string)
```

CHR

Opposite of ASC. CHR returns the character whose ANSI code is num (0-255). Its main use is to add nonprintable characters to a message, such as BEEP, which is code number 7. Its syntax is

```
CHR(num)
```

FORMAT

Converts a number, string, or date value (N_D_S_expr) into a string and formats it according to the given format string. If the format string is omitted, FORMAT has the same functionality as STR, which simply converts the given expression to a string. The format string is either a literal string enclosed in double quotes or a string variable containing the format string. Its syntax is

FORMAT(NumDateStr_expr [, fmt])

The following tables display the characters to create the fmt string, depending on whether you are formatting a number, date, or string.

The format string for numbers can be in four parts separated by semicolons (;). If only one part is used, it applies to all numbers. If you use two parts, the first is used for positive numbers and zeros, the second for negative numbers. When using three parts, the first is for positive numbers, the second is for negative numbers, and the third is for zeros. If you use the fourth part, the first three parts are as above, and the fourth part is used for empty and NULL values. For numbers, use the following format characters.

Symbols	Explanation
0	The 0 displays a digit if it exists or 0 if none is specified. Therefore, 0000.00 displays 123.4 as 0123.40.
#	Similar to the 0, the pound sign displays a digit if it exists; otherwise, it doesn't display anything. ####.### displays 123.4 as 123.4.
,	This adds commas as thousands separators in strings with # or 0. ###,###.00 displays 12345.6 as 12,345.60.
.	The period places a decimal point in strings with # or 0. ###.## displays 123.4 as 123.4.
$	This displays the local currency symbol. $###,###.00 displays 12345.6 as $12,345.60.
$$	The double dollar signs are similar to the $, but they display an international currency symbol for the present locale. In England $$###,###.00 displays 12345.6 as £12,345.60.
%	The percent converts the value to a percentage (i.e., multiplies the value by 100) and displays the percentage symbol after the value. ###.00% displays .12345 as 12.35%. Note that the number is truncated and rounded up.
8	The number 8 displays octal digits.
-,+,$,(), space	Displays a literal character. To force display of a character not included in this list, precede the character with a backslash (\).

"cccc",'cccc' (any characters; literal strings)	Displays the specified string, represented here as cccc within double or single quotes, as a literal.
X, x	X displays uppercase hexadecimal digits, while x displays lowercase hexadecimal digits.
R, r	R displays uppercase Roman numerals, while r displays lowercase Roman numerals.
E+, e+	These display a value in scientific format with a sign for both positive and negative exponential notation. #.###E+0 displays 0.12345 as 1.2345E-1 and #.###e+0 displays 1234.5 as 1.2345e+3.
E-, e-	These display a value in scientific format with a sign for only negative exponential notation. #.###E-0 displays 0.12345 as 1.2345E-1 and #.###e-0 displays 1234.5 as 1.2345e3.
/x	This truncates the number if it is too long to the left of the decimal for the format. Displays the literal character x in all digit positions if truncation occurs.
*x	It fills the number if it is too short for the format. Filling in from the left, the application adds the literal character x as needed to fill the space.

For strings, a format expression can have up to two parts separated by semicolons (;). If you use just one part, it applies to all strings, otherwise the second part applies to NULL values and zero-length strings. You use the following format characters for string data.

Symbol	**Explanation**
@	This defines a character if it exists or places a space for the specified position in the string if none is specified. Therefore, (@@@) @@@–@@@@ displays 8001234567 as (800) 123–4567. Note that because the hyphen (-) is a string formatting character, you should use an en-dash (-) instead of the hyphen for formatting text.
&	It defines a character if it exists; otherwise it doesn't display anything. (&&&) &&&–&&&& displays 1234567 as (123) 456–7.
!	Formats string using placeholders (specified by @ or &) from left to right rather than right to left.

/	Truncates the string if it is longer than the specified mask. Fills from the left until it runs out of placeholders and then truncates to the right.
<	Displays all subsequent characters in lowercase. &<&&&&&&& displays SABRA as Sabra.
>	Displays all subsequent characters in uppercase. &>&&&&&&& displays tyler as tYLER.
-	The hyphen does not change the case of subsequent characters. &<&&&-&&&& displays KRISTIAN as KristIAN.

There is only one part of the format string for dates. The table below lists the format characters for dates.

Symbol	**Explanation**
/	Use the date separator character defined in the Control Panel found when Oracle Power Objects began execution.
$	Use the time separator character defined in the Control Panel found when Oracle Power Objects began execution.
c	Date, as ddddd and time as ttttt, in that order. No fractional part to the date serial number means no time information is displayed; no integer portion means no date information is displayed.
d	Day, as a number: 1-31 (no leading zero).
dd	Day, as a number with a leading zero (01-31).
ddd	Day, as an abbreviation (Sun-Sat).
dddd	Day, as a full name (Sunday-Saturday).
ddddd	Date serial number, as a complete date (dmy) formatted with the Short Date setting. Default is m/d/yy.
dddddd	This displays a date serial number as a complete date (dmy), formatted according to the long date setting in the International section of the Windows Control Panel and the Macintosh Date & Time Control Panel. Default is mmmm dd, yyyy.
w	Day of the week, as a number (1 for Sunday through 7 for Saturday).
ww	Display the week of the year as a number (1-54).

m	Month, as a number: 1-12 (no leading 0). If m immediately follows h or hh, the minute is displayed, rather than the month.
mm	Month, as a number with a leading zero (01-12). If m immediately follows h or hh, the minute is displayed, rather than the month.
mmm	Month, as an abbreviation (Jan-Dec).
mmmm	Month, as a full name (January - December).
q	Quarter of the year, as a number (1-4).
y	Day of the year as a number (1-366).
yy	Year, as a two-digit number (00-99).
yyyy	Year as a four-digit number (0100-9999).
h	Hour, as 0-23 (no leading zero).
hh	Hour, as a number with leading zeros (00-23).
n	Minute, as 0-59 (no leading zero).
nn	Minute, as a number with leading zeros (00-59).
s	Second, as 0-59 (no leading zero).
ss	Second, as a number with leading zeros (00-59).
ttttt	Time serial number, as a complete time (hms) formatted using the time separator defined by the Time Format. A leading zero is displayed if the Leading Zero option is selected and the time is before 10:00 AM or PM. Default format is h:nn:ss (e.g., 1:23:45 AM).
AMPM	Default 12-hour clock value. Uses the Control Panel format for 12-hour clock display, that is, the localized AM suffix for hours between midnight and noon, and the localized PM suffix for hours between noon and midnight. AMPM can be either uppercase or lowercase, but the case of the string displayed matches the string as it exists in the configuration file.
AM/PM	12-hour clock value. Suffix is an uppercase AM for hours between midnight and noon or an uppercase PM for hours between noon and 11:59 PM.
am/pm	12-hour clock value. Suffix is a lowercase am for hours between midnight and noon, or a lowercase pm for all other hours. hh:nn am/pm displays 01:23 pm.

A/P	12-hour clock value. Suffix is an uppercase A for hours between midnight and noon, or an uppercase P for all other hours. h:nn A/P displays 1:23 A.
a/p	12-hour clock value. Suffix is a lowercase a for hours between midnight and noon, or a lowercase p for all other hours. h:nn am/pm displays 1:23 a.
0	If 0 immediately follows any 12-hour clock indicator (above), noon and midnight are displayed as 0:00 rather than as 12:00. For example, with a format mask of h:mm a/p0, noon displays as 0:00 p.
1123	A 24-hour clock version of AMPM for Macintosh, using localized suffixes for morning and afternoon/evening, taken from the Control Panel. (On Windows, which has no such facility, an empty string is displayed.)

INSTR

This function returns as an integer the character position of the first occurrence of string1 within another string2, starting the search at either the beginning of the string or at the given starting position, st_pos. It returns 0 if the entire string1 is not found in string2. The syntax for INSTR is

```
INSTR( [ st_pos, ] string1, string2 )
```

LCASE

Lcase returns a string where all letters of the given string have been converted to lowercase. Its syntax is

```
LCASE(string)
```

LEFT

LEFT returns a string containing the specified number of characters, substr_len, from the given string, taken from the left side of the string. Its syntax is

```
LEFT(string, substr_length)
```

LEN

LEN returns the integer length of the given string. Its syntax is

```
LEN(string)
```

LTRIM

LTRIM returns a copy of the given string with all leading white space characters (if any) removed. Its syntax is

```
LTRIM(string)
```

MID

MID returns a substring that is the part of the given string beginning at start_pos and continuing to the end of the string or the given sub_len (if given), whichever is shorter. Its syntax is

```
MID ( string, start_pos [ , sub_len ] )
```

RIGHT

RIGHT returns the part of the given string containing sub_len rightmost characters in the string. The syntax for RIGHT is

```
RIGHT(string, sub_len)
```

RTRIM

RTRIM returns a copy of the given string with all trailing white space characters (if any) removed. Its syntax is

```
RTRIM(string)
```

SPACE

SPACE returns a string consisting of the specified number of spaces. The syntax for SPACE is

```
SPACE(num_expr)
```

STRING

STRING returns a string of the specified length containing copies of the given single character. The character is designated by its ASCII code number or as the first character in a double-quoted string. The syntax for STRING is

```
STRING(str_len, ASCII_code)
```

or

```
STRING(str_len, string)
```

TRIM

TRIM returns a copy of the given string with leading and trailing white space characters (if any) removed. Its syntax is

```
TRIM(string)
```

UCASE

UCASE returns a string in which all letters of the given string have been converted to uppercase. Its syntax is

```
UCASE(string)
```

Conversion Functions

These are very useful functions to convert data of one datatype to another. They are particularly useful to convert the string data returned by the SQLLookup function and the GetColVal method to the appropriate datatype to match the actual datatype of the data retrieved. If the string given the numeric converters contains numeric and nonnumeric data, the converter skips to the first numeric character in the string and reads all following numeric data until the first nonnumeric character is encountered. It then converts the number read to the appropriate datatype.

CDBL

CDBL converts the given numeric or string containing numeric data to a double-precision value. If the string contains no numeric character, CDBL returns 0. If the string contains a mix of nonnumeric and numeric characters, CDBL returns the value of the first set of numeric characters in the string. Its syntax is

```
CDBL(string_or_num)
```

CINT

CINT converts the given string or number to an integer by rounding any fractional part of the number. If the fractional value is exactly .5, CINT rounds down for odd numbers and rounds up for even numbers. It rounds the absolute value of negative numbers, then returns the negative integer. The CINT syntax is

```
CINT(string_or_num)
```

CLNG

Same as CINT, except it converts the given string or number to a long integer. The syntax for CLNG is

```
CLNG(string_or_num)
```

CSNG

CSNG converts the given string or number to a single-precision value. It rounds double-precision values to single precision. Its syntax is

```
CSNG(string_or_num_expr)
```

CSTR

CSTR converts the given numeric (or string, but that is a little redundant) expression to a string. It is just like STR, except it does not leave a leading blank for positive numbers. Its syntax is

```
CSTR(num)
```

CVDATE

CVDATE converts the given string or numeric expression (which must evaluate to a date value) to a date. A string containing data that looks like a date, such as 21-oct-47 is convertible to a date. If the string looks like a number, it is first converted to a number and then to a date just as a number is converted. The range of numeric values acceptable as input values for date information is 2958465 (December 31, 9999 A.D.) through -657434 (January 1, 100 A.D.). Any fractional part of a number is converted to a time of day, beginning at midnight. The syntax for CVDATE is

```
CVDATE(string_or_num)
```

HEX

HEX returns a string that represents the hexadecimal value of the given decimal argument. The argument is first rounded to a whole number and then converted. If the argument is an integer, HEX returns four hexadecimal characters, and if it is a long integer, it returns eight characters. The syntax for HEX is

```
HEX(num_expr)
```

OCT

OCT returns a string that represents the octal value of the given decimal argument. Unlike HEX, any fractional part of the number is truncated rather than rounded. If the argument is an integer, it returns up to four octal characters, and if it is a long integer, it returns up to 11 octal characters. Its syntax is

```
OCT(num_expr)
```

STR

STR is similar to CSTR, except it leaves a space before positive numbers in the string it returns after converting the given number.

```
STR(num)
```

VAL

VAL returns the numeric value of the given string of numeric characters as a double-precision value. Its syntax is

```
VAL(string_expr)
```

Aggregate Functions

These functions operate on a repeated control in a form. For example, a text field that contains salaries in the primary panel of a repeater is such a form. In a report, any control in the detail part of the report is generally repeated and is a candidate for an aggregate function. The example report SalesByCust in Chapter 6 uses the

SUM function. The argument must contain at least one reference to a repeated control. It can contain other data as well, such as TotalCount=COUNT(6*myform.repeater1.emp_name). The container of the aggregate function must be outside the container of the repeated value.

AVG

AVG returns the arithmetic average (mean) of the given set of values as double-precision. Its syntax is

```
AVG(repeated_value)
```

COUNT

COUNT returns the number of expressions in the given repeated_value as double-precision. The syntax for COUNT is

```
COUNT(repeated_value)
```

MAX

MAX returns the maximum value among the set of given repeated values as double-precision. The syntax for MAX is

```
MAX(repeated_value)
```

MIN

MIN returns the minimum value among the set of given repeated values as double-precision. Its syntax is

```
MIN(repeated_value)
```

STDEV

STDEV returns the standard deviation for the set of given values as double-precision. The syntax for STDEV is

```
STDEV( repeated_value)
```

SUM

SUM returns the sum of the set of given repeated values as the datatype of the repeated value. The syntax for SUM is

```
SUM(repeated_value)
```

Date Functions

These functions all return a date value or a string that represents a date. Some of these functions take a time type argument. The time type is a string containing one of the following values.

Interval	Designator
Second	s (or S)
Minute	n (or N)
Hour	h (or H)
Day	d (or D)
Day of year	y (or Y)
Week	ww (or WW)
Weekday	w(or W)
Month	m (or M)
Quarter	q (or Q)
Year	yyyy (or YYYY)

DATE

DATE returns the current system date as a ten-character string in the mm-dd-yyyy format. Its syntax is

    DATE

DATEADD

The DATEADD function returns a time or date value calculated by adding the given number of time intervals of the type designated by the time type argument to the given date. The number of intervals can be negative to calculate a time in the past. The syntax for DATEADD is

    DATEADD(time_type, num_intervals, date)

DATEDIFF

DATEDIFF returns the number of designated time intervals (such as days or weeks) between the first_date and the second_date as double-precision. The syntax of DATEDIFF is

    DATEDIFF(time_type, first_date, second_date)

DATEPART

DATEPART returns the specified part (such as seconds or day) of the given date. If the date is 1/12/44 and you specify yyyy, DATEPART returns 2044. If the year is greater than 44, (e.g., 1/12/45) it returns 1945. The syntax for DATEPART is

    DATEPART(time_type, date)

DATESERIAL

DATESERIAL returns the date represented by the given integer argument for the year, month, and day. The year must be explicit for years 100 to 1899 and greater than 2000. For years beginning with 19, you can use just the last two digits. The month must be between 1 and 12, and the day must be appropriate for the given month. The syntax for DATESERIAL is

DATESERIAL(year, month, day)

MONTH

MONTH returns an integer between 1 and 12, inclusive, that represents the month of the given date. The date can be a string that is recognizable as a date. The syntax for MONTH is

MONTH(date_expr)

SYSDATE; NOW

SYSDATE and NOW are identical functions. They return the computer's system date and time as a date. The date returned can be used in any function that requires an argument of date datatype. It can also be converted to a string to display the current date and time according to the system's default date format. Its syntax is

SYSDATE
NOW

Time Functions

Time functions are similar to the date functions, except they return time or parts of time data as strings or dates.

TIME

TIME returns the current system time in an eight-character string in the format hh:mm:ss. The syntax for TIME is

TIME

TIMER

This function returns as an integer the number of seconds elapsed since midnight on the current day. Its syntax is

TIMER

TIMESERIAL

TIMESERIAL returns a date that represents the time of the given integer arguments representing the desired hour (0-23), minute (0-59), and second (0-59). Its syntax is

TIMESERIAL(hour,minute,second)

TIMEVALUE

TIMEVALUE returns a date that represents the time of the given string argument, which must look like a date or the time portion of a date. Its syntax is

```
TIMEVALUE(time_val)
```

ISDATE

ISDATE is a test function that identifies whether the value supplied could be converted to a date. It returns TRUE if it can; otherwise, it returns FALSE.

```
ISDATE(n_d_or_string)
```

DAY

DAY returns an integer between 1 and 31, inclusive, that represents the day portion of the given date, which may either be a string or number that represents a date. The syntax is

```
DAY(date_expr)
```

HOUR

HOUR returns an integer (0-23) that represents the hour portion of the specified date, which may be either a string or number that represents a date. The syntax for HOUR is

```
HOUR(date_expr)
```

MINUTE

MINUTE returns an integer between 0 and 59, inclusive, representing the minutes portion of the given date, which may be a string or number that represents a date. The syntax for MINUTE is

```
MINUTE(date_expr)
```

SECOND

SECOND returns an integer between 0 and 59, inclusive, that represents the seconds portion of the given date, which may be a string or number that represents a date. Its syntax is

```
SECOND(date_expr)
```

YEAR

YEAR returns an integer above 99 and below 10,000 representing the year portion of the given date, which may be a string or number that represents a date. The syntax for YEAR is

```
YEAR(date_expr)
```

WEEKDAY

WEEKDAY returns an integer between 1 (Sunday) and 7 (Saturday) representing the day of the week portion of the given date, which may be a string or number that represents a date. The syntax for WEEKDAY is

```
WEEKDAY(date_expr)
```

Financial Functions

These functions are very useful for developers of financial applications. They are built-in functions to calculate the most common types of monetary calculations. Several of these functions require a cash_flow_array, which is an array of cash outlays and cash receipts representing the cost to do business. Generally, there must be at least one expense (negative numbers) and one receipt (positive numbers) in the array. The number of items in the array is simply the number of expenses and receipts. Several calculations take into account whether the payment is due at the beginning (1) or end of the month (0) using the due_end argument.

DDB

DDB returns the depreciation of an asset's value for a single period using the straight-line method as a double-precision number. The arguments are the initial value, resale value, and the expected life of the asset and the depreciation period. Its syntax is

```
DDB( init_cost , resale_value , expected_life , depreciation_period )
```

FV

FV returns the future value for an investment, such as an annuity, using a constant interest rate and regular periodic payments of a constant amount. The return value is double-precision. The present value is the amount currently on hand. Its syntax is

```
FV(rate_per_period , num_of_periods , payment_each_period , present_value ,
due_end)
```

IPMT

IPMT returns a value as double-precision representing the amount applied to interest from the payment for the specified period (an integer) based on the life (num_of_periods) of the loan or saving plan. The last three arguments represent the original amount of money on hand, the desired amount to be on hand (0 for a mortgage) at the end of the period, and whether the payment is made at the beginning of the month (1) or at the end of the month (0). The syntax for IPMT is

```
IPMT ( rate_per_period , which_period , num_of_periods , present_value ,
future_value , due_end )
```

IRR
IRR is an iterative function—you generally must run the function several times, each time with a new estimate of the rate of return. When your estimate is in the ballpark, it returns as a double-precision value the interest rate represented by a series of periodic cash outlays, including both payments and receipts. Otherwise, it fails and returns a NULL. You then supply a new estimate and start again. The syntax for IRR is

```
IRR( cash_flow_array , estimate )
```

MIRR
MIRR returns the interest rate represented by a series of periodic cash flows, both payments and receipts, when the interest rate for payments (interest_paid) differs from that for receipts (interest_received). Its syntax is

```
MIRR(cash_flow_array , interest_paid , interest_received)
```

NPER
NPER returns as a double-precision the number of periods required for an annuity based on the interest rate, the periodic payment, the amount on hand, the desired final amount on hand, and whether the payment is made at the beginning of the month (1) or at the end of the month (0). The syntax for NPER is

```
NPER(interest , payment , present_value , final_value , due_end)
```

NPV
NPV returns as double-precision the net present value for an investment using a discount rate that applies over the entire period and the series of cash-flow values representing the payments and receipts for that period. The difference between NPV and PV is that the cash flow for NPV is variable and the values apply at the end of each period. Cash flow for PV is constant and the values can be applied at the beginning or end of each period. Its syntax is

```
NPV( discount_rate , cash_flow_array )
```

PMT
PMT returns as a double-precision the constant periodic payment to be expected from an investment with a constant interest rate. Its syntax is

```
PMT(rate_per_period , total_periods , present_value , future_value , due_end)
```

PPMT
PPMT returns a double-precision value representing the amount applied to principal in the given period for an investment such as a mortgage or an annuity. It is the complement to IPMT. The syntax for PPMT is

```
PPMT(rate_per_period , which_period , total_periods , present_value ,
future_value , due_end)
```

PV

PV returns the present value for an investment, such as an annuity, using a constant interest rate and regular identical payments. The future value represents the desired amount at the end of the transaction (0 for mortgages or final amount for an annuity). Its syntax is

PV(rate_per_period , num_of_periods , payment , future_value , due_end)

RATE

RATE returns as double-precision the interest rate per period for an investment, such as a mortgage or an annuity based on the total number of periods the payment is made, the payment amount, the beginning balance, the expected end amount (0 for mortgages), when the payment is made, and an estimate of the RATE. This function is iterative and repeatedly calculates the interest rate using the estimate. If it fails in 20 tries, it returns NULL, and you need to start it again with a different estimate. Its syntax is

RATE(num_of_periods , payment , present_value , future_value , due_end , estimate)

SLN

SLN returns the depreciation of an asset's value for a single period using the straight-line method based on its initial cost and its final value at the end of the expected life of the asset. The syntax for SLN is

SLN(asset_cost , salvage_value , expected_life)

SYD

SYD returns as double-precision the depreciation of an asset over a given period using the sum-of-the-years'-digits method based on the assets initial cost and its final value at the end of the expected life of the asset. Its syntax is

SYD(asset_cost , salvage_value , expected_life , depreciation_period)

APPENDIX C

Oracle, Oracle SQL, and Oracle Basic Reserved Words and Keywords

When creating Oracle Basic or Exec SQL scripts there are certain words that you cannot use and other words that you should avoid using as the name of any database object or part. The Oracle Reserved Words list contains words reserved for use by Oracle and cannot be used in statements. The SQL Keyword list consists of Oracle SQL keywords that you should avoid in scripts, because using these keywords would make statements difficult to read. Words followed by an asterisk (*) are ANSI SQL reserved words or keywords.

The last two sections, Oracle Basic Command Reserved Words and Oracle Basic Function Reserved Words are reserved in Oracle Basic for special values. You cannot use any of these words as variable or object names in Oracle Basic statements.

Oracle Reserved Words

ACCESS
ADD
ALL*
ALTER
AND*
ANY*
AS*
ASC*
AUDIT
BETWEEN*
BY*
CHAR*
CHECK*
CLUSTER
COLUMN
COMMENT
COMPRESS
CONNECT
CONSTRAINT
CREATE*
CURRENT*
DATE
DECIMAL*
DEFAULT*
DELETE*
DESC*
DISTINCT*
DROP
ELSE
EXCLUSIVE
EXITS*
FILE
FLOAT*
FOR*
FOREIGN
FROM*
GRANT*
GROUP*
HAVING*
IDENTIFIED
IMMEDIATE
IN*
INCREMENT
INDEX
INITIAL
INSERT*
INTEGER*
INTERSECT
INTO*
IS*
LEVEL
LIKE*
LOCK
LONG
MAXEXTENTS
MINUS
MODE
MODIFY

NOAUDIT
NOCOMPRESS
NOT*
NOWAIT
NULL*
NUMBER
OF*
OFFLINE
ON*
ONLINE
OPTION*
OR*
ORDER*
PCTFREE
PRIMARY
PRIOR
PRIVILEGES*
PUBLIC*
RAW
RENAME
RESOURCE
REVOKE
ROW
ROWID
ROWLABEL
ROWNUM
ROWS
SELECT*
SESSION
SET*
SHARE
SIZE
SMALLINT*
START
SUCCESSFUL
SYNONYM
SYSDATE
TABLE*
THEN
TO*
TRIGGER
UID
UNION*
UNIQUE*
UPDATE*
USER*
VALIDATE
VALUES*
VARCHAR
VARCHAR2
VIEW*
WHENEVER*
WHERE*
WITH*

Oracle SQL Keywords

ADMIN
AFTER
ALLOCATE
ANALYZE
ARCHIVE
ARCHIVELOG
AUTHORIZATION*
AVG*
BACKUP
BEGIN*
BECOME
BEFORE
BLOCK
BODY
CACHE
CANCEL
CASCADE
CHANGE
CHARACTER*
CHECKPOINT
CLOSE*
COBOL*

COMMIT*
COMPILE
CONSTRAINT
CONSTRAINTS
CONTENTS
CONTINUE*
CONTROLFILE
COUNT*
CURSOR*
CYCLE
DATABASE
DATAFILE
DBA
DEC*
DECLARE*
DISABLE
DISMOUNT
DOUBLE*
DUMP
EACH
ENABLE
END*
ESCAPE*
EVENTS
EXCEPT
EXCEPTIONS
EXEC*
EXECUTE
EXPLAIN
EXTENT
EXTERNALLY
FETCH*
FLUSH
FREELIST
FREELISTS
FORCE
FOREIGN*
FORTRAN*
FOUND*
FUNCTION
GO*
GOTO*
GROUPS
INCLUDING
INDICATOR*
INITRANS
INSTANCE
INT*
KEY*
LANGUAGE*
LAYER
LINK
LISTS
LOGFILE
MANAGE
MANUAL
MAX*
MAXDATAFILES
MAXINSTANCES
MAXLOGFILES
MAXLOGHISTORY
MAXLOGMEMBERS
MAXTRANS
MAXVALUE
MIN*
MINEXTENTS
MINVALUE
MODULE*
MOUNT
NEXT
NEW
NOARCHIVELOG
NOCACHE
NOCYCLE
NOMAXVALUE
NOMINVALUE
NONE
NOORDER
NORESETLOGS
NORMAL
NOSORT
NUMERIC*
OFF
OLD

ONLY
OPEN*
OPTIMAL
OWN
PACKAGE
PARALLEL
PASCAL*
PCTINCREASE
PCTUSED
PLAN
PLI*
PRECISION*
PRIMARY*
PRIVATE
PROCEDURE*
PROFILE
QUOTA
READ
REAL*
RECOVER
REFERENCES*
REFERENCING
RESETLOGS
RESTRICTED
REUSE
ROLE
ROLES
ROLLBACK*
SAVEPOINT
SCHEMA*
SCN
SECTION*
SEGMENT
SEQUENCE
SHARED
SNAPSHOT
SOME*
SORT
SQL*
SQLCODE*
SQLERROR*
STATEMENT_ID
STATISTICS
STOP
STORAGE
SUM*
SWITCH
SYSTEM
TABLES
TABLESPACE
TEMPORARY
THREAD
TIME
TRACING
TRANSACTION
TRIGGERS
TRUNCATE
UNDER
UNLIMITED
UNTIL
USE
USING
WHEN
WRITE
WORK*

Oracle Basic Command Reserved Words

BEEP
CALL
CASE
CHDIR
CHDRIVE
CLOSE
CONST
DECLARE

DIM
DO
END
ERASE
EXEC SQL
EXIT
FOR
FUNCTION
GET
GLOBAL
GOSUB
GOTO
IF
INPUT #
INPUTBOX
KILL
LET
LINE INPUT #
LOCK
MID
MKDIR
MSGBOX
NAME ... AS
ON
ON ERROR
OPEN
PRINT #
PUT
RANDOMIZE
REDIM
REM
RESET
RESUME
RETURN
RMDIR
SEEK
SELECT
STATIC
STOP
SUB
WHILE
WIDTH #
WRITE #

Oracle Basic Function Reserved Words

ABS
ASC
ATN
AVG
CDBL
CHOOSE
CHR
CINT
CLNG
COS
COUNT
CSNG
CSTR
CURDIR
CVDATE
DATE
DATEADD
DATEDIFF
DATEPART
DATESERIAL
DAY
DDB
ENVIRON
EOF
ERR
EXP
FIX
FORMAT
FREEFILE
FV
HEX
HOUR

IIF
INPUT
INSTR
INT
IPMT
IRR
ISDATE
ISNULL
ISNUMERIC
LBOUND
LCASE
LEFT
LEN
LOC
LOF
LOG
LTRIM
MAX
MID
MIN
MINUTE
MIRR
MONTH
MSGBOX
NOW
NPER
NPV
NVL
OCT
PMT
PPMT
PV
RATE
RIGHT
RND
RTRIM
SECOND
SEEK
SGN
SIN
SLN
SPACE
SPC
SQR
STDEV
STR
STRING
SUM
SWITCH
SYD
SYSDATE
SYSTEMNAME
TAN
TIME
TIMER
TIMESERIAL
TIMEVALUE
TRIM
UBOUND
UCASE
VAL
VARTYPE
WEEKDAY
YEAR

Index

D

G

Q

R

T

U

V

W

Y

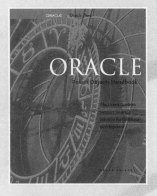

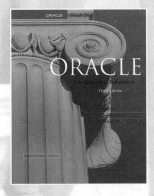

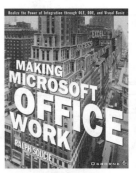

ORDER BOOKS DIRECTLY FROM OSBORNE/McGRAW-HILL

For a complete catalog of Osborne's books, call 510-549-6600 or write to us at 2600 Tenth Street, Berkeley, CA 94710

Call Toll-Free: ***1-800-822-8158***
24 hours a day, 7 days a week in U.S. and Canada

Mail this order form to:
McGraw-Hill, Inc.
Customer Service Dept.
P.O. Box 547
Blacklick, OH 43004

Fax this order form to:
1-614-759-3644

EMAIL
7007.1531@COMPUSERVE.COM
COMPUSERVE GO MH

Ship to:

Name ______________________________

Company ______________________________

Address ______________________________

City / State / Zip ______________________________

Daytime Telephone: ______________________________
(We'll contact you if there's a question about your order.)

ISBN #	BOOK TITLE	Quantity	Price	Total
0-07-88				
0-07-88				
0-07-88				
0-07-88				
0-07-88				
0-07088				
0-07-88				
0-07-88				
0-07-88				
0-07-88				
0-07-88				
0-07-88				
0-07-88				
0-07-88				
	Shipping & Handling Charge from Chart Below			
	Subtotal			
	Please Add Applicable State & Local Sales Tax			
	TOTAL			

Shipping & Handling Charges

Order Amount	U.S.	Outside U.S.
Less than $15	$3.50	$5.50
$15.00 - $24.99	$4.00	$6.00
$25.00 - $49.99	$5.00	$7.00
$50.00 - $74.99	$6.00	$8.00
$75.00 - and up	$7.00	$9.00

Occasionally we allow other selected companies to use our mailing list. If you would prefer that we not include you in these extra mailings, please check here: ❑

METHOD OF PAYMENT

❑ Check or money order enclosed (payable to Osborne/McGraw-Hill)

❑ AMERICAN EXPRESS ❑ DISCOVER ❑ MasterCard ❑ VISA

Account No. ______________________________

Expiration Date ______________________________

Signature ______________________________

In a hurry? Call 1-800-822-8158 anytime, day or night, or visit your local bookstore.

Thank you for your order

Code BC640SL